G000150184

TED HUGHES

Ted Hughes
A Bibliography

Second Edition
1946–1995

by

Keith Sagar and Stephen Tabor

MANSELL
London and New York

Mansell Publishing Limited, *A Cassell Imprint*
Wellington House, 125 Strand, London WC2R 0BB, England
370 Lexington Avenue, New York, NY 10017-6550, USA

First edition published 1983
Second edition first published 1998

British Library Cataloguing in Publication Data
A catalogue record for this book is available from the British Library.

ISBN 0-7201-2337-2

Library of Congress Cataloging-in-Publication Data
Sagar, Keith M.
    Ted Hughes, a bibliography, 1946–1995 / by Keith Sagar and
Stephen Tabor. — 2nd ed.
        p. cm.
    Includes bibliographical references (p.   ) and index.
    ISBN 0-7201-2337-2 (hardcover)
    1. Hughes, Ted, 1930-   —Bibliography.   I. Tabor, Stephen.
II. Title.
Z8423.43.S23   1998
[PR6058.U37]
016.821'914—dc21   97-48709
                                                                CIP

Frontispiece: Ted Hughes. Photograph by Jane Bown.

Typeset by BookEns Ltd, Royston, Herts.
Printed and bound in Great Britain by
Bookcraft Limited, Midsomer Norton

CONTENTS

INTRODUCTION TO FIRST EDITION

To describe Ted Hughes as the greatest living English poet hardly does justice to his stature. He is surely the greatest imaginative writer now writing in English, the natural successor to W. B. Yeats, D. H. Lawrence and T. S. Eliot. Hughes was fifty in August 1980. It seemed an appropriate time to begin the task of compiling a thorough list of his publications and of what has been written about him, up to the end of 1980. Hughes has been prolific, and many of his works have appeared only in obscure periodicals or anthologies, or in limited editions long unobtainable. Those poems which are available in trade editions are usually different from the earlier forms in which they appeared, since Hughes rarely misses the opportunity to revise at every stage.

Hughes' work has proved unusually stimulating to artists and composers, which has led to a profusion of prints and settings, as well as full-scale collaborations with, for example, the artist Leonard Baskin, the photographer Fay Godwin, and the composer Gordon Crosse.

The BBC was fortunate in that several of its producers recognized at an early stage Hughes' gifts as speaker and reader, and these were fully exploited on radio, particularly during the 1960s. Much of this material has never been published. Many Hughes works were first heard of on radio; this is therefore a more accurate guide to their dating than first publication.

Unlike Stephen Tabor I have had no training in bibliography. The division of labour between us has therefore been that Stephen has taken responsibility for sections A and B, where strict bibliographical conventions must be observed, while I have given what help I could with these, provided the lists of reviews, and compiled the rest of the book. The book is, of course, intended for bibliophiles, collectors and dealers, as well as for critics, students and readers; but my own interest is largely in the needs of the latter. We have tried to give as much useful information as possible, and to make it as accessible as possible. The contents and conventions of each section are described at the head of it. Full cross-referencing is unnecessary, since the index provides at a glance the publishing history of each item.

Keith Sagar

INTRODUCTION TO
SECOND EDITION

The last fifteen years have more than confirmed Hughes' pre-eminence among living English writers. In *River* (1983) Hughes produced what many believe to be his finest poetic work, a sacramental and totally unsentimental absorption in the natural world. In *Wolfwatching* (1989) his poetry moved into fascinating new modes, including a deeply personal mode which he has since developed, particularly in the previously unpublished poems in *New Selected Poems* (1995). Without ceasing to be prolific as a poet, and as a writer of stories for children, Hughes has also, with *Shakespeare and the Goddess of Complete Being* (1992) and *Winter Pollen* (1994) (especially the substantial new essays on Coleridge and Eliot), achieved a similar pre-eminence as a literary critic. He has also published translations (or 'versions') of Ovid and Wedekind (and there are translations of Lorca and Aeschylus in the pipeline).

Perhaps rather less has been published about Hughes in these years in the UK and the USA (in line with the steep decline in the publishing of all literary criticism here), but this has been more than compensated for by the increase in work on him worldwide (especially in Germany and Japan).

As well as extending the record up to the end of 1995, this edition enables us to correct some of the mistakes and omissions in the first edition, but we have retained the original numbering, except in sections D, F and J. As in the first edition, Stephen Tabor has carried the main responsibility for sections A and B, and I have compiled the rest, including a new section on the main locations of manuscripts. There are now enough in university libraries to enable the serious study of them to begin.

In sections A and B an asterisk (*) against an item number indicates that this is a new entry inserted into the sequence of the first edition. In addition, typefaces have been omitted in section A, because of the proliferation of digital fonts and the difficulty in keeping up with them. Also, because of the mass of new material needed to be added to section B and the time constraints, reviews have been omitted from this section.

Keith Sagar

ACKNOWLEDGEMENTS

We should like to thank many people for their help in providing information and copies of items for inspection. In particular Ted and Olwyn Hughes; Rosemary Goad and the staff of Faber and Faber; Fred Rue Jacobs, Challis Reed and the staff of the BBC Script Library; and Moira Doolan and the BBC Schools Department. We are also indebted to Alan Anderson; The Arvon Foundation; Anne Askwith; Muriel F. Austen; Jonathan Barker; Gillian Bate; Adam and Charles Black (Publishers); B. C. Bloomfield; Alan Brilliant; Martin Booth; Susan Brailove; James Budenholzer; Katie Burgess; Will Carter; Eric Cleave; John Commander; R. L. Cook; Seamus Cooney; Julia Cox; Robert Creffield; Barbara A. Dicks; Thomas J. Eastwood; Patricia Fairfield; D. R. Forbes; Bob Forster; Colin Franklin; Norman Franklin; Malcolm Fry; Terry Gifford; Richard Gilbertson; Rebecca Greenberg; Hugh Halman; Janelle Hardin; Marcia Harris; Mark Haworth-Booth; Antony R. Howell; Helen Huckle; Derek Hyatt; Indiana University Press; Noboru Iwata; Ben Kane; Jean Karl; Terry Karten; Richard Kot; Gerald Lacy; Trudy Lee; R. Lewis; Diana Lillig; Catheryn Lobbenberg; Heidemarie Luckert; Madeleine Lysley; Frances McCullough; Edward A. Mainzer; John Martin; Peter J. Matthews; Michele Medinz; Elaine N. Miller; Murray Mindlin; Jean Mossop; F. L. Mountford; George Murphy; John Murray Ltd.; Melissa Mytinger; Julian Nangle; New London Press; Charles Osborne; Rosalind J. Platt; Rita Platzman; Kate Raggett; E. M. Reid; Mary Remnant; Craig Robinson; Anthony Rudolf; Carolyn Ryder; St. Martin's Press; Gertrude P. Schafer; Michael Schmidt; Charles Seluzicki; Jacqueline Simms; Reresby Sitwell; Christopher and Robin Skelton; Charles Skilton; Ann C. Smit; Sara Smith; Sotheby Parke Bernet; Ralph Steadman; Laurie Stearns; P. W. Stockman; Brenda Stones; J. G. Studholme; Susan Suffes; Valerie

Sutherland; Alan Tarling; Pam Taylor; Vanessa Terry; Diana Thomas; Mrs. M. Thomas; Grete Ullstrup; the Interlibrary Loan Department of the Research Library at the University of California, Los Angeles; George Vay; Sarita Vellani; Katsuo Wakiyama; Sam Wanamaker; Mandy Wiltsher; and R. N. Wood.

We should like to repeat our thanks to those of the above who were also able to help with the second edition; and to express our thanks to the following, who have given generously of their time and knowledge: David Albahari; Nicholas Albery; Zoran Ančevski; Bloodaxe Books; Michael Brazilly; Clare Brown; Piers Burnett; Alan Clodd; Ann Crawley; Jenifer Entwistle; Aisling FitzPatrick; Matthew Frost; Nick Gammage; Hilary Hale; Stella Halkyard; Steven Halliwell; Paul Henderson; Mark Hinchliffe; Meredith Howard; Brian Hulme; Takeo Iida; Clare Johnson; Claas Kazzer; George Lawson; Joanna Legg; R. J. Lloyd; Rupert Loydell; Dr. Andrew McAllister; Frances McDowall; D. J. Mackenzie; Charles McNamara; David Milner; Joanny Moulin; Jemima Oakley; Pacific Books; David Pease; Anita Perala; Roger Pringle; John Randle; Colin Raw; Neil Roberts; Jean Rose; Leonard Scigaj; Ann Skea; Virginia Sleep; Apollonia Lang Steele; Maria Stella; Bernard Stone; Stephen Stuart-Smith; Alberta T. Turner; University of Georgia Press; Viking Press; Pamela Webb; Daniel Weissbort; Victoria Wells; Trevor Weston; Sara Williams; Kit Yee Wong; Penny Worms; and Elizabeth Wright.

LIST OF SOURCES

Accent (Urbana, Ill.)
Agenda (London)
Ambit (London)
America (New York)
American Book Review (New York)
American Poetry Review
   (Philadelphia, Pa.)
Anglo-Welsh Review (Tenby,
   Dyfed)
Antaeus (New York)
Aquarius (London)
Archiv für das Studium der neueren
   Sprachen und Literaturen
   (Braunschweig, Germany)
Argo (Stirling)
Ariel (Calgary)
Arion (Boston, Mass.)
Arizona Quarterly (Tucson, Ariz.)
Art Teacher (Reston, Va.)
Artful Reporter (Manchester)
Atlantic Monthly (Boston, Mass.)
Audience (Cambridge, Mass.)
Baltimore Evening Sun (Baltimore,
   Md.)
Bananas (London)
Best Sellers (Scranton, Pa.)
Birmingham Post (Birmingham)
Book Report (Worthington, Ohio)

Book Week (New York)
Book World (Washington Post)
   (Washington, D.C.)
Booklist (Chicago, Ill.)
Books and Bookmen (London)
Books and Issues (London)
Books for Keeps (London)
Books for Your Children
   (Birmingham)
Books from Borders
Books, Plays, Poems (London)
Boston University Journal (Boston,
   Mass.)
British Book News (London)
British Book News, Children's Books
   (London)
Buffalo News (Buffalo, N.Y.)
Bulletin of Bibliography (Westwood,
   Mass.)
Cambridge Evening News
   (Cambridge)
Cambridge Quarterly (Cambridge)
Canadian Forum (Toronto)
Carleton Miscellany (Northfield,
   Minn.)
Cencrastus (Edinburgh)
Center for Children's Books, Bulletin
   (Chicago, Ill.)

Chequer (Cambridge)
Chicago Review (Chicago, Ill.)
Chicago Tribune (Chicago, Ill.)
Children's Literature Association Quarterly (West Lafayette, Ind.)
Children's Literature in Education (London)
Choice (Middletown, Conn.)
Christian Century (Chicago, Ill.)
Christian Science Monitor (Boston)
Church Times (London)
Clio (Fort Wayne, Ind.)
Commonweal (New York)
Concerning Poetry (Bellingham, Wash.)
Connoisseur (Red Oak, Iowa)
Contemporary Literature (Madison, Wis.)
Contemporary Poetry (Bryn Mawr, Pa.)
Contemporary Review (Avenel, N.J.)
Country Life (London)
Coventry Evening Telegraph (Coventry)
Cricket (La Salle, Ill.)
Critic (Chicago, Ill.)
Critical Inquiry (Chicago, Ill.)
Critical Quarterly (Manchester)
Critical Survey (Hull)
Daily Mail (London)
Daily Telegraph (London)
Delap's F. & S. F. Review (West Hollywood, Calif.)
Delta (Cambridge)
Discourse (Moorhead, Minn.)
Don and Dearne (Mexborough Grammar School)
Dublin Magazine (Dublin)
Dutch Quarterly Review of Anglo-American Letters (Amsterdam)
Eastern Daily Press (Norwich)
Eigo Seinen (Tokyo)
Encounter (London)
English Journal (Urbana, Ill.)
English Studies (Lisse, Netherlands)

Erasmus Review (Bayside, N.Y.)
Essays in Criticism (Oxford)
Essence (New Haven, Conn.)
Études Anglaises (Paris)
Evening Standard (London)
Evidence (Oxford)
Explicator (Washington, D.C.)
Far Point (Winnipeg, Manitoba)
Financial Times (London)
Gemini (Cambridge)
Georgia Review (Athens, Ga.)
Glasgow Herald (Glasgow)
Granta (Cambridge)
Grapevine (Durham)
Grecourt Review (Northampton, Mass.)
Growing Point (Northampton)
Guardian (London)
Guardian Weekly (New York)
Halifax Courier (Halifax, Yorks.)
Hampstead and Highgate Express (London)
Harper's Magazine (New York)
Hartford Courant (Hartford, Conn.)
Helix (Ivanhoe, Australia)
Horn Book (Boston, Mass.)
Horn Book Guide (Boston, Mass.)
Houston Chronicle (Houston, Tex.)
Hudson Review (New York)
Human World (Swansea, Wales)
Illustrated London News (London)
Independent (London)
Independent on Sunday (London)
International Herald Tribune (New York)
Iowa Review (Iowa City, Iowa)
Irish Independent (Dublin)
Irish Times (Dublin)
Isis (Oxford)
Jack and Jill (Philadelphia, Pa.)
Jewish Chronicle (London)
John O'London's (London)
Junior Bookshelf (Huddersfield, Yorks.)
Kentish Gazette (Canterbury, Kent)

Kenyon Review (Fort Lee, N.J.)
Kingfisher (Sheffield)
Kirkus (New York)
Književne reč (Belgrade)
Lady (London)
Language and Literature
Language Arts (Urbana, Ill.)
Lettore di Provincia (Ravenna)
Library Journal (New York)
Listen (Hessle, Yorks.)
Listener (London)
Listening and Writing (London)
Literary Review (London)
Literary Review (Madison, N.J.)
Literatur in Wissenschaft und Unterricht (Neumünster, Germany)
Literature and History (London)
Living Language (London)
London Magazine (London)
London Review of Books (London)
Londoner (London)
Los Angeles Times (Los Angeles, Calif.)
Louisville Times (Louisville, Ky.)
Lyrikvännen (Stockholm)
Mademoiselle (New York)
Magpies (Victoria Park, Western Australia)
Malahat Review (Victoria, B.C.)
Manchester Guardian (Manchester)
Mars (London)
Massachusetts Review (Amherst, Mass.)
Mediterranean Review (Orient, N.Y.)
Michigan Quarterly Review (Ann Arbor, Mich.)
Minnesota Review (Bloomington, Ind.)
Miss London (London)
Modern Poetry in Translation (London)
Modern Poetry Studies (Buffalo, N.Y.)
Moderna Språk (Stockholm)

The Month (London)
Music and Musicians (London)
Musical Opinion (Bournemouth)
Musical Times (London)
Nation (New York)
National Observer (Salisbury, Zimbabwe)
National Review (New York)
New American Review (Cranford, N.J.)
New Blackfriars (Oxford)
New Departures (Bisley, Glos.)
New Republic (Washington, D.C.)
New Review (London)
New Statesman (London)
New Statesman & Society (London)
New Times (Phoenix, Ariz.)
New Universities Quarterly (Oxford)
New York Herald Tribune (New York)
New York Review of Books (New York)
New York Times (New York)
New York Times Book Review (New York)
New Yorker (New York)
Newsweek (New York)
Northern Broadsheet (Edinburgh)
Northern Review (Comber, N. Ireland)
Northwest Review (Eugene, Ore.)
Notes and Queries (London)
Notes on Contemporary Literature (Carrollton, Ga.)
Oberon (Japan)
Observer (London)
Observer Colour Supplement (London)
Opera (London)
Ord och Bild (Stockholm)
Outposts (Walton on Thames, Surrey)
Overland (Melbourne)
Oxford Magazine (Oxford)
Oxford Poetry Magazine (Oxford)
Oxford Times (Oxford)

Paris Review (Paris)
Parnassus (New York)
Partisan Review (New York)
Performance (New York)
Platform (Luddendenfoot, Yorks.)
Plays and Players (London)
Ploughshares (Cambridge, Mass.)
P.N Review (Manchester)
Poetry (Chicago, Ill.)
Poetry and Audience (Leeds)
Poetry Australia (Five Dock, NSW)
Poetry Book Society Bulletin
   (London)
Poetry Dial (South Bend, Ind.)
Poetry London/Apple Magazine
   (London)
Poetry Nation (Manchester)
Poetry Nation Review (Manchester)
Poetry Review (London)
Poetry Wales (Swansea)
Prairie Schooner (Lincoln, Neb.)
Publishers Weekly (New York)
Punch (London)
Quarry (Kingston, Ontario)
Quarterly Review of Literature
   (Princeton, N.J.)
Quarto (London)
Quill & Quire (Markham,
   Ontario)
Raritan (New Brunswick, N.J.)
Réalités (Paris, New York,
   London)
Resurgence (Hartland, Devon)
Review (London)
Sad Traffic (Barnsley, Yorks.)
St. Botolph's Review (Cambridge)
St. Louis Globe-Democrat (St. Louis,
   Mo.)
San Francisco Review of Books (San
   Francisco)
Saturday Review (New York)
School Librarian (Oxford)
School Library Journal (New York)
Scotsman (Edinburgh)
Sewanee Review (Sewanee, Tenn.)

Sheffield Morning Telegraph
   (Sheffield)
Sheffield Star (Sheffield)
Shenandoah (Lexington, Va.)
South West Review (Exeter)
Southern Arts (Winchester, Hants.)
Southern Humanities Review
   (Auburn, Al.)
Southern Review (Adelaide)
Southwest Review (Dallas, Tex.)
Spectator (London)
Spectrum (Amherst, Mass.)
Sphinx (Regina, Saskatchewan)
Stage and Television Today (London)
Stand (Newcastle upon Tyne)
Stanford Daily (Stanford, Calif.)
Straight Lines (London)
Studies in English Literature (Tokyo)
Sunday Correspondent (London)
Sunday Telegraph (London)
Sunday Times (London)
Sunday Times Colour Supplement
   (London)
Sydney Morning Herald (Sydney)
Sydney Studies in English (Sydney)
Tablet (London)
Tatler (London)
Teacher (London)
Teachers' World (London)
Temenos (Dulverton, Somerset)
Tempo (London)
Texas Arts Journal (Dallas, Tex.)
Texas Quarterly (Austin, Tex.)
Thames Poetry (Harrow,
   Middlesex)
Theatre Quarterly (London)
Theoria (Pietermaritzburg, South
   Africa)
Thought (Bronx, New York)
Threepenny Review (Berkeley,
   Calif.)
Time (New York)
Time and Tide (London)
Time Out (London)
Times (London)

Times Educational Supplement (London)
Times Higher Education Supplement (London)
Times Literary Supplement (London)
Today (London)
Tomorrow (Bedfont, Middlesex)
Transatlantic Review (London and New York)
Tri-Quarterly (Evanston, Ill.)
Tribune (London)
Tulsa Home and Garden (Tulsa, Okla.)
Twentieth Century Literature (Hempstead, N.Y.)
Two Cities (Paris)
Twórczość (Warsaw)
UNISA English Studies (Pretoria)
Universe (Manchester)
Use of English (St. Albans, Herts.)
Virginia Quarterly Review (Charlottesville, Va.)
Vogue (London)
Voice of Youth Advocates (Metuchen, N.J.)
Voices (Vinalhaven, Me.)
Weekend Financial Times (London)
Weekend Telegraph (London)
West Coast Review (Burnaby, B.C.)
Western Daily Press (Bristol)
Wilson Library Bulletin (New York)
Windless Orchard (Fort Wayne, Ind.)
Workshop (London)
World and I (Washington, D.C.)
World Literature Today (Norman, Okla.)
Yearbook of English Studies (London)
Yorkshire Post (Leeds)
Your Environment (London)

A. BOOKS, PAMPHLETS AND BROADSIDES BY TED HUGHES

The descriptions in this book are intended to follow conventions as given by Philip Gaskell in *A New Introduction to Bibliography* (Oxford University Press, 1972). While we have adopted a degressive approach to the descriptions in Section B, the conventions used there are for the most part the same; the differences will be explained at the beginning of Section B.

Although we have made every attempt to avoid ambiguity, some assumptions should nevertheless be pointed out.

Reference notation
The numbering of items in the first two sections of the bibliography follows the format 'A[B]x.y.z'. A [or B] stands for the section; x is the number of the specific work, which is ordered chronologically; y is a letter indicating the edition, also ordered chronologically. The number z is used in special cases where a distinction below the edition level is useful—for instance, reprints of a work in a different format, or a slightly altered printing of an English edition intended for sale in America. The precise meaning of this last field of the item number, when it is used, is therefore somewhat flexible, but the body of the entry will make clear the item's bibliographical status. We strictly differentiate between the terms 'edition' and 'printing'; the term 'state' here denotes any variation within a printing.

Title page transcription
Words not appearing on the title page are set apart by square brackets. Such a note referring to type style, borders, or similar special features

1

applies to *all* title page lines following the note, unless a later note specifies otherwise. For instance, '[freehand lettered; within a ruled border]' means that the entire title consists of a design reproduced from a hand-drawn original, and is contained within the border; this assumption is 'undone' by a later note such as '[type]' or '[outside the border]'. 'Flush to left [or right]' means that the left [or right] margin is straight while the other has been left ragged, and it has not been indented. 'Flush *at* left [or right]' means the margin is straight, but has been indented with respect to the full type measure. No attempt is made to show the differences among sizes of type, even different sizes used on the same line, except to distinguish between large and small caps within a line. Rules go the full type measure of the page unless a measurement is given.

If no separate title page is present, the transcription is taken from the front cover and the fact noted.

Collation and pagination

We have used parentheses to indicate interpolations or extrapolations in collation and pagination; by contrast, square brackets indicate that we have supplied the entire numbering scheme in the absence of any printed numbers in the book. Unnumbered pages within the main run of the text (i.e., that block noted in the collation as 'text') are not indicated thus in the formula, but are listed at the end of the section. Verso title material, if bibliographically important, is transcribed in quasi-facsimile. Elisions are indicated by the sign '[...]'. The number of illustrations includes the frontispiece, if any, but not cover or dust-wrapper illustrations.

The term 'printing code' refers to the string of numbers printed by some publishers on either the verso title or the last page of text to indicate the year of a particular printing. The number on one end is generally the number of the printing; on the other end are the last two digits of the year date. More recently it is common to give the number of the printing only, this being the lesser of the two numbers on either end of the string. We quote the code here as the two numbers separated by a dash, ignoring the numbers between.

Binding

All books are sewn in signatures unless otherwise described. No attempt has been made to distinguish various types of binding cloth in a consistent manner; however, we use the term 'coated cloth' to denote a cloth which has been treated with a material to give it a smooth, glossy finish suitable for receiving illustrations. We have made no attempt to distinguish between genuine gilt and imitation gold foil; likewise, 'silver' denotes a colour not a material. Lettering in colours other than gold and silver is in non-reflective pigments unless foil is specified. Spine lettering always reads down, and variations of type size within lines are not noted, as with the title page. In this section, and in all others except the title page transcription, we have supplied quotation marks when quoting material from the book; in no case are these present in the original.

Dust-wrapper

In so far as possible, quasi-facsimile transcription is used for the front of dust-wrappers, though the style of justification is not noted; lettering on the spines is recorded in the same way as that on the books themselves. Prices, when printed on the wrapper, may be assumed to be the same as the first-mentioned price in the section on publication data. In some cases the printed price will be higher, and though one may generally assume that such dust-wrappers constitute later states, we have made no systematic investigation of these changes. The paper used in the dust-wrapper is described using the same conventions given below.

Text paper

We make no attempt to distinguish among paper colours, textures, or finishes unless they are particularly pronounced. No designation means the item is printed on one of the variety of anonymous, machine-made, unmarked woves used in most modern books. The term 'laid', when used in quotes, refers to a machine-made paper with artificial chain lines.

Page and watermark measurements are given with the vertical dimension first. As a rule, various copies of the same book show variations of two or three millimetres in page size; we give an average dimension. When the range of variation is five millimetres or more, the fact is noted. Measurement of bulk excludes endpapers and binder's leaves.

We distinguish three types of page trim. 'Deckle' is used only with hand-made paper with the deckle still present. 'Trimmed' is applied to machine-made paper to denote the uneven effect imitative of having been opened with a paper-knife. 'Cut' refers to leaf edges cut absolutely straight, including cases in which the edges do not line up with each other.

Endpapers are understood to be white unless otherwise indicated. When a colour is given it means that the endpaper material was made of coloured 'stuff'; the qualifications 'coated' (for colours) and 'printed' (for designs) imply that colour or designs were applied to a white sheet— to the visible side of the paste-down and the facing surface of the free flyleaf unless otherwise mentioned.

Publication data

Publication dates are derived in the majority of cases from the publishers' data as found in printed sources, though many of the publishers were kind enough to send us more exact or corrected information. In most instances when the sources conflict we have taken the publisher's word as the final authority. However, it should be borne in mind that, particularly in America, the official publication date is interpreted very loosely indeed, and many follow the actual release of the book by two months or more. Thus, much as we have striven to provide definitive publication dates, few of those here can be taken as hard and fast.

The problem of determining the number of copies printed has proved even more thorny. Some publishers have kept no records on this, particularly for reprints; others could not take the time to extricate the figures from their files. Some publishers have a policy, observed with varying degrees of consistency, of not revealing this information, and these cases are noted. The figures that publishers do send for trade editions are by necessity approximate; we do not restate this qualification in the entries.

We include information on whatever reprints we were able to trace, but have not tried to be complete. The chief sin we have tried to avoid is allowing misidentification of a reprint as a first impression.

The Rainbow Press

Between 1971 and 1979 much of Hughes' writing was first collected in limited editions printed for the Rainbow Press, a publishing imprint owned by Hughes and his sister Olwyn. While the books were executed by outside printers and binders, Olwyn Hughes determined some of their general design features, such as dimensions, typography, style of binding, and type of paper used. The name of the press is related to an early plan (defeated by vagaries in the availability of materials) to have each smaller-format title bound in a different shade of leather so that the book spines would form a 'rainbow' along the shelf. Several of the books are printed on unmarked, Amatruda mould-made paper, all from a single large lot (containing two or three slightly differing batches) which Olwyn Hughes bought at the inception of the Press. The decorated stock used as endpapers was obtained through Akira Minami, the translator of Hughes' and Plath's works in Japan. Hughes himself made contributions to the design of the books; several are set in Bodoni—his favourite printing type—and a depiction of the goddess Isis which used to hang on his wall provided the front cover design to the *Poems* with Fainlight and Sillitoe.

Olwyn Hughes had a few copies of each title printed up out of series. She had one of these bound up in the edition binding to send to the British Library; most of the others were cheaply bound and distributed to the other copyright libraries. The published copies themselves were often bound up in batches as the need dictated; this practice accounts for the two states of the slipcase of *Eat Crow*, for example.

A1   THE HAWK IN THE RAIN   1957

a. First edition:

The Hawk in the Rain | [five-pointed star, half-shaded] | TED HUGHES | FABER AND FABER | 24 Russell Square | London

(A)⁸B–D⁸ = 32 leaves. Pages (i–ii)(1–8)9–59(60–62), consisting: (i–ii) blank; (1) half-title; (2) blank; (3) title page; (4) *'First published in mcmlvii | by Faber and Faber Limited | 24 Russell Square London W.C.1 | Printed in Great Britain by | Latimer Trend & Co Ltd Plymouth | All rights reserved'*; (5) 'To Sylvia'; (6) blank; (7) acknowledgements and notice that the book was chosen to receive the YM-YWHA's First Publication Award; (8) blank; 9–10 table of contents; 11–59 text; (60–62) blank.

Blue cloth over boards. Spine round, stamped in yellow: 'THE HAWK IN THE RAIN — TED HUGHES   FABER'.

Dust-wrapper yellow 'laid' (chain lines vertical, 2.7 cm.). Front: in upper left, in blue, bounded right and bottom by red rules, 'THE | HAWK | IN | THE | RAIN'; outside this box, vertical blue rules spaced .7 cm. which form background for printing in red: 'poems | by | Ted Hughes'. Back: list of other Faber poetry books, in blue. Spine, in blue and red: 'The Hawk in the Rain   TED HUGHES   [red line from front] Faber'. Issued with a yellow band 2.6 cm. wide, wrapping around the dust-wrapper, printed in red on the front: 'The Choice of the | POETRY BOOK SOCIETY'; on the back: 'THE HAWK IN THE RAIN | by Ted Hughes'; on the rear flap: 'Faber'.

21.9 × 13.8 cm., bulk .4 cm.; all edges cut. Printed letterpress.

CONTENTS: The Hawk in the Rain—The Jaguar—Macaw and Little Miss—The Thought-Fox—The Horses—Famous Poet—Song—Parlour-Piece—Secretary—Soliloquy of a Misanthrope—The Dove Breeder—Billet-Doux—A Modest Proposal—Incompatibilities—September—Fallgrief's Girl-Friends—Two Phases—The Decay of Vanity—Fair Choice—The Conversion of the Reverend Skinner—Complaint—Phaetons—Egg-Head—The Man Seeking Experience Enquires His Way of a Drop of Water—Meeting—Wind—October Dawn—Roarers in a Ring—Vampire—Childbirth—The Hag—Law in the Country of the Cats—Invitation to the Dance—The Casualty—Bayonet Charge—Griefs for Dead Soldiers—Six Young Men—Two Wise Generals—The Ancient Heroes and the Bomber Pilot—The Martyrdom of Bishop Farrar.

Published 13 September 1957 at 10s. 6d.; 2000 copies printed. There were reprints on 1 February 1960, 27 January 1964, and 19 July 1967, each of 1500 copies. The first paperback printing, an offset reduction of the first edition, appeared 22 May 1968 in 7000 copies. Paperback reprints were done in 1970 (7000 copies); 1972 (two printings, 2000 and 8000 copies); 1976 (8000 copies); 1979 (8000 copies); etc. All reprints we have seen are so noted on the verso title. This typesetting was still in use in 1993.

Hughes dedicated his first book to Sylvia Plath, whom he had married in June 1956. In a letter postmarked 24 May 1957 Plath wrote: 'We were stunned this week to get the proofs of Ted's book, not from Harper's [who had first accepted the manuscript], but from Faber & Faber, one week after they'd accepted it! We've gone through and through it with a little, but incomplete, handbook page on proofreading marks and put in endless commas. Ted has made some alterations, which I've limited. He would rewrite a poem to eternity and stop the presses.' (*Letters Home*, p. 313).

Berthold Wolpe designed the dust-wrapper.

See the note to item A1b for further information.

b. First American edition:

[double-page title; left:] [publisher's torch symbol] | HARPER & BROTHERS PUBLISHERS NEW YORK [right:] TED HUGHES | [script] *The Hawk in the Rain*

$[1–2]^{16}$ = 32 leaves. Pages (i–viii)ix–x(xi–xii)1–52, consisting: (i) half-title; (ii–iii) title spread; (iv) 'THE HAWK IN THE RAIN | Copyright © 1956, 1957, by Ted Hughes | Printed in the United States of America | [...] | First Edition | H–G | [acknowledgements]'; (v) 'TO SYLVIA'; (vi) blank; (vii) notice that the book was chosen to receive the YM-YWHA's First Publication Award; (viii) blank; ix–x table of contents; (xi) half-title; (xii) blank; 1–52 text.

Black, coated cloth over boards. Front: at lower right, stamped in gold, a double circle enclosing a torch and the letters 'HB'. Spine flat, stamped in gold: 'THE HAWK IN THE RAIN   TED HUGHES   HARPER'.

Dust-wrapper yellow, printed in dull greyish-blue. Front: paint-spatter design on upper two-thirds, signed 'ceh' (Caroline Harris); lower third: '[in script] *the hawk in the rain* | [regular type] TED HUGHES'; in lower left, 'Chosen by Marianne Moore, | W. H. Auden, and Stephen Spender | to receive the Poetry Center's | First Publication Award.' Spine: '*the hawk in the rain* HUGHES [typography as on front of dust-wrapper] Harper'. Back blank.

19.0 × 13.1 cm., bulk .55 cm.; fore-edge trimmed, top and bottom cut. Printed letterpress.

The contents are the same as in the English edition, but with the order changed except for the first poem and the last two.

Published 18 September 1957 at $2.75; 750 copies printed. A second printing of 750 copies was done in September (probably issued in October). These copies lack the 'First Edition' notice on the verso title and have the printing code 'I–G' (September 1957). A third printing, also of 750 copies, lacks both the first edition notice and the printing code, and collates $(1-4)^8$. The change in imposition was probably made because the bulky gatherings in the earlier copies tend to pull out of the casing. Around 2900 copies of this edition had been sold by 1965, when the book went out of print in the United States.

The Hawk in the Rain won the First Publication Award in a contest sponsored in early 1956 by the Young Men's and Young Women's Hebrew Association of New York; the 287 entries were judged by W. H. Auden, Marianne Moore, and Stephen Spender. Sylvia Plath typed the manuscript and persuaded Hughes to submit it. On 24 February 1957 a telegram notified the Hugheses that it had won; the prize was immediate publication by Harper, with the opportunity to negotiate independently with a British publisher. Faber accepted the manuscript around 10 May, and returned proofs in about a week. Harper's proofs arrived in early June, and it was apparently some time between these two points that the decision was made to rearrange the order of the poems. Hughes himself cannot remember now why the order was changed, but apparently he did not ask Faber to follow the new order themselves.

The University of Southern California's copy of the American first printing has '8/27/57' pencilled on the front fly; it is possible that bound copies were in circulation by this time.

REVIEWS: *Birmingham Post*, 26 Nov. 1957 (Sir Ifor Evans); *Booklist*, 15 Oct. 1957; *Books and Bookmen*, Nov. 1957 (J. C. Hall); *Church Times*, 28 Mar. 1958; *Critical Quarterly*, Summer 1960 (Alun Jones); *Daily Telegraph*, 4 Oct. 1957 (Kenneth Young); *Delta*, Spring 1958 (W. I. Carr); *Encounter*, Nov. 1957 (Graham Hough); *English*, Spring 1958 (Howard Sergeant); *Gemini* 3, 1957 (Roger Hubank); *Halifax Courier*, 6 Dec. 1957; *Irish Times*, 14 Sept. 1957 (Austin Clarke); *Isis*, 23 Oct. 1957 (Judith Spink); *Kirkus*, 15 July 1957; *Library Journal*, 1 Dec. 1957; *Listen*, Spring 1958 (Alan Brownjohn); *Listener*, 23 Jan. 1958; *London Magazine*, Jan. 1958 (Roy Fuller); *Manchester Guardian*, 4 Oct. 1957 (Robin Skelton); *New Statesman*, 28 Sept. 1957 (Edwin Muir); *New York Times*, 6 Oct. 1957 (W. S. Merwin); *Observer*, 6 Oct. 1957 (A. Alvarez); *Oxford Magazine*, 22 May 1958 (G. J. Warnock); *Oxford Times*, 20 Sept. 1957 (E.E.); *Poetry*, June 1958 (Galway Kinnell); *Saturday Review*, 9 Nov. 1957 (Philip Booth); *Spectator*, 11 Oct. 1957 (Robert Conquest); *Sunday Times*, 3 Nov. 1957 (John Press); *Time and Tide*, 19 Oct. 1957 (John Heath-Stubbs); *Times*, 23 Jan. 1958; *Times Literary Supplement*, 18 Oct. 1957; *Voices* 165, Jan.–Apr. 1958; *Yorkshire Post*, 30 Apr. 1959 (Leonard Clark).

A2   PIKE   1959

[Broadside:] [in red] PIKE [in black] A POEM BY TED HUGHES
WOODCUT BY ROBERT BIRMELIN | [woodcut of pikes, green and
black (two blocks), 14.1 × 26.7 cm.] | [the poem, two columns, 44 lines
total] | 150 COPIES PRINTED BY E. & L. BASKIN & RICHARD
WARREN AT THE GEHENNA PRESS NORTHAMPTON
MASSACHUSETTS 1959

In some copies the word 'PIKE' is printed in black.

Paper rough wove, probably handmade ('Shogun'), about 53.1 × 40.7
cm.; right and bottom deckle, top and left cut. Printed letterpress.

Published 1959 at $5.00; 150 copies printed. The price was raised to
$20.00 in 1963. The publisher could supply no further information.

Reproduced on the back of Sotheby's (London) catalogue for the sale of
21–22 July 1983.

A3   LUPERCAL   1960

a.1. First edition:

[outline letters] LUPERCAL | [outline Maltese cross, rotated 45°] |
[solid letters] TED HUGHES | FABER AND FABER | 24 Russell
Square | London

$(A)^8B-D^8 = 32$ leaves. Pages (1–4)5(6)7–63(64), consisting: (1) half-title;
(2) *'by the same author* | ★ | THE HAWK IN THE RAIN'; (3) title page;
(4) *'First published in mcmlx* | *by Faber and Faber Limited* | 24 *Russell Square
London WC*1 | *Printed in Great Britain* | *at the Bowering Press Plymouth* | To
Sylvia | © *Ted Hughes* | 1960'; 5, acknowledgements; (6) blank; 7–8
table of contents; 9–63 text; (64) blank.

Dull violet cloth over boards. Spine flat, stamped in gold: [outline
letters] 'LUPERCAL [outline Maltese cross, unrotated] [solid letters]
TED HUGHES FABER'.

Dust-wrapper pale green 'laid' (chain lines horizontal, 2.75 cm.). Front:
right 3 cm. separated from rest by vertical red rule; in this space
'● TED ● HUGHES ●' [reading up, circles in red]; to left of rule,
'LUPERCAL' printed eight times, one above the other, in outline
letters; one letter in each line printed solid red to spell title diagonally
down the front. Spine: '● LUPERCAL ● TED HUGHES ● Faber'
[title in outline, circles in red]. Back: list of Faber poets.

21.6 × 13.9 cm., bulk .5 cm.; all edges cut. Printed letterpress.

CONTENTS: Things Present—Everyman's Odyssey—Mayday on Holderness—February—Crow Hill—A Woman Unconscious—Strawberry Hill—Dick Straightup—Fourth of July—A Dream of Horses—Esther's Tomcat—Historian—Pennines in April—Hawk Roosting—Nicholas Ferrer—To Paint a Water Lily—Urn Burial—Of Cats—Fire-Eater—Acrobats—The Good Life—The Bull Moses—Cat and Mouse—View of a Pig—The Retired Colonel—The Voyage—Relic—Wilfred Owen's Photographs—An Otter—Witches—November—The Perfect Forms—Thrushes—Singers—Bullfrog—Crag Jack's Apostasy—Pike—Snowdrop—Sunstroke—Cleopatra to the Asp—Lupercalia.

Published 18 March 1960 at 12s. 6d.; 2250 copies printed. The second printing was exported to the United States (see next entry). English reprints were as follows: June 1960 (1500 copies); 1961 (1500 copies); 1965 (1000 copies); 1967 (1500 copies); and 1971 (1500 copies). The first paperback printing, an offset reduction of the first edition, was published on 6 May 1970 in 6000 copies; there were paperback reprints in 1971 (8000 copies), 1973 (8000 copies), and 1976 (6000 copies). All of the English reprints show small revisions in the acknowledgements (e.g. the insertion of "(under the title 'Tomcat')" in line 12, and the deletion of the page number); all of the English reprints are identified on the verso title. By the seventh printing, probably in the late 1980s, Faber had redesigned the title page and covers to its new standard double-rule frame format, but the poems remain in their original setting.

Hughes received his six author's copies of the book on 23 February 1960, though official publication was 24 days later. The dust-wrapper was originally planned to be of blue paper; it was designed by Berthold Wolpe. Sylvia Plath wrote that 'the red on the jacket and the purple on the cover are a bit of a clash to my morbidly sensitive eye, but looking at the book without the jacket, it is a handsome affair.' (*Letters Home*, p. 368).

a.2. First printing for America:

[outline letters] LUPERCAL | [outline Maltese cross, rotated 45°] | [solid letters] TED HUGHES | HARPER & BROTHERS | *Publishers* | New York

Collation same as in the first English printing, except: (4) 'LUPERCAL | copyright © 1960 by Ted Hughes | *Printed in Great Britain*'.

Binding same as first English printing, except 'FABER' on spine replaced by '*Harper*'.

Dust-wrapper same as first English printing, except:
1. on spine, in place of 'Faber', is 'Harper'
2. back blank

3. front flap blurb omits 'by a young English poet'
4. back flap carries excerpts from American reviews.

Paper same as first English printing.

CONTENTS same as first English printing except for acknowledgements (see above).

Published 3 August 1960 at $3.00; 750 copies printed.

Some copies with the American title page deviate from the above in the following respects: the *'Harper'* on the spine is replaced by 'HARPER'; the paper is whiter and bulks .4 cm.; and page 5 is unnumbered as in the later English printings. These are almost certainly copies of a second printing sent to America, though neither Harper nor Faber could verify this. About 1300 copies of this edition had been sold in America by 1965, when the book went out of print in the United States.

REVIEWS: *Atlantic*, Nov. 1961 (Peter Davison); *Audience*, Summer 1960; *Booklist*, 15 Nov. 1960; *Christian Science Monitor*, 25 Aug. 1960 (John Holmes); *Critical Quarterly*, Summer 1960 (Alun Jones); *Daily Telegraph*, 14 Apr. 1960 (Kenneth Young); *Delta*, Winter 1961 (J. M. Newton); *English*, Autumn 1960 (Ralph Lawrence); *Essence*, Winter 1960; *Granta*, 30 Apr. 1960; *Guardian*, 18 Mar. 1960 (Robin Skelton); *Halifax Courier*, 8 Mar. 1960; *Harper's*, Sept. 1960 (Stanley Kunitz); *Hudson Review*, Winter 1960 (John Thompson); *Irish Times*, 9 Apr. 1960 (Austin Clarke); *Isis*, 11 May 1960 (Greysteil Ruthven); *Kirkus*, 1 June 1960; *Library Journal*, Aug. 1960 (B. A. Robie); *Listener*, 28 July 1960 (Graham Hough); *New Statesman*, 9 Apr. 1960 (Donald Hall); *New York Herald Tribune*, 22 Jan. 1961 (Paul Engle); *New York Times*, 14 Aug. 1960 (Philip Booth); *Observer*, 27 Mar. 1960 (A. Alvarez); *Oxford Times*, 15 Apr. 1960 (E.E.); *Partisan Review*, Jan./Feb. 1961 (Kenneth Koch); *Poetry*, June 1961 (Thom Gunn); *Poetry Dial*, Winter 1961; *Poetry Review*, July 1960 (Robert Armstrong); *Prairie Schooner*, Fall 1962; *Sewanee Review*, Spring 1962 (E. Lucas Myers); *Spectator*, 22 Apr. 1960 (Norman MacCaig); *Sunday Times*, 3 Apr. 1960 (John Press); *Time and Tide*, 14 May 1960; *Times*, 25 Aug. 1960; *Times Literary Supplement*, 15 Apr. 1960; *Tomorrow*, 4, 1960 (Clive Jordan); *Twentieth Century*, Nov. 1960 (Christopher Williams); *Virginia Quarterly*, Winter 1961; *Voices* 174, Jan.–Apr. 1961; *Yorkshire Post*, 24 Mar. 1960 (Leonard Clark).

A4   MEET MY FOLKS!   1961

a. First edition:

Meet My Folks! | *by* | TED HUGHES | *illustrated by* | GEORGE ADAMSON | FABER AND FABER | 24 Russell Square | London

$(A)^8B^8C^6 = 22$ leaves. Pages (1–10)11(12)13–42(43–44), consisting: (1–2) blank; (3) half-title; (4) other books by Hughes (*Hawk in the Rain* and *Lupercal*); (5) title page; (6) '*First published in mcmlxi | by Faber and Faber Limited | 24 Russell Square London W.C.1 | Printed in Great Britain by | Latimer Trend & Co Ltd Plymouth | All rights reserved |* ©1961 *by Ted Hughes*'; (7) 'For | FRIEDA REBECCA'; (8) blank; (9) table of contents, headed 'Contents | [half-shaded star]'; (10) blank; 11, introductory verse ('I've heard so much about other folks' folks [...]'); (12) drawing; 13–42 text; (43–44) blank. Text pages 15, 16, 19, 20, 23, 24, 27, 28, 31, 32, 35, 36, 39, 40 unnumbered. Eight illustrations, line cuts.

Paper over boards; background yellow, printed in blue and red. Front: picture of people peering out of a door, signed 'Adamson'; freehand lettering: 'meet | my folks! | TED HUGHES'. Spine flat, lettered as on front 'meet my folks! TED HUGHES FABER ['FABER' in light yellow]'. Back: picture from p. (16) of text, blue on red, signed as on front.

Dust-wrapper front and spine same design as cover; on back, blue on white, list of other Faber children's verse.

20.9 × 15.4 cm., bulk .3 cm.; all edges cut. Printed letterpress.

CONTENTS: I've heard so much about other folks' folks—My Sister Jane—My Grandpa—Grandma—My Brother Bert—My Aunt—My Uncle Dan—My Mother—My Father.

Published 7 April 1961 at 10s. 6d.; 5000 copies printed. A second printing of 3145 copies was done offset in 1967. It is identified on the verso title, and collates $[1–3]^8$, with the four outer leaves serving as paste-downs and free endpapers. The third and fourth printings were issued in 1970 (4000 copies) and 1974 (5000 copies); each is identified on the verso title.

Two pages of the first printing come in more than one state:

Title page A. Space between 'GEORGE ADAMSON' and 'FABER AND FABER' is 10.4 cm.
B. Space is 9.6 cm.
Page 33 A. Bearing signature mark 'C'; star is point up.
B. Lacking signature mark; star is point down.

The compilers have seen copies containing three of the four possible combinations of these states, and we consider it likely that the fourth (state B of each page) also exists. The evidence points to the use of duplicate plates, with no priority assignable, though Faber was not able to verify this. There is no reason to prefer one version of the title over the other, though it is true that state B of page 33 is inconsistent both with Faber's house style and with the format of the rest of the book. However, later printings have title B, with page 33 a combination of states A and B (no signature mark, but star point *up*); this fact discourages interpretation of the evidence assuming an orderly and sequential alteration of a single set of plates. Page 33 for the reprints was most likely derived from state A.

The book is dedicated to the Hugheses' first child, who was born on 1 April 1960.

These poems were set to music by Gordon Crosse and published in this form in 1965 (see item I1).

b. First American edition (1973):

[title within a ruled rectangle] MEET MY FOLKS | by Ted Hughes | *illustrated by Mila Lazarevich* | THE BOBBS-MERRILL COMPANY, INC. | *Indianapolis   New York*

[1–3]^8 = 24 leaves; outer leaves form paste-downs and free endpapers both front and back. Pages [1–48], consisting: [1–2] paste-down; [3–4] free endpaper; [5] title page; [6] '*For Frieda Rebecca* | [notes regarding contents of this and 1961 edition] | [...] | POEMS COPYRIGHT © 1961, 1973 BY TED HUGHES | ILLUSTRATIONS COPYRIGHT © 1973 BY MILA LAZAREVICH | TYPE DESIGN BY JACK JAGET | PRINTED IN THE UNITED STATES OF AMERICA | ALL RIGHTS RESERVED | ISBN 0-672-51797-3 | [...] | [printing code (0–1)]'; [7] introductory verse ('I've heard so much about other folks' folks [...]') and table of contents; [8] illustration; [9–43] text; [44] capsule biographies of author and artist; [45–46] free endpaper; [47–48] paste-down. Eighteen illustrations, line cuts.

Coated yellow-brown cloth over boards. Front, stamped in blue foil: 'MEET MY FOLKS'. Spine flat, stamped in blue foil: 'HUGHES/ LAZAREVICH   MEET MY FOLKS   BM ['BM' reading across spine] Bobbs-Merrill'. Gatherings are side-stitched. Endpapers printed with formalized flower pattern.

Dust-wrapper: front, illustration of people behind a white fence with sunflowers and lion; blue border continues across spine to back; printed 'MEET MY FOLKS | by TED HUGHES | *illustrated by* MILA LAZAREVICH'. Spine printed in black, same as book spine. Back plain blue; at lower left, '51797'.

19.0 × 22.8 cm., bulk .35 cm.; all edges cut. Printed offset.

CONTENTS same as the first edition except: 'My Grandpa' and 'Grandma' are dropped; 'My Aunt' is retitled 'My Aunt Dora'; 'My Uncle Mick', 'My Aunt Flo', 'My Granny', and 'My Own True Family' have been added. All the illustrations are new.

Published 13 June 1973 at $4.50; 4000 copies printed.

c. First paperback edition (1977):

TED HUGHES | MEET MY | FOLKS! | *Illustrated by George Adamson* | [puffin logo in oval frame] | PUFFIN BOOKS | *in association with Faber and Faber*

'Perfect-bound', pages (1–12)13–14(15–16)17–19(20–22)23–24(25–26)27–28(29–30)31–32(33–34)35–36(37–38)39–40(41–42)43–44(45–46) 47–48(49–50)51–52(53–54)55–57(58–60)61(62–64), consisting: (1) 'PUFFIN BOOKS | *Editor: Kaye Webb* | MEET MY FOLKS! | [two lines of verse and a prose synopsis]'; (2) blank; (3) title page; (4) '[...] | First published by Faber and Faber 1961 | Published in Puffin Books 1977 | [short rule] | Text copyright © Ted Hughes, 1961, 1977 | Illustrations facing pp. 17, 31, 47 and 61 copyright © George Adamson, 1977 | All other illustrations copyright © Faber and Faber, 1961 | [short rule] | Made and printed in Great Britain | by Richard Clay (The Chaucer Press) Ltd | Bungay, Suffolk | Set in Monotype Bembo | [...]'; (5) 'For | FRIEDA REBECCA'; (6) blank; (7) table of contents; (8) blank; (9) introductory verse ('I've heard so much about other folks' folks [...]'); (10) blank; (11)–(62) illustrations and text; (63) picture of puffin carrying a letter, and ad for the Puffin Club; (64) blank. Each poem begins on a recto, facing a drawing; on each preceding recto is a detail from the larger drawing enclosed in an oval frame.

Wrappers, printed in colour with Adamson illustration of characters in the poems, on a dull orange background. Printed with the picture, on front cover: '[upper left, puffin logo as on title, yellow background] | meet | my folks! [lettering in yellow from the front cover of the Faber edition, reduced and with exclamation point re-done] | [lower left, in white] TED HUGHES | Illustrated by George Adamson'. Spine: '[in white:] Ted Hughes [in yellow:] Meet My Folks! [in black:] ISBN 0 14 03.0865 2 [puffin logo, black and white]'. Back: '[in white:] A Puffin Book | Published by Penguin Books | [in black] United Kingdom 30p | Canada $1.50 | [in yellow:] Here is a wildly improbable family, described | in twelve fantastic, extravagant, funny poems, | by the author of 'The Iron Man' and 'How | the Whale Became'. | [in black, lower right] ISBN 0 14 | 03.0865 2'.

18.1 × 11.1 cm., bulk .4 cm.; all edges cut. Printed offset.

CONTENTS the same as the first edition, with the addition of 'My Fairy Godmother', 'My Other Granny' ['My Granny' in A4b], 'My Uncle Mick', and 'My Own True Family', with their respective illustrations.

Published August 1977 at 30p.; 32,000 copies printed. There was a reprint of 12,000 copies in November 1980.

d. Second paperback edition (1987):

[within a double-rule frame] MEET | MY | FOLKS! | [rule, 2.6 cm.] | *Ted Hughes* | [below frame] ff | *faber and faber* | LONDON · BOSTON

32 leaves, 'perfect-bound'. Pages (1–10)11–61(62–64), consisting: (1–2) blank; (3) half–title; (4) 'Also by Ted Hughes | [26 titles]'; (5) title page; (6) 'First published in 1961 | by Faber and Faber Limited | 3 Queen Square London WC1N 3AU | Reprinted 1967, 1970 | This revised edition first published as a Faber Paperback in 1987 | Phototypeset by Wilmaset, Birkenhead, Wirral | Printed in Great Britain by | Redwood Burn Ltd, Trowbridge, Wiltshire | All rights reserved | Text copyright © Ted Hughes 1961, 1977, 1987 | Illustrations copyright © George Adamson, 1961, 1977, 1987 | [Net Book Agreement note, CIP data, and ISBN]'; (7) 'for | FRIEDA REBECCA'; (8) blank; (9) table of contents; (10) blank; 11, introductory verse ('I've heard so much about other folks' folks [...]'); 12, drawing; 13–61 text; (62–64) blank. Text pages 15, 23, 27, 31, 35, 39, 43, 47, 51, 55, 59 unnumbered.

Wrappers, printed in blue, with overall 'ff' pattern in dark purple halftone; text printed on white panels. Front: the frame and its enclosed text, same setting as title page; coloured illustration from 'My Father' overlapping right side of frame. Spine: '[reading across, thin-thick rule] [reading down] MEET MY FOLKS!   *Ted Hughes* [reading across] ff | [thick-thin rule]'. Back: '[within double-rule frame] ff | *faber and faber* | [blurb] | UK £2.95 net | US $6.95 | AUST. $10.95 (recommended) | CANADA $7.95 | [bar code]'.

19.8 × 12.6 cm., bulk .4 cm.; all edges cut. Printed offset.

CONTENTS same as A4c, with the addition of 'My Aunt Flo' and its illustration.

Published April 1987 at £2.95; number of copies undetermined.

REVIEWS: *Christian Science Monitor*, 7 Nov. 1973; *Kirkus*, 1 Aug. 1973; *Library Journal*, 15 Sept. 1973; *Publishers Weekly*, 22 Oct. 1973; *Saturday Review*, 4 Dec. 1973 (William Cole); *Tablet*, Oct. 1961 (Terence M. Cluderay); *Times Educational Supplement*, 22 Jan. 1988; *Times Literary Supplement*, 19 May 1961.

A5   SELECTED POEMS WITH THOM GUNN   1962

SELECTED POEMS | by | THOM GUNN | and | TED HUGHES | FABER AND FABER | 24 Russell Square | London

32 leaves, 'perfect-bound'. Pages (1–6)7–64, consisting: (1) half-title; (2) list of books by the same authors (three apiece); (3) title page; (4) *'First*

published in this edition mcmlxii | by Faber and Faber Limited | 24 Russell Square London W.C.1 | Printed in Great Britain by | R. MacLehose and Company Limited | All rights reserved | [Net Book Agreement note] | © This selection Faber and Faber Ltd., 1962'; (5–6) table of contents; 7–64 text.

Wrappers, printed as follows on a light green background. Front cover: at left edge, reading up in red, 'SELECTED'; across top, in red, 'POEMS'; in centre of front cover, in black, 'Thom | Gunn | & | Ted | Hughes | [in white on black panel] FABER'; at fore-edge, a 1.5 cm. black strip with white lettering reading down: 'FABER paper covered EDITIONS'. Rear cover: continuation (from inside back cover) of a list of Faber Paper Covered Editions in black; at fore-edge, a 1.5 cm. black strip with white lettering reading up: 'FABER paper covered EDITIONS'. Spine: 'THOM GUNN [red dot] TED HUGHES [red dot] [in red:] SELECTED POEMS [in white on black panel:] FABER'.

18.4 × 12.0 cm., bulk .6 cm.; all edges cut. Printed letterpress.

CONTENTS [poems by Hughes start on page 34, following the section by Gunn]: Song—The Thought-Fox—Wind—Macaw and Little Miss—Soliloquy of a Misanthrope—Six Young Men—The Dove-Breeder—The Jaguar—The Hag—Roarers in a Ring—The Horses—The Martyrdom of Bishop Farrar—October Dawn—Meeting—Witches—Crow Hill—Thrushes—Cleopatra to the Asp—An Otter—The Retired Colonel—November—Relic—The Good Life—Snowdrop.

Published 18 May 1962 at 5s.; 7500 copies printed. There were reprints on 10 July 1963 (6000 copies), 19 November 1964 (8000 copies), 12 December 1966 (8000 copies), 18 March 1968 (12,000 copies), 14 July 1972 (15,000 copies), and 19 October 1973 (25,000 copies), according to information supplied by Faber. In a 1974 printing, however, the verso title lists the reprints as 1963, 1965, 1967, 1968, 1971, 1972 (twice), and 1974. By this time the wrappers are white, with printing in black, red, and green.

REVIEW: *Agenda*, Feb./Mar. 1962 (Peter Dale).

A6 HOW THE WHALE BECAME 1963

a. First edition:

How the Whale Became | [rule, broken in middle by oval ornament] | TED HUGHES | *illustrated by* | GEORGE ADAMSON | FABER AND FABER | 24 Russell Square | London

(A)⁸B–D⁸E⁴ = 36 leaves. Pages (1–4)5(6)7–72, consisting: (1) half-title, 'How the Whale Became | FOR | FRIEDA AND NICHOLAS'; (2) list of four other books by Hughes; (3) title page; (4) '*First published in mcmlxiii* | *by Faber and Faber Limited* | *24 Russell Square London W.C.1* | *Printed in Great Britain by* | *Latimer, Trend & Co Ltd Plymouth* | *All rights reserved* | © *Ted Hughes* | *1963*'; 5, table of contents; (6) lion drawing; 7, introduction ('Long['L' three lines high] ago when the world was brand new [...]'); 8–72 text. Text pages 17, 29, 38, 52, 63 unnumbered. Six illustrations, line cuts.

Bicolour cloth (dark blue and light blue threads) over boards. Spine flat, stamped in gold: 'How the Whale Became ★ TED HUGHES ★ Faber'.

Dust-wrapper: front: trees in light orange-brown, signed 'Adamson', framing a blue space containing freehand lettering in white and black: 'How *the* | Whale *Became* | *and other stories by* | TED | HUGHES | *Drawings by George Adamson*'. Spine, illustration continued from front, lettered as on front: 'How *the* Whale *Became* TED HUGHES FABER'. Back: blurbs for other Faber children's books.

20.9 × 15.3 cm., bulk .43 cm.; all edges cut. Printed letterpress.

CONTENTS: Why the Owl Behaves as it Does—How the Whale Became–How the Fox Came to be where it is—How the Polar Bear Became—How the Hyena Became—How the Tortoise Became—How the Bee Became—How the Cat Became—How the Donkey Became—How the Hare Became—How the Elephant Became.

Published 8 November 1963 at 13s. 6d.; 5000 copies printed. Reprints in 1972 (2500 copies) and 1974 (4000 copies) are identified on the verso title.

b. First American edition (1964):

Ted Hughes | [swelled rule, 6.35 cm.] | [outline letters] HOW THE | [drawing of a whale] | [solid letters] WHALE | BECAME | *Drawings by Rick Schreiter* | [swelled rule, 6.35 cm.] | *Atheneum New York 1964*

[1–2]^{16}[3]^8[4]^{16} = 56 leaves. Pages (i–x)(1–2)3–100(101–102), consisting: (i) half-title, 'How *the Whale Became* | [swelled rule, 10.1 cm.]'; (ii) blank; (iii) title page; (iv) '*Copyright* © *1963 by Ted Hughes* | *All rights reserved* | [...] | *Published simultaneously in Canada by McClelland & Stewart Ltd* | *Manufactured in the United States of America* | *Composition by Clarke & Way, New York* | *Printed by The Murray Printing Company, Forge Village, Massachusetts* | *Bound by H. Wolff, New York* | *Designed by Harry Ford* | *First American Edition*'; (v) '*For Frieda and Nicholas* | [swelled rule, 6.3 cm.]'; (vi) blank; (vii) table of contents; (viii) blank; (ix) half-title, as above; (x) Schreiter whale drawing; (1) introduction ('Long ['L' two lines high] ago when the world was brand new [...]'); (2) Schreiter owl drawing; 3–100 text; (101) blank; (102) capsule biography of Hughes. Text pages 14, 21, 22, 31, 32, 39, 40, 46, 57, 58, 66, 73, 74, 83, 84, 91, 92 unnumbered. Twelve illustrations, black and white halftone.

Very dark-blue cloth over boards. Front blind-stamped with whale design as on title page. Spine round, stamped in gold: '*Ted Hughes* HOW THE WHALE BECAME *Atheneum*'. Endpapers yellow. Some copies of the first printing were bound in light blue-green cloth; the compilers could establish no priority.

Dust-wrapper: brick-red line drawing, extending around from front to back, of animals riding on a whale's back. Front, at top, yellow lettering on red rectangle: '*Ted Hughes* | [swelled rule] | [outline letters] HOW | THE | WHALE | BECAME'. Spine red, lettered in yellow as on book spine.

23.5 × 14.6 cm., bulk .8 cm.; all edges cut. Printed offset.

CONTENTS the same as the first edition.

Published 8 September 1964 at $3.50; 7500 copies were printed in June. A second printing of 3000 copies was ordered in March 1966 and was probably published in June; a third printing of 5000 copies was ordered in September 1967 and was probably published in December. The reprints bear changed dates on the title page and reprint notices on the verso title. Jean Karl of Atheneum states that about 12,360 copies of the book were sold, and that the unbound remainder of the third printing was probably destroyed when sales dropped off.

c. First paperback edition (1971):

[flush to left] Ted Hughes | How the Whale Became | and Other Stories | *Illustrated by George Adamson* | Penguin Books

'Perfect-bound', pages (1–8)9–107(108–112), consisting: (1) 'PUFFIN BOOKS | Editor: Kaye Webb | HOW THE WHALE BECAME | [introduction ('Long ago, when the world was brand new [...]') and short blurb]'; (2) blank; (3) title page; (4) 'Penguin Books Ltd, Harmondsworth, | Middlesex, England | [...] | First published by Faber & Faber 1963 | Published in Puffin Books 1971 | [...] | Made and printed in Great Britain by | Cox & Wyman Ltd, | London, Reading and Fakenham | Set in Monotype Bembo | [...]'; (5) 'FOR *Frieda and Nicholas*'; (6) blank; (7) table of contents; (8) drawing of a lion; 9–107 (108) text and illustrations; (109–112) blurbs for other Puffin Books.

Wrappers, printed in colour with illustration of animals in fantastic landscape. Printed with the picture, on front cover: '[upper left corner, puffin logo, black and white on blue ground within white oval; underneath, 'A YOUNG | PUFFIN' in white] How the | Whale Became | and Other Stories | Ted Hughes' [title in yellow freehand letters, author in white sans serif]. Spine: '[in white:] Ted Hughes [in yellow:] How the Whale Became and Other Stories [in black:] 14 030482 7 [puffin logo, black and white]'. Back: 'Published by Penguin Books | For copyright reasons this edition is not for sale in the U.S.A. | [abridged introduction, and price schedule; at lower right, ISBN]'.

Paper plain white, 19.6 × 12.9 cm., bulk .8 cm.; all edges cut. Printed offset.

CONTENTS the same as the first edition.

Published April 1971 at 20p.; the publisher has no record of the number printed. The edition was reprinted May 1976 (15,000 copies), December 1976 (30,000 copies), March 1978 (16,000 copies), April 1979 (18,000 copies), and February 1980 (20,000 copies).

d. First Japanese edition (1980):

First printing not seen.

An English-language text, edited and with notes by Yuichi Midzunoe. Published by the Hokuseido Press, Tokyo. Contains the same text as the first edition, with these stories omitted: How the Fox Came to be where it is—How the Cat Became—How the Hare Became. Also contains four illustrations done in Japan, one an imitation of a drawing by Adamson.

Published 20 October 1980 at 750 yen; 2500 copies printed. There was a reprint of 2500 copies on March 1981. The reprint has two groups of characters, printed side by side in Japanese, just below the first rule on the colophon; the left group contains the numbers 55, 10 and 20, separated by characters; the right group contains the numbers 56, 3 and 25. These numbers refer to the publication dates.

e. Second English paperback edition (1989):

[flush to left] TED HUGHES | *How the Whale Became* | *Illustrated by George Adamson* | [indented] ff | [flush to left] *faber and faber* | LONDON · BOSTON

48 leaves, 'perfect-bound'; pages (i–x)1–84(85–86), consisting: (i–ii) blank; (iii) half-title, flush to left; (iv) *'by the same author* | [28 titles]'; (v) title page; (vi) 'First published in 1963 | by Faber and Faber Limited | 3 Queen Square London WC1N 3AU | Reprinted in 1972 and 1974 | This paperback edition first published in 1989 | Printed in Great Britain by | Richard Clay Ltd, Bungay, Suffolk | All rights reserved | © Ted Hughes, 1963 | [notes on Net Book Agreement and CIP data, and ISBN]'; (vii) '[flush to left] For Frieda and Nicholas'; (viii) blank; (ix) table of contents; (x) illustration of lion; 1–84 text; (85–86) blank.

Wrappers, printed front and back with colour illustration of animals, text on white panels partly behind and partly in front of illustrations. Front: '[in double-rule frame] ff | How the | Whale Became | and Other |

Stories | [rule, 2.4 cm.] | *Ted Hughes* | Illustrated by | George Adamson'. Spine: '[reading across, thin-thick rule] [reading down] How the Whale Became and Other Stories   *Ted Hughes* [reading across] ff | [thick-thin rule]'. Back: '[in double-rule frame] ff | *faber and faber* | [blurb] | UK £1.99 net   Canada $4.95 | [bar code]'.

19.7 × 12.5 cm., bulk .6 cm.; all edges cut. Printed offset.

CONTENTS the same as the first edition.

Published November 1989 (the British Library copy is stamped 27 November) at £1.99; number of copies undetermined.

REVIEWS: *Birmingham Post*, 26 Nov. 1963; *Book Week*, 22 Nov. 1964 (M. S. Libby); *Guardian*, 6 Dec. 1963 (Robert Nye); *Horn Book*, Oct. 1964 (E.L.H.); *Irish Times*, 7 Dec. 1963; *Library Journal*, 15 Oct. 1964 (W. M. Crossley); *Listener*, 21 Nov. 1963 (Elizabeth Brewer); *New Statesman*, 8 Nov. 1963 (Christopher Ricks); *New York Review of Books*, 3 Dec. 1964 (J. A. Smith); *New York Times Book Review*, 8 Nov. 1964 (Gloria Vanderbilt); *School Librarian*, Mar. 1964 (Laurence Adkins); *Sunday Telegraph*, 24 Nov. 1963; *Sunday Times*, 24 Nov. 1963 (Oscar Turnhill).

A7   THE EARTH-OWL AND OTHER   1963
MOON-PEOPLE

THE EARTH-OWL | and other moon-people | by | TED HUGHES | *illustrated by* | R. A. BRANDT | FABER AND FABER | 24 Russell Square | London

(A)⁸B–C⁸ = 24 leaves. Pages (1–4)5(6)7–46(47–48), consisting: (1) half-title, 'The Earth-Owl | and other moon-people | FOR | FRIEDA AND NICHOLAS'; (2) list of four other books by Hughes; (3) title page; (4) '*First published in mcmlxiii | by Faber and Faber Limited | 24 Russell Square London W.C.1 | Printed in Great Britain by | Latimer Trend & Co Ltd Plymouth | All rights reserved | © 1963 by Ted Hughes*'; 5, table of contents; (6) blank; 7–46 text; (47–48) blank. Text pages 8, 12, 14, 21, 22, 26, 30, 32, 36, 38, 42 unnumbered. Eleven illustrations, line cuts.

Blue cloth over boards. Spine flat, stamped in gold: 'The Earth Owl and Other Moon People—TED HUGHES   Faber' ['Faber' reads across spine].

Dust-wrapper cream-coloured 'laid' (chain lines horizontal, 2.75 cm.), marked '*Arnold Signature*' (3.6 × 6.1 cm.), decorated front and back with light brick-red drawing. On front, in black: 'the earth-owl | and other | moon-people | BY TED HUGHES | with drawings by R. A. BRANDT'. Spine, in black and light brick-red: 'THE EARTH-OWL   TED HUGHES FABER'.

Paper plain white, 20.9 × 15.3 cm., bulk .4 cm.; all edges cut. Printed letterpress.

CONTENTS: The Earth-Owl—The Adaptable Mountain Dugong—Moon-Roses—Moon-Cloud Gripe—Moon-Horrors—Music on the Moon—Moon-Nasturtiums—The Armies of the Moon—Moon-Dog-Daisies—Moon-Hops—Cactus-Sickness—Crab-Grass—Tree-Disease—The Burrow Wolf—Moon-Tulips—Foxgloves—Moon-Transport—Moon-Freaks—The Snail of the Moon—Moon-Cabbage—The Silent Eye—The Dracula Vine—A Moon Man-Hunt.

Published 22 November 1963 at 15s.; 3000 copies printed. Reprints were published in 1970 (1500 copies); 1973 (2000 copies); and 1977 (2500 copies); they are identified on the verso title. The second-printing dust-wrapper bears a price of £1.00 or £1.20.

These poems did not appear in the United States until their publication in *Moon-Whales* in 1976.

REVIEWS: *Agenda*, Dec.–Jan. 1963–4 (Anita Auden); *Birmingham Post*, 26 Nov. 1963 (Pauline Smith); *English*, Summer 1964 (Howard Sergeant); *Guardian*, 22 Nov. 1963 (Richard Keel); *Hudson Review*, Autumn 1964 (Ian Hamilton); *Irish Times*, 4 April 1964 (Michael Longley); *New Statesman*, 6 Dec. 1963 (Christopher Ricks); *Observer*, 22 Dec. 1963 (A. Alvarez); *Outposts*, Spring 1964 (Philip Hobsbaum); *Review*, Jan. 1964 (P. Marsh); *Scotsman*, 4 Jan. 1964 (Martin Seymour-Smith); *Spectator*, 27 March 1964 (Elizabeth Jennings); *Teacher*, 24 Jan. 1964 (Ray Sparkes); *Times*, 5 Dec. 1963; *Times Literary Supplement*, 27 Feb. 1964; *Tribune*, 7 Feb. 1964 (Jeremy Robson); *Western Daily Press*, 18 Nov. 1963 (Keith Turner).

A8   NESSIE THE MANNERLESS MONSTER   1964

a. First edition:

[double-page title, freehand lettering integral with black-and-white illustration of the monster and fishes] [left:] NESSIE THE | BY TED HUGHES | PICTURES BY GERALD ROSE [right:] MANNERLESS | MONSTER | FABER AND FABER LIMITED · LONDON. | [standard type] *First published in mcmlxiv by Faber and Faber Limited, 24 Russell Square, London W.C.1. Printed in Great Britain by W. S. Cowell Ltd, Ipswich. Text © 1964 by Ted Hughes.*

[1–4]⁴ = 16 leaves. Pages [1–32], consisting: [1] half-title, 'Nessie | the Mannerless | Monster'; [2–3] title spread; [4–32] text. All pages illustrated in halftone, some in colour.

Paper over boards. Colour illustration of the monster with boats of sightseers, continued across spine to back. Front, freehand lettering in yellows and oranges: 'NESSIE | THE | MANNERLESS | MONSTER | BY TED HUGHES | PICTURES BY GERALD ROSE'. Spine flat, freehand lettered in orange and black: ' · NESSIE THE MANNERLESS MONSTER · HUGHES · FABER'.

Dust-wrapper same design as cover. Later examples of the dust-wrapper bear the price 15s./£0.75.

Paper plain white, 17.9 × 24.8 cm., bulk .3 cm.; all edges cut. Printed offset.

Published 24 April 1964 at 13s. 6d.; 10,000 copies printed. There was a 1973 reprint of 8750 copies, which lack the small type on the title page and bear a reprint notice opposite the last page of type. The dust-wrapper of the latter bears the price £1.40 or £1.60.

*b. First American edition, 1974 (*Nessie the Monster*):*

NESSIE THE MONSTER | by TED HUGHES | illustrated by Jan Pyk | The Bobbs-Merrill Company, Inc. | Indianapolis   New York | [illustration of the monster, two shades of green]

$[1-2]^8 = 16$ leaves. Pages [1–32], consisting: [1] title page; [2] illustration continued from title page, and '[...] | Text first published by Faber and Faber Ltd in Great Britain in 1964 | under the title *Nessie the Mannerless Monster* | Text copyright © 1964 by Ted Hughes | Illustrations copyright © 1974 by Jan Pyk | Printed in the United States of America | All rights reserved | ISBN 0-672-51798-1 | [...] | [printing code (0–1)]'; [3] background note on the Loch Ness Monster ('Loch Ness, a twenty-four-mile-long lake [...]'); [4] illustration of the monster, continued on next page; [5–32] text. Each page illustrated in two shades of green and black, halftone.

Green cloth over boards. Spine flat, stamped in blue: 'NESSIE THE MONSTER Hughes | /Pyk BM ['BM' reading across spine] Bobbs- | Merrill'. Endpapers printed with swirls, two shades of green.

Dust-wrapper printed in blue, two shades of green, and black, lettered in white. Front: illustration of the monster underwater with fishes and kelp (continued across spine to back) lettered: 'NESSIE | THE | MONSTER | by TED HUGHES | illustrated by Jan Pyk'. Spine lettered in white as on book spine.

Paper plain white, 15.3 × 22.8 cm., bulk .3 cm.; all edges cut. Printed offset.

CONTENTS the same as the English edition, with the addition of the background note which was written by an editor at Bobbs-Merrill.

Published 2 January 1974 at $4.95; 5000 copies printed on an October 1973 printing order. A second printing of 2000 copies was ordered in August 1975; reprints bear the printing code '9–1' on the verso title.

c. First paperback edition (1992):

Nessie the | Mannerless Monster | Ted Hughes | *illustrated by Gerald Rose* | [illustration of a bobby directing Nessie] | ff | *faber and faber* | LONDON · BOSTON

32 leaves, 'perfect-bound'. Pages (1–64), consisting: (1) half-title, 'Nessie the Mannerless Monster' | [illustration of Nessie diving]' (2) *'also by Ted Hughes* | [30 titles]'; (3) title page; (4) 'First published in 1964 | by Faber and ·Faber Limited | 3 Queen Square London WC1N 3AU | This paperback edition first published in 1992 | Phototypeset by Parker Typesetting Service, Leicester | Printed in England by Clays Ltd, St Ives plc | All rights reserved | © Ted Hughes, 1964 | Illustrations © Gerald Rose, 1992 | [notes on authorship, Net Book Agreement, and CIP data, and ISBN]'; (5) half-title; (6–63) text and illustrations; (64) blank. Illustrated throughout, black-and-white halftone.

Wrappers with all-over colour illustration; text printed on white panels. Front: '[within double-rule frame] ff | Nessie | the | Mannerless | Monster | [rule, 2.5 cm.] | *Ted Hughes* | Illustrated | by Gerald Rose'. Spine: '[reading across, thin-thick rule] [reading down] Nessie the Mannerless Monster *Ted Hughes* [reading across] ff | [thick-thin rule]'. Back: '[within double-rule frame] ff | *faber and faber* | [blurb] | UK £2.99 net | US $4.95 | Canada $5.99 | [bar code]'.

19.8 × 12.6 cm., bulk .4 cm.; all edges cut. Printed offset.

Gerald Rose provided a new set of illustrations for this edition.

Published April 1992 (the British Library copy is stamped 11 March) at £2.99; number of copies undetermined. A reprint has printing code 2–3 on title verso; the cover is partly redesigned with Hughes' name in red.

REVIEWS: *Book World (Washington Post)*, 19 May 1974; *Booklist*, 1 April 1974; *Christian Science Monitor*, 1 May 1974; *Coventry Evening Telegraph*, 30 April 1964 (Susan Hill); *Guardian*, 10 July 1964 (Robert Nye); *Junior Bookshelf*, July 1964; *Kirkus*, 1 Feb. 1974; *Library Journal*, 15 Sept. 1974; *Listener*, 28 May 1964 (Anthony Thwaite); *New Statesman*, 15 May 1964 (Mary Scrutton); *Sunday Telegraph*, 29 Nov. 1964 (Ian Serraillier); *Teacher*, July 1964, Feb. 1975; *Times Literary Supplement*, 9 July 1964.

A9 THE BURNING OF THE BROTHEL 1966

[flush to left] THE | BURNING | OF | THE | BROTHEL | TED HUGHES

[1]^8; pages [1–16], consisting: [1–2] blank; [3] title page; [4] blank (pronounced print-through from title); [5] blank save for Hughes' signature in copies 1–75; [6] blank; [7–11] poem; [12–14] blank; [15] '[two flowers] *Published by TURRET BOOKS* | *in October 1966. in an edition of 300 copies* | *of which the first 75 are numbered and signed* | *by the author.* © *1966 Ted Hughes.* [two flowers, as above] | [flower, as above] *Designed &* *Printed for Turret Books* | *at the GOLIARD PRESS London.* [flower, as above] | *Number.* [number] *of 300* | *TURRET* [publisher's device, tower with flag bearing white T] *BOOKS* | *5 Kensington Church Walk London W8'*; (16) blank. Text illustrated with five colour cuts of Elizabethan characters.

Sewn into plain heavy white paper wrappers. Five copies were bound in burgundy wrappers.

Dust-wrapper dark blue, lightweight, soft 'laid' paper (chain lines horizontal, 3.5–4.0 cm., some 1.2 cm.). Front lettered as on title. The University of North Carolina reports a copy with a purple dust-wrapper.

Paper: Sheets 1.8, 3.6, and 4.5 are heavy cream-coloured 'laid' (chains vertical, 2.4 cm.) marked '[crown] | *Glastonbury*' (6.1 × 12.3 cm.). Sheet 2.7 is handmade Japanese tissue paper (*ōsu chirigami*) with bits of *kōzo* bark embedded. Overall dimensions 28.8 × 22.7 cm., all edges cut. In some copies sheet 1.8 is of heavy cream-coloured wove, unmarked. Printed letterpress.

Published late October or November 1966 at 30s. for the unsigned copies; the compilers could not determine the original price of the signed copies, or even whether any of the latter were actually offered for sale. There were at least some copies out of series and unnumbered.

A10 RECKLINGS 1966

RECKLINGS | by | TED HUGHES | TURRET | publisher's logo, tower with flag bearing white T] BOOKS

[1–4]^4[5]^6 = 22 leaves. Pages (1–6)7–44, consisting: (1) half-title; (2) blank; (3) title page; (4) '150 signed and numbered copies of this book have been printed. | This is number [number] | Published in 1966 by Turret Books | 5 Kensington Church Walk | London, W8 | © 1966, Ted Hughes | [signature] | Printed by Villiers Publications Ltd | Ingestre Road, London, NW5'; (5) table of contents; (6) blank; 7–44 text.

Bicolour cloth (black and white threads) over boards. Spine round, stamped in gold: 'RECKLINGS   TED HUGHES'. Endpapers yellow-green 'laid' (chain lines horizontal, 2.4 cm.), marked '[crown] | *Glastonbury*' (6.1 × 12.3 cm.).

Dust-wrapper light grey 'laid', marked same as endpapers, printed in brown. Front: '*RECKLINGS* | [swelled rule, 10.1 cm.] | TED HUGHES'. Spine lettered same as book spine.

Paper white 'laid', marked same as endpapers; 23.0 × 15.7 cm., bulk .4 cm.; all edges cut. Printed letterpress.

CONTENTS: On the Slope—Water—Fishing at Dawn—Dully Gumption's Addendum—Guinness—Flanders—Keats—Beech Tree—Toll—Memory—Heatwave—Fallen Eve—The Toughest—Thaw—Plum-Blossom—Public Bar T.V.—As Woman's Weeping—Trees—A Colonial—Don Giovanni—A Match—Small Events—To be a Girl's Diary—Stealing Trout on a May Morning—Humanities—Tutorial—Poltergeist—Last Lines—Logos—The Lake—Unknown Soldier—Bawdry Embraced.

Published January 1967 at £5.6.0.; 150 copies printed.

A11   SCAPEGOATS AND RABIES   1967

[red and black, flush to left] Scapegoats And Rabies a poem in | five parts written by Ted Hughes | & | published in March sixty-seven | by Poet & Printer London England

[1]⁸; pages (1–5)6–14(15–16), consisting: (1) half-title, in red; (2) 'The text of *Scapegoats And Rabies* is | the copyright of its author Ted Hughes; | the printing of this edition was completed | in March 1967 by Alan Tarling at | 30 Halstead Road London E11.'; (3) title page; (4) blank; (5)6–14 poem; (15–16) blank.

Stapled pamphlet, back page glued into maroon wrappers with flaps. Wrappers printed on front, flush to left: 'SCAPEGOATS AND RABIES | by Ted Hughes | Two shillings | Published by Poet & Printer | London England'.

Paper plain white Mellotex, 17.8 × 12.7 cm., bulk .1 cm.; all edges cut. Wrappers Old Rose Abbey Mills Greenfield 'laid' (chain lines horizontal, 2.6 cm.), marked '[crown] | [gothic letters] Abbey Mills | Greenfield'; cut flush top and bottom. Printed letterpress.

Published 7 April 1967 at 2s.; a little more than 400 copies printed. Twenty-six of these had a special colophon and were lettered. Tarling sent these to Hughes, who used copies A through T for presentation;

copies U through Z were signed by Hughes and returned to Tarling, who eventually sold them. The unsigned copies sold out over the next month or two.

A copy has been reported with a laid-in printed notice on glossy card stock, 7.5 × 7.3 cm., reading 'Ted Hughes' *Scapegoats &* | *Rabies* represents the fourth | and last edition in one year's | verse pamphleteering | [rule, 1.8 cm.] | *Poet and Printer* | *Spring Sixty-seven*'.

The original typescript of this poem had a dash between 'it' and 'home' in the fourth-to-last line of the poem. It is here omitted. Regarding this, Tarling later wrote, 'I don't see how anyone could look kindly on the arrogant deletion of a dash in … S&R. I hope I was a very different person then.' (Letter to Fred Jacobs, 31 July 1977.) The change is perpetuated in the American *Wodwo*, where the poem was first collected.

REVIEWS: *New Statesman*, 16 June 1967 (Julian Symons); *Spectator*, 28 July 1967 (C. B. Cox).

A12 WODWO 1967

a.1. First edition:

TED HUGHES | WODWO | FABER AND FABER | 24 Russell Square | London

$(A)^8B–I^8K–L^8M^4 = 92$ leaves. Pages (1–8)9(10)11–12(13–16)17–184, consisting: (1–2) blank; (3) half-title; (4) list of eight other books by Hughes; (5) title page; (6) '*First published in mcmlxvii* | *by Faber and Faber Limited* | *24 Russell Square London WC1* | *Printed in Great Britain* | *by The Bowering Press Plymouth* | *All rights reserved* | © *1967 by Ted Hughes*'; (7) 'To my Mother and Father'; (8) blank; 9, '*Author's Note* | The stories and the play in this book may be read as notes […]'; (10) blank; 11–12 table of contents; (13) quotation from *Sir Gawayn and þe Grene Knyght*; (14) blank; (15) 'PART I'; (16) blank; 17–183 text; 184 acknowledgements. Text pages 42–44, 147–148 unnumbered.

Quarter red cloth, light grey-green cloth sides over boards. Spine round, stamped in gold: ' WODWO [title and box in freehand design] Ted Hughes Faber ['Faber' reads across spine]'. Some copies of the first printing bound up later have the spine stamped in silver; the publisher could supply no information on the number thus issued.

Dust-wrapper: front: red bars and white freehand-design lettering on dark-grey background: '[bar] | WODWO | [bar] | TED | HUGHES | [bar]'. Spine: red bars continued from front, else black printing on white: '[bar] WODWO [bar] TED HUGHES FABER ['Faber' reads across spine] [bar]'. Back: list of Faber poets.

Paper plain white, 21.6 × 13.8 cm., bulk 1.35 cm.; all edges cut. Printed letterpress.

CONTENTS: [poems] Thistles—Still Life—Her Husband—Cadenza—Ghost Crabs—Boom—Ludwig's Death-Mask—Second Glance at a Jaguar—Public Bar TV[1]—Fern—A Wind Flashes the Grass—A Vegetarian[2]—Sugar Loaf—Bowled Over—Wino—Logos[3]—Reveille—The Rescue—Stations—The Green Wolf—The Bear.
[short stories] The Rain Horse—Sunday—Snow—The Harvesting—The Suitor.
[radio-play] The Wound.
[poems] Theology—Gog: I, II and III—Kreutzer Sonata—Out: I, II and III—New Moon in January—The Warriors of the North—Karma—Song of a Rat: I, II and III—Heptonstall—Ballad from a Fairy Tale—Skylarks—Mountains—You Drive in a Circle—Wings: I, II and III—Pibroch—The Howling of Wolves—Gnat-Psalm—Full Moon and Little Frieda—Wodwo.

Published 18 May 1967 at 25s.; 3000 copies printed. Hughes inscribed a copy to his brother Gerald on 27 April. There were reprints in August 1967 (2500 copies) and 1971 (2000 copies). The first paperback printing, an offset reduction of the first edition consisting of 6000 copies, was published 31 May 1971; it was reprinted in 1972, 1973, 1985, and 1989. For one or both of these last two printings Faber redesigned the title page and covers to its new standard double-rule frame format, but the poems remain in their original setting. All reprints are identified on the verso title.

The dust-wrapper was designed by Berthold Wolpe.

a.2. First American printing:

WODWO | by | TED HUGHES | [publisher's torch symbol, with date 1817, squared oval border] | HARPER & ROW, PUBLISHERS | New York and Evanston

[1–6]^{16} = 96 leaves. Pages (1–6)7(8)9–10(11–14)15–184(185–192), consisting: (1) half-title; (2) other books by Hughes (*Lupercal* and *Hawk in the Rain*); (3) title page; (4) '[acknowledgements] | *Wodwo*. Copyright © 1959, 1960, 1961, 1962, 1963, 1964, 1965, 1966, 1967 by Ted | Hughes. Printed in the United States of America [...] | [...] | FIRST U.S. EDITION | [...]'; (5) 'To my Mother and Father'; (6) blank; 7, '*Author's Note* | The stories and the play in this book may be read as notes

---

[1] Not the poem of the same name in *Recklings*.
[2] 'Vegetarian' in the table of contents.
[3] A revision of the poem of the same name in *Recklings*.

[...]'; (8) blank; 9–10 table of contents; (11) quotation from *Sir Gawayn and þe Grene Knight*; (12) blank; (13) 'PART I'; (14) blank; 15–184 text; (185) biographical note; (186–192) blank. Text pages 47, 48, 151, 152 unnumbered.

Quarter blue cloth (5 cm. on to sides), brown paper sides over boards. Front, near lower right, stamped in silver, the Harper symbol as on title page. Spine round, stamped in silver: 'TED HUGHES [floral figure] *WODWO* [floral figure, reversed] HARPER | & | ROW [publisher reads across spine]'.

Dust-wrapper: Front brown, lettered in very light blue and slightly darker blue: 'WODWO | TED HUGHES'. Spine brown, lettered as above: 'HUGHES WODWO HARPER | & ROW [publisher reads across spine]'. Back white, printed in brown: '[photo of Hughes sitting on a doorstep, credited to Ander Gunn] | TED HUGHES'. At front flap, lower right, '1167'.

Paper plain white, 20.4 × 13.7–14.1 cm., bulk 1.4 cm.; all edges cut.

Printed offset from plates made from film of the English edition. The contents are the same as in the first English printing except:
1. In place of 'Logos' is 'Root, Stem, Leaf', a three-part piece composed of 'A Match', 'On the Slope', and 'To Be a Girl's Diary' from *Recklings*.
2. 'Scapegoats and Rabies' (see A11) is added after 'The Green Wolf'.
3. Parts II and III of 'Gog' have been deleted.
4. The subsidiary poems of 'Wings' lack titles.

Additionally, pages have been re-numbered and at least one typo corrected (the wrong-font *r* in 'Kreutzer', page 154 of the English printing). Only pages (1), (3), (4), 9, 10, 32, 33, and 40–45 are new.

Published 22 November 1967 at $4.95; 3000 copies printed.

REVIEWS: *Birmingham Post*, 17 June 1967 (Barbara Lloyd-Evans); *Booklist*, 15 Feb. 1968; *Books and Bookmen*, Nov. 1967 (Michael Baldwin); *Book World*, 24 Dec. 1967 (Chad Walsh); *Cambridge Evening News*, 8 July 1967; *Cambridge Quarterly*, Autumn 1967 (J. M. Newton); *Carleton Miscellany*, Summer 1968 (D. Galler); *Church Times*, 15 Sept. 1967 (Norman Nicholson); *Critical Survey*, Winter 1967 (C. B. Cox); *Delta*, Feb. 1968 (Sydney Bolt); *English*, Spring 1968 (Howard Sergeant); *English Studies*, June 1968 (M. Thorpe); *Far Point*, Fall 1968 (John Ferns); *Glasgow Herald*, 17 June 1967 (Charles Senior); *Guardian*, 19 May 1967 (Donald Davie); *Hudson Review*, Spring 1968 (A. Hecht); *Irish Times*, 20 May 1967 (Eavan Boland); *Kentish Gazette*, 18 July 1967 (R.A.F.); *Kenyon Review* 30, 1968 (Robin Skelton); *Kirkus*, 15 Sept. 1967; *Library Journal*, 1 Nov. 1967 (Jerome Cushman); *Listener*, 6 July 1967

(Graham Martin); *New Statesman*, 16 June 1967 (Julian Symons); *New Yorker*, 30 March 1968 (Louise Bogan); *New York Review of Books*, 1 Aug. 1968 (John Thompson); *Northwest Review*, Summer 1968 (R. Mariels); *Observer*, 21 May 1967 (A. Alvarez); *Poetry*, Sept. 1968 (H. Carruth); *Poetry Review*, Autumn 1967 (L. Clark); *Publishers Weekly*, 25 Sept. 1967; *Punch*, 5 July 1967 (John Press); *Scotsman*, 24 June 1967 (Martin Seymour-Smith); *Sheffield Star*, 1 July 1967 (Byron Rogers); *Spectator*, 28 July 1967 (C. B. Cox); *Sunday Times*, 28 May 1967 (Jeremy Rundale); *Tablet*, 8 July 1967 (John Juniper); *Times*, 13 July 1967 (Derwent May); *Times Literary Supplement*, 6 July 1967; *Tribune*, 30 June 1967 (Jeremy Robson); *Virginia Quarterly*, Summer 1968 (S. F. Morse); *Yorkshire Post*, 6 July 1967 (Leonard Clark).

A13   ANIMAL POEMS   1967

Animal Poems | by | Ted Hughes

Collation of copies 37–100: [1]^{12}. Pages (i–iv)1–18(19–20), consisting: (i) blank save for Hughes' signature; (ii) blank; (iii) title page; (iv) blank; 1–18 text; (19) 'Published by | RICHARD GILBERTSON | BOW, CREDITON, DEVON | in a limited edition consisting of one hundred copies. | 1–6. Interleaved throughout with blank paper, on which the | poet has written out each of the thirteen poems in full, to face the | printed text. Bound in full dark green levant morocco gilt by | Sangorski & Sutcliffe. | 7–16. Interleaved with three manuscript poems. Bound in half | morocco gilt by Sangorski & Sutcliffe. | 17–36. Contains one poem in manuscript—these vary and include | *The Thought Fox, Pike, The Hawk in the Rain, Jaguar*. Bound in | decorative wrappers. | 37–100. Copies Signed by the author. | [number] | [at bottom of page] Suttons, Paignton—17177'; (20) blank.

Copies 17–36 have an extra bifolium between sheet 1.12 and sheet 2.11; a poem in manuscript appears on the first page of this (in effect p. (iii) if the pages were re-numbered), the other pages of the bifolium are blank. The other states mentioned in the colophon were not seen.

Sewn into light maroon wrappers of heavy, embossed paper. Front printed same as title page.

Paper plain white, 25.4 × 19.0 cm., bulk .2 cm.; all edges cut. Printed letterpress.

CONTENTS: An Otter—Pike—Gnat-Psalm—The Jaguar—The Howling of Wolves—Skylarks—The Bear—The Bull Moses—A Dream of Horses—Gog—Wodwo—Second Glance at a Jaguar—Lineage—Hawk Roosting.

Published August 1967. Details on the prices and number of copies of each series are now blurred, but according to Gilbertson only three copies were finally produced with all the poems in manuscript, and only two of these bound. The unbound copy was offered for sale by Gilbertson some time later at £60. It is possible that not all of copies 7–16 (with three poems in manuscript) were printed, and Gilbertson was later offering unbound copies of this series for £18.18.0. Copies 17–37 were originally priced at £5.5.0; the remaining copies, with Hughes' signature only, originally sold for £2.2.0. No unsigned copies have been noted.

A14   POETRY IN THE MAKING   1967

a. First edition:

Poetry in the Making | [rule] | An Anthology of Poems and Programmes | from *Listening and Writing* | TED HUGHES | FABER AND FABER | 24 Russell Square | London

$(A)^8B-H^8 = 64$ leaves. Pages (1–6)7–124(125–128), consisting: (1) half-title; (2) list of Faber Poetry Books for the Middle School; (3) title page; (4) *'First published in mcmlxvii | by Faber and Faber Limited | 24 Russell Square London WC1 | Printed in Great Britain by | Latimer Trend & Co Ltd Plymouth | All rights reserved | © This anthology Ted Hughes | 1967'*; (5) 'To | Pauline Mayne | and | John Edward Fisher'; (6) blank; 7–9 table of contents; 10, acknowledgements; 11–13 'INTRODUCTION | In this book I have collected together [...]'; 14, poem 'The Small Box' by Vasco Popa; 15–124 text; (125–128) blank.

Clear plastic over printed white paper over boards. Front printed in red and black: 'TED HUGHES | *Poetry in the* | *Making* | An Anthology of | Poems and | Programmes from | *Listening and* | *Writing*'. Spine round, printed '*Poetry in the Making* TED HUGHES FABER ['FABER' reads across spine]'. Back: '*Faber* | Educational Books'.

Issued without a dust-wrapper.

Paper plain white, 20.0 × 13.2 cm., bulk .8 cm.; all edges cut. Printed letterpress.

CONTENTS: Capturing Animals—Wind and Weather—Writing About People—Learning to Think—Writing About Landscape—Writing a Novel: Beginning—Writing a Novel: Going on—Meet My Folks[1]—Moon Creatures[2]—Words and Experience. Nineteen Hughes poems are included, all previously published.

---

[1] Incorporates 'Nessie' and poems from *Meet My Folks!*
[2] Incorporates eight poems from *The Earth-Owl.*

Published 6 December 1967 at 7s. 6d.; 4000 copies printed. There was a reprint in 1968 (6250 copies). The first paperback printing of 6000 copies, an offset reproduction of the first edition, was published 14 July 1969. It was reprinted in 1970 (8000 copies), 1973 (10,000 copies), 1975 (10,214 copies), 1978, 1982, 1986, etc. Probably for the 1986 printing Faber redesigned the title page and covers to its new standard double-rule frame format, but the text remains in the original setting. Reprints are identified on the verso title; the latest the compilers have seen is the tenth.

*b. First American edition, 1970 (*Poetry Is*):*

[flush to left] POETRY IS | *by Ted Hughes* | *Doubleday & Company, Inc., Garden City, New York 1970*

[1]¹²[2]⁶[3]¹²[4]⁶[5]¹²[6–7]⁶ = 60 leaves.* Pages (i–viii)ix(x)xi–xvi(xvii–xviii)1–101(102), consisting: (i) half-title; (ii) blank; (iii) title page; (iv) '[…] | *Copyright © 1967 by Ted Hughes. All Rights Reserved | Printed in the United States of America | First Edition in the United States of America |* [acknowledgements]'; (v) acknowledgements continued; (vi) blank; (vii) '*To* | PAULINE MAYNE | *and* | JOHN EDWARD FISHER'; (viii) blank; ix, poem 'The Small Box' by Vasco Popa; (x) blank; xi–xiv table of contents; xv–xvi 'PREFACE | The idea behind the first of these talks […]'; (xvii) half-title, as above; (xviii) blank; 1–101 text; (102) capsule biography of Hughes.

Black cloth over boards. Spine round, stamped in silver: 'POETRY IS [ornament] *Ted Hughes* DOUBLEDAY'. Endpapers coated brick red. Also found in coated white cloth printed with the design of the dust-wrapper (see below). The latter copies were intended for libraries and were sold without their own dust-wrappers.

Dust-wrapper white, printed in red and black. Front: 'POETRY IS | [drawing of a bird atop a four-footed beast, signed 'Baskin'] | TED | HUGHES'. Spine: 'TED HUGHES POETRY IS DOUBLEDAY'. Back: drawing from front.

Paper plain white, 20.7 × 13.8 cm., bulk .9 cm.; all edges cut. Printed offset.

CONTENTS the same as the English edition with the omission of three chapters (Writing a Novel: Beginning—Writing a Novel: Going On—Words and Experience). The first and last paragraphs of Hughes' introduction have also been cut.

*There is some doubt as to the accuracy of this collational formulary. The page-block was crimped during the binding process in such a way that even cutting away the spine of one copy failed to show an unambiguous structure.

Published 2 October 1970; 10,000 copies printed. Of these, 2000 were hardbound as above and sold at $3.95; 5000 were bound in wrappers and sold at $1.95; and 3000 were given a library binding of coated white cloth printed with the design of the dust-wrapper above. (The library copies lack dust-wrappers.) There was a reprint of 2000 hardbound trade copies at an undetermined later date; these lack the date on the title page and the first edition notice on the verso title, though the price on the dust-wrapper is still $3.95. The hardbound trade copies went out of print in February 1974, the paperbound in December 1972. The library-bound copies went into three further printings of 2000 copies each.

c. First Japanese edition (1980):

[flush to left] Nan'un-do's Contemporary Library | [rule] | POETRY IN THE | MAKING | TED HUGHES | *Edited with Notes by* | Masaaki Yoshino | [rule] | Tokyo | NAN'UN-DO | [publisher's logo: radiant eagle in circle] | C-H61

58 leaves, 'perfect-bound'. Pages (i–ii)iii–vi(vii–viii)1–71(72)73–106(107–108), consisting: (i) title page; (ii) 'Reprinted from POETRY IN THE MAKING by Ted Hughes | Copyright © Ted Hughes 1967 | English language textbook with Japanese annotations rights | arranged with Faber and Faber Ltd., Publishers, London | through Tuttle-Mori Agency, Inc., Tokyo'; iii–vi introduction to Hughes, his work, and this book, in Japanese; (vii) table of contents; (viii) blank; 1–71 text, with line numbers; (72) blank; 73–106 English–Japanese glossary and notes; (107) colophon, in Japanese; (108) ads for other books, in Japanese.

Plastic-covered embossed wrappers; front: 'Nan'un-do's Contemporary Library | [on a yellow background] POETRY | IN THE MAKING | TED HUGHES | Tokyo | NAN'UN-DO | [publisher's logo: radiant eagle in circle] | [under yellow field] C-H61'. Spine: '*T. Hughes* POETRY IN THE MAKING «C-H61»'. Back: '[on a yellow background, Japanese characters for Nan'un-do inside letters NUD] | «C-H61»'. Endpapers of a lighter colour than the text paper inserted, tipped onto inside of wrappers front and back.

Paper plain white, 18.2 × 12.8 cm., bulk .75 cm.; all edges cut. Printed letterpress.

CONTENTS: Capturing Animals—Wind and Weather—Writing About People—Learning to Think—Writing About Landscape.

Published 25 January 1980 at 780 yen; 3000 copies printed. There was a reprint of 2000 copies on 15 April 1980; this can be identified by the presence in the colophon of two lines beginning '1980'.

REVIEWS: *Book World*, 8 Nov. 1970; *Booklist*, 15 Dec. 1970; *Center for Children's Books, Bulletin*, Jan. 1971; *English Journal*, March 1971; *Horn Book*, Feb. 1971; *Kentish Gazette*, 23 Jan. 1970 (C.R.E.P.); *Kirkus*, 1 Oct. 1970; *Library Journal*, 15 Dec. 1970 (M. A. Dorsey); *New Statesman*, 9 Feb. 1968 (Julian Symons); *New Yorker*, 5 Dec. 1970; *New York Times Book Review*, 8 Nov. 1970 (Thomas Lask); *Publishers Weekly*, 16 Nov. 1970; *Saturday Review*, 14 Nov. 1970 (Zena Sutherland); *Times Literary Supplement*, 14 March 1968; *Tribune*, 12 Sept. 1969 (Robert Nye).

A15	GRAVESTONES	1967

a.1. First edition:

Six linocut broadsides by Gavin Robbins. Order arbitrary. Paper apparently handmade laid, chain lines 3.1 cm., horizontal in the four upright prints, vertical in the others. Measurements approximate owing to the uneven deckle edges and variations from one copy to another. Each signed at bottom, in pencil: 'G. Robbins 67 [number]/40 [title] [Hughes' signature]'.

'Theology'. In green and black, 49 × 62 cm.
'Fern'. In green and black, 62 × 49 cm.
'Still Life'. In dark blue and black, 85 × 62 cm.
'Thistles'. In red and black, 62 × 49 cm.
'As Woman's Weeping'. In dark blue and black, 92 × 62 cm.
'Bowled Over'. In red and black, 52 × 80 cm.

Published some time in 1967; 40 sets printed. The publication history of these broadsides is very hazy; it is unlikely that there was a formal date of publication or a fixed price.

*a.2. First printing in book form, 1968 (*Poems: Ted Hughes, Linocuts: Gavin Robbins*):*

Poems: Ted Hughes | Linocuts: Gavin Robbins | [illustration of a handprint] | Bartholomew Books Exeter College of Art 1968

[1]¹⁰. Pages [1–20], consisting: [1] title page; [2] '© Poems: Ted Hughes 1968 | © Linocuts: Gavin Robbins 1968 | Printed and made in England | by James Townsend and Sons Limited | Exeter'; [3] at left, Hughes' signature; at right: 'Bartholomew Print Workshop was formed in 1966 | by the Printmaking Department at Exeter College of Art. | Apart from the production of individual prints, | members of the workshop are encouraged to work with | poets and writers to produce folios of their combined work | Where suitable a book version of the original folio | will be produced, this volume is the result | of such a collaboration | Alan Richards *Exeter 1968*'; [4] blank; [5–16] the six prints, versos blank; [17]

'School of Fine Prints and Graphic Design | Head of Department: Alan Richards | Designed by vocational course students | under the teacher of typographic | design: George Webb'; [18] blank; [19] 'The illustrations in this book are printed letterpress from line blocks | made from proofs of the original linocuts. | The inks used are Fishburn's Colour-Finder system and | Fishburn's black letterpress AP 3189. | The paper is Wiggins Teape All British Fluorescent shade smooth | s/o 22 × 30 200 gsm. | The case is printed letterpress on Tumba Tre Kronor cover paper | No. 10338 with Fabriano Ingres Blue Laid end papers. | Typeface: Monotype Univers Light (685).'; [20] blank.

Violet paper over boards, front printed: 'POEMS: TED HUGHES | LINOCUTS: GAVIN ROBBINS [title in freehand-design letters] | Bartholomew Books | [hand-print as on title page]'. Spine flat, printed 'Poems: Ted Hughes Linocuts: Gavin Robbins Bartholomew Books'. Endpapers blue.

Issued without a dust-wrapper.

Pages 21.2 × 32.8 cm., bulk .3 cm.; all edges cut.

CONTENTS: The prints from *Gravestones*, photographically reduced.

Probably published in 1968, at an unknown price; 300 copies printed. Though most copies were unnumbered, Sagar's copy has a note by Hughes on the colophon: 'No. 1 of 300 | 23rd March 1969'. The publication of this book partook of the informality of the distribution of the *Gravestones* broadsides. Hughes, in a letter to Sagar (6 October 1981), said '[Robbins] made it as a project on his art course, so there was never actually a publication date. It's just that at some point we began to sell them. Even the sale was a total fiasco—I've no idea where most of them went, or how they went ... I daresay your copy—March 69—was a little after some of them had been sold, though I'm not sure. I sold very few of the books.'

A16   SENECA'S OEDIPUS   1968

a. Early working script (unpublished):

OEDIPUS | [rule, 1.9 cm.] | by | Seneca | translated by | Ted Hughes

[56] single sheets, printed one side only, consisting: leaf [1] title page; leaves [2–55] text; leaf [56] 'Scripts printed by: | FRANELL ENTERPRISES, | 54 Uxbridge Road, | Shepherds Bush Green, | London, W.12. | [...]'.

Bound in light blue report wrappers, with a rectangle cut out on front to show 'OEDIPUS' and rule from title page.

Paper plain white, 28.0 × 21.5 cm., watermarked 'CROXLEY | SCRIPT' (4.0 × 8.0 cm.), bulk .6 cm.; all edges cut.

Typewritten; mimeographed.

See the note to item b below.

b. Later working script (unpublished):

OEDIPUS | [rule, 2.2 cm.] | by | Seneca | adapted by Ted Hughes | from a translation | by | David Anthony Turner

Collation, binding, paper, and printing as above.

This item and the one above were two versions of the rehearsal script for the National Theatre Company's production of *Oedipus* during the winter of 1967–68. The introductions which Hughes and Turner wrote for the Faber edition (item c, below) give a good account of the evolution of the production. Although Hughes was originally called in to rework Turner's translation into a form closer to director Peter Brook's concept of the play, Hughes ended up by making a completely new start at translation. (Turner's name appears on the title page of the second version because of contractual obligations.) The version of the play printed in these scripts differs substantially from both Turner's and Seneca's.

Though both scripts are undated, the first one described here (which we will call Edition A) is clearly earlier. It contains much material that was deleted in Edition B, mostly descriptions and references to mythology. The final published versions (see below) follow Edition B closely. Nevertheless, the typist of Edition B attempted to follow Edition A page for page whenever possible, and many pages were simply copies of A, sometimes with small corrections. Olwyn Hughes believes there may have been more than two acting scripts, but these are the only ones located so far.

As the leaves of both versions are single sheets bound up loose, leaves from the two versions could conceivably become intermixed. The following table gives one feature of each page which will enable differentiation. Pages that were copied for Edition B look fuzzier than the originals, but this is difficult to see without side-by-side examination. Pagination follows that of the originals.

	Edition A	*Edition B*
	Leaf following title begins Act I	Leaf has Prologue
I–1	First speaker is Oedipus	First speaker is Chorus
I–2	Left column reads 'OEDIPUS	(contd.)'	Duplicate, except '(contd.)' removed

I–3	First line begins 'these atrocities'	First line begins 'our lungs scorch'
I–4		Duplicate
I–5	Top line of dialogue ends 'visitor'	Top line of dialogue ends 'away'
I–6	Third line ends 'for the throne'	Third line ends 'for the | throne'.
I–7		Duplicate
I–8	Page contains two speeches	Page contains four speeches
I–9	Left column reads 'OEDIPUS | (contd.)'	Duplicate, except '(contd.)' removed
I–10	Contains five 'paragraphs'	Contains four 'paragraphs'
I–11	First line ends 'There's'	First line ends 'grass'
I–12	Page ends 'Weeping and shouting for death.'	Page ends 'Shouting for death.'
II–1	Oedipus's second speech begins 'now which'	Oedipus's second speech begins 'now I shall'
II–2	Creon's speech is two 'paragraphs' before indention	Creon's speech is three 'paragraphs' before indention
II–3	First line 'you murderer'	First line 'murderer'
II–4	Last line 'the valley … '	Last line 'lay before Laius'
II–5	First line 'at a ford … '	First line 'he expected'
II–6		Duplicate
II–7		Duplicate
II–8		Duplicate
II–9	Jocasta's speech is three lines	Jocasta's speech is two lines
II–10	Top line ends 'Oedipus'	Top line ends 'name'
II–11	Not present	Chorus to Bacchus
II–12	Not present	Chorus to Bacchus (contd.)
III–1	Last line 'kingdom … '	Last line 'the speech'

III–2	Creon's second speech begins 'you have forced'	Creon's second speech begins 'prepare yourself'
III–3	Left column reads 'CREON: | (contd.)'	Left column reads 'CREON'
III–4	First line begins 'I saw armies'	First line begins 'the roaring of dogs'
III–5		Duplicate
III–6	At middle of page: 'he'll want to get away as fast as his legs can carry him'	At middle of page: 'he'll want to get away fast'
III–7	Creon's speech begins 'Me'	Creon's speech begins 'would I drive …'
III–8	Last line 'what if I am innocent'	Last line 'guard him'
III–9	Page contains dialogue	Page contains chorus
III–10	Chorus	Not present
III–11	Chorus	Not present
III–12	Chorus	Not present
IV–1		Duplicate
IV–2	Line 7 'and death'	Line 7 'and more death'
IV–3	First line 'I know …'	First line 'there is …'
IV–4	Fourth line from the bottom: 'with their greatest secrets'	Duplicate; fourth line from the bottom altered to read 'even with their greatest secrets'
IV–5		Duplicate
IV–6	First line 'living | give'	First line 'the | living'
IV–7		Duplicate
IV–8	Last line 'bring torches …'	Duplicate; last line altered to read 'I shall …'
IV–9	First line 'will you tear …'	First line 'will you destroy …'
IV–10		Duplicate
IV–11	Last line 'a splash …'	Last line 'he kept …'

IV–12	Not present	Chorus (contd.)
V–1	Line 8 from the bottom has 'gripping'	Duplicate; line 8 from the bottom altered to read 'griping'
V–2		Duplicate
V–3	Line 7 from the bottom has 'agony | desperation'	Duplicate; the word 'desperation' has been removed
V–4		Duplicate
V–5	Last line 'frenzy ... '	Last line 'out of her mind ... '
V–6	Oedipus has final lines	Jocasta has final lines
V–7	Jocasta has final lines	Chorus has final lines
V–8	Last word on page 'faces'	Page ends with stage direction
V–9	Ends the play	Not present
Last leaf	Phone number is '01 743–6749'	Phone number is '01–743–6749'

c. First published edition (1969):

Seneca's | OEDIPUS | adapted by | TED HUGHES | London | FABER & FABER

(A)⁸B–C⁸D⁴ = 28 leaves. Pages (1–4)5(6)7–9(10–12)13–55(56), consisting: (1) half-title; (2) list of thirteen other books by Hughes; (3) title page; (4) *'First published in 1969 | by Faber and Faber Limited | 24 Russell Square London WC1 | Printed in Great Britain by | Latimer Trend & Co Ltd Plymouth | All rights reserved | SBN 571 09223 3 (paper bound edition) | SBN 571 09175 X (hard bound edition) | [...] | © 1969 by Ted Hughes'*; 5, 'The first performance of *Oedipus* was given at the Old Vic | Theatre [...] [notice followed by cast and production lists]'; (6) blank; 7–8 introduction by Hughes, unsigned; 9, introduction by David Anthony Turner, signed; (10) blank; (11) the introductory verse, 'show us | show us | a simple riddle [...]'; (12) blank; 13–55 text; (56) blank.

Orange-brown cloth over boards. Spine flat, stamped in gold: 'Seneca's OEDIPUS *adapted by* Ted Hughes   Faber'.

Dust-wrapper: front: left half, photo of John Gielgud and Irene Worth; right half, 'SENECA'S | OEDIPUS ['OEDIPUS' reading down] | adapted by | TED | HUGHES | [heavy rule, 4.8 cm.]'. Spine:

'SENECA'S OEDIPUS adapted by TED HUGHES Faber'. Back: blurbs for other Faber classics editions.

Paper plain white, 20.1 × 12.0 cm., bulk .4 cm.; all edges cut. Printed letterpress.

Published 8 December 1969 at 18s.; 2000 copies printed. A paperback printing of 5000 copies was done offset and published simultaneously, issued in plain stiff wrappers pasted into a dust wrapper. It was reprinted in 1974 (3000 copies). In 1983 Faber published a paperback 'reissue' at £1.95/$4.95. This is in fact the same setting of the text with the preliminaries revised and the covers redesigned.

d. First American edition (1972):

[flush to left] SENECA'S | OEDIPUS | Adapted by Ted Hughes | *Introduction* [*I* swash] *by Peter* [*P* swash] *Brook* [*B* swash] | *Illustrated* [*I* swash] *by Reginald* [*R* swash] *Pollack* [*P* swash] | DOUBLEDAY & COMPANY, INC., | Garden City, New York 1972

$[1–6]^8 = 48$ leaves. Pages (1–4)5–9(10–11)12–13(14)15(16)17–90(91–96), consisting: (1) half-title; (2) drawing; (3) title page; (4) *'Note:* SENECA'S OEDIPUS is the sole property of the author | [...] | ISBN: 0–385–00574–1 Trade | ISBN: 0–385–00662–4 Paperback | [...] | INTRODUCTION AND ILLUSTRATIONS COPYRIGHT © 1972 | BY DOUBLEDAY & COMPANY, INC. | TEXT COPYRIGHT © 1969 BY TED HUGHES | ALL RIGHTS RESERVED | PRINTED IN THE UNITED STATES OF AMERICA | FIRST EDITION'; 5–9 introduction by Peter Brook, 'Seneca's play has no external action whatsoever [...]', dated December 1970; (10) blank; (11) half-title, as above; 12, 'The first performance of *Oedipus* was given at the Old Vic Theatre, | London, by the National Theatre Company on March 19, 1968. The | cast was as follows: | [...]'; 13, production crew list; (14) drawing; 15, the introductory verse, 'show us | show us | a simple riddle [...]'; (16) drawing; 17–90 text; (91) drawing; (92–96) blank. Text pages 24, 32, 41, 45, 53, 58, 59, 64, 65, 68, 74, 75, 85, 91 unnumbered. Fourteen illustrations, line cuts.

Light green cloth over boards. Spine flat, stamped in blue: 'SENECA'S OEDIPUS *Adapted by Ted Hughes* DOUBLEDAY'. Endpapers coated aqua.

Dust-wrapper: colour painting continuous across front, spine, and back. Front: depiction of Oedipus, top lettered in orange shaded with white: 'Seneca's | Oedipus'; at lower right, in white: 'Adapted by | Ted Hughes | Introduction by Peter Brook | Illustrated by Reginald Pollack'. Spine lettered in white: 'Seneca's Oedipus   Adapted by Ted Hughes   Doubleday'.

Paper plain white, 20.8 × 13.8 cm., bulk .6 cm.; all edges cut. Printed offset.

CONTENTS the same as the Faber edition, except that Turner's note is replaced by Brook's.

Published 20 October 1972 at $4.95; 2000 copies printed. There was a simultaneous paperback printing of 5000 copies, lacking the first edition notice, and 'perfect-bound'.

REVIEWS: *Arion* 7, Autumn 1968 (Ian Scott-Kilvert); *Daily Mail*, 20 Mar. 1968 (Peter Lewis); *Daily Telegraph*, 20 Mar. 1968 (Eric Shorter); *Guardian*, 20 Mar. 1968 (Philip Hope-Wallace); *Illustrated London News*, 30 Mar. 1968; *Lady*, 4 Apr. 1968 (J. C. Trewin); *Listener*, 1 Jan. 1970 (Christopher Ricks); *Londoner*, 6 Apr. 1968 (Roger Baker); *Observer*, 24 Mar. 1968 (Ronald Bryden) and 25 Jan. 1970; *Plays and Players*, May 1968 (Martin Esslin); *Spectator*, 21 Mar. 1970 (Martin Seymour-Smith); *Sunday Telegraph*, 24 Mar. 1968 (Rosemary Say); *Sunday Times*, 24 Mar. 1968 (Harold Hobson); *Times*, 20 and 23 Mar. 1968 (Irving Wardle).

A17   THE IRON MAN   1968

a.1. First edition:

The Iron Man | A Story In Five Nights | *by* | TED HUGHES | *Illustrated by* | GEORGE ADAMSON | FABER AND FABER | 24 Russell Square | London

$(A)^8B-D^8 = 32$ leaves [D_7 forms the rear free endpaper, D_8 the rear paste-down]. Pages (1–10)11(12)13–59(60–64), consisting: (1–2) blank; (3) half-title; (4) list of nine other books by Hughes; (5) blank; (6) frontispiece, right side view of Iron Giant; (7) title page; (8) '*First published in mcmlxviii* | *by Faber and Faber Limited* | *24 Russell Square London W.C.*1 | *Printed in Great Britain by* | *Latimer Trend & Co Ltd Plymouth* | *All rights reserved* | © 1968 *by Ted Hughes*'; (9) 'TO FRIEDA, NICHOLAS AND SHURA'; (10) blank; 11, table of contents; (12) blank; 13–59 text; (60) blank; (61–62) free fly-leaf; (63–64) paste-down. Text pages 28, 36, 42, 50 unnumbered. Five illustrations, line cuts.

Paper over boards. Front red; picture of Iron Man (from frontispiece of text) in blue, red, and black. Bottom left, freehand lettered in red, blue, and white: '*The* | IRON | MAN | *by* | TED HUGHES | *Drawings by George Adamson*'. Spine flat, red; freehand lettered in blue, white, and black: '*The* IRON MAN · TED HUGHES · *Faber*'. Back plain blue.

Dust-wrapper front and spine same design as cover. Back has blurbs for other Faber children's books, printed black on white.

Paper plain white, 20.8 × 15.3 cm., bulk .5 cm.; all edges cut. Printed letterpress.

Published 26 February 1968 at 13s. 6d.; 6000 copies printed. There were reprints in 1969 (4000 copies); 1971 (5000 copies), 1973 (10,000 copies), 1976 (10,850 copies), and 1981. The first paperback printing, offset from the first edition, was published in 25,000 copies on 11 October 1971. It was reprinted in 1972 (15,000 copies), 1973 (25,000 copies), 1975 (25,000 copies), 1977 (50,000 copies), and 1980. The information on the title versos of various reprints are not consistent with each other or with Faber's dates as given above.

a.2. Japanese printings (1980):

First printing not seen.

Offset reprints of the first English edition, slightly reduced, with preliminaries, notes, and line numbers added. Notes and editing by Yuuichi Hashimoto. Published by Shinozaki Shorin, Tokyo.

Published 7 January 1980 at 500 yen; number of copies unknown. There was a second printing on 15 January 1980. The reprint has two lines of characters in Japanese, just below the first double-rule on the colophon; the first line contains the numbers 55, 1 and 7, separated by characters; the second line contains the numbers 55, 1 and 15. These numbers refer to the publication dates.

b. First American edition:

[flush to left] THE IRON GIANT | A Story in Five Nights | by Ted Hughes | Drawings by Robert Nadler | Harper & Row, Publishers · New York, Evanston, and London

$[1–4]^8$ = 32 leaves. Pages (i–viii)1–56, consisting: (i) half-title, 'THE IRON GIANT | A Story in Five Nights'; (ii) frontispiece, the giant surveying a railroad yard, taken from illustration on p. (50); (iii) title page; (iv) 'THE IRON GIANT: A Story in Five Nights. | Text copyright © 1968 by Ted Hughes. Drawings copyright © 1968 by Robert Nadler. | Printed in the United States of America [...] | [...]'; (v) 'To Frieda, Nicholas, and Shura'; (vi) blank; (vii) table of contents; (viii) blank; 1–56 text. Text pages 3, 7, 12, 15, 18, 25, 27, 29, 33, 36, 38, 44, 47, 50, 54 unnumbered. Fifteen illustrations, plus duplicate frontispiece; line cuts.

Dark blue paper over boards. Front, in white, Iron Man drawing; at top, in lighter blue: 'THE IRON GIANT | A Story in Five Nights | by Ted Hughes | Drawings by Robert Nadler'. Spine flat, printed in lighter blue: 'Hughes   THE IRON GIANT   Harper & Row'. Back plain dark blue.

Dust-wrapper same design as cover. No copy seen with original price. At bottom left flap '1068'.

Paper plain white, 22.8 × 17.7 cm., bulk .5 cm.; all edges cut. Printed offset.

CONTENTS the same as the English edition, except that 'Iron Giant' is everywhere substituted for 'Iron Man'. Harper made the change to avoid confusion with a cartoon series running at the time on American television.

Published 23 October 1968 at $2.95; the publisher prefers not to reveal the number printed. Harper also issued a 'library edition', part of the same printing but bound in dark blue coated cloth over boards, printed as above; the dust-wrapper bears the price $2.92. The prices of these two forms were soon raised to $3.95 and $3.79. The book was reprinted in December 1969, possibly coinciding with the price rise; according to Harper, 30% of the second printing was bound up as trade copies, the rest in library bindings. The compilers have seen no copy of the book bearing the words 'first edition' on the verso title; but this is not unusual because Harper's Junior Department had no policy regarding the inclusion of such wording at the time the book was printed.

Copies of the book are found with either white or dark blue endpapers. According to Harper, the former were used in the trade bindings, with the blue reserved for library copies. This practice was not carried out consistently, however, as some copies of the second printing bearing the $3.95 trade price were bound up with blue endpapers. In any event, the distinction has no bearing on priority.

c. First English paperback edition, 1973 (abridged):

[no title page; cover title:] [in white, on multi-coloured background] LISTENING AND READING | THE IRON MAN | ADAPTED FROM PART OF THE STORY | BY TED HUGHES | [colour drawing of Iron Man's head] | [at lower left, Penguin logo]

[1]^{16}. Pages 1–32, consisting of the story, with 6 illustrations printed colour halftone. Pages 2, 6, 10, 16, 18, 22, 30 unnumbered.

Stapled into wrappers of heavier paper, linen-embossed outside. Front printed as above. Back cover printed with the front cover design rotated 90° clockwise; at bottom left, four columns containing the following, in white: (1) penguin as on front cover; (2) 'Published by | Penguin | Education | ISBN 0 14 08.1222 9'; (3) 'United Kingdom 25p | New Zealand $0.85 | Canada $1.15 | Australia $0.85 | (recommended)'; (4) 'For copyright | reasons this edition | is not for sale | in the USA'. Inside front cover: 'Listening and Reading | Stage One | THE IRON MAN | Adapted from part of the story by Ted Hughes | Illustrations by Colin

Smithson | [the remainder in two columns; left:] Penguin Education | by arrangement with the British Broadcasting Corporation | Penguin Education, | A Division of Penguin Books Ltd, | [...] | First published by the BBC 1971 | Published by Penguin Education 1973 | Copyright © British Broadcasting Corporation, 1971, 1973 | Illustrations copyright © Penguin Education, 1973'; right column: 'Filmset in Monophoto Apollo by | Oliver Burridge Filmsetting Ltd, Crawley | Colour reproduction and printing by | W. S. Cowell, 8 Butter Market, Ipswich | [conditions of sale notice]'. Inside back cover: 'The full story of *The Iron Man*, with more adventures, is | published in hardback and paperback by Faber & Faber. | [in three columns, note about the *Listening and Reading Series* and list of titles]'.

Paper plain white, 14.8 × 20.9 cm., bulk .2 cm.; all edges cut. Printed offset.

An abridgement of chapters 1 and 2 of *The Iron Man*, done by one of the publisher's staff.

Published 30 August 1973 at 25p.; 3000 copies printed. The publishers believe there was a second printing, though the compilers have not seen a copy with the marks of one.

d.1. Third English edition, 1985:

[within a rule frame] ff | [rule] | THE | IRON MAN | [rule] | Ted Hughes | [below frame] illustrated by | Andrew Davidson | *faber and faber* | LONDON · BOSTON

[1–2⁸ 3⁴ 4⁸] = 28 leaves. Pages (1–10)11–53(54–56), consisting: (1–2) blank; (3) half-title; (4) '*by Ted Hughes* | [25 titles]'; (5) title page; (6) 'First published in 1968 | by Faber and Faber Limited | 3 Queen Square London WC1 3AU | Reprinted in 1969, 1971, 1976, and 1981 | First published in this edition in 1985 | Printed in Great Britain by | Jolly & Barber Ltd Rugby | All rights reserved | © 1968 by Ted Hughes | [CIP data]'; (7) 'TO FRIEDA, NICHOLAS AND SHURA'; (8) blank; (9) table of contents; (10) blank; 11–53 text; (54–56) blank. Text page 34 unnumbered. The illustrations are halftone reproductions of coloured wood-engravings.

Black cloth. Front blind-stamped with outline of Iron Man's head and right shoulder. Spine flat, stamped in silver: 'THE IRON MAN Ted Hughes [reading across, at foot] ff'. Endpapers light blue.

Dust-wrapper printed (back continuing to front) with colour illustration of the Iron Man in the scrap-metal yard. Front, in white compartment, upper left, the title and author as on the title page. Spine black, printed in white as on book spine. Back, near top, in white, 'ff | *faber and faber*'.

Paper medium glossy, 23.4 × 15.5 cm., bulk .5 cm.; all edges cut. Printed offset.

Published October 1985 at £7.95; number of copies undetermined.

d.2. Replating of 1985 English edition (paperback, 1985):

Title page the same as d.1, but space above imprint reduced.

32 leaves, 'perfect-bound'. Pages (1–10)11–62(64–65), consisting: (1–4) same as d.1; (5) title page; (6) same as d.1, except '[...] | Printed in Great Britain by | Richard Clay (The Chaucer Press Ltd, | Bungay, Suffolk | [...]', and addition of Net Book Agreement note before the CIP data; (7–10) same as d.1; 11–62 text, same keyboarding as d.1, but the lines shortened for this format; (63–64) blank. The illustrations are uncoloured.

Wrappers, same illustration as d.1 dust-wrapper, but only the Iron Man's eyes are coloured. Front and spine printed the same as d.1, but spine is white. Back: '[on white panel] ff | *faber and faber* | [rule] | THE IRON MAN | *A Children's Story in five Nights* | Ted Hughes | [reviews and blurb] | Cover illustration by Andrew Davidson | £1.95 net | [ISBN] | [bar code]'.

19.8 × 12.5 cm., bulk .4 cm.; all edges cut. Printed offset.

Published October 1985 at £1.95; number of copies unknown. There were two reprintings. In April 1989 Faber published a so-called 'reissue' at £1.99, which is the same internally as the 1985 paperback but the wrappers are illustrated in colour.

e. Second American edition (1988):

[in white, on recto, over double-page illustration of the Iron Man nearing top of sea cliff] THE IRON GIANT | *A Story in Five Nights* | *by* TED HUGHES | *illustrations by Dirk Zimmer* | Harper & Row, Publishers

[1–2]^{16} = 32 leaves. Pages (i–vi)1–58, consisting: (i) half-title; (ii–iii) title spread; (iv) '*To Frieda, Nicholas, and Shura* | The Iron Giant | Text copyright © 1968 by Ted Hughes | Illustrations copyright © 1988 by Dirk Zimmer | Printed in the U.S.A. All rights reserved. | [printing code, 10–1] | First Edition | [CIP data]'; (v) table of contents; (vi) illustration of the Iron Man at top of sea cliff; 1–58 text. Text pages 5, 8, 9, 20, 21, 27, 30, 32, 36, 44, 45, 48, 50, 54, 55 unnumbered.

Quarter white cloth (2.8 cm. onto boards), black paper sides over boards. Spine stamped in silver: 'Hughes/Zimmer THE IRON GIANT Harper & Row'. Endpapers grey.

Dust-wrapper not seen.

22.8 × 17.8 cm., bulk .5 cm.; all edges cut. Printed offset.

Published by 1 March 1988 (the date stamped in the Library of Congress copy) at $11.95; number of copies undetermined. Also issued in a 'library binding' at $11.89. A paperback printing was issued simultaneously at $3.95; it is the same internally except for the following:

1. Title page imprint reads 'A HARPER TROPHY BOOK | Harper & Row, Publishers'.
2. Glued, not sewn.
3. Verso title has '[. . .] All rights reserved | First Harper Trophy edition, 1988. | [CIP data]'.

A presumed later printing has front wrapper priced $4.95 with other small changes; title page imprint is '[publisher's logo: top of a flaming torch] | HarperTrophy | *A Division of* HarperCollins *Publishers*'; verso title has '[. . .] | Printed in Mexico. | All rights reserved. | [CIP data] | First Harper Trophy edition, 1988'.

REVIEWS: *Book World*, 23 Feb. 1969, 13 Mar. 1988; *Booklist*, 1 Jan. 1969, 1 May 1992; *Books and Bookmen*, Dec. 1971; *Books for Keeps*, Nov. 1988, Nov. 1989; *Books for Your Children*, Autumn 1985; *British Book News, Children's Books*, June 1986; *Center for Children's Books, Bulletin*, June 1988; *Connoisseur*, Sept. 1990; *Guardian*, 29 Mar. 1968 (J.R.T.); *Horn Book*, Dec. 1968 (V.H.); *Junior Bookshelf*, Feb. 1986 (M.C.); *Library Journal*, 15 Dec. 1968 (Elva Harmon); Listener, 16 May 1968 (Naomi Lewis); *New York Times Book Review*, 3 Nov. 1968 (Robert Nye); *Observer*, 5 Jan. 1986; *School Librarian*, July 1968 (Timothy Rogers); *Spectator*, 14 June 1968 (Colin MacInnes), 7 Dec. 1985; *Tablet*, 27 Apr. 1968 (Janet Bruce); *Teacher*, 13 Sept. 1968 (Margery Fisher); *Teachers' World*, 19 Apr. 1968; *Times*, 13 April 1968 (Robert Nye); *Times Educational Supplement*, 8 Mar. 1968; *Times Literary Supplement*, 14 Mar. 1968.

A18   FIVE AUTUMN SONGS FOR   1968
                    CHILDREN'S VOICES

Five Autumn Songs | for | Children's Voices | [ornament, white square within black diamond] | Ted Hughes

Collation of copies 38–500: [1]^6. Pages (i–ii)1–9(10), consisting: (i) title page; (ii) 'These poems were written for the 1968 Harvest Festival at | Little Missenden.'; 1–6 text; 7 blank; 8, 'THE MANUSCRIPT SERIES | [rule, 1 cm.] | *Autumn Songs* is No. 4 in *The Manuscript Series*. Previous | publications have been *Animal Poems*, by Ted Hughes [. . .] | [. . .] | August, 1967. | [two others]'; 9, 'Published by | RICHARD GILBERTSON | Bow | Nr. Crediton | Devonshire | Copy No. 1. With the whole of the poem *Who's killed the leaves?* | in the author's manuscript, and with a complete | set of the drawings by Philidor [sc.

Phillida] Gili, and having | the original corrected typescript and printer's | proof. | Copies 3–11 [sic]. Each having one verse of the poem *Who's killed | the leaves?* in the author's manuscript, and each | having an original watercolour drawing by Philidor | Gili. | Copies 12–37. Each having one verse, in manuscript, of the | poem *Who's killed the leaves?* | Copies 38–188. Signed by the author. | Copies 189–500. Numbered. | [number] | December, 1968.'; (10) blank.

Stapled into light-weight paper wrappers, outside coated intense pink. Front, in script: '*Five Autumn Songs | for | Children's Voices* | [ornament resembling eight-pointed snowflake] | *Ted Hughes* | [ornament, as above]'.

Paper plain white, 24.1–24.6 × 18.25–18.5 cm., bulk .1 cm.; all edges cut. Printed letterpress.

CONTENTS [poems untitled; first lines]: Who's Killed the Leaves? [Leaves]—The First Sorrow of Autumn [The Seven Sorrows]—With the Apple in his Strength [The Defenders]—There Came a Day that Caught the Summer [There Came a Day]—While the Rain Fell on the November Woodland Shoulder of Exmoor [The Stag].

Published 3 January 1969. Copy 1 was not for sale. Copies 2–11 were issued at £10.10.0, copies 12–37 at £4.10.0, copies 38–188 at £2.2.0, and the unsigned copies at 10s.6d. The compilers have seen signed copies dated by Hughes 3 January, 13 February, and undated. Copies 38–188 are signed and dated on the title page; the compilers have not seen an example of the first 37 copies.

Hughes wrote these poems at the request of Pat Harrison, a teacher in Little Missenden. She assigned various children to read them in the festival, and Richard Drakeford was asked to provide some interlude music. A catalogue issued by Richard Gilbertson says that the poems were first published in the Festival programme. In fact the texts arrived too late for inclusion, so this booklet constitutes their first appearance.

A19   I SAID GOODBYE TO EARTH   1969

Broadside, printed in red, green, and black with stylized representation of trees, fire, cross, and snowflake; poem in black; border red. At lower left, in pencil, 'G. Robbins 69 [number]/75'; at lower right, Hughes' signature.

Paper plain white, 58.4 × 45.7 cm.; all edges cut.

Published some time in 1969; 75 copies printed. Original price unknown. Turret Books (Bernard Stone) sold a few copies for the collaborators.

A20   A CROW HYMN   1970

[no title page; cover title:] A CROW HYMN | Ted Hughes

[1]^6. Pages [1–12], consisting: [1] '[publisher's mark, radiant eagle atop sceptre] | The Sceptre Press | Frensham | Farnham . Surrey'; [2] 'This issue is limited to 100 copies, | nos. 1 to 74, printed on laid paper, | with 26 lettered A to Z, and signed by | the poet. | Copy [number] | ~ | © 1970'; [3–4] blank; [5] half-title; [6] blank; [7] the poem; [8–11] blank; [12] capsule biography followed by heavy rule, 6.1 cm.

Stapled into white, heavy paper wrappers; front printed as above.

Paper: Sheets 1.6 and 3.4 white 'laid' (chain lines horizontal, 2.6 cm.), marked 'CONQUEROR | [castle] | LONDON | C[?]'; mark crosses the fold. Sheet 2.5 is heavy brown unmarked paper. Overall 20.0 × 13.2 cm., bulk .1 cm.; all edges cut. Printed letterpress.

Published 1 March 1970 at 63s. for signed copies and 5s. unsigned. There were about 8 copies out of series. According to Martin Booth of Sceptre Press, of the 100 copies in series only 21 signed and 64 unsigned were for sale, the remainder being taken by Hughes. Six of the eight out-of-series copies were sent to the copyright libraries, while the remaining two were sold in 1975 to raise money for the press.

The booklet was set by hand and printed at the Bourne Valley Printing Company, Farnham, Surrey.

A21   THE MARTYRDOM OF BISHOP FARRAR   1970

a.1. First separate printing:

The Martyrdom of | Bishop Farrar | by Ted Hughes

[1]^4. Pages [1–8], consisting: [1] facsimile of an account of the martyrdom, with woodcut, from a 16th-century edition of Foxe's *Book of Martyrs*; [2] 'Burned by Bloody Mary's men at Caermarthen. | "If I flinch from the pain of burning, believe not | the doctrine that I have preached." (His words on | being chained to the stake).'; [3] title page; [4–5] the poem; [6–7] blank; [8] 'Printed with the kind consent of Messrs. Faber and | Faber Ltd. | This is one of 100 copies, signed and dated, of which | this is | No [short dotted line] | [rule, 3.35 cm.] | Number Seven in *THE MANUSCRIPT SERIES* | Published by Richard Gilbertson, | Bow, Crediton, Devon. | PHILLIPS & CO., PRINTERS, CREDITON.'

Bound with two metal rivets into red and blue marble-printed wrappers, front and back printed 'The cruell burning of Maiſter Farrar, Martyr. | [woodcut from page [1]]'.

Paper brownish, poor quality, 25.3 × 18.0 cm., bulk .1 cm.; all edges cut.

The poem appeared previously in *The Hawk in the Rain.* Lines 2 and 3 of the third stanza are transposed, reading '... Thus their shepherd she seized / In their eyes ...'.

Published March 1970 at 10s. 6d. Exact number of copies unknown, but probably somewhat more than 100.

This version is much more commonly found than the corrected second printing, and there is little doubt that the whole printing was sold despite the defects. Most copies are unnumbered and unsigned. However, a copy has been noted with Hughes' signature and his manuscript notes and corrections, dated 25 September 1971, and with a note probably in Hughes' hand reading 'One of 6 out of series'.

Richard Gilbertson wrote (letter, 2 February 1981): 'My original intention was to have the woodcut blown up & to do a broadside in the style of those broadsides that were done, admittedly at a later date, and handed out at 'important' executions. [In fact he advertised the broadside in a catalogue at £9.9.0.] Then I found the marbled paper & changed my plans, for it seemed to me that if the woodcut were imposed on the flames-and-blue-sky of the paper that it could be very effective. But unfortunately it reminded Ted of an old school exercise book! And this, combined with the fact that the local printer transposed two of the lines of the poem, made it necessary to do it again.'

a.2. Second printing (corrected):

CONTENTS the same as above with the following changes:

1. The title page bears Hughes' signature and a date.

2. The transposed lines appear in their proper order ('... Thus their shepherd she seized / And knotted him ...'), but tilted.

3. A number has been written in the blank on the colophon page, and a printed slip of white paper, approximately 5.4 × 13.8 cm., is pasted in under the printer's name, reading as follows: 'Copies numbered 1–5 with the whole poem in the authors [sic] | fair manuscript. Signed and Dated. | Copies 6–12. Each having one of the seven verses in the | authors fair manuscript. Signed and Dated. | Copies 13–100. Signed and Dated'.

Paper same as the first printing, but 24.4 × 18.0–18.3 cm.

Stapled into light brown paper wrappers, front printed as in the first printing, back blank.

Published 4 March 1970. Gilbertson, in a catalogue issued just before publication, advertised copies 1–4 [sic] unbound at £20, and copies 5–100 (signed and dated only) at £6.6.0. A copy at the University of

Windsor (Ontario) has manuscript alterations to the pasted-in limitation slip, apparently in Hughes' hand, changing the series numbers to 1–6, 7–13, and 14–100. The compilers have not seen a copy with all or part of the poem in manuscript.

A22   [FOUR CROW POEMS]   1970

Four broadsides, each with poem printed in black with abstract designs coloured as noted below. All but the first on plain heavy white paper. Each numbered by hand and signed by R. J. Lloyd.

'That Moment'. Illustration in brown and black on yellow-brown 'laid' paper (chain lines vertical, 2.5 cm.) with fine black fibres; 45.6 × 31.5 cm.

'King of Carrion'. Illustration in light brown and dark brown; 54.4 × 41.8 cm.

'Crow and the Birds'. Illustration in grey; 63.1 × 52.2 cm.

'Crow's Last Stand'. Illustration in grey, brown, black and red; 55.8 × 77.0 cm., folded across the long side.

Issued without a portfolio.

Published 25 August 1970; about 20 numbered copies of each broadside were sold at £4 each, plus an undetermined number of artist's proofs at varying prices. At least some of the broadsides were signed by Hughes as well. Copies have been reported with Lloyd's signature dated either 1970 or 1978, and Hughes' 1978.

A23   THE COMING OF THE KINGS   1970
                  AND OTHER PLAYS

a. First edition:

THE COMING | OF THE KINGS | *and Other Plays* | [ornament, four-pointed snowflake] | TED HUGHES | London | FABER & FABER

$(A)^8B–F^8 = 48$ leaves. Pages (1–4)5(6–10)11–96, consisting: (1) half-title, '*The Coming of the Kings* | [snowflake, as on title page]'; (2) list of eleven other books by Hughes; (3) title page; (4) '*First published in 1970* | *by Faber and Faber Limited* | *24 Russell Square London WC1* | *Printed in Great Britain by* | *Latimer Trend & Co Ltd Plymouth* | *All rights reserved* | *ISBN 0 571 09518 6 (cloth)* | *ISBN 0 571 09562 3 (paper)* | *[. . .]* | *© 1970 by Ted Hughes*'; 5, table of contents; (6) blank; (7) '*Author's Note* | These plays were originally | written for broadcasting [. . .]'; (8) blank; (9) divisional title, same as half-title; (10) cast of characters for first play; 11–96 text. Text pages 33, 34, 58–60, 78–80 unnumbered.

Calico-grain blue paper over boards. Spine round, stamped in gold: '[four-pointed snowflake, as on title page] *The Coming of the Kings* TED HUGHES FABER [snowflake, as above]'.

Dust-wrapper white, printed in blue and black: 'TED HUGHES | The Coming | of the Kings | [drawing, in brown, blue, and black, of king flourishing an urn before befuddled citizenry] | & other plays [title in freehand-designed letters]'. Spine printed in brown and black: 'TED HUGHES The Coming of the Kings [drawing continued from front] Faber [title and publisher in freehand-designed letters]'. Back: blurbs for other Faber children's books.

Paper plain white, 20.1 × 13.1 cm., bulk .8 cm.; all edges cut. Printed letterpress.

CONTENTS: The Coming of the Kings—The Tiger's Bones—Beauty and the Beast—Sean, the Fool, the Devil, and the Cats.

Published 1 September 1970 at £1.00; 2000 copies printed. A paperback printing of 3000 copies was printed offset and issued simultaneously. There was a 1977 reprint of 2000 hardbound copies. The paperback was reprinted in 1972 (5000 copies), 1973 (5000 copies), 1976 (6038 copies), and 1979 (6000 copies). Reprints are identified on the verso title.

b. First American edition, 1974 (The Tiger's Bones *):*

[flush to left] TED HUGHES | *THE TIGER'S BONES* | *and Other Plays for Children* | *Illustrated by* ALAN E. COBER | THE VIKING PRESS NEW YORK [background drawing, covering both pages, of a tiger, a telescope, and a disappearing man]

$[1]^8[2-4]^{16}[5-6]^8 = 72$ leaves. Pages $(1-11)12-141(142-144)$, consisting: (1) half-title, '*THE TIGER'S BONES* | *and Other Plays for Children*'; (2) half of title-spread drawing; (3) title page, with other half of drawing; (4) '*First Edition* | Copyright © 1974 by Ted Hughes. Illustrations © 1974 by The | Viking Press, Inc. All rights reserved. First published in 1974 by | The Viking Press, Inc. [...] | [printing code (1– 74) and CIP data] | Four of these plays were published under the title *The Coming of* | *the Kings* by Faber and Faber (London) in 1970, © 1970 by Ted | Hughes. "Orpheus" was published by the British Broadcasting | Corporation in 1971, © 1971 by Ted Hughes. | [...]'; (5) '*Author's Note* | These plays were originally | written for broadcasting [...]'; (6) blank; (7) table of contents; (8) drawing of men, bones, and syringes; (9) divisional title '*The Tiger's Bones*'; (10) cast of characters for the first play; (11) 12–141 text; (142) blank; (143) capsule biographies of Hughes and Cober; (144) blank. Text pages 41–45, 68–71, 92–95, 109–113 unnumbered. Six illustrations, halftone.

Paper over boards. Front, in red and black, drawing of telescope, tiger, and man (not same as title page); printed 'TED HUGHES | *THE TIGER'S BONES* | *and Other Plays for Children* | *Illustrated by* ALAN E. COBER'. Background continues across spine to back. Spine: '*THE TIGER'S BONES* HUGHES VIKING [author and publisher in white on black background]'. Back: signature 'Alan E. Cober' and 'SBN 670-71263-9'.

Dust-wrapper same design as cover. At top of front flap: '*Reinforced Binding* $5.95 | 0174'.

Paper plain white, 21.2 × 14.2 cm., bulk 1.0 cm.; all edges cut. Printed offset.

CONTENTS the same as the English edition, with the addition of 'Orpheus'. The latter was first published separately in 1973, in the U.S. only (item A38).

Published January 1974 at $5.95; 10,000 copies printed. Copies shipped later have a sticker over the dust-wrapper price, changing it to $7.95.

REVIEWS: *Booklist*, 1 Apr. 1974; *Children's Literature*, vol. 3, 1974 (Stephen Howard Foreman); *Horn Book*, Apr. 1974; *Junior Bookshelf*, Dec. 1970; *Kirkus*, 1 Jan. 1974; *Library Journal*, 15 Mar. 1974; *Observer*, 27 Sept. 1970; *Publishers Weekly*, 11 May 1974; *Spectator*, 5 Dec. 1970; *Teacher*, May 1975; *Teachers' World*, 19 Feb. 1971 (Sidney Robbins); *Times Literary Supplement*, 30 Oct. 1970; *Use of English*, Spring 1971 (David A. Male).

A24   A FEW CROWS   1970

[in black and dark violet] *Ted Hughes* | A FEW CROWS | *Illustrated by* | *Reiner Burger* | 1970 | THE ROUGEMONT PRESS · EXETER

$[1]^8[2]^6 = 14$ leaves. Pages (i–vi)1–19(20–22), consisting: (i) half-title; (ii) drawing; (iii) title page; (iv) blank; (v) table of contents; (vi) blank; 1–19 text; (20) blank; (21) 'THIS LIMITED EDITION OF ONE HUNDRED AND FIFTY | COPIES WAS PRINTED BY ERIC CLEAVE AT THE | ROUGEMONT PRESS EXETER | 1970 | SET IN 10pt BEMBO BOLD, THE FIRST | SEVENTY-FIVE COPIES ARE SIGNED BY THE AUTHOR | THIS COPY BEING | NUMBER | [number] | [signature in copies 1–75] | The Rougemont Press was founded in 1969, and is directed by | Eric Cleave, Ted Hughes, Moelwyn Merchant, & Paul Merchant'; (22) blank. Text pages 3, 6, 9, 14, 17 unnumbered. Six illustrations, line cuts.

Pigskin-grained dark blue plastic over boards. Front stamped in gold, 'A FEW CROWS'. Spine round. Endpapers coated dark blue.

Dust-wrapper very light blue 'laid' (chain lines horizontal, 2.4 cm.), marked '[crown] | Glastonbury' (5.9 × 12.2 cm.). Front printed in blue-black: '*Ted Hughes | A FEW CROWS*'.

Paper plain white Huntsman cartridge, 18.7 × 19.4 cm., bulk .2 cm.; all edges cut. Text printed letterpress on a Cropper treadle press; illustrations printed by lithography on an R30/95 press.

CONTENTS: Crow's First Lesson—A Kill—Notes for a Little Play—A Grin—The Battle of Osfrontis[1]—Crow Tyrannosaurus[2]—A Childish Prank—That Moment—Carnival—Crow's Last Stand.

Published around 1 October 1970 at £5 signed / £1.10.0 unsigned; 150 copies printed.

A25   CROW: FROM THE LIFE AND SONGS   1970
                   OF THE CROW

a.1. First edition:

[flush to left] CROW | From the Life and Songs | of the Crow | TED HUGHES | FABER AND FABER | London

(A)[8]B–E[8] = 40 leaves. Pages (1–6)7–80, consisting: (1) half-title; (2) list of twelve other books by Hughes; (3) title page; (4) '*First published in 1970 | by Faber and Faber Limited | 24 Russell Square London WC1 | Printed in Great Britain by | The Bowering Press Plymouth | All rights reserved | ISBN 0 571 09563 1 |* Grateful acknowledgement is made to the | Abraham Woursell Foundation | © *1970 by Ted Hughes*'; (5) 'In Memory | of Assia and Shura'; (6) blank; 7–8 table of contents; 9–80 text.

Black cloth over boards. Spine round, stamped in gold: 'CROW   TED HUGHES   FABER'.

Dust-wrapper cream-coloured, marked 'BASINGWERK' (1.0 × 6.5 cm.), printed in black and brick red. Front: 'CROW | TED HUGHES | [crow drawing, front view, signed '·BASKIN·'] | [between crow's legs] From the Life | and Songs of | the Crow'. Spine: 'CROW   From the Life & Songs of the Crow   TED HUGHES   Faber'. Back: list of six other books by Hughes. Olwyn Hughes reports seeing a dust-wrapper printed on white paper.

Paper plain white, 21.6 × 13.8 cm., bulk .7 cm.; all edges cut. Printed letterpress.

---

[1] 'The Battle of Osfrontalis' in *Crow*.
[2] A stanza was omitted by the printer. The full poem appears in *Crow*.

CONTENTS: Two Legends—Lineage—Examination at the Womb-door—A Kill—Crow and Mama—The Door—A Childish Prank—Crow's First Lesson—Crow Alights—That Moment—Crow Tyrannosaurus—Crow's Account of the Battle—The Black Beast—A Grin—Crow Communes—Crow's Account of St. George—A Disaster—The Battle of Osfrontalis—Crow's Theology—Crow and the Birds—Criminal Ballad—Crow on the Beach—Oedipus Crow—Crow's Vanity—A Horrible Religious Error—Crow's Nerve Fails—In Laughter—Crow Frowns—Magical Dangers—Robin Song—Conjuring in Heaven—Crow Goes Hunting—Owl's Song—Crow's Undersong—Dawn's Rose—Crow's Playmates—Crowego—The Smile—Crow Improvises—Crow's Battle Fury—Crow Blacker Than Ever—Revenge Fable—A Bedtime Story—Crow's Song of Himself—Crow Sickened—Song for a Phallus—Apple Tragedy—Crow's Last Stand—Crow and the Sea—Truth Kills Everybody—Crow and Stone—Fragment of an Ancient Tablet—Notes for a Little Play—Snake Hymn—Lovesong—Glimpse—King of Carrion—Two Eskimo Songs: I. Fleeing from Eternity, II. How Water Began to Play—Littleblood.

Published 12 October 1970 at 20s.; 4000 copies printed. There were two reprints the same year of 4000 copies each, and two in 1971 of 4000 and 3000 copies respectively. Reprints are identified on the verso title.

a.2. Sixth printing, augmented (1972):

Faber's sixth printing of *Crow* is referred to as a new edition on the verso title and on the front flap of the dust-wrapper. It is actually a reprint from the original edition with the addition of seven poems: Crow Hears Fate Knock on the Door—Crow's Fall—The Contender—Crow Tries the Media—Crow's Elephant Totem Song—Crowcolour—Crow Paints Himself into a Chinese Mural. All but 'Crowcolour' appeared previously in the American edition of *Crow*; 'The Contender' appeared also in *Crow Wakes*.

Published 11 December 1972 at £1.40; 4000 copies printed. This augmented text was reprinted in 1973 (5000 copies). The first English paperback printing, offset from the augmented text, was published 14 October 1974 in 20,000 copies; a further 20,000 paperbound copies were printed in 1976. In the mid- to late 1980s Faber redesigned the title page and covers to its new standard double-rule frame format, but the text remains in the setting of a.2. Reprints are identified on the verso title; the latest the compilers have seen is the eighth.

b. First American edition (1971):

[double-page title; left page, flush to right:] *From the Life and | Songs of the Crow* | HARPER & ROW, PUBLISHERS | NEW YORK,

EVANSTON, SAN FRANCISCO, LONDON [right page, flush to right:] [crow drawing, same as on dust-wrapper of first English edition] | CROW | by Ted Hughes

$[1–3]^{16}$ = 48 leaves. Pages (i–vi)vii–viii(ix–x)1–84(85–86), consisting: (i) half-title; (ii) blank; (iii) list of nine other books by Hughes; (iv–v) title spread; (vi) 'IN MEMORY | OF ASSIA AND SHURA | [acknow-ledgements] | CROW. Copyright © 1971 by Ted Hughes. All rights reserved. Printed in the | United States of America [...] | [...] | FIRST U.S. EDITION | STANDARD BOOK NUMBER: 06-011989-6 | [...]'; vii–viii table of contents; (ix) half-title, as above; (x) blank; 1–84 text; (85) capsule biography; (86) blank save for printing code, lower right (71–1).

Quarter black cloth, pale yellow linen-grain paper sides over boards. Front, stamped in black, crow drawing as on title page, reduced. Spine flat, stamped in red: 'Ted Hughes CROW HARPER & ROW'. Endpapers black.

Dust-wrapper cream-coloured. Front printed in red and black, letters in freehand design: 'CROW | [Baskin crow, watercolour, left profile, reproduced black-and-white halftone] | *TED HUGHES*'. Spine lettered as on front: 'CROW *TED HUGHES* Harper & Row [publisher in standard type]'. Back: photo of Hughes by Fay Godwin. On front flap, lower right, '0371'.

Paper plain white, 20.9 × 13.8 cm., bulk .75 cm.; all edges cut. Printed offset.

CONTENTS same as the first English printing, with the addition of the following: Crow's Fall—Crow Tries the Media—The Contender—Crow Paints Himself into a Chinese Mural—The Lovepet—Crow Hears Fate Knock on the Door—Crow's Elephant Totem Song.

Published 3 March 1971 at $5.95 (publisher's review slip gives 17 March); 5000 copies printed. The second printing, also 1971, lacks the first edition notice, and the printing code on the last page is changed to 71–2. The first paperback printing, simultaneous with the first hardbound printing and priced at $2.95, is identical internally. A later paperback printing, also priced at $2.95, has the last line of the left-hand side of the title reset to read 'New York, Hagerstown, San Francisco, London'. The lower left corner of the front cover bears the code 'TD 119'. All paperback reprints the compilers have seen lack the 'FIRST U.S. EDITION' note and are identified with a printing code.

c. Second English edition (limited, 1973):

CROW | [swelled rule, 13.9 cm.] | From the Life and Songs of the Crow

| [swelled rule, 12.6 cm.] | TED HUGHES | With twelve drawings by | LEONARD | BASKIN | Faber and Faber 3 Queen Square | LONDON

[1–16]⁴ = 64 leaves. Pages (1–8)9–11(12–14)15–123(124–128), consisting: (1–2) blank; (3) half-title, '[swelled rule, 13.9 cm.] | CROW | [swelled rule, 12.6 cm.]'; (4) blank; (5) title page; (6) 'Published in 1973 | by Faber and Faber Limited | 3 Queen Square London WC1 | All rights reserved | ISBN 0 571 10294 8 | © Text copyright Ted Hughes 1970, 1972, 1973 | © Illustrations copyright Leonard Baskin 1973'; (7) 'IN MEMORY | OF | ASSIA AND SHURA | [swelled rule, 9.2 cm.]'; (8) blank; 9–11 table of contents; on p. 11 'PUBLISHER'S NOTE | This limited edition of CROW contains | three new poems which did not appear in | the previous Faber editions. They are: | Crow Rambles | Crow's Courtship | Crow's Song about Prospero and Sycorax'; (12) blank; (13) Baskin crow's head, left profile; (14) blank; 15–123 text; (124) blank; (125) 'Set by hand in Pegasus type | designed by Berthold Wolpe, | printed by the John Roberts Press | Clerkenwell, London | on T. H. Saunders mould-made paper | in a limited edition of 400 copies | Number [number] | [signatures of Hughes and Baskin]'; (126–128) blank. Text pages 19, 20, 27, 28, 39, 40, 47, 48, 57, 58, 67, 68, 79, 80, 89, 90, 101, 102, 109, 110, 117, 118 unnumbered. Twelve illustrations, line cuts.

Quarter coated black cloth, blue cloth sides over bevelled boards. Spine round, stamped in gold: 'Ted Hughes [right double brackets] CROW [left double brackets] Drawings by Leonard Baskin Faber'. Endpapers maroon.

Slip-case, black paper over heavy black-coated cardboard. On front, maroon paper label, 10.2 × 13.7 cm., printed: 'CROW | [swelled rule, 12.6 cm.] | TED HUGHES | With drawings by Leonard Baskin | Limited edition'.

Paper: Saunders 'NOT' mould-made drawing paper, ca. 32.7 × 24.1 cm., bulk 1.95 cm.; top edge cut, coloured red; fore- and bottom edges uncut. Printed letterpress.

CONTENTS the same as the augmented Faber trade edition (A25a.2), with the addition of three poems: 'Crow Rambles'[1] and 'Crow's Courtship', which appeared previously in *Poems* with Fainlight and Sillitoe (A29); and 'Crow's Song about Prospero and Sycorax',[2] which appeared previously in *Shakespeare's Poem* (A30).

---

[1] Collected in *Moortown* as 'Life is Trying to be Life'.
[2] Collected in *Moortown* as 'Prospero and Sycorax'.

Published 10 December 1973 at £30. A copy lettered 'A' was displayed at a Berthold Wolpe retrospective, and more lettered copies may exist in addition to the 400 in series.

Berthold Wolpe designed the book as well as the type; it was printed by Harry Upson on a Polygraph press under the supervision of Bernard Roberts and Wolpe.

d. Third English edition (1995):

[flush to left] TED HUGHES Crow | *From the Life and Songs of the Crow* | THE FABER LIBRARY | [indented] ff | [flush to left] *faber and faber*

[A^{16} B–C^{12} D^{16}] = 56 leaves (glued binding, not sewn). Pages (i–xiv) 1–89(90–98), consisting: (i–ii) blank; (iii) '[flush to left] THE FABER LIBRARY 5'; (iv) '*by the same author* | [37 titles]'; (v) title page; (vi) 'First published in 1970 | by Faber and Faber Limited | 3 Queen Square, London, WC1N 3AU | Faber Library edition first published in 1995 | Photoset by Parker Typesetting Service, Leicester | Printed in England by Clays Ltd, St Ives plc | All rights reserved | © Ted Hughes, 1970, 1972 | [notes on identification of author, CIP record, and ISBN] | [printing code, 10–1]'; (vii) '[flush to left] In Memory of Assia and Shura'; (viii) blank; (ix–xi) table of contents; (xii) blank; (xiii) '[flush to left] Publisher's note | This Faber Library edition follows the text of the 1972 | edition and includes the following seven poems which did | not appear in the original edition: | [...]'; (xiv) blank; 1–89 text; (90–98) blank.

Black calico-grain paper over boards. Spine round, stamped in gold: 'TED HUGHES   Crow [at foot, reading across] ff'. Endpapers blue.

Dust-wrapper light blue, printed in black and darker blue: '[flush to left] TED HUGHES | Crow | *From the Life and Songs | of the Crow* | [blurb by Peter Porter] | 1970   ff | THE FABER LIBRARY 5'. Spine printed like book spine, title in blue. Back: 'THE FABER LIBRARY | [6 titles] | [bar code] UK £8.95 net'.

12.7 × 9.75 cm., bulk .8 cm.; all edges cut. Printed offset.

CONTENTS same as A25a.2.

Published November 1995 at £8.95; number of copies undetermined.

REVIEWS: *Agenda*, Spring–Summer 1971 (Peter Dale); *Ambit* 46, 1971 (Martin Bax); *Birmingham Post*, 17 Oct. 1970 (Barbara Lloyd-Evans); *Book World*, 2 Jan. 1972; *Books and Bookmen*, Dec. 1970 (Derek Stanford); *Cambridge Quarterly*, Autumn 1971 (J. M. Newton); *Christian Science Monitor*, 29 Apr. 1971 (Victor Howes); *Church Times*, 27 Nov. 1970 (Norman Nicholson); *Commonweal*, 17 Sept. 1971 (B. Wallenstein);

Contemporary Literature, Winter 1973 (Marjorie G. Perloff); *Critical Quarterly*, Spring 1971 (David Lodge); *Delta*, Spring 1972 (N. Roberts); *Encounter*, March 1971 (Douglas Dunn); *English*, Spring 1971 (Howard Sergeant); *English Studies*, Dec. 1971 (F. M. Kuna); *Erasmus Review* 1, 1971 (Lee J. Richmond); *Guardian*, 15 Oct. 1970 (Peter Porter); *Hudson Review*, Summer 1971 (H. Carruth); *Human World*, Nov. 1972 (I. Robinson and D. Sims); *Irish Press*, 31 Oct. 1970 (Dannie Abse); *Irish Times*, 31 Oct. 1970 (Eavan Boland); *Kirkus*, 1 Feb. 1971; *Library Journal*, July 1971 (Sanford Dorbin); *Listener*, 29 Oct. 1970 (Derwent May); *London Magazine*, Jan. 1971 (Tony Harrison); *Malahat Review*, Apr. 1971 (R.S.); *Mediterranean Review*, Fall 1971 (Dabney Stuart); *Nation*, 16 Mar. 1974; *National Observer*, 31 May 1971; *New Statesman*, 16 Oct. 1970 (Alan Brownjohn); *Newsweek*, Apr. 1971 (J. Kroll); *New York Review of Books*, 22 July 1971 (Stephen Spender); *New York Times*, 18 Mar. 1971; *New York Times Book Review*, 18 Apr. 1971 (Daniel Hoffman), 2 June 1971, 12 Jan. 1974; *Observer*, 11 Oct. 1970 (A. Alvarez); *Outposts*, Summer 1971 (Ralph Meredith); *Parnassus*, 14:1, 1987 (Calvin Bedient); *Partisan Review*, Winter 1971/2 (G. S. Fraser); *Platform*, Summer 1971 (Luke Spencer); *Poetry*, Feb. 1972 (C. Kizer); *Prairie Schooner*, Fall 1972 (Mordecai Marcus); *The Review*, Dec. 1970 (John Fuller); *Saturday Review*, 2 Oct. 1971 (J. Kessler); *Scotsman*, 31 Oct. 1970 (Martin Seymour-Smith); *Sewanee Review*, July 1976; *Shenandoah*, Winter 1972 (Peter Cooley); *Southern Arts*, Jan. 1971 (John Fairfax); *Southern Review*, Spring 1975 (Steve Utz); *Spectator*, 6 Mar. 1971 (Christopher Hudson); *Stand*, Vol. 12, No. 2, 1971 (Anne Cluysenaar); *Sunday Telegraph*, 11 Oct. 1970 (C. B. Cox); *Sunday Times*, 25 Oct. 1970 (Lyman Andrews); *Sydney Morning Herald*, 5 June 1971 (Philip Roberts); *Tablet*, 21 Nov. 1970 (Damian Grant); *Time*, 5 April 1971 (Christopher Porterfield); *Times*, 17 Dec. 1970 (Richard Holmes); *Times Literary Supplement*, 8 Jan. 1971 (Ian Hamilton); *Tribune*, 11 Dec. 1970 (Jeremy Robson); *Use of English*, Vol. 22, No. 3, 1971 (Sandy Cunningham); *Wilson Library Bulletin*, Feb. 1974.

A26   FIGHTING FOR JERUSALEM   1970

[broadside:] [on a background of green flies rising from the eyeholes of a reddish-brown head] FIGHTING FOR JERUSALEM | [the poem] | *Ted Hughes | graphics, Ron Brown; midNAG poetry poster No. 7*

Paper brownish, 59.4 × 41.8 cm.; all edges cut. Printed offset.

Published around 20 October 1970 at an unknown price by the Mid Northumberland Arts Group; number of copies unknown, but George Stephenson of midNAG has written that 'the poetry poster editions are normally 400' [letter to Seamus Cooney].

A27   AMULET   1970

[Not seen by the compilers; described from a photocopy, and a description provided by the University of Calgary] Ted Hughes | *Amulet* | Published by A & G | Woodford Green | Christmas 1970

[1–2⁴] = 8 leaves. Pages [1–16], consisting: [1–2] blank; [3] half-title, 'Ted Hughes | AMULET'; [4] *'Printed and bound by Alan and Gemma | at 44 Westview Drive Woodford Green | December 1970'*; [5] title page; [6] blank; [7] *'for Eric and Dodo'*; [8] blank; [9] the poem; [10] blank; [11] *'This edition of one is published by A & G | for Eric and Dodo and with sincere acknowledgment to | Ted Hughes, marking the occasion of | Christmas and the prolonged | generosity of Eric and Dodo | to the publishers'*; [12–16] blank.

The unique copy is inscribed by Hughes on the half-title: 'To Dodo & Eric | [printed half-title text] | affectionately Ted | These are badger's whiskers | to bring you good lucks | briskers'. Two badger whiskers are taped to the page. P. [13] is inscribed 'Best wishes for Christmas & | the New Year | Love from Alan & Gemma'.

Simulated vellum 'Elephant Hide' (a synthetic paper) over boards; spine stamped in purple: 'TED HUGHES   AMULET'. Endpapers red, openings printed in an Oriental pattern.

Paper cream-coloured, 13.1 × 8.9 cm.; top edge cut, fore- and bottom edge trimmed.

Printed letterpress.

Alan and Gemma Tarling were the producers, and Eric and Dorothy White the recipients of this little book. The poem was part of the batch which was excluded from *Crow* and published as *Crow Wakes*. The original is now at the University of Calgary; a photostat of the same, before the inscriptions and the badger hairs were added, is at Harvard.

A27*   THIS GAME OF CHESS   ca. 1970

One fold; pages (1–4), consisting: (1) within a pea-green rule frame, colour reproduction of a photograph of three Elisabeth Frink sculptures of heads; (2) within a pea-green rule frame, Hughes' poem (untitled, first line 'This Game of Chess is played for Love.') printed in blue in two columns with undated copyright statement; below, in black: 'Three Elisabeth Frink heads at 40 Castelnau, Barnes, London SW13'; (3) within a pea-green rule frame, in black: 'Wishing you a very merry Christmas from | Nicky, Madeleine, Benedict & Peter Marsh'; (4) 'Photograph by Michael Joseph'.

Paper medium glossy, 20.4 × 26.3 cm.; all edges cut. Printed offset.

Possibly published in 1970, though this date could be off by two or three years; number of copies undetermined.

Peter Marsh, who owned the sculptures, had them photographed and commissioned Hughes to write a poem based on the photograph.

A28   CROW WAKES   1971

Ted | Hughes | CROW | WAKES | Poet & | Printer

[1–2]⁸ = 16 leaves. Pages (1–6)7–27(28–32), consisting: (1) half-title, 'CROW WAKES | TED HUGHES'; (2) blank; (3) title page; (4) *'Two hundred copies of | this book were printed and bound | for April 1971, a hundred each going to poet | and printer, by Alan Tarling at 44 Westview Drive | Woodford Green Essex UK where the imprint | Poet & Printer is registered. Copyright | is retained by the poet |* Ted Hughes © 1971'; (5) table of contents; (6) blank; 7–27 text; (28–32) blank.

Quarter cream-coloured Elephant Hide; red, patterned Elephant Hide sides over boards. Front: 'Ted | Hughes | CROW | WAKES | Twelve | Poems'. Spine round, printed: 'TED HUGHES CROW WAKES'. Endpapers 'laid' (chain lines vertical, 2.6 cm.), marked '[crown] | *Glastonbury*' (6.1 × 11.3 cm.).

Issued without a dust-wrapper.

Paper plain white (Grosvenor Chater cream cartridge), 19.5–20.0 × 12.2 cm., bulk .2 cm.; all edges cut. Handset, printed letterpress on an Adana 8 × 5 platen press.

CONTENTS: Crow Wakes[1]—Bones—Amulet—Crow's Table Talk[2]—In the Land of the Lion—I See a Bear—Anecdote—Song against the White Owl—The Ship—Lullaby—Snow Song—The Contender. 'Amulet' is in the same setting as its separate printing (A27).

Published April 1971 at £2.25; about 230 copies printed. Regarding this book, Mr. Tarling writes as follows: 'These poems were excluded for personal reasons from [Hughes'] *Crow* opus and he offered them to me in March 1970. The printing and casing-in lasted until April 71 when I began sending off copies. There were 200, a hundred each going to poet (TH) and printer (me) plus 30 review or academic copies. None of mine was signed and each cost £2.25, though I gave some to friends and relatives. All the "academic" copies were gratis, and said as much in an extra colophon ... I don't know how TH's copies were distributed or whether or not they were signed. My hundred copies

[1] An extract from *Eat Crow*.
[2] Collected in *Moortown* as 'Tiger-psalm'.

seemed to sell fairly quickly over six months or so.' [Letter, 2 November 1976.] Copies numbered and signed by Hughes have been seen, and some of these contain manuscript corrections to the last two lines of 'The Ship' (page 22). Tarling reportedly used two differing manuscript versions of this poem, one later than the other; however, Hughes' corrections vary from copy to copy, and it might be difficult at this point to establish final intention. Most likely the intended reading is 'Or be dragged from your bag of nerves, beyond your last howls / Into the Paradise of the Crow.'

A29   POEMS [WITH RUTH FAINLIGHT   1971
        AND ALAN SILLITOE]

POEMS | RUTH | FAINLIGHT | TED | HUGHES | ALAN | SILLITOE | [ark, dove and rainbow drawing, 3.8 × 5.2 cm.] | RAINBOW PRESS | LONDON 1971

[1–5]^4 = 20 leaves. Pages (i–viii)1–28(29–32), consisting: (i) half-title, (ii) blank; (iii) title page; (iv) '© RUTH FAINLIGHT 1971 | © TED HUGHES 1971 | © ALAN SILLITOE 1971'; (v) table of contents: (vi) blank; (vii) divisional title 'RUTH FAINLIGHT | [two-part swelled rule]'; (viii) blank; 1–28 text; (29–30) blank; (31) 'Published by the RAINBOW PRESS in April 1971 | in an edition of 300 copies | all numbered and signed by the three authors | Set in Bembo and Poliphilus types and printed at | Daedalus Press, Stoke Ferry, Norfolk on | Saunders mould made rag paper, not finish | Fully bound by Davis & Hodges, London, in olive green | leather, blocked in real gold front, spine and back, | with hand-printed Japanese endpapers, | in slip case of olive green leather | This is number [number] | [the three signatures]'; (32) blank. Text pages 8–10, 19, 20 unnumbered.

Bound in full olive-green leather, stamped in gold. Front: illustration of Isis from an early printed book, surrounded by text, headed 'ISIDIS | Magnæ Deorum Matris | APULEIANA DESCRIPTIO.'. Spine: 'POEMS * FAINLIGHT HUGHES SILLITOE RAINBOW PRESS'. Back: 'POEMS | [ornament as on half-title and divisional titles] | RUTH FAINLIGHT | TED HUGHES | ALAN SILLITOE'. Endpapers of decorated Japanese paper pasted to a sheet of the text paper; several types of Japanese paper were used.

In a cardboard slip-case covered with the same type of leather as the book, lined with decorated paper.

Paper mould-made 'wove', marked 'SAUNDERS' in open-face letters, but most of mark cropped. Overall 22.7 × 13.2 cm., bulk .4 cm.; all edges cut, top edge coloured green. Printed letterpress.

CONTENTS [poems by Hughes begin on page 11, preceded by Fainlight's section and followed by Sillitoe's]: Crow Rambles[1]—Genesis of Evil—Crow's Song About England—Crow's Courtship—Crow's Song About God—Crow the Just.

Published April 1971 at £18; slightly over 300 copies printed (see above, 'The Rainbow Press', p. 4).

A30   SHAKESPEARE'S POEM   1971

[no title page; cover title:] [within a ruled border, flush to left] Shakespeare's | Poem | Ted Hughes

Stab-bound bifolia, folds at fore-edge, outer leaves single. Printed in numbered columns two to a page; bifolia are here considered single leaves. [1–16] pages, consisting: [1] blank; [2] poem, 'Crow's Song about Prospero and Sycorax', 17 lines; [3–13] text, columns numbered 1–22; [14] 'This first edition is limited to one hundred and fifty copies, of which | seventy-five numbered copies, signed by the author are for sale. | The remaining seventy-five copies not for sale are for the author's use. | [signature and number] | *First published March 1971 by Lexham Press 1 Lexham Walk London W8* | *Printed in England by Trigram Press London* | © *Copyright 1971 Ted Hughes*'; [15–16] blank.

Last page pasted into black paper wrappers printed as above.

Laid into a black paper portfolio, front printed as wrappers above.

Paper: Main text paper stiff brown 'laid' ('wire' lines only, vertical), glossy on the printed side. Outer, single leaves heavy violet paper. 18.6 × 22.6 cm., bulk .18 cm.; top and bottom edges cut; wrappers project beyond contents. Printed letterpress.

Published May or June 1971 at £10; 150 copies printed.

This essay was included in Hughes' Shakespeare anthology (*A Choice of Shakespeare's Verse* in England and *With Fairest Flowers while Summer Lasts* in America, both 1971). It was printed for Judith J. Taylor by Asa Benveniste at the Trigram Press. Both individuals were unavailable to provide details on the publication.

[1] Collected in *Moortown* as 'Life is Trying to be Life'.

A31 EAT CROW 1971

TED HUGHES | EAT | CROW | LONDON | RAINBOW PRESS |
1971

[1–4]^4 = 16 leaves. Pages (i–viii)1–21(22–24), consisting: (i) half-title;
(ii) blank; (iii) crow drawing; (iv) blank; (v) title page; (vi) blank; (vii)
'Text [wrong-font 'x'] © Ted Hughes 1971 | Drawing © Leonard
Baskin 1971 | *The drawing by Leonard Baskin is greatly reduced | from its
original size* | All rights reserved'; (viii) blank; 1–21 text, at end '(1964)';
(22) blank; (23) 'This edition of 150 copies, numbered and signed | by
the author, was set in Bodoni types and printed at | Daedalus Press,
Stoke Ferry, Norfolk, on Italian | hand-made paper and bound by |
Zaehnsdorf, London. | This is copy number | [number] | [rule, 1.7 cm.] |
[signature] | [publisher's device, ark and rainbow, 38 × 52 mm.] |
Published by the RAINBOW PRESS, | 10 Arkwright Road, London
NW3.'; (24) blank.

Full black calf over boards. Spine flat, stamped in gold: 'TED HUGHES
★ EAT CROW Rainbow Press'.

Slip-case cardboard, covered outside with black cloth, lined with
marbled paper. Some copies bound up later come with slip-cases covered
with embossed linen-grain black paper.

Paper Italian mould-made wove, rough, unmarked, approx. 20.0 ×
15.2 cm., bulk .3 cm.; top edge cut, gilt; fore- and bottom edges deckle.
Printed letterpress.

Part of this work appeared earlier in the year as the title poem of *Crow
Wakes*.

Published November 1971 at £16.80/$45.00; slightly over 150 copies
were printed (see above, 'The Rainbow Press', p. 4), of which 135 were
for sale, the remainder for presentation.

A32 AUTUMN SONG 1971

[broadside:] [outline of large leaf on an orange ground; inside, on
background of leaves and forest debris, the poem on white leaf shapes
(one stanza per leaf); at head, in white on a black leaf] AUTUMN
SONG | from 5 poems for children | by | TED HUGHES | [at lower left]
NC 1971 [at lower right, in white on a black leaf, an advertisement for
another broadside] | drawn by Nina Carroll | available from | Nina
Steane | 31 Headlands | Kettering, Northants | England

Paper white, medium-high finish. 59.4 × 42.7 cm.; all edges cut.

Done in freehand-design letters; printed silk-screen.

A separate publication of 'Who's Killed the Leaves?' from *Five Autumn Songs for Children's Voices*.

Published 1971; price and number of copies unknown.

A33   THE POETRY OF TED HUGHES   1971

[Cover title:] The poetry of | Ted Hughes | A personal interpretation by Jill Lewin | [line of eight abstract decorations]

3, (8) separate sheets, consisting: 1–3 text by Lewin on white paper, each sheet printed in two columns one side only; (4–11) broadsides.

In a black paper portfolio, front printed in brown as above.

Printed on heavy unmarked paper of various colours (see contents); 38.0 × 12.9 cm.; all edges cut.

CONTENTS (order arbitrary, each broadside bearing an abstract lithograph printed on variously coloured paper, with the poem in letterpress): Crow Blacker Than Ever [purple on grey]—Fern [brown on tan]—New Moon in January [silver on light brown]—Relic [yellow on grey]—Still Life [grey on blue]—Sugar Loaf [brown on blue]—Thistles [purple on tan]—Wodwo [dark olive on brown].

Published 1971; price and number of copies unknown.

A34   IN THE LITTLE GIRL'S ANGEL GAZE ...   1972

Single sheet, 50.7 × 35.4 cm., folded, printed on one half of one side with fold at top. Within a heavy ruled border: illustration of crow, bones, blood, and two little girls' heads; poem at lower left. Outside border: at lower left, signature of Ralph Steadman; at lower right, Hughes' signature.

In a black paper folder, right flap with a blind-stamp: 'STEAM PRESS' between two concentric circles (outer measure 3.9 cm.). Inside left flap, printed in white: 'Edition limited to 50 copies only | numbered & signed by the author | & artist | This is No. | [number] | :c: 1972 Ted Hughes | and Ralph Steadman | Designed & printed by | Ralph Steadman on Chrome Coat | Art Paper at Steam Press | Kensington Church Walk | London W8 | [facsimile wood-engraving of steam press, 3.2 × 5.0 cm.] | Broadsheet No.8'.

Printed letterpress in black, brown and red.

Published early March 1972; 50 numbered copies were distributed. Of these, 40 were sold as singles at £3.15, packaged as described above. The first 10 were included in a ten-portfolio edition of broadside poems by various authors, called 'Ralph Steadman Poetry Broadsheets, Portfolio 1'. In the prospectus to the latter the present poem is called 'Crow Goes out to Play'. In addition, approximately 142 unnumbered copies were distributed as follows:

6 sent to the copyright libraries

12 copies, in folders, signed by both Hughes and Steadman for Hughes' use

6 copies, in folders, signed by both for Steadman's use

1 signed by Hughes to Steadman

1 signed by Steadman to Hughes

2 signed by both to personnel of Turret Books

16 copies, in folders, signed by Steadman only, retained by Steadman

17 copies, in folders, unsigned, retained by Steadman

29 copies, no folders, unsigned, retained by Steadman

52 spare half-sheets, no folders, unsigned, retained by Steadman.

Because the job was too complicated for Steadman's small press, the broadsides were actually printed by another press under Steadman's supervision. Steadman signed the *bon à tirer* on 10 January 1972, and the joint signing of the finished copies was done on 11 March.

A35 THE COMING OF THE KINGS 1972

First separate edition:

[line of type ornaments] | [wavy rule, 8.9 cm.] | A CHRISTMAS PLAY IN ONE ACT | The Coming of the Kings | by | TED HUGHES | [publisher's cuneiform device] | THE DRAMATIC PUBLISHING COMPANY | CHICAGO | [wavy rule, 8.9 cm.] | [line of type ornaments, as above]

[1]¹⁶. Pages (1–2)3–30(31–32), consisting: (1) title page; (2) '[double rule] | NOTICE | [rule] | The royalty fee, payable in advance [...] | [royalty information] | [rule] | © MCMLXXII By | TED HUGHES | Printed in the United States of America | All Rights Reserved | (THE COMING OF THE KINGS) | [rule]'; 3 '[double rule] | THE COMING OF THE KINGS | *A Christmas Play in One Act* | For Ten Men and Two Women | [rule] | [cast]'; 4, chart of stage positions and directions, with rule at top; 5–29 text; 30 '[double rule] | PROPERTIES | [rule] | [...]'; (31–32) blank save for running title 'DIRECTOR'S NOTES'.

Stapled into heavy orange-brown paper wrappers. Front: stylized star with rays, printed 'The Coming of the Kings | by Ted Hughes | [double rule, broken in middle by publisher's cuneiform device] | THE

DRAMATIC PUBLISHING COMPANY'. Back blank save for 'THE COMING OF THE KINGS' reading down near spine.

Paper plain white, 18.4 × 12.5 cm., bulk .2 cm.; all edges cut.

Composed on a typewriter, except for the title page, head title, and wrappers; contents printed offset, wrappers letterpress.

Contains the single play, which appeared originally in the Faber collection of the same name (A23).

Published 27 September 1972 at $1.00; 1025 copies printed. In 1975 the performance royalties were lowered from $15/$10 to $10/$7.50, and slips showing the change were pasted onto the verso title of some, but not all, copies distributed after this date.

A36   SELECTED POEMS 1957–1967   1972

a. First edition:

Selected Poems | 1957–1967 | Ted Hughes *| Faber & Faber | London*

[1–2]^{16}[3]^{8}[4]^{16} = 56 leaves. Pages (1–8)9–109(110–112), consisting: (1) half-title; (2) list of thirteen other books by Hughes; (3) title page; (4) '*This selection first published* 1972 *| by Faber and Faber Limited | 3 Queen Square London WC*1 *| Printed and bound by | Straker Brothers Ltd Whitstable |* ISBN 0 571 08926 7 | © Copyright Ted Hughes 1972 | [Conditions of Sale note]'; (5–7) table of contents; (8) blank; 9–109 text; (110–112) blank.

Wrappers. Front: '[on yellow field] Ted Hughes | [green band] | [on blue field] Selected | POEMS | 1957–1967'; at right margin, vertical black band with printing in white, reading down: 'FABER paper covered EDITIONS'. Spine: colours continued from front, printed 'TED HUGHES [green band] Selected Poems FABER' ('FABER' in white on a black field). Back: blurbs for other Hughes books; at left margin, vertical black band with printing in white, as on front but reading up. Inside covers: ads and critical comment on other books by Hughes.

Paper plain white, 18.5 × 12.3 cm., bulk .7 cm.; all edges cut. Printed offset.

CONTENTS: [From *The Hawk in the Rain*] The Thought-Fox—Song— The Jaguar—Famous Poet—Soliloquy[1]—The Horses—Fallgrief's Girl-Friends—Egg-Head—The Man Seeking Experience Enquires His Way

---

[1] = 'Soliloquy of a Misanthrope'.

of a Drop of Water—Meeting—Wind—October Dawn—Bayonet
Charge—Six Young Men—The Martyrdom of Bishop Farrar.
[From *Lupercal*] Mayday on Holderness—Crow Hill—A Woman
Unconscious—Strawberry Hill—Fourth of July—Esther's Tomcat—
Wilfred Owen's Photographs—Hawk Roosting—Fire-Eater—The Bull
Moses—Cat and Mouse—View of a Pig—The Retired Colonel—
November—Relic—An Otter—Witches—Thrushes—Snowdrop—
Pike—Sunstroke—Cleopatra to the Asp.

[From *Wodwo*] Thistles—Still Life—Her Husband—Cadenza—Ghost
Crabs—Boom[2]—Second Glance at a Jaguar—Fern—A Wind Flashes
the Grass—Bowled Over—Root, Stem, Leaf[3]—Stations[4]—The Green
Wolf—Scapegoats and Rabies[3]—The Bear—Theology—Gog[5]—
Kreutzer Sonata—Out—New Moon in January—The Warriors of the
North—The Rat's Dance[6]—Heptonstall—Skylarks[7]—Mountains—
Pibroch—The Howling of Wolves—Kafka[8]—Gnat-Psalm—Full Moon
and Little Frieda—Wodwo.

It was in this edition that the misprint 'hand' for 'band' in line 17 of
'November' first appeared, and it has persisted in all subsequent
collections.

Published 23 October 1972 at £0.60; 12,000 copies printed. There were
reprints in 1974 (10,000 copies), 1975 (10,000 copies), 1977 (15,167
copies), 1978 (20,000 copies), and 1979 (30,000 copies). Reprints are
identified on the verso title.

b. First American edition (1973):

[double-page title; printing in white against a predominantly black
drawing of a bear; left, flush to right:] TED | HUGHES | NEW YORK |
EVANSTON | SAN FRANCISCO | LONDON [right, flush to left:]
Selected | *Poems* | *1957–1967* | Drawings by Leonard Baskin | HARPER &
ROW, PUBLISHERS

[1–4]^{16} = 64 leaves. Pages [*i–ii*](i–vi)vii–ix(x–xii)1–111(112–114), consisting: one blank leaf: (i) half-title; (ii) blank; (iii) list of ten other books
by Hughes; (iv–v) title spread; (vi) '[acknowledgements] | SELECTED
POEMS: 1957–1967. Copyright © 1972 by Ted Hughes. Drawings
copyright | © 1973 by Harper & Row, Publishers, Inc. All rights

---

[2] Composed of three poems from *Wodwo*: 'Boom', 'Public Bar TV', and 'Wino'.
[3] From the U.S. printing of *Wodwo*.
[4] A new part, taken from the last third of 'Karma', is added in the middle.
[5] Part I only, as in the U.S. printing of *Wodwo*.
[6] = 'Song of a Rat', part I.
[7] A section has been added after part III, another at the end.
[8] = part II of 'Wings'.

reserved. Printed in the | United States of America [...] | [...] | FIRST
U.S. EDITION | DESIGNED BY GLORIA ADELSON | [rule] | [CIP
data; ISBN 0-06-011991-8] | [rule]'; vii–ix table of contents; (x) blank;
(xi) half-title, as above; (xii) drawing of fox; 1–111 text; (112–113)
blank; (114) blank save for printing code (73–1), lower right. Text pages
23, 24, 37, 54, 64, 104 unnumbered. Six illustrations, line cuts.

Quarter white cloth, black cloth sides over boards. Spine flat, stamped in
black: 'TED | HUGHES *Selected Poems 1957–1967* HARPER & ROW'.
Endpapers dark grey.

Dust-wrapper: Front: same drawing as on title page, reversed, signed
'Baskin 1973', lettered in white: 'TED | HUGHES | Selected | Poems |
1957–1967 | Drawings by Leonard Baskin' (typography as on title page).
Spine white, lettered as book spine except 'HARPER | & ROW' reads
across. Back black, photo of Hughes by Edward Lucie-Smith, labelled in
white 'TED HUGHES'; at bottom right, ISBN. On front flap, lower
right, '0174'.

Paper plain white, 23.3 × 16.0 cm., bulk 1.0 cm.; top and bottom edges
cut, fore-edge trimmed. Printed offset.

CONTENTS the same as the English edition, except the order is changed
somewhat, and 'Kafka' from the first edition (formerly part II of
'Wings') now appears untitled as the fourth part of 'Boom'.

Published September 1973 at $7.95; 7500 copies printed. The dust-
wrapper code is for January 1974. Second and third printings are bound
in all-white cloth, lack the first edition notice on the verso title, and are
identified by the printing code on the last page. The compilers have seen
a dust-wrapper on a copy of the second printing in which the back cover
has blurbs instead of the photograph, and the price is raised to $8.95,
though the date code is still for January 1974.

REVIEWS: *America*, 16 Mar. 1974 (Thomas Kinsella); *Baltimore Evening
Sun*, 13 Mar. 1974 (Jane Conly); *Book World (Washington Post)*, 10 Feb.
1974; *Booklist*, 15 Feb. 1974; *Buffalo News*, 2 Mar. 1974 (Jeff Simon);
Choice, May 1974; *Dublin Magazine*, Winter/Spring 1973 (R. Weber);
Hartford Courant, 3 Mar. 1974 (Paul H. Stacey); *International Herald
Tribune*, 20 Feb. 1974 (Marjorie Perloff); *Kirkus*, 1 Nov. 1973; *New
Republic*, 16 Feb. 1974; *New York Review of Books*, 7 Mar. 1974 (Karl
Miller); *New York Times Book Review*, 13 Jan. 1974 (Calvin Bedient), 2
June 1974; *St. Louis Globe-Democrat*, 30 Mar. 1974 (Brian Taylor);
Saturday Review World, 20 Nov. 1973; *Sewanee Review*, July 1976; *Southern
Humanities Review*, 1974, pp. 551–2 (John M. Ditsky); *Virginia Quarterly*,
Spring 1974; *Wilson Library Bulletin*, Feb. 1974.

A37 SUNDAY 1972

[cover title; flush at left] Leopards | Edited by Denys Thompson and Christopher Parry | Sunday | Ted Hughes | Illustrated by Graham Humphreys | [illustration in green and black of a group walking next to a canal, with a boat]

[1]^8. Pages (1)2–7(8)9–14(15–16), consisting: (1) title page; 2, capsule biography of Hughes, with mention that the story comes from *Wodwo*; 3–14 text; (15) blank; (16) on green background with white border: '[stylized leopard, in white] | 'Sunday' from *Wodwo* by Ted Hughes is reprinted by permission | of Faber and Faber Ltd. © Ted Hughes 1967. Notes, illustrations | and design © Cambridge University Press 1972. | ISBNs: | 0 521 08335 4 the pamphlet | 0 521 08378 8 Series B | Cambridge University Press | Printed in Great Britain by | Ebenezer Baylis & Son Ltd | Leicester and London'. Text page 8 unnumbered. One illustration, line cut in black and green.

Stapled pamphlet, front printed as above.

Paper plain white, 20.9 × 14.8 cm., bulk .1 cm.; all edges cut. Printed offset.

Contains the single story from *Wodwo*.

Published 21 February 1972; 20,000 copies printed at 88p. per pack of 10.

A38 ORPHEUS 1973

[line of type ornaments, with one of a different sort at each end] | [script] Orpheus | [roman] by | TED HUGHES | [publisher's cuneiform device] | THE DRAMATIC PUBLISHING COMPANY | CHICAGO | [line of type ornaments, as above]

[1]^{16}. Pages (1–2)3(4)5–18(19–32), consisting: (1) title page; (2) '[double rule] | NOTICE | [rule] | The royalty fee, payable in advance [...] | [royalty information] | [rule] | © MCMLXXIII By | TED HUGHES | Printed in the United States of America | *All rights reserved* | (ORPHEUS) | [rule]'; 3 '[double rule] | ORPHEUS | For Six Men and Two Women | [rule] | [cast]'; (4) blank; 5–18 text; (19–32) blank save for running title 'DIRECTOR'S NOTES'.

Stapled into heavy yellow paper wrappers. Front: '[Grecian harp] | [bold-face script] Orpheus | [roman] by TED HUGHES | [publisher's cuneiform device] | THE DRAMATIC PUBLISHING COMPANY'. Back blank save for 'ORPHEUS—Hughes' reading down near spine. Some copies were bound in brown wrappers printed as above. The publisher in a letter has said 'All copies were printed at the same time.

Our records say the covers ordered were gold. What probably happened is that the printer ran out of the gold and ran the rest of the covers brown.'

Paper plain white, 17.9 × 12.7 cm., bulk .2 cm.; all edges cut.

Composed on a typewriter, except for title page, head title and wrappers; printed offset.

Contains the single play.

Published 11 July 1973 at $1.00; 1023 copies printed.

A39   PROMETHEUS ON HIS CRAG   1973

[in red and black] *PROME* | *THEUS* | *ON HIS CRAG* | 21 POEMS BY TED HUGHES | WITH A DRAWING BY LEONARD BASKIN | LONDON | THE RAINBOW PRESS

[1–5]⁴ = 20 leaves. Pages [1–40], consisting: [1–2] blank; [3] half-title; [4] drawing of Prometheus and the vulture, signed 'Baskin'; at lower left, Baskin's signature in pencil; [5] title page; [6] blank; [7–28] text; [29–30] blank; [31] '[publisher's device: within a rectangle, 3.7 × 7.6 cm., a rainbow, sun, and outlined vine in black and green; under rainbow, in red: '● THE ● | ● RAINBOW PRESS ●']' | 'This edition of 160 numbered copies, signed by | the author and by the artist, was set in | Bodoni types, printed on Italian paper | at Daedalus Press, Stoke Ferry, | Norfolk, and bound by | Zaehnsdorf, London. | The colophon is by | Leonard Baskin. | This is copy number | [number and Hughes' signature]'; [32] blank; [33] '*Published by the* RAINBOW PRESS, | *10 Arkwright Road, London NW3* | *All rights reserved* | Text © Ted Hughes 1973 | Drawing © Leonard Baskin 1973'; [34–40] blank. All copies examined have a blank bifolium between the front free fly and the first gathering, which we have considered as binder's leaves and not noted in the collation.

Full purple morocco over boards. Spine flat, stamped in gold: 'TED HUGHES ★ PROMETHEUS ON HIS CRAG   Rainbow Press'. An unknown number of copies were bound in blue leather. The edition, however, was completely pre-subscribed, and as all copies would have been bound up at approximately the same time, no significant priority would be involved.

Slip-case, boards covered with bi-colour cloth (white and dark brown threads).

Paper Italian mould-made wove, rough, unmarked, about 19.4 × 15.2 cm., bulk .5 cm.; top edge cut, gilt; fore- and bottom edges deckle. Printed letterpress.

CONTENTS: [The poems are identified by number only. All but four begin 'Prometheus on his crag', with variations in capitalization]
  His voice felt out the way. 'I am' he said
  Prometheus . . . Relaxes
  Prometheus . . . Pestered by birds roosting and defecating
  Prometheus . . . Spotted the vulture coming out of the sun
  Prometheus . . . Knew what was coming and his eyes closed
  Prometheus . . . Has bitten his prophetic tongue off
  Prometheus . . . Lay astonished all his preparations
  Now I know I never shall
  Prometheus . . . Began to admire the vulture
  Prometheus . . . Tried to recall his night's dream
  Prometheus . . . Had begun to sing
  Prometheus . . . Can see Io fleeting across the map
  Prometheus . . . Heard the cry of the wombs
  Prometheus . . . Sees the wind
  Prometheus . . . Had such an advantageous prospect
  Prometheus . . . Too far from his people to tell them
  Prometheus . . . Was himself the fire
  The character neglected in this icon
  Prometheus . . . Shouts and his words
  Prometheus . . . Pondered the vulture. Was this bird
  His mother covers her eyes.

Published November 1973 at £18.40/$50.00; slightly over 160 copies printed (see above, 'The Rainbow Press', p. 4), of which 130 were for sale.

A40 THE STORY OF VASCO 1974

THE STORY OF VASCO | *Opera in three acts* | *Music by* | GORDON CROSSE | *Libretto based on* | *an English version by* | TED HUGHES | *of the play* | L'Histoire de Vasco *by* | GEORGES SCHEHADÉ | Music Department | OXFORD UNIVERSITY PRESS | 44 Conduit Street, London W1R 0DE | 1974

[1]^{28}. Pages (i–viii)1–46(47–48), consisting: (i) half-title; (ii) blank; (iii) title page; (iv) '© Oxford University Press, 1974 | [notes on royalties and the first performance] | PRINTED IN GREAT BRITAIN'; v, notes on the origins of the libretto, signed 'G.C.'; vi, synopsis; vii, list of characters; (viii) '*This opera is affectionately dedicated to* | COLIN GRAHAM'; 1–46 text; (47–48) blank.

Stapled into wrappers; outside pink, printed in red. Front: 'THE STORY OF | VASCO | Opera in three acts | GORDON CROSSE'. Back: 'OXFORD UNIVERSITY PRESS | 0 19 335702 X | PRINTED BY | G. W. DRAY & SON LTD. | BARKING, ESSEX'.

Paper plain white, 18.5 × 11.7 cm., bulk .3 cm.; all edges cut. Printed letterpress.

Published 21 February 1974 at 70p.; 500 copies printed.

REVIEWS of the first performance by Sadler's Wells Opera at the London Coliseum, 13 March 1974: *Birmingham Post*, 15 Mar. 1974 (John Falding); *Country Life*, 11 Apr. 1974 (Hugo Cole); *Daily Mail*, 14 Mar. 1974 (David Gillard); *Daily Telegraph*, 14 Mar. 1974 (Peter Stadlen); *Eastern Daily Press*, 16 Feb. 1974 (C.V.R.); *Evening Standard*, 14 Mar. 1974 (Christopher Grier); *Financial Times*, 15 Mar. 1974 (Ronald Crichton); *Guardian*, 13 Mar. 1974 (Lee Langley); *Jewish Chronicle*, 22 Mar. 1974 (Arthur Jacobs); *Listener*, 14 Mar. 1974 (Stephen Walsh); *Music & Musicians*, Mar. 1974 (Stephen Walsh); *Musical Opinion*, May 1974 (L.S.); *Musical Times*, Mar. 1974 (Hugo Cole), May 1974 (Winton Dean); *New Statesman*, 22 Mar. 1974 (Bayan Northcott); *Observer*, 10 Mar. 1974, 17 Mar. 1974 (Peter Hayworth); *Opera*, Mar. 1974 (Bayan Northcott), May 1974 (Harold Rosenthal); *Scotsman*, 15 Mar. 1974 (Conrad Wilson); *Spectator*, 23 Mar. 1974 (Rodney Milnes); *Stage and Television Today*, 21 Mar. 1974 (A.M.); *Sunday Telegraph*, 17 Mar. 1974 (Jeremy Noble); *Sunday Times*, 17 Mar. 1974 (Desmond Shawe-Taylor); *Tatler*, May 1974 (David Fingleton); *Tempo*, June 1974 (John Andrewes); *Times Educational Supplement*, 26 Apr. 1974 (Patrick Carnegy); *Tribune*, 22 Mar. 1974 (David Simmons); *Yorkshire Post*, 15 Mar. 1974 (Ernest Bradbury).

A41　　　BEAUTY AND THE BEAST　　　1974

[line of type ornaments] | A PLAY IN ONE ACT | BEAUTY AND THE BEAST | by | TED HUGHES | [publisher's cuneiform device] | THE DRAMATIC PUBLISHING COMPANY | CHICAGO | [line of type ornaments, as above]

[1]^{16}. Pages (1–2)3–26(27–32), consisting: (1) title page; (2) '[double rule] | NOTICE | [rule] | The royalty fee, payable in advance [...] | [royalty information] | [rule] | © MCMLXXIV By | TED HUGHES | Printed in the United States of America | All Rights Reserved | (BEAUTY AND THE BEAST) | [rule]'; 3 '[double rule] | BEAUTY AND THE BEAST | *A Play in One Act* | For Five Men and Two Women | [rule] | [cast]'; 4, chart of stage positions and directions, with rule at top; 5–25 text; 26 '[double rule] | PRODUCTION NOTES | [rule] | [...]'; (27–31) blank save for running title 'DIRECTOR'S NOTES'; (32) blank.

Stapled into heavy paper wrappers. Front: '[geometric design with comic mask] | BEAUTY AND | THE BEAST | by TED HUGHES |

[publisher's cuneiform device, at lower left] | [geometric design with tragic mask; within, in white letters:] THE DRAMATIC PUBLISHING COMPANY'. Back: 'BEAUTY AND | THE BEAST | a variant on the folk tale | of a bewitched young man | who regains his human | form when a girl says | she loves him. | [clown's mask]'; near spine, reading down: 'BEAUTY AND THE BEAST—Hughes'.

Paper plain white, 18.1 × 12.6 cm., bulk .15 cm.; all edges cut.

Composed on a typewriter, except for title page, head title, and wrappers; printed offset.

Published 30 July 1974 at $1.00; 1045 copies printed. This play appeared originally in *The Coming of the Kings* (A23).

A42   SEAN, THE FOOL, THE DEVIL   1974
            AND THE CATS

[line of type ornaments] | A PLAY IN ONE ACT | Sean, the Fool, the Devil | and the Cats | by | TED HUGHES | [publisher's cuneiform device] | THE DRAMATIC PUBLISHING COMPANY | CHICAGO | [line of type ornaments, as above, but inverted]

[1]¹⁶. Pages (1–2)3–25(26–32), consisting: (1) title page; (2) '[double rule] | NOTICE | [rule] | The royalty fee, payable in advance [...] | [royalty information] | [rule] | © MCMLXXIV By | TED HUGHES | Printed in the United States of America | All Rights Reserved | (SEAN, THE FOOL, THE DEVIL AND THE CATS) | [rule]'; 3, cast of characters, lengthy heading with two rules above and one below; 4, chart of stage positions and directions, with rule at top; 5–23 text; 24–25 '[double rule] | PRODUCTION NOTES | [rule] | [...]'; (26–32) blank save for running title 'DIRECTOR'S NOTES'.

Stapled into heavy paper wrappers. Front mostly black, with white Grecian column at right; lettering in white rectangle: 'Sean, the Fool, | the Devil and | the Cats | by | TED HUGHES | [below, in separate white rectangle] THE DRAMATIC PUBLISHING COMPANY | [publisher's cuneiform device, white on black]'. Back white, with lettering: 'Sean, the Fool, the Devil | and the Cats | Sean is able to outwit | the Devil because ... | [drawing of devil, signed 'mp']'; near spine, reading down: 'SEAN, the FOOL, the DEVIL and the CATS—Hughes'.

Paper plain white, 18.1 × 12.6 cm., bulk .2 cm.; all edges cut.

Composed on a typewriter, except for title page, head title and wrappers; printed offset.

Published 30 July 1974 at $1.00; 1036 copies printed. This play appeared originally in *The Coming of the Kings* (A23).

A43 THE TIGER'S BONES 1974

[line of type ornaments] | A PLAY IN ONE ACT | The Tiger's Bones | by | TED HUGHES | [publisher's cuneiform device] | THE DRAMATIC PUBLISHING COMPANY | CHICAGO | [line of type ornaments, as above, but inverted]

[1]^{16}. Pages (1–2)3–31(32), consisting: (1) title page; (2) '[double rule] | NOTICE | [rule] | The royalty fee, payable in advance [...] | [royalty information] | [rule] | © MCMLXXIV By | TED HUGHES | Printed in the United States of America | All Rights Reserved | (THE TIGER'S BONES) | [rule]'; 3 '[double rule] | THE TIGER'S BONES | *A Play in One Act* | For Eight Men and Extras* | [rule] | [cast]'; 4, chart of stage positions and directions, with rule at top; 5–30 text; 31 '[double rule] | PRODUCTION NOTES | [rule] | [...]'; (32) blank.

Stapled into heavy paper wrappers. Design uniform with *Beauty and the Beast* (A41). Front: '[geometric design with comic mask] | The | Tiger's | Bones | by | TED HUGHES | [publisher's cuneiform device] | [geometric design with tragic mask; within, in white letters:] THE DRAMATIC PUBLISHING COMPANY'. Back: 'The Tiger's Bones | a modern fable | The Master Scientist can make | the most elaborate calculations | but is unable to grasp the | essential point of any situation. | [clown's mask]'; near spine, reading down: 'THE TIGER'S BONES—Hughes'.

Paper plain white, 18.1 × 12.7 cm., bulk .15 cm.; all edges cut.

Composed on a typewriter, except for title page, head title, and wrappers; printed offset.

Published 30 July 1974 at $1.00; 1007 copies printed. This play appeared originally in *The Coming of the Kings* (A23).

A44 SEASON SONGS 1974

a. First edition (Spring Summer Autumn Winter):

[double-page title, in black and green; left:] SPRING SUMMER [right:] TED HUGHES | AUTUMN WINTER | Rainbow Press

[1–5]^6 = 30 leaves. Pages (i–ii)(1–4)5(6–8)9–54(55)56(57–58), consisting: (i–ii, 1) blank; (2–3) title spread; (4) 'to Carol'; 5, table of contents; (6) blank; (7) divisional title 'SPRING' in green; (8) blank; 9–54 text, with divisional titles 'SUMMER' in yellow, 'AUTUMN' in brown, and 'WINTER' in blue; (55) blank; 56 'Published by the Rainbow Press, 10 Arkwright Road, London NW3 | The poems are collected here for the first time except for the Autumn | poems which were published in 1968 in a small paper-bound edition | by Richard Gilbertson, Bow, as *Five Autumn songs* | © TED HUGHES 1973 | This edition is limited to 140 copies, numbered and signed by the author | Designed and printed by Sebastian Carter at the Rampant Lions Press, | Cambridge, in 14 point Centaur, on Barcham Green Dover laid | This is copy number [number] | [signature] | *Printed and made in Great Britain*'; (57–58) blank. Text pages 20–22, 31–32, 43–44 unnumbered.

Full natural calf over boards. Front stamped in gold: 'SPRING | SUMMER | AUTUMN | WINTER | Ted Hughes'. Spine round. The binding was by John P. Gray. Charles Seluzicki reports having sold a copy of the book bound in leather as above, but without the underlying boards.

Slip-case, boards covered with cork veneer.

Paper rough, brownish handmade 'laid' (chain lines horizontal, 3.5 cm.), unmarked, about 20.5 × 21.7 cm., bulk .4 cm.; top-edge cut, fore- and bottom edges deckle. Printed letterpress.

CONTENTS: Spring: April Birthday—Spring Nature Notes—The River in March—A March Calf—Deceptions.
Summer: Hunting the Summer—Mackerel Song—The Golden Boy—Work and Play—The Harvest Moon.
Autumn: Leaves—The Defenders—The Seven Sorrows—The Stag—There Came a Day.
Winter: The Warrior of Winter—Solstice Song—New Year Song—Snow and Snow—The Warm and the Cold.

Published September 1974 at £32/$78.00; a little over 140 copies printed (see above, 'The Rainbow Press', p. 4), of which 120 were for sale.

Carol Orchard, to whom the book is dedicated, married Hughes in 1970.

b. First American edition (1975):

TED | HUGHES | SEASON SONGS | Pictures | by | Leonard | Baskin | THE | VIKING | PRESS | NEW YORK | 19·75

$[1–2]^8[3–4]^4[5–6]^8 = 40$ leaves. Pages (1–8)9–77(78–80), consisting: (1) half-title; (2) blank; (3) title page; (4) '*First Edition* | *Text copyright* © *1968, 1973, 1975 by Ted Hughes* | Illustrations copyright © *1975 by Leonard Baskin* | *All rights reserved* | *Published in 1975 by The Viking Press, Inc.* | [. . .] | *Published simultaneously in Canada by* | *The Macmillan Company of Canada Limited* | *Printed in U.S.A.* | [printing code (1–75) and CIP data] | *ISBN 0-670-62725-9*'; (5) '*FOR CAROL*'; (6) blank; (7) divisional title '*SPRING*'; (8) pen, ink, and wash drawing of a calf; 9–77 text; (78) blank; (79) index of titles; (80) blank. Text pages 13, 16, 18, 19, 23, 26, 31, 36, 37,

40, 41, 43, 47, 49, 56, 57, 61, 65, 68, 72, 73, 76 unnumbered. Sixteen illustrations, halftone (fourteen in colour).

Quarter green cloth, olive-green paper sides over boards. Front blind-stamped 'SEASON | SONGS'. Spine flat, stamped in gold: 'HUGHES · BASKIN   SEASON SONGS   VIKING'.

Dust-wrapper front and back: pen, ink, and green wash drawing of rabbit, lettered in white: 'SEASON | SONGS | TED HUGHES | PICTURES BY | LEONARD BASKIN'. Spine white, lettered in black as on book spine. On front flap, upper right, '0975'. An uncommon form of the dust-wrapper has the illustration on the front printed in blue rather than green; the back cover is normal. The publisher and printer could supply no further information on this.

Paper plain white, 28.5 × 19.6 cm., bulk .7 cm.; all edges cut. Printed offset.

CONTENTS the same as *Spring Summer Autumn Winter* except that 'Hunting the Summer' is omitted and the following are added: Swifts—Hay—Sheep—Autumn Nature Notes—December River.

Published 6 October 1975 at $10.00; 10,000 copies printed. There was a reprint of 7500 copies in 1976 or 1977.

c. First English trade edition (1976):

Season Songs | [8.4 cm. rule broken by four-point snowflake ornament] | TED HUGHES | FABER AND FABER LTD | London

(A)⁸B–E⁸ = 40 leaves. Pages (1–8)9–10(11–12)13–75(76–80), consisting: (1–2) blank; (3) half-title; (4) list of sixteen other books by Hughes; (5) title page; (6) '*First published in 1976 | by Faber and Faber Limited | 3 Queen Square London WC1 | Printed in Great Britain by | Ebenezer Baylis and Son, Limited | The Trinity Press, Worcester, and London | All rights reserved | ISBN 0 571 10890 3 | © Ted Hughes, 1976*'; (7) 'To Carol'; (8) blank; 9–10 table of contents; (11) divisional title '*Spring* | [four-point snowflake ornament]'; (12) blank; 13–75 text; (76–80) blank. Text pages 25, 26, 41, 42, 62–64 unnumbered.

Blue calico-embossed paper over boards. Spine round, stamped in silver: '*Season Songs* TED HUGHES   Faber'.

Dust-wrapper printed with Baskin water-colour of a stag (from pp. (56–57) of the American edition), continuing across spine to back, with lettering in white. Front: 'TED HUGHES | Season Songs'. Spine: 'TED HUGHES Season Songs   Faber'.

Paper plain white, 21.6 × 13.4 cm., bulk .6 cm.; all edges cut. Printed letterpress.

CONTENTS the same as the American edition, with 'The Defenders' omitted, and with the following additions: March Morning Unlike Others—Icecrust and Snowflake—Apple Dumps—A Cranefly in September—Two Horses. 'Solstice Song' is retitled 'Christmas Card'.

Published 13 May 1976 at £2.40; 10,000 copies printed. There was a reprint of 5000 copies in 1979, identified as such on the verso title.

d. Second English trade edition, expanded (1985):

[within a triple rule frame] SEASON | SONGS | [rule, 2.1 cm.] | *Ted Hughes* | [below frame] ff | *faber and faber* | LONDON · BOSTON

[1¹⁶ 2⁸ 3⁴ 4¹⁶] = 44 leaves. Pages (1–8)9–10(11–12)13–88, consisting: (1–2) blank; (3) half-title; (4) *'also by Ted Hughes* | [24 titles]'; (5) title page; (6) 'First published in 1976 | by Faber and Faber Limited | 3 Queen Square London WC1N 3AU | This revised edition first published 1985 | Photoset by Wilmaset Birkenhead Wirral | Printed in Great Britain by | Redwood Burn Ltd Trowbridge Wiltshire | All rights reserved | © Ted Hughes, 1976, 1985 | [CIP data]'; (7) 'To Carol'; (8) blank; 9–10 table of contents; (11) divisional title *'Spring'*; (12) blank; 13–88 text. Text pages 31, 32, 53, 54, 71, 72 unnumbered.

Calico-grain orange paper over boards. Spine slightly rounded, stamped in gold: '[reading across, thin-thick rule] [reading down] SEASON SONGS *Ted Hughes* | [reading across] ff [thick-thin rule]'.

Dust-wrapper coated outside, printed yellow with all-over pattern of 'ff' in black. On both front and back: on a white panel, blue panel in double-rule frame; on the blue panel, 'SEASON | SONGS | [rule, 2.4 cm.] | *Ted Hughes*'. Superimposed slantwise on bottom part of panel, an illustration of a deer by Kathleen Lindsley. Spine printed like book spine, black on white panel. Dust-wrapper designed by Pentagram.

19.8 × 12.8 cm., bulk .6 cm.; all edges cut. Printed offset.

CONTENTS: adds the following poems to A44c: He Gets Up in Dark Dawn—A Swallow[1]—Evening Thrush[2]—A Dove[2]—Barley—Pets—Starlings Have Come. 'The Stag' and 'Two Horses' have been omitted.

Published October 1985 at £7.95; number of copies undetermined. A paperback printing of unknown size was published simultaneously at £2.95. The paperback was reprinted in 1985 and 1988, as indicated by notes on the verso title; and the compilers have seen a fourth paperback printing according to the printing code on the verso title.

---

[1] = 'The Swallow' from *A Primer of Birds*.
[2] Originally published in *A Primer of Birds*.

REVIEWS: *Art Teacher*, Spring 1976; *Booklist*, 15 Dec. 1975 (B. Hearn); *Cambridge Quarterly*, Vol. 7 No. 1 (John Newton); *Center for Children's Books, Bulletin*, Feb. 1976; *Chicago Tribune*, 26 Oct. 1975 (Susan Fromberg Schaeffer); *Children's Literature Association Quarterly*, Winter 1988; *Choice*, Feb. 1976; *Daily Mail*, 20 May 1976; *Economist*, 30 Nov. 1985; *Encounter*, Nov. 1976 (Douglas Dunn); *English*, Autumn 1976 (John Stokes); *Growing Point*, Oct. 1976, Jan. 1986; *Guardian*, 20 May 1976 (Martin Dodsworth); *Horn Book*, Apr. 1976 (P.H.); *Junior Bookshelf*, Aug. 1976; *Kirkus*, 15 Oct. 1975; *Listener*, 20 May 1976 (Ronald Blythe); *New Times*, 28 Nov. 1975 (Geoffrey Wolff); *New York Times Book Review*, 21 Dec. 1975 (Thomas Lask); *Northwest Review*, Vol. 15 No. 3 (A. K. Weatherhead); *Observer*, 4 July 1976 (Peter Porter); *Parnassus*, 14:1, 1987 (Calvin Bedient); *PN Review*, 1, 1976 (David Day); *Publishers' Weekly*, 6 Oct. 1975 (Jean F. Mercier); *Saturday Review*, 29 Nov. 1975; *School Library Journal*, Dec. 1975 (Merrie Lou Cohen); *Scotsman*, 29 May 1976 (George Mackay Brown); *Sewanee Review*, July 1976; *Spectator*, 17 July 1976 (Nick Totton); *Sydney Morning Herald*, 28 May 1977 (R. Gray); *Times Educational Supplement*, 25 June 1976 (Peter Fanning), 14 Feb. 1986; *Times Literary Supplement*, 29 Nov. 1985 (Alan Brownjohn), 16 July 1976 (Edwin Morgan); *Tribune*, 6 Feb. 1976 (Martin Booth).

A45   THE INTERROGATOR: 1975
                         A TITLED VULTURESS

The Interrogator | *A Titled Vulturess* | Poem by Ted Hughes: Drawing by Leonard Baskin | from the sequence 'Cave Birds' | THE ILKLEY LITERATURE FESTIVAL: 1975

Single sheet, French fold, pages [1–4], consisting: (1) title page; (2) left half, mounted facsimile of an early draft of the poem, 21.5 × 12.9 cm., half-tone blue and black; right half, the printed poem; (3) drawing of a vulture, left profile; (4) '*The Interrogator* and its attendant drawing by Leonard Baskin form part of the | Cave Birds sequence of poems written by Ted Hughes for the Ilkley Literature Festival, 1975. | Poem and drawing are here published for the first time by permission of poet and artist. | This sheet and the facsimile of an early draft of *The Interrogator* have been printed for the Festival by | The Scolar Press, Ilkley in an edition of 250 copies of which this is number | [number] | Manuscript and poem © copyright Ted Hughes, 1975 | Drawing © copyright Leonard Baskin, 1975'.

Paper apparently mould-made wove, 72.0 × 50.4 cm. unfolded (folded size 25.3 × 36.5 cm.); one edge 'deckle', one edge trimmed, two edges cut. Printed offset.

Published 24 May 1975; about 300 copies were printed, of which 250 were for sale at £1.40. Regarding this publication, John Commander of the Scolar Press writes as follows: '*The Interrogator* folder [was] put on sale coincidentally with the opening of the 1975 Ilkley [Literature] Festival. This ran from 24–31 May ... [It was] I believe sold by the ... Festival at the performance of *Cave Birds* on Friday 30 May. I do not know whether copies were sold previously by the Festival committee ... The Scolar Press provided them with 250 copies without charge as a contribution to the Festival. I suggested that they could easily ask £2.00 per copy but my recollection is that they chose to sell them for something less ... In addition to the 250 numbered copies ... we produced perhaps 50 additional copies. Some of these were provided to Messrs Baskin and Hughes: others have been retained by ourselves as specimens and for promotional purposes. Where these have passed out of our hands they have been inscribed "out of series".'

A46   CAVE BIRDS   1975

a. First edition:

Cave Birds | *Poems by Ted Hughes* | *Drawings by Leonard Baskin* | The Scolar Press | 1975

Poems printed on ten disjunct sheets, each folded once; laid, with another sheet similarly folded and bearing colophon, contents list etc., into a folder. Folder composed of dark brown paper over boards, backed with white paper. On front, light brown tissue-paper label reading 'Cave Birds | *Poems by Ted Hughes*'. Folder lined with same type of tissue paper.

The poems in the folder are in turn laid into a well in a larger folding box, with the ten drawings and a tissue guard placed on top. Case is dark brown burlap over boards, 72.5 × 52.5 cm. On front, light brown tissue-paper label reading 'Cave Birds | *Poems by Ted Hughes* | *Drawings by Leonard Baskin*'. The box has two sets of ribbon ties.

Collation: Tissue guard. Title sheet. Ten prints, each numbered '[number]/125'. Poem folder; sheets unsewn, $[1–11]^2 = 22$ leaves. Pages [1–44], consisting: [1] half-title; [2] 'The titles of the drawings relate to the poems as follows: | [contents note] | Poems © copyright Ted Hughes 1975 | Drawings © copyright Leonard Baskin 1975'; [3] 'The ten poems here printed for the first time form part of | *Cave Birds*, a sequence of twenty poems written 1974–5 | by Ted Hughes to drawings by Leonard Baskin. | The poems are here published together with prints from the | related drawings and each poem is accompanied by a facsimile | of a draft selected from the poet's working papers. | The poems have been set in Times New Roman and printed | letterpress by Balding and Mansell, Wisbech, on paper handmade | by F. Amatruda, Amalfi. | The facsimiles have been made and printed by The Scolar Press, | Ilkley, as have the prints which are on 'Crisbrook' | lithographic paper made by Barcham Green. | Published 1975 by The Scolar Press, 39 Great Russell Street, WC1 | the edition is limited to one hundred copies for sale, | each signed by Ted Hughes and Leonard Baskin | of which this is number | [number] | [signatures]'; [4] blank; [5–44] poems. The four pages of each poem sheet are composed as follows: (a) poem title; (b) blank; facsimile of an early draft tipped on, varying types of paper; (c) the printed poem; (d) blank.

Paper: Poems and title printed on cream-coloured handmade wove, about 70.4 × 50.0 cm. unfolded, marked 'F. AMATRUDA | AMALFI'; all edges deckle. Drawings printed on heavy white handmade paper, unmarked, about 50.2 × 69.8 cm.; top and right edges cut, bottom and left edges trimmed. Illustrations and facsimiles printed offset, the remainder letterpress.

CONTENTS [illustration title preceding poem title]: A Death-Stone Crow of Carrion: The Knight—A Maze Pelican: The Baptist—A Flayed Crow: The Hall of Judgement—A Double Osprey: The Gatekeeper—A Sunrise of Owl: A Loyal Mother—A Monkey-Eating Eagle: Incomparable Marriage—A Stud Cockerel Hunted in a Desert: The Culprit—A Scarecrow Swift: The Guide—A Crow of Prisms: Walking Bare—An Owl Flower: The Good Angel.

Published around 24 May 1975 at £125; about 125 copies printed, of which 100 were for sale. Regarding this publication, John Commander of the Scolar Press writes as follows: 'Both the *Cave Birds* portfolio and *The Interrogator* folder [A45] were put on sale coincidentally with the opening of the 1975 Ilkley [Literature] Festival. This ran from 24–31 May. Advance copies of the *Cave Birds* portfolio were on display at the stand taken by The Scolar Press in the festival book mart and I believe that orders were taken at that time for subsequent fulfilment ... [The copies] numbered 101–125 have been taken up by Ted Hughes, Leonard Baskin and ourselves. The Scolar Press have used perhaps five copies for promotional display and record purposes.'

Of the approximately 25 out-of-series copies, ten were embellished in March 1979 with three original water colours by Baskin and three holograph poems by Hughes, and lettered A to J. The sets were offered for sale in 1980 by Colin Franklin, who says that 'poems and watercolours are quite different in each of my copies'. The poems are as follows:

Copy A: 'Bride and Groom Lie Hidden for Three Days', 'After There was Nothing There was a Woman', 'The Hen'.
Copy B: 'The Advocate', 'Two Dreams in the Cell', 'Pheasant'.
Copy D: 'The Swans', 'The Executioner', 'A Dove'.
Copy E: 'Buzzard', 'The Fierce Osprey', 'Heron'.

Copy G: 'Caprimulg', 'Grabbery as Usual', 'His Legs Ran About'.
Copy J: 'Cuckoo's', 'Starling', 'Tern', 'Evening Thrush', 'Black Back'.

One of the remaining copies contains 'The Macaw', 'Kingfisher', and 'Sparrow'. Another contains 'Snipe', 'Shrike', and 'The Lame Flamingo Bathes its Knees'. We have no information on the other two.

The bird poems here are early drafts of poems intended for *A Primer of Birds*.

b.1. First trade edition (1978):

[flush at left] CAVE BIRDS | An Alchemical Cave Drama | [heavy rule] | Poems by Ted Hughes and | drawings by Leonard Baskin | [rule] | Faber and Faber · London & Boston

[1–4]^8 = 32 leaves. Pages (1–7)8–60(61–64), consisting: (1) half-title; (2) Baskin eagle drawing from p. (31); (3) title page; (4) *'First published in 1978 | by Faber and Faber Limited | 3 Queen Square, London WC1 | Printed in Great Britain | by Scolar Press, Ilkley | © 1978 Ted Hughes | © 1978 Leonard Baskin | [CIP data] | ISBN 0 571 10976 4'*; (5) table of contents; (6) 'To | ERIC WALTER WHITE'; (7) introductory poem 'The Scream'; 8–60(61) text and illustrations, with text on versos, paginated, and illustrations on rectos, unpaginated; (62) 'Finale | At the end of the ritual | up comes a goblin.'; (63) drawing of small bird's head; (64) blank. Twenty-eight illustrations, line cut and halftone.

Black cloth. Spine flat, stamped in gold: 'CAVE BIRDS ● Ted Hughes & Leonard Baskin ● Faber'.

Dust-wrapper brown 'laid' (chain lines horizontal, 2.6 cm.), marked '[crown] | Abbey Mills | Greenfield' (black letter, 9.7 × 11.7 cm.), printed in red and black. Front: 'CAVE BIRDS | an alchemical cave drama | [drawing from p. (27)] | Poems by TED HUGHES | and drawings by | LEONARD BASKIN'. Spine: same as book spine, printed in black with dots in red. Back: 'CAVE BIRDS | [drawing from front cover, reversed]'. On front flap, lower right, price £5.95 above black square printed over price £6.95.

Paper plain white 'laid' (chain lines horizontal, 2.8 cm.), 22.0 × 28.0 cm., bulk .5 cm.; all edges cut. Printed offset.

CONTENTS: This edition is so expanded and revised from the limited edition as to constitute in effect a new work. The poems only are titled: The Scream—The Summoner—After the First Fright—The Interrogator^1—She Seemed so Considerate—The Judge—The

---

^{1} Originally published separately (A45).

Plaintiff—In These Fading Moments I Wanted to Say—The
Executioner—The Accused—First, the Doubtful Charts of Skin—The
Knight[2]—Something was Happening—The Gatekeeper[3]—A Flayed
Crow in the Hall of Judgement[3]—The Baptist[3]—Only a Little Sleep, a
Little Slumber—A Green Mother[4]—As I Came, I Saw a Wood—A
Riddle[5]—The Scape-goat[6]—After There Was Nothing There Was a
Woman—The Guide[3]—His Legs Ran About—Walking Bare[2]—Bride
and Groom Lie Hidden for Three Days—The Owl Flower[7]—The
Risen—Finale.

Published 2 September 1978 at £5.95; 5700 copies printed.

Two types of defective copies are found, one due to a binding error, the
other to a wrong imposition:
1. In the first quire, the inner four leaves duplicate the outer four; i.e.,
   the pages run (1–4,1–4)13–16,13–16.
2. In the third quire, pages 38–39 are interchanged with 42–43.

b.2. First printing for America (1979):

Manufactured in England using the same or duplicate plates from the
English trade edition (previous entry). The title page is the same setting
of type except for the imprint line, which reads 'The Viking Press · New
York'; the type is also positioned higher on the page.

The binding is the same, except with 'Viking' instead of 'Faber' on the
spine.

The dust-wrapper has the following changes:
1. The second line on the front reads 'An Alchemical Cave Drama'.
2. The spine has 'Viking' in place of 'Faber'.
3. Copy on both flaps is completely re-written. On the back flap,
   lower right: 'PRINTED IN GREAT BRITAIN | ISBN 0-670-
   20927-9 | 1178'.

The contents are the same except for page (4): '*Text Copyright © Ted
Hughes, 1978 | Illustrations Copyright in all countries | of the International
Copyright Union | by Leonard Baskin, 1978 | Published in 1978 by The Viking
Press | 625 Madison Avenue, New York, N.Y. 10022 | [CIP data] | Printed in
Great Britain*'.

---

[2] From the limited edition.
[3] From the limited edition, with some revision.
[4] = 'A Loyal Mother' from the limited edition.
[5] A rewriting of 'Incomparable Marriage' from the limited edition.
[6] = 'The Culprit' from the limited edition.
[7] = 'The Good Angel' from the limited edition, with slight revision.

Published January 1979 at $14.95; 10,400 copies printed along with the printing for England.

REVIEWS: *Best Sellers*, May 1979 (David Bianco); *Booklist*, 1 Dec. 1978; *Books and Bookmen*, Dec. 1978 (Anthony Thwaite); *Books and Issues*, vol. 1, no. 1, 1979 (Aidan Coen); *British Book News*, Dec. 1978; *Choice*, July/Aug. 1979; *Critical Quarterly*, Summer 1980 (Bill Hutchings); *Encounter*, Nov. 1978 (Alan Brownjohn); *English*, Spring 1980 (E. Neill); *Horn Book*, Apr. 1979; *Kirkus*, 15 Nov. 1978; *Library Journal*, 15 Sept. 1978 (D. L. Guillory); *Listener*, 7 Sept. 1978 (Edwin Morgan); *Nation*, 21 Jan. 1978; *New Review*, Autumn 1978 (Christopher Reid); *New Statesman*, 5 Jan. 1979 (Craig Raine); *New York Review of Books*, 10 June 1982 (Richard Murphy); *Observer*, 1 Oct. 1978 (Peter Porter); *Parnassus*, Spring/ Summer 1980 (B. Howard); *Poetry*, Aug. 1981 (Julian Moynahan); *Prairie Schooner*, Fall 1979 (K. C. Mason); *Sewanee Review*, Summer 1980 (Calvin Bedient); *Stand*, vol. 20, no. 4 (Desmond Graham); *Sunday Times*, 26 Nov. 1978 (Julian Symons); *Times*, 7 Sept. 1978 (Robert Nye); *Tribune*, 13 Oct. 1978 (Martin Booth); *Use of English*, Summer 1979 (Stephen Tunnicliffe); *Virginia Quarterly Review*, Summer 1979; *World Literature Today*, Autumn 1979.

A47   [POEM PRINTS,   1975
                ILKLEY LITERATURE FESTIVAL]

Ten broadsides by staff and students of the Department of Communication Design, Leeds Polytechnic Institute. Each numbered and signed by the artist. Order arbitrary.

'Crow's Account of the Battle', by David Pike. Lithograph, 35.8 × 48.7 cm. Mediaeval battle scene in green and sepia; at bottom right, ten-line excerpt from 'Crow's Account of the Battle'. Edition of 20 copies, sold at £3.00 apiece.

'Esther's Tomcat', by Katharine E. Fendyke. Lithograph, 22.9 × 27.5 cm., in a hand-made envelope 23.6 × 28.0 cm. Background black; at left, the poem in white; at right, four white cats. Some copies possibly hand-tinted. Edition of 7 copies, sold at £2.00 apiece.

'Fern', by Frances Stevens. Etching hand-tinted in sepia, 39.4 × 30.4 cm. Head and shoulders of a knight in armour with fern and a mouse on helmet. Edition of 10 copies, sold at £3.00 apiece.

'The Rain Horse', by Jane Kay. Soft-ground etching, 45.0 × 29.2 cm. A horse in blue, sepia, and green; underneath, one sentence from 'The Rain Horse'. Edition of 20 copies, sold at £4.00 apiece.

'Crow', by Wilton Priestner. Lithograph, 41.0 × 56.2 cm., incorporating the title and two lines from 'Crow Hears Fate Knock on the Door'. Edition of 20 copies, sold at £6.00 apiece.

'Wodwo', by Derek Hyatt. Triptych etching, total 40.0 × 69.2 cm., with the complete text of the poem 'Wodwo'. Edition of 20 copies, sold at £8.00 apiece.

'The Dracula Vine', by Alyce Mininch. Lithograph, 52.5 × 69.2 cm. In black, brown, and red, four hippopotamus heads growing out of a tree; among the roots a sleeping hedgehog and snake; between them the text. Edition of 19, sold at £6.00 apiece.

'Hawk Roosting', by Vivian van der Toorn. Lithograph, 46.6 × 35.5 cm. In black, a hawk with a mechanical interior, perching on a stump around which the text is arranged. Edition of 15 copies, sold at £5.00 apiece.

'The Warriors of the North', by Paul V. Phillips. Lithograph, 67.3 × 45.2 cm. In silver, a frontal view of a Viking helmet; beneath, the title and one line from 'The Warriors of the North'. Edition of 21 copies, sold at £3.00 apiece.

'Moon Roses', by Anne Randall. Photolithograph, hand-coloured, 44.9 × 29.3 cm. Moon-roses and a turkey, with the full text of 'Moon-Roses'. Edition of 20 copies, sold at £3.00 apiece.

Issued without a portfolio.

Paper for lithographs: white offset litho cartridge. Paper for etchings: white Bockingford. All edges cut.

Published 24 May 1975 to coincide with the opening of the Ilkley Literature Festival, and sold in the Bookmart there. The etchings were printed one at a time as they were sold, and in most cases never reached the stated limitation number. All poems previously collected.

[Several weeks later an eleventh print was added, 'The Warriors of the North', by Paul V. Phillips. Lithograph, 53.2 × 36.6 cm. In several colours, a side-view of a Viking helmet; underneath, the complete text of 'The Warriors of the North'. Edition of 8 copies, price unknown.]

A48   EARTH-MOON   1976

[flush to left, in black and blue] *Ted Hughes | Earth ● moon | Illustrated by the author | Rainbow Press*

$[1–6]^6 = 36$ leaves. Pages (i–iv)(1–2)3–4(5–6)7–65(66–68), consisting: (i–ii) blank; (iii) half-title, in blue; (iv) blank; (1) title page; (2) blank; 3–4 table of contents; (5) drawing of wolves; (6) blank; 7–65 text and drawings; (66) drawing of monsters; (67) 'Published by the Rainbow Press | 100 Chetwynd Road, London NW5 | © Ted Hughes 1976 | This edition is limited to 226 copies, illustrated | numbered and signed by the author, of which 26 | copies, numbered A–Z, were printed for the author. | It was designed and printed by Sebastian Carter at | the Rampant Lions Press, Cambridge | in 9pt Century Schoolbook Bold, | on paper hand-made by J. Barcham Green, | and bound by Davis & Hodges. | This is copy number [number] | [signature] | Printed and made in Great Britain'; (68) blank. Text pages 20 and 25 unnumbered. Ten illustrations, line cuts, printed in blue.

Copies 1–100 bound in full blue calf, stamped in silver. Front: illustration of whales from page 47 of text. Spine stamped '*Earth-moon   Ted Hughes*'. Copies 101–200 bound in slate-blue Japanese paper over boards; on front, 8.3 cm. round cork inlay. Spine stamped as above. Copies A–Z not seen.

Slip-case cardboard, covered with blue Japanese paper.

Paper handmade 'laid' (chain lines vertical, 3.9 cm.), marked '[saint's head on a plaque] | 1399' (8.4 × 5.0 cm.). Overall 12.8 × 12.5 cm., bulk .6 cm.; top edge cut and silver-coated, fore-edge cut, bottom edge uncut. The fore-edge was meant to be left deckle, but was accidentally cut by the binder. Printed letterpress.

CONTENTS: A Moon-Lily—Moon-Weapons—Moon-Mirror—The Moon-Oak—Mushrooms on the Moon—The Moon-Bull—Moon-Ways—Moon-Walkers—Moon-Wind—Moon-Ravens—Moon-Witches—The Moon-Hyena—Moon-Bells—Moon-Heads—Moon-Thorns—Singing on the Moon—Moon-Marriage—Moon-Wings—Moon-Shadow-Beggars—The Moon-Mourner—Moon-Whales—Moon-Theatre—Moon-Thirst—Moon-Clock—A Moon-Witch—Visiting the Moon—The Moon-Mare—The Moon-Haggis—Moony Art—A Moon-Hare—Earth-Moon.

Published May 1976 at £22 for copies 1–100 and £18 for copies 101–200. Slightly over 225 copies printed (see above, 'The Rainbow Press', p. 4).

A49   ECLIPSE   1976

Eclipse | [swelled rule, 6.3 cm.] | Ted Hughes | THE SCEPTRE PRESS | Knotting · Bedfordshire

[1]⁴. Pages [1–8], consisting: [1] title page; [2] blank; [3] '*This edition is limited to 250 numbered copies | printed on Abbey Mills laid paper | Nos. 1–50 are signed by the poet | COPY [number] | [signature in copies 1–50] | © Ted Hughes 1976 | Printed by Skelton's Press, Wellingborough, Northamptonshire*'; [4] blank; [5–8] poem.

Stapled into blue-violet wrappers, front printed 'ECLIPSE | [swelled rule, 6.3 cm.] | TED HUGHES'.

Paper plain white 'laid' (chain lines vertical, 2.6 cm.) marked '[crown] | Abbey Mills | Greenfield' (in black letter, 10.2 × 11.8 cm.). Overall 20.9 × 12.6 cm., bulk .1 cm.; all edges cut. Printed letterpress.

Published 30 July 1976 at £6.25 for signed copies and £1.45 for unsigned. Hughes retained 10 signed and 20 unsigned copies, and the publisher took 6 apiece of signed and unsigned. A further 10 copies out of series were given away.

A50   MOON-WHALES   1976
                 AND OTHER MOON POEMS

a. First edition:

[rule, 9.7 cm.] | MOON- | WHALES | *and Other Moon Poems* | TED HUGHES | *Drawings by* | LEONARD BASKIN | THE VIKING PRESS | New York | 19 · 76 | [rule, 9.7 cm.]

[1–6]^8 = 48 leaves. Pages (i–viii)1–86(87–88), consisting: (i) 'MOON- | WHALES | ALSO BY TED HUGHES | *The Tiger's Bones* | *and Other Plays for Children* | *Season Songs*'; (ii) blank; (iii) title page; (iv) 'FIRST EDITION | *Copyright* © *Ted Hughes, 1963, 1976* | *Illustrations Copyright* © *Leonard Baskin, 1976* | *All rights reserved* | *First published in 1976 by The Viking Press* | *625 Madison Avenue, New York, N.Y. 10022* | *Printed in U.S.A.* | [printing code (1–76) and CIP data] | *ISBN 0-670-48864-X*'; (v–vi) table of contents; (vii) '*For Frieda and Nicholas*'; (viii) blank; 1–83 text and illustrations; (84) blank; 85–86 index of first lines; (87) blank; (88) biographical notes about Hughes and Baskin, and note on the book. Text pages 3, 4, 11, 12, 17, 18, 29, 30, 35, 36, 43, 44, 53, 54, 61, 62, 69, 70, 79, 80 unnumbered. Ten illustrations, one printed halftone, the others line cuts.

Quarter rust-coloured cloth, light blue paper over boards, stamped in silver. Front: reading down, at upper left paper area, 'MOON-WHALES'. Spine stamped 'MOON-WHALES   HUGHES   VIKING'.

Dust-wrapper coloured dark maroon. Front: '[within a ruled border, on a white ground, drawing of bird, moon and sun from page (11)] | [below border, in blue] MOON-WHALES | [remainder in white] *and Other Moon Poems* | TED HUGHES | DRAWINGS BY LEONARD BASKIN'. Spine lettered in white: 'HUGHES   MOON-WHALES   VIKING'. Back, within a ruled border, on white ground: '[in blue] MOON-WHALES | [remainder in black] and Other Moon Poems | [excerpt from a London *Times* review of *The Earth-Owl*]'. On front flap, upper right, '7.95 | 0976'.

Paper plain white, 23.2 × 14.0 cm., bulk .8 cm.; all edges cut. Printed offset.

CONTENTS: Combines the contents of *The Earth-Owl* and *Earth-Moon*. 'Moon Transport' is here called 'Untitled Poem'.

Published officially on 8 November 1976 at $7.95, though copies were being sold a month before; 7500 copies printed. A later state of the dust-wrapper has printed price $9.95. By February 1985, copies with this dust-wrapper had an adhesive sticker raising the price to $12.95.

The halftone illustration on page (3) is smudged in all the copies examined.

b. First English edition (1988):

[within a rule frame] ff | [rule] | MOON-WHALES | [rule] | Ted Hughes | [rule] | *illustrated by Chris Riddell* | [below frame] [illustration of moon-hyena] | ff | *faber and faber* | LONDON · BOSTON

$[1-6^8] = 48$ leaves. Pages (1–9)10–90(91–93)94–95(96), consisting: (1) half-title, 'MOON-WHALES | [illustration of whale tail protruding from moon]'; (2) 'Also by Ted Hughes | [26 titles]'; (3) title page; (4) 'First published in the USA in 1976 | First published in Britain in this revised edition 1988 | by Faber and Faber Limited | 3 Queen Square, London WC1N 3AU | Photoset by Parker Typesetting Service Leicester | Printed in Great Britain by | Redwood Burn Ltd Trowbridge Wiltshire | All rights reserved | © Ted Hughes, 1963, 1976, 1988 | Illustrations © Chris Riddell, 1988 | [CIP data] | [illustration, continuing to next page]'; (5) 'For Frieda and Nicholas | [illustration of a moon-walker]'; (6) [illustration of moon-knight]; (7–8) table of contents; (9) [illustration of moon-darker]; 10–90 text; (91) [illustration to 'Earth-Moon']; (92–93) printed solid black; 94–95 index of first lines; (96) blank. Text pages 11, 20, 21, 25, 31, 38, 41, 49, 51, 54, 62, 63, 65, 69, 73, 76, 87 unnumbered.

Black calico-grain paper over boards. Spine nearly flat, stamped in white: 'MOON-WHALES Ted Hughes [at foot of spine, reading across] ff'.

Dust-wrapper coated outside, colour illustration of moon-creatures continuous across front, spine, and back. Front, in white, the rule frame with included text as on title page. Spine printed like book spine, in white. Back: in white, at lower left, 'ff | *faber and faber*'; bottom middle, in black on white panel: bar code.

24.6 × 18.9 cm., bulk .7 cm.; all edges cut. Printed offset.

CONTENTS same as the American edition, omitting 'Moon-Theatre',

'Moon-Roses', 'The Moon-Mare', 'A Moon Man-Hunt', 'Moon-Freaks', and 'The Moon-Bull'. 'Moony Art' is retitled 'Moon Art'; 'Untitled Poem' is once again titled 'Moon Transport'.

Published June 1988 (the British Library copy is stamped 17 May) at £7.50; number of copies undetermined.

c. First paperback edition (1991):

Moon-Whales | Ted Hughes | *illustrated by Chris Riddell* | [illustration of moon-hyena] | ff | *faber and faber* | LONDON · BOSTON

48 leaves, 'perfect-bound'. Pages (1–9)10–93(94–96), consisting: (1) same as b; (2) *'Also by Ted Hughes* | [30 titles]'; (3) title page; (4) 'First published in 1976 | Revised edition first published in 1988 | This paperback edition first published in 1991 | by Faber and Faber Limited | 3 Queen Square, London WC1N 3AU | Photoset by Parker Typesetting Service Leicester | Printed in Great Britain by Cox & Wyman Ltd, Reading Berkshire | All rights reserved | © Ted Hughes, 1963, 1976, 1988 | Illustrations © Chris Riddell, 1988 | [notes on Net Book Agreement and CIP data, and ISBN] | [part of illustration from next page]'; (5–6) same as b; (7–8) table of contents, reset; (9) same as b; 10–91 text and illustrations; 92–93 index of first lines; (94–96) blank. Text pages 20, 23–27, 30, 31, 34, 40, 41, 45-47, 50, 51, 53-55, 62-71, 74-77, 90, 91 unnumbered.

Wrappers, outside linen-textured and printed blue with all-over pattern of 'ff' in black; text printed on white panels. Overlapping the panels, colour illustrations of moon creatures. Front: '[in double-rule frame] MOON- | WHALES | [rule, 2.6 cm.] | *Ted Hughes* | Illustrated by Chris Riddell'. Spine: 'MOON-WHALES *Ted Hughes* [at foot, reading across] ff [thick-thin rule]'. Back: '[in double-rule frame] ff | *faber and faber* | MOON-WHALES | *Ted Hughes* | [blurb] | Cover design by Chris Riddell | UK £3.50 net Canada $5.99 | [bar code]'.

19.8 × 12.6 cm., bulk .6 cm.; all edges cut. Printed offset.

CONTENTS same as b.

Published November 1991 (the British Library copy is stamped 31 October) at £3.50; number of copies undetermined. It is possible that this 'edition' derives from the same keyboarding as the 1988 edition. However, lines are turned where they were not before, and some illustrations are printed in negative or vignetted. Lacking information from the publisher, we call it a new setting.

REVIEWS: *Book World*, 7 Nov. 1976 (Joseph McLellan); *Booklist*, 1 Jan. 1977; *Center for Children's Books, Bulletin*, May 1977; *Children's Literature Association Quarterly*, Spring 1988; *Choice*, June 1977; *Delap's F. & S. F.*

Review, Apr. 1977 (Mary S. Weinkauf); *Growing Point*, Sept. 1988; *Horn Book*, Apr. 1977; *Hudson Review*, Summer 1977 (David Bromwich); *Junior Bookshelf*, Aug. 1988 (M.C.); *Kirkus*, 15 Oct. 1976; *Language Arts*, Nov. 1977; *Listener*, 8 Dec. 1988; *New York Times Book Review*, 9 Jan. 1977 (William Stafford); *Poetry*, Apr. 1978; *Poetry Review*, Autumn 1988 (W. Magee); *Publishers Weekly*, 13 Dec. 1976; *School Library Journal*, Dec. 1976; *Times*, 1 Oct. 1988; *Times Educational Supplement*, 15 July 1988; *Virginia Quarterly*, Autumn 1977.

A50*   MOON-HOPS   1976?

[calligraphy] MOON-HOPS | [the poem, in capitals throughout] | TED HUGHES

At foot of verso, in type: '*Designed by* LESLEY DUFF   *Printed at Skelton's Press, Wellingborough*'.

A yellow card, 21.6 × 15.4 cm. Paper 'laid' (chains vertical, 1.9–2.8 cm.).

The recto is printed offset, the verso letterpress.

CONTENTS: the single poem, previously collected in *The Earth-Owl*.

Published ca. 1976; price and number of copies unknown. Produced as a print-making and lettering exercise.

A51   GAUDETE   1977

a.1. First edition:

[flush to left except for 'by'] GAUDETE | by | Ted Hughes | FABER AND FABER LIMITED | 3 Queen Square London

[1–5]^{16}[6]^{4}[7]^{16} = 100 leaves. Pages (1–4)5–9(10)11–200, consisting: (1) half-title; (2) list of fifteen other books by Hughes; (3) title page; (4) '*First published in 1977 | by Faber and Faber Limited | 3 Queen Square London WC1 | Printed in Great Britain by | Western Printing Services Ltd Bristol | All rights reserved | © Ted Hughes, 1977 |* [within a ruled border, CIP data. ISBN 0-571-11076-2]'; 5–7 table of contents; 8, quotations from Heraclitus and Parzival; 9, Argument, twelve lines; (10) blank; 11–200 text. Text pages 21, 22, 171, 172 unnumbered.

Black cloth over boards. Spine stamped in gold and red, title and author in freehand-designed letters by Leonard Baskin: 'GAVDETE   TED HVGHES   FABER'.

Dust-wrapper cream-coloured, printed in red and black, author and title in freehand-designed letters by Leonard Baskin. Front: 'GAVDETE [outlined in black] | TED HUGHES | [drawing of man's head half-submerged]'. Spine: 'GAVDETE [outlined in black] TED HUGHES FABER'. Back: list and reviews of other books by Hughes.

Paper plain white, 21.5 × 13.7 cm., bulk 1.4 cm.; all edges cut. Printed letterpress.

CONTENTS: I, Prologue. II, Main section, divided into 56 subsections, identified in the contents by their first lines which are sometimes duplicated. III, Epilogue, a prose section followed by 45 poems identified by their first lines: What Will You Make of Half a Man—I Hear Your Congregations at Their Rapture—Who Are You?—At the Top of my Soul—A Lark Sizzles in my Ear—I Watched a Wise Beetle—In a World Where all is Temporary—Collision with the Earth has Finally Come—Trying to be a Leaf—I Heard the Screech, Sudden—Once I Said Lightly—Music, that Eats People—The Rain Comes Again—This is the Maneater's Skull—I See the Oak's Bride in the Oak's Grasp—She Rides the Earth—The Huntsmen, on Top of their Swaying Horse-Towers—A Primrose Petal's Edge—Waving Goodbye, from your Banked Hospital Bed—I Said Goodbye to Earth[1]—The Swallow [dash] Rebuilding—The Night Wind, Muscled with Rain—The Viper Fell from the Sun—A Doctor Extracted—The Coffin, Spurred by its Screws—The Grass-blade is not Without—Churches Topple—I Know Well—The Sun, Like a Cold Kiss in the Street—Sometimes it Comes, a Gloomy Flap of Lightning—Having First Given Away Pleasure—Looking for her Form—A Man Hangs on—When the Still-Soft Eyelid Sank Again—The Sea Grieves all Night Long—Hearing Your Moan Echo, I Chill. I Shiver—Faces Lift out of the Earth—I Skin the Skin—What Steel was it the River Poured—Calves Harshly Parted from their Mamas—A Bang [dash] a Burning—The Dead Man Lies, Marching Here and There—Every Day the World Gets Simply—Your Tree [dash] your Oak—Glare Out of Just Crumpled Grass.

Published 18 May 1977 at £4.50; 5000 copies printed. There was a reprint of 2500 copies in 1978. The first paperback printing, an offset reduction, was published in 8000 copies on 19 February 1979. These paperback copies have the expanded version of the Argument (here 29 lines) from the first American printing, but in a different setting of type. There were further printings, the last noted by the compilers being the fourth, as indicated by the printing code on verso title.

---

[1] Published previously as a broadside (A19).

a.2. First American printing of English edition:

[flush to left except for 'by'] GAUDETE | by | Ted Hughes | HARPER & ROW, PUBLISHERS | New York, Hagerstown, San Francisco, London

[1–4]^{16}[5]^8[6–7]^{16} = 104 leaves. Pages (i–iv)(1–4)5–9(10)11–200(201–204), consisting: (i–ii) blank; (iii) half-title; (iv) blank; (1) list of eleven other books by Hughes; (2) blank; (3) title page; (4) 'GAUDETE. Copyright © 1977 by Ted Hughes. All rights reserved. Printed | in the United States of America [...] | [...] | FIRST U.S. EDITION | [rule] | [CIP data] | [rule] | [printing code (77–1)]'; 5–8 same as corresponding pages in the English printing; 9, Argument, twenty-eight lines; 10–200, same as corresponding pages in the English printing; (201–204) blank.

Quarter white cloth, brown paper over boards. Front blind-stamped with publisher's torch symbol in rectangle, with '1817'. Spine stamped in black: 'GAUDETE   Ted Hughes   Harper | & Row' [publisher's name reading across spine]. Endpapers brown.

Dust-wrapper cream-coloured, printed in red and black. Front: same as English dust-wrapper, but somewhat enlarged. Spine: 'TED HVGHES GAVDETE [outlined in black]   HARPER & ROW' [author and title in Baskin-designed letters, but of different proportions than on English dust-wrapper]. Back: '[photograph of Hughes, credited to Layle Silbert] | TED HUGHES | [three-line blurb from London *Times*] | ISBN: 0–06–012007–X'. On front flap, lower right, '1277'.

Paper plain white, 23.4 × 15.7 cm., bulk 1.4 cm.; top and bottom edges cut, fore-edge trimmed.

An offset reprint from the English edition, on larger paper. The Argument has been expanded to 28 lines, and the verso title and the bottom half of the title page reset.

Published officially on 14 December 1977 at $10.00; the publisher prefers not to reveal the number printed. Copies were actually in the shops by late November, and proof copies were circulating in early October.

REVIEWS: *Agenda*, vol. 15, nos. 2–3, 1977 (Peter Dale); *Ambit* 71, 1977 (Edwin Brock); *American Book Review*, vol. 1, no. 3, Summer 1978 (Rochelle Ratner); *Booklist*, 1 Feb. 1978; *Book World*, 18 Dec. 1977 (Donald Hall); *Books and Bookmen*, Apr. 1979 (Derek Stanford); *British Book News*, Aug. 1977 (Shirley Toulson); *Cambridge Quarterly*, vol. 7, no. 4, 1977 (J. M. Newton); *Canadian Forum*, Mar. 1978; *Chicago Review*, Spring 1979 (L. Lee); *Chicago Tribune*, 12 Feb. 1978 (Susan Fromberg Schaeffer); *Choice*, Apr. 1978; *Church Times*, 1 July 1977 (Norman Nicholson); *Critical Quarterly*, Summer 1977 (C. B. Cox); *Daily Telegraph*, 26 May 1977 (Elizabeth Jennings); *Delta* 57, 1977 (Neil Roberts);

Encounter, Jan. 1978 (Douglas Dunn); *English*, Autumn 1977 (W. W. Robson); *Financial Times*, 7 July 1977 (Anthony Curtis); *Guardian*, 19 May 1977 (Martin Dodsworth); *Houston Chronicle*, 25 Dec. 1977 (T. R. DeG.); *Kirkus*, 1 Oct. 1977; *Library Journal*, 1 Dec. 1977 (Seamus Cooney); *Listener*, 2 June 1977 (John Bayley); *London Magazine*, Nov. 1977 (Craig Raine); *Nation*, 21 Jan. 1978 (William H. Pritchard); *New Republic*, 28 Jan. 1978 (Joyce Carol Oates); *New Statesman*, 27 May 1977 (Peter Conrad); *New Yorker*, 23 Aug. 1993; *New York Review of Books*, 17 Aug. 1978 (Irvin Ehrenpreis); *New York Times*, 19 July 1978; *New York Times Book Review*, 25 Dec. 1977 (Robert Pinsky); *Observer*, 22 May 1977 (Philip Toynbee); *Parnassus* 6, Spring/Summer 1978 (Geraldine Moyle); *Poetry*, Aug. 1981 (Julian Moynahan); *St. Louis Globe-Democrat*, 31 Dec. 1977 (Brian Taylor); *Spectator*, 11 June 1977 (Peter Ackroyd); *Spectrum* 2, Huddersfield New College, 1977 (Mark Hinchliffe); *Stand*, vol. 19, no. 2, 1978 (Terry Eagleton); *Sunday Telegraph*, 21 Aug. 1977 (Shirley Toulson); *Sunday Times*, 29 May 1977 (Julian Symons); *Thames Poetry*, Nov. 1977 (A. A. Cleary); *Times*, 7 July 1977 (Robert Nye); *Times Educational Supplement*, 10 June 1977 (Herman Peschmann); *Times Literary Supplement*, 1 July 1977 (Oliver Lyne); *Tribune*, 3 June 1977 (Martin Booth); *Virginia Quarterly Review*, Summer 1978; *World Literature Today*, Summer 1978 (Robert Holkeboer).

A52   CHIASMADON   1977

[in black and blue] Ted Hughes Chiasmadon with a relief print | by Claire Van Vliet and printed at The Janus Press | Vermont for Charles Seluzicki, Poetry Bookseller

[1]^8. Pages [1–16], consisting: [1–2] leaf of blue paper, blank; [3] title page; [4] printed in grey, 'COPYRIGHT © 1977 BY TED HUGHES'; [5] relief print of the head of a chiasmadon, protected by a sewn-in tissue leaf; [6] blank; [7–11] text, printed rectos only, leaves headed by Roman numerals in blue; [12] blank; [13] [printed in blue] 'This book initiates a series of fine press poetry | published by Charles Seluzicki, Poetry Booksel- | ler in care of The John Gach Bookservice at 3012 | Greenmount Avenue, Baltimore, Maryland 21218 | and has been printed by Susan Johanknecht and | Claire Van Vliet at The Janus Press, West Burke | in February 1977. The edition is limited to one | hundred & seventy-five signed copies, of which | numbers 1–120 are for sale and I–LV are *hors commerce* | This is copy number [number] | [Hughes' signature] | [Van Vliet's signature]'; [14] blank; [15–16] sheet of blue paper, blank.

Sewn into heavy, rough, blue wrappers (Newport Blue Strathmore Beau Brilliant), pasted into wrappers of the same material. On front of outer wrapper, 'Chiasmadon' printed in silver.

Paper heavy white Rives BFK, 24.2 × 19.0 cm., bulk .2 cm.; top and fore-edge cut, bottom edge trimmed. Outer leaves blue 'laid' Fabriano Miliani Ingres (chain lines vertical, 2.3 cm.) marked 'INGRES COVER-FABRIANO' (1.3 × 15.0 cm.).

Printed on a Vandercook SP15 hand cylinder press. The etching was printed on dampened paper on a Meeker-McFee power-driven etching press.

Published in early June 1977 at $25.00. There were ten copies out of series. Of these, six were special copies for the participants in the project, each containing an extra line printed with the recipient's name and bound in decorated boards with black leather spines. Hughes did not sign these special copies, possibly through an oversight. Of the four remaining out-of-series copies, two were signed.

After printing, the sheets were sent to Hughes' sister Olwyn in London for him to sign. A number of them were accidentally smudged by Miss Hughes' cleaning lady, but Claire Van Vliet was able to clean up most of them after their return. Of the in-series copies, numbers I–X and 101–120 were retained by Janus Press, and the latter twenty copies were soon sold. The remainder were sent to Charles Seluzicki on 26 May.

A53 SUNSTRUCK 1977

Sunstruck | Ted Hughes | THE SCEPTRE PRESS | Knotting · Bedfordshire

[1]⁴. Pages [1–8], consisting: [1] title page; [2] blank; [3] 'SUNSTRUCK *is published by Martin Booth | at Sceptre Press, Knotting, Bedfordshire, | in an edition of 300 numbered copies, | the first 100 of which are signed by the poet. | Printed by Christopher Skelton | in 'Monotype' Baskerville | on Glastonbury Laid paper, | in August 1977. |* THIS IS COPY NO: [number] | [signature, in copies 1–100] | *Fifty copies of the signed one hundred are | retained by the poet, in whom copyright remains. |* © Ted Hughes 1977.'; [4] blank; [5–7] poem; [8] '*Skelton's Press, Wellingborough, Northamptonshire*'.

Light brown wrappers. Front printed in dark maroon: 'SUNSTRUCK | *TED HUGHES*'. Copies 1–100 sewn, others stapled.

Paper cream-coloured 'laid' (chain lines horizontal, 2.5 cm., watermark incomplete in copies examined), 15.5 × 14.8 cm., bulk .1 cm.; all edges cut. Printed letterpress.

Published August 1977 at £10.00 signed/£2.00 unsigned. Six of the ordinary copies and six of the signed were retained by the publisher. Ten copies out of series were given away. The printer also kept at least a few copies, probably defective.

A54   MOON-BELLS AND OTHER POEMS   1978

a. First edition:

Moon-Bells and Other Poems | BY | TED HUGHES | 1978 | CHATTO &
WINDUS | LONDON

[1–2]⁸ = 16 leaves. Pages (1–6)7–32, consisting: (1) 'CHATTO POETS
FOR THE YOUNG | *Moon-Bells and Other Poems*'; (2) list of thirteen
other books in the series; (3) title page; (4) 'Published by | Chatto and
Windus Ltd | 40 William IV Street | London WC2N 4DF | * | Clarke,
Irwin & Co. Ltd | Toronto | [...] | [CIP data] | © Ted Hughes 1978 |
Printed in Great Britain by | Redwood Burn Ltd | Trowbridge & Esher';
(5) table of contents; (6) blank; 7–32 text.

White plastic-covered paper over boards, printed in dark blue and light
blue, with red in the drawing. Front: 'Chatto Poets for the Young | [the
remainder within a ruled border] Moon-Bells | and other poems | TED
HUGHES | [in all three colours, drawing of a moon and bells]'. Spine:
'Ted Hughes   Moon-Bells and Other Poems   Chatto & Windus'.
Back: 'Chatto Poets for the Young | [the remainder within a ruled
border] [blurbs for the series] | [notice of Hughes' other children's
books] | *Cover design by Charles Keeping* | ISBN 0 7011 2274 9 | [...]'.

Issued without a dust-wrapper.

21.5 × 12.7 cm., bulk .3 cm.; all edges cut. Printed letterpress.

CONTENTS: Pets—Nessie—Fox-Hunt—I See a Bear[1]—A Moon-Witch—
Roe-Deer—Tigress—Moon-Whales[2]—Coming Down Through
Somerset—Amulet[3]—Birth of Rainbow—Bullfinches—Moon
Walkers[2]—A Mountain Lion, Her Alarmed Skulk—He Gets Up in
Dark Dawn—Water[4]—Moon-Wind[2]—Moon-Bells[2]—Moon-Ravens[2]—
Horrible Song—Off-Days—Earth-Moon[2].

Published 2 February 1978 at £1.95; 6000 copies printed.

All copies seen have a price sticker on the lower left back cover.

b. Second edition, expanded (1986):

MOON-BELLS | and Other Poems | by | TED HUGHES | Illustrated
by Felicity Roma Bowers | THE BODLEY HEAD | London

---

[1] Originally published in *Crow Wakes*.
[2] Originally published in *Earth-Moon*.
[3] Originally published as a separate (A27).
[4] Originally published in *Recklings*.

$[1–3]^8 = 24$ leaves. Pages (1–6)7–46(47–48), consisting: (1) half-title, 'MOON-BELLS | and Other Poems | [illustration of a bird]'; (2) blank; (3) title page; (4) 'The illustrations reproduced within | *Moon-Bells and Other Poems* are monoprints. | [illustration of birds] | [CIP data] | Poems © Ted Hughes 1978, 'Ants' 1986, 'The Moorhen' 1986, | 'Sketching a Thatcher' 1983 | Illustrations © Felicity Roma Bowers 1986 | Printed in Great Britain for | The Bodley Head Ltd | 32 Bedford Square, London WC1B 3EL | by William Clowes Ltd, Beccles | *First published by Chatto & Windus 1978* | *This edition, with three additional poems, 1986*'; (5) table of contents; (6) illustration, continuing to 7; 7–47 text; (48) index of first lines. Text pages 8, 9, 11, 12, 15, 19, 22, 23, 25, 28, 30, 32, 34–39, 43, 45, 47 unnumbered. Twenty-three illustrations, halftone reproductions of monoprints.

Dark blue calico-embossed paper over boards. Spine flat, stamped in silver: 'TED HUGHES   Moon-Bells and Other Poems   [at foot, reading across] B | H'.

Dust-wrapper printed (front continuing to back) with colour illustration of bells and faces on the moon. Front: '[yellow] TED HUGHES | Moon-Bells | and Other Poems | [white] Illustrated by Felicity Roma Bowers'. Spine lettered like book spine, in yellow except for 'B | H' in white. On back, lower right, on white panel: bar code.

Paper medium glossy, 21.0 × 14.9 cm., bulk .3 cm.; all edges cut. Printed offset.

CONTENTS same as first edition, with the addition of 'The Moorhen', 'Ants', and 'Sketching a Thatcher'. 'The Moorhen' was previously published in *A Primer of Birds*.

Published October 1986 at £5.95; number of copies undetermined.

REVIEWS: *Books and Bookmen*, Dec. 1986; *British Book News*, June 1978; *British Book News, Children's Books*, March 1987; *Guardian*, 30 Mar. 1978 (Martin Dodsworth); *Listener*, 9 Nov. 1978; *Observer*, 14 Dec. 1986; *School Librarian*, June 1978 (M. Crouch); *Times*, 8 Mar. 1978; *Times Educational Supplement*, 18 Jan. 1980, 13 Feb. 1987; *Times Literary Supplement*, 7 Apr. 1978 (John Mole); *Tribune*, 19 May 1978 (Martin Booth).

A55   A SOLSTICE   1978

A Solstice | * | Ted Hughes | THE SCEPTRE PRESS | Knotting · Bedfordshire

$[1]^6$. Pages [1–12], consisting: [1] title page; [2] blank; [3] 'A SOLSTICE *is published by Martin Booth | at Sceptre Press, Knotting, Bedfordshire, | in an edition of 350 numbered copies, | the first 100 of which are signed by the poet. |*

Printed by Christopher Skelton | in 'Monotype' Bembo on Abbey Mills paper, | at Skelton's Press, Wellingborough, England | in July, 1978. | THIS IS COPY | [number] | [signature, in copies 1–100] | *Fifty copies of the signed one hundred are | retained by the poet in whom copyright remains.* | © *Ted Hughes 1978*'; [4] blank; [5–12] poem.

Stapled into heavy yellow wrappers. Front printed 'TED HUGHES | A Solstice'.

Paper white 'laid' (chain lines vertical, 2.5 cm.), marked '[crown] | Abbey Mills | Greenfield' [in black letter; no complete mark present in copies examined]. 21.0 × 12.6 cm., bulk .1 cm.; all edges cut. Printed letterpress.

Published July 1978 at £10.50 signed / £2.75 unsigned. The publisher retained six ordinary and six signed copies, and ten copies out of series were given away.

A56   ORTS   1978

[in red and black] *ORTS* | [rule, 4.2 cm.] | BY TED HUGHES | WITH A DRAWING BY | LEONARD BASKIN | [rule] | LONDON · RAINBOW PRESS · 1978

$[1–5]^8 = 40$ leaves. Pages [1–80], consisting: [1–2] blank; [3] half-title; [4] drawing of man's head in wolf's mouth, dated 1976; [5] title page; [6] blank; [7–9] table of contents; [10] blank; [11–73] text; [74] blank; [75] 'This edition of 200 numbered copies signed by the author | was set in Bodoni types, printed on Italian paper | at the John Roberts Press, London | and bound by Zaehnsdorf, London | This is copy number | [number] | [signature]'; [76] '*Published by the* RAINBOW PRESS | *100 Chetwynd Road, London* | *All rights reserved* | Text © Ted Hughes 1977 | Drawing © Leonard Baskin 1977'; [77–80] blank. There is an extra fly leaf front and back, not included in this collation.

Full black calf, spine stamped in gold: 'TED HUGHES ★ ORTS Rainbow Press'. At both front and back are a fold of decorated Japanese paper, and a fold of Italian paper like that used for the text, but with the chain lines vertical and all edges cut. One leaf of the Japanese fold forms the paste-down; the other is pasted to the outer leaf of the Italian fold to form the free fly; the remaining fold of Italian paper forms another fly leaf. Several types of Japanese paper were used, with varying patterns. Some copies were probably bound in indigo leather; a bookseller catalogued such a copy, but the compilers have not seen one.

In a slip-case covered with black cloth, lined with flocked fabric.

Paper Italian mould-made 'laid' (chain lines horizontal, 2.2 cm.), 18.7

× 15.2 cm., bulk .8 cm.; top edge cut and gilt, others deckle. Printed letterpress.

CONTENTS: The Fallen Oak Sleeps Under the Bog—Let That One Shrink Into Place—The Queen of Egypt—You Have Come Down From the Clouds—Skin—Air—At Some Juncture the Adult Dies—So Much Going On—Huge Global Trouble All to Earn—The Earth is Strong, Faithful, True and—Ophelia—The Express With a Bang—Look Back—Sunday Bells—The Volcano—He Hears Lithe Trees and Last Leaves Swatting the Glass—The White Shark—Eye Went Out to Hunt You—He Sickened—Are They Children or Are They Senile—Searching, I Am Confronted Again—In the M5 Restaurant—At the Bottom of the Arctic Sea, They Say—The Buzzard Mews—For Weights of Blood—Where Shall I Put My Hand?—Words Bring Wet Lumps of Earth—Sitting Under the Downpour—They Brought You a Lit-Up Flying City—The Mother of the Tree—If Searching Can't Find You—Before I Was Born, You Were a Spirit—Where You Wait—Stilled at His Drink—Children, New to the Blood—Hathershelf—Your Eyes are Poor—Better, Happier, to Stay Clear of the Pure—The Cathedral, For All Its Defiance—After Years of Methodical, Daily—Like the Future Oak Invisible—The Bulging Oak is Not as Old—A Cry is Coming Closer—He Did All That He Thought He Wanted to Do—Why Do You Take Such Nervy Shape to Become—You Have Made Me Careless—Each New Moment My Eyes—Does it Matter how Long—The Salmon's Egg Winters the Gouging Floods—Your Touch Jerks Me—Churches Darken Like Scabs—As Often as I Affirm—In the Zoo—The Engine Under the Car-Bonnet—By the Splitting, Spilling, Fly-Crazing—The Cat, Craning Over the Long Grass—The Cut Stone—Lucretia—Ophiuchos—Twisted Mouths—A Wild Drop Flies in Space—He Sits Grinning, He Blurts Laughter—Before Dawn Twilight, A Sky Dry as Talc.

Published around 1 August 1978 at £50; slightly over 200 copies printed (see above, 'The Rainbow Press', p. 4), of which 150 were for sale.

'Orts' means 'leavings' (especially of food). A typescript of *Orts* carries the epigraph 'The lady's leavings are the dog's dainties'. Many of these poems were left over from 'Lumb's Remains', an early version of the *Gaudete* epilogue.

A57 MOORTOWN ELEGIES 1978

a.1. First edition:

TED HUGHES | Moortown | Elegies [title in rust-coloured calligraphic letters] | THE RAINBOW PRESS

$[1-4]^6[5]^8 = 32$ leaves. Pages (i–ii)(1–9)10–56(57–62) [page 37 misnumbered 35], consisting: (i–ii) blank; (1) half-title; (2) blank; (3) title page; (4) 'Published by The Rainbow Press | 100 Chetwynd Road, London NW5 1DH | Poems © Ted Hughes 1978 | Drawing © Leonard Baskin 1978 | *Printed and made in Great Britain*'; (5) 'Dedicated to the memory of | JACK ORCHARD'; (6) blank; (7) table of contents; (8) blank; (9) half-title; 10–56 text; (57) Baskin drawing of plants and insects, dated 1977; (58) blank; (59) publisher's device by Baskin, similar to that in *Prometheus On His Crag*, but 4.9 × 10.6 cm., vine leaves coloured solid, and red letterpress beneath rainbow: 'THE | RAINBOW PRESS'; (60) 'This edition of one hundred and seventy five copies | signed by the author | was designed and printed by | Will Carter at the Rampant Lions Press, Cambridge | on Barcham Green handmade paper. | The type is Monotype Ehrhardt. | Six author's presentation copies | and twenty six further copies, lettered A to Z | were bound in full morocco by Sangorski & Sutcliffe, London | and one hundred and forty three numbered copies in | full limp white goat vellum by Zaehnsdorf, London. | The work was finished in the summer of 1978. | This is copy | [number or letter] | [signature]'; (61–62) blank. Text pages 36 and 44 unnumbered.

Copies A–Z and the six presentation copies bound in full brown morocco, edges bevelled, four raised bands on spine irregularly spaced. Front stamped in gold with a bull drawn by Hughes, 9.15 cm. from tip of nose to tip of tail. Spine stamped in gold 'MOORTOWN ELEGIES TED HUGHES'. In a slip-case of rust-coloured cloth over bevelled boards, lined with cloth. Decorated Japanese endpapers and extra binder's leaves inserted as in *Orts* (A56).

Copies 1–143 bound in full stiff vellum, fore-edges turned over; front stamped in gold with Hughes bull as above, but measuring 10.4 cm. Spine stamped in gold 'Ted Hughes MOORTOWN ELEGIES Rainbow Press'. In a slip-case of rust-coloured cloth over boards. After the printing of the book was completed, Olwyn Hughes decided to have the vellum binding done not by Zaehnsdorf but by W. T. Morrell of Covent Garden. An advertisement leaflet, issued by Rainbow Press after the lettered copies had been exhausted, announced this change.

Paper handmade laid (chain lines horizontal, 1.8 cm.), marked with an interlocked B and G in open-face script, and '1975' (5.7 × 4.4 cm.); or 'W & SC HAND-MADE' (1.3 × 17.4 cm.). Overall 33.2 × 23.5 cm., bulk .9 cm.; top edge cut and gilt, others deckle. Printed letterpress.

CONTENTS: Rain—Dehorning—Struggle—Poor Birds—Feeding Out-Wintering Cattle at Twilight—Foxhunt[1]—New Year Exhilaration[2]—Snow Smoking as the Fields Boil—Bringing in New Couples—Tractor—Couples Under Cover—Surprise—Last Night—Ravens—February 17th—Roe-Deer—March Morning Unlike Others—Turning Out—She has Come to Pass—Birth of Rainbow—Orf—Happy Calf—

Coming Down Through Somerset[1]—Little Red Twin—Teaching a Dumb Calf—Last Load—While She Chews Sideways—Sheep, Parts 1 and 2[3]—A Monument—A Memory[4]—The Day he Died—Now You Have to Push—The Formal Auctioneer—Hands.

Published October 1978 at £175 for lettered copies, £140 for the numbered; slightly over 175 copies printed (see above, 'The Rainbow Press', p. 4).

a.2. Broadside poems from Moortown Elegies *(1979):*

[Four broadsides; format for each:] [title] | [poem] | [in pen] [number]/100 [in type] PRINTED FOR THE RAINBOW PRESS BY WILL CARTER 1979 [Hughes' signature]

Paper the same as that used in *Moortown Elegies*, about 47.5 × 32.7 cm.; left edge cut, others deckle.

CONTENTS: Couples Under Cover—Teaching a Dumb Calf—February 17th—Ravens.

Published early in 1979 at £40 for the set or £12 each; 100 sets printed. Olwyn Hughes does not remember exactly when copies were first offered for sale, but both she and Will Carter have remarked that it was several months after the publication of *Moortown Elegies*.

Printed from the standing type of *Moortown Elegies*, with the titles reset.

*b. First trade edition (*Moortown Diary, *1989):*

[within a double-rule frame] TED | HUGHES | [rule, 1.9 cm.] | *Moortown* | *Diary* | [below frame] ff | *faber and faber* | LONDON · BOSTON

[1[16] 2[8] 3[16]] = 40 leaves. Pages (i–iv)v(vi)vii–xi(xii),1–68, consisting: (i) half-title; (ii) '*Also by Ted Hughes* | [30 titles]'; (iii) title page; (iv) '*Moortown* first published in 1979 | by Faber and Faber Limited | 3 Queen Square London WC1N 3AU | This selection of poems from | *Moortown* with notes first published in | this edition in 1989 | Phototypeset by Wilmaset, Birkenhead, Wirral | Printed in Great Britain by | Richard Clay Ltd, Bungay, Suffolk | © Ted Hughes, 1979, 1989 | [notes on Net Book Agreement and CIP data, and ISBN

---

[1] Previously published in *Moon-Bells*; small changes.
[2] Misspelled 'Exhileration' in the text.
[3] The first and third parts only from the poem in *Season Songs*; minor changes.
[4] Not the poem 'Memory' from *Recklings*; begins 'Your bony white bowed back'.

numbers]'; v, table of contents; (vi) 'In memory of Jack Orchard'; vii–xi preface by Hughes; (xii) blank; 1–60 text; 61–68 notes.

Black calico-grain paper over boards. Spine round, stamped in white: '[reading across, thin-thick rule] [reading down] TED HUGHES *Moortown Diary*   [reading across] ff | [thick-thin rule]'.

Dust-wrapper printed reddish brown with all-over 'ff' pattern; white panels on front, spine, and back. In front panel, the double-rule frame and its contents from title page; beneath, but still within the frame, a drawing of a bull by Hughes, coloured in reddish brown. Spine panel bears lettering like the book spine, in black. Back panel: '[within double-rule frame] ff | *faber and faber* | *Also by Ted Hughes* | [7 titles] | [bar code]'.

19.7 × 12.9 cm., bulk .7 cm.; all edges cut. Printed offset.

CONTENTS same as *Moortown Elegies*, the order somewhat altered. Dates of composition have been added.

Published 18 September 1989 (the British Library copy is stamped 16 August) at £8.99; number of copies undetermined. A paperback printing of unknown size was issued simultaneously, 'perfect-bound', at £3.99 ($9.95 Canadian). It is identical internally to the hardbound printing.

REVIEWS: *American Book Review*, June 1991; *Financial Times*, 23 Sept. 1989 (Bernard McGinley); *Listener*, 9 Nov. 1989 (Dannie Abse); *Month*, Jan. 1990; *Tablet*, 21 Oct. 1989 (Elizabeth Jennings); *Times*, 16 Sept. 1989 (Robert Nye); *Times Literary Supplement*, 20 Oct. 1989 (John Lucas); *Weekend Telegraph*, 21 Oct. 1989 (Derek Walcott).

A58   THE THRESHOLD   1979

[freehand-designed title by Ralph Steadman, abstract design in black and red with lettering:] THE THRESHOLD by Ted Hughes | Illustrated by Ralph Steadman

12 disjunct leaves, side-stitched. Pages [1–24], consisting: [1] title page; [2] part of illustration from next page; [3–21] text, all but two pages illustrated, with full-page colour lithographs at pages [5], [10], and [18]; [22] blank; [23] colophon printed over full-page enlargement, in light red, of an illustration of a steam press. In three columns; left: 'A numbered limited edition of 100 copies signed by the author and artist. | This is No. [number, in pencil]/100 [in pencil] [Steadman's signature in pencil] | [Hughes' signature in ink]'. Middle column, steam press illustration, 3.2 × 5.0 cm. Right column: '© Copyright: Ted Hughes & Ralph Steadman 1979 | Published by Ralph Steadman at the Steam Press, 43 Floral Street, Covent Garden, London WC2E 9DW | Designed

by Richard Saunders and printed at the Dawes Press, 68 Dawes Road, Fulham, London SW6 7EJ | The text is set in 10pt Rockwell Light'. Page [24] blank.

Black coated buckram over boards. Spine stamped in gold 'HUGHES-STEADMAN THE THRESHOLD STEAM PRESS'. Endpapers black.

Paper glossy, 29.8 × 42.8 cm., bulk .2 cm; all edges cut and gilt. Printed letterpress, with illustrations done by lithography.

Published January 1979 at £105; 100 copies printed.

Steadman gave half the edition to Hughes for his own use. The copies which Steadman distributed have the Steam Press blind-stamp (two concentric circles, outer diameter 3.9 cm., with 'Steam Press' between them) on the lower right colophon; those distributed by Hughes lack the stamp.

A59   ADAM AND THE SACRED NINE   1979

[in black and blue] TED HUGHES | ADAM | AND THE | SACRED | NINE | WITH A DRAWING BY | LEONARD BASKIN | THE RAINBOW PRESS

[1–4]^4 = 16 leaves. Pages (i–ii)(1–6)7–23(24–30), consisting: (i–ii) blank; (1) half-title; (2) drawing of a phoenix rising from the flames; (3) title page; (4) '*Printed in Great Britain*'; (5) table of contents; (6) blank; 7–23 text; (24) blank; (25) '[publisher's device by Baskin, similar to that in *Prometheus* except vine leaves are in yellow-brown outline and letterpress under rainbow reads 'THE | RAINBOW PRESS' in blue] | This edition of 200 copies | signed by the author | and with a drawing by | Leonard Baskin | was set in Monotype Bodoni | designed and printed at the | Rampant Lions Press, Cambridge | by Will Carter | and bound by Gray | of Cambridge | This copy is number [number] | [signature]'; (26) blank; (27) 'Published by The Rainbow Press | 100 Chetwynd Road, London, NW5 1DH | Text copyright Ted Hughes 1978 | Drawing copyright Leonard Baskin 1978'; (28–30) blank. Text pages 15 and 16 unnumbered. There is an extra fly leaf front and back, not included in this collation.

Full blue calf, raised band at top and bottom of spine; spine stamped in gold, reading up, 'TED HUGHES ★ ADAM AND THE SACRED NINE'. Endpapers of decorated Japanese paper sandwiched with binder's leaves as in *Orts*.

In a slip-case covered with blue cloth, lined with white ribbed fabric.

Paper mould-made wove, but with horizontal chain lines spaced 2.2 cm., marked 'L AMATRUDA | AMALFI' (4.1 × 11.0 cm.); 19.6 × 15.0 cm., bulk .3 cm.; top edge cut and gilt, fore- and bottom edges deckle. Printed letterpress.

CONTENTS: The Song—Adam—Awake!—All This Time His Cry—He had Retreated—And the Falcon Came—The Skylark Came—The Wild Duck Got Up With a Cry—The Swift Comes the Swift—The Unknown Wren—And Owl—The Dove Came—The Crow Came to Adam—And the Phoenix has Come—Light—Bud-Tipped Twig—The Sole of a Foot. Abbreviated titles are given in the table of contents.

Published Spring 1979 at £50; slightly over 200 copies printed (see above, 'The Rainbow Press', p. 4), of which 150 were for sale. The prospectus gave February for publication, but later copies of the prospectus have the month crossed out and 'Spring' inserted by hand.

A60   REMAINS OF ELMET   1979

a. First edition:

[double-page title in brown outline letters and black; left:] Remains | Photographs by Fay Godwin [right:] TED HUGHES | of Elmet | RAINBOW PRESS · 1979

$[1–4]^4[5]^6[6–11]^4 = 46$ leaves, not counting plates. Pages (i–ii)(1–6)7(8)9–11(12)13–87(88–90), consisting: (i–ii) blank; (1) half-title; (2–3) title spread; (4) blank; (5) 'In memory of Edith Farrar'; (6) blank; 7, introductory poem 'Six years into her posthumous life'; (8) blank; 9–11 table of contents; (12) blank; 13–87 text; (88) 'Published by the Rainbow Press | 100 Chetwynd Road, London NW5 | The text © Ted Hughes 1979 | The photographs © Fay Godwin 1979 | This book was designed and the letterpress printed by | Sebastian Carter at the Rampant Lions Press, Cambridge, | in 14 pt Ehrhardt semi-bold; the photographs were | printed by screenless offset lithography at The Stellar Press, | Hatfield, Herts; and the binding was by W. T. Morrell. | The edition is limited to 180 copies numbered and signed | by the author, divided as follows: numbers 1–70 are printed | on Barcham Green Charing hand-made paper, bound in | full treed calf, and also signed by the photographer, and | 71–180 on T. H. Saunders laid mould-made, bound in | quarter buckram. | This copy is number [number] | [signature of Hughes, and of Godwin in copies 1–70] | Printed and made in Great Britain'; (89–90) blank. A sheet with two photographs is wrapped around leaves $[4_{2.3}]$, and another around leaves $[10_{1.4}]$; the four photographs face pages 24, 28, 74, and 82, with the versos being blank.

Copies 1–70 bound in full natural calf, treed on both covers. Spine stamped in gold 'TED HUGHES · REMAINS OF ELMET'. In a slip-case of brown cloth over boards. Copies 71–180 bound in marbled boards, brown buckram spine. On front cover, a paper label printed '[two rough rules in brown] | REMAINS OF ELMET | TED HUGHES | [two rules as above]'. In a folding case of brown buckram over boards, lined with marbled paper matching book cover; spine stamped in gold 'REMAINS OF ELMET · TED HUGHES'.

Paper in copies 1–70 handmade wove, marked 'J GREEN & SON' (2.0 × 20.6 cm.), countermarked 'HAND MADE' (1.0 × 7.7 cm.). Overall 29 × 23 cm., bulk .9 cm.; top edge cut and gilt, fore- and bottom edges deckle. Paper in copies 71–180 mould-made 'laid' (chain lines vertical, 2.5 cm.), 28.3 × 22.1 cm., bulk 1.0 cm.; top edge gilt, all edges cut. The photographs in both versions are printed on machine-made white paper, 28.3 × 22.1 cm. Printed letterpress, photographs printed by screenless offset.

CONTENTS: *Six Years into her Posthumous Life*—Remains of Elmet—Wild Rock—Heather—Churn-Milk Joan—Dead Farms, Dead Leaves—For Billy Holt—First, Mills—Where the Mothers—Spring-Dusk—The Word that Space Breathes—Mill Ruins—Grouse-Butts—The Sluttiest Sheep in England—These Grasses of Light—Willow-Herb—Under the World's Wild Rims—The Sheep Went on Being Dead—Two—Mount Zion, Parts I and II—Hill Walls—Haworth Parsonage—Long Screams—Walls—The Canal's Drowning Black—Tick Tock Tick Tock—When Men got to the Summit—It is All—Rhododendrons—Top Withens—The Weasels we Smoked out of the Bank—Light Falls Through Itself—Heptonstall[1]—Tree—Hardcastle Crags—Football at Slack—The Big Animal of Rock—Hill-Stone was Content—Open to Hugh Light—Auction—Moors—Lumb Chimneys—Where the Millstone of Sky—The Long Tunnel Ceiling—Bridestones—Heptonstall Old Church—Widdop—Heptonstall Cemetery—Emily Brontë—Cock-Crows—Wycoller Hall—A Tree—High Sea-Light—Rock has not Learned—Curlews, Parts I and II—Sunstruck[2]—In April—Crown Point Pensioners—There Come Days to the Hills—You Claw the Door[3]—The Trance of Light—The Angel[4].

Published April 1979 at £140 for the leather-bound copies, £48 for the others. Slightly over 180 copies printed (see above, 'The Rainbow Press', p. 4), of which 150 were for sale.

---

[1] A different poem from the one of the same title in *Wodwo*.
[2] Published separately in 1977 (A53); slight revision.
[3] Previously published as 'Hathershelf' in *Orts*; slight revision.
[4] A rewriting of 'Ballad from a Fairy Tale' from *Wodwo*.

The leather binding was by W. T. Morrell, the boards and cloth binding by Wetherby Woolnough, contrary to the colophon's statement.

b.1. First trade edition:

[flush to left] *Remains of Elmet* | A Pennine Sequence | *Poems by* Ted Hughes | *Photographs by* Fay Godwin | Faber and Faber | London & Boston

[1–8]⁸ = 64 leaves. Pages (1–9)10–125(126–128) consisting: (1) half-title; (2) blank; (3) title page; (4) *'Photographs printed by Fiona Hall | The book designed by Yvonne Skargon* | First published in 1979 | by Faber and Faber Limited | 3 Queen Square London WC1N 3AU | Printed in Great Britain by | The Scolar Press, Ilkley | All rights reserved | © Ted Hughes 1979 | Photographs © Fay Godwin 1979 | [CIP data] | ISBN 0-571-11395-8 | ISBN 0-571-11426-1 Pbk'; (5) 'Poems in Memory of Edith Farrar | *The photographs are for Ted*'; (6) blank; 7, introductory poem 'Six years into her posthumous life'; (8) twelve-line note by Hughes, 'The Calder valley, west of Halifax, was the last ditch of Elmet ...'; (9) table of contents, two columns; 10–125 text and photographs; (126) blank; (127) list of locations of photographs, two columns; (128) blank. Sixty-three photographs.

Quarter off-white cloth, black paper over boards. Spine stamped in black 'REMAINS OF ELMET Ted Hughes · Fay Godwin FABER'. Endpapers 'laid' (chain lines vertical, 2.7 cm.), coated black both sides.

Dust-wrapper paper coated outside, coloured black except for photographs and white letters. Front: 'Remains of Elmet | Poems by Ted Hughes | Photographs by Fay Godwin | [photograph of Heptonstall from page 123]'. Spine same as book spine, but letters in white. Back: photograph of Top Withens from page 102. The front flap has Hughes' introduction from page (8).

Paper glossy, 25.3 × 21.5 cm., bulk .9 cm.; all edges cut. Printed offset.

CONTENTS: the same as the limited edition, with the following changes: lacking 'Wycoller Hall'; 'Grouse Butts' is shortened by 10 lines owing to a printer's error; 'Curlews, Parts I and II' is split into 'Curlews in April' and 'Curlews Lift'; 'Mount Zion, Parts I and II' is split into 'Mount Zion' and 'The Ancient Briton Lay Under His Rock'; order of poems changed (determined by Fay Godwin), and minor changes to many; 59 photographs are added to the 4 previous ones.

Published 21 May 1979 at £7.95; 3000 copies printed. There was a simultaneous paperback printing of 7000 copies at £3.95, identical internally save for the conditions of sale note on the verso title.

b.2. First printing for America:

[flush to left] *Remains of Elmet | Poems by* Ted Hughes | *Photographs by* Fay Godwin | Harper & Row, Publishers | New York, Hagerstown, San Francisco, London

Collation the same as the first English printing except for page (4), beginning third line: 'Copyright © 1979 by Ted Hughes. Photographs copyright © 1979 by | Fay Godwin. Printed in Great Britain [...] | [...] | ISBN 0-06-011953-0 | [...]'.

Binding the same as the first English printing, except 'HARPER & | ROW' in place of 'FABER'.

Dust-wrapper the same as the first English printing except for the following:
1. Substitution of publisher on the spine as above
2. Paper only coated part way onto flaps
3. Subtitle removed from front flap copy, and price changed
4. Rear flap copy removed except for the new ISBN.

Published officially on 31 October 1979, though copies were in the shops by the middle of the month; price $16.95. 15,000 copies were printed at the same time as those for Faber. Of these, 4000 copies were shipped from England already bound, the remainder as unbound sheets. Except as noted above the contents are identical to those in the first English printing.

*c. Second trade edition, expanded (*Elmet, *1994):*

[flush at left] ELMET | *Poems by* TED HUGHES | *Photographs by* FAY GODWIN | [indented] ff | [flush at left] *faber and faber* | LONDON · BOSTON

[1⁴ 2–9⁸] = 68 leaves. Pages (1–8)9–132(133)134–135(136), consisting: (1) half-title; (2) '[in two columns; left] *by the same author* | TED HUGHES | [33 titles] [right] FAY GODWIN | [14 titles]'; (3) title page; (4) '[flush at left] First published as *Remains of Elmet* in 1979 | by Faber and Faber Limited | 3 Queen Square London WC1N 3AU | This revised edition first published in 1994 | Photoset in Monotype Apollo by | Datix International Limited, Bungay, Suffolk | Printed in England by Jackson Wilson Ltd, Leeds | All rights reserved | © Ted Hughes, 1979, 1994 | Photographs © Fay Godwin, 1979, 1994 | [notes on identity of authors and CIP record, and ISBN numbers] | [printing code, 10–1]'; (5) '[flush at left] In memory of Edith Farrar and William Hughes | The photographs are for Ted'; (6) blank; (7–8) table of contents; 9–11 note initialled by Hughes; 12 blank except for page number; 13–132 text;

(133) blank; 134–135 list of locations of photographs; (136) blank. 60 photographs.

Charcoal-grey cloth over boards. Spine round, stamped in very light green: '[reading across] [rule] | ff | [rule] [reading down] ELMET   Ted Hughes   Fay Godwin'. Endpapers light greenish-grey.

Dust-wrapper outside coated and coloured grey, front and spine printed with words in white and rules in black. Front: '[in a rule frame] ff | [rule] | ELMET | [rule] | *Poems by* | Ted Hughes | [rule] | *Photographs by* | Fay Godwin | [below frame, in a white heavy rule frame, photograph of Heptonstall from p. 123]'. Spine printed like book spine with an additional rule across near foot. Back: '[in a white heavy rule frame, photograph of Lumb Valley from p. 43] | [on white panel, bar code]'.

Copies were shipped in an unprinted corrugated cardboard slip-case.

Paper glossy, 25.0 × 20.0 cm., bulk .8 cm.; all edges cut. Printed offset, with illustrations in duotone (unlike A60b).

CONTENTS: The Dark River[1]—Abel Cross, Crimsworth Dean[2]—Football at Slack—Two Photographs of Top Withens[3]—Stanbury Moor[4]—Two Trees at Top Withens[5]—First, Mills—Hill-Stone Was Content—The Weasels We Smoked out of the Bank—Leaf Mould[3]—Heptonstall—Wild Rock—Moors—Tick Tock Tick Tock—There Come Days to the Hills—Shackleton Hill[6]—Chinese History of Colden Water[7]—Rhododendrons—Auction at Stanbury[8]—Curlews in April—Curlews Lift—On the Slope[9]—For Billy Holt—Sunstruck—When Men Got to the Summit—Churn-Milk Joan—Heather—Alcomden[10]—The Canal's Drowning Black—The Sheep Went on Being Dead—Bridestones—Cock-Crows—Walls at Alcomden[11]—The Long Tunnel Ceiling—Two—Mount Zion[12]—What's the First Thing You Think of?[3]—Tree—Dick Straightup[13]—The Sluttiest Sheep in England—

---

[1] = 'Six Years into her Posthumous Life'.
[2] = 'Where the Mothers'.
[3] Here first collected.
[4] = 'These Grasses of Light'.
[5] = 'Open to Huge Light'.
[6] = 'Dead Farms, Dead Leaves'.
[7] = A revision of 'The Trance of Light'.
[8] = 'Auction'.
[9] Previously published in *Recklings* &c.
[10] = 'Rock Has Not Learned'.
[11] = 'Hill Walls'.
[12] Part I only.
[13] From *Lupercal*.

Wadsworth Moor[14]—Familiar—Heptonstall Old Church—Crown Point Pensioners—West Laithe Cobbles[15]—Widdop—Emily Brontë—Walt[3]—The Horses[16]—The Beacon[17]—Wind[16]—Roarers in a Ring[16]—Pennines in April[13]—Six Young Men[16]—Slump Sundays—Climbing into Heptonstall[3]—Heptonstall Cemetery—Heptonstall[18]—Sacrifice[3]—Telegraph Wires[3]—For the Duration[3]—Anthem for Doomed Youth[3].

Hughes' note on Elmet is rewritten.

Published October 1994 at £30.00 ($75.00 in Canada, $45.00 in U.S.); number of copies undetermined. A simultaneous paperback printing of unknown size was issued at £14.99 ($40.00 in Canada, $29.99 in U.S.), identical internally except for the addition of a Net Book Agreement note on title verso. The back cover lacks the photograph, bearing instead blurbs and prices.

REVIEWS: *Agenda*, Summer/Autumn 1981 (Humphrey Clucas); *American Poetry Review*, Sept./Oct. 1980 (D. Smith); *British Book News*, Nov. 1979 (S. Toulson); *Church Times*, 27 July 1979 (Norman Nicholson); *Clio*, Winter 1985; *Concerning Poetry*, 14:1, 1981 (Carol Bere); *Daily Telegraph*, 26 July 1979 (Elizabeth Jennings); *Delta* 60, 1980 (Neil Roberts and Terry Gifford); *Encounter*, Aug. 1979 (Alan Brownjohn); *English*, Spring 1980 (E. Neill); *Guardian*, 24 May 1979 (Glyn Hughes); *Hampstead and Highgate Express*, 25 May 1979 (Liz Sagues); *Irish Independent*, 21 June 1979 (A.M.L.); *Listener*, 26 July 1979 (Geoffrey Grigson); *London Magazine*, Aug./Sept. 1979 (Alan Ross); *Louisville Times*, 7 June 1980 (Julie Ardery); *Miss London*, 21 May 1979 (Angela Coles); *New Statesman*, 8 June 1979 (Andrew Motion); *New Statesman & Society*, 2 Dec. 1994; *New York Review of Books*, 10 June 1982 (Richard Murphy); *Observer*, 15 July 1979 (Peter Porter); *Parnassus*, Spring/Winter 1980 (B. Howard); *Poetry Wales*, Spring 1980 (P. F. Robinson); *Punch*, 27 June 1979; *School Librarian*, Sept. 1979 (Margaret Meek); *Sewanee Review*, July 1980 (Calvin Bedient); *Sheffield Morning Telegraph*, 26 May 1979 (Malcolm Pain); *Spectator*, 15 Sept. 1979 (Emma Fisher); *Tablet*, 27 Aug. 1979 (John Heath-Stubbs); *Times*, 20 Dec. 1979 (Richard Holmes); *Times Literary Supplement*, 18 Jan. 1980 (Edna Longley); *Use of English*, Autumn 1979 (S.T.); *World Literature Today*, Summer 1980 (David Rogers).

[14] = 'Where the Millstone of Sky'.
[15] = 'It is All'.
[16] From *Hawk in the Rain*.
[17] = 'You Claw the Door'.
[18] First line 'Black village of gravestones'; from *Wodwo*.

A61 THE FIRST PUBLICATIONS OF 1979
THE MORRIGU PRESS

[Three broadsides:]

NIGHT ARRIVAL OF SEA-TROUT | [poem] | [Hughes' signature] | [in yellow-brown] *30 Numbered copies hand-printed by THE MORRIGU PRESS 25.3.1979* | [number in manuscript]

THE IRON WOLF | [poem] | [Hughes' signature] | [in yellow-brown] *30 Numbered copies hand-printed by THE MORRIGU PRESS 13.4.1979* | [number in manuscript]

PUMA | [poem] | [Hughes' signature] | [in yellow-brown] *30 Numbered copies hand-printed by THE MORRIGU PRESS 4.14.1979 | Copy No.* [number in manuscript]

In a folder of decorative Japanese paper with white printed label: 'The First Publications Of | THE MORRIGU PRESS | Single | Unpublished Poems By | TED HUGHES | In editions of 30 numbered | copies only, signed by the author. | Hand-set in Centaur type on | Italian paper. | No 1 NIGHT ARRIVAL OF SEA | TROUT | No 2 THE IRON WOLF | No 3 PUMA'.

Paper Italian mould-made 'laid', 29.7 × 20.0 cm.; chain lines vertical, 2.3 cm. All edges cut.

Published May 1979 at £15.00; 30 sets printed.

Printed by Hughes' son Nicholas on an Albion hand press belonging to Olwyn Hughes.

A62 BROOKTROUT 1979

[Half-sheet broadside:] Brooktrout | [drawing of four leaping trout by Ted Hughes] | [poem] | [Hughes' signature] | [in yellow-brown] *60 Numbered copies hand-printed hy* [sic] *THE MORRIGU PRESS 28.5.1979 | Copy No* [number in pen]

Paper handmade laid (chain lines vertical, 3.8–4.1 cm.), 39.5 × 26.2 cm., marked '[saint's head on shield] | 1399'. Torn along one long edge, the other three deckle.

Published early June 1979 at £15; 60 copies printed.

Printed by Hughes' son Nicholas on an Albion hand press.

A63 FOUR TALES TOLD BY AN IDIOT 1979

Four Tales | told by an Idiot | [outline swelled rule, 2.5 cm.] | Ted Hughes | THE SCEPTRE PRESS | Knotting · Bedfordshire

[1]⁴. Pages [1–8], consisting: [1] title page; [2] blank; [3] 'FOUR TALES TOLD BY AN IDIOT | *is published by Martin Booth* | *at Sceptre Press, Knotting, Bedfordshire,* | *in an edition of 450 numbered copies,* | *the first 100 of which are signed by the poet.* | *Printed by Christopher Skelton* | *in 'Monotype' Bembo on Bewick Text paper,* | *at Skelton's Press, Wellingborough, England,* | *in August, 1979.* | THIS IS COPY | [number] | [signature in copies 1–100] | *Fifty copies of the signed one hundred are* | *retained by the poet in whom copyright remains.* | © *Ted Hughes 1979*'; [4] blank; [5–8] text. Erratum slip laid in.

Stapled into heavy grey paper wrappers (paper 'laid', chain lines vertical, 1.2 cm.). Front cover printed '*Four Tales* | *told by an Idiot* | *TED HUGHES*'.

16.6 × 14.9 cm., bulk .1 cm.; all edges cut. Printed letterpress.

Contains four numbered poems; first lines: I Woke in the Bed of the Rains—I was Tied to a Stake, in a Tectite Desert—Night-Wind, a Freedom—That Star.

Published August 1979 at £12.50 signed / £3.50 unsigned; 460 copies printed. The publisher retained 6 regular and 6 signed copies, and 10 copies out of series were given away.

The erroneous substitution of 'fruit' for 'krait' in line 5 of the first poem was only noticed after the publisher's 28 standing orders had been mailed out. Erratum slips were therefore printed up, included in subsequent shipments, and set separately to most (but not all) of the standing orders.

A64 PAN 1979

[Half-sheet broadside:] Pan | [drawing of two scorpions by Frieda Hughes Dawes] | [poem] | [Hughes' signature] | [in yellow-brown] *60 Numbered copies hand-printed by THE MORRIGU PRESS August the fourteenth 1979* | *Copy No* [number in pen]

Paper handmade laid (chain lines vertical, 3.8–3.9 cm.), marked either with a hand and sleeve, with flower growing from second finger, or with '[saint's head on shield] | 1399' and '[script] FJH[ead]'. Ca. 39.5 × 26.0–26.5 cm. Torn along one long side, the other three deckle.

Published August 1979 at £15; 60 copies printed.

Printed by Nicholas Hughes on an Albion hand press.

A65　　　　　WOODPECKER　　　　1979

[Broadside:] [in red] WOODPECKER | [poem, the first letter in each of the three stanzas in red] | [Hughes' signature] | [in blue] 60 *numbered copies hand-printed by THE MORRIGU PRESS August the nineteenth* 1979 | [number in pen]

Paper mould-made, 28.7 × 20 cm. All edges 'deckle'.

Published August 1979 at £15; 60 copies printed.

Printed by Nicholas Hughes on an Albion hand press.

A66　　　　IN THE BLACK CHAPEL　　　1979

a. First edition:

[Broadside: within a ruled border] [pen and water-colour illustration by Leonard Baskin, reproduced in halftone, of a bird atop a man's head | [rule] | [poem, 9 lines, all but the last in double columns separated by a line] | [at bottom, outside the border, in halftone grey:] DRAWING BY LEONARD BASKIN [vertical line] POEM BY TED HUGHES | PUBLISHED ON THE OCCASION OF THE EXHIBITION ILLUSTRATIONS TO TED HUGHES POEMS AT THE | VICTORIA AND ALBERT MUSEUM 12 SEPTEMBER UNTIL 28 OCTOBER 1979. PRODUCED WITH THE ASSISTANCE | OF THE ASSOCIATES OF THE V & A. | [in black] Drawing # Leonard Baskin 1979. Poem © Ted Hughes 1979. Printed by UDO Litho Ltd.

76.0 × 50.5 cm.; all edges cut. Printed offset.

Published for the exhibition at £1.50; 1500 copies printed.

b. Second edition (limited, 1980):

Differs from the first edition in that the text of the poem has been reset and the colour of the drawing improved. An additional line at the bottom reads: THIS POSTER HAS BEEN PRINTED IN A SPECIAL EDITION LIMITED TO 150 COPIES SIGNED BY THE POET AND THE ARTIST. Signed under the drawing, Ted Hughes on the left, Baskin on the right. Copies numbered in pencil in bottom left-hand corner. Published December 1980 at £20.00.

A67　　　　　MOORTOWN　　　　1979

a. First edition:

[flush at left] TED HUGHES | MOORTOWN | FABER AND FABER | LONDON BOSTON

[1–4]^{16}[5]^8[6]^{16} = 88 leaves. Pages (1–6)7–11(12–14)15–170(171–176), consisting: (1–2) blank; (3) half-title, with Hughes' bull drawing from the cover of *Moortown Elegies*; (4) list of eighteen other books by Hughes; (5) title page; (6) '*First published in 1979* | *by Faber and Faber Limited* | *3 Queen Square London WC1N 3AU* | *Typeset by Robert MacLehose & Co Ltd Glasgow* | *Printed in Great Britain by* | *Unwin Brothers Limited* | *Old Woking Surrey* | *All rights reserved* | © *Ted Hughes 1979* | Drawings on pages 12 and 171 | © Leonard Baskin 1979 | Drawing on the half-title page | by the author | ISBN 0 571 11453 9 (cased) | ISBN 0 571 11518 7 (paperback)'; 7–11 table of contents; (12) snake drawing; (13) divisional title 'MOORTOWN | To the memory of | JACK ORCHARD'; (14) blank; 15–170 text; (171) phoenix drawing, previously used as frontispiece to *Adam and the Sacred Nine*; (172–176) blank. Text pages 69, 70, 93, 94, 157, 158 unnumbered. Errata slip laid in.

Red cloth over boards, spine stamped in gold and green foil: 'MOORTOWN TED HUGHES FABER'.

Dust-wrapper coloured green and plastic-coated except for flaps, printed in red and black. Front: snake drawing in black, from p. (12) of book, with printing arranged around: 'MOORTOWN | BY | TED | HUGHES'. Spine: 'MOORTOWN TED HUGHES FABER' ('FABER' reading across). Back: '[phoenix drawing in black, from p. (171) of book] | MOORTOWN'. Regarding the dust-wrapper drawings, Hughes wrote to Sagar: 'The whole drift is an alchemising of a phoenix out of a serpent.'

Paper poor-quality, 21.4 × 13.8 cm., bulk 1.0 cm.; all edges cut. Printed letterpress.

CONTENTS:
Moortown
    [The 34 poems published previously as *Moortown Elegies*]
Prometheus On His Crag
    [From the book of the same title. Three poems have been deleted:
    Prometheus ... Knew What Was Coming and His Eyes Closed
    Prometheus ... Can See Io Fleeting Across the Map
    Prometheus .:. Was Himself the Fire.
       Three new poems have been added:
    Prometheus ... Dreamed He Had Burst the Sun's Mass
    Prometheus ... Arrested Half-Way From Heaven
    No God—Only Wind on the Flower]
Earth-Numb
    Earth-Numb—That Girl—Here is the Cathedral—Postcard from
       Torquay—Old Age Gets Up—Nefertiti—A Motorbike—Deaf

School—Photostomias, 1, 2, and 3[1]—The Lovepet[2]—Second Birth—
Song of Longsight—Life is Trying to be Life[3]—A Citrine Glimpse,
1 and 2

Four Tales Told by an Idiot [The four poems from A63]

Actaeon

Seven Dungeon Songs: (1) The Wolf—(2) Dead, She Became Space-
Earth—(3) Face was Necessary [dash] I Found Face—(4) The
Earth Locked Out the Light—(5) I Walk—(6) The Oracle—(7) If
Mouth Could Open its Cliff

A Knock at the Door

Orts: (1) Each New Moment My Eyes[5]—(2) Are They Children[5]—
(3) For Weights of Blood[5]—(4) Heatwave—(5) In the M5
Restaurant[5]—(6) Poets—(7) *Grosse Fuge*—(8) Lucretia[5]—(9)
The Cathedral[5]—(10) Pan[11]—(11) Speech Out of Shadow—(12)
Everything is Waiting—(13) Night Arrival of Sea-Trout[1]—(14)
Flight From Egypt—(15) Beeches, Leafless[6]—(16) Look Back[5]—
(17) Buzz in the Window—(18) Lumb[7]—(19) The Express[5]—(20)
T.V. Off[8]—(21) Ophiuchos[5]—(22) Funeral—(23) Children[5]—
(24) Prospero and Sycorax[9]—(25) Before-Dawn Twilight, a Sky
Dry as Talc[5]

Tiger-Psalm[10]—The Stone

Stained Glass: (1) The Virgin—(2) The Womb—(3) The Virgin Knight

A God

Adam and the Sacred Nine
[From the book of the same title. Five poems are omitted:
Awake!—All This Time His Cry—He Had Retreated—Light—Bud-
Tipped Twig]

Published 22 October 1979 at £5.25; 2000 copies printed. There was a
simultaneous paperback printing of 20,000 copies at £1.95, 'perfect-bound'
but internally identical save for the conditions of sale note on the verso title.

Both printings were issued with an errata slip, printed offset and listing
three corrections.

---

[1] Previously published separately as *Chiasmadon*.
[2] From the American edition of *Crow*, last line omitted.
[3] Previously published as 'Crow Rambles' in *Poems* with Fainlight and Sillitoe.
[4] Previously published as one of *The First Publications of the Morrigu Press*.
[5] Previously published in *Orts*; a few revisions.
[6] A revision of 'The Earth is Strong, Faithful, True and' from *Orts*.
[7] = 'At the Bottom of the Arctic Sea, They Say' from *Orts*.
[8] = 'He Hears Lithe Trees and Last Leaves Swatting the Glass' from *Orts*.
[9] = 'Crow's Song About Prospero and Sycorax' from *Shakespeare's Poem*.
[10] = 'Crow's Table Talk' from *Crow Wakes*.
[11] Previously published separately.

b.1. First American edition:

[thick-thin rule, 5.9 cm.] | Ted Hughes | [rule, 5.9 cm.] | MOORTOWN | Drawings by Leonard Baskin

$[1-4]^{16}[5]^4[6-7]^{16} = 100$ leaves. Pages (i–vii)viii–xi(xii)(1–2)3–182(183–188), consisting: (i) half-title; (ii) blank; (iii) list of fifteen other books by Hughes; (iv) 'HARPER & ROW, PUBLISHERS | [rule, 5.3 cm.] | [publisher's logo, a torch in a square frame over '1817'; between two columns with the names of eight other cities]'; (v) title page; (vi) ' "Bride and Groom Lie Hidden for Three Days" first appeared in | *Cave Birds: An Alchemical Cave Drama* published by The Viking | Press. | MOORTOWN. Copyright © 1979 by Ted Hughes. Drawings copy- | right © 1979 by Leonard Baskin. All rights reserved. Printed in | the United States of America [...] | [...] | FIRST U.S. EDITION | *Designer: Gloria Adelson* | [rule] | [CIP data] | [rule] | [printing code, 80–1]'; (vii)viii–xi table of contents, (xii) snake drawing; (1) '[thick-thin rule] | MOORTOWN | [light rule] | TO THE MEMORY OF | JACK ORCHARD'; (2) blank; 3–182 text; (183) phoenix drawing; (184–188) blank.

Quarter black cloth, brown paper over boards. Front blind-stamped at bottom with Hughes bull drawing from the cover of *Moortown Elegies* (measuring 7.9 cm. from nose to tip of tail). Spine stamped in copper-coloured foil: 'Ted Hughes MOORTOWN Harper | & Row' (publisher's name reads across spine). Endpapers black, embossed with leather grain.

Dust-wrapper brown 'laid' (chain lines vertical, 2.0–2.2 cm.). Front: Baskin snake, as above; at top, 'TED HUGHES'; between coil and tail, 'MOORTOWN'. Spine: 'TED HUGHES MOORTOWN [reading across: publisher's torch logo, lacking date] | Harper | & Row'. Back: '[Baskin phoenix drawing, as above] | MOORTOWN | [lower right] 0-06-012016-9'. At lower right of front flap, '0580'; on rear flap, photograph of Hughes by Jim Kalett.

23.4 × 15.5 cm., bulk 1.5 cm.; all edges cut. Printed offset.

CONTENTS the same as the English edition, with the addition of 'Bride and Groom Lie Hidden for Three Days' (previously published in the trade edition of *Cave Birds*), and the omission of 'The Lovepet'.

Published 28 May 1980 at $10.95; the publisher prefers not to reveal the number printed.

b.2. First American paperback printing (1983):

[Same setting as b.1, reduced] [thick-thin rule, 5.3 cm.] | Ted Hughes | [rule, 5.3 cm.] | MOORTOWN | Drawings by Leonard Baskin | [remainder newly set:] [publisher's logo, stylized lighted lamp] |

HARPER COLOPHON BOOKS | Harper & Row, Publishers | New York, Cambridge, Philadelphia, San Francisco | London, Mexico City, São Paulo, Sydney

96 leaves, 'perfect-bound'. Pages (i–iii)iv–vii(viii),(1–2)3–182(183–184), consisting: (i) title page; (ii) '*Also by Ted Hughes* | [15 titles] | "Bride and Groom Lie Hidden for Three Days" first appeared in *Cave Birds:* | *An Alchemical Cave Drama* published by The Viking Press. | A hardcover edition of this book is published by Harper & Row, Publishers, Inc. | MOORTOWN. Copyright © 1979 by Ted Hughes. All rights reserved. Printed in the | United States of America. [...] | [...] | First HARPER COLOPHON edition published 1983. | [rule] | [CIP data, including printing code 83-1] | [rule]'; (iii)iv–vii(viii)(1–2)3–182(183–184) same setting as b.1 (vii)viii–xi(xii)(1–2)3–182(183–184) but reduced, pre-liminaries renumbered.

Wrappers coloured yellow-brown. Front printed like dust-wrapper of b.1, but reduced; reading up from bottom near spine: '*HARPER* [publisher's logo, as above] *COLOPHON BOOKS/CN 1017/$5.95*'. Spine: 'TED HUGHES   MOORTOWN   *HARPER* | *COLOPHON BOOKS* [reading across] [publisher's logo, as above] *CN* | *1017*'. Back: blurbs; at lower left: 'HARPER & ROW, PUBLISHERS | *Cover drawing by Leonard Baskin*'; at lower right, ' > > $5.95 | ISBN 0-06-091017-8 | 03057283'.

Paper highly acidic, 20.3 × 14.4 cm., bulk 1.0 cm.; all edges cut. Printed offset.

Published in 1983 at $5.95; number of copies undetermined.

REVIEWS: *Agenda*, Summer/Autumn 1981 (Humphrey Clucas); *American Poetry Review*, Jan./Feb. 1982 (S. McPherson); *Argo*, Autumn 1979 (Aline Fairweather); *Atlantic*, June 1980; *Best Sellers*, Sept. 1980; *Book World*, 7 Sept. 1980; *Booklist*, 15 May 1980; *British Book News*, Feb. 1980 (Shirley Toulson); *Chicago Tribune*, 22 Feb. 1981 (Joseph Parisi); *Christian Century*, 24 Dec. 1980 (Tony Stoneburner); *Church Times*, 25 Jan. 1980 (Norman Nicholson); *Critical Quarterly*, Summer 1980 (W. Hutchings); *Encounter*, Nov. 1980 (Alan Brownjohn); *English*, Spring 1980 (Edward Neill); *Guardian*, 28 Nov. 1979 (Charles Causley); *Hudson Review*, Winter 1980 (Dana Gioia); *Kirkus*, 1 May 1980; *Library Journal*, 15 May 1980 (Charles Warren); *Listener*, 17 Apr. 1980 (John Harvey); *Literary Review*, 16 Nov. 1979 (Keith Sagar); *Literary Review* (Madison, N.J.), Spring 1981 (C. Bere); *London Review of Books*, 21 Feb. 1980 (John Bayley); *Los Angeles Times*, 10 Aug. 1980 (Peter Clothier); *National Review*, 19 Sept. 1980 (Selden Rodman); *New Statesman*, 4 Jan. 1980 (Blake Morrison); *New York Review of Books*, 10 June 1982 (Richard Murphy); *New York Times Book Review*, 20 July 1980 (Christopher Ricks); *Observer*, 27 Jan. 1980 (Peter Porter); *Outposts*, Summer 1980 (Michael Ferguson);

Parnassus, Spring/Winter 1980 (B. Howard), 14:1, 1987 (Calvin Bedient); *PN Review* 15, 1980 (Dick Davis); *Poetry*, Aug. 1981 (Julian Moynahan); *Poetry Wales*, Spring 1980 (P. F. Robinson); *Publishers Weekly*, 4 Apr. 1980; *Quarto*, Feb. 1980 (Lachlan Mackinnon); *Sewanee Review*, Spring 1981; *Southwest Review*, Spring 1981 (G. Burns); *Stand*, vol. 21, no. 3, 1980 (Terry Eagleton); *Sunday Telegraph*, 13 Jan. 1980; *Sunday Times*, 9 Dec. 1979 (John Carey); *Tablet*, 1 Dec. 1979 (David Wright); *Thought*, June 1987; *Threepenny Review*, Winter 1981 (Paul Lake); *Times*, 17 Jan. 1980 (Robert Nye); *Times Educational Supplement*, 23 Nov. 1979 (Myra Barrs); *Times Higher Education Supplement*, 29 Feb. 1980 (Eric Homberger); *Times Literary Supplement*, 4 Jan. 1980 (Peter Scupham); *Tribune*, 30 Nov. 1979 (Martin Booth); *Tulsa Home and Garden*, Sept. 1980 (Thomas F. Staley); *Yorkshire Post*, 27 Mar. 1980 (Robert Welch).

A68   HENRY WILLIAMSON   1979

[flush to left] HENRY | WILLIAMSON | A tribute by Ted Hughes | given at the Service of Thanksgiving | at the Royal Parish Church of | St Martin-in-the-Fields | 1 December 1977 | Rainbow Press

[1]^{10} (not counting wrappers). Pages [1–20], consisting: [1–4] blank; [5] half-title; [6] blank save for two small guide marks; tipped on, a halftone reproduction, in green, of a pencil sketch of Williamson by William Thompson, 19.3 × 13.3 cm.; [7] title page; [8] blank; [9–16] text; [17] blank; [18] '*The* [*T* swash] *Rainbow* [*R* swash] *Press · 100 Chetwynd Road · London NW5 | Copyright Ted Hughes 1979 | Frontispiece portrait by Bill Thomson* [*T* swash] *| 200 copies, of which 125 are for sale, designed and printed by | Sebastian Carter at the Rampant* [*R* swash] *Lions Press, Cambridge, England, | in 18 pt Palatino on Zerkall* [*Z* swash] *mould-made paper, and bound in | Fabriano covers; the frontispiece printed by the Stellar Press. | This* [*T* swash] *copy is number* [number] *| signed by* [signature]'; [19–20] blank.

Sewn into wrappers of the same paper as the text.

Pasted, by a strip of paste on the back near the spine, into a maroon dust-wrapper, handmade laid by Fabriano (chain lines horizontal, 3.5–4.5 cm.), marked with a wolf suckling Romulus and Remus within an oval border 7.2 × 9.5 cm. Front printed (flush to left) 'HENRY | WILLIAMSON'. Will and Sebastian Carter report that some copies had brown wrappers—the compilers have not seen one of these.

Text paper mould-made by Zerkall, marked with a P and Z superimposed (3.1 × 1.6 cm.). Overall 26.0 × 18.5 cm., top edge cut, fore- and bottom edge 'deckle'. Portrait printed on machine-made medium-finish paper. Text printed letterpress, portrait offset.

Published November 1979 at £24; slightly over 200 copies printed (see above, 'The Rainbow Press', p. 4), of which 125 were for sale.

This text was also published in *Henry Williamson: The Man, The Writings*, Tabb House, Padstow, 1980.

A69   WOLVERINE   1979

[Half-sheet broadside:] [in red] WOLVERINE | [in dark brown, drawing of wolverine by Ted Hughes] | [poem in black] | [Hughes' signature] | [in red] 75 *numbered copies hand-printed by THE MORRIGU PRESS December the twentyseventh* 1979 | [number in pen]

Paper handmade, marked 'HAND MADE 6', or with a shield bearing indistinct symbols, torn along one long side, other edges deckle. Ca. 40.0 × 28.0–28.5 cm.

Published December 1979 at £20; 75 copies printed.

Printed by Nicholas Hughes on an Albion hand press.

A70   EAGLE   1980

[Broadside:] [drawing of eagle's talons in yellow-brown by Ted Hughes] | [in red] EAGLE | [poem in black] | [Hughes' signature] | [in red] 75 *numbered copies hand-printed by THE MORRIGU PRESS July the twenty seventh* 1980 | [number in pen]

Paper handmade laid (chain lines vertical, 3.9 cm.), 40 × 26 cm., marked '[hand and sleeve, with flower growing from second finger]'. All edges deckle.

Published July 1980 at £20; 75 copies printed.

Printed by Nicholas Hughes on an Albion hand press.

A71   MOSQUITO   1980

[Broadside:] [in red] MOSQUITO | [drawing of mosquito in dark green by Ted Hughes] | [poem in black] | [Hughes' signature] | [in red] 75 *numbered copies hand-printed by THE MORRIGU PRESS August the twenty fifth* 1980 | *Copy number* [number in pen]

Paper handmade laid (chain lines vertical, 3.3 cm.), 46.5 × 30 cm., marked 'F J Head'. All edges deckle.

Published August 1980 at £20; 60 copies printed.

Printed by Nicholas Hughes on an Albion hand press.

A72   TAPIR'S SAGA   1980

[Broadside:] [in red] TAPIR'S SAGA | [in black] *When Iceland's deserted by Tapir, he'll be happier.—Tapir* | [poem] |15 *numbered copies hand-printed by* THE MORRIGU PRESS *August* 1980

Paper handmade laid (chain lines horizontal, 3.7–4.0 cm.), 26 × 20 cm., marked '[saint's head on shield] | 1399'. All edges deckle.

Printed on an Albion hand press by Nicholas Hughes, who, being unhappy with the typeface, never issued the broadside. The copies still exist, and some have been given away. The copy seen is unnumbered.

A73   SKY FURNACE   1980

Broadside: a reproduction in colour of an oil painting by Roger Vick. Underneath in four columns a facsimile of the poem in manuscript. At bottom '*Sky-Furnace* Painting by Roger Vick. Poem by Ted Hughes © 1980 [number in pencil]'. Signed in pencil under the painting, on the left by Roger Vick and on the right by Ted Hughes.

Mounted and framed by Holsworthy Art Products. Size framed 69 × 83 cm.

Published by Caricia Fine Arts, Court Green, North Tawton, Devon. Edition limited to 150 copies. Probably not distributed until January 1981. Price £98.50

The order form, which carries a colour miniature reproduction of the broadside, states: 'Caricia Fine Arts are pleased to offer the first collaboration by painter Roger Vick and poet Ted Hughes in an edition limited to 150 prints of *Sky Furnace* each signed and numbered by artist and author. Ted Hughes' holograph is the first publication of this poem and the picture which has been finely printed by the Scolar Press is the sole reproduction of the original oil painting by Roger Vick.'

A74   UNDER THE NORTH STAR   1981

a.1. First edition:

[watercolour lettering by Baskin] UNDER THE ['N' and 'D', and 'H' and 'E' share downstrokes] | NORTH | STAR | [regular type, black halftone screen over solid red] TED HUGHES | DRAWINGS BY | LEONARD BASKIN | [black] A STUDIO BOOK [small solid diamond] THE VIKING PRESS [small solid diamond] NEW YORK

[1–3⁸] = 24 leaves. Pages (1–8)9(10–11)12–44(45–48), consisting: (1) half-title, a reduced version of title-page title; (2) '[flush to left] *Also by*

Ted Hughes and Leonard Baskin | [centred under this, 3 titles]'; (3) title page; (4) '[flush to left] Text Copyright © Ted Hughes, 1981 | Illustrations Copyright © Leonard Baskin, 1981 | All rights reserved | First published in 1981 by The Viking Press (A Studio Book) | 625 Madison Avenue, New York, N.Y. 10022 | Published simultaneously in Canada by | Penguin Books Canada Limited | [CIP data] | [...] | Printed in Japan by Dai Nippon Printing Co., Ltd., Tokyo | Set in Palatino'; (5) '[flush to right] To Lucretia'; (6) blank; (7) table of contents; (8) blank; 9, the poem 'Amulet'; (10) blank; (11) half-title, same as title-page title; 12–44(45–47) text and illustrations; (48) blank. Text pages 13, 15, 17, 21, 23, 25, 29, 31, 35, 37, 43, 45–47 unnumbered.

Brownish-orange cloth over boards. Spine flat, stamped in gold: 'HUGHES [small solid diamond] BASKIN   UNDER THE NORTH STAR   VIKING'. Endpapers green.

Dust-wrapper coated outside. Front: '[watercolour of a raptor] | [title and authorship statement as on title page]'. Spine printed like book spine, black halftone screen over solid blue except for diamond which is black halftone screen over solid red. Back: '[watercolour from front] | [poem titles, in 12 lines] | [ISBN]'. Front flap has date code 0381.

28.0 × 19.4 cm., bulk .4 cm.; all edges cut. Printed offset.

Published by 9 March 1981 (the date stamped in the Library of Congress copy) at $14.95; 14,000 copies printed. There was a second printing in September 1982, identified as such on the verso title.

CONTENTS: Amulet[1]—The Loon—The Wolverine—The Snowy Owl—The Black Bear—An Evening Seal—The Muskellunge—A Lynx—The Snow-Shoe Hare—Woodpecker—The Musk-Ox—The Heron—The Grizzly Bear[2]—Brooktrout[3]—The Wendigo—The Osprey—Mooses—The Arctic Fox—Puma—Skunk—Goose—Wolf[4]—The Mosquito[5]—Eagle.

a.2. First printing for England:

Same as above except:
1. Title page imprint is 'FABER AND FABER | LONDON BOSTON';
2. P. (2) has '[flush to left] Also by Ted Hughes | [19 titles]';
3. P. (4) has '[...] | All rights reserved | First published 1981 in Great

---

[1] Previously published as a separate, then twice collected.
[2] = 'I See a Bear'.
[3] Previously published as a separate (A62).
[4] Previously published as 'The Iron Wolf' in A61.
[5] Previously published as a separate (A71).

Britain by Faber and Faber Limited | 3 Queen Square, London WC1N 3AU | [CIP data] | [. . .]'.

Same binding as American copies, but publisher's name on spine is 'FABER AND FABER'.

Dust-wrapper front, spine, and back same as the American edition, except publisher's name on spine is 'FABER AND FABER', and back lacks ISBN. Text on the flaps is different, and front flap lacks the date code.

28.0 × 19.4 cm., bulk .4 cm.; all edges cut. Printed offset.

Published 27 April 1981 at £5.95; number of copies undetermined.

REVIEWS: *Atlantic*, May 1981 (P.-L. Adams); *Booklist*, 15 May 1981; *British Book News, Children's Books*, Autumn 1981 (N. Philip); *Christian Science Monitor*, 14 Dec. 1981 (M. Lenhart); *Growing Point*, Sept. 1981 (Margery Fisher); *Horn Book*, Nov./Dec. 1986; *Junior Bookshelf*, Aug. 1981; *Kirkus*, 15 June 1981; *Library Journal*, 1 April 1981 (D. L. Guillory); *London Review of Books*, 2 July 1981 (Claude Rawson); *New Statesman*, 26 June 1981 (Graham Martin); *New York Review of Books*, 10 June 1982 (Richard Murphy); *New York Times Book Review*, 14 March 1982 (D. Donoghue); *Northwest Review*, 20:1 (A. K. Weatherhead); *Publishers Weekly*, 6 Feb. 1981; *Punch*, 24 June 1981; *School Librarian*, Dec. 1981 (G. Maunder); *Stand*, 23:3 (John Saunders); *Times Educational Supplement*, 5 June 1981 (Kevin Crossley-Holland); *Times Literary Supplement*, 24 July 1981 (Roger Garfitt); *Tribune*, 26 June 1981 (Martin Booth).

A75   THREE RIVER POEMS   1981

A portfolio of three broadsides:

A) [in red] CATADROME | [in black, the poem framed by Ted Hughes' drawing of an eel] | [Hughes' signature] | [in red] 75 copies hand-printed by THE MORRIGU PRESS February the first 1981 | Copy number [number]
Ca. 51.0–51.5 × 32.0–32.5 cm.
Light blue handmade laid paper (chain lines vertical, 3.2–3.3 cm.), marked with a hand and a cross, and 'HAND-MADE'; or a saint's head on a shield and '[intertwined script 'BG'] | 1979' [i.e. Barcham Green]. Deckle edges.

B) [two drawings of caddisflies] | [in red] CADDIS | [in black, the poem] | [three drawings of caddisfly larvae] | [Hughes' signature] | [in red] 75 copies hand-printed by THE MORRIGU PRESS April the twenty seventh 1981 | Copy number [number]
Ca. 50.5–51.5 × 32.5 cm.

Handmade laid paper (chain lines vertical, 3.2–3.5 cm.), marked with '[intertwined script 'BG'] | 1980' or 'hand-made'. Deckle edges.

C) [in red] VISITATION | [in black, Ted Hughes drawing of four paw-prints] | [the poem] | [drawing of four different paw-prints] | [in red] 75 copies hand-printed by THE MORRIGU PRESS April the twenty ninth 1981 | Copy number [number] | [Hughes' signature] Ca. 51.5 x 32.0 cm.
Handmade paper, marked with saint's head on a shield and '[intertwined script 'BG'] | 1979'; or a hand and a cross, and 'HAND-MADE'. Deckle edges.

The three broadsides in a folder of light-green paper; on front, white printed label, ca. 8.5–9.5 × 13.5–14.0 cm.: 'THREE RIVER POEMS | [in red] CATADROME | CADDIS | VISITATION'.

Printed letterpress.

Published probably in May 1981 at an undetermined price; 75 copies printed.

A76   A PRIMER OF BIRDS   1981

TED HUGHES | A | PRIMER | OF | [red] BIRDS | [black] WOODCUTS BY | LEONARD BASKIN | THE | GEHENNA | PRESS | 19 · 81

$[1–3^8] = 24$ leaves. Pages (1–48), consisting: (1) half-title; (2) blank; (3) title page; (4) blank; (5) poem, 'For Leonard & Lisa'; (6) blank; (7–40) text; (41) colour woodcut of phoenix; (42) blank; (43) '[woodcut of a bird, with initials at the four corners (letters in red, raised periods in black), clockwise from upper left: '·B·C·', '·R·W·', '·L&L·B·', '·J&M·D·'] | Two hundred and fifty copies of this book were | printed at The Gehenna Press, Lurley in Devon. | The woodcuts were printed from the blocks; | the paper is Dover, handmade at Maidstone, Kent, | these copies are signed by the poet and the artist | and are numbered one to two hundred twenty five. | Twenty five copies have an additional suite of the | woodcuts printed on a Japanese paper, signed and | numbered I–XXV by the artist. The work was | achieved on the press' nineteenth century | Columbian and finished during June MCMLXXXI. | This is copy number [number in pencil] | [signatures of Baskin and Hughes]'; (44–48) blank. Except for the phoenix, the woodcuts are all printed in black.

Special copies I–XXV (not seen) bound in boards, morocco spine. With a suite of separate prints from the blocks printed on Japanese paper, each signed and numbered by Baskin.

Copies 1–225 bound in marbled paper over boards. Front: cream-coloured paper label printed 'TED HUGHES | [red] A PRIMER OF BIRDS | [black] WOODCUTS BY | LEONARD BASKIN'. Spine round, cream-coloured paper label printed '·T·H· A PRIMER OF BIRDS ·L·B·' (initials in red).

Paper handmade laid 'Dover' (chain lines vertical, 2.7–2.9 cm., marked with intertwined script 'BG' [Barcham Green] and '1981'), brownish, ca. 27.5 × 15.0 cm., bulk .4 cm.; top edge cut, fore- and bottom edges deckle.

Printed letterpress. The compositor and pressman was D. R. Wakefield.

CONTENTS: For Leonard & Lisa—Cuckoo's[1]—Swans—Buzzard—Black Back Gull—Snipe[1]—The Swallow—Sparrow—The Macaw[1]—The Hen[1]—Mallard—Kingfisher—Whiteness—A Sparrow-Hawk—Evening Thrush[1]—Magpie—Shrike[1]—Starlings Come Suddenly—Bullfinch[2]—Nightjar—A Rival—Wren—Tern[1]—Treecreeper—Nightingale—A Dove[1]—The Moorhen—The White Owl[3]—Pheasant[1]—Phoenix.

Published probably in July 1981 at £450.00 or $900.00 for copies I–XXV, and £175.00 or $350.00 for copies 1–225.

A77   COWS   1981

[Half-sheet broadside:] [in red] COWS | [in dark brown, illustration of three cows by Hughes] | [in black, the poem] | [signature of Hughes] | [in red] 26 lettered and 50 numbered copies hand-printed by Nicholas Hughes on the Twenty First of September 1981 | for the benefit of | Farms for City Children | Copy [number]

Paper handmade laid (chain lines vertical, 3.7–4.5 cm. with tranche-file 2.4–2.5 cm.), ca. 48.5 × 30.0–32.0 cm., watermark '[in oval] [Romulus and Remus suckling the wolf] | ROMA'; countermark 'C. M. FABRIANO ITALIA'. Torn along one long edge, the other three deckle.

With a tissue guard, in a folder of dark brown laid paper (chain lines indistinct), label printed in red on white laid paper (chain lines vertical, 3.8–4.6 cm.) pasted to front: 'COWS | BY | TED HUGHES'.

Published September 1981 at an undetermined price; 76 copies printed on an Albion hand press.

[1] Later draft of a manuscript poem in the special copies of *Cave Birds* (A46a).
[2] = 'Bullfinches' from *Moon-Bells*.
[3] = 'Song Against the White Owl' from *Crow Wakes*.

a. First edition:

NEW | SELECTED | POEMS | [outline swelled rule, gap in middle with two halves sealed off] | Ted Hughes | [publisher's logo: torch in rectangle] | *1817* | HARPER & ROW, PUBLISHERS, New York | Cambridge, Philadelphia, San Francisco | London, Mexico City, São Paulo, Sydney

[1–8^{16}] = 128 leaves (glued not sewn). Pages (i–x)xi–xii(xiii–xiv)1–242, consisting: (i) half-title; (ii) '*Also by Ted Hughes* | [16 titles], | (iii) title page; (iv) 'Some of the poems in this collection appeared in *The Hawk in the Rain*, Copyright © 1956, | 1957 by Ted Hughes; [...] | [...] | [...] Reprinted by permission of Harper & Row, Publishers, Inc. | Grateful acknowledgment is made to Viking Penguin, Inc., for permission to reprint "The | Executioner," "The Knight," "The Risen," and "Bride and Groom Lie Hidden for Three | Days" from *Cave Birds*, Copyright © 1978 by Ted Hughes; "A March Calf," "Swifts," and | "The Harvest Moon," from *Season Songs*, Copyright © 1973, 1975 by Ted Hughes; "Goose" | and "Eagle" from *Under the North Star*, Copyright © 1981 by Ted Hughes. | NEW SELECTED POEMS. Copyright © 1982 by Ted Hughes. All rights reserved. Printed in the | United States of America. [...] | [...] | FIRST EDITION | *Designer: Ruth Bornschlegel* | [rule] | [CIP data, and two lines of ISBN numbers and printing codes (for hardback and paperback, both 82–1)] | [rule]'; (v–x) table of contents; xi–xii foreword; (xiii) half-title; (xiv) blank; 1–239 text; (240) blank; 241–242 table of contents.

Black cloth, spine round, stamped in copper-coloured foil: 'Ted Hughes NEW SELECTED POEMS HARPER & ROW'.

Dust-wrapper cream-coloured, front and spine printed in three colours of grey with yellow-brown strips in rectangular compartments. Front: 'Ted Hughes | [yellow-brown] NEW | SELECTED | POEMS'. Spine: 'Hughes [yellow-brown] NEW SELECTED POEMS [reading across, at foot] Harper & Row'. Back, on light-grey ground: blurbs, photograph by Layle Silbert, two-sentence biography, and ISBN. Dust-wrapper designed by Gloria Adelson.

23.4 × 15.6 cm., bulk 1.8 cm.; all edges cut. Printed offset.

CONTENTS:[1] [From *The Hawk in the Rain*] The Thought-Fox—Song—The Jaguar—Famous Poet—Soliloquy—The Horses—Fallgrief's Girlfriends—Egg-Head—Wind—The Man Seeking Experience

---

[1] Sources are given as in table of contents, but some poems are dropped into these groupings from other sources.

Enquires His Way of a Drop of Water—Meeting—October Dawn—
Bayonet Charge—Six Young Men—The Martyrdom of Bishop
Farrar.
[From *Lupercal*] Mayday on Holderness—Crow Hill—A Woman
Unconscious—Strawberry Hill—Esther's Tomcat—Fourth of
July—Wilfred Owen's Photographs—Hawk Roosting—Fire-
Eater—The Bull Moses—Cat and Mouse—View of a Pig—The
Retired Colonel—November—Relic—An Otter—Witches—
Thrushes—Snowdrop—Pike—Sunstroke—Cleopatra to the Asp.
[From *Wodwo*[2]] Thistles—Still Life—Her Husband—Cadenza—Ghost
Crabs—Boom (I. And Faces at the Glutted Shop-Windows; II. Bar-
Room TV[3]; III. Tutorial; IV. Wino; V. Kafka)—Second Glance at
a Jaguar—Fern—A Wind Flashes the Grass—Bowled Over—Root,
Stem, Leaf—Stations—Scapegoats and Rabies—Stealing Trout on a
May Morning—Theology—Gog—Kreutzer Sonata—Out—New
Moon in January—The Warriors of the North—The Rat's
Dance—Heptonstall—Skylarks—Mountains—Pibroch—The Howl-
ing of Wolves—Gnat-Psalm—The Green Wolf—Full Moon and
Little Frieda—Wodwo.
[From *Crow*] Examination at the Womb-Door—A Childish Prank—
Crow's First Lesson—That Moment—The Black Beast—A Horrible
Religious Error—Owl's Song—The Contender—Dawn's Rose—
Apple Tragedy—Crow's Last Stand—Lovesong—Notes for a Little
Play—The Lovepet—How Water Began to Play—Littleblood—You
Hated Spain.
[From *Cave Birds*] The Executioner—The Knight—Bride and Groom
Lie Hidden for Three Days—The Risen.
[From *Season Songs*] A March Calf—Apple Dumps—Swifts—The
Harvest Moon—A Cranefly in September.
[From *Under the North Star*] Goose—Eagle—Do Not Pick Up the
Telephone.
[From *Gaudete*] Collision with the Earth Has Finally Come—Once I
Said Lightly—This is the Maneater's Skull—I See the Oak's Bride in
the Oak's Grasp—A Primrose Petal's Edge—Waving Goodbye, from
Your Banked Hospital Bed—The Swallow [dash] Rebuilding—The
Grass-Blade is Not Without—I Know Well—Sometimes It Comes, a
Gloomy Flap of Lightning—Calves Harshly Parted from their
Mamas—A Bang [dash] a Burning—At the Bottom of the Arctic
Sea, They Say—Your Tree [dash] Your Oak.

[2] Except as noted, poems in this section follow the American text of *Selected Poems 1957–1967*.
[3] = 'Public Bar T.V.'.

[From *Remains of Elmet*[4]] An October Salmon—Wadsworth Moor
—Moors—Curlews Lift[5]—Curlews in April[6]—Rock Has Not
Learned—When Men Got to the Summit—For Billy Holt—It Is
All—Widdop—Football at Slack—Dead Farms, Dead Leaves—
Emily Brontë—Heptonstall Old Church—Heptonstall Cemetery.
[From *Moortown*] Tractor—Roe Deer—Birth of Rainbow—Couples
under Cover—Ravens—February 17th—Sheep[7]—Coming Down
Through Somerset—Now You Have to Push—The Formal Auction-
eer.
[From *Prometheus on His Crag*] Now I Know I Never Shall—Prometheus
on His Crag Began to Admire the Vulture—Prometheus on His Crag
Pondered the Vulture.
[From *Adam and the Sacred Nine*] And the Falcon Came—The Wild
Duck[8]—The Swift Comes the Swift—And Owl—The Dove Came—
And the Phoenix Has Come—The Song.
[From *Earth-Numb*[9]] Earth-Numb—A Motorbike—Deaf School—Life
Is Trying to Be Life—Speech out of Shadow—Night Arrival of Sea-
Trout—From *Seven Dungeon Songs*[9] (Dead, She Became Space-
Earth—Face Was Necessary [dash] I Found Face—The Earth
Locked Out the Light—I Walk—If Mouth Could Open its Cliff)—
TV Off—Prospero and Sycorax—Tiger Psalm—The Stone—The
Virgin Knight—A God.
[From *River*] Salmon Eggs—That Morning.

Published 24 February 1982 at $15.50; number of copies undetermined.
There was a simultaneous paperback printing of unknown size at $6.95;
these are identical internally to the hardbound copies. The catalogue
number at the bottom of both the front and spine of the wrapper is
printed as CN 900, and the ISBN on the back is 0-06-090900-5. In most
copies seen, some or all of these are cancelled by printed adhesive strips
bearing the number CN 925 or ISBN 0-06-090925-5.

*b. First English edition (*Selected Poems 1957–1981*):*

[flush to left] Selected Poems | [indented] 1957–1981 | [flush to left]
TED HUGHES | [indented] ff | [flush to left] *faber and faber*

120 leaves (glued binding, no quire structure remaining). Pages (1–6)7–
238(239–240), consisting: (1–2) blank; (3) half-title, '[flush to left]

---

[4] Texts follow the trade edition.
[5] = 'Curlews', part II.
[6] = 'Curlews', part I.
[7] First and third parts only.
[8] = 'The Wild Duck Got Up with a Cry'.
[9] Never published as a separate group; a subsection of *Moortown*. Some poems
are borrowed from other sections.

Selected Poems | [Leonard Baskin drawing of a bird]'; (4) 'BY TED HUGHES | [22 titles]'; (5) title page; (6) '*This selection first published in 1982 | by Faber and Faber Limited | 3 Queen Square London WC1N 3AU | Filmset by King's English Typesetters Ltd Cambridge | Printed in Great Britain by | Richard Clay (The Chaucer Press) Ltd | Bungay Suffolk | All rights reserved | © Ted Hughes, 1982* | [CIP data]'; 7–12 table of contents; 13–235 text; (236) blank; 237–238 'Note' by Hughes (same as the Foreword in the American edition); (239–240) blank.

Calico-grain dark green paper over boards. Spine round, stamped in silver: '[reading across, thin-thick rule] [reading down] TED HUGHES *Selected Poems 1957–1981* [reading across] ff | [thick-thin rule]'.

Dust-wrapper machine-made 'laid' (only faint vertical wire lines visible), coated outside, printed with all-over pattern of 'ff' on dark-green ground; text printed in dark green on very light green panels (a light halftone screen). Front: '[in double-rule frame] TED | HUGHES | [rule, 2.7 cm.] | *Selected Poems* | *1957–1981* | [Baskin drawing of a hawk]'. Spine printed same as book spine. Back: '[within double-rule frame] ff | *faber and faber* | [rule, 2.7 cm.] | *Also by Ted Hughes* | [11 titles]'.

21.5 × 13.4 cm., bulk 1.7 cm.; all edges cut. Printed offset.

CONTENTS: same as the American edition, in a slightly different order, except for the following: adds 'Crow and the Birds', 'Mount Zion', and 'The Woman in the Valley'; omits 'Moors' and 'The Virgin Knight'; 'It Is All' is retitled 'West Laithe'.

Published April 1982 at £4.95; number of copies undetermined. There was a simultaneous paperback printing of unknown size at £2.50. The setting of the paperback copies is identical except for the addition of the Net Book Agreement note below the copyright statement on the title page verso. The cover design is the same as the dust-wrapper of the hardcover version except, on the back cover, the titles of other Hughes books are replaced by: '[blurb] | Cover design by Pentagram | Illustration by Leonard Baskin | £2.50 net ISBN 0571 11916 6'. For one or more later paperback printings Faber redesigned the title page to its new standard double-rule frame format and reset the preliminaries, but the poems remain in their original setting. The compilers have seen a paperback printing having *The Iron Woman* (1993) in the list of titles on p. (4) and a code '10' on the verso title, priced at £5.99, but not explicitly identified as a reprint.

REVIEWS: *America*, 27 Nov. 1982 (David Rogers); *Booklist*, 1 Feb. 1982; *British Book News*, Aug. 1982 (Neil Philip); *Glasgow Herald*, 15 May 1982 (Douglas Dunn); *Irish Times*, 10 July 1982 (Medbh McGuckian); *Library Journal*, 15 Feb. 1982 (Michael Hennessy); *Los Angeles Times*, 4 April 1982 (Nancy Shiffrin); *New York Review of Books*, 10 June 1982 (Richard

Murphy); *New York Times*, 14 March 1982 (Denis Donoghue); *Stand*, 24:4 (John Saunders); *Sunday Times*, 9 May 1982 (Christopher Reid); *Tablet*, 10 July 1982 (Emelie FitzGibbon); *Time Out*, 10 Sept. 1982; *Times*, 17 June 1982 (Robert Nye); *Times Educational Supplement*, 27 Aug. 1982 (Hermann Peschmann); *Times Literary Supplement*, 25 June 1982 (Anthony Thwaite); *Virginia Quarterly Review*, Winter 1983; *Washington Post*, 18 July 1982.

A79   WOLF-WATCHING [separate poem]   1982

[in red] WOLF-WATCHING | TED HUGHES

[1⁶] = 6 leaves. Pages (1–12), consisting: (1) half-title, in red; (2) blank; (3) title page; (4) blank; (5–8) text; (9) blank; (10) 'This work was printed | during July 1982 on | our Albion hand-press. | The type face is Centaur, | the paper is Michaelangelo, | in covers of Del-Sarto. | Both papers are hand-made | by Milano Fabriano. | The edition is limited to | seventy five copies. | The Colophon was drawn | for the press by | Leonard Baskin. | [line-cut of a large bird in circle] | [red] THE MORRIGU PRESS | [in Ted Hughes' hand] Number [number] | [signature]'; (11–12) blank.

Sewn into wrappers of greyish-brown handmade laid paper (chain lines vertical, 3.6–4.4 cm.); on front a pasted-on label of white laid paper printed in red: 'WOLF-WATCHING'.

Paper handmade laid (chain lines vertical, 3.8–4.3 cm., with one tranche-file 2.4–2.6 cm., the other 2.6–2.8 cm.), watermark '[in oval] [Romulus and Remus suckling the wolf] | ROMA'; countermark 'C. M. FABRIANO ITALIA'; overall ca. 24.7 × ca. 17.0 cm., bulk .2 cm.; top edges trimmed, fore- and bottom edges deckle.

Printed letterpress by Nicholas Hughes.

Contains the single poem.

Published July 1982 at £20.00; 75 copies printed.

A80   GIANT DREAM OF ELEPHANTS   1982

[in red] GIANT | DREAM OF | ELEPHANTS | TED HUGHES

[1⁶] = 6 leaves. Pages (1–12), consisting: (1) half-title, '[in red] GIANT | DREAM OF | ELEPHANTS'; (2) blank; (3) title page; (4) blank; (5–7) text; (8–9) blank; (10) 'This work was printed | during July 1982 on | our Albion hand-press. | The type face is Centaur, | the paper is Michaelangelo, | in covers of Tiziano. | Both papers are hand-made | by Milano Fabriano. | The edition is limited to | seventy five copies. | The

Colophon was drawn | for the press by | Leonard Baskin. | [line-cut of a large bird in circle] | [red] THE MORRIGU PRESS | [number] | [signature]'; (11–12) blank.

P. (10) was printed mostly from type left standing from *Wolf-Watching*.

Sewn into wrappers of grey handmade laid paper (chain lines vertical, 3.9–4.5 cm.); on front a pasted-on label of white laid paper printed in red: 'GIANT | DREAM OF | ELEPHANTS'.

Paper handmade laid (chain lines vertical, 3.8–4.2 cm., with one tranche-file 2.4–2.6 cm., the other 2.6–2.8 cm.), watermark '[in oval] [Romulus and Remus suckling the wolf] | ROMA'; countermark 'C. M. FABRIANO ITALIA'; overall ca. 25.0 × 17.0 cm., bulk .2 cm.; all edges deckle.

Printed letterpress by Nicholas Hughes.

Published July 1982 at £20.00; 75 copies printed.

A81   THE GREAT IRISH PIKE   1982

Not seen. 6 separate sheets, each with a lithograph by Barrie Cooke and a reproduction of a section of Hughes' holograph of the poem. Printed by David Tomlin at the Appledore Press, Devon. Each set numbered, and signed by Cooke and Hughes. Distributed from Jerpoint, Thomastown, Co. Kilkenny, Ireland. The prospectus also gives Hughes' address in Devon; this is crossed out by hand in the copy seen.

Paper handmade by Barcham Green, ca. 80.0 × 58.5 cm.

Published in 1982 at £300 (£400 Irish); 26 copies printed.

A82   MICE ARE FUNNY LITTLE CREATURES   1983

[in red] MICE ARE | FUNNY LITTLE | CREATURES | [black, drawing of a mouse by Ted Hughes] | [in red] TED HUGHES

One fold (2 leaves). Pages (1–4), consisting: (1) title page; (2–3) the poem; (4) 'This work was printed | during January 1983 on | our Albion hand-press, | in 14 point Perpetua. | The paper is Roma, | hand-made by | Milano Fabriano. | The edition is limited to | seventy five copies, | signed by the author. | [line-cut of Baskin drawing of a large bird in circle] | [in red] THE MORRIGU PRESS | [number] | [signature]'.

Sewn into wrappers of brown handmade laid paper (chain lines vertical, 3.6–4.6 cm.), watermarked '[in oval] [Romulus and Remus suckling the wolf] | ROMA' or 'C. M. FABRIANO ITALIA'. On front, a pasted-on label of white laid paper printed in red: 'MICE ARE | FUNNY LITTLE | CREATURES'.

Paper handmade laid (chain lines vertical, 3.6–4.6 cm. with tranche-file of 2.6–2.7 cm.), marked as above; overall ca. 24.5 × 16.5 cm., edges torn or deckle.

Printed letterpress by Nicholas Hughes.

Printed January 1983 (but possibly not issued until mid-March) at £28.00; 75 copies printed. Also sold with *Fly Inspects* and *Weasels at Work* at £79.00 for the three. The colophon of each is in the same setting.

A83   WEASELS AT WORK   1983

[in red] WEASELS | AT WORK | [black, drawing of weasels by Ted Hughes] | [in red] TED HUGHES

One fold (2 leaves). Pages (1–4), consisting: (1) title page; (2–3) the poem; (4) 'This work was printed | during January 1983 on | our Albion hand-press, | in 14 point Perpetua. | The paper is Roma, | hand-made by | Milano Fabriano. | The edition is limited to | seventy five copies, | signed by the author. | [line-cut of Baskin drawing of a large bird in circle] | [in red] THE MORRIGU PRESS | [number] | [signature]'.

Sewn into wrappers of reddish-brown handmade laid paper (chain lines vertical, 3.8–4.4 cm.), watermarked '[in oval] [Romulus and Remus suckling the wolf] | ROMA' or 'C. M. FABRIANO ITALIA'. On front, a pasted-on label of white laid paper printed in red: 'WEASELS | AT WORK'.

Paper handmade laid (chain lines vertical, 3.6–4.6 cm. with tranche-file of 2.6–2.7 cm.), marked as above; overall ca. 24.5 × 16.5 cm., edges torn or deckle.

Printed letterpress by Nicholas Hughes.

Printed January 1983 (but possibly not issued until mid-March) at £28.00; 75 copies printed. Also sold with *Fly Inspects* and *Mice are Funny Little Creatures* at £79.00 for the three. The colophon of each is in the same setting.

A84   FLY INSPECTS   1983

[in red] FLY | INSPECTS | [black, drawing of a fly by Ted Hughes] | [in red] TED HUGHES

One fold (2 leaves). Pages (1–4), consisting: (1) title page; (2–3) the poem; (4) 'This work was printed | during January 1983 on | our Albion hand-press, | in 14 point Perpetua. | The paper is Roma, | hand-made by | Milano Fabriano. | The edition is limited to | seventy five copies, | signed by the author. | [line-cut of Baskin drawing of a large bird in circle] | [in red] THE MORRIGU PRESS | [number] | [signature]'.

Sewn into wrappers of blue handmade laid paper (chain lines vertical, 3.6–4.6 cm.), watermarked '[in oval] [Romulus and Remus suckling the wolf] | ROMA'. On front, a pasted-on label of white laid paper printed in red: 'FLY | INSPECTS'.

Paper handmade laid (chain lines vertical, 3.6–4.6 cm. with tranche-file of 2.6–2.7 cm.), marked as above; overall ca. 24.5–25.0 × 16.5–17.0 cm., edges torn or deckle.

Printed letterpress by Nicholas Hughes.

Published mid-March 1983 at £28.00; 75 copies printed. Also sold with *Mice are Funny Little Creatures* and *Weasels at Work* at £79.00 for the three. The colophon of each is in the same setting.

A85   RIVER   1983

a. First edition:

[flush at left] *River* | [rule projecting further left] | Poems by Ted Hughes | Photographs by Peter Keen | [indented] ff | [flush with other text] *faber and faber* LONDON · BOSTON in association with JAMES & JAMES

$[1-8^8] = 64$ leaves. Pages (1–7)8–128, consisting: (1) half-title, 'River | [projecting left, rule, 11.0 cm.]'; (2) photograph of a river; (3) title page; (4) two columns, each flush at left; left column: 'First published in 1983 | by Faber and Faber Limited | 3 Queen Square London WC1N 3AU | In association with James & James | 6 Rona Road London NW3 2JA | Colour origination by Wensum Graphics, Norwich | Printed in Great Britain by | Jolly & Barber Limited, Rugby | All rights reserved | © Poems, Ted Hughes, 1983 | © Photographs, Peter Keen, 1983 | [...]'. Right column: CIP data and advertisement for British Gas; (5) 'For Andrea and for Nicholas'; (6) photograph of fish; (7) table of contents; 8–125 text and photographs; 126–128 notes on the photographs. Text pages 67, 73, 97, 105 unnumbered.

Blue calico-grain paper over boards. Spine flat, stamped in silver: '*River* [smaller letters] Poems by Ted Hughes Photographs by Peter Keen [at foot, reading across] ff | [rule] | J&J'.

Dust-wrapper coated outside, printed with river scenes in colour front and back. Front: [in white, flush at left] *River* [smaller letters] Poems by

Ted Hughes | Photographs by Peter Keen'. Spine printed same as book spine, in black. Back, lower left, in white, 'ff | *faber and faber*'.

Paper medium glossy, 24.1 × 26.2 cm., bulk 1.0 cm.; all edges cut. Printed offset.

CONTENTS: The Morning Before Christmas—Japanese River Tales—Flesh of Light—New Year—Whiteness[1]—Four March Watercolours—Dee—The Merry Mink—Salmon-taking Times—Under the Hill of Centurions—A Cormorant—Stump Pool in April—Go Fishing—Milesian Encounter on the Sligachan—Ophelia[2]—Creation of Fishes—River Barrow—West Dart—Strangers—After Moonless Midnight—An August Salmon—The Vintage of River is Unending—Night Arrival of Seatrout[3]—The Kingfisher[1]—That Morning—River—Last Night—Gulkana—In the Dark Violin of the Valley—Low Water—A Rival[1]—August Evening—Last Act—September Salmon—Eighty and Still Fishing for Salmon—September[4]—An Eel—Fairy Flood—Riverwatcher—October Salmon—Visitation[5]—Torridge—Salmon Eggs.

Published September 1983 at £10.00; number of copies undetermined. A simultaneous paperback printing of unknown size was issued at £4.95, identical internally except for the addition of the Net Book Agreement note on verso title. The back cover has a blurb at the bottom. Faber first announced the book for June 1983 as *October Salmon: River Poems and Photographs*, to sell for £10.95. Later the date was set back to July, and then to September; but copies were in circulation by 20 August.

b. First American edition (1984):

[flush at left, but indented] TED | HUGHES | *RIVER* | [rule, not indented] | [publisher's logo: torch and '1817'; at right] HARPER & ROW, PUBLISHERS, New York | *Cambridge, Philadelphia, San Francisco, London | Mexico City, São Paulo, Singapore, Sydney*

[1^{16} 2^8 3^{16}] = 40 leaves (glued, not sewn). Pages (1–4)5–79(80), consisting: (1) half-title, flush to left; (2) blank; (3) title page; (4) 'For Andrea and for Nicholas | RIVER. Copyright © 1983 by Ted Hughes. All rights reserved. Printed in | the United States of America. [...] | [...] | FIRST U.S. EDITION 1984 | *Designer: Sidney Feinberg* | [rule] | [CIP

---

[1] Previously published in *A Primer of Birds*.
[2] Previously published in *Orts*.
[3] Previously published in *The First Publications of the Morrigu Press*.
[4] Begins 'There's another river'; a different poem from the one of the same title in *Hawk in the Rain*.
[5] Previously published in *Three River Poems*.

data, and two lines of ISBN numbers and printing codes (for hardback and paperback, both codes 84–1)] | [rule]'; 5–6 table of contents; 7–79 text; (80) blank.

Blue-green cloth over boards. Front cover, blind-stamped at lower right, publisher's logo as on title page. Spine flat, stamped in gold: 'Ted Hughes RIVER *HARPER & ROW*'.

Dust-wrapper coated outside; front: '[to left] Ted | Hughes | [flush to right, shaded letters filled with green halftone photograph of river water] RIVER | [regular type] New | Poems'. Spine: 'Ted Hughes RIVER [at foot, reading across] Harper | & Row'. Back: in dark green, poem 'Low Water'; in black, blurb and ISBN. Dust-wrapper designed by William Graef.

23.5 × 15.5 cm., bulk .7 cm.; all edges cut. Printed offset.

CONTENTS same as the first edition, in a slightly different order.

Published officially on 6 June 1984, though copies were in the stores at least two days earlier; price $12.95; number of copies undetermined. There was a simultaneous paperback printing of unknown size at $6.95.

REVIEWS: *American Poetry Review*, Sept./Oct. 1984 (Mary Kinzie); *Books from Borders*, July 1984 (Emil Efthimides); *British Book News*, Feb. 1984 (Martin Booth); *Christian Century*, 1 May 1985; *Devon Life*, Oct. 1983 (John Cairns); *Encounter*, Mar. 1984 (John Mole); *English in Education*, Spring 1984 (Terry Gilliam); *Études Anglaises*, Jan.–Mar. 1986 (P. Lagayette); *Exeter Express*, 10 Sept. 1983 (N.J.W.); *Guardian*, 15 Sept. 1983 (Glyn Hughes); *Jerusalem Post*, 23 Dec. 1983 (Aloma Halter); *Library Journal*, July 1984 (Stephen H. Cape), Jan. 1985; *Listener*, 12 Jan. 1984 (Dick Davis); *Litmus* 4 (Peter Reading); *London Magazine*, Feb. 1984 (Herbert Lomas); *London Review of Books*, 16 Feb. 1984 (John Kerrigan); *New Republic*, 3 Sept. 1984 (J. D. McClatchy); *New York Times Book Review*, 30 Sept. 1984 (A. Poulin); *New Yorker*, 31 Dec. 1984 (Helen Vendler); *Observer*, 4 Sept. 1983 (Blake Morrison); *Parnassus*, 14:1, 1987 (Calvin Bedient); *Poetry Review*, Jan. 1984 (Edna Longley); *San Francisco Review of Books*, Spring 1986 (Ron Smith); *Scotsman*, 17 Sept. 1983 (Alan Bold); *Stand*, Spring 1985 (John Saunders); *Stanford Daily*, 7 Aug. 1984 (Bradley Rubidge); *Sunday Times*, 23 Oct. 1983 (Christopher Reid); *Tablet*, 31 March 1984 (Roger Sharrock); *Time Out*, 26 July 1984 (Steve Grant); *Times Literary Supplement*, 11 Nov. 1983 (Peter Redgrove); *Universe*, 9 Sept. 1983 (Rowanne Pasco); *Virginia Quarterly Review*, Autumn 1984; *West Coast Review*, April 1984 (R. B. Hatch); *World Literature Today*, Winter 1985 (Manly Johnson).

A86   CORMORANTS   1983

Single sheet, printed on one side from a line cut of Hughes' autograph of the poem.

Paper handmade laid (chain lines horizontal, 4.0 cm.), marked '[saint's head on shield] | 1399'; ca. 26.0 × 20.0 cm. Some edges deckle, some torn.

Printed by Nicholas Hughes at the Morrigu Press. A few copies were sent out as Christmas cards in December 1983. The intention had been to use the facsimile in a Morrigu publication, 'but then the poem seemed so bad, and the imposition of my script so offensive, we dropped it' (Hughes, letter to Sagar, 14 Dec. 1983).

A87   WHAT IS THE TRUTH?   1984

a.1. First edition:

[hand-drawn letters] WHAT IS THE TRUTH? | A FARMYARD FABLE FOR THE YOUNG | TED HUGHES | [illustration of a country road] | DRAWINGS BY R.J. LLOYD | [regular type] ff | *faber and faber* | LONDON · BOSTON

$[1-4^{16}] = 64$ leaves. Pages (1–8)9–127(128), consisting: (1) blank; (2) illustration of a bull; (3) half-title, in hand-drawn letters; (4) illustration of a mouse; (5) title page; (6) double columns; left: 'First published in 1984 | by Faber and Faber Limited | 3 Queen Square London WC1N 3AU | Printed in Great Britain by | Redwood Burn Ltd, Trowbridge, Wiltshire. | All rights reserved | © Ted Hughes, 1984 | Drawings © R. J. Lloyd, 1984 | [CIP data]'. Right column: '*by Ted Hughes* | [24 titles]'; (7) 'For Clare and Michael | [illustration of a bird]'; (8) illustration of a magpie; 9–127 text and illustrations, printed partly in double columns; (128) blank. Text pages 122–125 unnumbered.

Brown calico-grain paper over boards. Spine flat, stamped in gold on a dark-brown panel: '[reading across, thin-thick rule] [reading down, flush at left] WHAT IS THE TRUTH? *A farmyard fable for the young* | Ted Hughes, *illustrated by R J Lloyd* [at foot, reading across] ff | [thick-thin rule]'. Endpapers yellowish-brown 'laid' (chain lines vertical, 2.6–2.7 cm., marked '[crown] | [black-letter] Abbey Mills | Greenfield').

Dust-wrapper coated outside, coloured olive green, printed with all-over pattern of 'ff' in black, text on white panels within double-rule frames. Front: '[hand-done lettering as on title page] [rule] | WHAT IS THE TRUTH? | [drawing of a magpie] TED HUGHES | [larger drawing of a magpie] | DRAWINGS BY R. J. LLOYD | [rule]'. Spine printed like book spine, in black. Back: '[regular type] ff | *faber and faber* | [rule, 3.4 cm.] | [blurb]'. Dust-wrapper designed by Pentagram.

21.9 × 27.6 cm., bulk .8 cm.; all edges cut. Printed offset.

A series of untitled poems connected by narrative. The poems on the hen, the bullfinch, and the treecreeper were previously published in *A Primer of Birds*. The one on the bullfinch was originally published in *Moon-Bells*.

Published June 1984 (the British Library copy is stamped 4 May) at £7.95; number of copies undetermined. Faber first announced the book for October 1983.

a.2. First printing for America:

As above except:
1. Imprint on title page is '[publisher's logo: torch in rectangle] | *1817* [to right:] HARPER & ROW, PUBLISHERS, New York | Cambridge, Philadelphia, San Francisco, London, | Mexico City, São Paulo, Singapore, Sydney'.
2. Title page verso reads: '[flush at left] Text copyright © 1984 by Ted Hughes. | Drawings copyright © 1984 by R. J. Lloyd. | All rights reserved. Printed in Great Britain. [...] | [...] | FIRST U.S. EDITION | [Library of Congress and ISBN numbers]'.
3. Imprint on book and dust-wrapper spine is '[reading across] 'Harper | & | Row'. The dust-wrapper lacks the all-over 'ff' pattern.

Published September 1984 at $17.95; an undetermined number of copies was printed and hardbound in England. Further copies, identical internally, were paperbound in England and sold in the U.S. for $12.95. In these the spine lettering is reduced, and the imprint reads '[reading down] HARPER | COLOPHON BOOKS [reading across] [publisher's logo, stylized lighted lamp] | CH1180'.

a.3. First English paperback printing (1986):

The same internally as a.1 except for p. (6). Left column: 'First published in 1984 | by Faber and Faber Limited | [...] | First published as a Faber Paperback in 1986 | [...] | [at bottom of column, Net Book Agreement note]'. Right column lists 25 titles.

Wrappers follow the design of the dust-wrapper of a.1, but back cover panel contains a shortened version of the blurb and reviews, prices, and bar code.

21.7 × 27.4 cm., bulk .85 cm.; all edges cut. Printed offset.

Published November 1986 at £4.95 ($14.95 in Australia, $12.95 in Canada); number of copies undetermined.

Note: for 1995 edition see *Collected Animal Poems* (A112(B)).

REVIEWS: *Children's Literature in Education,* Mar. 1991; *Guardian,* 22 June 1984 (Alex Hamilton), 29 Mar. 1985 (Stephanie Nettell); *Junior Bookshelf,* Oct. 1984 (M.C.); *Listener,* 29 Nov. 1984 (Paul de la Sautée); *Los Angeles Times,* 11 Nov. 1984 (Richard Eder); *Parnassus,* 14:1, 1987 (Calvin Bedient); *Punch,* 16 Jan. 1985; *School Librarian,* Dec. 1984 (Margaret Meek); *Stand,* Summer 1986 (John Saunders); *Tablet,* 29 Nov. 1986 (Sydney Carter); *Time Out,* 26 July 1984 (Steve Grant); *Times Educational Supplement,* 2 Nov. 1984 (Neil Philip), 13 Feb. 1987; *Times Literary Supplement,* 13 July 1984 (George Szirtes).

A88   MOKOMAKI   1985

[on a red grid] MOKOMAKI | thirteen etchings | of shrunken & tattooed | Maori heads | by | Leonard Baskin | & | three poems | by | Ted Hughes

$[1^{10}] = 10$ leaves, + [14] prints. Composed of a variety of handmade papers, some whole sheets guarded, some folded and quired, in a way that is quite indescribable and possibly unique for each copy. The quire of 10 leaves consists of pp. (1–4) blank; (5) engraved decorative half-title, on a red background; (6) blank; (7) title page; (8) blank; (9–13) poems; (14) blank; (15) half-title '*MOKOMAKI*'; (16–18) blank; (19) engraving; (20) blank. Following the remaining engravings is a fold of blue paper with colophon on first page: '[in red, drawing by Baskin] [in black] *Fifty copies of Mokomaki were printed & | issued during 1985 by The Eremite Press, | Leeds, Massachusetts. The etchings were | printed from the original plates on a variety | of hand-made papers by Bruce Chandler. | The type matter was printed photo-litho- | graphically by Gail Alt and Lou Bannister | at Amherst. The binding is by Gray Parrot | of Easthampton. The edition is arranged as | follows: copies numbered one to ten have a | second set of the etchings printed on other | papers & in different colors. The remainder | of the edition is numbered eleven to fifty. | This is copy no.* [number] | [Baskin's signature]'.

Copies 1–10 (not seen) bound in full morocco by Gray Parrot. Accompanied by the second set of etchings, a cancelled plate, and an original drawing or watercolour (the latter in a folder) in a vellum chemise. The whole in a clamshell case of leather and marbled paper.

Copies 11–50 bound in limp vellum stamped in gilt. Front: Maori design. Spine: 'MOKOMAKI'. Label of Gray Parrot pasted at foot of rear paste-down. In a clamshell case covered with brown cloth. Spine vellum, stamped in gilt reading across: 'MOKO | MAKI | [solid diamond] | BASKIN | [rule, .9 cm.] | HUGHES'.

Ca. 38 × 28 cm., bulk ca. 1 cm.; most edges deckle. Printed offset. A few sets of etchings were printed on vellum.

CONTENTS: Aspiring Head—Halfway Head—Landmark Head.

Published in 1985, probably at $2700 for copies 11–50; 50 copies printed.

A89   THE BEST WORKER IN EUROPE   1985

a.1. Numbered proof state:

[drawing of a leaping salmon] | The Best Worker | in Europe | TED HUGHES | With three drawings by | Charles Jardine

$[1^6]$ = 6 leaves. Pages (1–12), consisting: (1) cover title: '[drawing of salmon swimming] | The Best Worker | in Europe | TED HUGHES | Proof copy'; (2) blank; (3) title page; (4) 'Published by The Atlantic Salmon Trust | Copyright Ted Hughes 1985 | The drawings copyright Charles Jardine 1985 | Printed & made in Great Britain'; (5–8) text (at end, drawing of three salmon); (9) 'Designed and printed by Sebastian Carter | at the Rampant Lions Press, Cambridge; | hand-set in Hunt Roman and printed on | Saunders Laid mould-made paper. | This Edition is limited to 156 numbered | copies, each signed by Author and Artist. | [in Hughes' manuscript, copy number over '30'] | [signatures of Hughes and Jardine]'; (10–12) blank.

Self-wrappers, sewn with blue thread.

24.8 × 18.0 cm., bulk .1 cm.; all edges cut. Printed letterpress.

Apparently all thirty copies were given away.

a.2. Published state:

$[1^8]$ = 8 leaves. Pages (1–16), consisting: (1–4) blank; (5) title page, as above but drawing printed in green; (6–11) same as pp. (4–9) of a.1, except illustrations printed in green, and colophon has a single number in Hughes' hand; (12–16) blank.

Self-wrappers, sewn with white thread.

In a brown dust-wrapper, front printed like p. (1) of a.1, but illustration in green. Pasted to the pamphlet by a line of weak adhesive.

Paper Saunders mould-made 'laid' (chains vertical, 2.6–2.8 cm.), 25.0 × 16.8 cm., bulk .2 cm.; top edge cut, fore- and bottom edges 'deckle'.

Published in 1985 at an undetermined price; 156 copies printed. Copies were still available in April 1997.

A90 FFANGS THE VAMPIRE BAT 1986
AND THE KISS OF TRUTH

a. First edition:

[within rule frame] ff | [rule] | TED HUGHES | [rule] | Ffangs the
Vampire Bat | and the Kiss of Truth | [rule] | *illustrated by Chris Riddell* |
[below frame] [illustration of a rat] ff | *faber and faber* |
LONDON · BOSTON

[1–3^{16}] = 48 leaves. Pages 1–96 (only pages 14, 30–32, 39, 44, 46, 57, 58,
64, 66, 72, 89, 91, 94, and 96 are numbered), consisting: (1) half-title,
'*Ffangs the Vampire Bat and the Kiss of Truth* | [illustration of Ffangs]'; (2)
'*Also by Ted Hughes* | [24 titles]'; (3) title page; (4) 'First published in
1986 | by Faber and Faber Limited | 3 Queen Square London WC1N
3AU | Photoset by Parker Typesetting Service, Leicester | Printed in
Great Britain by | Clark Constable, Edinburgh & London | All rights
reserved | © Ted Hughes 1986 | [CIP data] | [part of illustration from
facing recto]'; (5) table of contents, with back view of Ffangs; (6)
illustration of rooster; 7–96 text and illustrations.

Black linen-grain paper over boards. Spine flat, stamped in silver: 'TED
HUGHES Ffangs the Vampire Bat and the Kiss of Truth [at foot of
spine, reading across] ff'.

Dust-wrapper medium glossy, coated outside, printed with colour
illustrations front and back. Front: illustration of Ffangs; near top, on
white panel, the rule frame with included text as on title page. Spine
white, printed as on book, in black. Back: illustration of Ffangs facing an
aghast crowd; at bottom, bar code on white panel.

24.5 × 18.8 cm., bulk .6 cm.; all edges cut. Printed offset.

Published August 1986 (the British Library copy is stamped 14 August)
at £5.95; number of copies undetermined.

b. First paperback edition (1990):

[within double-rule frame] ff | Ffangs | The Vampire Bat | and the | Kiss
of Truth | [rule, 2.5 cm.] | *Ted Hughes* | Illustrated by | Chris Riddell |
[illustration of a rat] *faber and faber* | LONDON · BOSTON

80 leaves, 'perfect-bound'. Pages (i–viii) (1)2–150(151–152), consisting:
(i–ii) blank; (iii) half-title, 'Ffangs the Vampire Bat and the Kiss of
Truth | [illustration of Ffangs]'; (iv) '*Also by Ted Hughes* | [31 titles
including this one]'; (v) title page; (vi) 'First published in 1986 | by
Faber and Faber Limited | 3 Queen Square London WC1N 3AU | This
paperback edition first published in 1990 | Photoset by Parker
Typesetting Service, Leicester | Printed in Great Britain by | Cox and

Wyman Ltd Reading Berkshire | All rights reserved | © Ted Hughes 1986 | Illustrations © Chris Riddell 1986 | [note about Net Book Agreement] | [CIP data] | [part of illustration from facing recto]'; (vii) table of contents, with back view of Ffangs; (viii) blank; (1) divisional title, '[flush to left] Chapter One | Trials of Attila | [illustration of rooster]'; 2–150 text and illustrations; (151–152) blank. Text pages 18–21, 30, 31, 37, 38, 46, 47, 52, 53, 76, 77, 86–89, 99, 100, 120, 121, 126, 127 unnumbered.

Wrappers, printed (front continuing to back) with colour illustration of Ffangs in front of a bus. Front: '[on white panel lying partly over and partly under illustration, in double-rule frame:] ff | Ffangs | The Vampire Bat | and the | Kiss of Truth | [rule, 2.5 cm.] | *Ted Hughes* | Illustrated by | Chris Riddell'. Spine, in white panel over illustration: '[reading across, thin-thick rule] [reading down] Ffangs the Vampire Bat and the Kiss of Truth   *Ted Hughes*   [reading across] ff | [thick-thin rule]'. Back: on white panel lying partly over and partly under illustration, in double-rule frame: 'ff | *faber and faber* | FFANGS THE VAMPIRE BAT | AND THE KISS OF TRUTH | *Ted Hughes* | [blurb] | UK £2.50 net | [bar code]'.

19.8 × 12.6 cm., bulk 1.0 cm.; all edges cut. Printed offset.

Published April 1990 (the British Library copy is stamped 19 April) at £2.50; number of copies undetermined. There is a chance that this was plated from the same keyboarding as the first edition, but Faber could not confirm this.

REVIEWS: *Books for Keeps*, Sept. 1990; *Books for Your Children*, Autumn 1986; *British Book News, Children's Books*, Sept. 1986; *Junior Bookshelf*, Dec. 1986 (M.H.); *New Statesman*, 12 Sept. 1986; *Time Out*, 3 Sept. 1986 (Jeff Nuttall); *Times Educational Supplement*, 13 July 1990; *Times Literary Supplement*, 28 Nov. 1986 (George Szirtes).

A91   FLOWERS AND INSECTS   1986

a.1. First edition:

[within a double-rule frame] *Flowers and Insects | Some Birds and a Pair of Spiders* | TED HUGHES | With drawings by | LEONARD BASKIN | ff | *faber and faber* | LONDON · BOSTON

[1–4⁸] = 32 leaves. Pages (1–8)9–61(62–64), consisting: (1–2) front paste-down (blank); (3) half-title, '*Flowers and Insects | Some Birds and a Pair of Spiders*'; (4) '*for Frieda and Lucretia*'; (5) title page; (6) 'First published in 1986 | by Faber and Faber Limited | 3 Queen Square London WC1N 3AU | Designed and produced for the publishers | by

Pilot Productions Limited | 59 Charlotte Street London W1P 1LA | Poems copyright © Ted Hughes, 1986 | Drawings copyright © Leonard Baskin, 1986 | [acknowledgements of prior publication, CIP data, and Net Book Agreement note] | Typeset by Rowland Phototypesetting (London) Ltd | Colour origination by RCS Graphics Leeds LS28 5LY | Printed by Mandarin Offset Marketing (H.K.) Ltd | FIRST EDITION'; (7) table of contents; (8) blank; 9–61 text; (62–64) blank (last leaf being the rear paste-down). Text pages 15, 42, 43 unnumbered.

Dark blue calico-grain paper over boards. Spine flat, stamped in gold: '[reading across, thin-thick rule] [reading down] TED HUGHES *Flowers and Insects* [reading across] ff | [thick-thin rule]'.

Dust-wrapper coated outside, printed with all-over pattern of 'ff' on dark blue, with lettering on white panels. Front: '[on yellow panel, within double-rule frame on white panel] TED | HUGHES | *Flowers* | *and Insects* | [illustration of flower] | With Drawings by | LEONARD BASKIN'. Spine printed like book spine, on white panel. Back: '[on white panel, within double-rule frame] *Also by Ted Hughes* | [10 titles] | [bar code]'.

Paper glossy, 21.0 × 11.9 cm., bulk .4 cm.; all edges cut. Printed offset.

CONTENTS: Narcissi—A Violet at Lough Aughrisburg—Brambles—Daffodils—Two Tortoiseshell Butterflies—Cyclamens in a Bowl—Saint's Island—Where I Sit Writing My Letter—Tern[1]—Sketch of a Goddess—The Honey Bee—In the Likeness of a Grass-hopper—Sunstruck Foxglove—Eclipse[2]—Big Poppy—Nightjar[3]—An Almost Thornless Crown. In the text the latter is subtitled 'Titania Choreographs a Ballet, Using Her Attendants'.

Published October 1986 (the British Library copy is stamped 29 October) at £7.95; number of copies undetermined.

a.2. First printing for America:

Same as above except:
1. Title page imprint is '[borzoi logo] | ALFRED A. KNOPF | New York'.
2. Title page verso reads: 'This is a Borzoi Book | First published in the United States of America | by Alfred A Knopf Incorporated |

---

[1] Originally appeared in manuscript in copy J of the Scolar Press *Cave Birds* (A46a); subsequently printed in *A Primer of Birds*. The last stanza is revised here.
[2] Originally published separately (A49).
[3] Previously printed in *A Primer of Birds*.

201 East 50th Street New York NY 10022 | Designed and produced for the publishers | [etc., through acknowledgements as in first edition] | [flush at left] All rights reserved under International and Pan-American | Copyright Conventions | [CIP data, different from English edition] | Typeset by Rowland Phototypesetting [etc., as in first edition]'.

3. Spine stamped in gold: '*FLOWERS* AND *INSECTS* [the initials *F* and *I* are larger]   TED HUGHES   [borzoi logo] KNOPF'.

4. Dust-wrapper coated outside. Front: on light-green panel, '[painting of flowers from pp. 22–24] | [flush to right, in dark brown] *FLOWERS* | AND *INSECTS* [the initials *F* and *I* are larger] | SOME BIRDS AND | A PAIR OF SPIDERS | [rule, 8.6 cm.] | TED HUGHES | WITH DRAWINGS BY | LEONARD BASKIN | [rule, 8.6 cm.]'. Spine printed like book spine, in black. Back: on light green panel, text of 'The Honey Bee'; at foot, ISBN; at outer margin, reading up, 'Printed in Hong Kong © 1986 Alfred A. Knopf, Inc.'. On back flap, '10/86'. Dust-wrapper designed by Sara Eisenman.

Published by 17 September 1986 (the date stamp in one Library of Congress copy) at $14.95; number of copies undetermined.

REVIEWS: *Booklist*, 15 Feb. 1987; *British Book News*, Jan. 1987 (Gavin Ewart); *Critical Quarterly*, Autumn 1987 (William Scammell); *Encounter*, March 1987 (John Mole); *Glasgow Herald*, 20 Dec. 1986 (James Aitchison); *Guardian*, 19 Oct. 1986 (Martin Dodsworth); *Listener*, 8 Jan. 1987 (A. Coles); *Los Angeles Times Book Review*, 14 Dec. 1986; *Observer*, 14 Dec. 1986; *Poetry Review*, Apr. 1987 (Edna Longley); *Spectator*, 29 Nov. 1986; *Sunday Telegraph*, 14 Dec. 1986 (Ronald Blythe); *Sunday Times*, 2 Nov. 1986 (David Profumo); *Tablet*, 29 Nov. 1986 (Sydney Carter); *Times*, 8 Jan. 1987 (Robert Nye); *Times Literary Supplement*, 6 Mar. 1987 (Grevel Lindop); *Today*, 28 Dec. 1986 (Michael Horovitz); *World Literature Today*, Summer 1987.

A92   THE CAT AND THE CUCKOO   1987

a. First edition (prints):

A series of 28 separate offset-printed colour illustrations of animals by R. J. Lloyd, each with a Hughes poem printed below.

Paper cream-coloured 'laid' (chain lines vertical, 2.6 cm.), 29.8 × 22.0 cm.

CONTENTS: Cat—Shrew—Hen[1]—Crow—Squirrel—Goat—Pike[2]—Donkey—Mole—Fantails—Sparrow—Dog—Pig—Peacock—Cow—Robin—Toad—Stickleback—The Red Admiral—Ram—Snail—Dragonfly—Hedgehog—Owl—Otter[3]—Thrush—Worm—Cuckoo.

Published May 1987 (per publisher's prospectus) at £450.00 for the set or £20.00 apiece. 200 copies of each sheet were printed, and signed as required.

b. First book edition:

[hand-done letters, within a double-rule border] THE CAT | AND THE | CUCKOO | BY TED | HUGHES | WITH PAINTINGS BY | R·J· LLOYD

[1–4⁸] = 32 leaves. Leaves (i–iii)1–28(29), consisting: (i)ʳ half-title, '[in hand-done letters resembling type] THE CAT | AND THE | CUCKOO'; (i)ᵛ illustration of a cuckoo; (ii)ʳ title page; (ii)ᵛ 'For | Daniel Hews | Sebastian Clarke | Hugh and Toby Norton-Smith | and | for all the children who visit | FARMS FOR CITY CHILDREN'; (iii)ʳ table of contents; (iii)ᵛ illustration of a cat; 1–28ʳ text, each poem facing a colour illustration within a halftone grey rule frame; 28ᵛ '*This edition of two thousand copies of 'The | Cat and the Cuckoo' is the first publication of | the Sunstone Press | Two hundred and fifty copies are numbered | and signed by artist and author |* [in numbered copies only:] This copy is number .... [number written over periods] | [signatures of Lloyd and Hughes]'; (29)ʳ pressmark of Sunstone Press; (29)ᵛ '© Ted Hughes 1987 | © Paintings, R. J. Lloyd 1987 | ISBN 1 870641 05 1 | Printed by Sydney Lee (Exeter) Ltd'.

Blue cloth over boards, front stamped in gold with title-page design. Spine round. Endpapers beige 'laid' (chains 2.7–2.8 cm.), marked '[crown] | [black-letter] Abbey Mills'.

Dust-wrapper coated outside, coloured orange-brown. Front: within rule frame containing a white border, illustration of a cat; outside frame: '[top] TED HUGHES [the neighbouring 'H' and 'E' share a vertical stroke]; [bottom] R. J. LLOYD [left, reading up] THE CAT AND [right, reading down] THE CUCKOO'. Spine: ' · THE CAT AND THE CUCKOO · HUGHES · LLOYD · '. Back: within rule frame containing a white border, illustration of a cuckoo.

The numbered copies have a slip-case covered with very light-green cloth.

---

[1] First line 'Dowdy the Hen'; not the same as 'The Hen' in *A Primer of Birds*.
[2] First line 'I am the Pike'; not the same as the poem in *Lupercal*.
[3] First line 'An Otter am I'; not the same as 'An Otter' in *Lupercal*.

14.9 × 10.5 cm., bulk .5 cm.; all edges cut. Printed offset.

The text settings, or at least the layout and spacing, are different from the separate print version.

Published September 1987 at £20.00 for the numbered copies and £7.95 for the rest; 2000 copies printed.

REVIEWS: *Books for Your Children*, Spring 1991; *British Book News, Children's Books*, Mar. 1988; *Junior Bookshelf*, Feb. 1991; *Times Educational Supplement*, 23 Dec. 1988.

A93   T. S. ELIOT: A TRIBUTE   1987

[in blue-black] T.S. ELIOT: | A TRIBUTE | [in grey] By the Poet Laureate | TED HUGHES | Privately Printed by | FABER AND FABER

[1⁸] = 8 leaves. Pages (1–16), consisting: (1) title page; (2) blank; (3) '[in grey] FABER AND FABER LIMITED | 3 Queen Square London WC1N 3AU | Printed by the Salient Seedling Press | Photograph by Caroline Forbes | Copyright :1987: Ted Hughes | All rights reserved | [ornament]'; (4) blank; (5) '[pasted-on halftone photograph of the plaque to Eliot] | An address on the occasion of the unveiling of a | blue plaque at 3 Kensington Court Gardens | London W8, on the 26th September 1986.'; (6) blank; (7–11) text; (12) blank; (13) '[in grey] TWO HUNDRED FIFTY COPIES | were printed using Baskerville foundry and | monotype on Frankfurt Cream paper | with Fabriano Roma wrappers. | Completed in August, 1987. | [ornament] | [Hughes' signature]'; (14–16) blank.

Sewn into two nested sheets of dark blue Fabriano handmade paper ('Roma', chain lines vertical, 3.9–4.4 cm.).

Dust-wrapper of the same Fabriano paper (watermark '[in oval] [Romulus and Remus suckling the wolf] | ROMA'; countermark 'C. M. FABRIANO ITALIA'). Front: 'T.S. ELIOT: | A TRIBUTE'.

Packaged in a translucent synthetic paper folder sealed with a square of gummed paper. Around this, a folder of very light green 'laid' paper (chain lines horizontal, 2.8 cm.); on front, a pasted-on paper label, 7.4 × 8.9 cm., printed: 'T.S. ELIOT: | A TRIBUTE | By the Poet Laureate | TED HUGHES'.

Paper mould-made 'laid' (Frankfurt Cream), chain lines vertical, chain and wire lines wavy and irregularly spaced; overall 24.1 × 16.0 cm., bulk .2 cm.; top edge cut, fore- and bottom edges 'deckle'. Printed letterpress.

Published probably in August 1987 at an undetermined price; 250 copies printed.

a.1. First edition:

[within a rule frame] ff | [rule] | TED HUGHES | [rule] | Tales of the | Early World | [rule] | *Illustrated by Andrew Davidson* | [below frame] *faber and faber* | LONDON · BOSTON

[1–4^{16}] = 64 leaves. Pages (i–vi)1–121(122), consisting: (i) half-title; (ii) '*Also by Ted Hughes* | [28 titles]'; (iii) title page; (iv) 'First published in 1988 | by Faber and Faber Limited | 3 Queen Square, London WC1N 3AU | Photoset by Parker Typesetting Service Leicester | Printed in Great Britain by | Mackays of Chatham Ltd, Kent | All rights reserved | Text © Ted Hughes, 1987, 1988 | Illustrations © Andrew Davidson, 1988 | 'The Guardian' was first published in *Guardian Angels,* | edited by Stephanie Nettell, Viking Kestrel, 1987 | [CIP data] | For Carol'; (v) table of contents; (vi) blank; 1–121(122) text. Text pages 50, 94 unnumbered.

Black calico-grain paper over boards. Spine round, stamped in white: 'TED HUGHES Tales of the Early World [at foot, reading across] ff'.

Dust-wrapper coloured black and coated outside; front and back with colour illustrations of eyes. Front, upper left, in white, the rule frame with included text as on title page. Spine printed like book spine, in white. Back, in white, at top: 'ff | *faber and faber*'; at bottom, in black on a white panel, bar code.

23.4 × 15.5 cm., bulk .8 cm.; all edges cut. Printed offset.

CONTENTS: How Sparrow Saved the Birds—The Guardian—The Trunk—The Making of Parrot—The Invaders—The Snag—The Playmate—The Shawl of the Beauty of the World—Leftovers—The Dancers.

Published June 1988 (the British Library copy is stamped 13 June) at £5.95; number of copies undetermined.

a.2. First paperback printing (1990):

Same setting as above except:
1. The list on p. (ii) is reset and contains 30 titles.
2. P. (iv) reads: 'For Carol | First published in 1988 | by Faber and Faber Limited | 3 Queen Square London WC1N 3AU | This paperback edition first published in 1990 | Photoset by Parker Typesetting Service Leicester | Printed in Great Britain by | Cox and Wyman Ltd, Reading, Berkshire | All rights reserved | Text © Ted Hughes, 1987, 1988 | Illustrations © Andrew Davidson, 1988 | 'The Guardian' was first published in *Guardian Angels,* | edited by

Stephanie Nettell, Viking Kestrel, 1987 ⁋ [authorship and Net
Book Agreement notes, reference to CIP data, and ISBN]'.

64 leaves, 'perfect-bound'.

Wrappers printed with coloured version of illustration on p. 55,
extending across spine to back. Front, upper right, in white: '[on black
panel] ff | [on red panel] TALES OF THE | EARLY WORLD | [on
green panel] Ted Hughes | [on yellow-brown panel] Illustrated by |
Andrew Davidson'. Spine, in white: '[on black panel, reading across]
ff [reading down, in white] [on red panel] TALES OF THE EARLY
WORLD [on green panel] Ted Hughes'. Back, to left, in white: '[on
black panel] ff | *faber and faber* | [on red panel] TALES OF THE
EARLY WORLD | Ted Hughes | [on green panel] [blurb] | UK
£1.99 net | Canada $4.95 | [on white panel on the green, bar code in
black]'. In one copy seen, Hughes' name on the front cover is on a blue
panel.

Paper poor-quality white, 19.8 × 12.6 cm., bulk .8 cm.; all edges cut.
Printed offset.

Published September 1990 at £1.99; number of copies undetermined.

a.3. First American printing (1991):

[within a rule frame] [arched] TALES | [straight] OF THE | EARLY |
WORLD | [rule, 7.0 cm.] | TED HUGHES | PICTURES BY |
ANDREW DAVIDSON | [rule, 7.0 cm.] | FARRAR, STRAUS AND
GIROUX | NEW YORK

64 leaves (no structure discernible; apparently a glued binding). Pages
(i–vi)1–121(122), consisting: (i) half-title; (ii) 'BOOKS FOR
CHILDREN | BY TED HUGHES | [11 titles]'; (iii) title page; (iv)
'*For Carol* | Text copyright © 1987, 1988 by Ted Hughes | Pictures
copyright © 1988 by Andrew Davidson | All rights reserved | First
published in 1988 by Faber & Faber Ltd., London | First American
edition, 1991 | Library of Congress catalog card number: 90-50454 |
Printed in the United States of America | 'The Guardian' was first
published in *Guardian Angels*, | edited by Stephanie Nettell (Viking
Kestrel, 1987)'; (v) table of contents, same setting as a.1 except for
heading 'CONTENTS'; (vi) blank; 1–121(122) same setting as a.1
except for the following:
1. All story titles reset.
2. Running titles reset; they and page numbers repositioned.
3. Each opening paragraph has a heavy initial with a deep indent,
   with text flowed to accommodate.
4. Text on p. 34 and illustration on p. 35 interchanged.
5. First line of p. 39 shifted to bottom of p. 38; three dots added at

end of p. 38 as a division marker.

6. All text on p. 90 moved to p. 91. Remains out of step with a.1 to the end of this story, where a smaller illustration is substituted.

7. Page numbers deleted on pp. 7, 15, 22, 29, 34, 36, 44, 55, 61, 66, 71, 81, 84, 90, 99, 109, and 113.

Quarter white cloth (4 cm. onto boards), black paper sides over boards. Spine round, stamped in black: 'HUGHES [solid diamond] TALES OF THE EARLY WORLD [solid diamond] DAVIDSON   FSG'.

Dust-wrapper coated outside, printed with same black background with eyes as a.1. Front: '[printed in yellow and light peach, within white rule frame] [arched] TALES | [straight] OF THE | EARLY | WORLD | [rule, 5.5 cm.] | TED HUGHES | PICTURES BY | ANDREW DAVIDSON'. Spine printed like book spine, in light peach except for diamonds in light blue.

23.4 × 14.5 cm., bulk .9 cm.; all edges cut. Printed offset.

Published March 1991 at $13.95; number of copies undetermined. A second printing (1992) of unknown size is identified as such on verso title.

REVIEWS: *Booklist*, 15 Apr. 1991, 15 Jan. 1992, 15 Mar. 1992; *Book Report*, Nov. 1991; *Books for Keeps*, Jan. 1991; *Horn Book Guide*, Fall 1991; *Center for Children's Books, Bulletin*, June 1991; *Junior Bookshelf*, Oct. 1988 (M.C.); *Kirkus*, 15 Feb. 1991; *Observer*, 7 Aug. 1988; *Poetry Review*, Autumn 1988 (W. Magee); *Publishers Weekly*, 29 March 1991; *School Library Journal*, May 1991; *Times*, 14 July 1988; *Times Educational Supplement*, 15 July 1988, 15 Feb. 1991; *Voice of Youth Advocates*, June 1991; *Wilson Library Bulletin*, Sept. 1991.

A95   WOLFWATCHING   1989

a. First edition:

[within a double-rule frame] TED | HUGHES | [rule, 2.1 cm.] | *Wolfwatching* | [below frame] ff | *faber and faber* | LONDON · BOSTON

[1–2^{16}] = 32 leaves. Pages (i–vi)vii(viii)1–55(56), consisting: (i) half-title; (ii) '*Also by Ted Hughes* | [30 titles including this one]'; (iii) title page; (iv) 'First published in 1989 | by Faber and Faber Limited | 3 Queen Square London WC1N 3AU | Phototypeset by Wilmaset, Birkenhead, Wirral | Printed in Great Britain by | Richard Clay Ltd, Bungay, Suffolk | All rights reserved | © Ted Hughes, 1989 | [notes about Net Book Agreement and CIP data, and ISBN numbers]'; (v) 'For Hilda'; (vi) blank; vii table of contents; (viii) blank; 1–54 text; 55 note to 'The Black Rhino'; (56) blank.

Black calico-grain paper over boards. Spine flat, stamped in white: '[reading across, thin-thick rule] | [reading down] TED HUGHES *Wolfwatching* [reading across] ff | [thick-thin rule]'.

Dust-wrapper coated outside, printed dark blue with 'ff' pattern in black. Text on front, spine, and back printed on white panels. Front: '[within a double-rule frame] TED | HUGHES | [rule, 2.5 cm.] | *Wolfwatching* | [photograph of *netsuke* of a wolf]'. Spine printed like book spine, in black. Back: '[within a double-rule frame] ff | *faber and faber* | *Also by Ted Hughes* | [7 titles] | [bar code]'.

19.7 × 12.9 cm., bulk .5 cm.; all edges cut. Printed offset.

CONTENTS: A Sparrow Hawk[1]—Two Astrological Conundrums (I. The Fool's Evil Dream; II. Tell)—Slump Sundays—Climbing into Heptonstall—Macaw[1]—Dust as We Are—Wolfwatching—Telegraph Wires—Source—Sacrifice—For the Duration—Anthem for Doomed Youth—The Black Rhino—Leaf Mould—Manchester Skytrain—Walt (I. Under High Wood; II. The Atlantic)—Take What You Want But Pay For It—Us He Devours—Little Whale Song—On the Reservations (I. Sitting Bull on Christmas Morning; II. Nightvoice; III. The Ghost Dancer)—A Dove[1]—*Note to* The Black Rhino.

Published 18 September 1989 (the British Library copy is stamped 16 August) at £8.99; number of copies undetermined. A paperback printing of unknown size was issued simultaneously, 'perfect-bound', at £3.99 ($9.95 Canadian). The cover design is the same as the dust-wrapper except for the back cover.

b.1. First American edition (1991):

[flush to left] Ted Hughes | Wolfwatching | Farrar, Straus and Giroux | New York

40 leaves, 'perfect-bound'. Pages (i–xii)(1–2)3–66(67–68), consisting: (i–iii) blank; (iv) '[flush to left] *Poetry by Ted Hughes* | [13 titles including this one]'; (v) half-title, flush to left; (vi) blank; (vii) title page; (viii) '*Copyright © 1989 by Ted Hughes* | *All rights reserved* | *First published by Faber and Faber Ltd., London* | *First American edition, 1991* | *Library of Congress catalog card number: 90-50453* | *Printed in the United States of America* | *Designed by Cynthia Krupat*'; (ix) '[flush to left] *For Hilda*'; (x) blank; (xi) table of contents; (xii) blank; (1) half-title, flush to left; (2) blank; 3–62 text; (63) '[flush to left] Notes'; (64) blank; 65–66 notes to 'The Black Rhino' and 'On the Reservations'; (67–68) blank.

---

[1] Previously published in *A Primer of Birds.*

Red cloth over boards. Spine flat, stamped in black: 'TED HUGHES /
WOLFWATCHING / FSG'.

Dust-wrapper: front: '[green band] | [black rule] | [on beige ground,
freehand lettered in red] TED HUGHES | [black rule] | [shamanistic
design in black and white] | [freehand, in black] WOLF- | WATCH- |
ING | [rule] | [green band]'. Spine: '[green band and rule continued
from front] [on beige ground, freehand] TED HUGHES [small solid red
diamond] [black freehand] WOLFWATCHING [small solid red
diamond] [black freehand] FSG [rule and green band continued from
front]'. Back: between rules and bands continued across spine,
photograph of Hughes by Jane Bown. Both dust-wrapper and book
designed by Cynthia Krupat.

22.8 × 15.1 cm., bulk .6 cm.; all edges cut. Printed offset.

CONTENTS: same as the first edition, but here 'Macaw' is named 'A
Macaw' in the contents, and the text of the poem itself bears the title
'*The Punishment of Iago, Re-incarnated as Malvolio in the Form of* A Macaw'.
A note to 'On the Reservations' is added at the end.

Published 17 January 1991 at $18.95; number of copies undetermined.

b.2. First American paperback printing (1992):

[flush to left] Ted Hughes | Wolfwatching | *The Noonday Press* | *Farrar,
Straus and Giroux* | *New York*

40 leaves, 'perfect-bound'. Collation the same as b.1, and printed from
the same setting of type except for the title page and three lines on the
title verso: '*First American edition, 1991*' has been replaced with '*First
American edition published by* | *Farrar, Straus and Giroux, 1991* | *First Noonday
Press edition, 1992*'.

Wrappers. Front and spine same design as dust-wrapper of b.1, but spine
lettering replaced with type, and publisher is 'NOONDAY'. Back:
blurbs and bar code.

22.8 × 15.2 cm., bulk .6 cm.; all edges cut. Printed offset.

Published in 1992 at $9.00; number of copies undetermined.

REVIEWS: *American Book Review,* June 1991; *Booklist,* 15 Nov. 1990; *Choice,*
June 1991; *Economist,* 23 Sept. 1989; *Financial Times,* 23 Sept. 1989
(Bernard McGinley); *Georgia Review,* Summer 1991; *Glasgow Herald,* 23
Sept. 1989 (James Aitchison); *Guardian,* 15 Sept. 1989 (Hugh Herbert),
19 Oct. 1989 (Carol Ann Duffy); *Independent,* 23 Sept. 1989 (Peter
Forbes); *Library Journal,* Dec. 1990; *Listener,* 9 Nov. 1989 (Dannie Abse);
London Magazine, June/July 1990 (Sean O'Brien); *London Review of Books,*
22 Mar. 1990 (Edna Longley); *Month,* Jan. 1990; *New Republic,* 24 June

1991 (Mary Jo Salter); *New Statesman & Society*, 27 Oct. 1989 (Jo Shapcott); *New Yorker*, 23 Aug. 1993; *New York Times Book Review*, 21 April 1991 (William Logan); *New York Times (Late Edition)*, 23 Jan. 1991; *Observer*, 17 Sept. 1989 (Mick Imlah); *Poetry Review*, Winter 1989/90 (P. Gross); *Spectator*, 30 Sept. 1989 (Peter Levi); *Sunday Correspondent*, 17 Sept. 1989 (Dick Davis); *Sunday Times*, 8 Oct. 1989 (Peter Reading); *Tablet*, 21 Oct. 1989 (Elizabeth Jennings); *Times*, 16 Sept. 1989 (Robert Nye); *Times Educational Supplement*, 29 Sept. 1989; *Times Literary Supplement*, 20 Oct. 1989 (John Lucas); *Virginia Quarterly Review*, Summer 1991; *Weekend Telegraph*, 21 Oct. 1989 (Derek Walcott); *World Literature Today*, Winter 1993.

A96   CAPRICCIO   1990

[within two concentric woodcut frames, illustration of human figure across top printed in four colours] CAPRICCIO | POEMS BY | TED HUGHES | ENGRAVINGS BY | LEONARD | BASKIN | [outside the inner frame] THE GEHENNA PRESS | MCMXC

$[1^4\ 2\text{--}21^2] = 46$ leaves, unpaginated. Quire [1] consists of pages (1–4) blank; (5) half-title, engraved, with red overprinted by woodcut, epigraphic lettering on a *tabula ansata*: 'CAPRCICIO' [sic; the I's are within the C's]'; (6) blank; (7) title page; (8) blank. Quires [2–20] each have the following composition: p. (1) poem title; p. (2) the poem; p. (3) an illustration by Baskin (woodcut or engraved), most printed on a separate sheet and mounted; (4) blank, or continuation of the poem, or another illustration. Most of these quires have guards at the inner fold to increase the spine thickness. Of quire [21] only the first recto is printed: '[pasted-on coloured engraving of spider] | Fifty copies of Capriccio | were issued in the unsettled Spring of | 1990. The papers throughout were handmade | in Italy & France. Jan van Krimpen's Spectrum types | were supplied by the Berliner Typefoundry at Nevada City, | Ca. The composition & printing of the letterpress was achieved | by Arthur Larson & Daniel Keleher of Hadley, Mass. The copper- | plates were printed by D. R. Wakefield of Humberside, Eng^d. and | by Michael Kuch of Northampton, Ma. The edition is arranged | as follows: ten copies, numbered 1–10 have a second suite of the | engravings printed variously & on different papers; these copies | also contain a page of Ted Hughes' manuscript & a drawing | by Leonard Baskin; they also carry one of the copper- | plates. Copies numbered 11–50 comprise the | regular edition. All copies are signed | by the poet & the artist. | [number] | [Hughes' signature] | [Baskin's signature]'. Pages with illustration have tissue guards laid in.

Full morocco, leather hinges; front and back covers trisected into vertical panels (outer ones green, inner one brown). Black leather strips demarcate the panels and run along top and bottom. Front: '[in black leather onlay]: CAPRICCIO'. Spine stamped in gilt on brown panel bordered in black, with black leather strips at head and tail: ' · CAPRICCIO · TED HUGHES · LEONARD BASKIN   · '. Back: '[in black leather onlay]: *GP* | [gilt] 1990'. The only copy seen of numbers 11–50 lacks the raised periods on spine, and the date on the back. Inside the back cover is a light-green label printed in gold: '[double rule] | BOUND BY | [rule] | GRAY PARROT | · & CO · | [double rule]'.

Copies 1–10 with a separate folder of prints on various papers in various sizes, each hinged to a backing sheet 51.0 × 35.5 cm. In a clamshell case of khaki cloth over boards, a green morocco strip at fore-edge of each cover. Spine of green morocco gilt with fillets top and bottom; between two other fillets parallel to these: '[reading down] [fillet] | · CAPRICCIO · | [fillet] | · *HUGHES · BASKIN* · | [fillet]'. An original plate for one of the engravings is laid into a well in the bottom of the case, covered by a hinged board.

Copies 11–50 have a similar case, lacking the well. The spine lacks the fillets above the title and below the names.

Papers handmade, marked variously '[crown] | UMBRIA | ITALIA | C. M. | F.', 'ZECCHI | FIRENZE [at left, a floral figure in a square]', or '[in oval frame] 1526 | [heart] | [in ornamental oval frame] RICHARD BAS'. Ca. 51 × 35.5 cm., bulk ca. 2 cm.; some edges deckle.

Printed letterpress.

CONTENTS: Capriccios—The Locket—The Mythographers—Systole Diastole—Descent—Folktale—Fanaticism—Snow—Rules of the Game—Possession—The Coat—Smell of Burning—The Pit and the Stones—Shibboleth—The Roof—The Error—Opus 131—Familiar—Flame—Chlorophyl.

Published in the spring of 1990 at an undetermined price; 50 copies printed.

A97   SHAKESPEARE AND THE GODDESS   1992
OF COMPLETE BEING

a.1. First edition:

SHAKESPEARE | AND THE GODDESS OF | COMPLETE BEING | [drawing of head of goddess] | TED HUGHES | ff | *faber and faber*

[1–17¹⁶] = 272 leaves. Pages (i–vi)vii–ix(x)xi–xiii(xiv)xv(xvi–xx)1–

499(500)501–511(512)513–517(518–524), consisting: (i) half-title,
'SHAKESPEARE | AND THE GODDESS OF | COMPLETE
BEING'; (ii) '*Also by Ted Hughes* | [31 titles]'; (iii) title page; (iv) 'First
published 9 March 1992 | by Faber and Faber Limited | 3 Queen Square
London WC1N 3AU | Photoset by Wilmaset Ltd, Birkenhead, Wirral |
Printed in England by | Clays Ltd, St Ives plc | All rights reserved | ©
Ted Hughes, 1992 | [notes regarding identity of author and CIP record,
and ISBN] | [identification of title-page drawing, in roman type]'; (v)
'For Donya Feuer | who provided the occasion and encouragement | and
for Peter Brook | who provided the key to the key | and for Roy Davids |
who provided the moral support and the books'; (vi) blank; vii–ix table
of contents; (x) blank; xi–xiii foreword by Hughes; (xiv) blank; xv,
acknowledgements; (xvi) blank; (xvii) quotation by Yeats; (xviii) blank;
(xix) four quotations; (xx) blank; 1–499 text; (500) blank; 501–504
postscript; 505–511 Appendix I; (512) blank; 513–517 Appendix II;
(518–524) blank. Text pages 44–48, 93, 94, 208–210, 224–226, 280–282,
321, 322, 332–334, 376–378 unnumbered.

Dark blue calico-grain paper over boards. Spine round, stamped in gold
reading across: '[in a rule frame] ff | [rule] | TED | HUGHES | [rule] |
Shakespeare | and the | Goddess of | Complete | Being'.

Dust-wrapper coated outside, front and front flap printed with detail of
coloured woodcut of a boar by Andrew Davidson. Front, at upper left,
on gold panel: '[in a rule frame] ff | [rule] | TED | HUGHES | [rule] |
Shakespeare | and the | Goddess of | Complete Being'. Spine and back
printed gold; spine: '[reading across] [rule] | ff | [rule] | [reading down,
flush at left] TED HUGHES | Shakespeare and the Goddess of
Complete Being [reading across: rule]'. Back: 'ff | *faber and faber* | [colour
reproduction of Islamic depiction of the 'Lotus World'] | [on white
panel, bar code]'. On the rear flap the last line of the blurb reads 'vision
of life and death in season.' An early state contains the error 'life in death
and season.' The compilers do not know whether the error was caught
before copies were shipped.

23.3 × 15.5 cm., bulk 3.8 cm.; all edges cut. Printed offset.

Published 13 April 1992 (the British Library copy is stamped 2 March)
at £18.99; number of copies undetermined.

a.2. First American printing of English edition, corrected and expanded:

Typesetting the same as above except:
1. Imprint on title page is 'FARRAR STRAUS GIROUX | NEW
    YORK'.
2. P. (iv): '*Copyright* © *1992 by Ted Hughes* | *All rights reserved* | *First
    published, in slightly different form,* | *by Faber and Faber Limited, London,*

1992 | *Printed in the United States of America* | *First American edition, 1992* | [Library of Congress catalog card number] | [identification of title-page drawing, in italic]'.

3. Pages (i–vi)vii–ix(x)xi–xiv(xv–xx)1–499(500)501–511(512)513–517(518)519–524. After p. xiii the preliminaries are: xiv, acknowledgements; (xv) quotations by Yeats; (xvi) blank; (xvii) six quotations (including the original four); (xviii) blank; (xix) half-title, 'SHAKESPEARE | AND THE GODDESS OF | COMPLETE BEING'; (xx) blank. The headings of the table of contents, foreword, and acknowledgements are reset from roman capitals to upper- and lowercase italic. There are major revisions to pp. 17, 83, 92, 161, 220, 221, 270, 502, and 504, and more minor ones to pp. 16, 32, 60, 162, 201, 236, 271, 272, 328, 368, 396, 401, 402, and 433. Pages 519–524 contain 'Appendix III: The Equation in *The Merchant of Venice*', which is now listed in the table of contents.

Same signatures as above, but glued, not sewn.

Black calico-grain paper over boards. Front blind-stamped with drawing of head of goddess from title page. Spine stamped in gold, reading across: 'SHAKE- | SPEARE | AND THE | GODDESS | OF | COMPLETE | BEING | [rule, 1.6 cm.] | TED | HUGHES | FARRAR | STRAUS | GIROUX'.

Dust-wrapper coated outside. Front: boar illustration as in English version; flush at left: '[yellow letters, each line on a separate red strip] SHAKESPEARE | AND THE GODDESS | OF COMPLETE BEING [centred at foot, in black on white background] TED HUGHES'. Spine, reading across: '[yellow letters, each line on a separate red strip] SHAKESPEARE | AND THE GODDESS | OF COMPLETE BEING [black on white background] TED HUGHES | [grey] FARRAR | STRAUS | GIROUX'. Back: blurbs and bar code. Designed by Cynthia Krupat.

23.3 × 15.5 cm., bulk 3.5 cm.; all edges cut. Printed offset.

Published November 1992 at $35.00; number of copies undetermined.

a.3. First English printing of expanded text (paperback, 1993):

Typesetting the same as a.1 (though reduced) except:
1. Half-title includes a capsule biography.
2. P. (iv): 'First published in 1992 | by Faber and Faber Limited | 3 Queen Square London WC1N 3AU | This revised paperback edition first published in 1993 | Photoset by Wilmaset Ltd, Birkenhead, Wirral | Printed in England by Clays Ltd, St Ives plc | All rights reserved | © Ted Hughes, 1992, 1993 | [notes regarding identity of

author, Net Book Agreement and CIP record, and ISBN] |
[identification of title-page drawing, in roman] | [printing code, 2–
1]'.

3. Pagination, and all after p. xiii, same as a.2, but one line is
dropped between pp. 17 and 18.

272 leaves, 'perfect-bound'.

Wrappers. Front: colour reproduction of a late medieval painting of
Richard de Vere attacked by a boar; on a gold panel: '[in a double-rule
frame] ff | [rule] | TED HUGHES | [rule] | Shakespeare and | the
Goddess of | Complete Being'. Spine and back coloured black. Spine:
'[on gold panel, reading across] [rule] | ff | [rule] | [reading down] TED
HUGHES | Shakespeare and the Goddess of Complete Being | [reading
across, rule]'. Back, in white lettering: 'ff | *faber and faber* | [reviews] |
[identification of cover illustration] | UK £9.99 net Canada
$22.99 US $15.95 | [black on white panel, bar code]'.

21.6 × 13.4 cm., bulk 4.0 cm.; all edges cut. Printed offset.

Published March 1993 at £9.99; number of copies undetermined.

REVIEWS: *Atlantic*, Jan. 1993; *Cambridge Quarterly*, 22:4, 1993 (David
Gervais); *Commonweal*, 6 Nov. 1992; *Economist*, 11 Apr. 1992; *Financial
Times*, 11 Apr. 1992 (A. L. Rowse); *Guardian*, 2 Apr. 1992 (Terry
Eagleton); *Guardian Weekly*, 19 Apr. 1992; *Hudson Review*, Summer 1993;
Independent, 11 April 1992 (Lachlan Mackinnon); *Independent on Sunday*, 19
Apr. 1992 (Michael Hoffman); *Library Journal*, Dec. 1992; *Literary Review*
(London), Apr. 1992 (Mary McGowan); *London Review of Books*, 9 Apr.
1992 (Tom Paulin); *New Statesman & Society*, 17 April 1992 (Geoff Dyer);
Observer, 12 Apr. 1992 (Anthony Burgess); *Publishers Weekly*, 26 Oct.
1992; *Raritan*, Winter 1994 (William Kerrigan); *Resurgence*, Jan./Feb.
1993 (John Moat); *School Librarian*, Aug. 1992; *Spectator*, 18 Apr. 1992
(Hilary Mantel), 21 Nov. 1992; *Stand*, Summer 1993; *Sunday Telegraph*, 5
Apr. 1992 (Frank Kermode); *Sunday Times*, 5 Apr. 1992 (John Carey),
30 Apr. 1992 (Harvey Porlock); *Temenos* 13, 1992 (Joseph Milne); *Times*,
9 Apr. 1992 (Eric Griffiths); *Times Educational Supplement*, 9 Apr. 1992, 1
May 1992; *Times Literary Supplement*, 17 Apr. 1992 (Marina Warner);
Weekend Telegraph, 11 Apr. 1992 (Peter Levi); *World and I*, June 1993.

A98   RAIN-CHARM FOR THE DUCHY   1992

a.1. First edition:

[Two volumes; volume 1:]

[flush to left] RAIN-CHARM FOR THE DUCHY | AND OTHER
LAUREATE POEMS *by* Ted Hughes | *faber and faber*

$[1-4^8] = 32$ leaves. Pages (i–viii)1–54(55–56), consisting: (i) half-title, flush to left; (ii) blank; (iii) title page; (iv) 'Published in 1992 by Faber and Faber Limited | 3 Queen Square London WC1N 3AU | Photoset by Wilmaset Birkenhead Wirral | Printed and bound in Great Britain by | Smith/Settle, Otley, West Yorkshire | All rights reserved | The poems © Ted Hughes, 1984, 1985, 1986, 1988, 1990 | This collection © Ted Hughes, 1992 | [note regarding identity of author and CIP record, and ISBN]'; (v) table of contents; (vi) blank; (vii) poem, 'Solomon's Dream'; (viii) blank; 1–41 text; (42) blank; (43) ['flush to left] NOTES'; (44) blank; 45–54 notes; (55) blank; (56) 'This edition of | *Rain-Charm for the Duchy* | is limited to | two hundred and eighty copies | each signed by the author. | Thirty copies numbered I–XXX | are reserved for the author. | Two hundred and fifty copies | numbered 1–250 are for sale. | This is copy number | [number] | [signature]'. Text pages 8, 22 unnumbered.

Maroon 'laid' paper over boards (chain lines vertical, 2.7–2.8 cm.), black cloth spine stamped in gold: 'RAIN-CHARM FOR THE DUCHY   Ted Hughes'. Endpapers brownish-yellow 'laid' (chain lines vertical, 2.6 cm.).

Paper white 'laid' (chain lines vertical, 2.7 cm.), 26.8 × 17.8 cm., bulk .5 cm.; all edges cut. Printed offset.

CONTENTS: Rain-Charm for the Duchy—Two Poems for Her Majesty Queen Elizabeth the Queen Mother (1. The Dream of the Lion; 2. Little Salmon Hymn)—A Birthday Masque (1. The First Gift; 2. An Almost Thornless Crown[1]; 3. The Second Gift; 4. The Ring; 5. The Third Gift; 6. Candles for the Cake)—The Song of the Honey Bee—Two Songs (1. For Her Royal Highness Princess Beatrice of York; 2. For the Christening of Her Royal Highness Princess Beatrice of York)—A Masque for Three Voices.

[Volume 2:]

[flush to left] THE UNICORN *by* Ted Hughes | *faber and faber*

$[1^6] = 6$ leaves. Pages (1–12), consisting: (1) title page; (2) '© Ted Hughes, 1992'; (3–7) text; (8–11) notes; (12) 'This edition of 'The Unicorn', | published by Faber and Faber Limited | as a supplement to | *Rain-Charm for the Duchy*, | is limited to | two hundred and eighty copies | each signed by the author. | Thirty copies numbered I–XXX | are reserved for the author | This is copy number | [number] | [signature]'.

Sewn into plain white paper wrappers.

Dust-wrapper dark maroon 'laid' paper (chain lines vertical, 2.7 cm.).

---

[1] A revision of the poem in *Flowers and Insects*.

Same text paper and dimensions as vol. 1, bulk .1 cm.; all edges cut. Printed offset.

CONTENTS: The Unicorn (1. X-Ray; 2. Falstaff; 3. The Unicorn; 4. A Unicorn Called Ariel; 5. Envoi).

The two volumes in a slip-case covered with yellow 'laid' paper (only wire lines discernible).

Published June 1992 at £75.00; 280 copies printed.

a.2. First trade printing:

Title page same setting as above, but imprint is '[indented] ff | [flush to left] *faber and faber*'.

$[1^{16} 2^8 3^{16}] = 40$ leaves. Pages (i–x)1–47(48–50)51–64(65–70), consisting: (i–ii) blank; (iii) half-title, flush to left; (iv) '*Also by Ted Hughes* | [32 titles]'; (v) title page; (vi) 'First published in 1992 by Faber and Faber Limited | 3 Queen Square London WC1N 3AU | Photoset by Wilmaset Birkenhead Wirral | Printed in England by Clays Ltd St Ives plc | All rights reserved | The poems © Ted Hughes, 1984, 1985, 1986, 1988, 1990, 1992 | This collection © Ted Hughes, 1992 | [notes regarding identity of author and CIP record, and ISBN numbers]'; (vii) table of contents; (viii) blank; (ix) introductory verse, 'Solomon's Dream'; (x) blank; 1–47 poems; (48) blank; (49) divisional title: '[flush to left] NOTES'; (50) blank; 51–64 notes; (65–70) blank. Text pages 8, 22, 42 unnumbered.

Blue calico-grain paper over boards. Spine flat, stamped in gold: 'RAIN-CHARM FOR THE DUCHY   Ted Hughes [at foot, reading across] ff'.

Dust-wrapper printed dark blue with all-over pattern of 'ff' in gold; text in black on white panels. Front: '[in double-rule frame] RAIN-CHARM | FOR | THE DUCHY | and other | Laureate | Poems | [rule, 2.5 cm.] | *Ted Hughes*'. Spine: '[reading across: thin-thick rule] [reading down] RAIN-CHARM FOR THE DUCHY *Ted Hughes* [reading across] ff | [thick-thin rule]'. Back: '[in double-rule frame] ff | *faber and faber* | *Also by Ted Hughes* | [reviews] | [bar code]'.

23.4 × 15.4 cm., bulk .6 cm.; all edges cut. Printed offset.

CONTENTS: combines both volumes of the limited edition. The title page, title verso, and table of contents incorporate some of the typesetting of the limited edition; the text and notes are entirely the same setting except for the first page of 'The Unicorn' (p. 43). The latter shows a wider word-spacing in the trade printing, indicating at least a re-plating and possibly a re-keying of the text of 'X-Ray'.

Published June 1992 (the British Library copy is stamped 8 May) at

£12.99 ($19.95 U.S.; $25.99 Canadian); number of copies undetermined. A paperback printing of unknown size was issued simultaneously at £4.99. The paperback differs on p. (vi), which adds a Net Book Agreement note and printing code 10–1.

REVIEWS: *London Review of Books*, 9 July 1992; *New Statesman & Society*, 26 June 1992; *Observer*, 14 June 1992 (Andrew Motion); *Poetry Review*, Autumn 1992 (Peter Levi); *Spectator*, 20 June 1992; *Stand*, Summer 1993; *Sunday Times*, 28 June 1992 (Peter Reading); *Times Literary Supplement*, 26 June 1992 (Sean O'Brien); *World Literature Today*, Spring 1993.

A99   A DANCER TO GOD   1992

a.1. First edition:

A DANCER TO GOD | Tributes to | T.S. ELIOT | Ted Hughes | ff | *faber and faber* | LONDON · BOSTON

[1–2¹⁶] = 32 leaves. Pages (i–viii)(1–2)3–47(48–50)51–54(55–56), consisting: (i–ii) blank; (iii) half-title; (iv) '*Also by Ted Hughes* | [33 titles]'; (v) title page; (vi) 'First published in 1992 | by Faber and Faber Limited | 3 Queen Square London WC1N 3AU | Photoset by Wilmaset Ltd, Wirral | Printed in England by Clays Ltd, St Ives plc | All rights reserved | © Ted Hughes, 1992 | [note regarding authorship, acknowledgements, mention of CIP data, and ISBN] | [printing code, 2–1]'; (vii) 'For Valerie Eliot'; (viii) table of contents; (1) divisional title, 'I · THE TRULY GREAT | [...]'; (2) blank; 3–47 text; (48) blank; (49) divisional title, 'NOTES'; (50) blank; 51–54 notes; (55–56) blank. Text pages 8–10, 17, 18 unnumbered.

Blue calico-grain paper over boards. Spine flat, stamped in white: '[reading across, thin-thick rule] [reading down] A DANCER TO GOD   *Ted Hughes* [at foot, reading across] ff | [thick-thin rule]'.

Dust-wrapper coated outside, printed with all-over 'ff' pattern in dark blue, text in black on white panels. Front: '[in double-rule frame] A DANCER | TO GOD | Tributes to | T.S. Eliot | [rule, 2.6 cm.] | *Ted Hughes*'. Spine printed like book spine. Back: '[in double-rule frame] ff | *faber and faber* | Also by Ted Hughes | SHAKESPEARE AND THE | GODDESS OF COMPLETE BEING | [reviews]'.

21.5 × 13.7 cm., bulk .5 cm.; all edges cut. Printed offset.

CONTENTS: The Truly Great¹—The Song of Songs in the Valley of Bones—A Dancer to God.

---

¹ Originally published separately as *T. S. Eliot: A Tribute*.

Published September 1992 (the British Library copy is stamped 12 August) at £12.99 ($29.99. Canadian); number of copies undetermined.

a.2. First printing for America (1993):

Internally the same as a.1 except for the following:
1. Title page imprint is 'Farrar Straus Giroux | NEW YORK'.
2. P. (vi): 'Copyright © 1992 by Ted Hughes | All rights reserved | Printed in the United Kingdom | First published in 1992 | by Faber and Faber Limited | First American edition, 1993 | [acknowledgements and Library of Congress catalog card number]'.

Binding the same as a.1, except publisher's name at foot of spine is 'FSG' reading down.

Dust-wrapper coated outside, coloured blue with printing on white panels. Front panel contents same as in a.1. Spine printed like book spine, but space between '*Hughes*' and 'FSG' reduced. Back panel: '[within a double-rule frame] Also by Ted Hughes | SHAKESPEARE AND THE | GODDESS OF COMPLETE BEING | [reviews, same setting as a.1] | [bar code]'. On back flap, 'Printed in the United Kingdom'. No printed price.

Paper and dimensions same as a.1. Printed offset.

Published in 1993 at $16.00; number of copies undetermined.

REVIEWS: *Atlantic*, Jan. 1993; *Book World*, 22 Nov. 1992; *Commonweal*, 6 Nov. 1992; *Daily Telegraph*, 5 Mar. 1994 (Allan Massie), 4 Mar. 1995 (Stephen Spender); *Hudson Review*, Summer 1993; *Library Journal*, Dec. 1992, 15 May 1993; *Observer*, 29 Nov. 1992, 18 Apr. 1993; *Spectator*, 26 Nov. 1992 (Stephen Spender); *Stand*, Summer 1993; *Times Educational Supplement*, 9 Apr. 1993; *Times Literary Supplement*, 2 Oct. 1992 (Stephen Medcalf).

A100 THE MERMAID'S PURSE 1993

[double rule] | TED | HUGHES | [double rule] | THE | MERMAID'S | PURSE | [double rule] | watercolours | by | R. J. LLOYD | [double rule]

[1¹⁰ 2–3⁸ 4¹⁰] = 36 leaves. Leaves (i–vi)1–28(29–30), consisting: (i–ii) paste-down and free flyleaf, the first opening printed with a black-and-white halftone reproduction of a painting of kelp, (ii)ᵛ blank; (iii)ʳ half-title, '[double rule] THE | MERMAID'S | PURSE | [double rule]'; (iii)ᵛ colour illustration of a mermaid looking into a mirror; (iv)ʳ title page; (iv)ᵛ blank; (v)ʳ 'FOR | EMMA | FIRST EDITION | [pressmark of Sunstone Press] | MAY | 1993'; (v)^v blank; (vi)^r table of contents; (vi)^v colour illustration of a seal; 1^r–28^r text and illustrations; 28^v '*This first edition of 'The Mermaid's Purse' | has been designed, produced and published at the | Sunstone Press, Iffield House, Bideford, Devon, | in a limited edition of 100 signed and numbered copies | bound in full green cloth with slip case* | [signatures of Lloyd and Hughes] | [in manuscript, 'Number [number]'] | *Printed by Tony Lee of Exeter.* | © *Poems Ted Hughes.* | © *Watercolours R. J. Lloyd*'; 29^r blank; (30–31) paste-down and free flyleaves, the last opening printed with kelp painting as above.

Dark green cloth over boards. Spine flat, stamped in gold: 'TED HUGHES · THE MERMAID'S PURSE · R. J. LLOYD'.

In a slip-case covered with dark green cloth; on side, on a stamped inset, a colour-printed paper label showing a shark's egg capsule with lettering on its side 'The | Mermaid's | Purse'; reading up on the left side, 'TED HUGHES'; reading down on the right, 'R. J. LLOYD'.

21.0 × 14.8 cm., bulk .7 cm.; all edges cut. Printed offset.

CONTENTS: Seal—Sea Anemone—Gull—Starfish—Shell—Heron[1]— Limpet—Flounder—Blenny—Whelk—Sea Monster—Whale— Jellyfish—Ragworm—Pebbles—Cormorant—Bladderwrack—Conger Eel—Shrimp—Lobster—Wreck—Hermit Crab—Octopus—Sandflea— Crab—Mussel—The Mermaid's Purse—Mermaid.

Published May 1993 at £85.00; 100 copies printed.

A101   RECKLESS HEAD   1993

[flush with left margin of text] Reckless Head | [text] | © 1993 Ted Hughes | [centred] [publisher's device: tower with flag bearing black T] *Published by Bernard Stone and Raymond Danowski. The Turret Bookshop, London May 1993.*

Broadsheet, 29.7 × 20.95 cm.

Paper light green 'laid' (chain lines vertical, 2.75 cm.), marked 'conqueror | [portcullis]'. Printed offset.

Published May 1993 at an unknown price; number of copies undetermined.

---

[1] First line 'I am nothing'; a different poem from 'The Heron' in *Under the North Star*.

A102					THREE BOOKS					1993

[flush to left] TED HUGHES Three Books | *Remains of Elmet, Cave Birds, River* | [indented] ff | [flush to left] *faber and faber*

[1–3^{16} 4^8 5–7^{16}] = 104 leaves. Pages [1–2](i–iv)v–ix(x)(1–2)3–186(187–196), consisting: [1–2] blank; (i) '[flush to left] THREE BOOKS | [capsule biography of Hughes]'; (ii) '*Also by Ted Hughes* | [34 titles]'; (iii) title page; (iv) 'This edition first published in 1993 | by Faber and Faber Limited | 3 Queen Square London WC1N 3AU | Photoset by Wilmaset Ltd, Wirral | Printed in England by Clays Ltd, St Ives Plc | All rights reserved | This edition © Ted Hughes, 1993 | *Cave Birds* © Ted Hughes, 1978 | *Remains of Elmet* © Ted Hughes, 1979 | *River* © Ted Hughes, 1983 | [notes regarding authorship, Net Book Agreement, and CIP record] | [printing code, 10–1]'; v–ix table of contents; (x) blank; (1) divisional title to *Remains of Elmet*; (2) blank; 3–179 text; (180) blank; 181–186 notes; (187–196) blank. Text pages 62–64, 102–104 unnumbered.

Wrappers, printed gold, with all-over 'ff' pattern in dark blue, text printed in black on white panels. Front: '[in a double-rule frame] TED | HUGHES | [rule, 2.6 cm.] | Three Books | [rule, 2.6 cm.] | *Remains of Elmet | Cave Birds | River* | [Baskin drawing of an eagle]'. Spine: '[reading across, thin-thick rule] [reading down] TED HUGHES Three Books [reading across, at bottom of white panel:] ff | [thick-thin rule]'. Back: '[in a double-rule frame] ff | *faber and faber* | [blurb] | Cover drawing by Leonard Baskin | UK £8.99 net Canada $19.99 US $13.95 | [bar code]'.

19.7 × 12.7 cm., bulk 1.6 cm.; all edges cut. Printed offset.

CONTENTS: *Remains of Elmet:* the same selection published in *Elmet* (A60c), with the following omissions: Dick Straightup—Walt—The Horses—Wind—Roarers in a Ring—Pennines in April—Six Young Men—Slump Sundays—Climbing into Heptonstall—Heptonstall ('—old man ...')—Sacrifice—Telegraph Wires—For the Duration—Anthem for Doomed Youth.
Cave Birds: same as A46b. 'After There Was Nothing There Was a Woman' is retitled 'After There Was Nothing Came a Woman'.
River: a different selection from A85: Salmon Eggs—Japanese River Tales—Flesh of Light—The Merry Mink—Stump Pool in April—Whiteness—An August Salmon—Fairy Flood—The West Dart—1984 on 'The Tarka Trail'—Ophelia—Be a Dry-Fly Purist—A Rival—Dee—Salmon-Taking Times—Earth-Numb[1]—Caddis[2]—The Gulkana—Madly Singing in the Mountains—Go Fishing—If—

[1] From *Moortown*.
[2] From *Three River Poems*.

The Bear ('The day darkened in rain. ...')—The River[3]—Under the Hill of Centurions—Stealing Trout on a May Morning[4]—The Moorhen[5]—September Salmon—The Mayfly is Frail—A Cormorant —River Barrow—Catadrome[2]—Milesian Encounter on the Sliga-chan—High Water—Low Water—Night Arrival of Sea-Trout—An Eel—In the Dark Violin of the Valley—Strangers—The King-fisher—Visitation—Performance—Everything Is on its Way to the River—August Evening—Last Night—Eighty, and Still Fishing for Salmon—October Salmon—That Morning.

Published June 1993 (the British Library copy is stamped 11 May) at £8.99; number of copies undetermined.

REVIEWS: *Times*, 20 Jan. 1994.

A103   THE IRON WOMAN   1993

a.1. First edition:

THE IRON WOMAN | A Sequel to THE IRON MAN | *Ted Hughes* | Illustrated by ANDREW DAVIDSON | [woodcut of an otter] | ff | *faber and faber*

[1–3[16]] = 48 leaves. Pages (i–vi)1–87(88–90), consisting: (i) half-title, 'THE IRON WOMAN | A Sequel to | THE IRON MAN'; (ii) '*Also by Ted Hughes* | [33 titles]'; (iii) title page; (iv) 'First published in Great Britain on 7 September 1993 | by Faber and Faber Limited | 3 Queen Square London WC1N 3AU | Photoset by Parker Typesetting Service, Leicester | Printed in Great Britain by Clays Ltd, St Ives plc | All rights reserved | Text © Ted Hughes, 1993 | Illustrations © Andrew Davidson, 1993 | [notes regarding authorship and CIP data, and ISBN] | [printing code, 2–1]'; (v) 'For Frieda and Nicholas'; (vi) blank; 1–87 text; (88–90) blank. Text pages 6, 16, 34, 47, 50, 64, 72, 86 unnumbered.

Black calico-grain paper over boards. Spine round, stamped in white: 'THE IRON WOMAN   Ted Hughes [at foot, reading across] ff'.

Dust-wrapper glossy, coated outside, coloured black with coloured woodcut of the Iron Woman on front, continued on back, lettered in white and silver. Front: 'ff | TED HUGHES | THE IRON WOMAN | A sequel to *The Iron Man*'. Spine: on a black ground: 'THE IRON WOMAN   Ted Hughes [at foot, reading across] ff'. Back, at head, 'ff |

---

[3] = 'River'.

[4] From *Recklings*.

[5] From *Moon-Bells*, 2nd edn (A54b).

faber and faber'; at lower right, on white panel, bar code.

23.3 × 15.5 cm., bulk .8 cm.; all edges cut. Printed offset.

Published officially on 7 September 1993 (the British Library copy is stamped 6 August) at £9.99 ($19.99 in Canada); number of copies undetermined.

a.2. First paperback printing (1994):

THE IRON WOMAN | A Sequel to THE IRON MAN | *Ted Hughes* | *Illustrated by* ANDREW DAVIDSON | [woodcut of an otter] | ff | *faber and faber* | LONDON · BOSTON

48 leaves, 'perfect-bound'. Pages (i–vi)1–87(88–90), consisting: (i) blurb; (ii) '*by the same author* | [33 titles, a different arrangement from a.1]'; (iii) title page; (iv) 'First published in Great Britain in 1993 | by Faber and Faber Limited | 3 Queen Square London WC1N 3AU | This paperback edition first published in 1994 | Photoset by Parker Typesetting Service, Leicester | Printed in Great Britain by Clays Ltd St Ives plc | All rights reserved | Text © Ted Hughes, 1993 | Illustrations © Andrew Davidson, 1993 | [notes regarding authorship, Net Book Agreement and CIP data, and ISBN] | [printing code, 2–1]'; (v) 'For Frieda and Nicholas'; (vi) blank; 1–87 text, same setting as a.1, reduced; (88) blank; (89) advertisement for *The Iron Man* in paperback; (90) blank.

Wrappers, same illustration and basic design as the dust-wrapper to a.1 (silver lettering replaced by white on spine). Front and spine have same transcription. Back: 'ff | *faber and faber* | THE IRON WOMAN | A sequel to *The Iron Man* | [reviews] | Illustrated by Andrew Davison [sic] | [at bottom right] UK £3.99 net | Canada $6.99 | [on white panel, bar code]'.

19.7 × 12.5 cm., bulk .6 cm.; all edges cut. Printed offset.

Published September 1994 (the British Library copy is stamped 27 July) at £3.99 ($6.99 in Canada); number of copies undetermined.

b. First American edition (1995):

Ted Hughes | [flush to left] The [larger] Iron | Woman | [centred] *With Engravings by Barry Moser* | [publisher's logo, a sundial] | Dial Books · New York

[1–2^{16} 3^8 4^{16}] = 56 leaves (glued not sewn). Pages (1–9)10–109(110–112), consisting: (1) half-title; (2) blank; (3) '*Also by Ted Hughes* | [12 titles]'; (4) illustration of a bridge; (5) title page; (6) 'First published in the United States 1995 by | Dial Books | A Division of Penguin Books

USA Inc. | 375 Hudson Street | New York, New York 10014 | Published in Great Britain by Faber and Faber Limited | Text copyright © 1993 by Ted Hughes | Pictures copyright © 1995 by Barry Moser | All rights reserved | Designed by Barry Moser | Printed in the U.S.A. | First Edition | [printing code, 1–2] | [CIP data] | The images in this book were engraved on Resingrave™, | a synthetic engraving medium.'; (7) 'For Frieda and Nicholas | —T.H. | *And for Leonard Baskin* | —B.M.'; (8) illustration of girl looking down from a bridge; (9)10–109 text and illustrations; (110) blank; (111) biographies of Hughes and Moser; (112) blank. Text pages 20, 33, 47, 57, 71, 87, 99, 107 unnumbered.

Quarter black cloth (2.5 cm. onto sides), charcoal paper sides over boards. Spine round, stamped in copper: 'Hughes/Moser   The Iron Woman [at foot, reading across, publisher's logo as above] | Dial'. Endpapers brownish orange.

Dust-wrapper coated outside. Front with colour illustration of the Iron Woman; overprinted: '[brown] The [larger] Iron | Woman | [black] Ted Hughes | *With Engravings by Barry Moser*'. Spine and back coloured blue; spine lettered like book spine with author's, illustrator's, and publisher's names in white, title in reddish brown, logo in black and reddish brown. Back: on white panel, reduced illustration from p. 47; at foot, on white panel, bar code.

22.8 × 15.2 cm., bulk .8 cm.; all edges cut. Printed offset.

Published 4 September 1995 at $14.99; 10,000 copies printed. There have been no reprints.

REVIEWS: *Booklist*, Aug. 1995; *Books for Keeps*, Nov. 1994; *Guardian*, 21 Sept. 1993 (Joanna Carey); *Guardian Weekly*, 3 Oct. 1993; *Independent*, 25 Sept. 1993 (Christina Hardyment); *Magpies*, July 1994; *Publishers Weekly*, 17 July 1995; *Quill & Quire*, Feb. 1994; *School Librarian*, Nov. 1993; *School Library Journal*, Sept. 1995; *Spectator*, 11 Sept. 1993; *Sunday Times*, 12 Sept. 1993; *Sydney Morning Herald*, 22 Jan. 1994 (Andrea Sutton); *Times*, 16 Aug. 1993 (Brian Alderson); *Times Educational Supplement*, 3 Sept. 1993 (John Mole), 2 Dec. 1994.

A104   WINTER POLLEN   1994

a.1. First edition:

WINTER POLLEN | Occasional Prose | TED HUGHES | [rule, 4.8 cm.] | EDITED BY | WILLIAM SCAMMELL | ff | *faber and faber* | LONDON · BOSTON

[1–15¹⁶] = 240 leaves. Pages (i–iv)v–xiv(1)2–465(466), consisting: (i) half-title; (ii) '*Also by Ted Hughes* | [36 titles]'; (iii) title page; (iv) 'For

Carol | First published in 1994 | by Faber and Faber Limited | 3 Queen Square London WC1N 3AU | Set in Linotype Sabon | by Wilmaset Ltd, Birkenhead, Wirral | Printed in England by Clays Ltd, St Ives plc | All rights reserved | © Ted Hughes, 1994 | Introduction © William Scammell, 1994 | [authorship and CIP information, and ISBN] | [printing code, 2–1]'; v–vi table of contents; vii–viii acknowledgements; ix–xiv introduction by Scammell; 1–465 text; (466) blank. Text pages 1, 4, 10, 25, 27, 33, 36, 40, 42, 45, 48, 51, 56, 60, 68, 70, 73, 79, 84, 85, 103, 122, 128, 136, 154, 161, 163, 170, 177, 212, 220, 229, 237, 239, 244, 249, 268, 293, 373 unnumbered.

Black calico-grain paper over boards. Spine round, stamped in white, reading across: '[within a rule frame] ff | [rule] | TED | HUGHES | [rule] | Winter | Pollen'.

Whole dust-wrapper printed with colour miniature from the Saray Album (Topkapi Palace Museum). Front cover, lower left, on black panel, printed in gold: '[within a rule frame] ff | [rule] | TED HUGHES | [rule] | Winter Pollen | [rule] | *Occasional Prose* | [rule] | Edited by William Scammell'. Spine, on black panel, printed in gold: 'ff | [rule] | TED | HUGHES | [rule] | Winter | Pollen | [rule] | *Occasional* | *Prose*'. Back cover, at bottom, on white panel: bar code.

21.6 × 13.7 cm., bulk 3.6 cm.; all edges cut. Printed letterpress.

CONTENTS: Context—Fantastic Happenings and Gory Adventures—The Burnt Fox[1]—Poetry in the Making: Three Extracts (Capturing Animals, Learning to Think, Words and Experience)—A Word about Writing in Schools—Concealed Energies—Strong Feelings—Quitting—Asgard for Addicts—Unfinished Business—Dr Dung—Opposing Selves—Superstitions—Regenerations—Revelations: The Genius of Isaac Bashevis Singer—Music of Humanity—National Ghost—Tricksters and Tar Babies—Heavenly Visions—The Hanged Man and the Dragonfly—The Great Theme: Notes on Shakespeare—Orghast: Talking without Words—The Environmental Revolution—Myth and Education—Emily Dickinson—Sylvia Plath: *Ariel*—Publishing Sylvia Plath—Collecting Sylvia Plath—Sylvia Plath and Her Journals—Sylvia Plath: The Evolution of 'Sheep in Fog'[1]—Keith Douglas[2]—Vasko Popa—János Pilinszky—Laura Riding—Crow on the Beach[1]—Inner Music—Keats on the Difference between the Dreamer and the Poet—Poetry and Violence[1]—The Poetic Self: A Centenary Tribute to T.S. Eliot—Shakespeare and Occult Neoplatonism—Myths, Metres, Rhythms[1]—The Snake in the Oak[1].

[1] Previously unpublished.
[2] The version from B23, with postcripts.

Published 7 March 1994 (the British Library copy is stamped 28 January) at £17.50; number of copies undetermined.

a.2. First American printing of English edition:

$[1-13^{16} \ 14^8 \ 15-16^{16}] = 248$ leaves (glued not sewn).

Same setting as above except:

1. Title page rule is 5.1 cm. and imprint is 'Picador USA | New York | [publisher's device]'.
2. P. (iv): 'For Carol | WINTER POLLEN. Copyright © 1994, 1995 by Ted Hughes. Introduction | copyright © 1994 by William Scammell. All rights reserved. Printed in the | United States of America. [...] | [...] | [...] For information, | address Picador USA, 175 Fifth Avenue, New York, NY 10010. | Picador® is a U.S. registered trademark and is used by St. Martin's Press | under license from Pan Books Limited. | [CIP data] | First published in Great Britain by Faber and Faber Limited | First Picador USA Edition: October 1995 | [printing code, 10–1]'.
3. Pp. 466–481 are added, containing 'Sylvia Plath's *Collected Poems* and *The Bell Jar*' (previously uncollected), with p. (482) blank. A corresponding entry is added to the table of contents on p. vi.

Quarter black cloth (2.5 cm. onto sides), blue paper sides over boards. Spine round, stamped in silver: '[reading across, publisher's device] [reading down] Hughes Winter Pollen [reading across, at foot] Picador USA'. Endpapers coated blue-grey, with overall pattern of '**PICADOR** USA' in white.

Dust-wrapper printed blue except as noted. Front: photograph of Hughes; superimposed, in green, part of a draft of Plath's 'Sheep in Fog'; superimposed on these: '[white, on black band] TED HUGHES | [black, on white band] Poet Laureate of England | [black, on green band] Winter Pollen | [white, on black band] OCCASIONAL PROSE | [black, on white band] Edited by William Scammell'. Spine white, printed in black: '[reading across, black band] [reading down] Ted Hughes WINTER POLLEN [reading across] PICADOR | [rule] | USA | [red band]'. Back: '[white, on black strip] ACCLAIM FOR WINTER POLLEN | [blurbs, white on blue]' | [black on white panel, bar code]'.

23.3 × 15.6 cm., bulk 3.1 cm.; all edges cut. Printed offset, with the paper grain horizontal.

Published by 12 October 1995 (the date stamped in the Library of Congress copy) at $27.50; number of copies undetermined.

a.3. First paperback printing (1995):

Internally the same as Faber's first edition (a.1) except:
1. P. (ii): '*by the same author* | [34 titles including this one]'.
2. P. (iv): after publisher's address a line is inserted: 'This paperback edition first published in 1995'. After identification of the author is inserted a note about the Net Book Agreement. ISBN changed. At foot of page, printing code 2–1.

240 leaves, 'perfect-bound'.

Wrappers coated outside, coloured yellow. Front: 'ff | Ted Hughes | Winter Pollen | *Occasional Prose* | Edited by William Scammell | [panel: miniature from the Saray Album, continuing across spine to back]'. Spine, reading across: 'ff | Ted | Hughes | Winter | Pollen | *Occasional* | *Prose* | [continuation of illustration]'. Back printed in two columns; left: '[photograph of Hughes] | Photo by Jane Bown | [on white panel] UK £8.99 net | Canada $19.99 | US $14.95 | [vertical bar code]'. Right column: 'ff | *faber and faber* | [reviews] | [continuation of illustration] | [identification of illustration]'.

21.6 × 13.5 cm., bulk 3.6 cm.; all edges cut. Printed offset.

Published March 1995 (the British Library copy is stamped 25 January) at £8.99; number of copies undetermined.

REVIEWS: *Agenda*, Winter 1994 (Kathleen Raine); *Daily Telegraph*, 5 Mar. 1994 (Allan Massie), 4 Mar. 1995 (Stephen Spender); *Economist*, 2 July 1994; *Independent on Sunday*, 6 Mar. 1994 (Blake Morrison); *Observer*, 6 Mar. 1994, 20 Nov. 1994, 5 Mar. 1995; *Poetry Nation Review*, July–Aug. 1995 (R. A. Page); *Poetry Review*, Autumn 1994 (Sean O'Brien); *Publishers Weekly*, 21 Aug. 1995; *Resurgence*, May/June 1994 (Keith Sagar); *Spectator*, 12 Mar. 1994, 18 Mar. 1995; *Sunday Telegraph*, 20 Mar. 1994 (Ian Hamilton); *Sunday Times*, 6 Mar. 1994; *Sydney Morning Herald*, 20 May 1995 (Rhyll McMaster); *Times*, 10 Mar. 1994; *Times Educational Supplement*, 11 Mar. 1994 (John Mole); *Times Literary Supplement*, 6 May 1994 (John Bayley); *World Literature Today*, Spring 1996 (Sudeep Sen).

A105 POETRY (ПОЕЗИЈА) 1994

Ted Hughes | Тед Хјуз | [blue-filled letters, shaded black] POETRY | ПОЕЗИЈА | [regular type] Selection, translation and preface by | ZORAN ANČEVSKI | Избор, препев и предговор: | ЗОРАН АНЧЕВСКИ | [in blue, hawk drawing by Leonard Baskin] | *Detska Radost* | Skopje, Macedonia | „Детска радост"| Скопје, Македонија, | 1994

[1–31⁶] = 186 leaves. Pages (1–3)4–5(6–10)11–27(28–30)31–48(49–51)52–349(350–352)353–370(371–372), consisting: (1) half-title: '[stylized bird sitting on letters qp (standing for 'детска радост')] | NIP

Nova Makedonija | Redakcija *Detska Radost* | НИП „Нова
Македонија" | Реиакција „Детска радост" | [rule, 7.6 cm.] | Struga
Poetry Evenings | Струшки вечери на поезијата | [ornament, globe
between laurel branches] | Golden Wreath of the SPE 1994 | Златен
венец на СВП | 1994'; (2) '[flush at left] Drawings in this book are by
LEONARD BASKIN, from *Cave Birds: An Alchemical Cave* | *Drama*,
poems by TED HUGHES | [the same in Macedonian] | Art and graphic
design by | ALEKSANDAR CVETKOSKI | [the same in
Macedonian]'; (3) title page; 4, 'A MESSAGE BY **TED HUGHES,** |
THE GOLDEN WREATH AWARD WINNER FOR 1994, | TO THE
STRUGA POETRY EVENINGS | [letter from Hughes, 2 April 1994]';
5, the same in Macedonian; (6–7) colour photo of Hughes; at left,
reproduction in blue of the holograph of the letter transcribed on p. 4;
(8) blank; (9) divisional title '*PREFACE*' in shaded outline letters with
bird drawing by Baskin; (10) blank; 11–27, 'Naming the Darkness in
the Self', signed by Zoran Ančevski; (28) blank; (29) divisional title,
'*ПРЕДГОВОР*' in shaded outline letters with bird drawing by Baskin;
(30) blank; 31–48, preface in Macedonian; (49) divisional title, '[outline
letters] Ted Hughes: | [shaded outline letters] POEMS | [drawing of
hawk by Baskin] | [outline letters] Тед Хјуз: | [shaded outline letters]
ПЕСНИ'; (50) small version of the drawing on previous page; (51)
divisional title, '[bird drawing by Baskin] | [shaded outline letters, flush
right] *From* | *THE HAWK IN THE RAIN* | [rule, 10.4 cm.] | *Од* |
СОКОЛ НА ДОЖДОТ'; 52–349 text, English facing Macedonian;
(350) same as (50); (351) divisional title, '[bird drawing by Baskin] |
[shaded outline letters, flush right] *ХРОНОЛОГИЈА* | *и* | *БЕЛЕШКИ*';
(352) blank; 353–358 chronology in Macedonian; 359–364 notes in
Macedonian; 365–370 table of contents, bilingual; (371) parallel texts in
Macedonian and English, each in rule frame; the English version (on right):
'NIP *Nova Makedonija* | General Manager: | Pande Kolomiševski |
[ornament, globe between laurel branches] | Publisher: Redakcija *Detska
Radost* | Director and Editor-in-Chief: | Petre Bakevski | and | Struga Poetry
Evenings | President of the SPE Council: | Atanas Vangelov | [ornament, as
above] | Editorial Director: | Zdravko Korveziroski | Editor: | Slavomir
Marinkoviќ | Proofreading: | Deniz Thestorides | [ornament, as above] |
Printed by | NIP *Nova Makedonija,* | RE *Pečatnica* | Skopje, 1994 | Republic
of Macedonia'; (372) '*This book has been completely financed by the Republic of
Macedonia Ministry of* | *Culture.* | [the same in Macedonian] | [in rule frame,
CIP data] *Според Мислењето на Министерството за култура број 21-*
3524/2 од | *13.6.1994 година, за книгата „Поезија" од Тед Хјуз се плаќа*
повластена | *даночна сталка*'. Text pages 60, 61, 78, 79, 110, 111, 178,
179, 190, 191, 202, 203, 216, 217, 230, 231, 240, 241, 254, 255, 266, 267,
276, 277, 296, 297, 328, 329 unnumbered.

Dark-blue imitation morocco over boards, stamped in gold and silver. Front: 'TED HUGHES | ТЕД ХЈУЗ'. Spine flat, stamped reading up: 'TED HUGHES ● ТЕД ХЈУЗ'. Endpapers printed at the first and last openings in dark pink with a coarse halftone of a bridge on the Drim River in Struga. Rear free endpaper recto printed in black with translator's acknowledgements, bilingual. A white silk bookmark is bound in.

Dust-wrapper very glossy, outside printed blue with lettering in yellow and white. Front: 'TED HUGHES | ТЕД ХЈУЗ | GOLDEN WREATH | ЗЛАТЕН ВЕНЕЦ | *1994* | STRUGA ● СТРУА'. Spine: '[reading up] TED HUGHES [in brown:] ● [in white] ТЕД ХЈУЗ'; at foot, reading across: '[ornament as on p. 371] | GOLDEN | WREATH | [double rule] | ЗЛАТЕН ВЕНЕЦ | 1994'. Back: '[colour illustration of arms of Macedonia] | GOLDEN | WREATH | [double rule, 3.9 cm.] | ЗЛАТЕН ВЕНЕЦ | 1994'.

Paper glossy, 22.0 × 22.9 cm., bulk 1.75 cm.; all edges cut. Printed offset.

CONTENTS:[1] [From *The Hawk in the Rain*] The Thought-Fox—The Jaguar.

[From *Lupercal*] Hawk Roosting—Relic—Thrushes—Pike.

[From *Wodwo* I] Thistles—The Green Wolf—Theology—Gog—Pibroch—Gnat-Psalm—Full Moon and Little Frieda—Wodwo.

[From *Crow*] Examination at the Womb-Door—A Childish Prank—Crow's First Lesson—Crow Hears Fate Knock on the Door—Crow Tyrannosaurus—The Black Beast—The Battle of Osfrontalis—Crow's Fall—Crow and the Birds—The Contender—Crow's Vanity—A Horrible Religious Error—Conjuring in Heaven—Crow Goes Hunting—Owl's Song—Revenge Fable—Apple Tragedy—Crow's Last Stand—Crow and the Sea—Fragments [sic] of an Ancient Tablet—Lovesong.

[From *Moortown* I]: The Lovepet—King of Carrion—Littleblood.

[From *Cave Birds*] The Knight—Bride and Groom Lie Hidden for Three Days.

[From *Season Songs*] Swifts—The Harvest Moon.

[From *Gaudete*] Collision with the Earth Has Finally Come—This is the Maneater's Skull—I See the Oak's Bride in the Oak's Grasp—Waving Goodbye, from Your Banked Hospital Bed—Your Tree [dash] Your Oak.

[From *Remains of Elmet*] When Men Got to the Summit—Widdop—Emily Brontë—Heptonstall Old Church.

[From *Moortown* II] Ravens—February 17th.

---

[1] Sources are given as in table of contents, but some poems are dropped into these groupings from other sources.

[From *Prometheus on His Crag*] Now I Know I Never Shall—Prometheus on His Crag Began to Admire the Vulture.

[From *Earth-Numb*] A Motorbike—Life Is Trying to Be Life.

[From *Seven Dungeon Songs*] Prospero and Sycorax—Go Fishing.

[From *River*] The River—Milesian Encounter on the Sligachan—An Eel—October Salmon—That Morning.

[Uncollected] Reckless Head[2]—Opus 131[3]—Lines about Elias—The Last of the 1st/5th Lancashire Fusiliers from the May 6th 1915 Landing—Anecdote[4].

Published 20 July 1994; 500 copies printed. The book was distributed free to participants, journalists, and guests of the Struga Poetry Festival in August; leftover copies were sent to libraries in Macedonia.

A106   EARTH DANCES   1994

[flush to left, in brown] EARTH | DANCES | [black] poems by | [indented] Ted Hughes | [flush to left] chosen & decorated by | [further indented] R. J. Lloyd | [flush to right, in brown, printer's mark, a stile] [black] The Old Stile Press

$[1-4^6] = 24$ leaves. Pages (1–6)7(8–10)11(12)13–43(44–48), consisting: (1–3) blank; (4) frontispiece illustration; (5) title page; (6) blank; 7, poem, 'Epigraph | *for Reg* | [...]'; (8) blank; (9) illustration; (10) blank; 11, table of contents; (12) illustration; 13–43 text; (44) 'Colophon | *Epigraph* is printed here for the first time. *Barley* is as yet | uncollected but the remaining poems are taken from the | collections referred to on page 11, and are reprinted here | with the permission of Faber & Faber Ltd. | poems © Ted Hughes 1994 | linocuts © R. J. Lloyd 1994 | type & layout © The Old Stile Press 1994 | ISBN: 0 907664 33 4 | The text was hand set in 18 point Bembo (with Bodoni) by | Nicolas McDowall, who completed the printing of the text | and of R. J. Lloyd's linocut images (which were printed from | the lino) in December 1994 at The Old Stile Press, Catchmays | Court, Llandogo, Monmouth, Gwent NP5 4TN. | The text paper is 160gsm Rivoli while the main images are | printed on papers handmade by Frances McDowall (they are | also used on the covers) which incorporate iris, nettle, onion, | Japanese knotweed, pampas grass and alkanet fibres. | The binding was designed at The Old Stile Press and was | executed at The Fine Bindery, Wellingborough. | The edition is limited to 250 copies. Each copy is numbered and signed by Ted Hughes and R. J. Lloyd. This is number [number] | [signatures]'; (45) blank; (46) illustration; (47–48) blank. Sheet 2.5 of each gathering is

---

[2] Published as a separate the previous year (A101).

[3] From *Capriccio*.

[4] From *Crow Wakes*.

handmade paper printed with illustrations in black, and these pages are unpaginated. The text pages also have linocuts printed in brown.

Handmade paper over boards, green cloth spine, flat, stamped in gold: 'TED HUGHES *EARTH DANCES* R. J. LLOYD'. Endpapers reddish brown.

In a slip-case covered with brown cloth, lined with reddish-brown paper, sides stamped in bluish-black with Lloyd designs.

Text paper plain white; interleaved illustrations on handmade laid paper (chains vertical, 2.8–3.9 cm.) watermarked '[stile] | fMcD'. Overall ca. 31.8 × 22.5 cm., bulk .6 cm.; top edge, and all edges of the white text paper, cut; fore- and bottom edges of handmade leaves deckle. Printed letterpress.

CONTENTS: Epigraph[1]—October Dawn—Fern—August Evening—Willow-Herb—Sugar Loaf—Low Water—Barley[1]—September—Bridestones—Thistles—Shackleton Hill[2]—Hill-Stone Was Content—Walls—Japanese River Tale[3]—Night Arrival of Sea Trout—Autumn Nature Notes 1[4]—Autumn Nature Notes 2[5]—Solstice [first 15 lines only]—The Morning before Christmas [first 8 lines only].

Published around Christmas 1994 at £195.00; 250 copies printed. An unknown number of copies were sold in sheets to design bookbinders.

A107   NEW SELECTED POEMS 1957–1994   1995

[flush to left] TED HUGHES | New Selected Poems | 1957–1994 | [indented] ff | [flush to left] *faber and faber*

[1–11^{16}] = 176 leaves. Pages (i–iv)v–xiii(xiv)(1–2)3–316(317–318)319–332(333–338), consisting: (i) half-title: flush to left, 'NEW SELECTED POEMS 1957–1994'; (ii) '[flush to left] *by the same author* | [35 titles]'; (iii) title page; (iv) 'This selection first published in 1995 | by Faber and Faber Limited | 3 Queen Square London WC1N 3AU | Typeset by Wilmaset Ltd, Wirral | Printed in England by Clays Ltd, St Ives plc | All rights reserved | © Ted Hughes, 1995 | [notes regarding authorship and CIP record, and ISBN numbers]'; v–xiii table of contents; (xiv) blank; (1) half-title, 'NEW SELECTED POEMS'; (2) blank; 3–316 text; (317) '[flush to left]

---

[1] Previously uncollected.
[2] = 'Dead Farms, Dead Leaves'.
[3] = 'Japanese River Tales', part 1.
[4] = 'Autumn Nature Notes', part 2.
[5] = 'Autumn Nature Notes', part 7.

INDEXES'; (318) blank; 319–332 indexes; (333–338) blank. Text pages 22, 44, 120, 130, 174, 192, 210, 222, 234, 242 unnumbered.

Dark blue calico-grain paper over boards. Spine round, stamped in light green, reading across: 'ff | Ted | Hughes | New | Selected | Poems | 1957–1994'.

Dust-wrapper medium glossy, coated outside. Front: 'ff | POETRY | Ted Hughes | New Selected Poems | 1957–1994 | [colour botanical illustration, continued to spine]'. Spine printed like book spine, in black. Back printed in two columns; left: '[photograph of Hughes] | Photo by Jane Bown | [in rule frame, vertical bar code]'. Right column: 'ff | *faber and faber* | Also by Ted Hughes | [reviews of *Elmet* and *Winter Pollen*] | [identification of botanical illustration]'.

21.6 × 13.7 cm., bulk 2.7 cm.; all edges cut. Printed offset.

CONTENTS:[1] [From *The Hawk in the Rain*] The Thought-Fox—Song—The Jaguar—Famous Poet—Soliloquy—The Horses—Fallgrief's Girlfriends—Egg-Head—Vampire—The Man Seeking Experience Enquires His Way of a Drop of Water—Meeting—Wind—October Dawn—The Casualty—Bayonet Charge—Six Young Men—The Martyrdom of Bishop Farrar—Song from *Bawdry Embraced*[2].

[From *Lupercal*] Mayday on Holderness—February—Crow Hill—A Woman Unconscious—Strawberry Hill—Fourth of July—Esther's Tomcat—Wilfred Owen's Photographs—Relic—Hawk Roosting—Fire-Eater—To Paint a Water Lily—The Bull Moses—Cat and Mouse—View of a Pig—The Retired Colonel—November—An Otter—Witches—Thrushes—Snowdrop—Pike—Sunstroke—Cleopatra to the Asp.

['Uncollected', but in fact published in limited editions:]
Recklings: Stealing Trout on a May Morning—Water—Memory—Tutorial—Trees—The Lake—A Match—Small Events.
Crow Wakes.

[From *Wodwo*] Thistles—Still Life—Her Husband—Cadenza—Ghost Crabs—Public Bar TV[3]—Kafka—Second Glance at a Jaguar—Fern—Stations—The Green Wolf—The Bear—Scapegoats and Rabies—Theology—Gog—Kreutzer Sonata—Out—New Moon in January—The Warriors of the North—Song of a Rat—Heptonstall—Skylarks—Pibroch—The Howling of Wolves—Gnat-Psalm—Full Moon and Little Frieda—Wodwo.

[From *Crow*] Two Legends—Lineage—Examination at the Womb-

---

[1] Sources are given as in table of contents, but some poems are dropped into these groupings from other sources.
[2] The last six stanzas from 'Bawdry Embraced', actually taken from *Recklings*.
[3] First line 'On a flaked ridge of the desert'.

Door—A Childish Prank—Crow's First Lesson—That Moment—
Crow Tyrannosaurus—The Black Beast—Crow's Account of the
Battle—Crow's Fall—Crow and the Birds—Crow on the Beach—
The Contender—Crow's Vanity—A Horrible Religious Error—In
Laughter—Robin Song—Conjuring in Heaven—Owl's Song—
Crow's Elephant Totem Song—Dawn's Rose—The Smile—Crow's
Battle Fury—Crow Blacker than Ever—Revenge Fable—Bedtime
Anecdote[4]—Apple Tragedy—Crow's Last Stand—Fragment of an
Ancient Tablet—Lovesong—Notes for a Little Play—The Love-
pet—How Water Began to Play—Littleblood.
[From *Cave Birds*] The Scream—The Executioner—The Knight—A
Flayed Crow in the Hall of Judgement—The Guide—His Legs Ran
About—Bride and Groom Lie Hidden for Three Days—The Risen.
[From *Season Songs*] A March Calf—The River in March—Apple
Dumps—Swifts—Sheep[5]—Evening Thrush—The Harvest Moon—
Leaves—from 'Autumn Notes'[6]—A Cranefly in September.
[From *Gaudete*] Collision with the Earth Has Finally Come—Once I
Said Lightly—This is the Maneater's Skull—I See the Oak's Bride in
the Oak's Grasp—A Primrose Petal's Edge—Waving Goodbye, from
Your Banked Hospital Bed—The Swallow [dash] Rebuilding—The
Grass-Blade is Not Without—I Know Well—Sometimes It Comes, a
Gloomy Flap of Lightning—Calves Harshly Parted from their
Mamas—A Bang [dash] a Burning—At the Bottom of the Arctic
Sea, They Say—Your Tree [dash] Your Oak.
[From *Remains of Elmet*] Football at Slack—Stanbury Moor[7]—Leaf
Mould—Moors—Chinese History of Colden Water[8]—Rhododendrons
—Sunstruck—Curlews [both parts]—For Billy Holt—When Men
Got to the Summit—The Canal's Drowning Black—Cock-Crows—
Mount Zion[9]—The Long Tunnel Ceiling—Tree—Heptonstall Old
Church—Widdop—Emily Brontë.
[From *Moortown Diary*] Rain—Dehorning—Bringing in New Couples—
Tractor—Roe-Deer—Sketching a Thatcher—Ravens—February
17th—Birth of Rainbow—Coming Down Through Somerset—The
Day He Died—A Memory[10].
[From *Earth-Numb*] Earth-Numb—A Motorbike—Deaf School—Life Is
Trying to Be Life—Speech out of Shadow.

---

[4] = 'Anecdote'.
[5] All three parts.
[6] Autumn Nature Notes', parts 3–6.
[7] = 'These Grasses of Light'.
[8] = A revision of 'The Trance of Light'.
[9] Part 1 only.
[10] Begins 'Your bony white bowed back'.

[From *Seven Dungeon Songs*[13]] Dead, She Became Space-Earth—Face Was Necessary [dash] I Found Face—The Earth Locked Out the Light—I Walk—If Mouth Could Open its Cliff.
Tiger-Psalm.

[From *Orts*] In the M5 Restaurant—That Star—Poets—Grosse Fuge—Children—Prospero and Sycorax.
The Beacon (I. The Stone—II. TV Off).
A God.

[Uncollected] Remembering Teheran—Bones[12]—Do Not Pick up the Telephone[13]—Reckless Head[14].

[From *Prometheus on His Crag*] Prometheus on His Crag Relaxes—Prometheus on His Crag Pestered by Birds Roosting and Defecating—Now I Know I Never Shall—Prometheus on His Crag Began to Admire the Vulture—Prometheus on His Crag Sees the Wind—Prometheus on His Crag Shouts and His Words.

[From *Flowers and Insects*] A Violet at Lough Aughresberg (sic)—Two Tortoiseshell Butterflies—Where I Sit Writing My Letter—Tern—The Honey Bee—Sunstruck Foxglove—Eclipse—In the Likeness of a Grasshopper.

[From *What Is the Truth?*] New Foal—The Hen—The Hare.

[From *River*] The River—Milesian Encounter on the Sligachan—Low Water—Japanese River Tales—Ophelia—Strangers—The Gulkana—Go Fishing—Salmon Eggs—A Cormorant—An Eel—Performance—Night Arrival of Sea-Trout—October Salmon—That Morning.

[From *Wolfwatching*] Astrological Conundrums (I. The Fool's Evil Dream; II. Nearly Awake; III. Tell)—Dust As We Are—Telegraph Wires—Sacrifice—For the Duration—Walt (I. Under High Wood; II. The Atlantic)—Little Whale Song—On the Reservations (I. Sitting Bull on Christmas Morning; II. Nightvoice; III. The Ghost Dancer).

[From *Rain-Charm for the Duchy*] Rain-Charm for the Duchy.

[Uncollected] Old Oats—The Last of the 1st/5th Lancashire Fusiliers[11]—Anniversary—Chaucer—You Hated Spain[13]—The Earthenware Head—The Tender Place—Black Coat—Being Christlike—The God—The Dogs Are Eating Your Mother—The Other—The Locket—Shibboleth[15]—Snow[15]—Folktale[15]—Opus[16]—Descent[15]—The Error[15]—Lines about Elias[11].

A Dove[17].

---

[11] Collected in 1994 in *Poetry* (*Поезија*) (A105).
[12] From *Crow Wakes*.
[13] Collected in *New Selected Poems*.
[14] Actually published as a separate in 1993 (A101).
[15] From *Capriccio*.
[16] = 'Opus 131' from *Capriccio*.
[17] From *A Primer of Birds*.

Published officially on 6 March 1995 at £14.99 ($35.00 in Canada, $22.95 in the U.S.); number of copies undetermined. A copy belonging to one of the compilers is signed and dated by Hughes 25 February; the British Library copy of the paperback is stamped 25 January. A second printing bears printing code 10–2 on verso title. The paperback printing was issued simultaneously at £7.99 ($18.99 in Canada, $12.95 in the U.S.); it is the same internally except for the addition of the Net Book Agreement note and printing code 10–1 on verso title.

REVIEWS: *Agenda*, Autumn 1994; *Contemporary Review*, June 1995; *Daily Telegraph*, 4 Mar. 1995 (Stephen Spender); *Independent on Sunday*, 26 Mar. 1995 (Hugh Haughton); *Literary Review* (Madison, N.J.), March 1995 (Robert Nye); *London Magazine*, June/July 1995 (Nick Gammage); *New Statesman & Society*, 14 Apr. 1995; *Observer*, 5 Mar. 1995; *Poetry Review*, Spring 1995 (Don Paterson); *Spectator*, 18 Mar. 1995; *Sunday Times*, 5 Mar. 1995; *Sydney Morning Herald*, 20 May 1995 (Rhyll McMaster); *Times*, 23 Mar. 1995 (Daniel Johnson); *Times Literary Supplement*, 21 Apr. 1995 (Simon Armitage); *World Literature Today*, Spring 1996 (Peter Firehow).

A108   THE DREAMFIGHTER   1995

The Dreamfighter | and Other | Creation Tales | TED HUGHES | ff | *faber and faber*

80 leaves, 'perfect-bound'. Pages (i–viii)1–150(151–152), consisting: (i) half-title, 'THE DREAMFIGHTER | AND OTHER CREATION TALES'; (ii) *'by the same author* | [35 titles]'; (iii) title page; (iv) 'First published in Great Britain in 1995 | by Faber and Faber Limited | 3 Queen Square London WC1N 3AU | in association with Jackanory | Typeset by Wilmaset Ltd, Wirral | Printed in England by Clays Ltd, St Ives plc | All rights reserved | © Ted Hughes, 1995 | [note on identity of author and CIP record, and ISBN] | [printing code, 2–1]'; (v) 'for Carol'; (vi) blank; (vii) table of contents; (viii) blank; 1–150 text; (151–152) blank.

Blue calico-grain paper over boards. Spine round, stamped in very light green: 'TED HUGHES   The Dreamfighter and Other Creation Tales [at foot of spine, reading across] ff'.

Dust-wrapper coated outside. Front: colour illustration of ant and space-beings by Chris Riddell; overprinted: 'ff | TED HUGHES | The Dreamfighter | and Other Creation Tales'. Spine printed like book spine, in black. Back: 'ff | *faber and faber* | Other Creation Tales by Ted Hughes: | [blurbs for *How the Whale Became* and *Tales of the Early World*] | Jacket illustration by Chris Riddell | [bar code]'.

19.8 × 12.6 cm., bulk .9 cm.; all edges cut. Printed offset.

CONTENTS: Goku—The Dreamfighter—Gozzie—How God Got His Golden Head—The Moon and Loopy Downtail—The Gambler—The Screw—Camel—The Grizzly Bear and the Human Child—The Last of the Dinosaurs—The Secret of Man's Wife.

Published March 1995 (the British Library copy is stamped 14 February) at £10.99 ($18.99 in Canada, $16.95 in the U.S.); number of copies undetermined. A paperback printing did not appear until 1996.

REVIEWS: *Junior Bookshelf*, June 1995; *Sunday Times*, 16 Apr. 1995; *Times Educational Supplement*, 10 Mar. 1995 (Leon Garfield).

A109   SPRING AWAKENING   1995

FRANK WEDEKIND | Spring Awakening | in a new version | by Ted Hughes | ff | *faber and faber* | LONDON · BOSTON

48 leaves, 'perfect-bound'. Pages (i–viii)1–84(85–88), consisting: (i–ii) blank; (iii) 'Frank Wedekind: Spring Awakening | in a new version by Ted Hughes | [capsule biographies of Wedekind and Hughes'; (iv) '*also by Ted Hughes* | [37 titles]'; (v) title page; (vi) 'First published in 1995 | by Faber and Faber Limited | 3 Queen Square London WC1N 3AU | Photoset by Parker Typesetting Service, Leicester | Printed in England by Clays Ltd, St Ives plc | All rights reserved | © Ted Hughes, 1995 | [notes regarding authorship, rights, Net Book Agreement, and CIP record, with ISBN] | [printing code, 2–1]'; (vii) 'This version of **Spring Awakening** was first performed by | the Royal Shakespeare Company at The Pit in the | Barbican, London, on 2 August 1995. The cast was as | follows: | [...]'; (viii) list continued; 1–84 text; (85–88) blank.

Wrappers, coated outside. Front: 'ff | PLAYS | Frank Wedekind | Spring Awakening | A new version by | Ted Hughes | [colour reproduction of *Puberty* by Edvard Munch]'. Spine: '[reading across] ff [reading down] Wedekind **Spring Awakening** Ted Hughes'. Back: 'ff | *faber and faber* | [blurb] | [in rule frame] UK £6.99 net | Canada $13.99 | US $10.95 | [vertical bar code] [to right, identification of cover painting]'.

19.7 × 12.7 cm., bulk .7 cm.; all edges cut. Printed offset.

Published by 29 August 1995 (the date stamped in the British Library copy) at £6.99; number of copies undetermined.

A110   SHAKESPEARE'S OVID   1995

[in black and pea green] TED HUGHES | SHAKESPEARE'S | OVID | CHRISTOPHER LE BRUN | [Blakean illustration of women with spinning-wheels] | ENITHARMON PRESS | MCMXCV

[1–6⁴] = 24 leaves. Pages [1–2](i–vi)vii–viii(ix–x)(1–2)3–30(31–36), consisting: [1–2] blank; (i) half-title; (ii) blank; (iii) title page; (iv) 'Published in 1995 | by Stephen Stuart-Smith | at the Enitharmon Press | 36 St George's Avenue | London N7 0HD | Text © Ted Hughes 1995 | Images © Christopher Le Brun 1995 | ISBN 1 870612 94 9 | Printed and made in Great Britain'; (v) '[table of contents] | Christopher Le Brun's drawings | 'Venus and Adonis' and 'Salmacis and Hermaphroditus' | are reproduced after their respective part-titles. | His original etching, 'Atalanta and Hippomenes', is contained | in a wallet in the slipcase of the de luxe edition | [star ornament] | This book is published in aid of | the Shakespeare Globe Trust and its appeal | to rebuild the Globe Theatre, | [...]'; (vi) blank; vii–viii(ix) introduction by Hughes; (x) blank; (1) divisional title, 'VENUS AND | ADONIS'; (2) blank; 3–30 text; (31–32) blank; (33) 'Ted Hughes's translations were commissioned | by Michael Hofmann and James Lasdun for *After Ovid:* | *New Metamorphoses* (Faber and Faber, 1994). | The text of *Shakespeare's Ovid* has been | designed and printed by Sebastian Carter of the | Rampant Lions Press, Cambridge. The introduction is | set in 14 pt Perpetua and the main text hand-set in | Eric Gill's Golden Cockerel roman. The paper is | 160 gsm Arches Vélin. The books have been | bound by The Fine Bindery, Northamptonshire, | who also made the slipcases for the de luxe edition. | Christopher Le Brun's etching has been printed | on 300 gsm Somerset TP at Hope Sufferance Press in | London, in an edition comprising fifty impressions | signed and numbered 1 to 50, fifteen *hors commerce* | impressions, signed and numbered i to xv, and twenty | artist's proofs, numbered AP 1 to 20. | The facsimiles of Christopher Le Brun's two drawings | have been printed by Expression Printers Ltd. | The de luxe edition consists of fifty copies and fifteen | *hors commerce* copies, slipcased and numbered 1 to 50 | and i to xv, all of which are signed by Ted Hughes | and Christopher Le Brun, and accompanied | by Le Brun's etching. A regular edition | of one hundred and fifty cloth-bound copies, | signed by Ted Hughes, is numbered 51 to 200. | This is number [number] | [Hughes' signature, in copies 51–200]'; (34–36) blank. Text pages 22–24 unnumbered. The drawings, printed in black-and-white halftone, are inserted after pp. (2) and (24).

Copies 51–200: light yellow-brown cloth over boards with printed labels on blind-stamped panels. Front: '[in black and pea green] TED HUGHES | SHAKESPEARE'S | OVID | CHRISTOPHER LE BRUN'. Spine (round): 'SHAKESPEARE'S OVID'. Special copies not seen.

Paper mould-made wove, marked 'ARCHES | FRANCE ∞ | T', ca. 32 × 25 cm., bulk .8 cm.; top edge cut, fore- and bottom edges 'deckle'. Printed letterpress.

CONTENTS: Venus and Adonis—Salmacis and Hermaphroditus.

Published 1 September 1995 at £450.00 for copies 1–50, £100.00 for the rest.

A111   DIFFICULTIES OF A BRIDEGROOM   1995

a.1. First edition:

Difficulties | of a Bridegroom | [rule, 2.1 cm.] | TED HUGHES | ff | *faber and faber*

$[1-2^{16}\ 3-4^{12}\ 5-6^{16}] = 88$ leaves. Pages [1–2](i–vi)vii–ix(x)1–159(160–164), consisting: [1–2] blank; (i) half-title; (ii) '*by the same author* | [36 titles]'; (iii) title page; (iv) 'This collection first published in 1995 | by Faber and Faber Limited | 3 Queen Square London WC1N 3AU | Typeset by Wilmaset Ltd, Wirral | Printed in England by Clays Ltd, St Ives plc | All rights reserved | © Ted Hughes, 1995 | [notes regarding authorship and CIP record, and ISBN] | [printing code, 2–1]'; (v) table of contents; (vi) blank; vii–ix foreword by Hughes; (x) blank; 1–159 text; (160–164) blank.

Dark blue calico-grain paper over boards. Spine round, stamped in very light green: '[reading across] ff [reading down, flush at left] Ted Hughes | Difficulties of a Bridegroom'.

Dust-wrapper medium glossy. Front: colour illustration of Zimbabwean rock paintings (predominantly brown) continuing across spine to back; overprinted: 'ff | Ted Hughes | Difficulties of a Bridegroom | Collected Short Stories'. Spine printed like book spine, in black. Back printed in two columns; left: '[photo of Hughes, copyright Niall McDiarmid] | [on white panel, vertical bar code]'. Right: 'ff | *faber and faber* | Other books by Ted Hughes: | [reviews of 7 titles] | [identification of cover illustration]'.

19.7 × 12.8 cm., bulk 1.3 cm.; all edges cut. Printed offset.

CONTENTS: The Deadfall—O'Kelley's Angel—Snow[1]—Sunday[1]—The Rain Horse[1]—The Harvesting[1]—The Wound[1]—The Suitor[1]—The Head.

Published September 1995 (the British Library copy is stamped 1 August) at £12.99 ($24.99 in Canada, $19.95 in U.S.); number of copies undetermined.

[1] Previously collected in *Wodwo*.

a.2. First American printing:

Same setting as a.1 except for the following:

1. Title page imprint is 'Picador USA | New York | [publisher's device]'.
2. Page facing title has 'Also by Ted Hughes | [37 titles]'.
3. Verso title has 'DIFFICULTIES OF A BRIDEGROOM. Copyright © 1995 by Ted | Hughes. All rights reserved. Printed in the United States of | America. [...] | [...] | [CIP data] | First published in Great Britain by Faber and Faber Limited | First Picador USA Edition: October 1995 | [printing code, 10–1]'.
4. Pages numbered (i–viii)ix–xi(xii–xiv)1–159(160–162).

Glued binding, no structure discernible.

Quarter white cloth, orange-brown paper over boards; spine stamped in red: '[reading across, publisher's device] [reading down] HUGHES Difficulties of a Bridegroom   Picador USA'. Endpapers coated blue-grey, with all-over pattern of '**PICADOR** USA' in white in three different sizes.

Dust-wrapper coated. Front: '[on blue panel, in white] Ted Hughes | [in orange] Poet Laureate *of* England | [below blue panel, white area; overlapping both, photograph by Henry Ausloos of horses running through shallow water, printed in red] | [black on white ground] DIFFICULTIES of | a BRIDEGROOM | [white on yellow-orange panel] COLLECTED STORIES'. Spine, black on white: 'Ted Hughes   DIFFICULTIES OF A BRIDEGROOM   PICADOR | USA'. Back: blurbs printed in white on blue panel; below panel, black on white in rule frame, bar code. Back flap has photograph of Hughes by Niall McDiarmid. Dust-wrapper designed by Henry Sene Yee and Debbie Bishop.

Published October 1995 at $20.00; number of copies undetermined.

REVIEWS: *Independent on Sunday*, 24 Sept. 1995 (Michelle Roberts); *Literary Review* (Madison, N.J.), Oct. 1995 (Sam Dutton); *Sunday Times*, 10 Sept. 1995; *Times Educational Supplement*, 15 Sept. 1995; *Times Literary Supplement*, 17 Nov. 1995 (M.I.); *Weekend Financial Times*, 30 Sept. 1995; *World Literature Today*, Spring 1996 (Sudeep Sen).

A112   COLLECTED ANIMAL POEMS   1995

a.1. Numbered proof copies:

Four volumes bound in one. A total of 207 leaves, 'perfect-bound', as follows:

A preliminary leaf printed on recto only: 'THESE ARE UNCOR-RECTED PROOFS. ALL QUOTATIONS OR | ATTRIBUTIONS

SHOULD BE CHECKED AGAINST THE | BOUND COPY OF THE BOOK. WE URGE THIS FOR THE SAKE | OF EDITORIAL ACCURACY AS WELL AS FOR YOUR LEGAL | PROTECTION. | No [number, stamped by machine] in a limited edition of 292 | [signature of Hughes]'.

The Iron Wolf: pages (iii–vi), (ix–xii (here numbered v–vii, last recto unnumbered)), and 1–85(86) of the published version (see a.2(A) below). The verso title has 'Cased version' at top. The illustrations are either sketches of the final versions, or absent.

What Is the Truth?: pages (i–iv), vii–viii (here numbered v–vi), and 1–114 of the published version (see a.2(B) below). The verso title bears the Net Book Agreement note from the paperback printing (a.3(B)); the page numbers in the table of contents are not yet filled in; the text is unpaginated. The illustrations are the final versions, but the last one is lacking.

A March Calf: pages (iii–vi), (ix–x), and 1–117(118) of the published version (see a.2(C) below). The verso title bears the Net Book Agreement note from the paperback printing (a.3(C)) and has 'Paperback version' at head; pages (ix–x) and 117 are differently formatted.

The Thought-Fox: pages (i–iv), (vii–viii), and 1–67 of the published version (see a.2(D) below). The verso title bears the Net Book Agreement note from the paperback printing (a.3(D)) and has 'Paperback version' at head; page (vii) is differently formatted; the verso of p. 67 is blank.

In all four parts the imprint on the title page is wholly or partly missing, and in all but *What Is the Truth?* the title page illustration is missing.

Wrappers, glossy. Front: 'ff | Collected Animal Poems | Volumes 1–4 | *published in four individual volumes* | [drawing of a hare, reduced from p. 93 of *What is the Truth?*] | UNCORRECTED PROOF'. Spine: '[reading across] ff [reading down] **Ted Hughes** Collected Animal Poems Volumes 1–4   UNCORRECTED PROOF'. Back: 'ff | *faber and faber* | [blurb, features of promotion, and prices] | 4 September 1995'; near foot, reading up at spine, 'Cover illustration by Lisa Flather from *What is the Truth?*'.

20.35 × 13.95 cm., bulk 2.15 cm.; all edges cut. Printed by an electrostatic process.

Published at an undetermined date in 1995.

a.2. First published edition:

Four volumes, each with the following characteristics:

[Title pages:] [indented] Ted Hughes | [flush to left] COLLECTED ANIMAL POEMS | VOLUME [number] | [indented, upper- and lowercase: volume title as given below] | [illustration] | ff | [flush to left] *faber and faber* | LONDON · BOSTON

Black calico-grain paper over boards. Spine flat, stamped in very light green: '[reading across] ff | [reading down] Ted Hughes [volume title as given below] | [at foot, reading across, volume number]'.

Dust-wrappers medium glossy, coated outside. Front: 'ff | POETRY | Ted Hughes | Collected Animal Poems: Volume [number] | [volume title] | [illustration]'. Spine lettered like book spine, in black. Back: 'ff | *faber and faber*'.

19.75 × 12.7–12.9 cm.; all edges cut. Printed offset.

The four volumes in a slip-case, boards covered with coated paper. With respect to the open end, the left side has illustration of a rabbit. Right side: 'ff | *faber and faber* | Ted Hughes | Collected Animal Poems | Volume 1 | The Iron Wolf | Volume 2 | What is the Truth? | Volume 3 | A March Calf | Volume 4 | The Thought-Fox'. Back: 'UK £35.00 net | Canada $75.00 | US $55.00 | [bar code] | Illustration by Lisa Flather'.

(A): The Iron Wolf

Title page has 'The Iron Wolf | Illustrated by Chris Riddell | [black-and-white version of dust-wrapper illustration of the iron wolf]'.

$[1^{16}\ 2\text{–}3^{12}\ 4^{16}] = 56$ leaves; pages (i–xii)1–85(86)87–89(90)91–93(94–100), consisting: (i–ii) blank; (iii) half-title, '[flush at left] COLLECTED ANIMAL POEMS VOLUME 1 | The Iron Wolf'; (iv) '[flush at left] COLLECTED ANIMAL POEMS | [list of volumes]'; (v) title page; (vi) 'First published in Great Britain in 1995 | by Faber and Faber Limited | 3 Queen Square London WC1N 3AU | Photoset by Wilmaset Ltd, Birkenhead, Wirral | Printed in England by Clays Ltd, St Ives plc | All rights reserved | This collection © Ted Hughes, 1995 | Illustrations © Chris Riddell, 1995 | [notes on identification of author and CIP record, and ISBN numbers] | [printing code, 10–1]'; (vii) 'to Olwyn and Gerald'; (viii) blank; (ix–x) table of contents; (xi) poem 'Amulet'; (xii) blank; 1–84 text; 85, list of sources; (86) blank; 87–89 index of first lines; (90) blank; 91–93 subject index; (94–100) blank. Text pages 33, 45, 71 unnumbered.

The dust-wrapper illustration of the iron wolf is in colour.

CONTENTS: Amulet—The Mermaid's Purse—Limpet—Whale—Conger Eel—Lobster—Sandflea—Cormorant—Whelk—Heron—Starfish—Sea Anemone—Crab—Jellyfish—Ragworm—Octopus—Blenny—Flounder—Shrimp—Gull—Hermit Crab—Mussel—Seal—The Osprey—Fantails—Worm—Thrush—Otter—Owl—Dragonfly—Snail—The Red Admiral—

Ram—Stickleback—Toad—Robin—Cow—Peacock—Pig—Sparrow—Mole—Donkey—Goat—Pike—Squirrel—Crow—Hen—Shrew—Cat—Cuckoo—The Heron—The Wolverine—Brooktrout—The Snow-shoe Hare—Ants—The Arctic Fox—Woodpecker—The Moorhen—Wolf—Eagle—Mooses—Puma—Phoenix—The Musk Ox—Goose—The Honey Bee—Grizzly[1]—In the Likeness of a Grasshopper—Spider—Crow's Elephant Totem Song.

All poems previously collected except for 'Ant' and 'Spider'. The others listed as 'uncollected' on p. 85 all appeared in *The Mermaid's Purse* (1993).

(B): What Is the Truth?

Title page has 'What is the Truth? | Illustrated by Lisa Flather | [illustration of a rabbit]'.

$[1-4^{16}] = 64$ leaves; pages (i–vi)vii–viii,1–113(114)115–119(120), consisting: (i) half-title, '[flush at left] COLLECTED ANIMAL POEMS VOLUME 2 | What is the Truth?'; (ii) '[flush at left] COLLECTED ANIMAL POEMS | [list of volumes]'; (iii) title page; (iv) 'First published in Great Britain in 1984 | by Faber and Faber Limited | 3 Queen Square London WC1N 3AU | This edition first published in 1995 | Photoset by Wilmaset Ltd, Birkenhead, Wirral | Printed in England by Clays Ltd, St Ives plc | All rights reserved | © Ted Hughes, 1984, 1995 | Illustrations © Lisa Flather, 1995 | [notes on identification of author and CIP record, and ISBN numbers] | [printing code, 10–1]'; (v) 'to Olwyn and Gerald'; (vi) blank; vii–viii table of contents; 1–113(114) text; 115–119 indexes; (120) blank. Text pages 4, 14, 19, 22, 42, 45, 49, 69, 93, 99, 112, 114 unnumbered.

The dust-wrapper illustration of a swallow is in colour.

CONTENTS: text the same as A87.

(C): A March Calf

Title page has 'A March Calf | [illustration of a calf]'.

$[1-2^{16}\ 3^8\ 4-5^{16}] = 72$ leaves; pages (i–x)1–117(118)119–121(122)123–125(126–134), consisting: (i–ii) blank; (iii) half-title, '[flush at left] COLLECTED ANIMAL POEMS VOLUME 3 | A March Calf'; (iv) '[flush at left] COLLECTED ANIMAL POEMS | [list of volumes]'; (v) title page; (vi) 'First published in Great Britain in 1995 | by Faber and Faber Limited | 3 Queen Square London WC1N 3AU | Photoset by Wilmaset Ltd, Birkenhead, Wirral | Printed in England by Clays Ltd, St Ives plc | All rights reserved | This collection © Ted Hughes, 1995 |

---

[1]   = 'I See a Bear'.

Illustration © Lisa Flather, 1995 | [notes on identification of author and CIP record, and ISBN numbers] | [printing code, 10–1]'; (vii) 'to Olwyn and Gerald'; (viii) blank; (ix–x) table of contents; 1–116 text; 117, list of sources; (118) blank; 119–121 index of first lines; (122) blank; 123–125 index of subjects; (126–134) blank.

The dust-wrapper illustration of a calf is in colour.

CONTENTS: A March Calf—A Swallow—The Canal's Drowning Black—Pets—Mackerel Song—Tigress—Off-Days—Waterlicked—Mosquito—Sheep—Sparrow—The Long Tunnel Ceiling—Song against the White Owl—Teaching a Dumb Calf—Cuckoo[1]—Visitation—Under the Hill of Centurions—Eclipse—Swans—Feeding Out-Wintering Cattle at Twilight—Black-Back Gull—Stealing Trout on a May Morning—Where I Sit Writing My Letter—Bringing in New Couples—Shrike—Caddis—Struggle—Snipe—Live Skull—Nightingale—Dehorning—Strangers—Mallard—The Weasels We Smoked out of the Bank—While She Chews Sideways—Magpie—The Bear[2]—Pheasant—The Bull Moses—Performance—Irish Elk—September Salmon—A Rival—Very New Foal—A Macaw—Whiteness—Curlews [both parts]—Couples under Cover—Starlings Have Come—A Cranefly in September—Birth of Rainbow—Tern—Buzz in the Window—The Kingfisher—An Eel—The Mayfly is Frail—A Mountain Lion—Two Tortoiseshell Butterflies—A Cormorant—Nightjar—Manchester Skytrain—February 17th—Evening Thrush—Coming down through Somerset—Tiger—Roe Deer—Bullfrog—Crow and the Birds—Macaw and Little Miss—Meeting—Happy Calf.

All poems previously collected except for 'Waterlicked', 'Cuckoo', 'Live Skull', 'Irish Elk', 'Very New Foal', and 'Tiger'. The others listed as 'uncollected' on p. 117 had all appeared in *A Primer of Birds* (1981) or in *Moortown* (1979).

(D): The Thought-Fox

Title page has 'The Thought-Fox | [illustration of two pawprints, same as on dust-wrapper]'.

$[1^{16}\ 2^8\ 3^{16}] = 40$ leaves; pages (i–viii)1–65(66)67–72, consisting: (i) half-title, '[flush at left] COLLECTED ANIMAL POEMS VOLUME 4 | The Thought-Fox'; (ii) '[flush at left] COLLECTED ANIMAL POEMS | [list of volumes]'; (iii) title page; (iv) 'First published in Great Britain in 1995 | by Faber and Faber Limited | 3 Queen Square

---

[1] First line 'Away, Cuckoo!'; a different poem from the one of the same title in *The Cat and the Cuckoo*.
[2] First line 'The day darkened in rain ...'.

London WC1N 3AU | Photoset by Wilmaset Ltd, Birkenhead, Wirral | Printed in England by Clays Ltd, St Ives plc | All rights reserved | This collection © Ted Hughes, 1995 | [notes on identification of author and CIP record, and ISBN numbers] | [printing code, 10–1]'; (v) 'to Olwyn and Gerald'; (vi) blank; (vii) table of contents; (viii) blank; 1–65 text; (66) blank; 67, list of sources; 68–72 indexes.

CONTENTS: Wodwo—Wolfwatching—The Bear[1]—Gnat-Psalm—And the Falcon Came—The Skylark Came—The Wild Duck—The Swift Comes the Swift—The Unknown Wren—And Owl—The Dove Came—Gog—The Gulkana—Song of a Rat—View of a Pig—Pike—The Jaguar—Hawk Roosting—The Horses—The Merry Mink—Bones—Swifts—The Howling of Wolves—Thrushes—An August Salmon—Skylarks—Tiger-Psalm—A Sparrow Hawk—The Black Rhino—An Otter—The Thought-Fox—Night Arrival of Sea-Trout—Second Glance at a Jaguar—Little Whale Song—A Dove—An October Salmon—That Morning.

All poems previously collected. 'Bones', listed as uncollected on p. 67, had appeared in *Crow Wakes* (1971).

The four volumes published as a unit, 4 September 1995, at £35.00; number printed undetermined.

a.3. Paperback printings:

The four volumes in a.2 were also issued singly in paperback, 'perfect-bound'. They are identical to the hardcover copies internally except for the addition of a Net Book Agreement note following the statement of authorship on the title verso.

Wrappers coloured and coated outside, with lettering in white. Fronts: 'ff | POETRY | Ted Hughes | [volume title] | [on a white panel, illustration from hardcover dust-wrapper]'. Spines printed like book spines, with less space between title and volume number. Back in two columns; left: '[photo of Hughes] | © Niall McDiarmid | [on white panel, prices as below, and vertical bar code]'; right: 'ff | *faber and faber* | Ted Hughes | Collected Animal Poems: Volume [number] | [volume title] | [in vols. 1 and 2] *Illustrated by* [1] *Chris Riddell* [2] *Lisa Flather* | [blurb] | [in vol. 3 only] Cover illustration by Lisa Flather'.

'Perfect-bound'.

(A): The Iron Wolf
Wrappers coloured dark red. Priced £3.99 ($7.99 in Canada, $5.95 in U.S.).

---

[1] First line 'In the huge …'.

(B): What Is the Truth?
Wrappers coloured dark blue. Priced £3.99 ($7.99 in Canada, $5.95 in U.S.).

(C): A March Calf
Wrappers coloured dark green. Priced £5.99 ($9.99 in Canada, $9.95 in U.S.).

(D): The Thought-Fox
Wrappers coloured grey. Priced £5.99 ($9.99 in Canada, $9.95 in U.S.).

Published 4 September 1995 (the British Library copy of each volume is stamped 15 August); number of copies printed unknown. Evidently not sold as a unit.

REVIEWS: *Independent on Sunday*, 24 Sept. 1995 (Michelle Roberts); *Literary Review* (Madison, N.J.), Oct. 1995 (Sam Dutton); *Spectator*, 30 Sept. 1995; *Sunday Times*, 10 Sept. 1995; *Times Educational Supplement*, 15 Sept. 1995.

A113 FOOTBALL 1995

[colour illustration of a footballer] | Football | *a new poem by* | TED HUGHES | *with illustrations by* | CHRISTOPHER | BATTYE | PROSPERO | POETS | 1995

A single long strip of paper, ca. 20.6 × 183.3 cm. Printed on one side in twelve panels and accordion folded, making pages ca. 14.9 cm. wide, the first and last with a narrow strip projecting at the outer edge. The cover has the structure of a dust-wrapper, and the two strips of the text are folded and pasted to the respective outer edges of the cover flaps. The entire structure folds up to resemble a traditional codex, but the text block is not secured at the spine and can be dumped out of the covers in a closed loop. In copies 60–199, two stiff boards are lightly pasted into this structure—one each inside the front and back covers—as stiffeners. In copies 200–499 these are replaced by a single oblong piece of light cardboard inserted loose. We have not seen one of copies I–L or 1–59.

Pages (1–12), consisting: (1, on a verso:) title page; (2–10) text; (11) blank (in copies 60–199, signatures of Hughes and Battye); (12) [recto] ''Football' | is copyright to Ted Hughes, | the illustrations | are copyright to Christopher Battye | Printed litho | by the Aldgate Press | on Scottish Mellotex paper | and bound with considerable difficulty | by Chris Hicks. | This edition of 499 copies | has 199 copies signed by the poet and artist | of these 60 [sic] copies, numbered 1–59 | have a loose additional print, signed by the artist. | 50 copies numbered I to L | have been reserved for the collaborators. | This copy is no. [number] | Trevor

Weston is the publisher | Simon Rae is the editor | Dennis Hall is the designer | Clarion Publishing   Neatham Mill   Holybourne   Alton England'.

The Clarion Press advertising matter gives a different breakdown of copies, i.e. I–L, 1–59, 60–149, and 150–499, but the numbers given in the colophon are correct.

Wrappers printed on front with larger version of the illustration from p. (8); at head, 'Football'.

Bulk .3 cm. Printed offset, the illustrations in colour with a glossy finish.

Published 15 November 1995 at £48.00 for copies 1–59, £32.00 for copies 60–199, and £18.50 for copies 200–499; 549 copies printed, the additional fifty (numbered I–L) being reserved for Hughes and Battye. The extra 'print' in the 59 copies is actually a lightweight beige card, 29.7 × 14.7 cm., on which are printed the entire poem (untitled) and two of the illustrations from the book, in black-and-white halftone. These were hand-coloured by Trevor Weston's wife, numbered to correspond with the accompanying book, and signed by both Hughes and Battye. Some extras of this were produced; the compilers have seen an uncoloured example.

B. Books, Pamphlets and Broadsides Edited or with Contributions by Ted Hughes

This section includes publications containing works by Hughes which appeared prior to their collection, or to their separate publication. Programme notes are treated separately in section H, Miscellaneous.

Our chief concern in this section of secondary books has been to allow the user to identify first printings, and to trace the printing history of Ted Hughes' writings prior to collection. For reasons of space we have therefore used a shortened form of description. While the entries are briefer, we have generally followed the conventions outlined in the introduction to section A; however, the rules for section B items differ in two respects:

1. The collation is meant to give an idea of the extent of a book, but not an exhaustive accounting of blank or unnumbered pages. We give the number of the last page of the book containing text *of consequence*, whether or not it actually bears a printed number in the book. Final unnumbered pages bearing only on-line imprints or publisher's marks are not included; indexes, colophons, and capsule biographies are. If preliminaries have a separate roman numeral sequence in the book, we give the number of the last *printed* page of the preliminaries as well, whether or not the page bears a number in the book. When none of the preliminaries has been numbered, and the text proper begins on page 1, we have supplied a roman numeral pagination in parentheses for the preliminaries, assuming their pagination to begin at the first printed

page of the book. Blank pages between preliminaries and text are not included or mentioned. When the entire work is unpaginated, the collation is given in square brackets, with the supplied numbering beginning on the first printed page and continuing straight through to the last, according to the criteria described above. The collation does not note which pages within a numbered sequence are blank, or indicate when printed pages are unnumbered.

2. The verso title transcription is shortened to include only the wording relevant to the identification of the printing at hand; text above or below the transcription is ignored.

While the page numbers of Hughes' contributions are given, these are not meant to be inclusive.

B1   POETRY FROM CAMBRIDGE 1952–4   1955

Poetry from Cambridge | 1952–4 | [rule, 1.9 cm., broken by diamond] | Edited by Karl Miller | Fantasy Press

44 pages; 19.0 × 12.0 cm.

Stapled into blue wrappers, front printed in black and red. Dust-wrapper blue, printed as on front cover.

The first printing is not identified as such.

Published 10 May 1955 at 5s.; 100 copies printed. Hagstrom and Bixby, in their Thom Gunn bibliography, state that there was a second printing of 199 copies, indistinguishable from the first 100, issued 26 May 1955; we are not able to confirm or clarify this.

CONTENTS: 'The Little Boys and the Seasons', p. 27; 'The Jaguar', p. 29; 'The Court-Tumbler and Satirist', p. 30.

B2   LANDMARKS AND VOYAGES   1957

[no title page; cover title:] LANDMARKS | AND | VOYAGES | *Poetry Supplement | edited by | VERNON WATKINS | for the Poetry Book Society | Christmas* 1957 | POETRY BOOK SOCIETY LTD | 4 ST JAMES'S SQUARE | LONDON SW1

[12] pages; 19.7 × 13.6 cm.

Stapled booklet, front printed as above.

The first printing is not identified as such; there was no reprint.

Published December 1957; 500 copies printed. Price unknown.

CONTENTS: 'Everyman's Odyssey', p. [12].

NEW POEMS 1958   1958

New Poems | [swelled rule, broken by '1958' in a decorative oval] | *Edited by* | BONAMY DOBRÉE | LOUIS MacNEICE | PHILIP LARKIN | [publisher's logo: mermaid within an oval] | *London* | MICHAEL JOSEPH

123 pages; 20.0 × 13.4 cm.

Quarter red cloth, decorative boards printed in yellow-green, dark grey and red. Dust-wrapper light grey, printed in red.

On verso title: '*First published by* | MICHAEL JOSEPH LTD. | [...] | 1958'.

Published 10 November 1958 at 13s. 6d.; 2600 copies printed. An unknown number of copies were distributed in the United States by Transatlantic at $3.75.

CONTENTS: 'Thrushes', p. 53.

B4   POETRY FROM CAMBRIDGE   1958

POETRY | FROM CAMBRIDGE | *Edited by* | CHRISTOPHER LEVENSON | THE FORTUNE PRESS | 15 BELGRAVE ROAD, LONDON, S.W.1

63 pages; 19.1 × 12.8 cm.

Quarter coated black cloth, black paper sides, spine stamped in gold. Dust-wrapper very light bluish green, printed in black.

On verso title: 'First Published in 1958'.

Published 22 December 1958 at 8s. 6d. The present owner of Fortune Press, Charles Skilton Ltd., has no record of the number printed. Timothy d'Arch Smith, author of *R. A. Caton and the Fortune Press*, wrote to Sagar, 'I would guess about 300 were done.' However, Philip Hobsbaum later wrote to Sagar, 'This must be one of the rarest books on earth since it was "published" by the legendary Caton who refused to issue any copies. I had to go on Levenson's behalf and extract copies for the contributors ... To the best of my knowledge the only copies issued were those I extracted from an immensely grudging Caton.'

CONTENTS: 'Thrushes', p. 25; 'The Good Life', p. 25; 'The Historian', p. 26; 'Dick Straightup', p. 27; 'Crow Hill', p. 28.

B5 POETRY 1960 1960

[cover title] A CRITICAL QUARTERLY SUPPLEMENT | [rule, in blue] | [in black] POETRY | [in blue] *An anthology of the best poems* | [in black] 1960 | [in blue] *by new writers in the '50s; new poems* | [in black] An Appetiser | [in blue] *by established poets; prize poems* | [rule, in blue] | [in black] Kingsley Amis   Elizabeth Jennings | J. M. Cameron   Philip Larkin | Donald Davie   Laurence Lerner | D. J. Enright   Christopher Levenson | Geoffrey Grigson   Christopher Logue | Thom Gunn   Robin Skelton | John Holloway   R. S. Thomas | Graham Hough   John Wain | Ted Hughes   Vernon Watkins | PRICE ONE SHILLING

24 pages; 21.9 × 14.2 cm.

Stapled in grey wrappers printed in blue and black.

The first printing is not identified as such; there were no reprints.

Published 1 February 1960 at 1s.; 12,000 copies printed.

CONTENTS: 'Hawk Roosting', p. 11.

B6 THE GOLDEN YEAR 1960

a.1. First edition:

[flush to left:] THE POETRY SOCIETY OF AMERICA | ANTHOLOGY (1910–1960) | [the remainder flush to right, title in red script:] *The* | *Golden Year* | edited by MELVILLE CANE, JOHN FARRAR, | and LOUISE TOWNSEND NICHOLL | foreword by CLARENCE R. DECKER | NEW YORK   THE FINE EDITIONS PRESS   1960

xxv, 370 pages 20.5 × 13.4 cm.

Red cloth, spine stamped in gold, top edge stained red. Dust-wrapper front and spine tan, lettered in white; back white with tan flower.

On verso title: '*First Printing*'. Colophon: '[publisher's logo: within two ovals, the outer dotted, the inner solid, two readers sitting on a stylized vine; around the ovals, in black-letter: 'The ·Fine ·Editions ·Press—New York—'] | *Of this first edition of* | THE GOLDEN YEAR | *2,500 copies were printed by The Davidson* | *Printing Corporation of New York in* | *the month of December, 1959*'.

Published 15 March 1960 at $6.00; 2500 copies printed.

CONTENTS: 'Thrushes', p. 145; 'Witches', p. 146.

a.2. Facsimile reprint of first edition (1969):

Title page as above, but in black only; in place of imprint: '*Granger Index Reprint Series* | BOOKS FOR LIBRARIES PRESS | FREEPORT, NEW YORK [at left, publisher's logo: stylized Greek temple]'.

xxv, 368 pages; 19.6 × 12.7 cm.

Green cloth, front stamped in blind with logo as above; spine stamped in gilt, with title on panel of darker green. Endpapers dark green.

On verso title: 'Reprinted 1969 by arrangement with | The Poetry Society of America'.

Published 1969 at $9.75; number of copies unknown.

B7   INTRODUCTION   1960

INTRODUCTION | [rule, 1.2 cm.] | [rule, .8 cm.] | *Stories by New Writers* | FABER AND FABER | 24 Russell Square | London

251 pages; 20.0 × 13.3 cm.

Black cloth, spine stamped in gold. Dust-wrapper printed in black, yellow and red, with freehand design on front.

On verso title: '*First published in mcmlx*'.

Published 7 October 1960 at 18s.; 3000 copies printed. The proof copies bear the date 21 July 1960.

CONTENTS: 'The Rain Horse', p. 111; 'Sunday', p. 121; 'Snow', p. 133.

B8   POETRY AT THE MERMAID   1961

[no title page; cover title, flush to left, on brown background, white letters outlined in black:] POETRY | AT THE | MERMAID | [in blue, mermaids blowing trumpets] | [white letters] SOUVENIR PROGRAMME THREE SHILLINGS AND SIXPENCE

96 pages (pages 25–(72) printed on green paper); 20.4 × 12.1 cm.

Wrappers printed in brown, black and blue.

The first printing is not identified as such; there was no reprint.

Published by the Poetry Book Society for the opening of the Festival, 16 July 1961, at 3s. 6d.; the Society has no record of the number printed.

CONTENTS: 'My Uncle's Wound', p. 41.

B9   NEW POEMS 1961   1961

[Two ornaments] | NEW POEMS | 1961 | A P.E.N. Anthology of | Contemporary Poetry | [two ornaments, as above] | *Edited by* | WILLIAM PLOMER | ANTHONY THWAITE | HILARY CORKE | HUTCHINSON OF LONDON

135 pages; 20.0 × 13.3 cm.

Decorated boards printed in pink and black; brown paper spine stamped in gold and white. Dust-wrapper printed with pink bands, lettered in black (some letters with white interiors).

On verso title: '*First* [sic] *published 1961*'.

Published 9 October 1961 at 18s.; publisher prefers not to reveal the number of copies printed. An unknown number of copies were distributed in the United States by Transatlantic at $4.50.

CONTENTS: 'Thistles', p. 47; 'Unknown Soldier', p. 48.

B10   GUINNESS BOOK OF POETRY 1960/61   1962

THE GUINNESS | *BOOK OF POETRY* | *1960/61* | [drawing of a wading bird among plants] | *PUTNAM* | *42 GREAT RUSSELL STREET* | *LONDON*

120 pages; 21.6 × 13.9 cm.

Blue cloth, spine gilt, top edge stained light blue. Dust-wrapper not seen.

The first printing is not identified as such; there was no reprint.

Published 16 April 1962 at 10s. 6d.; the publishers have no record of the number of copies printed, but Peter J. Matthews of Guinness Superlatives writes that 'it was a fairly limited quantity'.

CONTENTS: 'Unknown Soldier', p. 68.

This is the fifth of the Guinness books of poetry.

B11   THE NEW POETRY   1962

a. First edition:

THE NEW POETRY | AN ANTHOLOGY SELECTED AND INTRODUCED BY | A. ALVAREZ | PENGUIN BOOKS

191 pages; 18.0 × 11.1 cm.

Wrappers, printed in red, brown and black.

On verso title: 'This selection first published 1962'.

Published 19 April 1962 at 3s. 6d.; the publisher has no record of the number printed. A 1963 reprint is so identified on the verso title.

CONTENTS: 'Gog' (Part 1 only), p. 163; 'Pibroch', p. 164. There are also nineteen poems previously collected.

b. 'Revised edition' (1966):

First printing not seen.

All reprints seen of this edition are identified on the verso title.

Published 1966 at an undetermined price; number of copies printed unknown. There were reprints in April 1967 (35,000 copies), August 1968 (25,000 copies), August 1969 (18,000 copies), April 1970 (25,000 copies), May 1971 (23,000 copies), June 1972 (24,000 copies), October 1974 (20,000 copies), November 1976 (12,000 copies), 29 June 1978 (12,000 copies), and 31 July 1980 (10,000 copies). The most recent printing seen by the compilers is the nineteenth, as indicated by the printing code on verso title.

CONTENTS: The first three poems by Hughes from the first edition, 'The Jaguar', 'Macaw and Little Miss', and 'The Thought-Fox', were omitted at Hughes' request.

B12   LEONARD BASKIN   1962

[flush at left] **Leonard Baskin** / woodcuts and wood-engravings | An exhibition of the woodcuts and wood-engravings of | Leonard Baskin: a part of the Graven Image exhibition | of 1962, held at the RWS Galleries, 26 Conduit Street W1 | from May 1 to May 26, 1962 | [in red, Baskin engraving of porcupine]

[12] pages; 25.0 × 17.8 cm.

Green wrappers, front printed in dull gold.

Published for the exhibition. Robert Erskine, the organizer of the show, writes, 'I have no record of the number of copies of the catalogue we issued, but I doubt if it was more than 500, if that. We would have sold it for about two shillings, though I can't be sure of that, either.'

CONTENTS: 'Introduction', p. [3].

B13   NEW POETS OF ENGLAND   1962
AND AMERICA, 2

[title justified irregularly, the rest flush to left:] *NEW POETS | OF ENGLAND | AND AMERICA* | SECOND SELECTION | ENGLISH POETS EDITED BY Donald Hall | AMERICAN POETS EDITED BY Robert Pack | *Meridian Books* | THE WORLD PUBLISHING COMPANY | CLEVELAND AND NEW YORK

384 pages; 18.1 × 10.6 cm.

Wrappers, printed in black, blue and red with some lettering in white.

On verso title: 'First printing June 1962'.

Published June 1962 at $1.65 (the copyright is registered 24 July); the records on the number printed have apparently been lost. There were at least nine printings, identified by notes or printing codes on the verso title. Distribution of the edition in America passed to William Collins & World, and subsequently to the New American Library around 1978. An unknown number of copies were distributed in England by Trans-Atlantic Book Service on 14 October 1963, price 15s.; the compilers have not seen one of these. Distribution in England was taken over in 1978 by the New English Library, which imported 800 copies.

CONTENTS: 'Pibroch', p. 86. There are also nine poems previously collected.

B14   VOGUE'S GALLERY   1962

VOGUE'S GALLERY | The Condé Nast Publications Ltd., Vogue House, Hanover Square, London, W.1 [to right:] CONDÉ NAST | [publisher's logo, white V on a square of black] | PUBLICATIONS

255 pages; 25.4 × 16.6 cm.

Quarter white plastic, green boards, spine stamped in gold; pictorial endpapers. Pictorial dust-wrapper printed in colour.

The first printing is not identified as such; there was no reprint.

Published 1 October 1962 at 35s.; the publisher has no record of the number of copies printed. St. Martin's Press distributed copies in the United States at $7.95. A representative of St. Martin's writes, 'Our initial order from Condé Nast for *Vogue's Gallery* was 500 copies. The title was released on November 12, 1962. There was a further order of 250 copies, then another of 100.'

CONTENTS: 'Nessie' (the short poem), p. 165.

B15   NEW POEMS 1962   1962

[two ornaments] | NEW POEMS | 1962 | A P.E.N. Anthology of |
Contemporary Poetry | [ornaments as above] | *Edited by* | PATRICIA
BEER | TED HUGHES | VERNON SCANNELL | HUTCHINSON
OF LONDON

143 pages; 19.9 × 13.4 cm.

Decorative boards printed in black and aqua, maroon paper spine
stamped in gold and white. Dust-wrapper printed in blue and black.

On verso title: '*First published 1962*'.

Published 29 October 1962 at 21s.; the publisher prefers not to reveal the
number of copies printed. An unknown number of copies were
distributed in the United States by Transatlantic at $5.25.

The introduction is signed with all three editors' initials.

B16   POET'S CHOICE   1962

a. First edition:

POET'S | CHOICE | [ornamental rule, 4.6 cm.] | EDITED BY | Paul
Engle and Joseph Langland | [publisher's logo, cupid astride a lion] |
THE DIAL PRESS NEW YORK 1962

xx, 303 pages; 23.1 × 15.6 cm.

Reddish-brown cloth, spine stamped in gold, endpapers reddish-brown.
Dust-wrapper printed in black, red and gold.

The first printing is not identified as such.

Published 29 October 1962 at $6.00; 10,000 copies printed.

CONTENTS: 'Pibroch', p. 287; short note on his reasons for choosing it to
be printed here, p. 288.

b. First paperback edition (1966):

Not seen. Published by Dell (Delta Books), January 1966, at $1.95.

c. Second paperback edition (1966):

Not seen. Published by Time, New York, 9 August 1966, at $1.25 for
subscribers to the Time Reading Program; 80,000 copies printed. The
compilers have seen an impression with 'Reprinted 1982 by arrangement
with The Dial Press' on verso title.

B17   ENGLISH POETRY NOW   1962

[no title page; cover title, flush at left:] [in white] ENGLISH | POETRY
NOW | [in black] *Edited by C. B. Cox and A. E. Dyson* | [rule] | *A Selection
of the best poems by* | *modern British writers* | [the next three lines printed
over a drawing of a rose in white] CRITICAL QUARTERLY
POETRY SUPPLEMENT | NUMBER 3 | [rule] | PRICE ONE
SHILLING

24 pages; 21.8 × 14.0 cm.

Stapled into wrappers printed in red and black, with some lettering in
white, as above.

The first printing is not identified as such; there was no reprint. The
booklet is undated.

Published November 1962 at 1s.; 9000 copies printed.

CONTENTS: 'The Road to Easington', p. 6; and a poem previously
collected.

B17*   BEST POEMS OF 1961   1962

BEST POEMS | of 1961 | BORESTONE MOUNTAIN | POETRY
AWARDS | 1962 | *A Compilation of Original Poetry* | *published in* | *Magazines
of the English-speaking World* | *in 1961* | FOURTEENTH ANNUAL
I S S U E | V O L U M E   X I V | P A C I F I C   B O O K S,
PUBLISHERS • PALO ALTO, CALIFORNIA | 1962

(xii), 118 pages; 21.55 × 13.85 cm.

Light greenish-tan cloth, spine stamped in blue. No dust-wrapper seen.
Also issued in wrappers, coloured gold, printed in black.

The first printing is not identified as such.

Published November 1962; 1075 copies were issued hardbound at $3.50
and 610 paperbound at $1.50.

CONTENTS: 'Her Husband', p. 68.

B18   HERE TODAY   1963

Here Today | *Introduced by* | TED HUGHES | [publisher's bull logo] |
HUTCHINSON EDUCATIONAL

126 pages; 18.4 × 12.0 cm.

Pink boards printed in black with lettering in white. Issued without a dust-wrapper.

On verso title: '*First published 1963*'.

Published January 1963 at 6s. 6d.; 9000 copies printed. There were reprints in January and September 1964, March and July 1965, July 1966, August 1967, November 1969, 1971, 1975, 1976, 1978, and 1980; a total of 119,000 copies had been printed by December 1980. A paperback printing of 7500 copies was published in May 1975; a total of 26,000 paperback copies had been printed by December 1980. All reprints seen have been identified on the verso title.

CONTENTS: 'Introduction: Listening to Poetry', p. 11, and a previously collected poem.

B19   FIVE AMERICAN POETS   1963

Five | *American Poets* | [rule] | EDGAR BOWERS | HOWARD NEMEROV | HYAM PLUTZIK | LOUIS SIMPSON | WILLIAM STAFFORD | *edited by* | *Thom Gunn and Ted Hughes* | FABER AND FABER | 24 Russell Square | London

110 pages; 21.7 × 13.8 cm.

Dark blue cloth, spine stamped in gilt. Dust-wrapper light green, printed in black, blue and red.

On verso title: '*First published in mcmlxiii*'.

Published 31 May 1963 at 21s.; 2500 copies printed.

CONTENTS: The foreword is signed with both the editors' initials; the biographical notes were also a collaboration.

B20   NEW LINES 2   1963

NEW LINES—II | [decorative rule, 2.8 cm.] | *An Anthology* | *edited by* | ROBERT CONQUEST | LONDON | MACMILLAN & CO LTD | 1963

xxix, 136 pages; 21.7 × 13.9 cm.

Red cloth, spine stamped in gold. Dust-wrapper printed in black and grey.

The first printing is not identified as such.

Published 15 August 1963 at 21s.; the publisher prefers not to reveal the number printed.

CONTENTS: 'The Road to Easington', p. 58; and three previously collected poems.

B21   NEW POEMS 1963   1963

a. First edition:

[two ornaments] | NEW POEMS | 1963 | A P.E.N. Anthology of | Contemporary Poetry | [ornaments as above] | *Edited by* | LAWRENCE DURRELL | HUTCHINSON OF LONDON

161 pages; 20.0 × 13.3 cm.

Decorated boards, black paper spine stamped in gold and white. Dust-wrapper printed in black and red.

On verso title: '*First published 1963*'.

Published 18 November 1963 at 21s.; the publisher prefers not to reveal the number printed.

CONTENTS: 'Her Husband', p. 66; 'Wodwo', p. 67.

b. First American edition (1964):

Not seen.

Published 8 April 1964 by Harcourt, Brace & World, New York, at $3.95; 1500 copies printed.

B22   OF BOOKS AND HUMANKIND   1964

OF BOOKS AND | HUMANKIND | [rule] | Essays and Poems | Presented to | Bonamy Dobrée | [rule] | EDITED BY JOHN BUTT | *Assisted by J. M. Cameron | D. W. Jefferson and Robin Skelton* | [publisher's logo: medieval gate in circle] | Routledge and Kegan Paul | LONDON

Portrait frontispiece + x, 232 pages; 21.6 × 14.0 cm.

Maroon cloth, spine stamped in gold reading up. Dust-wrapper printed in light brown and black, with Dobrée's photograph on the front.

On verso title: '*First published 1964*'. There was no reprint.

Published 30 January 1964 at 35s.; the publisher prefers not to reveal the number printed. Later states of the dust-wrapper have a sticker changing the price to £2.00. Humanities Press distributed copies of the book in the United States in February 1964 at $6.00; they prefer not to reveal the number.

CONTENTS: 'Wodwo', p. 182.

B23   SELECTED POEMS, KEITH DOUGLAS   1964

a.1. First edition:

SELECTED POEMS | Keith Douglas | EDITED | WITH AN
INTRODUCTION | BY | *Ted Hughes* | FABER & FABER | 24
Russell Square | London

63 pages; 20.1 × 13.3 cm.

Dark maroon cloth, spine gilt. Dust-wrapper light blue, printed in black,
red and green.

On verso title: '*First published in mcmlxiv*'.

Published 14 February 1964 at 13s. 6d.; 2000 copies printed. There was
a second printing of 1500 copies on 28 April 1965, of which 750 copies
were exported to the United States (see below).

CONTENTS: 'Biographical Note', signed 'T .. H', p. 9; 'Introduction',
p. 11.

a.2. First printing for America (1965):

Title page as above, with imprint changed to '[publisher's logo; stylized
flying bird] | CHILMARK PRESS | NEW YORK'.

63 pages; 20.1 × 13.3 cm.

Binding and dust-wrapper as above, but with wording changes
appropriate to American distribution.

The first printing for America is not identified as such; on verso title:
'*Printed in Great Britain*'.

Published July 1965 at $3.50; 750 copies printed.

A reprint of the Faber edition, with changes necessary for export. It was
distributed by Random House.

B24   WRITERS ON THEMSELVES   1964

WRITERS | ON THEMSELVES | [swelled rule, 3.7 cm.] | NORMAN
NICHOLSON | REBECCA WEST | WILLIAM SANSOM |
EMANUEL LITVINOFF | VERNON SCANNELL | THOMAS
HINDE | JOHN BOWEN | RICHARD MURPHY | MICHAEL
BALDWIN | JULIAN MITCHELL | TED HUGHES | DAVID
STOREY | SYLVIA PLATH | with an introduction by | HERBERT
READ | British Broadcasting | Corporation

(x), 116 pages; 18.5 × 12.1 cm.

Blue boards, spine stamped in gold. Dust-wrapper printed in red and black.

On verso title: 'First Published 1964'. There was no reprint.

Published 15 September 1964 at 15s.; 3000 copies printed.

CONTENTS: 'The Rock', p. 86.

B25   **NEW POETRY 1964**   1964

[no title page; cover title:] [at right, white lettering] New | Poetry | 1964 [at left, and underneath the white lettering] Sylvia Plath | Philip Larkin | R. S. Thomas | Thom Gunn | Ted Hughes | Karen Gershon | Jon Stallworthy | William Stafford | Louis Simpson | Theodore Roethke | Adrienne Rich | Robert Bly | James Wright | Anne Sexton PRICE ONE SHILLING | CRITICAL QUARTERLY POETRY SUPPLEMENT NUMBER 5 | [abstract design]

24 pages; 22.0 × 14.1 cm.

Stapled into wrappers printed in green and black with some lettering in white.

The first printing is not identified as such; there was no reprint.

Published autumn 1964 at 1s.; 9000 copies printed.

CONTENTS: 'After Lorca', p. 11.

B26   **TODAY'S POETS**   1964

a. First edition:

Not seen. Edited by Chad Walsh.

Published 3 November 1964 by Charles Scribner's Sons, New York, at $3.50; the publisher has no record of the number printed. There were several printings in hardcover or paperback; these may be identified from the printer's code on the verso title. For instance, the code 'F–3.69[v]' indicates the sixth printing (F), done in March 1969.

CONTENTS: 'Wodwo', 'New Moon in January', and 'Encounter' (shortened by seven lines and retitled 'Full Moon and Little Frieda' in *Wodwo*). Also nine previously collected poems.

b. Second edition (1972):

Identified as such on the title page; on verso title: 'A–1.72[v]'. Published 10 January 1972. Contains eleven poems by Hughes, all previously collected.

B27   THE FABER BOOK OF TWENTIETH   1965
CENTURY VERSE (SECOND EDITION)

THE FABER BOOK | OF | TWENTIETH CENTURY VERSE |
Revised Edition | *edited by* | JOHN HEATH-STUBBS | *and* | DAVID
WRIGHT | FABER AND FABER | 24 Russell Square | London

366 pages; 18.4 × 11.8 cm.

Green cloth, spine stamped in gold. Dust-wrapper printed in black and
white on light blue.

On verso title: '*Second edition mcmlxv*'.

Published 11 February 1965 at 21s.; 4440 copies printed. There was a
reprint in 1966, identified on the verso title. A paperback printing of
12,000 copies was published 26 January 1967 at 15s. A third edition
appeared in 1975.

CONTENTS: 'The Lake', p. 175.

B28   ARIEL   1965

a. First edition:

ARIEL | by | SYLVIA PLATH | FABER AND FABER | 24 Russell
Square | London

86 pages; 21.7 × 13.9 cm.

Red cloth, spine stamped in gold; dust-wrapper yellow, printed in blue,
black, and red.

On verso title: '*First published in mcmlxv*'.

Published 11 March 1965 at 12s. 6d.; 3100 copies printed. There were
reprints on 14 January 1966 (3180 copies), 6 July 1967 (2500 copies),
and 20 March 1972 (2000 copies). The first paperback printing, from
the same edition, appeared 3 June 1968 in 10,000 copies; it was reprinted
8 October 1968 (10,000 copies), 17 March 1971 (12,000 copies), 25 July
1972 (20,000 copies), 13 December 1974 (25,000 copies), 5 October 1976
(25,000 copies), and 11 May 1979 (20,000 copies). The latest paperback
printing seen by the compilers is the sixteenth, as indicated by the
printing code on verso title.

Though not so stated, the book was edited by Ted and Olwyn Hughes.

b. First American edition (1966):

ARIEL | BY | SYLVIA PLATH | HARPER & ROW, PUBLISHERS |
New York

xii, 87 pages; 20.6 × 14.1 cm.

Black cloth, front and spine stamped in blue. Dust-wrapper cream-coloured, printed in black, violet, and orange-brown.

On verso title: 'FIRST EDITION'.

Published June 1966 at $4.95; the publisher prefers not to reveal the number of copies printed. There was also a paperback version, offset from the same American edition, which went into many printings, as indicated by the printing code at the foot of the last page.

CONTENTS: The English selection is here augmented by three poems.

B29   WINTER'S TALES FOR CHILDREN 1   1965

WINTER'S TALES | FOR CHILDREN 1 | EDITED BY | CAROLINE HILLIER | [drawing of dragon] | *Illustrated by* | *HUGH MARSHALL* | MACMILLAN | London · Melbourne · Toronto | [swelled rule, 4.5 cm.] | ST MARTIN'S PRESS | New York | 1965

vii, 200 pages; 23.7 × 17.5 cm.

Green boards, gilt dragon on front, spine stamped in gold. Dust-wrapper printed in orange, green, brown and black with dragons front and back.

The first printing is not identified as such.

Published 14 October 1965 at 21s.; the publisher prefers not to reveal the number printed. St. Martin's Press distributed the book in the United States at $4.95. A representative writes, 'Saint Martin's ordered its edition [sic] from Macmillan in August of 1965. It was released on January 5, 1966. We received 501 copies on the first shipment. Later we ordered 200 more copies and in March another 100. We do not know if it was all from the first printing or not.'

CONTENTS: 'Nessie', p. 19.

B30   MOMENTS OF TRUTH   1965

[line of hourglass and floral ornaments] | Moments of Truth | Nineteen Short Poems | by Living Poets | [line of ornaments as above, but shorter] | London | The Keepsake Press | 1965 | [line of ornaments as above]

24 pages; 17.2 × 10.8 cm.

Light brown wrappers printed in grey and brown. Issued with pages unopened.

Colophon: '[ornament] *First published in 1965* [ornament] *Hand set & hand* |

printed by Roy Lewis & Julius Stafford Baker at | The Keepsake Press, 26 Sydney Road, Richmond, | Surrey [...] | [...] | [...] Of this edition | each contributor receives 12 copies as keepsakes; 100 | are for sale.'

Published October 1965 at 5s.; about 328 copies printed.

CONTENTS: 'More Theology', p. 21 (collected as part II of 'Plum-Blossom' in *Recklings*).

B31   A TRIBUTE TO AUSTIN CLARKE   1966

A TRIBUTE TO | AUSTIN CLARKE | ON HIS SEVENTIETH BIRTHDAY | 9 MAY 1966 | DOLMEN EDITIONS

27 pages; 27.7 × 18.5 cm.

Plain stiff wrappers, grey dust-wrapper pasted on at spine; dust-wrapper printed in black and maroon.

Colophon: '*A Tribute to Austin Clarke* is set in Pilgrim type and printed and | published at the Dolmen Press Limited 8 Herbert Place Dublin 2 | in the Republic of Ireland, in an edition of one thousand copies. | May 1966'.

Probably published May 1966 at 15s.; 1000 copies printed. *Whitaker's Cumulative Book Index* gives November as the month of publication.

CONTENTS: 'Beech Tree', p. 16.

B32   THE ANIMAL ANTHOLOGY   1966

DIANA SPEARMAN | The | Animal | Anthology | FOREWORD BY | PETER SCOTT | [publisher's logo, solid black circle containing 'JOHN BAKER' and a horse in white] | JOHN BAKER | 5 ROYAL OPERA ARCADE | PALL MALL, LONDON, SW1

208 pages; 19.7 × 12.9 cm.

Green cloth; spine stamped with red panel with title in gold superimposed, publisher's logo in gold at foot. Dust-wrapper light grey, printed in black and red, with rhinoceros design by Dürer on front.

On verso title: '*First published 1966*'.

Published 25 October 1966 at 25s. Adam and Charles Black Ltd., who acquired John Baker in 1972, have no record of the number of copies printed.

CONTENTS: 'The Last Migration', p. 7. The first half of this poem became 'Irish Elk' (C354).

B33   NEW POEMS 1966   1966

[no title page; cover title:] CRITICAL QUARTERLY POETRY SUPPLEMENT NUMBER 7 | [in white] [rule] | *New Poems 1966* | [rule] | [in black] Thom Gunn, Robert Lowell, R. S. Thomas, Gary Snyder, Ted Hughes | Randall Jarrell, Seamus Heaney, Donald Davie, Louis Simpson | Charles Tomlinson, Edward Brathwaite, Sylvia Plath | Iain Crichton Smith, David Holbrook, Elizabeth Jennings | [in white, reverse silhouette of leaves and branches] | [lower right, in black] PRICE | ONE SHILLING

24 pages; 22.0 × 13.9 cm.

Stapled into wrappers printed in purple and black, with some lettering in white.

The first printing is not identified as such; there was no reprint.

Published autumn 1966 at 1s.; 9000 copies printed.

CONTENTS: 'Reveille', p. 19.

B34   CATALOGUE OF AN EXHIBITION   1967
            OF POETRY MANUSCRIPTS
            [POETRY IN THE MAKING]

a.1. First edition, trade state:

[flush to left] CATALOGUE OF AN EXHIBITION | OF POETRY MANUSCRIPTS IN | THE BRITISH MUSEUM | April–June 1967 | by | JENNY LEWIS | with contributions by | C. DAY LEWIS | T. C. SKEAT | PHILIP LARKIN | Published by TURRET BOOKS for | THE ARTS COUNCIL OF GREAT BRITAIN & | THE BRITISH MUSEUM

The half-title and cover call this publication *Poetry in the Making*.

68 pages + (4) leaves of plates; 23.8 × 15.0 cm. Paperbound copies 24.6 × 15.3 cm.

Green cloth, spine gilt, endpapers yellow-green. Dust-wrapper printed in two shades of green and black, with lettering in white. Also issued in wrappers with same design as dust-wrapper.

On verso title: 'Published in 1967 by Turret Books [...]'.

Published April 1967; 500 unsigned hardbound copies issued at 25s.; 1500 paperbound copies issued at 12s. 6d.

CONTENTS: 'Mountains' and a fragment of 'Sort' (facsimile of the original draft), plate VIII.

Copies were issued with a 7-page booklet (21.4 × 13.6 cm.) bearing the cover title 'POETRY IN THE MAKING | ILLUSTRATIVE MATERIAL | [swelled rule, 6.3 cm.] | TURRET BOOKS'. Accompanying both was a mimeographed sheet listing readings (one by Hughes included) to be given in conjunction with the exhibition.

a.2. Limited state:

Not seen. A hundred numbered and 26 lettered copies of the above edition were issued, bound in dark purple cloth. Each bore a printed limitation statement on the verso title and was signed by the four contributors mentioned on the title. The lettered copies were for the use of the contributors; the numbered copies were sold at a price not disclosed.

B35   JOURNAL OF CREATIVE BEHAVIOR   1967
POETRY SUPPLEMENT

[flush to left] [rule] | *The Journal of* | *Creative Behavior* | POETRY SUPPLEMENT | Volume 1 | Number 3 | Summer, 1967 | [rule] | [Journal logo] | Copyright © THE CREATIVE EDUCATION FOUNDATION, INC., 1967

(vi), 34 pages; 25.0 × 17.5 cm.

Wrappers, the front printed with an illustration of a man, the back with the same in negative; front printed in upper left, and reading upwards near spine.

The first printing is not identified as such.

Published summer 1967; included in the subscription to the magazine, also sold separately at $2.50.

CONTENTS: 'Three Legends', p. 18 (the first collected as the first of 'Two Legends' in *Crow*).

Edited by David Posner.

B36   POETRY 1900–1965   1967

Poetry 1900 to 1965 | *An anthology* | *selected and edited by* | George MacBeth | [publisher's logo: within an oval, a ship and '1724'] | Longmans | with | Faber and Faber

xxiv, 343 pages; 19.7 × 13.2 cm.

Boards, printed in violet and blue with white lettering. Issued without a dust-wrapper.

On verso title: '*First published 1967 in conjunction with Faber and Faber Ltd*'.

Published 27 November 1967 at 12s. 6d.; 10,000 copies printed. The book was reprinted in 1968 (10,000 copies), 1969 (15,000 copies), 1970 (20,000 copies), 1971 (20,000 copies), 1972 (20,000 copies), 1973 (20,000 copies), 1974 (25,000 copies), 1976 (20,000 copies), and 1978 (15,000 copies). The compilers have also seen a 1972 reprint in wrappers of the same design.

CONTENTS: 'The Brother's Dream', p. 326; and nine previously collected poems.

B37   A CHOICE OF EMILY DICKINSON'S VERSE 1968

A CHOICE OF | EMILY DICKINSON'S | VERSE | selected | with an introduction by | TED HUGHES | FABER AND FABER | 24 Russell Square | London

68 pages, 20.0 × 13.0 cm.

Red cloth, spine stamped in gold. Dust-wrapper printed in blue and black, with a drawing of Dickinson.

On verso title: '*First published in this edition in mcmlxviii*'.

Published 25 March 1968 at 16s.; 2825 copies printed. Six thousand copies of a paperbound printing of the same edition were issued 24 March 1969 at 7s. Copies of the hardback issued later have a Faber sticker over the price, raising it to £1.30.

CONTENTS: 'Introduction', p. 9.

B38   YEHUDA AMICHAI: SELECTED POEMS   1968

a. First edition:

[title distributed over the rectos of the first three leaves, printed in blue as follows:] [1:] [Amichai's holograph signature and copy number in black felt-tipped pen, copies 1–50] | *Yehuda Amichai* [2:] *Selected Poems* [3:] *Cape Goliard* | *Translated by Assia Gutmann*

[27] pages; 24.9 × 16.4 cm.

Blue boards, spine stamped in silver. Endpapers yellow-brown. Dust-wrapper blue, printed in lighter blue and red. Also issued in wrappers.

Colophon: '[…] | […] This First Edition has been | Designed, Printed & Published by Cape | Goliard Press, […] | […] & of this Edition 50 | Copies have been Signed & Numbered by | the Author […]'.

Published 11 July 1968 at 84s. for the signed copies, 21s. for the trade hardbound, and 12s. 6d. for the paperbound copies. The publisher prefers not to reveal the number of trade copies printed.

Though not credited in the book, Hughes collaborated on the translation.

*b. First American edition, expanded (*Poems, *1969):*

[irregularly justified] YEHUDA AMICHAI | POEMS | *Translated from the Hebrew by* | *Assia Gutmann* | *With an Introduction by Michael Hamburger* | [rule with a diamond ornament at left end] | HARPER & ROW, PUBLISHER   NEW YORK AND EVANSTON

xiii, 59 pages; 20.5 × 14.1 cm.

Blue cloth and white boards, spine stamped in silver; endpapers light blue. Dust-wrapper front printed in blue, with drawings of *shtetl* figures in black and lettering in white; back cover has negative image of the drawings.

On verso title: 'FIRST U.S. EDITION'.

Published 18 June 1969 at $4.95; the publisher prefers not to reveal the number of copies printed.

CONTENTS: Same as the first edition, with the addition of twenty-six poems.

c. Second English (first paperback) edition, further expanded (1971):

[flush to left] Selected Poems | Yehuda Amichai | *Translated by* | Assia Gutmann and | Harold Schimmel with | the collaboration of | Ted Hughes | [publisher's logo: penguin within oval] Penguin Books [to right:] *With an Introduction by* | Michael Hamburger

96 pages; 18.1 × 11.2 cm.

Wrappers, printed in yellow, green and black, with a picture of Amichai on the front.

On verso title: 'This selection first published 1971'.

Published 30 November 1971 at £0.25; 10,000 copies printed. There was no reprint.

CONTENTS: Same as above, with the addition of a section of thirteen poems translated by Harold Schimmel.

B39   WORD IN THE DESERT   1968

WORD | IN THE DESERT | *The Critical Quarterly* | *Tenth Anniversary Number* | edited by | C. B. COX and A. E. DYSON | *London* | OXFORD UNIVERSITY PRESS | NEW YORK TORONTO | 1968

(viii), 199 pages; 21.6 × 13.9 cm.

Orange cloth; spine stamped in gold, with title over a dark green panel. Dust-wrapper printed in green, orange and yellow, with lettering in white.

The first printing is not identified as such.

Published 25 July 1968 at 35s. / $4.95; 1978 copies printed.

CONTENTS: 'Dog Days on the Black Sea', p. 107; '?', p. 108; 'Second Bedtime Story', p. 109 (the latter collected in *Crow* as 'Lovesong').

The book is printed from the same setting of type as the *Critical Quarterly* Tenth Anniversary Number (X:1,2), with title page and other preliminaries added.

B40   WINTER'S TALES FOR CHILDREN 4   1968

Winter's Tales | *for Children* | 4 | EDITED BY | M. R. HODGKIN | *Illustrated by* | *GORDON G. CLOVER* | MACMILLAN | LONDON · MELBOURNE · TORONTO | 1968

(v), 182 pages + (4) colour plates; 23.6 × 17.2 cm.

Blue boards; spine stamped in gold with title on a red panel; endpapers illustrated in colour. Dust-wrapper front and spine printed with colour picture of the front of a house; back with picture of a running girl in black and blue.

The first printing is not identified as such.

Published 29 August 1968 at 30s.; the publisher prefers not to reveal the number of copies printed.

CONTENTS: 'Horrible Song', p. 135.

B41   HERE, NOW AND BEYOND   1968

[flush to right] NANCY MARTIN | Here, now and beyond | OXFORD UNIVERSITY PRESS 1968

240 pages; 21.0 × 15.8 cm.

Boards, printed in black and yellow with a photograph of a tree in cross-section; some lettering in white. Dust-wrapper, if any, not seen.

The first printing is not identified as such.

Published September 1968 at 10s. 6d.; regarding the number of copies printed, Oxford states, 'Our records are rather hazy.' There were reprints in 1970, 1972, 1974, 1976, and 1978. A paperback printing of the same edition appeared 20 April 1972; 7500 copies printed.

CONTENTS: 'The Price of a Bride', p. 124 (opening only), and a previously collected poem.

B42   POETRY GALA   1968

[no title page; cover title, in blue and orange:] POETRY GALA | Presented by The Poetry Society | With: Basil Bunting, Spike Hawkins, Ted | Hughes, Christopher Logue, Hugh | MacDiarmid, Brian Patten, Tom Pickard, | William Plomer, Stevie Smith | and Ezra Pound | [drawing of a mouth]

48 pages; 22.7 × 15.1 cm.

Wrappers, front printed as above.

The first printing is not identified as such.

Published late 1968 at 5s. The Poetry Society has not retained records of the exact date or the number. The Festival itself took place on 3 February 1969.

CONTENTS: 'Crowquill', p. 7; 'Crow and the Birds', p. 8.

B43   VASKO POPA, SELECTED POEMS   1969

[flush at left] Vasko Popa | Selected Poems | [two columns; at left:] *Translated by* | Anne Pennington [at right:] *With an Introduction by* | Ted Hughes | [at bottom, publisher's logo: penguin within oval] | Penguin Books

128 pages; 17.9 × 11.1 cm.

Wrappers, printed in black and red.

On verso title: 'First published 1969'.

Published 27 February 1969 at 20p.; the publisher has no record of the number printed.

CONTENTS: 'Introduction to the Poetry of Vasko Popa', p. 9.

B44   POETRY 1969   1969

[cover title] [in two columns; left] Jon Stallworthy, Seamus Heaney |
Tony Connor, Louis Simpson | D. J. Enright, Elizabeth Jennings |
Norman MacCaig, Derek Mahon | Edward Lowbury, Roy Fuller |
Douglas Dunn, Ian Hamilton | David Harsent, Ruth Miller | Molly
Holden, Ted Hughes | R. S. Thomas [right column; in white] *Poetry 1969*
| *Edited by Damian Grant* | [in black] CRITICAL QUARTERLY |
POETRY SUPPLEMENT | NUMBER 10 | Price One Shilling | [below
both columns, abstract design]

24 pages; 21.8 × 14.1 cm.

Stapled into wrappers printed in purple and black, with some lettering
in white.

The first printing is not identified as such; there was no reprint.

Published September 1969; 12,000 copies printed.

CONTENTS: 'Second Bedtime Story', p. 21 (collected in *Crow* as
'Lovesong'); 'Notes for a Little Play', p. 22.

B45   THE ART OF SYLVIA PLATH   1970

a.1. First edition:

The art of | SYLVIA PLATH | [swelled rule, 4.2 cm.] | *A Symposium* |
Edited by Charles Newman | *Selected criticism, with a complete* | *bibliography,*
checklist of criticism, | *and an appendix of uncollected* | *and unpublished work.* |
FABER AND FABER | London

Portrait frontispiece + 320 pages; 21.6 × 13.7 cm.

Black cloth, spine stamped in gold. Dust-wrapper printed in blue and
black.

On verso title: '*First published in 1970*'.

Published 5 January 1970 at 50s./£2.50; 2500 copies printed.

CONTENTS: 'The Chronological Order of Sylvia Plath's Poems', p. 187.

a.2. First American printing:

Same title as above except, substituted for last two lines, 'Indiana
University Press | Bloomington & London'.

Portrait frontispiece + 320 pages; 20.8 × 14.0 cm.

Maroon cloth, front stamped in blind, spine stamped in gold. Dust-
wrapper printed in red and black, with some lettering in white.

On verso title: '*First published in the United States 1970*'.

Published 16 March 1970 at $6.50; 3041 copies printed. Of these, 2005 were bound in January, the remainder in May 1972. The first paperback printing of 5080 copies (not seen) was issued in 1971; it was reprinted in 1973 (3090 copies) and 1975 (3061 copies).

An offset printing done from film of the English edition.

B46 TWELVE TO TWELVE 1970

a.1. Limited state:

[flush to left] TWELVE | TO | TWELVE | EDITED BY JENI COUZYN | POETRY D-DAY | CAMDEN FESTIVAL 1970 | POETS TRUST LONDON 1970

51 pages, the first two leaves being used as front paste-down and fly-leaf; 23.6 × 18.3 cm.

Orange-brown boards. Dust-wrapper orange-brown, printed in black.

On the page preceding the title: '*This edition, signed by the poets,* | *is limited to 100 copies of which* | *this is number* [number] | [signatures of the twelve poets]'. On verso title: 'First Published 1970 by the Poets Trust'.

Issued with a laid-in, [4]-page leaflet printed with the schedule for Poetry D-Day; Hughes is among the readers.

Published for Poetry D-Day, 9 May 1970, at an undetermined price; 100 copies thus issued.

CONTENTS: 'Apple Tragedy', p. 13.

a.2. Trade state:

The same edition, probably the same printing as above. Lacking the limitation notice and the poets' signatures. Bound in wrappers, front black, front and spine lettered in red. Published simultaneously with the limited state at 10s. 6d.; The Poetry Society, who published the book, has not retained records of the number printed.

B47 A BRITISH FOLIO 1970

[no title page; folder title:] UNICORN FOLIO | *Series Three Number Two* | A BRITISH FOLIO | [unicorn head silhouette in red and white stripes]

14 separate sheets, as follows: contents; introduction by Edward Lucie-

Smith; capsule biographies of the poets; ten broadsides, each a different colour and size and by a different poet; colophon.

In a folder of blue paper, folded size 50.7 × 33.2 cm. Front printed as above.

Colophon: 'Three hundred and seventy-five numbered | copies of this folio of British Poetry were | published as the tenth Unicorn Folio in a | series of twelve. Typography by Alan Bril- | liant. Printed by Noel Young. Bindery by | Donald Rojo. Copyright MCMLXX. Unicorn | Press books are published in Santa Barbara | by Alan Brillant [sic] and Teo Savory. | No. [N swash] [number written in white ink over a series of printed horizontal lines]'.

Published 22 May 1970 at $5.00. According to Alan Brilliant, in addition to the 375 sets, 25 extra copies of all the broadsides were printed for the use of their respective authors. Bernard Stone reports some lettered sets which were apparently in addition to the 25 extras. 'There may well have been 26 copies. A few were sold and a few given to the contributors.'

CONTENTS: 'Though the Pubs are Shut', printed on pink paper, 45.8 × 30.7 cm.

According to Olwyn Hughes, 'Though the Pubs are Shut' was not considered by Hughes to be ready for publication, and was included here without his knowledge.

B48   BRITISH POETRY SINCE 1945   1970

British Poetry | *since 1945* | [star ornament] | EDITED WITH AN INTRODUCTION BY | *Edward Lucie-Smith* | [publisher's logo, penguin in an oval] | PENGUIN BOOKS

412 pages + (2) pages of ads; 18.1 × 11.2 cm.

Wrappers, printed in black with an abstract design in colour.

On verso title: 'First published 1970'.

Published 24 September 1970 at 10s.; the publisher has no record of the number printed. There were reprints in September 1971 (18,000 copies), February 1973 (15,000 copies), September 1974 (14,000 copies), August 1976 (11,000 copies), 23 February 1978 (10,000 copies), and 24 April 1980 (10,000 copies).

CONTENTS: 'Fifth Bedtime Story', p. 161 (collected in *Crow* as 'A Bedtime Story').

B49   POETRY 1970   1970

[no title page; cover title:] [in two columns; left] W. H. Auden | Edward
Brathwaite | W. S. Graham, Sylvia Plath | Ted Hughes, Tony Connor |
R. S. Thomas | John Berryman | Christopher Levenson | Glyn Hughes
and | Norman MacCaig [right column] [in white] *Poetry 1970* | *Edited by*
Damian Grant | CRITICAL QUARTERLY | POETRY
SUPPLEMENT | NUMBER 11 | *Price Two Shillings* | [below both
columns, in white, designs resembling interlocked planetary orbits]

24 pages; 21.8 × 14.1 cm.

Stapled into wrappers printed in purple and black, with some lettering
in white.

The first printing is not identified as such; there was no reprint.

Published September 1970 at 2s.; 12,000 copies printed.

CONTENTS: 'Owl's Song', p. 9; 'Crow Alights', p. 9; 'Crow's Song of
Himself', p. 10.

B50   YOUNG WINTER'S TALES 1   1970

YOUNG | WINTER'S TALES | EDITED BY | M. R. HODGKIN |
['1' within a frame of Garamond ornaments] | MACMILLAN

167 pages; 20.2 × 13.0 cm.

Blue boards, spine stamped in gold. Dust-wrapper illustrated in colour
with fantastic characters, lettered in white and black.

On verso title: 'First published 1970 [...]'.

Published October 1970 at 30s.; the publisher prefers not to reveal the
number of copies printed.

CONTENTS: 'Wild West', p. 82.

B51   WORKS IN PROGRESS 2   1971

[flush to right] WORKS IN | PROGRESS | NUMBER TWO | Book
trade distribution by | Doubleday & Company, Inc. | The Literary
Guild of America, Inc. | New York, N.Y.

237 pages; 18.2 × 10.6 cm.

Wrappers, front and spine with colour illustration of wood type on
burlap, printed in black; back black, lettered in white.

The first printing is not identified as such; there was no reprint.

Published by the Literary Guild of America on 8 January 1971; the number of copies printed was not available. Anchor Books (a Doubleday imprint) bought 1000 copies from the Literary Guild on 7 December 1970 and published them simultaneously with the Literary Guild's copies. It bought a further 1500 copies on 22 January 1971. The book was declared out of print by the Literary Guild on 21 July 1971.

CONTENTS: 'Crow Totem', p. 32, collected in the American *Crow* as 'Crow's Elephant Totem Song'.

B52   NEW POEMS 1970–71   1971

[two ornaments] | NEW POEMS | 1970–71 | A P.E.N. Anthology | of Contemporary Poetry | [two ornaments as above] | *Edited by* | ALAN BROWNJOHN | SEAMUS HEANEY | JON STALLWORTHY | HUTCHINSON OF LONDON

113 pages; 19.6 × 12.8 cm.

Black boards, spine stamped in gold; endpapers grey. Dust-wrapper printed in green and black, lettered in white on front and spine.

On verso title: '*First published 1971*'.

Published 19 April 1971 at £1.50; the publisher prefers not to reveal the number of copies printed.

CONTENTS: 'The Space-Egg was Sailing', p. 49 (incorporating 'Crow's Song of Himself', which was previously collected in *Crow*).

B53   WITH FAIREST FLOWERS WHILE   1971
                    SUMMER LASTS

a. First edition:

[at left, drawing of a flower by Leonard Baskin; all lettering except for imprint in Baskin calligraphy] WITH | FAIREST FLOWERS | WHILE SVMMER LASTS | POEMS FROM | SHAKESPEARE | EDITED & | INTRODVCED | BY TED HVGHES | [in type] DOUBLEDAY & COMPANY, INC., | GARDEN CITY, NEW YORK | 1971

xxv, 140 pages; 20.7 × 13.6 cm.

White boards, front and back lettered in red and black and with a painting of a flower by Baskin. Dust-wrapper of same design. The only copy of the dust-wrapper seen has a gold adhesive label around spine reading 'A Doubleday reinforced library edition'. Also issued in wrappers of the same design.

On verso title: 'First Edition'. Hardbound copies have 'M9' at the bottom right corner of p. 140. Paperbound copies lack the 'First Edition' statement, and the code on p. 140 varies (see below).

Published 7 May 1971 at $4.95 for the hardbound copies and $1.95 for the paperbound. The publisher prefers not to reveal the number of copies printed, but states there was one printing only. The book went out of print in May 1976.

CONTENTS: 'Introduction', p. v. The Introduction alone was published earlier in the year as *Shakespeare's Poem* (item A30). This edition contains 180 selections.

The copies in wrappers come in two states:
1. Price '$1.95' printed on front cover, upper right corner; p. 140 has 'M9' like the hardbound copies.
2. Lacking the price; p. 140 lower right corner has 'M45'. At least some of these were issued as Christmas keepsakes by Doubleday. They were packaged in a folding heavy red paper wrapper with raised green script reading 'MERRY | CHRISTMAS | FROM | DOUBLEDAY' on the flap. With the book are a blank insert of the same red stock, which was used for presentation signatures, and a semi-transparent sheet printed in green with a Shakespearean quotation.

Two different types of paper appear to have been used as well in the paperbound copies, though the compilers have not seen enough copies to tell whether there is a definite connection with the states above. The evidence would indicate separate printings, but this is at odds with the publisher's statement to us (letter, 13 January 1982).

Hughes wrote to Peter Redgrove that he was not responsible for the title, which had been 'foisted' on him.

*b. First English edition (*A Choice of Shakespeare's Verse*):*

A CHOICE OF | SHAKESPEARE'S | VERSE | selected | with an introduction by | TED HUGHES | FABER AND FABER | 3 Queen Square | London

212 pages; 19.6 × 12.8 cm.

Red cloth, spine stamped in gold. Dust-wrapper printed in black and red. Also issued in wrappers.

On verso title: '*First published in 1971*'.

Published 22 November 1971; 9500 copies printed, of which 1500 were issued hardbound at £2.50 and 8000 in wrappers at 80p.

Contains the same 180 selections as above. Most of Hughes' introduction is moved to the back.

c. Second English edition (1991):

A CHOICE OF | Shakespeare's Verse | *Selected | and with an introduction by* | TED HUGHES | ff | *faber and faber* | LONDON · BOSTON

(viii), 216 pages; 19.7 × 12.9 cm.

Wrappers, linen-grained, printed with all-over pattern of 'ff', with text in white panels. Droeshout portrait of Shakespeare on front.

On verso title: 'This new revised edition first published in 1991', and printing code 2–1.

Published November 1991 (the British Library copy is stamped 2 October) at £4.99 ($9.95 in U.S., $12.99 in Canada); number of copies undetermined.

Contains 218 selections. Both Hughes' introduction and the final essay are new.

*d.1. Second American edition (*The Essential Shakespeare, *1991):*

[rule with three pendent solid diamonds in V formation at either end] | The Essential | SHAKESPEARE | Selected and with an | Introduction by | TED HUGHES | The Ecco Press | [rule with a single solid diamond above either end]

(ix), 230 pages; 20.2 × 12.6 cm.

Quarter black cloth, blue paper sides; front blind-stamped with fanciful human figure in square frame; spine stamped in gold. Dust-wrapper printed in light orange-brown, lettered in dark blue and black.

On verso title: 'FIRST EDITION'.

Published December 1991 at $18.95 ($22.99 Canadian). The Library of Congress copy is stamped 13 December. 4500 copies printed. There has been no reprint.

Contains 219 selections. Hughes' new introduction and essay (both from B53c) are printed together at the beginning.

d.2. Paperback printing of d.1 (1992):

Same internally as above, but verso title has 'FIRST PAPERBACK EDITION' instead of 'FIRST EDITION'.

16.45 × 11.6 cm.

Wrappers, printed in light orange-brown, red, and black.

Published October 1992 at $8.00; 5100 copies printed. There has been no reprint.

B54   CROSSING THE WATER   1971

a. First edition:

CROSSING | THE WATER | by | Sylvia Plath | FABER AND FABER | 3 Queen Square | London

64 pages; 21.6 × 13.5 cm.

Blue cloth, spine stamped in gold. Dust-wrapper printed in black and blue.

On verso title: '*First published in 1971*'.

Published 31 May 1971 at £1.25; 7000 copies printed. There was a second printing of 30,000 copies in 1972. The first paperback printing, consisting of 10,000 copies, was issued 15 September 1975 at 75p.; a second, also of 10,000 copies, appeared in 1976. The compilers have seen a paperback copy with 'Reprinted ... 1991' and printing code 8–9 on verso title.

The dust-wrapper states this book to have been edited by Hughes.

b. First American edition:

[double-page title, irregularly justified; left:] *Sylvia Plath* | [publisher's logo: torch in rectangle with '1817'] HARPER & ROW, PUBLISHERS | *New York, Evanston, San Francisco, London* [right:] *Crossing the Water* | TRANSITIONAL POEMS

vii, 56 pages; 20.5 × 14.0 cm.

Quarter yellow-brown cloth, grey paper over boards, spine stamped in silver. Dust-wrapper: aerial photograph of waves on a beach front and back, lettered in white.

On verso title: 'FIRST U.S. EDITION'; at foot of p. 56, printing code '71–1'.

Published September 1971 at $5.95; the publisher prefers not to reveal the number printed. There were two reprintings in the same year, and a fourth printing in 1975; these are indicated by the printing numbers on p. 56. The first paperback printing, from the same edition, was issued in 1975 at $2.95; there were five printings of this through 1980, each noted by the printing numbers on p. 56.

A substantially different selection of poems from the one in the English edition.

B55 FIESTA MELONS 1971

[in red and black:] FIESTA MELONS | [ornament] | SYLVIA PLATH | Introduction by TED HUGHES | 1971 | THE ROUGEMONT PRESS · EXETER

(vi), 23 pages; 26.9 × 21.6 cm.

Red cloth, front and spine stamped in gold. Dust-wrapper light brown, printed in red on front and spine.

Colophon: 'This book was designed and printed in May 1971 at | The Rougemont Press Exeter by Eric Cleave and | handbound by Alan Constance. The text is set in | 12pt Plantin and the paper is Glastonbury Antique Laid. | This edition is limited to 150 copies the introduction | of the first 75 copies being signed by Ted Hughes. | [number]'.

Published May 1971 at £7.00 for copies 1–75, £3.00 for copies 76–150. In addition to copies accounted for in the colophon, one has been offered for sale marked 'Out of Series', and the compilers have seen another, unsigned, numbered '26/30'.

CONTENTS: 'Introduction', p. (i).

B56 CORGI MODERN POETS IN FOCUS I 1971

a.1. First edition:

Corgi Modern Poets | in Focus: I | Edited by | DANNIE ABSE | [publisher's logo: in white on a circle of solid black, a head of a dog holding a book in its mouth] | CORGIBOOKS | TRANSWORLD PUBLISHERS LTD | A National General Company

144 pages; 17.7 × 11.0 cm.

Wrappers, printed with a razor-blade pattern in colour.

On verso title: 'First publication in Great Britain | PRINTING HISTORY | Corgi edition published 1971'.

Published 24 September 1971 at 30p; 20,000 copies printed.

CONTENTS: 'Existential Song', p. 52; also nine other poems and two prose excerpts previously collected.

a.2. First hardbound printing (1973):

MODERN POETS | IN FOCUS: 1 | Edited by | DANNIE ABSE | [publisher's logo] | THE WOBURN PRESS : LONDON

145 pages; 21.6 × 15.6 cm.

Red boards, spine stamped in gold. Dust-wrapper printed in red, blue, and black.

On verso title: 'This edition first published in 1973 [...]'.

Published June 1973 at £1.90. The publisher's records do not go back this far, but the Financial Director of Frank Cass & Co., the current owner of Woburn Press, says 'the print-run was likely to have been around 1000 copies'.

Same setting as a.1, the type-pages enlarged and reimposed with divisional titles.

B57   WINTER TREES   1971

a. First edition:

WINTER TREES | by | Sylvia Plath | FABER AND FABER | 3 Queen Square | London

55 pages; 21.5 × 13.9 cm.

Blue cloth, spine lettered in silver. Dust-wrapper coloured blue front and spine, lettered in white and grey; back white, with blurbs in black.

On verso title: '*First published in 1971*'.

Published 27 September 1971 at £1.00; 5000 copies printed. It was reprinted later in 1971 (3000 copies), 1972 (4000 copies), and 1975 (1500 copies). Reprints are so identified on the verso title. The first paperback printing, 10,237 copies, was issued 15 September 1975 at 75p.; further paperbound printings were issued in 1976 (10,000 copies) and 1978 (12,000 copies). The compilers have seen a ninth paperback printing, as indicated by the code on verso title.

CONTENTS: Edited by Hughes, and with a note signed 'T.H.', p. 7.

b. First American edition:

[double-page title, flush at inner margin; left:] [silhouette landscape with bare trees, printed in grey] | Sylvia Plath [right:] [illustration reversed] | WINTER TREES | Harper & Row, Publishers | New York, Evanston, San Francisco, London vii, 64 pages; 21.0 × 14.4 cm.

Quarter grey cloth, violet paper over boards, spine stamped in black. Dust-wrapper coloured silver, printed in black, with illustration from title page front and back.

On verso title: 'FIRST U.S. EDITION'; at foot of p. 64, printing code '72–1'.

Published September 1972 at $5.95; the publisher prefers not to reveal the number of copies printed. In the reprints the 'FIRST U.S. EDITION' note is removed; there was one later in 1972, and a third in 1973, as indicated by the printing code on p. 64.

CONTENTS: A slightly different selection of poems. 'The last nine months' in Hughes' note has been changed to 'The last year'.

B58   SOUTH BANK POETRY AND MUSIC   1971

[no title page; front cover dark blue with lettering in white:] SOUTH | BANK | POETRY | AND | MUSIC | Presented by | The Poetry Society and | The National Book League | with | TED HUGHES | TONY HARRISON | SEAMUS HEANEY | VERNON SCANNELL | music | JEREMY TAYLOR | and friends | [to right, yellow crescent moon over water]

[16] pages; 21.0 × 14.9 cm.

Wrappers, printed as above.

The first printing is not identified as such.

Published October 1971 at 20p. The Poetry Society has not retained records of the exact date or number.

CONTENTS: 'Prometheus ... spotted the vulture', p. [2].

B59   NEW POEMS 1971–72   1972

[two ornaments] | NEW POEMS | 1971–72 | A P.E.N. Anthology | of Contemporary Poetry | [two ornaments as above] | *Edited by* | PETER PORTER | HUTCHINSON OF LONDON

184 pages; 19.8 × 12.9 cm.

Red-orange boards, spine stamped in gold; endpapers grey. Dust-wrapper printed in red and black.

On verso title: '*First published 1972*'.

Published 26 June 1972 at £2.00; the publisher prefers not to reveal the number printed.

CONTENTS: 'Existential Song', p. 90; and three previously collected poems.

B60   THE THREE CHOIRS FESTIVAL   1972

UNDER ROYAL PATRONAGE | THE THREE CHOIRS FESTIVAL | *c.* 1715–1972 | *PROGRAMME* | *of the* | WORCESTER | MUSIC MEETING | for the benefit of the Widows and Orphans | of clergymen in the Dioceses of Worcester, | Hereford, and Gloucester | IN ASSOCIATION WITH THE ARTS COUNCIL OF GREAT BRITAIN | August 27th to September 1st, 1972 | Being the Two Hundred and Forty-fifth | Annual Meeting of the Three Choirs | of Worcester, Hereford and Gloucester | SUBJECT TO ALTERATION

126 pages + (8) leaves of plates; 24.3 × 18.5 cm.

Wrappers, front coloured orange with printing in blue.

Published for the Festival at an undetermined price; 4010 copies printed.

CONTENTS: 'The New World', p. 69, consisting of six poems: It is Not Long You'll be Straddling the Rocket—When the Star was on Her Face—A Star Stands on Her Forehead—I Said Goodbye to Earth—The Street was Empty and Stone—Where Did We Go?

B61   TED HUGHES   1972

a. First edition:

TED HUGHES | by | KEITH SAGAR | *Edited by Ian Scott-Kilvert* | PUBLISHED FOR | THE BRITISH COUNCIL | BY LONGMAN GROUP LTD

Frontispiece portrait + 50 pages and (2) pages of ads; 21.6 × 13.8 cm.

Wrappers, printed in green and black with some lettering in white.

On verso title: '*First published 1972*'.

Published 23 October 1972 at 20p.; 7000 copies printed.

CONTENTS: 'Existential Song', p. 38; 'Song of Woe', p. 39; 'I Said Goodbye to Earth', p. 41.

b. Second edition (1981):

TED HUGHES | by | KEITH SAGAR | [gryphon emblem] |

PUBLISHED BY | PROFILE BOOKS LTD. | WINDSOR, BERKSHIRE, ENGLAND

57 pages; 21.1 or 21.6 × 13.3 cm.

Wrappers, printed in green and black with some lettering in white, based on the design of the first edition.

On verso title: 'First Published 1981'.

Published December 1981 at £1.20; number of copies undetermined. The copies measuring 21.1 cm. high may be a later printing or binding; the compilers have seen one such with a publisher's price sticker of £1.50. In February 1997 the book was still in print, being distributed by Northcote House Publishers at £2.99. Their representative believes there were no reprints.

CONTENTS: Heavily revised from the first edition. This edition contains 'Barley', p. 93, not heretofore collected.

B62   ORGHAST AT PERSEPOLIS   1972

a.1. First edition:

[flush to left except for title] [rule] | ORGHAST AT PERSEPOLIS | [rule] | A. C. H. SMITH | *an account of the experiment* | *in theatre directed by* PETER BROOK | *and written by* TED HUGHES | [publisher's logo: a crowned lion's head within a hexagon] | EYRE METHUEN · LONDON

264 pages; 19.7 × 13.3 cm.

Green boards, spine stamped in gold. Dust-wrapper printed in orange, green, and black, with some lettering in white; front and back printed with photographs from the play. Also published in paperback (not seen).

On verso title: '*First published 1972*'. The book was not reprinted in England.

Published 16 November 1972; 3500 copies printed. Of these, 2500 were initially bound up in hard covers as above and sold at £3.25. The remaining 1000 sets of sheets were published in wrappers in March 1975 at £1.75. The compilers have seen a hardbound copy with a wrap-around band advertising a price reduction to £1.25.

CONTENTS: An outline of the Orghast mythology and a drawing of Orghast, p. 92; an excerpt from the play, with translation, p. 116. Short summaries of sections and ideas are found throughout the book.

a.2. First American printing (1973):

[flush at left except for rules which go further left] *ORGHAST | AT PERSEPOLIS* | [rule] | BY A. C. H. SMITH | *An International Experiment in Theatre* | *Directed by* PETER BROOK *and written by* TED HUGHES | A RICHARD SEAVER BOOK | *The Viking Press/New York*

264 pages; 20.2 × 13.7 cm. The same typesetting as the English edition, but the illustrations were re-screened to a better quality, and their position slightly adjusted on the page.

Green cloth, spine stamped with purple foil, top edge coloured green; pea-green endpapers. Dust-wrapper printed with different photographs than the first edition, with lettering in black, green, and purple (one line in white).

On verso title: 'Published in 1973 by The Viking Press, Inc. | [...] | Printed in U.S.A.'.

Published 25 April 1973 at $7.95 (soon raised to $8.95); 3000 copies printed. There was no reprint, and the book went out of print in America on 7 November 1975.

B63   SAY IT ALOUD   1972

Say It Aloud | [swelled rule, 4.6 cm., broken by an ornament] | EDITED FOR THE POETRY SOCIETY BY | NORMAN HIDDEN | [publisher's logo, bull within an oval] | HUTCHINSON EDUCATIONAL

168 pages; 21.6 × 13.7 cm.

Black boards, spine stamped in gold; no dust-wrapper seen. Also issued in wrappers.

On verso title: '*First published 1972*'; there was no reprint.

Published November 1972; 5000 copies printed. Of these, 1500 were issued hardbound at £2.50 and 3500 in wrappers at £1.00.

CONTENTS: 'A Lucky Folly', p. 90; and two previously collected poems.

B63*   WORKS IN PROGRESS 5   1972

[flush to right] WORKS IN | PROGRESS | NUMBER FIVE | Book trade distribution by | Doubleday & Company, Inc. | The Literary Guild of America, Inc. | New York, N.Y.

396 pages; 18.1 × 10.5 cm.

Wrappers, front printed with colour montage, lettering in black.

The first printing is not identified as such.

Published in 1972 at $1.95; number of copies undetermined.

CONTENTS: Interview of Hughes by Ekbert Faas, p. 369.

B64   STONES   1973

[flush at left, printed in red and black:] STONES | POEMS BY | PAUL
MERCHANT | LITHOGRAPHS BY | BARBARA HEPWORTH |
Introduction by | Ted Hughes | 1973 | THE ROUGEMONT PRESS |
EXETER

30 pages; 28.4 × 18.9 cm.

Light brown cloth, front and spine stamped in gold (spine lettered up).
Endpapers light olive.

Colophon: 'This book was designed and printed | in January 1973 at the
| Rougemont Press Exeter | by Eric Cleave | and handbound by Alan
Constance | The edition is limited to 150 copies | the first 75 copies being
signed | by the author and artist | this copy being | number | [number] |
[signatures, first 75 copies]'.

Published January 1973 at £7.50 signed / £3.50 unsigned.

CONTENTS: Introduction, p. (7).

B65   POEMS FOR SHAKESPEARE 2   1973

a.1. Limited state:

[flush at right] *Poems for | Shakespeare 2 | Edited with an | Introduction by |
Graham Fawcett* | The Globe Playhouse | Trust Publications | London
1973

80 pages; 20.1 × 13.6 cm.

Quarter calf, red cloth sides, gilt, all edges gilt. In a slip-case covered
with the same red cloth.

Colophon: 'A limited, numbered edition of 100 copies, signed by the |
poets and specially bound, has been printed (hors | commerce) in
advance of the first edition [...]'. Signed by the poets opposite the title
page.

Published 23 April 1973 at £40.00; 100 copies thus issued. The price on
the unsold copies was raised to £75.00 some time before 1978.

CONTENTS: 'An Alchemy', p. 13.

a.2. Trade state:

Same typesetting, and probably the same printing as the above.

20.3 × 13.1 cm.

Cream-coloured wrappers, printed in red and black, with a Picasso drawing of Shakespeare on front. The compilers have seen one copy with a laid-in mimeographed slip expressing thanks to Sir Jack and Lady Lyons for permission to reproduce this drawing.

Published 20 May 1973 at 40p.; 1000 copies thus issued.

B66   LET THE POET CHOOSE   1973

[flush to right, in dark green] *Let the* | *Poet Choose* | edited by | JAMES GIBSON | [publisher's logo: Pegasus within a double circle] | HARRAP LONDON

191 pages; 21.6 × 13.6 cm.

Orange boards, spine stamped in black. Dust-wrapper printed in brown and yellow, lettered in white. Also issued in wrappers (not seen).

On verso title: 'First published in Great Britain 1973'.

Published 14 May 1973; 2000 hardbound copies issued at £1.70, 10,000 paperbound at 80p. There was a second paperback printing of 5000 copies on 5 May 1976, and a third (number not disclosed) in 1978.

CONTENTS: Short notes on 'Second Glance at a Jaguar' and 'Full Moon and Little Frieda', p. 87, in which Hughes gives his reasons for choosing the poems.

B66*   ACCENT: AN ANTHOLOGY, 1940–60   1973

[flush to left] ACCENT | AN ANTHOLOGY, 1940–60 | Edited by | DANIEL CURLEY | GEORGE SCOUFFAS | CHARLES SHATTUCK | UNIVERSITY OF ILLINOIS PRESS Urbana Chicago London

xix, 507 pages; 22.7 × 15.2 cm.

Blue cloth, spine stamped in darker blue, ISBN on back cover. Dust-wrapper not seen.

The first printing is not identified as such.

Published 1973 at $12.50; number of copies undetermined.

CONTENTS: 'The Little Boys and the Seasons', p. 290.

B67   NEW POEMS 1973–74   1974

NEW POEMS | 1973–74 | A P.E.N. Anthology | of Contemporary
Poetry | *Edited by* | STEWART CONN | [publisher's logo, bull within an
oval] | HUTCHINSON OF LONDON

184 pages; 19.7 × 12.7 cm.

Red-orange boards, spine stamped in gold. Dust-wrapper orange,
printed in black, with blue cherubs on the front.

On verso title: '*First published 1974*'.

Published August 1974 at £2.00; the publisher prefers not to reveal the
number printed.

CONTENTS: 'New Year Song', p. 79; 'The Warm and the Cold', p. 81;
'His Mother Covers Her Eyes', p. 82 (a revised version of poem 21 of
Prometheus on His Crag, from C276).

B68   WORLDS   1974

WORLDS | SEVEN MODERN POETS | CHARLES CAUSLEY |
THOM GUNN | SEAMUS HEANEY | TED HUGHES | NORMAN
MacCAIG | ADRIAN MITCHELL | EDWIN MORGAN |
Photographs by | Fay Godwin, Larry Herman and Peter
Abramowitsch | [rule] | Edited by Geoffrey Summerfield | Penguin
Education

288 pages; 21.0 × 14.8 cm.

Wrappers, linen-grained, printed in black, brown and orange and
including the poets' pictures.

On verso title: 'First published 1974'.

Published 26 September 1974 at 80p.; 20,000 copies printed. A second
printing of 13,000 copies was issued 29 June 1976; it is identified on verso
title.

CONTENTS: 'The Rock', p. 122. Of the ten photographs by Fay Godwin
in the Hughes section, seven were collected in the trade edition of
Remains of Elmet. Also included here are twenty previously collected
poems.

B69   NEW POETRY 1974   1974

[no title page; cover title, flush to left:] new | poetry | 1974 | *Critical Quarterly* poetry supplement No. 15 | EDITED BY C. B. COX | [silhouette of a tree] [at upper right: '*20p*']

23 pages; 21.6 × 14.1 cm.

Stapled into orange-brown wrappers printed in blue-grey.

The first printing is not identified as such; there was no reprint.

Published September 1974 at 20p.; 12,000 copies printed.

CONTENTS: 'The Harvest Moon', p. 22.

B70   MENCARD 2ND SERIES   1974

A pack of 15 blue cards, 15.2 × 10.2 cm., containing 16 poems in translation. Five hundred sets published by the Menard Press, London, at 75p.; the publisher has no record of the date.

CONTENTS: On one card, 'Under the Winter Sky' by János Pilinszky, translated by Hughes and János Csokits (here misspelt 'Czokits').

B71   THE ART OF TED HUGHES   1975

a. First edition:

THE ART OF | TED HUGHES | KEITH SAGAR | *Senior Staff Tutor in Literature* | *Extra-Mural Department, University of Manchester* | CAMBRIDGE UNIVERSITY PRESS | CAMBRIDGE | LONDON · NEW YORK · MELBOURNE

Portrait frontispiece + (vii), 213 pages; 21.6 × 13.6 cm.

Black boards, spine stamped in gold. Dust-wrapper printed in black and red, with Baskin crow illustration on front.

On verso title: 'First published 1975'.

Published 28 August 1975 at £5.90; 3000 copies printed.

CONTENTS: 'Existential Song', p. 132; 'Song of Woe', p. 136; 'I Said Goodbye to Earth', p. 140; 'His Mother Covers Her Eyes', p. 155 (the revised version of poem 21 of *Prometheus on His Crag*, previously published in B67); 'Quest', p. 161; 'Bride and Groom Lie Hidden for Three Days', p. 167.

b. Second edition (1978):

Identified as such on the title page, spine, and dust-wrapper. Chapters for *Season Songs*, *Gaudete*, and *Cave Birds* were added, and the bibliography brought up to date. (viii), 277 pages.

Published 2 November 1978; 4000 copies printed, of which 1000 were issued hardbound at £12.50, and 3000 paperbound at £3.95.

CONTENTS: 'Existential Song', p. 132, 'Song of Woe', p. 136; 'Where Did We Go?', p. 140; 'His Mother Covers Her Eyes', p. 154 (revised version); 'In the Little Girl's Angel Gaze', p. 159; 'Quest', p. 228; 'A Lucky Folly', p. 236.

B72   POETRY DIMENSION ANNUAL 3   1975

Edited by DANNIE ABSE | POETRY DIMENSION | ANNUAL 3 | The Best of the Poetry Year | [publisher's logo: two books] Robson Books

223 pages; 19.8 × 12.7 cm.

Cloth, binding not seen. Also issued in wrappers, printed in yellow and orange with some lettering in white.

On verso title: 'FIRST PUBLISHED IN GREAT BRITAIN IN 1975'.

Published October 1975; 4500 copies printed. Of these, 1500 were hardbound and issued at £3.50; 3000 were issued in wrappers at £1.60. The book was distributed in the United States in 1976 by St. Martin's Press, price $8.95. St. Martin's has no records regarding the number or exact date, and the compilers have not seen an imported copy.

CONTENTS: 'Sheep', p. 153; 'Swifts', p. 156.

B73   NEW POEMS 1975   1975

[two ornaments] | NEW POEMS | 1975 | A P.E.N. Anthology | of Contemporary Poetry | [two ornaments, as above] | *Edited by* | PATRICIA BEER | HUTCHINSON OF LONDON

185 pages; 19.8 × 12.6 cm.

Orange-brown boards, spine stamped in gold. Dust-wrapper green, printed in black, with an old woodcut of a printer on the front.

On verso title: 'First published 1975'.

Published 17 November 1975 at £3.25; the publisher prefers not to reveal the number printed.

CONTENTS: 'Six Poems', p. 144, untitled, first lines as follows: 'In the M5 Restaurant'; 'Before-Dawn Twilight, A Sky Dry as Talc'; 'Let That One Shrink Into Place'; 'Stilled at His Drink'; 'The Bulging Oak is Not as Old'; 'Why do You Take Such Nervy Shape to Become'.

B74   CHILDREN AS WRITERS 2   1975

Children as Writers 2 | *Award-winning entries from the* | *16th Daily Mirror Children's* | *Literary Competition* | [publisher's logo: in a squared oval, '[windmill] | H·E·B'] | HEINEMANN | LONDON

xiv, 113 pages; 21.6 × 13.7 cm.

Red boards, spine gilt. Dust-wrapper printed in colour with pens on the front. Also issued in wrappers.

On verso title: 'First published 1975'.

Published December 1975 at £2.80; the publisher prefers not to reveal the number printed. Issued simultaneously in wrappers at 95p.

CONTENTS: 'Foreword', p. iii.

B75   POETRY BOOK SOCIETY SUPPLEMENT   1975

Poetry Supplement | COMPILED BY | DANNIE ABSE | FOR THE | POETRY BOOK | SOCIETY | *CHRISTMAS* [*T* swash] | 1975

[56] pages; 21.6 × 14.0 cm.

Green wrappers, printed in black and red.

The first printing is not identified as such; there was no reprint.

Published December 1975 at 50p.; 2000 copies printed.

CONTENTS: 'X', p. [27]. Collected in *Orts* and *Moortown* as 'Each New Moment My Eyes'.

B76   CAMBRIDGE BOOK OF ENGLISH VERSE,   1976
1939–1975

CAMBRIDGE | *BOOK OF* | *ENGLISH VERSE* | *1939–1975* | *Edited by* | *ALAN BOLD* | [shield] | *CAMBRIDGE UNIVERSITY PRESS* | *CAMBRIDGE* | *LONDON · NEW YORK · MELBOURNE*

xii, 248 pages; 20.9 × 11.5 cm.

Brown boards, spine stamped in gold. Dust-wrapper printed in brown and black with lettering in white. Also issued in wrappers.

On verso title: 'First published 1976'.

Published 4 March 1976; 6500 copies printed. Of these, 1500 were issued hardbound at £7.50, and 5000 paperbound at £2.50.

CONTENTS: 'Song of Woe', p. 145, and nine previously collected poems. On p. 234 the editor quotes from an unpublished letter from Hughes about *Crow*.

B77   21 YEARS OF POETRY & AUDIENCE   1976

[flush to left:] *21 YEARS | of | POETRY & AUDIENCE | Edited by | Tom Wharton & Wayne Brown* | [eagle stooping] | aquila poetry

72 pages; 20.3 × 15.4 cm.

Brown plastic over boards, endpapers orange; dust-wrapper brown, stamped in gold. Also issued in wrappers.

The first printing is not identified as such.

Published May 1976 at £3.25; the compilers have been unable to contact the publisher for further information. There was a simultaneous paperback printing at £1.50.

CONTENTS: 'Look Back', p. 67.

B78   WRITERS, CRITICS, AND CHILDREN   1976

a.1. First edition:

[flush to left except for editors' names] WRITERS, CRITICS, | AND CHILDREN | Articles from | *Children's literature in education* | Edited by | Geoff Fox | Graham Hammond | Terry Jones | Frederic Smith | Kenneth Sterck | AGATHON PRESS | New York | HEINEMANN EDUCATIONAL BOOKS | London

ix, 245 pages; 20.8 × 14.0 cm.

Green cloth, spine stamped in blue. Dust-wrapper blue and green with some white lettering.

On verso title: 'First published in the United States, 1976 [...]'.

Published 12 July 1976 at $12.00; 1150 copies printed.

CONTENTS: 'Myth and Education', p. 77. This is a different essay from the one of the same title published in *Children's Literature in Education* (C240).

a.2. First printing for England:

Copies of the edition above were printed in America and sent to England.

They are identical except for an altered verso title, which states in part 'First published in Great Britain, 1976 [...]'.

Published October 1976 at £4.95; 1500 copies printed. 2500 copies in wrappers were issued simultaneously at £1.95 (not seen by the compilers). As there was no paperback version in the United States, this might have consisted of unbound sheets bound up in England. A second paperback printing of 4000 copies was issued in 1978.

B79 JÁNOS PILINSZKY: SELECTED POEMS 1976

a. First edition:

[flush to left] JÁNOS | PILINSZKY | Selected Poems | translated by | TED HUGHES | & JÁNOS CSOKITS | Carcanet New Press

67 pages; 21.5 × 13.5 cm.

Blue paper over boards, spine stamped in gold. Dust-wrapper yellow, printed in blue.

On verso title: 'First published in 1976'.

Published September 1976 at £2.25; 1000 copies printed. Persea Books distributed part of this printing without change in the United States at $8.95. They also advertised a paperback version at $3.95, which the compilers have not seen.

CONTENTS: In addition to being a co-translator, Hughes provides an introduction, p. 7. One of these poems, 'Under the Winter Sky', was previously published in B70.

b. Second edition (The Desert of Love, 1989):

János Pilinszky | THE DESERT OF LOVE | Selected Poems | Translated by | János Csokits and Ted Hughes | Introduced by Ted Hughes | with a memoir by | Ágnes Nemes Nagy | Anvil Press Poetry

Grey boards; spine stamped in gold. Endpapers light purplish-grey. Dust-wrapper printed black, illustration of sculpture of hands on front, photograph of Pilinszky on back, lettering in white, light grey, and black. Also issued in wrappers (not seen).

79 pages; 21.5 × 13.7 cm.

On verso title: 'Revised and enlarged edition published in 1989'.

Published 18 May 1989 (the British Library copy is stamped 9 May); 1100 copies printed, of which 400 hardbound copies were issued at £9.95 and 700 paperbound at £4.95.

CONTENTS: Adds three poems; Hughes' introduction is revised.

B80   WORDS BROADSHEET TWENTY-FIVE   1976

Words Broadsheet | TWENTY FIVE | [drawing of men at a window] | *Drawing by Patricia Moynagh* | *CONTRIBUTORS* | LYMAN ANDREWS · TED HUGHES | EDWIN MORGAN · JEREMY REED | [rule] | *Published in a limited edition of 200 copies, of which* | *numbers 1–50 are signed by the contributors.* | *NUMBER* | [number] | © *with the authors* | WORDS PRESS: 89 THEBERTON STREET : LONDON N1

A single light brown sheet, 42.1 × 28.0 cm., folded twice, a quarter of one side printed as above.

Published around September 1976 at £3.50; the publisher has no record of the exact date or the price of the signed copies.

CONTENTS: 'The Virgin Knight' printed on a quarter of one side.

B81   NEW POEMS 1976–77   1976

[two ornaments] | NEW POEMS | 1976–77 | A P.E.N. Anthology | of Contemporary Poetry | [two ornaments, as above] | *Edited by* | HOWARD SERGEANT | HUTCHINSON OF LONDON

168 pages; 19.9 × 12.7 cm.

Orange-brown boards, spine stamped in gold. Dust-wrapper brown, printed in darker brown with an old woodcut of men and women at a table.

On verso title: 'First published 1976'.

Published 1 November 1976 at £3.50; the publisher prefers not to reveal the number printed.

CONTENTS: 'His Legs Ran About', p. 61; 'A God', p. 140.

B82   NEW POETRY 2   1976

[flush to left] New poetry 2 | An anthology edited by | Patricia Beer & Kevin Crossley-Holland | The Arts Council of Great Britain

284 pages; 21.0 × 13.1 cm.

Grey boards, printed in black on front and spine; endpapers black. Dust-wrapper printed in red and black with lettering in white. Also issued in wrappers.

On verso title: '*New Poetry 2* published 1976'.

Published 18 November 1976; 2500 copies printed. Of these, 1000 were issued hardbound at £3.80, and 1500 in wrappers at £2.00.

CONTENTS: 'Five Birds in Paradise', p. 126, consisting of 'And the Falcon Came', 'The Wild Duck Got Up With a Cry', 'The Unknown Wren', 'And the Owl Floats', 'And the Phoenix Has Come'. 'And the Owl Floats' was collected as 'And Owl' in *Adam and the Sacred Nine*.

B82*   THE BOOK OF CATS   1976

a.1. First edition:

THE | BOOK OF CATS | [two typographic flourishes mirroring each other] | *edited by* | GEORGE MACBETH | *and* | MARTIN BOOTH | SECKER & WARBURG | LONDON

ix, 288 pages; 27.8 × 21.6 cm.

Black cloth, spine stamped in gold, endpapers blue, top edge coloured blue. Dust-wrapper front printed with colour painting of cats, lettering in white, yellow, and black.

On verso title: '*First published in England 1976* [...]'.

Published November 1976 at £8.50; number of copies undetermined. At least some copies sold later have the bottom corner of the front flap clipped and a Heinemann Group sticker giving the price as £13.50.

CONTENTS: 'Pets', p. 276; and two others previously collected.

a.2. First printing for America (1977):

Title page same as above, but imprint is 'William Morrow and Co., Inc. | New York'.

ix, 288 pages; 27.8 × 21.3 cm.

Black cloth, spine stamped in gold, endpapers blue, top edge coloured blue. Dust-wrapper not seen.

On verso title: 'Published in the United States in 1977.'

The same setting as the 1976 edition, with changes appropriate to American publication.

Published in 1977; price and number of copies undetermined.

b. First paperback edition (1979):

Not seen. Published January 1979 by Penguin at £2.25; 55,000 copies printed.

c. Third edition (1992):

THE [silhouette of cat] | [rule] | BOOK OF CATS | [rule] | EDITED BY | George MacBeth | AND | Martin Booth | [publisher's logo, Eric Bloodaxe] | [hand-done letters] BLOODAXE BOOKS

360 pages + plates; 19.9 × 12.6 cm.

Wrappers, colour painting by Jane Lewis on front; spine and back coloured yellow-orange; lettering in black and red.

On verso title: 'This edition published 1992 [...]'.

Published January 1992 at £8.95; 7500 copies printed. This edition was not reprinted. Distributed in the United States for $19.95 by Dufour Editions.

B83   AMEN   1977

a.1. First edition:

AMEN | [rule, 6.8 cm.] | [drawing by Shalom of Safed, 'The Temptation in the Garden'] | [rule, 6.8 cm.] | YEHUDA AMICHAI | Translated from the Hebrew by | the author and Ted Hughes | HARPER & ROW, PUBLISHERS | NEW YORK, HAGERSTOWN, SAN FRANCISCO, LONDON

110 pages; 20.3 × 13.6 cm.

Brown boards, spine stamped in gold. Dust-wrapper coloured light red-brown, printed in brown, including illustration from title page. Also issued in wrappers (not seen).

On verso title: 'FIRST EDITION' and printing code 77–1.

Published June 1977 at $7.95 hardbound / $4.95 paperbound; the publisher prefers not to reveal the number of copies printed.

In addition to being a co-translator, Hughes provides an introduction, p. 9.

a.2. First English printing (1978):

YEHUDA AMICHAI | AMEN | Translated from the Hebrew | by the

author and Ted Hughes | with an Introduction by | Ted Hughes | [Oxford 500th anniversary logo] | OXFORD UNIVERSITY PRESS | *Oxford Melbourne*

110 pages; 21.5 × 13.3 cm.

Wrappers, printed in yellow and brown, with the drawing from the title page and dust-wrapper of the American edition on the front.

The first printing is not identified as such.

Published October 1978 at £2.75; 1000 copies printed.

An offset reprint of the American edition.

a.3. Milkweed Editions reprint (1987):

AMEN | *Poems* [P swash] *by* | YEHUDA AMICHAI | Translated from the Hebrew by | the author and Ted Hughes | [black oval with inscribed white oval frame; within, in white, a milkweed seed] | MILKWEED EDITIONS | MINNEAPOLIS, MINNESOTA

110 pages; 22.85 × 15.2 cm.

Wrappers; front mostly red, printed in gold, blue, and white, with illustration of the Tree of Life; spine and back mostly blue, printed in gold, white, and black.

On verso title: printing code 89–1 and 'SECOND EDITION'. There was only one Milkweed printing.

An offset reprint of a.1.

Published May 1987 at $7.95; 2000 copies printed.

B84   JOHNNY PANIC AND THE   1977
                      BIBLE OF DREAMS

a.1. First edition:

[flush to left except for italic line] Johnny Panic | and the Bible of Dreams | *and other prose writings* | SYLVIA PLATH | FABER AND FABER LIMITED | 3 Queen Square, London

250 pages; 19.6 × 12.6 cm.

Orange paper over boards, spine stamped in silver. Dust-wrapper coloured orange, lettered in white and black.

On verso title: '*First published in 1977*'.

Published 17 October 1977 at £4.95; 5000 copies printed. A 1978 reprint (so identified on the verso title) comprised 2000 copies.

CONTENTS: 'Introduction', p. 11. To this a 'Postscript' (p. 19) was added in proof after a further cache of Plath papers was discovered at the Lilly Library at the University of Indiana.

a.2. Augmented (first paperback) printing (1979):

Title as above.

352 pages; 19.8 × 12.8 cm.

Wrappers, front printed like the dust-wrapper of the first printing.

On verso title: '*This edition first published in 1979*'.

Published 23 April 1979 at £3.50; 8000 copies printed.

CONTENTS: The contents have been augmented by fourteen stories or articles and some journal fragments. Hughes' introduction is much shortened.

b. First American edition:

[within a half-tone floral frame] Sylvia Plath | [decorative rule] | JOHNNY PANIC AND THE | BIBLE OF DREAMS | [rule as above] | Short Stories, Prose | and Diary Excerpts | HARPER & ROW, PUBLISHERS | NEW YORK, HAGERSTOWN, SAN FRANCISCO, LONDON

vi, 313 pages; 23.5 × 15.8 cm.

Brown paper over boards, embossed with Harper torch logo on front, quarter darker brown cloth, spine stamped in copper-coloured foil. Dust-wrapper with floral pattern similar to title page, printed in full colour front and back, lettered in purple and black.

On verso title: 'FIRST EDITION'; printing code 79–1. A second printing from the same year lacks the 'FIRST EDITION' statement and has printing code 79–2.

Published January 1979 at $10.95.

CONTENTS: A comparable but somewhat different selection from a.2; each edition has a couple of pieces which the other lacks. Hughes' introduction is a revision of the a.1 version.

B85   HAND AND EYE   1977

HAND AND EYE | *An Anthology for* | *Sacheverell Sitwell* | Edited by | Geoffrey Elborn | *Privately Printed at* | THE TRAGARA PRESS | EDINBURGH | 1977

34 unnumbered pages; 22.3 × 14.4 cm.

Bound in green Fabriano boards with black cloth spine; title printed on spine. Issued in a plain white dust-wrapper.

Published 15 November 1977 (Sitwell's eightieth birthday) at £8.50; 175 copies printed and numbered. Copies 1–20 were signed by the sixteen contributors. There was also a copy for each of the contributors, and a few extra copies reserved for the use of the editor. The book was sold out immediately upon publication, and there was no reprint.

CONTENTS: 'Whiteness', p. [22].

B86   NEW POEMS 1977–78   1977

[two ornaments] | NEW POEMS | 1977–78 | A P.E.N. Anthology | of Contemporary Poetry | [two ornaments, as above] | *Edited by* | GAVIN EWART | HUTCHINSON OF LONDON

192 pages; 19.8 × 12.6 cm.

Black boards, spine stamped in silver. Dust-wrapper brown, printed in black, with an old woodcut of a hand holding a pen on the front.

On verso title: 'First published 1977'.

Published 21 November 1977 at £4.95; the publisher prefers not to reveal the number of copies printed.

CONTENTS: 'Nefertiti', p. 91; 'The Unknown Warrior', p. 92.

B87   BANANAS   1977

a.1. First edition:

[in a heavy black frame] BANANAS | EDITED BY EMMA TENNANT | ART EDITOR: JULIAN ROTHENSTEIN | Blond | & | Briggs | IN ASSOCIATION WITH QUARTET

221 pages; 21.6 × 13.7 cm.

Black boards, spine stamped in white. Dust-wrapper printed in black and red, with a hand with cards on the front.

On verso title: 'FIRST PUBLISHED 1977'.

Published November 1977 at £5.95; number of copies undetermined.

CONTENTS: 'February 17th', p. 138, here untitled.

a.2. First paperback printing:

Internally the same as a.1, but title page imprint is 'Q | *Quartet* | LONDON, MELBOURNE, NEW YORK | IN ASSOCIATION WITH BLOND & BRIGGS'.

Wrappers, printed like the dust-wrapper of a.1.

The compilers have not seen a copy with the 'FIRST PUBLISHED 1977' line on verso title.

Published by 21 November 1977 (the date stamped in the British Library copy) at £2.50; the publisher prefers not to reveal the number printed. An unknown number of copies were distributed in the United States by Horizon Press at $4.95; these have stickers covering the original price on the back cover.

B88 POETRY SUPPLEMENT 1977

Poetry Supplement | COMPILED BY | COLIN FALCK | FOR THE | POETRY BOOK | SOCIETY | *CHRISTMAS* | 1977

[56] pages; 21.5 × 13.9 cm.

Yellow wrappers printed in black and red-brown.

The first printing is not identified as such; there was no reprint.

Published 1 December 1977 at 50p.; 2500 copies printed.

CONTENTS: 'After the Grim Diagnosis', p. [32]; 'Old Age Gets Up', p. [33]; 'A Memory', p. [34].

B89 NIGHT RIDE AND SUNRISE 1978

Night Ride and Sunrise | An Anthology of New Poems | Edited | and introduced | by | EDWARD LOWBURY | CELTION POETRY

72 pages; 20.4 × 14.6 cm.

Black paper over boards, spine stamped in gold. Dust-wrapper printed red and black, with some white lettering. Also issued in wrappers.

The first printing is not identified as such.

Published 1 May 1978; 5000 copies printed. Of these, 1500 were issued in cloth at £3.99 and 3500 in wrappers at £1.99.

CONTENTS: 'A Citrine Glimpse', p. 27.

B90   VASKO POPA: 1978
                 COLLECTED POEMS 1943–1976

a.1. First edition:

VASKO POPA | Collected Poems | 1943 ∼ 1976 | [drawing of a vine] | translated by ANNE PENNINGTON | with an introduction by TED HUGHES | Carcanet/Manchester

xiii, 194 pages; 21.6 × 13.6 cm.

Blue boards, spine gilt. Dust-wrapper violet, printed in black.

On verso title: 'First published in 1978 [...]'.

Published June 1978 at £3.25; 1000 copies printed. Part of this edition was distributed without change in the United States by Persea Books at $12.50; a photocopied slip laid into these copies gives the publisher's name.

CONTENTS: 'Introduction', p. 1.

a.2. First American printing:

VASKO POPA | [rule] | Collected Poems | 1943 ∼ 1976 | translated by ANNE PENNINGTON | with an introduction by TED HUGHES | PERSEA BOOKS/New York

xiii, 194 pages; 21.6 × 13.3 cm.

Wrappers printed in blue and black, with a photograph of Popa on front.

On verso title: 'First American Edition'.

Published in 1978 at $5.95; 1050 copies printed.

This printing is internally identical to the one above except for the title and the verso title. There is no indication of where it was printed or bound.

B91   CONCEPT   1978

concept | An Anthology of Contemporary Writing | NEW LONDON PRESS | Dallas

204 pages; 27.4 × 21.2 cm.

White wrappers printed in black.

On verso title: ' "Concept" is also published as issues 2–4 of | *The Texas Arts Journal*'. No indication of first printing. See C353.

Published October 1978 at $9.95; 600 copies printed.

CONTENTS: 'Four Poems', p. 33, comprising 'Little Red Twin', 'It Is All', 'These Grasses of Light', and 'Hill-Stone Was Content'.

B91*   A SELECTION FROM POEMS   1978
                    FOR SHAKESPEARE

[within a quasi-Renaissance pictorial frame] A Selection from | Poems for | Shakespeare | Volumes 1 to 6 | *With original drawings* | *Edited by* Roger Pringle & Christopher Hampton | [below frame] GLOBE PLAYHOUSE PUBLICATIONS · LONDON 1978

103 pages, [2] folded plates; 21.6 × 14.1 cm.

White wrappers, printed in black and blue, with sketch portrait of Shakespeare on front.

On verso title: 'This edition is limited to 500 copies, all of which are numbered. | This copy is number [handwritten number above printed rule]'.

Published in 1978 at £2.25; 500 copies printed.

CONTENTS: 'An Alchemy', p. 24.

B92   TIME   1979

a.1. First edition:

TIME | [rule] | *Poems by Yehuda Amichai* | HARPER & ROW PUBLISHERS | New York, Hagerstown, | San Francisco, London

viii, 88 pages; 20.3 × 14.1 cm.

Grey paper over boards, black cloth spine stamped in silver; endpapers blue-grey. Dust-wrapper: front and spine with a colour photograph of an old man in an alley, lettered in white; back, photograph of Amichai. Also issued in wrappers (not seen).

On verso title: 'FIRST EDITION' and printing code 79–1.

Published 28 February 1979 at $9.95 hardbound / $4.95 paperbound; the publisher prefers not to reveal the number of copies printed.

Though Hughes is not credited in the book, he collaborated with the author on the translation.

a.2. First English printing:

YEHUDA AMICHAI | TIME | Translated from the Hebrew | by the

author | with Ted Hughes | Oxford Melbourne | OXFORD UNIVERSITY PRESS | 1979

viii, 88 pages; 21.7 × 13.4 cm.

Wrappers, front with a photograph of a section of the Old Wall at Jerusalem, lettered in white; spine and back printed brown, lettered in white.

The first English printing is not identified as such.

Published 4 October 1979 at £3.50; 1000 copies printed.

A reprint of the American edition, done in England.

B93   ALL AROUND THE YEAR   1979

[within a ruled border enclosing two pages] ALL ['A' two lines high] AROUND | THE YEAR [title within ruled border, on grey background] | Michael Morpurgo | Photographs by James Ravilious | Drawings by Robin Ravilious | NEW POEMS BY TED HUGHES | JOHN MURRAY

208 pages; 24.5 × 18.6 cm.

Green paper over boards, stamped with gold on spine. Dust-wrapper printed in maroon, yellow and black, with photographs front and back.

The first printing is not identified as such.

Published 26 April 1979 at £4.95; the publisher prefers not to reveal the number of copies printed.

CONTENTS: 'Barley', p. 13; 'Foal', p. 170; and ten poems previously collected or published separately.

B94   POETRY BOOK SOCIETY: 1979
          THE FIRST TWENTY-FIVE YEARS

Poetry | Book Society | THE FIRST | TWENTY-FIVE | YEARS | *edited by* | Eric W. White | *for members of* | *the Society* | LONDON | Poetry Book Society | 1979

72 pages; 21.5 × 13.6 cm.

Brown cloth, spine stamped in gold. Dust-wrapper light grey, printed in brown and red.

The first printing is not identified as such; there was no reprint.

Published May 1979 at £1.00; 2000 copies printed.

CONTENTS: 'Ariel by Sylvia Plath', p. 33, a reprint of 'Sylvia Plath' from C168.

B95   SOTHEBY CATALOGUE, 24 JULY   1979

CATALOGUE OF | VALUABLE AUTOGRAPH | LETTERS, | LITERARY MANUSCRIPTS AND | HISTORICAL DOCUMENTS | [...] | which will be sold by auction | by | SOTHEBY PARKE BERNET & CO. | [...] | MONDAY, 23 JULY, 1979 LOTS 1–175 | AT ELEVEN O'CLOCK PRECISELY | TUESDAY, 24TH JULY, 1979 LOTS 176–427 | AT ELEVEN O'CLOCK PRECISELY | [...]

308 pages; 24.5 × 17.9 cm.

Green wrappers, printed in black.

The first printing is not identified as such; there was no reprint.

Published June 1979 at £4.50; number of copies unknown.

CONTENTS: 'Black Bear' (facsimile of the manuscript), p. 169. 'Brooktrout' is also included.

B96   A FIRST POETRY BOOK   1979

[title in colour] A FIRST | POETRY | BOOK | [at left, the sun reading a book] | compiled by John Foster | illustrated by | Chris Orr | Martin White | Joseph Wright | Oxford University Press 1979

128 pages; 21.6 × 16.5 cm.

Plastic-coated boards, illustrated in colour. Also issued in wrappers.

The first edition is not identified as such.

A paperback printing of 15,000 copies, called a 'school edition' by the publisher, was issued 12 July 1979 at £1.25. The hardbound 'trade edition' of 5000 copies, actually the same edition and possibly the same printing as the other, was published 16 August 1979 at £2.50. The two versions were sold in the United States at $5.95 and $10.95.

CONTENTS: 'Roger the Dog', p. 56.

B97   SATURDAY NIGHT READER   1979

[within heavy rectangular frame] SATURDAY NIGHT | READER | [decorative rule, 4.6 cm.] | EDITED BY | EMMA TENNANT | W. H. ALLEN | LONDON 1979 | A HOWARD & WYNDHAM COMPANY

246 pages; 24.5 × 18.7 cm.

Plastic-coated boards, printed in red, yellow and black. Decorative endpapers. No dust-wrapper.

The first printing is not identified as such.

Published 22 October 1979 at £5.95; about 4000 copies printed.

CONTENTS: 'The Head' (short story), p. 81; 'Whiteness', p. 162.

B98   POETRY SUPPLEMENT 1979   1979

Poetry Supplement | COMPILED BY | DOUGLAS DUNN | FOR THE | POETRY BOOK | SOCIETY | *CHRISTMAS* [*T* swash] | 1979 | *The Poetry Book Society receives financial assistance* | *from the Arts Council of Great Britain*

[63] pages; 21.7 × 14.0 cm.

Yellow-brown wrappers printed in black and grey.

The first printing is not identified as such; there was no reprint.

Published December 1979 at 75p.; 1500 copies printed.

CONTENTS: 'Salmon Taking Times', p. [21]; 'You Hated Spain', p. [22].

B99   THE STORY-TELLER 2   1980

[flush to left] *The Story-Teller 2* | *Compiled by Graham Barrett and* | *Michael Morpurgo* | *Ward Lock Educational*

180 pages; 21.5 × 13.7 cm.

Coated orange boards printed in brown with lettering in white.

On verso title: 'First published 1979'.

Published February 1980 at £4.25; 3800 copies printed.

CONTENTS: 'The Tigerboy' (short story), p. 107.

B100   THE OXFORD BOOK OF   1980
                  CONTEMPORARY VERSE

The Oxford Book of | Contemporary Verse | 1945–1980 | Chosen by | D. J. Enright | Oxford Melbourne | OXFORD UNIVERSITY PRESS | 1980

xxxii, 299 pages; 21.6 × 12.9 cm.

Dark blue cloth, stamped in gold. Dust-wrapper printed in black with lettering in yellow and blue, with reproduction of Ben Nicholson painting. Also issued in wrappers.

The first printing not identified as such.

Published 15 May 1980; 26,000 copies printed. Of these, 11,000 were issued hardbound at £7.50 (6000 for Book Club Associates), and 15,000 paperbound at £3.50. There was a reprint in November 1980 of 1500 hardbound (500 for Book Club Associates) and 5000 paperbound.

CONTENTS: 'A Dove', p. 235, and eight previously collected poems.

B101   TED HUGHES: 1980
        THE UNACCOMMODATED UNIVERSE

a.1. First edition:

EKBERT FAAS | [in yellow-brown] TED HUGHES: | THE | UNACCOMMODATED | UNIVERSE | [in grey] With Selected | Critical Writings | by Ted Hughes | & Two | Interviews | Santa Barbara | [in black] BLACK SPARROW PRESS | [in grey] 1980

229 pages; 22.9 × 15.2 cm.

Grey paper over boards, printed in four colours; black cloth spine with printed paper spine label. Also issued in grey wrappers printed like the boards.

Colophon: '[Black Sparrow logo] | Printed May 1980 in Santa Barbara & Ann Arbor for the Black Sparrow | Press by Mackintosh and Young & Edwards Brothers Inc. This edition is | published in paper wrappers; there are 750 cloth trade copies; & 294 | numbered copies have been handbound in boards by Earle Gray & are | signed by Ted Hughes & Ekbert Faas'.

Published 16 June 1980; 750 hardbound copies issued at $14.00, 3059 paperbound copies issued at $7.50.

CONTENTS: 'Laura Riding' (excerpt from an unpublished article of 1970), p. 188; 'Ted Hughes and *Gaudete*' (interview with Faas, 1977), p. 208.
    Also, 'Ted Hughes and Crow: An Interview with Ekbert Faas' (E4); and excerpts from these previously published but uncollected works: 'Leonard Baskin' (B12); Introduction to Keith Douglas's *Selected Poems* (B23); Introduction to *A Choice of Emily Dickinson's Verse* (B37); 'Myth and Education' (second version, B78); Introduction to János Pilinszky's *Selected Poems* (B79); 'Ted Hughes Writes' (C31); 'Context' (C109); 'The Poetry of Keith Douglas' (C118); Review of Bowra's *Primitive Song* (C116); Review of Anderson's *Emily Dickinson's Poetry* (C145); Review of

Turville-Petre's *Myth and Religion of the North* (C152); Review of Lethbridge's *Ghost and Divining Rod* (C162); Review of Eliade's *Shamanism* (C163); Review of White's *Voss* (C151); Review of Greenaway's *Literature Among the Primitives* and *The Primitive Reader* (C181); 'The Genius of Isaac Bashevis Singer' (C171); 'Sylvia Plath' (C168 and B94); 'Notes on the Chronological Order of Sylvia Plath's Poems' (C195 and B45); Review of Thomas's *Selected Letters* (C201); 'Vasko Popa' (C207); Review of Nicholson's *Environmental Revolution* (C247); 'Orghast: Talking Without Words' (C272).

a.2. Limited state:

As above, but with the following differences:
1. An additional leaf bound in following the title, signed by Faas and Hughes and numbered by Hughes.
2. Hand-bound in grey boards printed as above, spine of yellow-brown linen with printed paper spine label.
3. The colophon numbered.

Published simultaneously with the trade copies at $30.00. In addition to the 294 copies in series there were six copies numbered 295 to 300 and marked 'Author's Copy', 'Editor's Copy', 'Publisher's Copy', 'Printer's Copy', 'Binder's Copy', and 'File Copy'.

B102   A GARLAND OF POEMS   1980
              FOR LEONARD CLARK

A GARLAND OF POEMS | for LEONARD CLARK on | his 75th birthday | as a tribute to his achievements | as a poet and in the cause of poetry | Compiled by | R. L. COOK | THE LOMOND PRESS, Kinnesswood and | THE ENITHARMON PRESS, London | 1980

35 pages; 21.0 × 14.9 cm.

Blue wrappers printed in black.

On verso title: 'Edition limited to 400 copies'.

Published 1 August 1980 at £2.50. R. L. Cook states in a letter, 'The publication date, which was strictly observed, was pre-determined and dictated by the fact that the dedicatee (Leonard Clark)'s 75th birthday fell on 1st August 1980.'

CONTENTS: 'Fort', p. 34.

B103   THE REEF AND OTHER POEMS   1980

[flush to left:] THE REEF | and other poems by | KEITH SAGAR |

with an introduction by | TED HUGHES | Published by Proem Pamphlets 1980

[20] pages; 21.1 × 14.7 cm.

Stapled into light blue wrappers, outside printed in green with photograph of a reef, lettered in green.

The first printing is not identified as such.

Published 3 October 1980; 750 copies printed. Fifty of these were signed by Sagar and Hughes and sold for £1.25; the remainder, unsigned, were sold for £.50.

CONTENTS: 'Introduction', p. 2.

B104   NEW POETRY 6   1980

[flush at left] New Poetry 6 | Edited by Ted Hughes | Hutchinson | London Melbourne Sydney Auckland Johannesburg | in association with the Arts Council | of Great Britain and PEN

217 pages; 21.5 × 13.7 cm.

Yellow paper over boards, spine stamped in silver. Dust-wrapper printed in light peach and black.

On verso title: 'First published 1980'.

Published 1980 at £5.95; number of copies unknown.

B105   A SECOND POETRY BOOK   1980

[green] A SECOND | POETRY | BOOK | [black] compiled by John Foster | illustrated by | Alan Curless | Paddy Mounter | Martin White | Joe Wright | Oxford University Press 1980

128 pages; 21.7 × 16.5 cm.

Plastic-coated boards illustrated in colour. Issued without dust-wrapper. Also issued in wrappers (not seen).

The first printing is not identified as such.

Published January 1981; 22,500 copies printed. Of these 7500 were issued hardbound at £3.50; the remaining 15,000 copies were designated the 'school edition' and issued in wrappers.

CONTENTS: 'Black Bear', p. 70; 'The Musk-Ox', p. 71; and a previously collected poem.

B106   TED HUGHES: A CRITICAL STUDY   1981

TED HUGHES: | A Critical Study | [four ornaments arranged in a square] | TERRY GIFFORD and | NEIL ROBERTS | FABER AND FABER | London Boston

288 pages; 21.6 × 13.7 cm.

Orange-brown cloth, spine stamped in gold. Dust-wrapper yellow-brown, printed in red-brown and black.

On verso title: '*First published in 1981*'.

Published April 1981 (the British Library copy is stamped 25 March) at £9.50; number of copies undetermined. Within about a year the price was raised to £10.50. At an undetermined date Faber issued the remaining sheets in wrappers with the all-over 'ff' pattern which they adopted around 1985; this version was priced at £7.50.

CONTENTS: 'Well, how fed up I am', p. 255; excerpts from letters, pp. 256, 259–60.

B107   COLLECTED POEMS by Sylvia Plath   1981

a.1. First edition:

Sylvia Plath | COLLECTED POEMS | Edited by Ted Hughes | FABER AND FABER | London · Boston

351 pages; 23.3 × 15.6 cm.

Blue boards, spine stamped in silver. Dust-wrapper printed in blue and black, with some lettering in white.

On verso title: 'First published in 1981'.

Published 28 September 1981 at £10.00; 2000 copies printed. There was a second printing of 1000 copies in 1983. A paperback printing of 10,000 copies was issued simultaneously; there was a second paperback printing of 8000 copies in 1982.

Includes an introduction by Hughes.

a.2. First American printing:

The | *Collected* | *Poems* [capitals swash] | [ornamental rule] | *Sylvia Plath* [*P* swash] | Edited by Ted Hughes | [publisher's logo, torch within a rectangle with '*1817*' below] | HARPER & ROW, PUBLISHERS, New York | Cambridge, Philadelphia, San Francisco, | London, Mexico City, São Paulo, Sydney

Contents as in a.1, with pp. (1), (3), and (4) reset. On verso title: 'FIRST U.S. EDITION' and printing code 81–1.

23.4 × 15.5 cm.

Black cloth, front blind-stamped, spine stamped in gold. Dust-wrapper printed in copper and black on a light grey field.

Published 25 November 1981 at $17.50; the publisher prefers not to reveal the number of copies printed. A paperback printing was issued simultaneously at $7.95. We have seen hardbound copies, apparently of the second and third printings, with the printing code changed to 82–2 and 82–3 respectively; in each case the 'FIRST U.S. EDITION' notice remains. In 1992 the imprint was changed to 'HarperPerennial', but the typesetting remains the same. The compilers have seen a 23rd paperback printing from 1994, as indicated by the printing code on verso title.

B108   LONDON REVIEW OF BOOKS   1981
ANTHOLOGY ONE

[heavy rule] | London Review | OF BOOKS | [light rule] | ANTHOLOGY ONE | [light rule] | WITH AN INTRODUCTION BY | KARL MILLER | JUNCTION BOOKS | LONDON | [heavy rule]

xi, 307 pages; 21.3 × 13.7 cm.

Black boards, spine stamped in gold. Dust-wrapper coloured light blue, lettering in white and black. Also issued in paperback (not seen).

On verso title: 'First published in Great Britain by | Junction Books Ltd'.

Published October 1981 at £12.50 hardback/£5.95 paperback; number of copies undetermined.

CONTENTS: 'The Earthenware Head', p. 140.

B109   INVISIBLE THREADS   1981

a.1. First edition:

[within rule frame] YEVGENY | YEVTUSHENKO | [rule, 16.6 cm.] | INVISIBLE THREADS | DESIGNED BY CRAIG DODD | [rule, 11.9 cm.] | SECKER & WARBURG · LONDON

64 + [65–192] pages; 27.9 × 22.8 cm.

Black boards, spine stamped in gold. Dust-wrapper primarily dark purple, colour photographs front and back, lettering in light blue and white.

On verso title: 'First published in England 1981 by | Martin Secker & Warburg Limited'.

Published October 1981 at £9.95 (raised after 31 December 1981 to £12.50); number of copies undetermined.

CONTENTS: 'Safari in Ulster' by Yevtushenko, translated by Hughes, p. 35.

a.2. First printing for America (1982):

The same internally as a.1, but title-page imprint is 'MACMILLAN PUBLISHING CO., INC. | NEW YORK'.

Quarter black cloth, grey boards. Spine round, stamped in silver. Dust-wrapper not seen.

27.7 × 22.8 cm.

The first printing is not indicated as such. Printed in England.

Published 1982 at $19.95; number of copies undetermined.

B110   A GARLAND FOR THE LAUREATE   1981

[within a wood-engraved floral oval printed in red-brown, text in black] A Garland | for the | Laureate | *Poems presented* | *to Sir John* | *Betjeman* | *on his 75th* | *birthday* | *The Celandine Press*

Edited by Roger Pringle and printed by the Whittington Press.

[49] pages; ca. 27.5 × 19.0 cm.

Colophon: '350 copies hand-set [...] | [...] | 150 copies are quarter-bound, of which 75 have | been signed by the contributors, and 200 | copies are bound in paper covers. | Printing completed in October 1981'.

The breakdown of copies was as follows:
> Copies 1–25 (not seen): signed by all the contributors. Quarter-bound in black Oasis morocco, marbled paper sides, spine gilt, red endpapers; in a black buckram-covered slip-case. Not for sale.
> Copies 26–50 (not seen): like copies 1–25. £75.00.
> Copies 51–75 (not seen): like copies 1–50, but quarter-bound in black buckram. £65.00.
> Copies 76–150 (not seen): unsigned; bound like copies 51–75, but no slip-case. £18.00.
> Copies 151–350: unsigned; bound in marbled wrappers, primarily maroon, with pasted-on printed label on front. £8.50.

Published 20 November 1981, the day after a private presentation ceremony to Betjeman.

John Randle writes in *The Whittington Press: A Bibliography 1971–1981*: 'The signing was put in hand before we had even started the setting, and our final task was to print the title-page opposite these priceless and already unrepeatable signatures (one of the contributors having already died in the interim).'

CONTENTS: 'That Morning', p. [42].

B111   POETRY BOOK SOCIETY SUPPLEMENT   1981

Poetry Supplement | COMPILED BY | ANDREW MOTION | FOR THE | POETRY BOOK | SOCIETY | *CHRISTMAS* [T swash] | 1981 | *The Poetry Book Society is subsidised by* | *the Arts Council of Great Britain*

[59] pages; 21.2 × 13.8 cm.

Light-blue wrappers, printed in black and dark grey.

The first printing is not identified as such; there was no reprint.

Published before 30 November 1981 at £1.25. The Society does not have records of the number printed, but their Director in 1997, Clare Brown, believes it would have been in the order of 1200 copies.

CONTENTS: 'River of Dialectics', p. [20].

B112   NEW POETRY 7   1981

[flush to left:] New Poetry 7 | an Arts Council anthology | edited by David Harsent | Hutchinson | London Melbourne Sydney Auckland Johannesburg | in association with | The Arts Council of Great Britain and PEN

114 pages; 21.4 × 13.7 cm.

Dark blue boards, spine stamped in silver. Dust-wrapper printed in dark blue with some lettering in white.

On verso title: 'First published 1981'.

Published November 1981 at £6.50; number of copies undetermined.

CONTENTS: 'Drove Six or So High Miles', p. 61; 'Plenty Coups', p. 62.

B113   THE WAY TO WRITE   1981

a.1. First edition:

[flush to left:] *The Way* | [flush to right:] *to Write* | JOHN FAIRFAX |

and JOHN MOAT | [flush to left:] *Foreword by Ted Hughes* | [flush to right:] [logo of Hamish Hamilton: tree flanked by two letters 'h', with '50' in roots] | ELM TREE BOOKS ● London

xix, 87 pages; 21.5 × 13.5 cm.

Orange boards, spine stamped in gold. Dust-wrapper printed in red, yellow, and black. Also issued in paperback.

On verso title: 'First published in Great Britain 1981'. The compilers have seen a paperback copy which retains this line but adds a printing code indicating the seventh printing.

Published in 1981 at £6.50. The publisher has no record of the number in the first printing, but says 'it is unlikely to have been an edition of more than 3,500'.

CONTENTS: 'Foreword', p. xi.

a.2. First American printing:

The same setting as a.1 except for the following:
  1. Title page imprint is 'ST. MARTIN'S PRESS | NEW YORK'.
  2. Verso title mostly reset; the first American printing is not identified as such.
  3. Preliminaries slightly rearranged.
  4. Pages 81–87 (the last chapter, 'Notes on Presentation and Submission') are not included.

(xv), 80 pages; 20.85 × 13.7 cm.

Grey wrappers, printed in dark blue and dark red-brown.

Published 1981 at $3.95; number of copies undetermined.

B114   THE JOURNALS OF SYLVIA PLATH   1982

a. First edition:

[ornament] | THE JOURNALS OF | [facsimile signature] Sylvia Plath | Foreword by Ted Hughes | Ted Hughes, Consulting Editor | and Frances McCullough, Editor | The Dial Press | New York | [logo, cupid astride lion]

xiii, 370 pages + plates; 23.3 × 15.5 cm.

Brown cloth, spine stamped in copper-coloured foil. Dust-wrapper printed in wallpaper pattern in browns, with lettering in black with cream-coloured shading.

On verso title: 'First printing'.

Published late March 1982 at $16.95. In advance promotional material, the book was announced for 23 April; copies were in the shops by 16 April; Smith College received its copy from Frances McCullough on 30 March; and the copy at Library of Congress is stamped 29 March. The first printing consisted of 35,000 copies. A second printing (also 1982) is identified as such on the verso title.

b. Literary Guild edition (1982):

Title page transcription as in the first edition, but reduced.

xi, 337 pages + plates; 20.8 × 13.8 cm.

Quarter dark-brown boards, dark orange-yellow sides, spine stamped in gold. No dust-wrapper seen.

Published as an October 1982 alternate choice of the Literary Guild (New York). The price to members was $12.79; the publisher prefers not to reveal the number of copies printed. Although this edition superficially resembles the Dial edition, it is entirely reset.

c. First paperback edition (1983):

The | *JOURNALS* | *of SYLVIA* | *PLATH* | Foreword by Ted Hughes | Ted Hughes, Consulting Editor | and Frances McCullough, Editor | BALLANTINE BOOKS ● NEW YORK

xv, 368 pages + plates; 17.4 × 10.5 cm.

Wrappers printed in yellow, letters printed in black and red.

On verso title: 'First Ballantine Books Edition: August 1983'.

Published August 1983 at $3.95; the publisher prefers not to reveal the number of copies printed.

B115   ARVON FOUNDATION POETRY   1982
              COMPETITION. 1980 ANTHOLOGY

Arvon | Foundation | Poetry Competition | 1980 ANTHOLOGY | Edited and introduced | by | TED HUGHES and | SEAMUS HEANEY | Kilnhurst Publishing Company

173 pages; 23.4 × 15.4 cm. With a laid-in errata slip bearing corrections to three pages.

Light-yellow wrappers printed in dark green.

On verso title: 'First published in Great Britain 1982'.

Published May 1982 (the British Library copy is stamped 27 April) at

£3.00; 5000 copies printed. The book was still in print in December 1996.

CONTENTS: Second half of the Introduction, p. 6. Hughes judged the competition with Heaney, Charles Causley, and Philip Larkin.

B116   WHAT RHYMES WITH 'SECRET'?   1982

What Rhymes with 'Secret'? | *Teaching children to write poetry* | Sandy Brownjohn | With a Foreword by Ted Hughes | [in box, a chess bishop] | HODDER AND STOUGHTON | LONDON SYDNEY AUCKLAND TORONTO

104 pages; 21.6 × 13.4 cm.

Textured wrappers coloured red, ships in bottles on front, lettering in black and white.

On verso title: 'First published 1982'.

Published 1 June 1982 at £2.75. The publisher has no record of the number of copies printed, but there were fourteen printings through 1996.

CONTENTS: Foreword, p. 5.

B117   POEMS FOR CHARLES CAUSLEY   1982

[flush to left] Poems for | Charles Causley | [two-column list of 26 contributors] | LONDON/THE ENITHARMON PRESS/1982

39 pages; 21.6 × 13.9 cm.

Black cloth, spine stamped in gold; endpapers blue-violet. Dust-wrapper blue, printed in darker blue and black. Also issued in blue wrappers of the same design as the dust-wrapper.

On verso title: 'Edition limited to five hundred and fifty copies | of which four hundred and fifty are for sale'.

Published for Causley's birthday on 24 August 1982; about 200 copies hardbound and 350 paperbound were issued. About 100 of these were distributed among the contributors. Steven Halliwell, who has done a bibliographical study of the Enitharmon Press, believes that approximately 30 of the latter were hardbound and 70 paperbound. The remainder were sold at £5.25 hardbound/£3.60 paperbound.

CONTENTS: 'Little Whale Song', p. 38. A note in the contents list says that Hughes' contribution was received too late for inclusion in alphabetical order.

B118   THE RATTLE BAG   1982

THE RATTLE BAG | [swelled rule, 2.2 cm.] | *An Anthology of Poetry* | *selected by* | SEAMUS HEANEY and TED HUGHES | ff | *faber and faber*

(1–4)7–498 pages; 21.6 × 13.9 cm.

Yellow boards, spine stamped in gold. Dust-wrapper coloured blue with all-over 'ff' pattern in darker blue, yellow panels with printing in black.

On verso title: '*First published in 1982*'.

Published October 1982 (the British Library copy is stamped 27 September) at £10.00; number of copies undetermined. There was a simultaneous paperback printing of unknown size at £4.95. The paperback was reprinted in 1983 and 1984, as indicated on the verso title. For the third printing Faber redesigned the title page to its new standard rule-frame format.

B119   NEW YEAR POETRY SUPPLEMENT   1982

New Year | *Poetry Supplement* | COMPILED BY | ALAN BROWNJOHN | FOR THE | POETRY BOOK | SOCIETY | *DECEMBER* | 1982 | *The Poetry Book Society is subsidised by* | *the Arts Council of Great Britain*

[64] pages; 21.6 × 14.0 cm.

Beige wrappers printed in brick red and black.

The first printing is not identified as such.

Published December 1982 at £1.50. The Society does not have records of the number printed, but their Director in 1997, Clare Brown, believes it would have been in the order of 1200 copies.

CONTENTS: 'Madly Singing in the Mountains', p. [33]; 'A Cormorant', p. [34].

B120   THE ACHIEVEMENT OF TED HUGHES   1983

a.1. First edition:

[flush to right] [two short rules one over the other] *EDITED BY* **KEITH SAGAR** | The Achievement | of Ted Hughes | [rule] | [rule, 2.9 cm.] MANCHESTER | UNIVERSITY PRESS [at right, publisher's logo: cypher of letters MUP]

(vi), 377 pages; 23.4 × 15.6 cm.

Dark khaki boards; spine stamped in gold. Dust-wrapper printed in blue with photograph of relief panel by Leonard Baskin, rules in brown and green, lettered in blue and brown.

The first printing is not identified as such.

Published 31 March 1983 at £27.50; 1800 copies printed. A paperbound printing of 1250 copies was published 12 January 1987 at £9.50; it is the same internally, and the wrappers have the same design as the dust-wrapper. The publisher believes there were no reprints.

CONTENTS: 'The Little Boys and the Seasons', p. 314; 'Quest', p. 315; 'Lines to a Newborn Baby', p. 316 (= 'Lines to a Newborn Baby' from C82 plus 'To F.R. at Six Months' from C130); 'O White Elite Lotus', p. 318; 'The Brother's Dream', p. 321; 'Birdsong', p. 324; 'Song of Woe', p. 326; 'Existential Song', p. 328; 'Crow Fails', p. 330; 'Crow Compromises', p. 330; 'A Lucky Folly', p. 331; 'The New World', p. 338; 'An Alchemy', p. 341; 'The Lamentable History of the Human Calf', p. 344; 'The Advocate', p. 346; 'Two Dreams in the Cell', p. 347; 'Your Mother's Bones Wanted to Speak, They Could Not', p. 348; 'She Is the Rock', p. 349.

a.2. First printing for America:

Title page as above, but imprint is '[rule] | [stylized Doric column] | [rule] | THE UNIVERSITY OF GEORGIA PRESS | Athens'.

Same setting as above, and printed in Hong Kong like the first English impression.

23.4 × 15.6 cm.

Same binding as above, with changes appropriate to American publication. Issued without a dust-wrapper.

The first printing is not identified as such.

Published May 1983 at $25.00; the publisher is not able to retrieve its record of the number of copies printed.

B121   WEST COUNTRY FLY FISHING   1983

a.1. First edition:

West Country | *Fly Fishing* [all capitals swash] | AN ANTHOLOGY EDITED BY | ANNE VOSS BARK | [reproduction of a Thomas Bewick wood-engraving] | B. T. BATSFORD LTD · *LONDON*

xi, 131 pages + plates; 23.0 × 15.5 cm.

Dark green boards, spine stamped in gold. Dust-wrapper with colour photo of fisherman on front, black-and-white photo of river on back.

On verso title: 'First published 1983'.

Published by 23 May 1983 (the date stamped in the British Library copy) at £9.95. The publisher has retained no records on this title. After about a year the price was raised to £10.95.

CONTENTS: 'Taw and Torridge', p. 25.

a.2. First paperback printing (1986):

Same setting as a.1; also published by Batsford.

23.25 × 15.5 cm.

Wrappers, front printed same as dust-wrapper of a.1, spine and back coloured green with lettering in white, blurbs on back.

On verso title: 'First published 1983 | First paperback edition 1986'.

Published by 18 June 1986 (the date stamped in the British Library copy) at £8.95; number of copies undetermined.

B122   MODERN POETRY IN TRANSLATION: 1983   1983

a.1. First edition:

[rule] | [flush at left] Edited by Daniel Weissbort | with an introduction by Ted Hughes | [further to left, grey halftone] Modern Poetry | in Translation: 1983 | [flush with second line, black] An Annual Survey | MPT/Carcanet | London/Manchester

214 pages; 22.6 × 13.7 cm.

Wrappers, printed in brick red and black.

On verso title: 'First published in Great Britain in 1983'

Published May 1983 at £6.95. Carcanet's records for this title were evidently destroyed in the Corn Exchange bombing in June 1996, but the editor, Daniel Weissbort, guesses the print run was between 1000 and 1500. Carcanet undertook the distribution for about half the edition. This was intended as the first of a series of annual surveys, a successor to the periodical of the same title which Weissbort and Hughes started in 1965. Only this issue was published.

CONTENTS: 'Modern Poetry in Translation', p. 9.

a.2. First printing for America:

Same as above except:
1. Imprint is 'MPT/Persea | New York'.
2. Verso title has changes appropriate to American publication, including 'First edition printed in Great Britain by Short Run Press Limited, Exeter'.
3. Wrappers have changes appropriate to American publication.

22.5 × 13.7 cm.

Published 1983 at $9.95; the publisher estimates 750 to 1000 copies were printed. The book was still in print in January 1997.

B123   PEOPLE   1983

People [first and last letters swash] | ESSAYS & POEMS | EDITED BY | SUSAN HILL | CHATTO & WINDUS | [rule, 5.4 cm.] | THE HOGARTH PRESS | LONDON

192 pages; 23.2 × 15.4 cm.

Grey boards, spine stamped in gold. Dust-wrapper with painting of boulevardiers front and spine, back cover yellow, lettering in violet and black.

The first printing is not identified as such; there was no reprint.

Published 12 September 1983 (the British Library copy is stamped 18 August) at £8.95; 5000 copies printed.

CONTENTS: 'Sketching a Thatcher', p. 65.

B124   TENFOLD   1983

[flush at left:] *Tenfold* | *Poems for* | FRANCES | HOROVITZ

Edited by Paul Hyland and Gillian Clarke.

[19] pages; 24.6 × 13.5 cm.

Cream or grey wrappers, front printed in red.

On p. [3]: 'TENFOLD is published by Martin Booth in October, | 1983, on behalf of the Frances Horovitz Benefit, in an | edition of 500 copies with an additional fifty copies | being numbered and signed by the contributors. It is | printed on St Cuthbert's Mill rag paper by Skelton's | Press, Wellingborough, Northamptonshire, and is | first published to coincide with a reading given by the | contributors at the Colston Hall, Bristol on October | 30th, 1983.'

Published 30 October 1983 at £3.50; 550 copies printed.

CONTENTS: 'Sunstruck Foxglove', p. [12].

B125 WINTER POETRY SUPPLEMENT 1983

Winter | Poetry Supplement | COMPILED BY | DAVID HARSENT | FOR THE | POETRY BOOK | SOCIETY | *DECEMBER* | 1983 | *The Poetry Book Society is subsidised by | the Arts Council of Great Britain*

[53] pages; 21.5 × 14.0 cm.

Wrappers, drawing of reader on front, lettered in dark green and black.

The first printing is not identified as such.

Published December 1983 at £1.50. The Society does not have records of the number printed, but their Director in 1997, Clare Brown, believes it would have been in the order of 1200 copies.

CONTENTS: 'Grace', p. [23]; 'Waste', p. [24].

B126 WHERE I USED TO PLAY ON THE GREEN 1984

GLYN HUGHES | [double rule, 1.7 cm.] | WHERE I USED TO PLAY | ON THE GREEN | *Introduction by Ted Hughes* | [penguin logo in oval frame] | A KING PENGUIN | PUBLISHED BY PENGUIN BOOKS

192 pages; 19.85 × 13.0 cm.

Wrappers, front coloured light yellow with coloured woodcut in oval; photo of author on back; lettered in black and dark maroon.

On verso title: 'First published by Victor Gollancz 1982 | Published in Penguin Books 1984'.

Published 26 April 1984 at £2.50; 10,000 copies printed. After about a year the price was raised to £2.95.

CONTENTS: 'Introduction', p. (5). The first edition (hardcover from Gollancz, 1982) lacked this.

B127 BETWEEN COMETS 1984

Between Comets | for Norman Nicholson at 70 | Edited by | WILLIAM SCAMMELL | TAXVS | [rule, 2.9 cm.] | 1984

66 pages; 21.7 × 13.3 cm.

Copies 1–50: dark red cloth, front and spine stamped in gold; endpapers light grey 'laid'. No dust-wrapper. A further 700 copies were issued in wrappers, landscape painting by Ian R. Steel on front, continued across spine to back; lettering along top in dark brown on yellow-brown ground.

On verso title: 'First published 1984. [...]'.

Published September 1984. The numbered copies were signed by Norman Nicholson and William Scammell and sold for £35.00; the paperbound copies sold for £5.00. There was also a single presentation copy bound in boards for Nicholson.

CONTENTS: 'A Tern', p. 25.

B128   BRITAIN: A WORLD BY ITSELF   1984

BRITAIN [*R* and *T* swash] | *A WORLD BY ITSELF* | *Reflections on the landscape by eminent British writers* | [rule, 9.6 cm.] | *WITH COMMENTARIES BY DR FRANKLYN PERRING* | [rule, 9.6 cm.] | *Photographs by Paul Wakefield* | *AURUM PRESS*

159 pages; 28.1 × 22.0 cm.

Brown boards, spine stamped in gold; endpapers tan. Dust-wrapper coloured brown, colour photograph of a mountain valley on front cover, lettering in white.

The first printing is not identified as such; there was no reprint.

Published November 1984 at £14.95; Aurum Press has not kept records on the number of copies printed. The book was distributed in America by Little, Brown at $27.50.

CONTENTS: 'A Devon River', p. 10, composed of 'Nymet' and a prose passage beginning 'During the last forty years ...'.

B129   THE COMPLETE PRINTS OF   1984
                    LEONARD BASKIN

[double-page title; left:] A CATALOGUE RAISONNÉ 1948–1983 [right:] THE COMPLETE PRINTS OF | LEONARD BASKIN | BY ALAN FERN AND JUDITH O'SULLIVAN | [Baskin woodcut] | INTRODUCTION BY TED HUGHES | A NEW YORK GRAPHIC SOCIETY BOOK | LITTLE, BROWN AND COMPANY   BOSTON

304 pages; 30.5 × 22.8 cm.

Quarter black cloth, grey boards; front cover blind-stamped, spine stamped in silver. Endpapers dark grey. Dust-wrapper printed in black and red, with Baskin illustrations front and back.

On verso title: 'First Edition'.

Published 1984 at $60.00; number of copies undetermined. Distributed in the U.K. at £35.00 by Hutchinson Books, beginning October 1984.

CONTENTS: 'The Hanged Man and the Dragonfly', p. 10.

B130   SYLVIA PLATH'S SELECTED POEMS   1985

[within a double-rule frame] SYLVIA | PLATH'S | SELECTED | POEMS | [rule, 2.4 cm.] | *chosen by Ted Hughes* | [below frame] ff | *faber and faber* | LONDON · BOSTON

85 pages; 19.6 × 12.6 cm.

Green-blue boards; spine stamped in silver. Dust-wrapper printed in green, with all-over 'ff' pattern in black; text printed in black on white panels.

On verso title: 'This selection first published in 1985'.

Published 8 July 1985 at £6.95; 2500 copies printed. A simultaneous paperback printing of 17,500 copies was issued at £2.95, identical internally except for the addition of a Net Book Agreement note on verso title. Later reprints of the paperback have a printing code on verso title; the latest the compilers have seen is the 11th.

B131   SOUTH WEST REVIEW: A CELEBRATION   1985

South West Review | *A Celebration* | *Edited by* | LAWRENCE SAIL | *Foreword by* | PATRICIA BEER | [publisher's logo: in rule frame: '[outline of southwest of England] | SOUTH WEST ARTS']

104 pages; 21.0 × 14.7 cm.

Wrappers, coloured blue, printed in red and light grey.

On verso title: 'First published in 1985 [...]'.

Published October 1985 at £2.95; the publisher has kept no records on this publication. Copies were still in print in January 1997.

CONTENTS: 'Conscripts', p. 65; and another poem previously collected.

B132   45 CONTEMPORARY POEMS   1985

*45 | CONTEMPORARY | POEMS | The Creative Process | Edited by |
Alberta T. Turner | Cleveland State University* | [ship logo] | Longman | New
York & London

ix, 246 pages; 23.4 × 16.1 cm.

Wrappers, printed in several shades of red, blue, and purple, lettering in
white and black.

On verso title: printing codes 9–1 and 92–85.

Published 1985 at $15.95; number of copies undetermined. The book
was not reprinted.

CONTENTS: 'Crow on the Beach' (poem and essay), p. 91.

B133   WILLIAM GOLDING   1986

William Golding | The Man and his Books | [thick-thin rule] | *A Tribute
on his 75th Birthday* | Edited by John Carey | ff | *faber and faber* |
LONDON · BOSTON

191 pages, plates; 21.5 × 13.7 cm.

Black boards, spine stamped in gold.

On verso title: 'First published in 1986'.

Published September 1986 (the British Library copy is stamped 3
September) at £12.50; number of copies undetermined. Copies issued
later have a sticker with Faber's logo on it, raising the price to £15.00.

CONTENTS: 'Baboons and Neanderthals: A Rereading of *The Inheritors*',
p. 161.

B134   SELECTED POEMS by Harry Fainlight   1986

HARRY FAINLIGHT | SELECTED POEMS | Introduction by | *Ruth
Fainlight* | a memoir by | Allen Ginsberg | and | a poem by | Ted Hughes |
TURRET [publisher's device: on black ground, a white tower bearing
flag with a T] BOOKS

v, 78 pages; 24.5 × 17.0 cm.

Blue morocco-grain plastic over boards, spine stamped in black. Dust-
wrapper printed in black, with Fainlight's name lettered by Ralph
Steadman.

On verso title: 'This edition [...] | is limited to 1,000 copies'.

Published 1986 at £12.50; 1000 copies printed.

CONTENTS: 'To be Harry', p. 5.

B135   THE POETRY BOOK SOCIETY   1986
ANTHOLOGY 1986/87

The | Poetry Book Society | Anthology 1986/87 | *Edited with an Introduction by* | *JONATHAN BARKER* | Hutchinson | London Melbourne Auckland Johannesburg

94 pages; 19.7 × 13.6 cm.

Wrappers, printed in violet and blue, with lettering in blue, white, red, and black.

On verso title: 'This edition first published in 1986 by Hutchinson Ltd, [...]'.

Published 1986 at £4.95; number of copies undetermined.

CONTENTS: 'Lovesick', p. 55; 'Devon Riviera', p. 56.

B136   GUARDIAN ANGELS   1987

a.1. First edition:

GUARDIAN | ANGELS | [heavy rule, 4.0 cm.] | Fifteen new stories by winners of the | *Guardian* Children's Fiction Award. | Edited by Stephanie Nettell | *Illustrated by Mike Daley* | VIKING KESTREL

195 pages; 21.6 × 13.5 cm.

Dark-green boards, spine stamped in silver. Dust-wrapper with colour drawings front and back, lettered in red, green, and black.

On verso title: 'First published 1987'. There was no reprint.

Published 26 March 1987 at £6.95; 5500 copies printed.

CONTENTS: 'The Guardian', p. 183.

a.2. First paperback printing (1988):

Same setting as a.1. Imprint on title page is '[publisher's logo, a puffin in an oval] | PUFFIN BOOKS'.

Adds [6] leaves of ads at end. 19.8 × 13.9 cm.

Wrappers, printed to same basic design as dust-wrapper of a.1.

On verso title: 'First published by Viking Kestrel 1987 | Published in Puffin Books 1988'.

Officially published 17 March 1988 (the British Library copy is stamped 26 February) at £2.50; 15,000 copies printed. There were reprints on 27 April 1989 (3000 copies) and 29 March 1990 (4000 copies), neither one seen by the compilers.

B137   MEET AND WRITE, BOOK 2   1987

[flush to left] Meet and Write | *A teaching anthology of* | *contemporary poetry* | book two | Edited by Sandy and Alan Brownjohn | [in box, a chess bishop] | HODDER AND STOUGHTON | LONDON SYDNEY AUCKLAND TORONTO

126 pages; 23.3 × 15.6 cm.

Wrappers, printed in grey, green, and black, with square panel on front shading from gold through green to blue.

On verso title: 'First published 1987'.

Published 1 March 1987 at £3.45; 4000 copies printed. After about a year the price was raised to £3.75. The book went out of print in April 1994.

CONTENTS: 'Ted Hughes', p. 90.

B138   THE BIGGEST EGG IN THE WORLD   1987

MARIN | SORESCU | The Biggest | EGG | in the World | [publisher's logo, Eric Bloodaxe] | [hand-done letters] BLOODAXE BOOKS

79 pages; 21.6 × 13.8 cm.

Wrappers; front: surrealistic colour photograph of breakfast utensils, continued to back; lettered in red, yellow, white, and blue.

On verso title: 'First published 1987 [...]'.

Published May 1987 at £4.95; 2000 copies printed. There was no reprint.

CONTENTS: Hughes' translations (with Joana Russell-Gebbett) of Sorescu's poems 'Destiny', p. 17; 'Looking for Hegel's Portrait', p. 21; 'Warning', p. 23; 'Ballad', p. 36; 'The Whistle', p. 43; 'The House', p. 48; 'Group', p. 57; 'Circuit', p. 78.

B139   POEMS FOR SHAKESPEARE 10   1987

[flush to left] Poems for | Shakespeare 10 | *Edited with an Introduction* | *by Charles Osborne* | Bishopsgate Press | Southwark 1987

62 pages; 21.6 × 13.4 cm.

Wrappers coloured light yellow, front with caricature portrait of Shakespeare, printed in black and red.

The first printing is not identified as such.

Published July 1987 at £3.50; number of copies undetermined. After about a year the price was raised to £4.95.

CONTENTS: 'Full House' (1. Queen of Hearts; 2. Queen of Spades; 3. Queen of Clubs; 4. Queen of Diamonds; 5. King of Hearts; 6. King of Spades; 7. King of Clubs; 8. King of Diamonds), p. 11.

B140   CAUSLEY AT 70   1987

[flush to left] Causley At 70 | Edited by Harry Chambers | [publisher's logo, man under umbrella] | PETERLOO POETS

119 pages; 21.5 × 13.8 cm.

Wrappers, cream-coloured, front with pen and water-colour portrait; lettered in blue.

On verso title: 'First published in 1987'.

Published 27 October 1987 at £4.95 (£3.30 to associate members of Peterloo Poets); number of copies undetermined.

CONTENTS: 'Birthday Greetings', p. 12.

B141   POETRY BOOK SOCIETY   1987
ANTHOLOGY 1987/88

The | Poetry Book Society | Anthology 1987/88 | *Edited with an Introduction by GILLIAN CLARKE* | Hutchinson | London   Melbourne   Auckland   Johannesburg

viii, 100 pages; 19.8 × 12.6 cm.

Wrappers, front with colour painting of a butterfly, lettered in red, white, and black.

On verso title: 'This edition first published in 1987 [. . .]'.

Published by 30 October 1987 (the date stamped in the British Library copy) at £5.95; number of copies undetermined.

CONTENTS: 'Kore', p. 53.

B142   ISLAND OF THE CHILDREN   1987

ISLAND THE | CHILDREN | [solid square] *An Anthology of New Poems*
[solid square] | COMPILED BY | ANGELA HUTH |
DECORATIONS BY | JANE RAY | [drawing of trees] |
ORCHARD BOOKS | London

128 pages; 25.1 × 18.6 cm.

Blue boards, spine stamped in gold. Endpapers reddish-brown. Dust-wrapper with colour illustrations front and back, lettered in red, dark purple, blue, and black. Also issued in wrappers with same design as the dust-wrapper.

On verso title: 'First published in Great Britain in 1987 [...]'.

Published October 1987; about 2800 hardback copies issued at £8.95, and 4300 paperback copies in two printings at £4.95. The publisher claims the paperback was published in March 1990 and reprinted in September 1990, but all copies seen are dated 1987 and carry ISBNs for both bindings.

CONTENTS: 'Hen', p. 38 (first line 'Dowdy the Hen').

B143   COMPLETE POEMS OF KEITH DOUGLAS   1987

a.1. First edition with Hughes' introduction:

KEITH DOUGLAS | [rule] | Complete Poems | PREFACE AND
EDITED BY | DESMOND GRAHAM | Oxford   New York |
OXFORD UNIVERSITY PRESS

xxvii, 145 pages; 21.5 × 13.4 cm.

Wrappers, photos of Douglas front and back printed in sepia, lettered in black. Back cover bears reviews, an excerpt from Hughes' introduction, and a short blurb.

On verso title: '*First published 1978 | First issued as an Oxford University Press paperback 1979 | Reissued, with Ted Hughes' Introduction, 1987 | [...] | Printed in Great Britain [...]*'.

Published 19 November 1987 (the British Library copy is stamped 6 November) at £5.95; 2500 copies printed. There was a reprint of 750 copies in 1990 (not seen).

CONTENTS: 'Introduction', p. xv. This was lacking in the 1978 and 1979 printings.

a.2. New plating, partly reset (1995):

KEITH DOUGLAS | *The Complete Poems* | *Edited and with a Preface by* | Desmond Graham | *Introduction by* | Ted Hughes | OXFORD UNIVERSITY PRESS

xxix, 146 pages; 21.6 × 13.7 cm.

Wrappers, photos of Douglas front and back printed in sepia, front cover over red panel lettered in white, black, and yellow, spine and back lettered in black. Back cover bears an excerpt from Hughes' introduction and a longer blurb than a.1.

On verso title: '*First published 1978* | *First issued as an Oxford University Press paperback 1979* | *Reissued, with Ted Hughes' Introduction, 1987*| *Reprinted 1990* | *Reissued 1995* | [. . .] | *Printed in Hong Kong*'.

The poems are in the same setting as in a.1, but the titles are set in a larger size. The preface and introduction are also set larger (though not necessarily re-keyboarded).

Published 4 May 1995 (the British Library copy is stamped 27 April) at £8.99; 890 copies printed.

B144   SINGING BRINK   1987

[within rule frame] SINGING BRINK | An *Anthology of* Poetry | *from* L*umb Bank* | [below frame] Edited by | Maura Dooley and David Hunter | With an introduction by | Ted Hughes | ARVON PRESS | 1987

80 pages; 21.0 × 14.7 cm.

Wrappers, printed with a colour manuscript map of Hebden Bridge. Green free flyleaves.

On verso title: 'SINGING BRINK is published in 1987 [. . .]'.

Published 1987 at £4.00; 2000 copies printed. The book was still in print in December 1996.

CONTENTS: 'Introduction', p. 8; 'A Chinese History of Colden Water', p. 24 (a revision of 'The Trance of Light').

B145   FOUR POETS FOR ST MAGNUS   1987

FOUR POETS | FOR ST MAGNUS | [red] George Mackay Brown | Ted Hughes | Seamus Heaney | Christopher Fry | [black] MCMLXXXVII

Published by the Breckness Press, Stromness, Orkney.

[48] pages; 31.2 × 23.5 cm.

From colophon: 'This edition is limited to one hundred copies | of which fifteen bearing the letters A–O | are not for sale | of the remaining, eighty-five copies | numbered 1–85, numbers 1–5 are individually bound'. Signed by all four poets.

Copies 1–5 (not seen) were bound according to specification, or in full vellum or calf. Copies A–O not seen. Copies 6–85 bound in reddish-brown boards, the front with an illustration of a church interior; vellum spine stamped in gold. Endpapers light brown. In a slipcase covered with green cloth, with paper label bearing an illustration inset on side.

Published in 1987 at £380.00 for copies 1–5, £250.00 for copies 6–85.

CONTENTS: 'The Zodiac in the Shape of a Crown', p. [12] (facsimile of manuscript), p. [14] (transcription).

B146   AN ANTHOLOGY OF POETRY   1988
                    FOR SHAKESPEARE

[flush at left] An Anthology | of Poetry | for Shakespeare | *Selected by Charles Osborne* | *Illustrated by Louis le Brocquy* | Bishopsgate Press | Southwark 1988

83 pages; 21.6 × 13.6 cm.

Blue boards, spine stamped in silver; dust-wrapper, if any, not seen. Also issued in wrappers, abstract colour portrait of Shakespeare on front, lettered in black, emblem on back partly printed in red.

The first printing is not identified as such.

Published August 1988 at an undetermined price for the hardbacks and £3.95 for the paperbacks; number of copies undetermined.

CONTENTS: 'Foreword', p. 5; 'A Full House', p. 8.

B147   PEARLS OF WISDOM   1988

PEARLS OF | WISDOM | —— Edited by —— | WENDY WILSON | —— Foreword by —— | SHEILA HANCOCK | —— Introduction by —— | DEREK NUTTALL | Darton, Longman and Todd | London | Published in association with CRUSE | [rule]

xii, 84 pages; 19.7 × 12.8 cm.

Red boards, spine stamped in gold. Dust-wrapper front: photograph of pearls on velvet, continued to back; lettering in white, yellow, and light blue.

On verso title: 'First published in Great Britain in 1988 [...]'.

Published October 1988 at £4.95; number of copies undetermined.

CONTENTS: Paragraph of explanation for choosing a quotation of Walt Whitman, p. 32.

B148   FIRST AND ALWAYS   1988

[in double-rule frame] | FIRST AND | ALWAYS | [rule, 2.0 cm.] | *Poems for The | Great Ormond Street | Children's Hospital* | [childish drawing of a crying child] | Compiled and edited by | Lawrence Sail | Introduction by Ted Hughes

Published by Faber and Faber.

ix, 69 pages; 19.8 × 12.5 cm.

Wrappers, printed with all-over pattern of 'ff' in red, blue, green, and yellow on black ground; white panels with lettering in black.

On verso title: 'First published in 1988'.

Published October 1988 (the British Library copy is stamped 17 October) at £5.95; number of copies undetermined.

CONTENTS: 'Foreword', p. vii; 'Under High Wood', p. 32.

B149   HILL FIELD   1989

[in blue] *Hill Field* | [in black] POEMS AND MEMOIRS FOR JOHN MONTAGUE | ON HIS SIXTIETH BIRTHDAY, 28 FEBRUARY 1989 | COMPILED AND EDITED BY THOMAS DILLON REDSHAW | Coffee House Press, Minneapolis :: Gallery Books, Oldcastle

(vii), 113 pages; 22.7 × 15.1 cm. (presentation copies); 22.3 × 14.9 cm. (paperback).

From the colophon: 'Of the run, 1,700 copies have been sewn and glued into paper wrappers; 150 have been cased in cloth over boards; and 26 lettered presentation copies have been bound by hand in quarter-linen [...]'.

Copies A–Z bound in marbled boards, white linen spine, printed spine label. The compilers have not seen one of the 150 hardbound copies. The remainder are bound in wrappers, coloured blue, lettered in white, with abstract colour illustration on front.

Published by June 1989 at $22.95 for the numbered copies and $11.95 for the paperbacks; 1876 copies total. Distributed in Ireland by the Gallery Press, Dublin, at £9.00 beginning June 1989.

CONTENTS: 'Madly Singing in the Mountains', p. 18.

B150   LETTERS TO AN EDITOR   1989

[flush at left] Letters | to an | Editor | [centred] Edited by Mark Fisher | CARCANET

xix, 290 pages; 21.6 × 13.7 cm.

Black boards, spine stamped in gold. Dust-wrapper: painting of a typewriter printed in purple on front; spine and back white; lettering in black and white.

On verso title: 'First published in 1989 [...]'. There was no reprint.

Published 26 October 1989 (the British Library copy is stamped 23 October) at £14.95; 1500 copies printed.

CONTENTS: Letters from Hughes, p. 143 (17 June 1979); p. 154 (undated, 1980).

B151   THE POETRY BOOK SOCIETY   1989
ANTHOLOGY 1989–1990

The | Poetry Book Society | Anthology 1989–1990 | *Edited with an introduction by* | CHRISTOPHER REID | Hutchinson | London Sydney Auckland Johannesburg

ix, 99 pages; 19.9 × 12.6 cm.

Wrappers, coloured maroon, photograph of sculpture of fighting rabbits on front, lettering in yellow and white.

On verso title: 'This edition first published in 1989 [...]'.

Published October 1989 (the British Library copy is stamped 22 September) at £6.95; number of copies undetermined.

CONTENTS: 'Mayday', p. 55.

B152   THE ORANGE DOVE OF FIJI   1989

THE ORANGE | DOVE OF FIJI | *Poems for the World Wide Fund for Nature* | *Edited by* | *Simon Rae* | *Preface by* | *H.R.H. The Duke of Edinburgh* | Hutchinson | London   Sydney   Auckland   Johannesburg xviii, 125 pages; 21.5 × 13.4 cm.

Wrappers, coloured black, colour painting by David Hockney on front, lettered in white and yellow.

On verso title: 'This edition first published in 1989 [...]'.

Published October 1989 (the British Library copy is stamped 24 October) at £9.95; number of copies undetermined.

ᵣCONTENTS: 'What the Serpent Said to Adam', p. 57.

B153   IN PRAISE OF TROUT   1989

[within a double-rule frame] IN PRAISE OF TROUT [the initial letters are slightly taller] | DAVID PROFUMO | [colour illustration of a fly] | *Foreword by Ted Hughes* | ILLUSTRATIONS BY ALAN JAMES ROBINSON | [below frame] VIKING

xxii, 90 pages; 22.9 × 29.6 cm.

Green boards, spine stamped in gold. Dust-wrapper blue with light-yellow panel on front and white panel on back, each containing a colour illustration of a trout.

On verso title: 'First published 1989 | [printing code, 1–2]'.

A hundred copies were bound in quarter dark-green morocco, lighter green cloth sides, with marbled endpapers. They contain an additional preliminary leaf bearing a limitation statement. Each is numbered, and signed by Profumo and Robinson.

Published 30 November 1989 (the British Library copy is stamped 24 November) at £25.00; 5000 copies printed. The special copies were published 13 November.

CONTENTS: 'Foreword', p. ix.

B154   SOTHEBY CATALOGUE, 14 DECEMBER   1989

English Literature | and History | including | The Trumbull Papers | Day of Sale | Thursday 14th December 1989 at 10:20 am | in the Grosvenor Gallery | Bloomfield Place, New Bond Street, London W1 | [...]

175 pages; 27.1 × 20.9 cm.

Wrappers, printed with brown fabric design, photograph of a corrected galley proof on front, corrected typescript on back, lettered in white and black.

The first printing is not identified as such; there was no reprint.

Published November 1989 at £15.00; number of copies undetermined.

CONTENTS: 'Crow Goes to the Films' or 'Crow Goes to the Movies', autograph drafts (lot 131), illustrated p. 73.

B155   GABBIANO   1990

GABBIANO | *e altri versi* | *Poems by Camillo Pennati – translated by Ted Hughes* | *ON EDGE* | *Drawings by Lester Elliot* | *EDIZIONI L'ARZANÀ ASSOCIAZIONE CULTURALE – TORINO 1990*

[48] pages; 27.9 × 20.8 cm.

Wrappers, front with an Elliot painting in colour, lettered in black, spine and back blank. Both front and back covers fold out.

Colophon: 'Finito di stampare nel | mese di aprile 1990 | [signature of Pennati] | Edizione limitata su carta Leykam Muerztaler (Austria) | COPIA N. [number, but no limitation given]'.

Published April 1990 at Lire 25,000/$30.00; number of copies undetermined.

Includes a facsimile of a letter from Hughes to the author, 10 August 1989.

B156   DEAR (NEXT) PRIME MINISTER   1990

DEAR [in script, inserted] Next [regular type] PRIME MINISTER | OPEN LETTERS TO | MARGARET THATCHER | & NEIL KINNOCK | EDITED BY NEIL ASTLEY | [publisher's logo, Eric Bloodaxe] | [hand-done letters] BLOODAXE BOOKS

x, 182 pages; 21.4 × 14.7 cm.

Wrappers; front, continued to back, montage of portraits in front of 10 Downing Street; lettered in white, red, and blue.

On verso title: 'First published in 1990 [...]'. There was no reprint.

Published July 1990 at £5.95; 3270 copies printed.

CONTENTS: Letter from Hughes, p. 96.

B157   SHAUN HILL'S GIDLEIGH PARK   1990
              COOKERY BOOK

SHAUN HILL'S | [rule, 9.7 cm.] | GIDLEIGH | [baseline rule, 2.5 cm.]

PARK [baseline rule, 2.5 cm.] | *Cookery Book* | Foreword by Ted Hughes | CENTURY | London Sydney Auckland Johannesburg

128 pages; 26.4 × 19.7 cm.

Green boards, spine stamped in gold. Dust-wrapper with out-of-focus green background with ferns, lettering in darker green outlined in black, colour photo of author on front, of Gidleigh Park Hotel on back.

On verso title: 'First published in 1990 [...]'.

Published 13 September 1990 at £15.99; 8,500 copies printed. The book was remaindered in April 1993, and by 1996 was out of print, with total sales of 7,200 copies.

CONTENTS: 'Foreword', p. (6), incorporating a poem (first line 'When you lift up your eyes').

B158   POETRY BOOK SOCIETY ANTHOLOGY 1:   1990 NEW SERIES

The Poetry Book Society | Anthology 1 | New Series | *Edited by* | Fraser Steel | Hutchinson | London Sydney Auckland Johannesburg

(xi), 114 pages; 19.8 × 12.7 cm.

Wrappers, printed black and light blue, with compass roses and lettering in red, white, and black.

On verso title: 'This edition first published in 1990 by Hutchinson Ltd [...]'.

Published October 1990 at £6.99; number of copies undetermined. The only copy seen has an adhesive label with a bar code pasted over the original one. The original bar code bears an ISBN which does not correspond to that on the verso title.

CONTENTS: 'Flame', p. 42.

B159   THREE CONTEMPORARY POETS   1990

[flush to right] Three Contemporary Poets | Thom Gunn | Ted Hughes | & | R. S. Thomas | A CASEBOOK | EDITED BY | A. E. DYSON | M | MACMILLAN

294 pages; 21.55 × 13.5 cm.

Blue boards, spine stamped in gold. Dust-wrapper front and back with text in black, blue, and red on yellow panels with blue and red rule borders. Also issued in paperback (not seen).

On verso title: 'First published 1990'. A 1991 reprint is identified as such on verso title.

Published October 1990 at £30.00; number of copies undetermined. There was a simultaneous paperback printing of unknown size at £9.50.

CONTENTS: Sections of interviews of Hughes by Ekbert Faas, p. 101; 'A Reply to Critics (1979)', p. 108; excerpt from letter on images in *Crow*, ca. 1980, p. 114.

B160   A GARLAND FOR STEPHEN SPENDER   1991

[green silk-screen: a garland containing the hand-formed words:] a garland for Stephen | [black letterpress] *Arranged by Barry Humphries* | The Tragara Press | EDINBURGH | 1991

[1–4⁸] = 32 leaves. 55 pages; ca. 24.9 × 16.8 cm. (edges uncut).

Green wrappers with flaps; on front: 'A GARLAND FOR | STEPHEN SPENDER | [portrait]'.

Colophon: '*Edition limited to 150 copies* | *(of which 75 are for sale)* | *hand-set in 12 point Bembo type* | *and printed on 'Character' laid paper.* | *[...]*'.

Published by 16 May 1991 (the date stamped in the British Library copy), probably at £21.00; 150 copies printed.

CONTENTS: 'Two Views of the Sea', p. 26.

B161   WINNING WORDS   1991

WINNING WORDS | Prizewinners | in the Faber and Faber | Write-A-Story | Competition | Chosen and with a Foreword by | *Ted Hughes* | Illustrated by Genevieve Webster | after ideas by the authors | ff | *faber and faber* | LONDON · BOSTON

(ix), 196 pages; 19.8 × 12.6 cm.

Wrappers, front with colour fantasy figures continuing to back; lettering in black on white panels.

On verso title: 'First published in 1991'.

Published 3 June 1991 (the British Library copy is stamped 26 April) at £3.99; number of copies undetermined.

CONTENTS: 'Foreword', p. (ix).

B162   SAVE THE EARTH   1991

[each letter in a different shade of grey to black] SAVE | [rule, 3.7 cm.] THE [rule, 3.8 cm.] | EARTH | [rule] | JONATHON PORRITT | [rule] | FOREWORD | HRH THE PRINCE OF WALES | [rule] | INTRODUCTION | SIR RICHARD ATTENBOROUGH | [colour photograph of the earth from space] | [publisher's logo, open book bearing letters DK] | DORLING KINDERSLEY | LONDON ● NEW YORK ● STUTTGART

208 pages; 28.85 × 22.7 cm.

Plastic-covered boards decorated with colour illustrations of natural objects, lettered in many colours. Endpapers coated green. Issued without a dust-wrapper.

On verso title: 'First published in Great Britain in 1991'.

Published September 1991 at £14.99; number of copies undetermined. Distributed in the United States by Turner Publications, Atlanta, at $29.95. As of May 1997, 379,163 copies had been distributed outside Britain.

CONTENTS: 'First Things First (an election duet, performed in the womb by foetal twins)', p. 192.

B163   CASTING A SPELL   1991

[bent upward in middle] CASTING | [straight] A SPELL | AND OTHER POEMS | *An Anthology of New Poems* | *Compiled by* | ANGELA HUTH | *Illustrations by* | JANE RAY | [illustration of a hen] | [drawing of trees] | ORCHARD BOOKS

96 pages; 25.15 × 18.6 cm.

Green boards, printed with shells in white, spine lettered in white. Endpapers coated green. Dust-wrapper with colour illustrations front and back, lettered in blue, green, and black.

On verso title: 'First published in Great Britain in 1991'.

Published October 1991 at £9.99; number of copies undetermined.

CONTENTS: 'Crab', p. 57; 'Jellyfish', p. 57.

B164   HOCKNEY'S ALPHABET   1991

a.1. First edition:

HOCKNEY'S ALPHABET | Drawings by David Hockney | & Written

contributions edited by | Stephen Spender | *faber and faber* | *for the* | Aids Crisis Trust

[117] pages (A⁴ B–H⁸); 32.1 × 24.3 cm. Printed offset.

On verso title: 'First published in 1991'.

Three versions:

REGULAR: bound in dark blue boards, spine stamped in gold. Dust-wrapper printed in red, blue, yellow, and green, spine and back lettered in black.

SPECIAL: with an additional leaf bound after the title leaf, bearing colophon: 'This edition of *Hockney's Alphabet* | is printed on Exhibition Fine Art Cartridge | and is specially bound in library buckram. | Each copy is signed by | the artist and the editor | [signatures of Spender and Hockney]'. Bound in yellow cloth, spine in gold on black panel. In a slip-case covered with grey cloth.

DE LUXE: not seen. With an additional leaf bound after the title leaf (transcription reported by Bertram Rota Ltd. without line endings): 'This edition [...] comprises 300 copies printed on Exhibition Fine Art Cartridge paper, specially bound in quarter vellum with handmade Fabriano Roma paper sides, signed by David Hockney, Stephen Spender and contributors. 250 numbered copies are for sale. A further 26 copies lettered A–Z are for the writers. In addition there are 24 copies numbered I–XXIV for William A. McCarty-Cooper, the artist and the editor. [...]'. The recto and verso of this leaf bear the signatures of all contributors. Top edge and spine gilt; in a matching slip-case with paper label.

Published 1991 at £25.00 regular/£175.00 special/£1000 de luxe; the number of 'regulars' and 'specials' is undetermined. The 'de luxe' and 'special' copies were distributed by Bertram Rota Ltd.

CONTENTS: 'S' (fantasia on the letter S in verse and prose), p. [85] of the regular copies.

a.2. First printing for America (1992):

Same typesetting as above, except title page imprint is '*Random House* | *in association with* | *the American Friends of* | *Aids Crisis Trust*'. Verso title has 'Manufactured in Great Britain | [printing code, 2–3] | Random House, Inc., 1992 Edition'. All copies seen have this code rather than the expected 2–1.

32.2 × 24.2 cm.

Black boards, spine stamped in gold; cream endpapers. Dust-wrapper as in a.1, with changes appropriate to American issue; on back flap,

'Printed in Great Britain. 9/92'. On front cover, a circular sticker specifying the charitable destination of the proceeds.

Published in the autumn of 1992 at $50.00 ($65.00 in Canada); number of copies undetermined.

B165   POETRY BOOK SOCIETY ANTHOLOGY 3   1992

The Poetry Book Society | Anthology 3 | *Edited by* | William Scammell | Hutchinson | London

x, 86 pages; 19.8 × 12.5 cm.

Wrappers, printed in shades of purple and black, with designs of dragonflies, lettering in white and light violet.

On verso title: 'This edition first published in 1992 [...]'.

Published October 1992 (the British Library copy is stamped 7 September) at £6.99; number of copies undetermined. Copies bought directly from the Society were later priced at £7.99, though the price printed on the book is unchanged.

CONTENTS: 'Laws of the Game', p. 37 (collected in *New Selected Poems* as 'The Other').

B166   NEW WRITING 2   1993

[heavy rule] | [flush at left, but indented] *New* | *Writing 2* | edited by | MALCOLM BRADBURY | and | ANDREW MOTION | Minerva in association with the | British Council

(viii), 392 pages; 19.7 × 12.5 cm.

Wrappers, illustrated front and back with abstract colour designs suggestive of Saturn; spine and part of back wrapper black; lettering in white, red, and yellow.

On verso title: 'First published in Great Britain 1993'.

Published 14 January 1993 (the British Library copy is stamped 4 December 1992) at £6.99 ($14.99 in Canada); 7500 copies printed.

CONTENTS: 'Three Poems for J.R.' (1. Waif; 2. Lovesick; 3. Atavist), p. 42.

B167   POEMS FOR ALAN HANCOX   1993

[in yellow-brown, wood-engraving of a hill by Miriam Macgregor] |

Poems for Alan Hancox | *Melvyn Bragg, D. J. Enright, U. A. Fanthorpe,* | *Michael Foot, Duncan Forbes, John Fuller, Seamus Heaney,* | *Michael Horovitz, Ted Hughes, Adrian Mitchell,* | *Jenny Joseph, P. J. Kavanaugh, Laurie Lee, Peter Levi,* | *Brian Patten, Lawrence Sail, Jon Silkin, Jon Stallworthy,* | *Charles Tomlinson* | [in yellow-brown, wood-engraving of hiking gear]

Variant: lacking the commas after 'Levi' and 'Stallworthy'.

[41] pages; 28.2 × 20.0 cm.

On verso title: 'Printed and published by The Whittington Press, | Lower Marston, Nr. Risbury, Herefordshire | [...]'. Colophon: 'This tribute to Alan Hancox was assembled by Alan Tucker, and set | in Goudy Modern type and printed at Whittington on Zerkall mould- | made paper in an edition of 350 copies. 50 copies are signed by the | contributors and quarter bound in Oasis leather, with a separate | proof of the title-page wood-engravings by Miriam Macgregor | March 1993 | This is copy no: [number in pen]'.

Copies 1–300 bound in decorated boards (printed at the Whittington Press), brown cloth spine stamped in gold, top edge gilt; endpapers brown 'laid'. Copies I–L have the same boards with brown morocco spine; a pocket inside the back cover contains two sheets, each with one of the woodcuts from the title page, printed in black and signed by Macgregor.

Copies I–L in a slip-case covered with brown paper, top and bottom covered with brown cloth.

Copies I–L are signed by all the contributors on the blank page opposite the title.

Published March 1993 at £175.00 for copies I–L, £42.50 for copies 1– 300. The signed copies sold out immediately; the regulars were 'a good deal slower to sell', according to *The Whittington Press: A Bibliography 1982–1993*, p. 123. 'Due to a slight altercation among some of the poets late in the evening while they were signing, a few of these precious frontispieces became slightly stained with beer, but by that time it was impossible to leave them out and so a few of these rather unusual copies must be in circulation somewhere.'

Regarding the commas on the title page, John Randle wrote to one of us (18 January 1997), 'I seem to remember noticing the 2 commas were missing during the run, so some copies will have them in, some won't and it won't be evenly split among specials and ordinaries.'

CONTENTS: 'The Bear', p. [22].

B168   SACRED EARTH DRAMAS   1993

SACRED EARTH | DRAMAS | An anthology | of winning plays | from the | 1990 competition | of the | Sacred Earth | Drama Trust | ff | *faber and faber* | LONDON · BOSTON

xii, 179 pages; 19.7 × 12.5 cm.

Wrappers, front with colour painting by Brent Linley, spine and back white; lettered in blue, white, and black.

On verso title: 'First published in Great Britain in 1993' and printing code 2–1.

Published September 1993 (the British Library copy is stamped 22 July) at £7.99 ($14.99 in Canada; $12.95 in the U.S.); number of copies undetermined.

CONTENTS: 'Foreword', p. vii.

B169   KLAONICA   1993

KLAONICA | [white on black panel] POEMS FOR BOSNIA | EDITED BY | KEN SMITH & JUDI BENSON | [publisher's logo, Eric Bloodaxe] | [hand-done letters] BLOODAXE BOOKS

128 pages; 21.4 × 13.9 cm.

Wrappers; colour illustration by Ralph Steadman on front, lettering in red and black.

On verso title: 'First published 1993 [...]'.

Published September 1993 at £7.95; 3000 copies printed. Distributed in the United States by Dufour Editions. The book has not been reprinted.

CONTENTS: 'Why the "21st Child" Could Not Be Lifted', p. 87.

B170   THE CHALLENGE OF TED HUGHES   1994

The Challenge of | Ted Hughes | [rule] | Edited by | Keith Sagar | *Reader in English Literature* | *University of Manchester* | M | [rule, 3.2 cm.] | St. Martin's Press

xv, 190 pages; 21.5 × 13.8 cm.

Black boards, spine stamped in gold. Dust-wrapper front coloured grey, reproduction of Baskin drawing of bird skeleton; spine red, back white; lettering in red, white, and black.

On verso title: 'First published in Great Britain 1994 by | THE

MACMILLAN PRESS LTD | [. . .] First published in the United States of America 1994 by | Scholarly and Reference Division, | ST. MARTIN'S PRESS, INC.,'.

Published 19 May 1994 (the British Library copy is stamped 6 April) at £35.00; number of copies undetermined. Of these, 200 were distributed in the United States by St. Martin's Press starting in April 1994. Within a couple of years the price on the English copies was raised to £37.50.

CONTENTS: 'The Dove', first draft of 'The Dove Came', facsimile p. 48, with editorial reconstruction p. 47.

B171   GHOSTLY HAUNTS   1994

a.1. First edition:

[on light yellow panel within dark blue rule frame] *Published in association with* | [small silhouette of leaves] | The National Trust | [over halftone grey flourishes] [small solid circle flanked by two 1.5-cm. rules] | [in red] GHOSTLY | HAUNTS | [below flourishes] EDITED BY MICHAEL MORPURGO | *Illustrated by Nilesh Mistry* | [below frame] [devilish mask resembling a leaf or a butterfly] | [publisher's logo: [hemispherical skylight] | PAVILION | [rule, 2.0 cm.]]

160 pages; 24.15 × 19.2 cm.

Red boards, spine stamped in white. Dust-wrapper with all-over colour illustration, lettering in black and red on cream-coloured panels.

On verso title: 'First published in Great Britain in 1994 [. . .]' and printing code 2–1.

Published 19 October 1994 at £12.99; 4000 copies printed. Distributed in the United States by Trafalgar at $22.95. A paperback printing was not issued by Pavilion until 1996.

CONTENTS: 'The Deadfall', p. 11.

a.2. First paperback printing (HarperCollins, 1995):

Not seen. Published by HarperCollins (sub-licensed from Pavilion); presumed to be the same setting as a.1.

Published 9 October 1995 at an undetermined price. The publisher prefers not to reveal the number of copies printed.

B172 **AFTER OVID** 1994

a.1. First edition:

AFTER OVID | NEW METAMORPHOSES | [Grecian decoration] | EDITED BY | MICHAEL HOFMANN | AND JAMES LASDUN | ff | *faber and faber*

[2], xiv, 298 pages; 21.5 × 13.6 cm.

Blue cloth, spine stamped in white. Dust-wrapper coloured blue with all-over pattern of 'ff'; text in black on white panels; colour illustration on front panel.

On verso title: 'First published in 1994'.

Published November 1994 (the British Library copy is stamped 12 October) at £14.99; number of copies undetermined. A paperback printing did not appear until 1996.

CONTENTS: Translations: 'Creation/Four Ages/Flood', p. 3; 'Bacchus and Pentheus', p. 94; 'Salamacis and Hermaphroditus', p. 114; 'Venus and Adonis', p. 245.

a.2. First American printing (1995):

The same setting as a.1 except:
1. Title page imprint is '*Farrar, Straus and Giroux* | NEW YORK'.
2. Preliminaries reordered, and verso title reset; with '*First American edition, 1995*'.
3. Type-page slightly larger throughout.

Grey cloth, spine stamped in black. Dust-wrapper front with photograph of Jacqueline Goddard by Man Ray; back black; both lettered in orange. Spine orange, lettered in black.

23.3 × 15.5 cm.

Published in 1995 at $25.00; number of copies undetermined.

B173 **POEM FOR THE DAY** 1994

Not seen. Edited by Nicholas Albery, with a foreword by Wendy Cope.

400 pages; 23.3 × 15.3 cm.

Wrappers, printed in navy blue and pink.

On verso title: 'First published in Great Britain by | The Natural Death Centre [...] | in association with | Sinclair-Stevenson [...]'. Reprints are identified as such on verso title.

Published December 1994 at £9.99 (£11.49 from the Centre, including postage and handling); number of copies printed undetermined. There were five printings in nine months totalling about 30,500 copies. A hardback and an American edition did not appear until 1996.

CONTENTS: Note on the writing of 'Thistles', p. 240.

B174   GIDLEIGH PARK   1995

[cover title, two columns on dark green background. Left column: colour photograph of Gidleigh Park Hotel. Right column, in white:] [monogram 'GP' in double oval] | [script] Gidleigh | Park | [modified fleur-de-lys flanked by two short rules near baseline] | [roman] RELAIS & | CHATEAUX

[16] pages including wrappers; 14.75 × 21.0 cm.

The first printing is not identified as such.

Published February 1995; number of copies undetermined. Distributed free by the hotel.

CONTENTS: Untitled poem, first line 'Older than the river the sea-wind', p. [14].

B175   MUCK AND MAGIC   1995

[hand-drawn letters] MUCK AND MAGIC | Stories from the Countryside | [drawing of boy with rooster on his head] | Edited by Michael Morpurgo | Foreword by HRH The Princess Royal | [regular type] HEINEMANN · LONDON

175 pages; 21.5 × 13.5 cm.

Dark green boards, spine stamped in gold. Dust-wrapper with colour drawings of children by Quentin Blake front and back (back is same as title page), lettering in black. Endpapers decorated with drawings.

On verso title: 'First published in Great Britain 1995 [...]'. The hardback was not reprinted.

Also issued in paperback, with wrappers of the same basic design as the dust-wrapper. In this printing the title page imprint is changed to 'MAMMOTH' in a rule frame, the Net Book Agreement is added to the verso title, and an advertisement added to the last page.

The hardback was published 17 November 1995 (the British Library copy was stamped the previous day) at £12.99; 1500 copies printed. The paperback was published 13 November 1995 at £3.99; 10,000 copies printed. The paperback was reprinted (copies not seen). It has been reported to the compilers that there were 200 copies, presumably hardbound, signed by all the contributors, selling for £100.

CONTENTS: 'Where is the Key to the Universe?', p. 41.

B176   YOUNG POETRY PACK   1995

A corrugated plastic satchel, ca. 31.5 × 22.5 × 3.0 cm., containing the following:
1. 'Reading and Writing Poetry' (cover title, white on black panel, reading up near bottom of spine). 32 pages; 23.9 × 17.6 cm. Front cover with colour illustration of an artichoke on a purple background; at upper right, a frame containing title 'Young Poetry Pack'. Back with a smaller artichoke on purple, with poem by Katie-Ellen McCrory.
   Contains 'Introduction' by Hughes, p. 1.

The remaining items have no contributions by Hughes:
2. 'Poetry Notebook' (cover title, white on black panel, reading up near bottom of spine). A pamphlet containing mostly blank pages.
3. 'Poetry Poster' (cover title, white on black panel, reading up near bottom of spine). A broadside, folded twice.
4. A separate sheet with advertisement and order form.
5. A cassette tape, 'Poetry in Performance'.
6. A biro printed with identifying logos and title of set.

Published by The Poetry Society and BBC Radio 4.

Published 1995 at £9.50 postpaid; number of copies undetermined.

C. Contributions to Periodicals

We have not included the reprinting in periodicals of works already collected. The title is the title under which the work was actually published, even though, especially in the case of book reviews, this may have been supplied editorially. In brackets, after the name of the periodical, is the volume number (or issue number when there is no volume number), followed by a colon, followed by the inclusive page numbers. Significant differences between this version of a text and others have been noted.

C1   WILD WEST [poem]

     HARVESTING [essay]

Don and Dearne (1:20–1, 26–7), Whitsuntide 1946.

The *Don and Dearne* was the school magazine of Mexborough Grammar School. These pieces are signed E. J. Hughes (V.C.).

'Harvesting', an apparently factual account, contains the seeds of 'The Harvesting' in *Wodwo*.

C2   SUB-EDITORIAL

     WHEN WARRIORS MEET

Don and Dearne (1:2–3, 40–2), July 1947.

The editor of *Don and Dearne* in 1947 and 1948 was Mr. J. E. Fisher, an English master who gave Hughes great encouragement in his writing. The sub-editors of this issue were Edward Hughes and his sister Olwyn. 'When Warriors Meet' is a comic account of a staff–student hockey match.

C3   THE IMPORTANCE OF BEING EARNEST [review]

WROT'S WRITINGS ON LOLPS [nonsense essay signed R.P.E. and Eeple Jote Hyewze]

TOO BAD FOR HELL [poem]

THE RECLUSE [poem]

INITIATION [poem]

HERE IN THE GREEN AND GLIMMERING GLOOM [poem]

Don and Dearne (1:15–16, 22–3, 27–30), July 1948.

The poems are signed E.J.H. (VI.A Arts).

C4   PASTORAL SYMPHONY NO. 1 [poem]

Don and Dearne (1:24), July 1950.

Hughes had left Mexborough Grammar School the previous summer and was now doing his National Service at Fylingdales.

C5   THE LITTLE BOYS AND THE SEASONS [poem]

Granta (57:1147), 8 June 1954.

This, the first poem Hughes published in Cambridge, appeared (under the pseudonym Daniel Hearing) in the month in which he graduated.

C5a   SONG OF THE SORRY LOVERS [poem]

Chequer (6), Summer 1954.

This poem appeared under the pseudonym Peter Crew.

C6   THE CASUALTY [poem]

THE JAGUAR [poem]

Chequer (7:2, 17), November 1954.

'The Jaguar' ends, here (and in B1):
    But what holds them, from corner to corner swinging,

    Swivelling the ball of his heel on the polished spot,
    Jerking his head up in surprise at the bars,
    Has not hesitated in the millions of years,
    And like life-prisoners they through bars stare out.

C7   THE WOMAN WITH SUCH HIGH HEELS SHE LOOKED DANGEROUS [poem]

Delta (5:12), Spring 1955.

C7a   COMMENT ON 'CHEQUER' [review]

Broadsheet (III:22), 8 June 1955.

The first piece of prose published by Hughes after leaving school appeared under the pseudonym Jonathan Dyce.

C8   FALLGRIEF'S GIRLFRIENDS [poem]

WHEN TWO MEN MEET FOR THE FIRST TIME IN ALL [poem]

WHENEVER I AM GOT UNDER MY GRAVESTONE [poem]

IF I SHOULD TOUCH HER SHE WOULD SHRIEK AND WEEPING [poem]

All collected in *The Hawk in the Rain*, the second as 'Law in the Country of the Cats', the third as 'Soliloquy of a Misanthrope', the fourth as 'Secretary'.

Saint Botolph's Review, February 1956. pp. 16–19.

This was the only number of the *Saint Botolph's Review*, so-called because several of the founders lodged at St. Botolph's Rectory. The editor was David Ross. At the party to launch the magazine, 25 February 1956, Ted Hughes met Sylvia Plath.

C9   SCENE WITHOUT AN ACT [poem]

Granta, 12 May 1956. p. 11.

This is a longer version of 'Parlour Piece'. Its last line:
    Under what black wilderness of waters weep.
becomes, slightly revised, the last line of 'Thrushes'.

C10   BAWDRY EMBRACED [poem]

Poetry (88:295–7), August 1956.

This was the first of Hughes' poems to be published beyond Cambridge. On 26 May Sylvia Plath had written to her mother: 'We spent a whole day out in the Whitstead gardens in the sun, me typing first copies and carbons of about 25 of his best poems, and he editing, to send off to *The New Yorker*, *Atlantic*, *Harper's* and *Poetry* magazines. ... I can't wait to see how he is received in America. He is going to be a brilliant poet; I know it with every critical fiber in me.'

C11   THE HAG [poem]

Nation (183:144), 18 August 1956.

C12   WIND [poem]

Nation (183:408), 10 November 1956.

C13   ROARERS IN A RING [poem]

Nation (183:543), 22 December 1956.

C14   THE HAWK IN THE STORM [poem]

Atlantic Monthly (199:53), February 1957.

This poem was later substantially revised as 'The Hawk in the Rain'. Here line 8 reads:
    Grasping small breaths, catching last sounds, as the wind

Lines 11–12 read:
    Like a rapt water-walker springs my dream
    With its sleeper staring from the eyes.

C15   THE DROWNED WOMAN [poem]
    Poetry (89:296–7), February 1957.

C16   THE LITTLE BOYS AND THE SEASONS [poem]
        BILLET-DOUX [poem]
    Accent (17:82–3), Spring 1957.

    Three lines have been omitted from this version of 'The Little Boys
    and the Seasons'.

C17   BARTHOLOMEW PYGGE ESQ. [story]
    Granta, 4 May 1957. pp. 23–5.

    Hughes' first published story.

C18   O'KELLY'S ANGEL [story]
        THE MARTYRDOM OF BISHOP FARRAR [poem] Broadcast 14
        April 1957.
        THE DOVE BREEDER [poem]
    Granta, 18 May 1957. pp. 3–4, 15.

C19   FAMOUS POET [poem]
        WIND [poem]
        MACAW AND LITTLE MISS [poem]
    Gemini (1:16–19), Summer 1957.

    On 7 March Sylvia had written to her mother: 'The next issue of
    Gemini (the new magazine) in May will carry three poems by Ted and
    a story and book review by me. We do love to appear together.'

    Sylvia's contributions were 'All the Dead Dears' and a long review of
    The Stones of Troy by C. A. Trypanis.

C20   SIX YOUNG MEN [poem]
    Delta (12:4–5), Summer 1957.

    There are small differences affecting three lines here.

C21   MEETING [poem]
    Spectator (199:111) 19 July 1957.

C22   INCOMPATIBILITIES [poem]
    Nation (185:34), 20 July 1957.

    The third stanza here begins:

But desire, outstripping the hands that mere touch fills,
  Has dived into the opposite eyes,
Plummeting ...

C23   THE CASUALTY [poem]

THE ANCIENT HEROES AND THE PILOT [poem] Collected in *The
Hawk in the Rain* as 'The Ancient Heroes and the Bomber Pilot'.

THE JAGUAR [poem]

THE MARTYRDOM OF BISHOP FERRAR [sic] [poem]

Poetry (90:279–83), August 1957.

C24   THE DOVE-BREEDER [poem]

Harper's Magazine (215:65), August 1957.

C25   PARTING [poem] Collected in *The Hawk in the Rain* as 'September'.

Spectator (199:166), 2 August 1957.

C26   THE HAG [poem]

Times Literary Supplement, 16 August 1957. p. xvii.

C27   SECRETARY [poem]

Spectator (199:279), 30 August 1957.

C28   THE THOUGHT-FOX [poem]

New Yorker, 31 August 1957. p. 28.

C29   FAMOUS POET [poem]

London Magazine (4:23), September 1957.

On 13 April Sylvia Plath had written to her mother about the rejection
of some of Ted's poems by John Ciardi at the *Saturday Review*: 'Well, we
weathered this news with typing and retyping sessions, sending five or
six more Mss. out, and this morning got our reward—again, in a twin
package—from, guess where—John Lehmann at the *London Magazine*!
Our first real professional 'British' acceptance, and it is the *Atlantic
Monthly* of England! They accepted two of my poems. ... They
accepted a longish one of Ted's, 'Famous Poet', and obviously felt they
could not resist the pressure of such about-to-be-world-celebrated
poets. At last! The halls of British conservatism have recognized us.'

C30   TWO WISE GENERALS [poem]

Spectator (199:311), 6 September 1957.

C31   TED HUGHES WRITES

TED HUGHES

Poetry Book Society Bulletin (15:1–2), September 1957.

The Hawk in the Rain, issued 13 September, was the Poetry Book Society Autumn Choice.

C32   LETTER [poem]

New Statesman (54:387), 28 September 1957.

C33   GROOM'S DREAM [poem] Collected in *Lupercal* as 'A Dream of Horses'.

Grecourt Review (1:32), November 1957.

The Grecourt Review is an undergraduate publication at Smith College, Northampton, Massachusetts, where Sylvia was teaching at the time.

The first line of the final stanza reads here:
   Let me, tied, be torn to quarters by these poor horses.

The Grecourt Review, like many other periodicals, provided contributors with offprints. Offprints of this poem and of C53 have been sold for high prices. They are identical with the magazine texts and of no bibliographical interest.

C34   QUEST [poem]

Grapevine (5:9), February 1958.

The Grapevine was an annual publication of creative writing by the University of Durham Institute of Education. 'Quest' was commissioned.

C35   THRUSHES [poem]

Encounter (10:45), March 1958.

C36   CROW HILL [poem]

New Statesman (15:352), 15 March 1958.

C37   THE GOOD LIFE [poem]
       THINGS PRESENT [poem]
       WITCHES [poem]
       EVERYMAN'S ODYSSEY [poem]

Sewanee Review (66:256–8), Spring 1958.

C37a   BAWDRY EMBRACED [poem]

Gemini 5, Spring 1958.

C38   OF CATS [poem]

Harper's Magazine (216:30), June 1958.

There are substantial differences in this text, and it carries the envoi:
   A cat on a shop doorstep gazes steadily through the thick
   Street-width of legs, wheels, exhaust: deep in his centuries as in
                                                              cushions,

From a shop doorstep a cat returns her look:
Thus, in the clutter of your brain, the eternals make their assignations.

C39   BILLY HOOK AND THE THREE SOUVENIRS [children's story]
Jack and Jill, July 1958. pp. 26–32.

C40   CRAG JACK'S APOSTASY [poem]
THE GOOD LIFE [poem]
Spectator (201:19), 4 July 1958.

C41   GROOM'S DREAM [poem]
CONSTANCY [poem]
London Magazine (5:17–18), August 1958.

C42   WITCHES [poem]
New Statesman (56:173), 9 August 1958.

C43   THE RETIRED COLONEL [poem]
Spectator (201:260), 22 August 1958.

C44   THINGS PRESENT [poem]
Spectator (201:454), 3 October 1958.

C45   OF CATS [poem]
New Statesman (56:564), 25 October 1958.

C46   RELIC [poem]
Harper's Magazine (217:36), November 1958.

C47   HISTORIAN [poem]
Nation (187:364), 15 November 1958.

C48   THRUSHES [poem]
Observer, 23 November 1958. p. 7.

C49   PENNINES IN APRIL [poem]
Spectator (201:922), 26 December 1958.

C50   PENNINES IN APRIL [poem]
Mademoiselle, January 1959. p. 35.

C51   WILFRED OWEN'S PHOTOGRAPHS [poem]
Spectator (202:22), 2 January 1959.

C52   FEBRUARY [poem]
THE BULL MOSES [poem]
THE VOYAGE [poem]
London Magazine (6:47–9), April 1959.

C53　ROOSTING HAWK [poem] Collected in *Lupercal* as 'Hawk Roosting'.

Grecourt Review (2:235), May 1959. *See* C33.

C54　SUNSTROKE [poem]

Observer, 17 May 1959. p. 21.

C55　CROW HILL [poem]

Paris Review (21:71), Spring–Summer 1959. p. 71.

C56　THRUSHES [poem]

THE BULL MOSES [poem]

THE VOYAGE [poem]

PIKE [poem]

NICHOLAS FERRER [poem]

Audience, Summer 1959.

C57　HAWK ROOSTING [poem]

STRAWBERRY HILL [poem]

NOVEMBER [poem]

Critical Quarterly (1:124–5), Summer 1959.

C58　DICK STRAIGHTUP [poem]

Northern Broadsheet, Summer 1959.

Lacks the Obit. which was added in *Lupercal* after the death of the original of Dick Straightup.

C59　HISTORIAN [poem]

Encounter (13:43), July 1959.

C60　A WOMAN UNCONSCIOUS [poem]

CAT AND MOUSE [poem]

TO PAINT A WATER LILY [poem]

LUPERCALIA [poem]

Poetry (94:296–300), August 1959.

C61　SHELLS [poem]

New Yorker, 1 August 1959. p. 61.

C62　VIEW OF A PIG [poem]

Times Literary Supplement (2997:xv), 7 August 1959.

C63　BULLFROG [poem]

New Yorker, 8 August 1959. p. 26.

C64   RELIC [poem]
Encounter (13:32), September 1959.

C65   FOURTH OF JULY [poem]
New Statesman (58:756), 28 November 1959.

C66   SNOWDROP [poem]
Observer, 29 November 1959. p. 1.

C67   DICK STRAIGHTUP [poem]
Atlantic Monthly (204:136–7), December 1959.
Lacks Obit. in *Lupercal*.

C67a   GULLS ALOFT [poem]
Christian Science Monitor, 12 December 1959.

C68   SNAILS [poem]
Christian Science Monitor, 15 December 1959. p. 8.

C69   CLEOPATRA TO THE ASP [poem]
New Statesman (58:884), 19 December 1959.

C70   THE RAIN HORSE [story]
Harper's Magazine (220:76–80), January 1960.
On 13 October 1959 Sylvia Plath wrote to her mother: 'Ted's proofs for his *Harper's* story have come—very exciting, and it reads marvellously. It will have black-and-white drawings with it, I gather. ... We are very proud of it.' The drawings were by Eileen Taber. The text differs slightly from all later printings.

C71   TOMCAT [poem] Collected in *Lupercal* as 'Esther's Tomcat'.
New Yorker, 9 January 1960. p. 102.

C72   MAYDAY ON HOLDERNESS [poem]
Spectator (204:113), 22 January 1960.

C73   SNOWDROP [poem]
       FOURTH OF JULY [poem]
Massachusetts Review (1:229), February 1960.

C74   THE RAIN HORSE [story]
London Magazine (7:14–21), February 1960.

C75   AN OTTER [poem]
       PIKE [poem]
Encounter (14:44–5), March 1960.

On 5 July 1958 Sylvia Plath had written to her mother: 'The Ouija board also told Ted to write about "Otters", so he is doing so, and the beginnings sound quite good.'

C76　THE PERFECT FORMS [poem]
　　　FIRE-EATER [poem]
　　　URN BURIAL [poem]
Sewanee Review (68:292–3), Spring 1960.

C77　HAWK ROOSTING [poem]
Partisan Review (27:271–2), Spring 1960.

C77a　LUPERCALIA [poem]
　　　THE ACROBATS [poem]
　　　TO PAINT A WATER LILY [poem]
　　　A WOMAN UNCONSCIOUS [poem]
　　　CAT AND MOUSE [poem]
Critical Quarterly (2:24–7), Spring 1960.

C78　ENGLAND'S TOUGHEST COMMUNITY [review of *Weekend in Dinlock* by Clancy Segal]
Nation (191:14–15), 2 July 1960.

Hughes' first published book review.

C79　THISTLES [poem]
　　　A FABLE [poem]
Times Literary Supplement, 9 September 1960. pp. xli, lxx.

C80　ARNOLD WESKER: 'A SORT OF SOCIALISM' [review of *The Wesker Trilogy* by Arnold Wesker]
Nation (191:402–4), 19 November 1960.

On 28 September 1960 Sylvia Plath wrote to her mother: 'He is also grunting over an article for *The Nation* on the Arnold Wesker trilogy of plays which we enjoyed seeing here this summer. He was originally going to refuse to do the article, but I felt it was because he, out of his great modesty, felt he didn't know enough about the American theatre of the 30's and Clifford Odets' plays (also, about Jews and Communists), so I very slowly persuaded him to take a day or two to read Odets at the British Museum and that his own instinctive reactions were better than most garbled criticism I had read.'

C81　POLTERGEIST [poem]
Spectator (205:859), 25 November 1960.

C82   THE CANING [story]
      LINES TO A NEWBORN BABY [poem]
   Texas Quarterly (3:27–37, 214), Winter 1960.

C83   PIBROCH [poem]
      UNKNOWN SOLDIER [poem]
   Critical Quarterly (2:322–3), Winter 1960.

C84   FOR FRIEDA IN HER FIRST MONTHS [poem]
   Western Daily Press, 22 February 1961.

C85   THISTLES [poem]
      A FABLE [poem]
   Mademoiselle, March 1961. pp. 204, 206.

C86   SHELLS [poem]
      DULLY GUMPTION'S COLLEGE COURSES: i. SEMANTICS; ii.
      POLITICAL SCIENCE; iii. THEOLOGY; iv. HUMANITIES [poems]
   London Magazine (8:19–21), March 1961.
   For the history of Dully Gumption see 'Dully Gumption's Adden-
   dum' in *Recklings*.

C87   HER HUSBAND [poem]
   Spectator (206:414), 24 March 1961.

C88   MY GRANDPA; MY BROTHER BERT; MY SISTER JANE [poems]
   Sunday Times, 26 March 1961. p. 37.

C89   THE HARVESTING [story]
   London Magazine (1:41–7), April 1961.

C90   LAST LINES [poem]
      SUGAR LOAF [poem]
      GOG [poem] Collected in *Wodwo* as 'Gog I'.
      WINO [poem]
      FLANDERS, 1960 [poem] Collected in *Recklings* as 'Flanders'.
      TOLL OF AIR RAIDS [poem] Collected in *Recklings* as 'Toll'.
   Observer, 16 April 1961. p. 31.

C91   GOG [poem] Collected in *Wodwo* as 'Gog I'.
   Nation (192:358), 22 April 1961.

C92   THE HOUSE OF ARIES [play]
   Audience (8:77–105), Spring 1961.

Part I only of a verse play in two parts, never published complete. See
C99 and C102.

C93   FISHING AT DAWN [poem]

New Statesman (61:838), 26 May 1961.

C94   FLANDERS [poem]

Spectator (206:768), 26 May 1961.

C95   FIVE TON PHANTOM [review of *Loch Ness Monster* by Tim
        Dinsdale]

New Statesman (61:887), 2 June 1961.

C96   TALK WITH JOURNALISTS [review of *Nimrod Smith* by Alan
        Wykes]

New Statesman (61:1015), 23 June 1961.

C97   MEMORY [poem]

Times Literary Supplement, 14 July 1961. p. i.

C98   STILL LIFE [poem]

New Yorker, 15 July 1961. p. 24.

C99   EXCERPTS FROM A PLAY IN VERSE: THE CAPTAIN'S SPEECH;
        SPEECH OF THE OUIJA; WIFE'S SONG

Two Cities, Summer 1961. pp. 12–13.

The play is *The House of Aries*. See C92 and C102.

C100   THE RAIN HORSE [story]

        CAPTURING ANIMALS [talk]

        WRITING A NOVEL: BEGINNING [talk]

Listening and Writing, Autumn 1961. pp. 4–9, 16–23, 29–34.

This version of 'The Rain Horse' is reduced to about two-thirds.
'Capturing Animals' is slightly longer than the version in *Poetry in the
Making*, but lacks the final 'Note'. 'Writing a Novel' lacks two
paragraphs and two of the sample beginnings. This was the first
pamphlet ever published for a BBC Schools English programme, and
the only one to print the entire script.

C101   WODWO [poem]

New Statesman (62:347), 15 September 1961.

C102   MISS MAMBRETT AND THE WET CELLAR [story]

        TWO POEMS FOR A VERSE PLAY: THE CAPTAIN'S SPEECH; THE
        GIBBONS

Texas Quarterly (4:46–55, 146–7), Autumn 1961.

The play is *The House of Aries*. This is a different Captain's speech from C99. See C92.

C103   SNOW [story]

Harper's Bazaar, October 1961. pp. 183, 216–17, 221.

C104   THE LAKE [poem]

New Yorker, 21 October 1961. p. 192.

C105   PUBLIC BAR T.V. [poem] Collected in *Wodwo*.

New Statesman (62:604), 27 October 1961.

This is a completely different poem from the poem of the same name in *Recklings*.

C106   THE RESCUE [a speech from a play]

Observer, 29 October 1961. p. 30.

C107   A FEW SWEET WORDS [review of *The Cat in the Hat Comes Back* by Dr. Seuss; *Barnaby and the Horses* by Lydia Pender; *Timba* by Lilli Koenig; *Gringolo* by Lilli Koenig; *The Cricket in Times Square* by George Selden]

ACCORDING TO ELSA [review of *Living Free* by Joy Adamson]

New Statesman (62:704–5, 712), 10 November 1961.

On 30 October 1961 Sylvia wrote to her mother: 'We've got about 50 children's books to review in all now, a real gift, because we can't review more than ten apiece—everything from *The Cat in the Hat Comes Back* to the story of Elsa, the lioness and her cubs. A good $50 to $60 worth. My acquisitive soul rejoices.'

C108   HER HUSBAND [poem]

Harper's Magazine (223:28), December 1961.

C108a   NESSIE [poem]

Vogue, December 1961.

C108b   LINES TO THREE MONTHS [poem]

Evidence (1:43), Winter 1961/2.

Identical with C84.

C109   STILL LIFE [poem]

CONTEXT [answer to questionnaire]

London Magazine (1:15, 44–5), February 1962.

C110   A BOOK TO REMEMBER 1: TED HUGHES TELLS YOU ABOUT A BOOK OF FANTASY

Sunday Times, 25 February 1962. p. 45.

This introduction to *The Little Prince* by Antoine de Saint-Exupéry was the first of a projected series of six introductions to children's classics. Apparently only five appeared. See C113, C119, C122, C129.

C111   THE RESCUE [poem]
Atlantic Monthly (209:65), March 1962.

C112   MAN AND SUPERBEAST [review of *The Nerve of Some Animals* by Robert Froman, and *Man and Dolphin* by J. C. Lilly]
New Statesman (63:420–1), 23 March 1962.

C113   THE WIND IN THE WILLOWS [introduction to an extract from *The Wind in the Willows* by Kenneth Grahame]. See C110.
Sunday Times, 15 April 1962. p. 34.

C114   DULLY GUMPTION'S ADDENDUM [poem]
Poetry (100:92–4), May 1962.
Contains an additional line after each stanza.

C115   SUGAR-LOAF [poem]
Atlantic Monthly (209:69), May 1962.

C116   PRIMITIVE SONG, BY C. M. BOWRA [review]
Listener (67:781), 3 May 1962.

C117   DR. SEUSS [review of *One Fish Two Fish Red Fish Blue Fish* by Dr. Seuss; *The Cat's Opera* by Eilis Dillon; *The Otter's Tale* by Gavin Maxwell; *Animals of the Forest* by Marcelle Vérité; *Close-Up of a Honeybee* by Virgil Foster; *Oddities of Animal Life* by Eric Roberts]
New Statesman (63:726), 18 May 1962.

C118   THE POETRY OF KEITH DOUGLAS [essay]
Listener (67:1069), 21 June 1962.
This is a different essay from C135 and B23.

C119   THE WAR OF THE WORLDS [introduction to an extract from *The War of the Worlds* by H. G. Wells]. See C110.
Sunday Times, 24 June 1962. p. 29.

C120   IMITATIONS, BY ROBERT LOWELL [review]
Listener (68:185), 2 August 1962.

C121   MOUNTAINS [poem]
Observer, 5 August 1962. p. 14.

C121a THE ROAD TO EASINGTON [poem]
Listener, 23 August 1962. p. 278.

C122 TARKA THE OTTER, BY HENRY WILLIAMSON [introduction]. See
    C110.
Sunday Times Colour Supplement, 16 September 1962. p. 18.

C123 WIND AND WEATHER [talk]
Listening and Writing, Autumn 1962. pp. 37–45.
This version ends with an additional poem, 'Pennines in April', and a
paragraph about it.

C124 BOWLED OVER [poem]
New Statesman (64:406), 28 September 1962.

C125 AN ANTHOLOGY OF WEST AFRICAN FOLKLORE, BY ALTA JABLOW
    [review]
Listener (68:629), 18 October 1962.

C126 TUTORIAL [poem]
New Statesman (64:628), 2 November 1962.
The third line here reads:
    What are those tilted tomes? Boards
The sixth begins:
    He is gone at the seams, this burst bearskin ...

C127 THE WARRIORS OF THE NORTH [poem]
    A VEGETARIAN [poem] Collected in *Wodwo* as 'Vegetarian'.
Observer, 4 November 1962. p. 27.

C128 BEASTS [review of *Everyman's Ark* by Sally Patrick Johnson; and
    Here Come the Elephants by Alice Goudey]
New Statesman (64:667), 9 November 1962.

C129 THE WORST JOURNEY IN THE WORLD, BY APSLEY CHERRY-
    GARRARD [introduction]. See C110.
Sunday Times Colour Supplement, 18 November 1962. p. 27.

C130 TO F. R. AT SIX MONTHS [poem] The same poem as C84.
    FLANDERS [poem]
    LAST LINES [poem]
    MEMORY [poem]
Sewanee Review (71:85–7), January–March 1963.

C131 WATER [poem]
   NEW MOON IN JANUARY [poem]
   DARK WOMEN [poem] Collected in *Wodwo* as 'The Green Wolf'.
   Observer, 6 January 1963. p. 19.
   Line 19 of 'Dark Women' has 'flaring' for 'smouldering'.

C132 FULL MOON AND LITTLE FRIEDA [poem]
   Observer, 27 January 1963. p. 23.

C132a LOVE [poem]
   Town (4 2:32), February 1963.

C133 IT WAS LIKE THIS [review of *I, Said the Sparrow* by Paul West]
   Guardian, 8 February 1963. p. 7.

C134 A WORLD OF MEN, DEATH ON A LIVE WIRE, ON STEPPING FROM A
   SIXTH STORY WINDOW, BY MICHAEL BALDWIN [review]
   Listener (69:346–7), 21 February 1963.

C135 THE POETRY OF KEITH DOUGLAS [essay]
   Critical Quarterly (5:43), Spring 1963.
   This version of the essay, different from C118, became the
   introduction to *The Selected Poems of Keith Douglas* (B23).

C136 SUNDAY EVENING [poem]
   Atlantic Monthly (211:59), May 1963.

C137 LEARNING TO THINK [talk]
   Listening and Writing, Summer 1963. pp. 10–16.
   Includes 'Wodwo'.

C138 THE LAKE [poem]
   London Magazine (3:5), July 1963.

C139 FOXGLOVES [poem]
   New Yorker, 27 July 1963. p. 28.

C140 IS POETRY YOUR HOBBY? [review of *Rule and Energy* by John
   Press]
   New Statesman (66:172), 9 August 1963.

C141 MUSIC ON THE MOON [poem]
   New Yorker, 10 August 1963. p. 24.

C142 KREUTZER SONATA [poem]
   New Statesman (66:230), 23 August 1963.

C143 WRITING ABOUT PEOPLE [talk] Includes 'Her Husband'.

   MOON CREATURES [talk]

Listening and Writing, Autumn 1963. pp. 10–17, 38–42.

This version of 'Writing About People' has a discussion of W. S. Merwin's poem 'Grandfather in the Old Men's Home' in place of Philip Larkin's 'Mr. Bleaney', and lacks the 'Note'. 'Moon Creatures' lacks the discussions of 'Civil War on the Moon', 'The Snail of the Moon' and 'A Moon Man-Hunt'.

C144 QUITTING [review of *Vagrancy* by Philip O'Connor]

New Statesman (66:293), 6 September 1963.

C145 EMILY DICKINSON'S POETRY BY CHARLES R. ANDERSON [review]

Listener (70:394), 12 September 1963.

C146 THE ROCK [talk in the BBC series 'The Writer and his Background']

Listener (70:421–3), 19 September 1963.

C146a REMEMBRANCE DAY [poem] Collected in *Wodwo* as 'Out III'.

Granta, 19 October 1963. p. 6.

C146b SYLVIA PLATH [introduction to 'Ten Poems by Sylvia Plath']

Encounter (XXI 4:45), October 1963.

C146c THE RAT UNDER THE BOWLER [essay]

Saturday Night (78:10:21–7), November 1963.

Saturday Night had invited Hughes to reply to a piece called 'England Revisited' by Arthur Hailey in the September issue.

C147 POEM TO ROBERT GRAVES PERHAPS [poem]

   ON WESTMINSTER BRIDGE [poem]

   AFTER LORCA [poem]

   HEATWAVE [poem]

   ERA OF GIANT LIZARDS [poem]

   SMALL HOURS [poem]

Poetry (103:152–6), December 1963.

'On Westminster Bridge' contains the lines:
   ... Let us all go down to exult
   Under the haddock's thumb, rejoice
   Through the warped mouth of the flounder, let us labour with God
                                          on the beaches!
In 'Public Speech' (later 'Karma') this becomes:
   They have gone into dumber service. They have gone down

To labour with God on the beaches. They fatten
Under the haddock's thumb. They rejoice
Through the warped mouth of the flounder.

In *Selected Poems 1957–1967* the final section of 'Karma' was substituted for the third and fourth sections of 'Stations'.

C148   FULL MOON [poem] Collected in *Wodwo* as 'Full Moon and Little Frieda'.

Atlantic Monthly (212:72), December 1963.

This version ('Encounter' in B26) contains a part II not in *Wodwo:*
The cows submerge.
The moon has opened you wide and bright like a pond.

The moon lifts you off the grass—
A cat's cradle of spider's web, where the stars are trembling into place.

The brimming moon looks through you and you cannot move.

Any minute
A bat will fly out of a cat's ear.

C149   FOLKTALES OF JAPAN. EDITED BY KEIGO SEKI. FOLKTALES OF ISRAEL. EDITED BY DOV NOY [review]

Listener (70:999), 12 December 1963.

C150   BAD NEWS GOOD! [poem]

Agenda (3:16), December–January 1963/4.

C151   PATRICK WHITE'S VOSS [essay]

Listener (71:229–30), 6 February 1964.

C152   ASGARD FOR ADDICTS [review of *Myth and Religion of the North* by E. O. G. Turville-Petre]

Listener (71:484–5), 19 March 1964.

C153   STEALING TROUT [poem] Collected in *Recklings* as 'Stealing Trout on a May Morning'.

New Yorker, 21 March 1964. p. 44.

There are several minor variations in this text.

C154   THE CRIME OF FOOLS EXPOSED [review of *The Collected Poems of Wilfred Owen* edited by C. Day Lewis]

New York Times Book Review, 12 April 1964. pp. 4, 18.

C155   THE SUITOR [story]

Encounter (22:35–9), May 1964.

C156   OUT OF AFRICA [review of *A Selection of African Prose* edited by W. H. Whiteley; *The Heroic Recitations of the Bahima of Ankole* edited by Henry F. Morris; *Somali Poetry* edited by B. W. Andrzejewski and I. M. Lewis]

Listener (71:892), 28 May 1964.

C157   CADENZA [poem]

New Yorker, 30 May 1964. p. 38.

C158   DICE [poem in 8 parts: 'Torture Chamber', 'Eclipse of Moon-Man', 'Fiesta', 'Statue of Atalanta', 'Porpoises at Brighton', 'Guinness', 'Durst', 'Upper Code']

Critical Quarterly (6:153), Summer 1964.

C159   THE RAIN HORSE [story]

CAPTURING ANIMALS [talk]

THE COMING OF THE KINGS [play]

Listening and Writing, Autumn 1964. pp. 7–12, 17–24, 44–60.

'The Rain Horse' and 'Capturing Animals' are reprinted from C100.

C160   DR. DUNG [review of *The Three Christs of Ypsilanti* by Milton Rokeach]

New Statesman (68:323–4), 4 September 1964.

C161   OPPOSING SELVES [review of *The Letters of Alexander Pushkin* edited by J. Thomas Shaw]

Listener (72:514–15), 1 October 1964.

C162   SUPERSTITIONS [review of *Astrology* by Louis MacNeice; *Ghost and Divining-rod* by T. C. Lethbridge]

New Statesman (68:500), 2 October 1964.

C163   SECRET ECSTASIES [review of *Shamanism* by Mircea Eliade; *The Sufis* by Idries Shah]

Listener (72:677–8), 29 October 1964.

C164   OPPUGNANCY [review of *Mysterious Senses* by Vitus Dröscher]

New Stateman (68:838–40), 27 November 1964.

C165   O WHITE ÉLITE LOTUS [poem]

Critical Quarterly (6:319), Winter 1964.

C166   A HERO'S HISTORY [review of *Heimskringla* and *The Prose Edda* by Snorri Sturluson; *Gods, Demons and Others* by R. K. Narayan]

New York Review of Books, 31 December 1964. pp. 6–7.

C167   THE HOWLING OF WOLVES [poem]
    Observer, 10 January 1965. p. 27.

C168   SYLVIA PLATH [substantial note on *Ariel*, the Poetry Book Society Spring Choice for 1965] Reprinted in B94.
    Poetry Book Society Bulletin 44, February 1965.

C169   HILL TOP [poem] Collected in *Wodwo* as 'Heptonstall'.
    New Yorker, 27 February 1965. p. 103.

    The second line here reads:
      Head of an idiot.

C170   ONE [poem] Collected in *Wodwo* as 'Bowled Over'.
      TWO [poem] Collected in *Recklings* as 'Tutorial'.
    Northern Review (1:4–5), Spring 1965.

C171   THE GENIUS OF ISAAC BASHEVIS SINGER [essay]
    New York Review of Books, 22 April 1965. pp. 8–10.

C172   CADENZA [poem]
      FALLEN EVE [poem]
    Agenda (4:28–9), April–May 1965.

C173   MUSIC OF HUMANITY [review of *The Faber Book of Ballads* edited by Mathew Hodgart]
    Guardian, 14 May 1965. p. 11.

C174   STEALING TROUT ON A MAY MORNING [poem]
    Books, Plays, Poems, Summer 1965. pp. 39–41.

C175   X [a dialogue from *Eat Crow*]
    Encounter (25:20–1), July 1965.

C176   TREES [poem]
    New Yorker, 17 July 1965. p. 30.

    The first line here reads:
      I asked the holly, 'What is your life if ...?'
    The eighth line reads:
      I asked the birch, 'How can you ...?'
    There is an additional line after the second stanza:
      Like a ghost I tried to fade.

C177   MEN WHO MARCH AWAY [review of *Men Who March Away, Poems of the First World War* edited by I. M. Parsons]
    Listener (73:208), 5 August 1965.

C178   WIND AND WEATHER [talk]

THE TIGER'S BONES [play]

Listening and Writing, Autumn 1965. pp. 30–38, 44–61.

'Wind and Weather' is reprinted from C123.

C179   'OUR POLICY IS TO CONCENTRATE ...' [unsigned, untitled editorial]

Modern Poetry in Translation (1:1), Autumn 1965.

Ted Hughes was co-editor of the first ten issues with Daniel Weissbort, who has confirmed that much of the unsigned editorial material in those numbers was written by Hughes.

C180   BEAUTY AND THE BEAST [play]

Living Language, Autumn 1965. pp. 22–6.

Only about the last third of the play is printed here.

C181   TRICKSTERS AND TARBABIES [review of *Literature Among the Primitives* and *The Primitive Reader* by John Greenaway]

New York Review of Books, 9 December 1965. pp. 33–5.

C182   CAROL [poem]

Sunday Times, 19 December 1965. p. 29.

C183   WARM MOORS [poem]

STATIONS [poem]

THE KNIGHT [poem] Collected in *Wodwo* as 'Gog III'.

FOLK-LORE [poem]

A MATCH [poem] Collected in *Recklings* and in American *Wodwo* as 'Root, Stem, Leaf I'.

Critical Quarterly (8:5–8), Spring 1966.

For a possibly earlier version of 'Warm Moors' see C450 [Gilbertson].

The text of 'A Match' corresponds to the version in *Recklings*. The last four lines of 'Warm Moors' are identical with the last four lines of Section IV of 'Skylarks' in *Wodwo*.

C184   GIBRALTAR [poem]

A COLONIAL [poem]

New Statesman (71:504), 8 April 1966.

C185   LEARNING TO THINK [talk]

Listening and Writing, Summer 1966. pp. 11–17.

Reprinted from C137.

C186   DON GIOVANNI [poem]

> DEATH MASK [poem] Collected in *Wodwo* as 'Ludwig's Death Mask'.

New Statesman (71:802), 17 June 1966.

C187   AS WOMAN'S WEEPING [poem]

> THE BEAR [poem]
>
> LOGOS [poem]

Critical Quarterly (8:108–9), Summer 1966.

C188   THE POETRY OF VASCO POPA [essay]

Critical Survey (2:211–14), Summer 1966.

This version is slightly different from B43 and C207.

C189   NIGHTFALL [poem] Collected in *Wodwo* as 'Ghost Crabs'.

Listener (76:89), 21 July 1966.

C190   THEOLOGY [poem]

Observer Colour Supplement, 14 August 1966. p. 13.

C191   A PAUSE FOR BREATH [poem] Collected in *Recklings* as 'On the Slope', and in the American *Wodwo* as 'Root, Stem, Leaf II'.

New Yorker, 27 August 1966. p. 90.

C192   MOON CREATURES [talk]

Listening and Writing, Autumn 1966. pp. 42–9.

Reprinted from C143.

C193   THE PRICE OF A BRIDE [verse play]

Living Language, Autumn 1966. pp. 4–5.

The opening only, as in B41. See C235.

C194   HEATWAVE [poem]

> EINSTEIN PLAYS BACH [poem] Collected in *Wodwo* as 'Wings III'.
>
> BIRDSONG [poem]
>
> GNAT-PSALM [poem]

London Magazine (6:60–6), September 1966.

C195   NOTES ON THE CHRONOLOGICAL ORDER OF SYLVIA PLATH'S POEMS [essay]

Tri-Quarterly (7:81–8), Fall 1966.

The opening and closing paragraphs are considerably longer here than in B45.

C196　PLUM BLOSSOM [poem]

Transatlantic Review (22:71–2), Autumn 1966.

The version in *Recklings* contains only the second and third of these six stanzas.

C197　SKYLARKS [poem]

Critical Quarterly (8:200–2), Autumn 1966.

C198　ON THE SLOPE [poem] Collected in the American *Wodwo* as 'Root, Stem, Leaf II'.

BEECH TREE [poem]

Poetry Review (57:148), Autumn 1966.

C199　BOOM [poem]

TO BE A GIRL'S DIARY [poem] Collected in the American *Wodwo* as 'Root, Stem, Leaf III'.

New Statesman (72:523), 7 October 1966.

C200　WINGS I, II [poem]

New York Review of Books, 3 November 1966. p. 12.

C201　DYLAN THOMAS'S LETTERS [review of *The Selected Letters of Dylan Thomas* edited by Constantine Fitzgibbon]

New Statesman (72:783), 25 November 1966.

C202　PUBLIC SPEECH [poem] Collected in *Wodwo* as 'Karma'.

A WIND FLASHES THE GRASS [poem]

Critical Quarterly (8:349–50), Winter 1966.

C203　SCAPEGOATS AND RABIES [poem]

New Statesman (73:50–2), 13 January 1967.

C204　TO W. H. AUDEN [poem]

Sunday Times, 19 February 1967. p. 28.

C205　SMALL EVENTS [poem]

YOU DRIVE IN A CIRCLE [poem]

THAW [poem]

FERN [poem]

New Yorker, 18 March 1967. p. 48.

'Fern' here has an additional stanza after the first:
 A dancer, leftover, among crumbs and remains
 Of God's drunken supper,
 Dancing to start things up again.

And they do start up—to the one note of silence.
The final stanza begins:

How many went under? Everything up to this point went under.
Now they start up again
Dancing gravely . . .

C206 SECOND GLANCE AT A JAGUAR [poem]

New Yorker, 25 March 1967. p. 52.

C207 VASCO POPA [essay]

Tri-Quarterly (9:201–5), Spring 1967.

The same version as B43.

C208 WATER AND LANDSCAPE [talk] Collected in *Poetry in the Making* as 'Writing about Landscape'.

Listening and Writing, Summer 1967. pp. 10–16.

This version ends:

Landscape is not just our surroundings, just dull land, just the face of the earth. In poems of this sort, it's a thing both beautiful in itself and a source of freshness. And of new strength. It lies there, everywhere around us, waiting for our observant eyes, and accurate words.

C208a THREE LEGENDS: BLACK WAS THE WITHOUT EYE; HOW DEEPLY THE STONE SLEPT; BLACK HAD SWALLOWED THE SUN [poems]

Journal of Creative Behavior, vol. 1, no. 3, July 1967.

C209 A DISASTER [poem]

Scotsman, 22 July 1967. p. 3.

C210 THE RAIN HORSE [story]

    CAPTURING ANIMALS [talk]

    THE COMING OF THE KINGS [play]

Listening and Writing, Autumn 1967. pp. 5–10, 15–20, 41–57.

'The Rain Horse' and 'Capturing Animals' are reprinted from C100, 'The Coming of the Kings' from C159.

C211 TV ON [poem]

Listener (78:387), 28 September 1967.

C212 A BATTLE [poem] Collected in *Crow* as 'Crow's Account of the Battle'.

Outposts (74:6–8), Autumn 1967.

There are minor variations in twelve lines of this version.

C213 CAPTURING ANIMALS [talk]
Listener (78:498–9), 19 October 1967.

C214 A MOTORBIKE [poem]
Listener (78:723), 30 November 1967.

C215 LOVESONG [poem]
       ANECDOTE [poem]
Northwest Review (9:56–9), Fall–Winter 1967–8.

Line 29 of 'Lovesong' here reads:
    Her love-tricks were clashing of jail-keys.
'Anecdote' has two additional lines. After line 21:
    Masticating food that was no food
and after line 25:
    And the weight of his head on the neck that was no neck
The last line has 'fever' for 'leopard'.

C216 REVENGE FABLE [poem]
Times Literary Supplement, 11 January 1968. p. 34.

C217 CROW'S FIRST LESSON [poem]
       THE BATTLE OF OSFRONTIS [poem] Collected in *Crow* as 'The
       Battle of Osfrontalis'.

       A CHILDISH PRANK [poem]

       THAT MOMENT [poem]

       CROW'S LAST STAND [poem]
Listener (79:118–19), 25 January 1968.

C218 IN LAUGHTER [poem]
Times Literary Supplement, 14 March 1968. p. 273.

Lines 28–9 are here conflated to:
    And finally sits up, exhausted.

C218a SEAN, THE FOOL, THE CATS AND THE DEVIL [play]
Living Language, Summer 1968.

C219 LORE ABIDING [review of *Folktales of Chile* edited by Richard M.
       Dorson; *Hindoo Fairy Legends* edited by Mary Frere; *The Glass Man
       and the Golden Bird* edited by Ruth Manning-Sanders; *The Black
       Monkey* edited by John Hampden]
New Statesman (75:699–700), 24 May 1968.

C220 CAUTIONARY TALE [poem] Collected in *Crow* as 'Criminal
       Ballad'.
Listener (79:743), 6 June 1968.

Line 8 has 'bleached' for 'drained'; line 14 'frowned' for 'gazed'; and line 34 'fragments' for 'splinters'.

C221   DOG DAYS ON THE BLACK SEA [poem]

    ? [poem]

    SECOND BEDTIME STORY [poem] Collected in *Crow* as 'Love-song'.

Critical Quarterly (10:107–10), Spring and Summer 1968.

The contents of this double issue are identical with B39.

C222   FIFTH BEDTIME STORY [poem] Collected in *Crow* as 'A Bedtime Story'.

Listener (80:78), 18 July 1968.

Lines 34–6 here come four lines later. Lines 49–51 are conflated to:
And saw what he could and did what he could

C223   BEAUTY AND THE BEAST [play]

Living Language, Autumn 1968. pp. 11–17.

A shortened version.

C224   WILD WEST [poem]

Scotsman, 14 September 1968.

C225   A LEGEND [poem] Collected in *Crow* as 'Two Legends II'.

    KING OF CARRION [poem]

Listener (80:415), 26 September 1968.

Line 10 of 'King of Carrion' reads:
Into the darkness and dumbness and blindness of the gulf

C226   THE OEDIPUS OF SENECA [play]

Arion (7:327–71), Autumn 1968.

This text is very close to A16c but there are minor differences.

C227   CROW'S FIRST LESSON [poem]

    A CHILDISH PRANK [poem]

Quarry (18:4–5), Fall 1968.

C228   EXAMINATION AT THE WOMB DOOR [poem]

Listener (81:21), 2 January 1969.

C229   A GRIN [poem]

    NOTES FOR A LITTLE PLAY [poem]

    CROW TYRANNOSAURUS [poem]

    A KILL [poem]

Observer, 12 January 1969.

Line 25 of 'Crow Tyrannosaurus' has 'of itself' for 'trapsprung'.

C230   LITTLEBLOOD [poem]

New Statesman (77:161), 31 January 1969.

C231   TWO ESKIMO SONGS: FLEEING FROM ETERNITY; HOW WATER
BEGAN TO PLAY [poems]

Listener (81:382), 20 March 1969.

C232   CROW'S FIRST LESSON [poem]

THE BATTLE OF OSFRONTIS [poem] Collected in *Crow* as 'The
Battle of Osfrontalis'.

A CHILDISH PRANK [poem]

THAT MOMENT [poem]

CROW'S LAST STAND [poem]

Quarterly Review of Literature (16:101–4), 1969.

C233   SONG FOR A PHALLUS [poem]

Transatlantic Review (32:35–7), Summer 1969.

C234   CROW ALIGHTS [poem]

TRUTH KILLS EVERYBODY [poem]

Listener (82:108), 24 July 1969.

Line 7 of 'Crow Alights' has 'rain-rotten' for 'rain-sodden'.
Line 16 of 'Truth Kills Everybody' has 'sinking' for 'dragging'.

C235   THE PRICE OF A BRIDE [verse play]

Living Language, Autumn 1969. pp. 4–9.

A different extract from C193, virtually the ending.

C236   CROW'S TABLE TALK [poem] Collected in *Moortown* as 'Tiger-
psalm'.

Sad Traffic (1:20–1), December 1969.

Several minor differences. The most important is line 32:
   Kills with the strength of madness, kills possessed.

C237   WATERSONG [poem] Collected in *Crow* as 'How Water Began to
Play'.

BALLAD OF BAUBLE-HEAD [poem]

FIFTH BEDTIME STORY [poem] Collected in *Crow* as 'Crow's
Account of the Battle'.

New American Review (8:40–3), January 1970.

Line 5 of 'Fifth Bedtime Story' has 'reach' for 'hold'.
Line 23 has 'tap' for 'drainpipe'. After line 46 is an extra line:
   People fell to bits too easily.

C238   PLAY THE GAME [review of *Children's Games in Street and Playground* by Iona and Peter Opie]

Sunday Times, 11 January 1970.

C238a   KING OF CARRION [poem]

     THAT MOMENT [poem]

     EXAMINATION AT THE WOMB DOOR [poem]

     CROW ALIGHTS [poem]

     CROW'S FEAST [poem]

     A DISASTER [poem]

     TRUTH KILLS EVERYBODY [poem]

Halifax Evening Courier, 30 January 1970.

Line 12 of 'Crow Alights' has 'ashes' for 'embers'.
Line 14 has a 'white' cup.

C239   FRAGMENT OF AN ANCIENT TABLET [poem]

     OWL'S SONG [poem]

     DAWN'S ROSE [poem]

Observer, 15 February 1970. p. 30.

Line 3 of 'Fragment of an Ancient Tablet' has 'famous' for 'notable'.

C240   MYTH AND EDUCATION [essay]

Children's Literature in Education (1:55–70), March 1970.

This essay is completely different from B78.

C241   AN IDEA WHOSE TIME HAS COME [review of *The Environmental Revolution* by Max Nicholson]

Spectator (224:378–9), 21 March 1970. See also C247.

C242   THE TIGER'S BONES [play]

Listening and Writing, Summer 1970. pp. 44–61.

C243   ROBIN SONG [poem]

     CROW HYMN [poem] A different poem from A20. Collected in *Crow* as 'Snake Hymn'.

Sunday Times, 24 May 1970. p. 35.

C244   CROW'S THEOLOGY [poem]

     A HORRIBLE RELIGIOUS ERROR [poem]

Spectator (224:717), 30 May 1970.

C245   THE BLACK BEAST [poem]
       CROWEGO [poem]
       Transatlantic Review (36:130–1), Summer 1970.

C246   CROW'S FIRST LESSON [poem]
       CROW ALIGHTS [poem]
       EXAMINATION AT THE WOMB DOOR [poem]
       THAT MOMENT [poem]
       CROW'S LAST STAND [poem]
       Michigan Quarterly Review (9:147–51), Summer 1970.

C247   THE ENVIRONMENTAL REVOLUTION [review of *The Environmental Revolution* by Max Nicholson]
       Your Environment (1:81–3), Summer 1970.

       A much longer version of C241.

C248   CROW'S SONG OF HIMSELF [poem]
       CONJURING IN HEAVEN [poem]
       CROW AND STONE [poem]
       CROW SICKENED [poem]
       SONG OF WOE [poem]
       CROW BLACKER THAN EVER [poem]
       Critical Quarterly (12:107–10), Summer 1970.

       Line 8 of 'Crow Sickened' has 'calling' for 'challenging'.

C249   THE PASSION OF RAVENSBRUCK; THE DESERT OF LOVE; INTROITUS [poems by János Pilinszky, translated by Peter Siklos and Ted Hughes]
       Modern Poetry in Translation (7:29), June 1970.

C250   CROW TRIES THE MEDIA [poem]
       MAGICAL DANGERS [poem]
       CROW FROWNS [poem]
       CROW'S UNDERSONG [poem]
       CROW AND MAMA [poem]
       New Yorker, 18 July 1970. pp. 30–1.

C251   CROW GOES HUNTING [poem]
       New Statesman (80:96), 24 July 1970.

C252   TED HUGHES'S CROW [talk]

     CROW COMMUNES [poem]

     CROW'S BATTLE FURY [poem]

     CROW'S NERVE FAILS [poem]

Listener (84:149, 156), 30 July 1970.

Line 18 of 'Crow's Battle Fury' has 'skull' for 'head'.
This version lacks lines 21–5. The last line here reads:
   He moves forward a step, then a step, then a step—

C253   CROW HEARS FATE KNOCK ON THE DOOR [poem]

     CROW'S ELEPHANT TOTEM SONG [poem]

     EXISTENTIAL SONG [poem]

     THE CONTENDER [poem]

     SONG AGAINST THE WHITE OWL [poem]

London Magazine (10:16–23), July/August 1970.

C254   A LUCKY FOLLY [poem]

Workshop (10:3), September 1970.

C255   THE HOUSE OF DONKEYS [play]

Living Language, Autumn 1970. pp. 6–10.

First half only. See C287.

C256   CROW AND THE SEA [poem]

New Statesman (80:389), 25 September 1970.

C257   OEDIPUS CROW [poem]

     CROW'S VANITY [poem]

     BONES [poem]

Listener (84:458), 1 October 1970.

C258   FIGHTING FOR JERUSALEM [poem]

Times Literary Supplement, 9 October 1970. p. 1152.

C258a   THE GOD BENEATH THE SEA [review of *The God Beneath the Sea* by Leon Garfield and Edward Blishen]

Children's Literature in Education (3:66–7), November 1970.

C259   CROWCOLOR [poem]

New Yorker, 14 November 1970. p. 144.

C260   COLLECTED BEINGS [review of *The Book of Imaginary Beings* by Jorge Luis Borges]

Guardian, 26 November 1970. p. 11.

C261 CROW'S FALL [poem]
New Yorker, 19 December 1970. p. 46.

C262 ORPHEUS [verse play]
Listening and Writing, Spring 1971. pp. 16–23. Reprinted Summer 1974.

C263 THE LOVEPET [poem]
New Yorker, 2 January 1971. p. 24.

C264 CROW PAINTS HIMSELF INTO A CHINESE MURAL [poem]
New Yorker, 23 January 1971. p. 38.

C265 CROW'S SONG ABOUT PROSPERO AND SYCORAX [poem]
Collected in *Moortown* as 'Prospero and Sycorax'.
CROW'S COURTSHIP [poem]
GENESIS OF EVIL [poem]
CROW RAMBLES [poem] Collected in *Moortown* as 'Life Is Trying To be Life'.
Vogue (128:81), 15 April 1971.

C266 SYLVIA PLATH'S CROSSING THE WATER: SOME REFLECTIONS [a revised version of G67]
Critical Quarterly (13:165–72), Summer 1971.

C267 PROMETHEUS ON HIS CRAG [poem] Collected in *Moortown* as 'Prometheus on his Crag 4'.
Workshop (13:11), September 1971.

C268 GENESIS OF EVIL [poem]
CROW'S COURTSHIP [poem]
Critical Quarterly (13:201–2), Autumn 1971.

C268a [Note on Plath's *Winter Trees*]
Poetry Society Bulletin 70, Autumn 1971.

C269 COMMENTARY [letter about *The Savage God* by A. Alvarez]
Times Literary Supplement, 19 November 1971. p. 1448.
Alvarez replied the following week.

C270 SYLVIA PLATH [letter about *The Savage God* by A. Alvarez]
Observer, 21 November 1971. p. 10.
A different letter from C269.

C271 THE BIRTH OF SOGIS [extract from *Orghast*]

Performance (1:64–5), December 1971.

The same piece (see J122) also contains comments by Hughes on *Orghast*, pp. 61–2, 66.

C272   ORGHAST: TALKING WITHOUT WORDS [essay]

Vogue (128:96–7), December 1971.

C273   A CONVERSATION WITH T. S. ELIOT [letter about Christopher Ricks' review of *A Choice of Shakespeare's Verse* the previous week]

Observer, 23 January 1972.

C274   SORCERER'S APPRENTICE [review of *A Separate Reality* by Carlos Castaneda]

Observer, 5 March 1972. p. 32.

C275   CHILDREN PLANT TREES FOR TOMORROW [letter]

Times Educational Supplement, 17 November 1972.

C276   FROM A PROMETHEUS SEQUENCE [poems] Collected in *Moortown* as 'Prometheus on his Crag 13, 21, 9, 12 and 10'.

Antaeus (12:62–6), Winter 1973.

In poem 9, line 6 reads here:
    Calculated for me—for a sea
Line 8 reads:
    What secret is it?
In poem 21, lines 4–5 read:
    Birth-hacked flesh-ripeness.
    The cry bulging, a slow mire
Lines 13–15 read:
    Cloud-bird
    Midwifes the upglare naphtha,
    Opening the shell.

C277   PROMETHEUS ON HIS CRAG [poems] Collected in *Moortown* as 'Prometheus on his Crag 10, 11 and 15'.

Réalités (268:42–3), March 1973.

C278   PROMETHEUS ON HIS CRAG [poem] Collected in *Moortown* as 'Prometheus on his Crag 20'.

Oxford Poetry Magazine (2:30–1), Summer 1973.

In line 2 this text has 'speculated about' for 'pondered'.

C279   NEW YEAR SONG [poem]

THE RIVER IN MARCH [poem]

A MARCH CALF [poem]

Listener (90:210–11), 16 August 1973.

Line 19 is missing from this text of 'A March Calf'.

C280   THE PRICE OF A BRIDE [verse play]
Living Language, Autumn 1973. pp. 4–9.
Reprinted from C235.

C281   THE WARM AND THE COLD [poem]
Listener (90:640), 8 November 1973.
Line 18 has 'giggle' for 'chuckle'.

C282   SPRING NATURE NOTES [poem]
Listener (91:48–9), 10 January 1974.
Part 2, lines 8–9 have 'disturb' for 'touch', and 'disturbed' for 'touched'.

C282a OCTOBER [poem]
NOVEMBER [poem]
Outposts (100:8–9), Spring 1974.
These became sections 5 and 7 of 'Autumn Nature Notes' in *Season Songs*.

C283   SHEEP [poem] Collected in *Season Songs* as 'Sheep 1 and 3' and in *Moortown* as 'Sheep 1 and 2'.
Listener (91:438), 4 April 1974.

C284   SWIFTS [poem]
Listener (91:633), 16 May 1974.

C285   DECEMBER RIVER [poem]
New Yorker, 24 June 1974. p. 42.

C286   THE STONE [poem]
New Statesman (88:319), 6 September 1974.

C287   THE HOUSE OF DONKEYS [play]
Living Language, Autumn 1974. pp. 4–13.
Unlike C255, this text is complete.

C288   AUTUMN NATURE NOTES [poem]
Listener (92:412–14), 26 September 1974.

C289   THE SUMMONER [poem]
THE EXECUTIONER [poem]

THE SENTENCED [poem] Collected in *Cave Birds* as 'The Risen'.
New Statesman (88:433), 27 September 1974.

C290   THAT GIRL [poem]
New Statesman (88:544), 18 October 1974.

C291   THE HARVEST MOON [poem]
Listener (92:611), 7 November 1974.

C292   THE DEAD MAN LIES, MARCHING HERE AND THERE [poem]
       THE NIGHT WIND, MUSCLED WITH RAIN [poem]
       A PRIMROSE PETAL'S EDGE [poem]
       CALVES HARSHLY PARTED FROM THEIR MAMAS [poem]
Boston University Journal (23:28-9), Winter 1975.
Line 8 of 'The Night Wind' has 'run' for 'scamper'.
'A Primrose Petal's Edge' lacks line 9.

C293   WELCOMBE [poem]
       EXITS [poem]
       FESTIVAL OF POETS [poem] Collected in *Moortown* as 'Poets'.
       APPLE DUMPS [poem]
       THE OAK [poem] Collected in *Gaudete* as 'Your tree—your oak'.
Bananas (1:10), January/February 1975.
'Festival of Poets' has the following differences:
Line 1: They fringe the earth, a corolla, wings
Line 5: They chorus a dawn
Lines 9-12:
    Or they absent
    Into the grass-blade glint-atom
    Fusing the globe
    With the light that fled
'The Oak' begins:
    A guard
    At the pure well of leaf
    A glare
    Of upward lightning
and ends with the additional line:
    With a crow in the top.

C294   IN THE M5 RESTAURANT [poem]
       BEFORE-DAWN TWILIGHT [poem]
       LET THAT ONE SHRINK INTO PLACE [poem]

STILLED AT HIS DRINK [poem]

THE BULGING OAK [poem]

WHY DO YOU TAKE SUCH NERVY SHAPE [poem]

Listener (93:375), 20 March 1975.

C295   MARCH MORNING UNLIKE OTHERS [poem]

New Statesman (89:422), 28 March 1975.

C296   THE GOOD ANGEL: AN OWL FLOWER [poem] Collected in *Cave Birds* as 'The Owl Flower'.

Times Literary Supplement, 30 May 1975. p. 597.

C297   A MOUNTAIN LION [poem]

New Statesman (90:17), 4 July 1975.

Line 2 has 'blended' for 'molten'.
Line 3 has 'the background' for 'shadows'.
Line 21 has 'wary and sudden' for 'suddenly'.

C298   MOON-BELLS [poem]

Encounter (45:36), September 1975.

C299   MOON-WHALES [poem]

MOON-MUSHROOMS [poem] Collected as 'Mushrooms on the Moon'.

MOON-RAVENS [poem]

Cricket (3:31–3), October 1975.

Illustrated by Michael Patrick Hearn.

C300   BEWARE OF THE STARS [poem] Collected in *Moortown* as 'That Star'.

THE LAMENTABLE HISTORY OF THE HUMAN CALF [poem]

New Departures (7/8, 10/11:29, 33–4), 1975.

Line 16 of 'Beware of the Stars': 'We are totally surrounded.' disappears in *Moortown*.

'The Lamentable History' derives from the play *Difficulties of a Bridegroom*.

C301   GREEN MOTHER [poem]

Boston University Journal (24:40), Winter 1976.

This is an early version of 'A Green Mother' in *Cave Birds*, but very different from it.

C302   YOU HAVE COME DOWN FROM THE CLOUDS [poem]

LOOK BACK [poem]

Poetry and Audience (22:1), 1976.

C303   THE INTERROGATOR [poem]
  THE PLAINTIFF [poem]
 Listener (95:188), 12 February 1976.

C304   ICECRUST AND SNOWFLAKE [poem]
  THE VIRGIN KNIGHT [poem]
 New Statesman (91:370), 19 March 1976.
 Line 11 of 'The Virgin Knight' has 'sgae bolg' for 'gae bulga'.

C305   HIS LEGS RAN ABOUT [poem]
 Listener (95:378), 25 March 1976.

C306   AS I CAME, I SAW A WOOD [poem]
  A FLAYED CROW IN THE HALL OF JUDGEMENT [poem]
 Critical Quarterly (18:41–2), Spring 1976.

C307   LIGHT [poem]
  AIR [poem]
  SKIN [poem]
 Granta, April 1976. pp. 14–15.
 In this text of 'Air' all the verbs in the second half are in the present tense.
 Line 11 of 'Skin' has 'rendings' for 'rippings'.

C308   AFTER THERE WAS NOTHING THERE WAS A WOMAN [poem]
  HE CALLED [poem]
  SOCRATES' COCK [poem] Collected in *Cave Birds* as 'The Accused'.
  FIRST, THE DOUBTFUL CHARTS OF SKIN [poem]
 London Magazine (16:5–7), April/May 1976.
 'After There was Nothing' has an additional line after line 18:
 She could see the excited wind flexing on the face of the water.
 'He Called' is a very different version of 'In These Fading Moments' in *Cave Birds*.

C309   TWO HORSES [poem]
 London Magazine (16:51–3), June/July 1976.
 Part 2, line 13 has 'bushy' for 'shaggy'.
 Part 5, line 6 has 'shaggy' for 'shag-haired'; line 8 has 'spring-wire' for 'wire-spring'; line 11 omits the phrase: 'In a steam of dung and sweat'.

C310 THE KNIGHT [poem]

THE GATEKEEPER [poem]

JÁNOS PILINSZKY [essay]

Critical Quarterly (18:5–7, 75–8), Summer 1976.

The essay corresponds to the radio script (G75) and differs slightly from B79.

C311 JÁNOS PILINSZKY: AN INTRODUCTION [essay]

Poetry Nation (6[= 3 2]:110–15), 1976.

A shorter version of B79.

C312 FEBRUARY 17TH [poem]

Bananas (5:25), Summer 1976.

Line 4 has 'bogged' for 'bobbed'.
Line 23 lacks 'baby'.

C313 ACTAEON [poem]

Atlantic Monthly (238:75), September 1976.

C314 THE FALLEN OAK [poem]

YOU HAVE COME DOWN FROM THE CLOUDS [poem]

Boston University Journal (24:34), Fall 1976.

C315 THE SCREAM [poem]

Stand (17:11), 1976.

Line 21 reads here:
He smiled, in half-coma, a smiling doll.

C316 POSTCARD FROM TORQUAY [poem]

New Statesman (92:607), 29 October 1976.

C317 YEHUDA AMICHAI: FOUR POEMS ['The Portuguese Synagogue in Amsterdam', 'A Dog After Love', 'Like the Inner Wall of a House', 'A Song About Rest', translated by Yehuda Amichai and Ted Hughes.]

Times Literary Supplement, 29 October 1976. p. 1354.

C318 THE WOMB [poem]

New Statesman (92:762), 26 November 1976.

C319 COLLISION WITH THE EARTH [poem]

A PRIMROSE PETAL'S EDGE [poem]

THIS IS THE MANEATER'S SKULL [poem]

THE GRASS BLADE IS NOT WITHOUT [poem]

CALVES HARSHLY PARTED FROM THEIR MAMAS [poem]

EVERY DAY THE WORLD GETS SIMPLY [poem]

Bananas (6:30), Autumn/Winter 1976.

C320   WHO LIVES IN MY SKIN WITH ME? [poem]

I WALK [poem]

IF YOU DOUBT THIS FACE [poem]

LUMB [extract from *Gaudete* pp. 77–83]

Mars (1:26, 34–8), 1977.

These three poems are from a projected sequence called *Caprichos*.

'I Walk' has an additional line after line 15 in *Moortown*:
    My futile stridings tangle it worse

C321   THE SONG [poem]

NEFERTITI [poem]

Poetry Australia (62:22–3), February 1977.

Line 8 of 'Nefertiti' reads:
    She can't say a thing.

C322   THE BAPTIST [poem]

A RIDDLE [poem]

THE SCAPEGOAT CULPRIT [poem] Collected in *Cave Birds* as 'The
Scapegoat'.

THE JUDGE [poem]

Transatlantic Review (58/9:55–8), February 1977.

C322a ROE-DEER [poem]

DEAF SCHOOL [poem]

South West Review (I:36–7), March 1977.

C323   DEAD, SHE BECAME SPACE-EARTH [poem]

Boston University Journal (25:23), Spring 1977.

C324   FOXHUNT [poem]

Listener (97:550), 28 April 1977.

C325   HE GETS UP IN DARK DAWN [poem]

Listener (97:787), 16 June 1977.

Line 22 lacks 'blue'.

C326   HEPTONSTALL OLD CHURCH [poem]

NEFERTITI [poem]

FOOTBALL AT SLACK [poem]

Times Literary Supplement, 24 June 1977. pp. 746, 749, 767.

Line 8 of 'Nefertiti' reads:
    She can't say a thing.

C327   COMING DOWN THROUGH SOMERSET [poem]
London Magazine (17:29–30), August/September 1977.

C328   HILL WALLS [poem]
Encounter (49:50), September 1977.

C329   THE WILD DUCK [poem]
       THE SWIFT COMES [poem]
       AND THE FALCON CAME [poem]
Poetry Australia (64:24–5), October 1977.

C330   FOOTBALL AT SLACK [poem]
Overland (68:34), 1977.

C331   EYE WENT OUT TO HUNT YOU [poem]
Aquarius (9:45), 1977.

C332   UNDER THE WORLD'S WILD RIMS [poem]
       THE WEASELS WE SMOKED OUT OF THE BANK [poem]
       HEATHER [poem]
       THE CANAL'S DROWNING BLACK [poem]
P.N Review (5:31), Winter 1977.

C333   MOUNT ZION [poem] Collected in *Remains of Elmet* as 'Mount
       Zion' and 'The Ancient Briton Lay Under His Rock'.
Encounter (49:40–1), December 1977.

Line 12 has 'hot' for 'stinging'.

C334   TRACTOR [poem]
       COCKCROW [poem] Collected in *Remains of Elmet* as 'Cock-
       crows'.
       BIRTH OF RAINBOW [poem]
       TEACHING A DUMB CALF [poem]
Antaeus (28:79–85), Winter 1978.

This version of 'Cockcrow' begins:
    You heard
    Out of deep middle-earth, in the valley cauldron
    The fire crests of the cocks
    Toss up flaring, sink back again dimming

> And toss harder and brighter and higher
> Talon-shouts hooking higher
> To hang smouldering from the night's fringes

C335   PETS [poem]
Overland (69:37), 1978.

C336   GROUSE-BUTTS [poem]
New Statesman (95:231), 17 February 1978.
Line 13 has 'strategy' for 'emplacements'.
Lines 14–15 read: Dedicated
> To the worship of beautiful guns.
The last third of this poem was inadvertently omitted in A60.

C337   THE EXPRESS, WITH A BANG [poem]
Straight Lines (1:1), March 1978.

C338   WYCOLLER HALL [poem]
HEPTONSTALL CEMETERY [poem]
WHERE THE MOTHERS [poem]
BRIDESTONES [poem]
Antaeus (30/31:99–103), Summer/Autumn 1978.

C339   TICK TOCK TICK TOCK [poem]
Times Literary Supplement, 7 April 1978. p. 367.

C340   THE FORMAL AUCTIONEER [poem]
Times Literary Supplement, 14 April 1978. p. 409.

C341   TIGER [poem]
London Magazine (18:31), May 1978.

C342   A NATION'S A SOUL [poem]
Times Literary Supplement, 23 June 1978. p. 704.

C343   RHODODENDRONS [poem]
Listener (99:743), 8 June 1978.

C344   MOORS [poem]
Times Literary Supplement, 30 June 1978. p. 743.

C345   THE HEAD [story]
Bananas (11:38–42), Summer 1978.

C346   LAST LOAD [poem]
London Magazine (18:6–7), July 1978.

C347 CROWN POINT PENSIONERS [poem]

Listener (100:27), 6 July 1978.

Line 19 reads:
   Ancient melody, wild improvisation.
Line 20 has 'proud' for 'stirred'.

C348 THERE COME DAYS TO THE HILLS [poem]

Times Literary Supplement, 21 July 1978. p. 811.

C349 TURNING OUT [poem]

   TEACHING A DUMB CALF [poem]

   THE FOAL HAS LANDED [poem] Collected in B93 as 'Foal'.
   Collected with revisions in *What is the Truth?*, untitled; and in
   New Selected Poems 1957–1994 as 'New Foal'.

Critical Quarterly (20:5–8), Autumn 1978.

C350 FIRST, MILLS [poem]

   ROCK HAS NOT LEARNED [poem]

   CROWN POINT PENSIONERS [poem]

Use of English (30:5–7), Autumn 1978.

The text of 'Crown Point Pensioners' here is as C347.

C351 HERE IS THE CATHEDRAL [poem]

Listener (100:452), 5 October 1978.

Line 13 has 'live' for 'hurt'.
Line 48 has 'do we have to tell you' for 'do you have to be told'.

C352 TIGER-PSALM [poem]

Listener (100:656), 16 November 1978.

Line 41 lacks 'Does not kill'.

C353 LITTLE RED TWIN [poem]

   IT IS ALL [poem]

   THESE GRASSES OF LIGHT [poem]

   HILL-STONE WAS CONTENT [poem]

Texas Arts Journal (2–4:33–5), 1978. [Also published as B91]

The last two lines of 'It Is All' are reversed here.

Line 10 of 'These Grasses of Light' has 'glare' for 'gleam'.

Line 15 of 'Hill-stone' reads:
   In their long, hopeless, darkening stand.

C354　IRISH ELK [poem]
Listener (101:121), 18 January 1979.
This poem derives from the first half of 'The Last Migration' [B32].

C355　HERE IS THE CATHEDRAL [poem]
Helix (3:24–5), February 1979.
The text is as C351.

C356　A DOVE [poem]
Listener (101:381), 15 March 1979.

C356a　A DOVE [poem]
Observer Colour Supplement, 20 May 1979.

C357　THE STONE [poem]
Listener (101:724), 24 May 1979.

C357a　SIX POEMS—YEHUDA AMICHAI [translations by Hughes]
Jewish Chronicle, 1 June 1979, p. vi.

C358　CHILDREN [poem]
New Yorker, 27 August 1979. p. 35.

C359　THE ROSE [poem]
　　　TOP WITHENS [poem]
　　　HAPPY CALF [poem]
Poetry London/Apple Magazine (1:28–9), Autumn 1979.
This version of 'Top Withens' begins:
　　Hope squared the stone
　　And laid these roof-slabs, and wore the way to them
　　With a pioneer eye.

　　How young that world must have looked!
　　The hills full of savage promise.

　　Here climbed the news
　　Of America's rich surrender—the wilderness
　　Blooming with cattle, wheat, oil, cities.

　　The dream's fort held—
　　Stones blackening with stubborn purpose.

C360　A KNOCK AT THE DOOR, YOU OPEN THE DOOR [poem]
Critical Quarterly (21:43), Autumn 1979.
Line 5 reads: Darkness of person, hairiness of a creature—
Line 19 has 'pieces' for 'bits'.

Line 24 reads: A mouth wet and red and agile
Line 43 has 'hot can's edge' for 'scalding can's metal'.
Line 59 is missing.
Line 60 has 'glistening' for 'shining'.
Additional penultimate line:
    Nobody's, humped where gravity glues it,

C361 NIGHT ARRIVAL OF SEA-TROUT [poem]
London Review of Books (1:8), 25 October 1979.

C362 WOODPECKER [poem]
Times Literary Supplement, 14 December 1979.

C363 PUMA [poem]
Listener (102:871), 20 and 27 December 1979.

C364 UNFINISHED MYSTERY [poem]
    THE EARTHENWARE HEAD [poem]
London Review of Books (2:4), 21 February 1980.

C365 THE IRON WOLF [poem]
Listener (103:281), 28 February 1980.

C366 NIGHTJAR [poem]
London Review of Books (2:10), 15 May 1980.

C367 YOU HATED SPAIN [poem]
    LILY [poem]
    A DOVE [poem]
    DO NOT PICK UP THE TELEPHONE [poem]
Ploughshares (6:82–7), 1980.

C368 THE SNOW-SHOE HARE [poem]
Listener (104:413), 25 September 1980.

C369 THE WORD RIVER [poem]
    MESSAGE FOR THE POETRY OLYMPICS [letter]
New Departures (12:3), 26 September 1980.

The 'Message' begins, in facsimile: 'It's so long now since those international poetry frolics passed away, this is probably a good time to start something fresh.' The next paragraph is taken from H1.

The final paragraph is new: 'It is not enough to say this once. It has to be said afresh year after year, in as many places and different languages as possible. And the effort of poets themselves to live up to their calling has to be renewed also, year after year ...'

C370 EAGLE [poem]
      LOW WATER [poem]
      London Review of Books (2:16), 2 October 1980.

C371 LAST ACT [poem]
      THE MOORHEN [poem]
      SEPTEMBER SALMON [poem]
      THE MERRY MINK [poem]
      Quarto (11:6), October 1980.

C372 THE ARCTIC FOX [poem]
      Listener (104:622), 6 November 1980.

C373 MOOSES [poem]
      Times Literary Supplement, 21 November 1980. p. 1329.

C374 NYMET [poem]
      London Review of Books (2:20), 4 December 1980.

C375 IN DEFENCE OF CROW [essay]
      Books and Issues (3–4:4–6), 1981.

C376 GOOSE [poem]
      New Statesman, 30 January 1981. p. 23.

C377 FIGHT ON THE BEACHES [letter]
      Times, 20 March 1981.

C378 FISHING THE ESTUARY [poem]
      Graffiti (3:18–19), Spring 1981.

C379 LYNX [poem]
      Times Literary Supplement, 27 March 1981. p. 347.

C380 AN OCTOBER SALMON [poem]
      London Review of Books, 16 April 1981. p. 6.
      Line 18 has 'fury' for 'power'.
      Line 44 has 'elation' for 'energy'.

C381 SKUNK [poem]
      Listener (105 2710:582), 30 April 1981.

C382 THE DEAD VIXEN [poem]
      Times Educational Supplement, 5 June 1981. p. 76.

C383 TREECREEPER [poem]
    GO FISHING [poem]
New Statesman, 26 June 1981.

C384 FAIRY FLOOD [poem]
Poetry Review (71:62), September 1981.

C385 AN ICON [poem]
    IN THE DARK VIOLIN OF THE VALLEY [poem]
    SALMON EGGS [poem]
Grand Street (I i:38–42), Autumn 1981.
Line 10 of 'In the Dark Violin' has 'steely limits', which becomes 'draughty limits' in *River*.
Line 2 of 'Salmon Eggs' has 'caressing' for 'touching'.
Line 40 has 'raw' for 'swollen'.

C386 THAT MORNING [poem]
London Review of Books (3:10), 3 December 1981.

C387 SING THE RAT [poem]
London Review of Books (4 iii:21), 18 February 1982.
In comparison with *What is the Truth?* line 29 has 'thousand' for 'million', and 'Sing him' between lines 29 and 30.

C388 FEELING FOR THE FATE OF EROS [review of *Where I Used to Play on the Green* by Glyn Hughes]
Arts Yorkshire, March 1982. p. 8.

C389 SYLVIA PLATH AND HER JOURNALS [essay]
Grand Street (I iii:86), Spring 1982.

C390 REMEMBERING TEHERAN [poem]
London Review of Books (4 xv:10), 19 August 1982.

C391 THE GREAT IRISH PIKE [poem]
London Review of Books (4 xxii–xxiii:6), 2–29 December 1982.

C392 COWS [poem]
Aquarius (XV/XVI:103), 1983.

C393 TO BE HARRY [poem]
New Departures (15:62), January 1983.

C394 STARLINGS HAVE COME [poem]
    NEW YEAR [poem]
Listener (109 2794:20–1), 13 January 1983.

C395   THE KINGFISHER [poem]

Observer, 16 January 1983. p. 46.

Corresponds with the text in *River*, which is slightly different from *A Primer of Birds*.

C396   A SPARROW-HAWK [poem]

London Review of Books (5 v:8), 17 March 1983.

Lines 11 and 12 have 'we' for 'you'.

C397   MILESIAN ENCOUNTER ON THE SLIGACHAN [poem]

Enter Rumour, Spring 1983. pp. 25–7.

Line 13 has 'scapulars' for 'scapulae'.
Line 18 has 'glimpse' for 'glance'.
Line 38 has 'searing' for 'searching'.

C398   SWALLOWS [poem]

Listener (109 2805:26–7), 21 April 1983.

The three sections are headed 'What The Schoolmaster Said:', 'What The Farmer's Wife Said:' and 'What The Vicar Said:', but the schoolmaster's poem does not appear in *What is the Truth?* It is the same as 'The Swallow' in A76 and 'A Swallow' in A44d, but lacking lines 1–2 and 16–20.
Line 9 of section 3 has 'propeller-blur, ponderous,' for 'putt-putting'.

C399   THE GULKANA [poem]

London Review of Books (5 ix:10), 19 May 1983.

Line 84 has 'dissolved' for 'melted'.
Line 85 has 'ecstasy' for 'sacrament'.
Line 91 has 'seized on'.

C400   EVENING THRUSH [poem]

Listener (109 2811:27), 2 June 1983.

Line 7 lacks 'head up'.

C401   OPHELIA [poem]

Times Literary Supplement (4194:875), 19 August 1983.

C402   DEE [poem]

Observer, 21 August 1983.

C403   JAPANESE RIVER TALES [poems]

Times Literary Supplement, 2 September 1983.

C404   THE MAYFLY [poem]

    AN AUGUST SALMON [poem]

AN EEL [poem]

THE PIGEON'S WINGS [poem]

AUGUST EVENING [poem]

London Magazine (23 vii:5–10), October 1983.

A few lines and phrases from 'The Mayfly' reappear in 'Saint's Island'. Despite the similarity of the first two lines, the rest of the poem has nothing in common with 'The Mayfly is Frail' in *Three Books*. 'An August Salmon' in *River* omits line 27:

On the torpedo launch of his poise—

C405   THE LIVE-BAIT [poem]

Outposts (138:58), Autumn 1983.

C406   SHEEP [poem]

Times Literary Supplement (4208:1315), 25 November 1983.

This poem, destined for *What is the Truth?* (p. 41), is completely different from 'Sheep' in *Season Songs*.

C407   [No entry]

C408   VIOLET [poem]

New Statesman (106 2751:25), 9 December 1983.

In *Flowers and Insects* as 'A Violet at Lough Aughrisburg'.
Line 3 has 'tree-full' for 'branch'.
Line 10 has 'protects it all' for 'holds it all, a moment,'.

C409   DAFFODILS [poem]

London Review of Books (6 iv:8), 1 March 1984.

Line 1 has 'bit' for 'patch'.
Line 4 begins 'It was'.
Line 5 has 'they kept on' for 'kept'.
Line 19 has 'wrappers' for 'rustlings'.
Line 21 has 'green' for 'dark'.
Line 28 has 'bright, scared' for 'scared, bright'.
Line 29 has 'gentler' for 'a defter'; 'A thousand' for 'So many'.
Line 31 reads:
    Felt deep into her chilly fountain of blades—
Lines 42–3 are reversed.
Line 45 reads:
    Had taken refuge inside me—
Line 61 lacks 'so'.
Line 65 has 'grass' for 'garden'.
Line 68 reads:
    With a grisly awe

C410 SUBSIDY FOR POETRY [essay]
Unesco Features 803, 1984.

C411 BIG POPPY [poem]
New Republic (190:34), 26 March 1984.

C412 FOX [poem]
    THE BAT [poem]
    HARE [poem]
Times Literary Supplement (4226:340), 30 March 1984.
Line 9 of 'Hare' has 'Bulge-eyed' for 'Huge-eyed'.

C413 WATERLICKED [poem]
Times Literary Supplement (4230:459), 27 April 1984.

C414 MY DONKEY [poem]
New Yorker (60:54), 7 May 1984.

C415 FAMILIAR [poem]
Times Literary Supplement (4233:539), 18 May 1984.

C416 LITTLE WHALE SONG [poem]
    DISARMAMENT [poem]
Critical Quarterly (26:44–5), Spring/Summer 1984.

C417 WALT [poem]
    A MACAW [poem]
London Review of Books, 15 November 1984. p. 27.

C418 RAIN-CHARM FOR THE DUCHY [poem]
Observer, 23 December 1984. p. 7.

C419 SACRIFICE [poem]
London Review of Books (7 i:16), 24 January 1985.

For the first two lines in *Wolfwatching* this version has:
    Little One Too Many—
    Born at the bottom of the heap.
    The baby daughter's doll.
    She trailed after the others, lugging him.

    Little One Too Many grew up
    With a strangely wrinkled brow—fold on fold
Line 14 has 'piled' for 'built'.
Line 16 has 'Little One Too Many's' for 'His fateful'.
Line 17 has 'shakes' for 'jars'.
Line 34 has 'four-inch' and 'sky' for 'five-inch' and 'skylines'.

C420   THE ANGEL CARVED IN WOOD [poem]
Twelve Times a Year, January/February 1985.

C421   THREE VOICES [poem]
Spectator (254 8169:24), 2 February 1985.

C422   CONSCRIPTS [poem]
South West Review (24:3), February 1985.

C423   SLUMP SUNDAYS [poem]
Times Literary Supplement (4275:247), 8 March 1985.
Line 15 is 'Decrepit mythology'.
Line 22 is 'Like a stone tipped from the overgrown quarry'.

C424   THE BEST WORKER IN EUROPE [poem]
Times, 18 March 1985.
First three stanzas only.

C425   REMEMBERING JENNY RANKIN [poem]
Rialto (2:19), Spring 1985.

C426   FOR THE DURATION [poem]
Listener, 9 May 1985. p. 28.
Line 19 has 'astounding' for 'appalling'.
Line 34 has 'laugh and marvel' for 'marvel and laugh'.

C427   HARDCASTLE CRAGS [poem]
Times Literary Supplement (4288:642), 7 June 1985.
Heavily revised version.

C428   CUCKOO [poem]
       WHERE I SIT WRITING MY LETTER [poem]
Listener (113 2913:30–1), 13 June 1985.
'Cuckoo' is a heavily revised version of 'Cuckoo's' in *A Primer of Birds*.

C429   PUTTING A VALUE ON U.K.'S SALMON RICHES [letter]
Times, 13 August 1985. p. 11.

C430   GROUSE BUTTS [poem]
Listener (114 2922:30), 15 August 1985.
Heavily revised version.

C431   EDITH [poem]
Listener (114 2925:26), 5 September 1985.

C432 RIGHTS [poem]

Arts Yorkshire (4 8:16), October/November 1985.

The poem also appeared in *Artful Reporter* (82:6), October 1985.

C433 RITES [poem]

Reverberations, Autumn 1985, front cover.

C434 SUNSTRUCK FOXGLOVE [poem]

TWO TORTOISESHELL BUTTERFLIES [poem]

London Magazine (25 8:25), November 1985.

Line 10 of 'Two Tortoiseshell Butterflies' continues:
, brocade of Daisies,
Embroidery of Dandelions.
Line 19 here reads:
Thick-fold throat, among plain glistenings
thus omitting, perhaps in error, two half-lines from the text in A91.
Line 22 has 'then flat open'.

C435 TELEGRAPH WIRES [poem]

Listener (114 2936:34), 21 November 1985.

Line 1 has 'empty' for 'lonely'.

C436 THE DREAM OF THE LION [poem]

Observer, 29 December 1985. p. 21.

C437 SACRIFICED HEAD [poem]

HALFWAY HEAD [poem]

LAMENTING HEAD [poem]

RECKLESS HEAD [poem]

Grand Street (6 1:14–17), Autumn 1986.

C438 CHILDREN AND SECRETLY LISTENING ADULTS [letter]

Signal (49:55–6), January 1986.

Extracts from a letter from Hughes to Lissa Paul, 1 May 1984.

C439 'DUST AS WE ARE' ... ETC. [poem]

Listener (115 2941:25), 2 January 1986.

Line 10 has 'veil' for 'curtain', and 'briskly' for 'deftly'.
Line 28 lacks 'a silence like'.
Line 33 has 'smallness' for 'fragility'.
Last line has 'sort' for 'kind'.

C440 MANCHESTER SKYTRAIN [poem]

London Review of Books (8 iv:6), 6 March 1986.

Line 1 reads: The nightmare is that last straight into the camera—
Line 19 has 'flings' for 'whirls'.
Line 32 has 'Salvaged from the crash' for 'Eased hot from the wreck'.

C441   THE CROWN OF THE KINGDOM [poem]

Times, 21 April 1986. p. 16.

'An Almost Thornless Crown' (the second of the six parts) is in
Flowers and Insects, with the sub-title 'Titania Choreographs a Ballet,
Using Her Attendants'.
Line 29 adds 'there'.
Lines 48–50 read:
    (An intricate, masterly Japanese brush-stroke
    Dabbed her identity signature)—
              now twine over
    And under hot and tipsy Honeysuckles,
Lines 64–5 read:
    Now weave in there
    The lofty Arum Lily. She hunches
    Her fleshless scapulae
Line 69 has 'nunnery' for 'seminary'.
Line 72 has 'utterance' for 'appeal'.
The whole poem was revised as 'A Birthday Masque' in Rain-Charm
for the Duchy.

C442   THE PIKE [poem]

       MAYDAY [poem]

Listener, 22 May 1986.

C443   CLIMBING INTO HEPTONSTALL [poem]

London Review of Books (8 xi:22), 19 June 1986.

Line 8 has 'drains' for 'weeps'.
Line 11 has 'condensed' for 'congealed'.
Line 33 has 'sole' for 'one'.
Line 40 has 'only' for 'barely'.
Line 42–5 has 'Of going without—of going without'.
Line 55 has 'With a sweep of the arm, as if he'd heard nothing:'.

C444   THE HONEY BEE AND THE THISTLE [poem]

Times, 23 July 1986. p. 16.

This poem appeared on the same date in the Guardian, the Daily
Express and the Daily Mail.

C445   THE WHISTLE; GROUP; CIRCUIT [poems by Marin Sorescu
       translated by Hughes]

Irish Review (1:76–8), 1986.

C446 SICK POEM [poem]
  Bookdealer (766:6), 9 October 1986.

C447 IN THE LIKENESS OF A GRASSHOPPER [poem]
  Literary Review, October 1986. p. 55.

C448 THOUGH THE OWL [poem]
  Bookdealer (769:6–7), 30 October 1986.

C449 IN 1955 OR SO [poem]
  Bookdealer (770:7), 6 November 1986.

C450 TO RICHARD [poem]
      WARM MOORS [poem]
      THE IMPALA [poem]
  Bookdealer (771:7–8), 13 November 1986.

Richard Gilbertson claims that this draft of 'Warm Moors' is 'the first draft of an unpublished poem'. In fact it was published in 1966 (C183). This draft is, however, slightly different, and may be earlier. Line 1 has 'faucet' for 'pane', and 'by' for 'to'; line 7 'squaring' for 'scoring'; line 8 'Step by step' for 'This is the way'.

C451 IN THE TIMES [poem]
      CROW'S EVERY MOVE [poem]
  Bookdealer (775:6), 11 December 1986.

C452 DESTINY [poem by Marin Sorescu translated by Hughes]
  The Catalogue, Bloodaxe Books, 1987.

C453 FIRST THINGS FIRST [poem]
  Times, 4 June 1987. p. 10.

C454 AN INTRODUCTION TO 'THE THOUGHT FOX' [essay]
  The English Programme 1987–8. p. 29.

C455 ON THE BRINK [poem]
  Daily Telegraph Weekend, 24 October 1987. p. 1.
  In *Wolfwatching* as 'Black Rhino'.
  Begins 'Here he is' instead of 'This is the Black Rhino'.
  In section III the rhino is here male and the White Egret female.
  Line 20 of section III has 'beneath' for 'between'; line 27 'VIPs' for 'bigshots'.
  Section IV here was omitted in *Wolfwatching*.

C456 TO PARSE OR NOT TO PARSE [letter]
  Sunday Times, 22 November 1987. p. 39.

C457 GLIMPSE [poem]
London Review of Books (10 3:19), 4 February 1988.

C458 ON SYLVIA PLATH'S BIOGRAPHERS [letter]
Sunday Times, 13 March 1988. p. A3.

C459 THE BLACK RHINO [poem]
Antaeus (60:176–82), Spring 1988.

Text identical with C454 except for the opening words: 'This is the Black Rhino'.

C460 ON THE RESERVATIONS [poem]
London Review of Books (10 11:8), 2 June 1988.

C461 NO CHANCE FOR FISHERY INTERESTS [letter]
Trout and Salmon, July 1988, p. 33.

C462 TAKE WHAT YOU WANT BUT PAY FOR IT [poem]
London Review of Books (10 17:8), 29 September 1988.

Line 15 has 'primaeval' for 'surrounding'.
Line 20 has 'sculpted' for 'finished'.

C463 UNDER HIGH WOOD [poem]
Times, 4 October 1988. p. 20.

C464 FOR THE CHRISTENING OF HER ROYAL HIGHNESS PRINCESS
BEATRICE OF YORK BORN: 8.18, 8–8–88 [poem]
Daily Telegraph, 20 December 1988. p. 13.

C465 THE PLACE WHERE SYLVIA PLATH SHOULD REST IN PEACE [letter]
Guardian, 20 April 1989. p. 22.

A reply to letters of 7 and 11 April.

C466 SYLVIA PLATH: THE FACTS OF HER LIFE AND THE DESECRATION
OF HER GRAVE [letter]
Independent, 22 April 1989. p. 19.

A reply to 'The poet and the unquiet grave' by Ronald Hayman, *Independent*, 19 April 1989, p. 19. There followed readers' letters on 24 and 26 April.

C467 CURLEWS LIFT [poem]
Birds, Summer 1989. p. 41.

This is the first occasion on which 'Curlews in April' becomes the second part of one poem with 'Curlews Lift'. In *New Selected Poems* and *Collected Animal Poems* the title of the combined poem becomes simply 'Curlews'.

C468   WHAT THE SERPENT SAID TO ADAM [poem]
     Sunday Correspondent, 17 September 1989. p. 33.

C469   WHERE RESEARCH BECOMES INTRUSION [letter]
     Observer, 29 October 1989. p. 47.

C470   FOR THE POETRY BOOK SOCIETY BULLETIN [notes on *Wolfwatching*]
     Poetry Book Society Bulletin, Autumn 1989. no. 142. pp. 1, 3.

C471   LINES ABOUT ELIAS [poem]
     PN Review (16 ii:44), 1989.

C472   [No entry]

C473   LITTLE SALMON HYMN [poem]
     Times, 18 July 1990.

C474   THREE VOICES FOR THE QUEEN MOTHER [poem]
     Daily Telegraph, 4 August 1990. pp. I–II.
The second line of part 2 has 'Wrapped in' for 'Lit with'.
Part 3, line 37 has 'This moment, this day' for 'This day, this moment'.
Part 3, line 54 has 'An ocean sliver' for 'A sliver of ocean'.
Part 3, line 60 has 'The moment, this,' for 'This moment, and this,'.
Part 6, line 10 has 'Re-named' for 'Re-styled'.
Part 6, line 15 has 'hurricane' for 'Hurricane'.
Guardian, 16 August 1990.

C475   DEVON-SENT [extract from foreword to B157]
     Sunday Express, 26 August 1990.

C476   FIRST THINGS FIRST [poem]
     Guardian, 27 September 1991. p. 29.

C477   THE FORTIETH ANNIVERSARY OF THE ACCESSION OF HER MAJESTY QUEEN ELIZABETH II [poem]
     Daily Telegraph, 6 February 1992. p. 7.

C478   THE INTERPRETATION OF PARABLES [article]
     Times Educational Supplement, 20 March 1992.

C478a   THE EYES OF LOVE [extract from A97]
     Independent on Sunday, 5 April 1992.

C479   LOBBY FROM UNDER THE CARPET [poem]
     Times, 9 April 1992.

C480 SHAKESPEARE AND THE GODDESS [reply to review]
Times, 16 April 1992.

C481 BATTLING OVER THE BARD [reply to review]
Sunday Times, 19 April 1992. Section 7, p. 6.

C482 TED HUGHES AND THE PLATH ESTATE [letter]
Times Literary Supplement, 24 April 1992.

C483 TYNDALE ANNIVERSARY COMMEMORATION [joint letter]
Times Literary Supplement, 1 May 1992. p. 15.

C484 THE LOCKET [poem]
Independent on Sunday, 7 June 1992.
Identical with the text in A107 except for lacking 'blueish' in line 14.

C485 THE INTERPRETATION OF PARABLES [essay]
Signal 69, September 1992. pp. 147–52.
A slightly expanded version of C478.

C486 YOUR WORLD [review article on *Your World*, HarperCollins 1992]
Observer Magazine, 29 November 1992. pp. 23–39.

C487 THE LAST OF THE 1ST/5TH LANCASHIRE FUSILIERS FROM THE
      MAY 6TH LANDING [poem]
Guardian, 23 November 1993.

C488 PLAYING WITH AN ARCHETYPE [poem]
Spectator, 24 September 1994. p. 33.

C489 T. S. ELIOT: THE DEATH OF SAINT NARCISSUS [introductory note]
Poetry Review (84 3:6), Autumn 1994.

C490 BEING CHRISTLIKE [poem]
Spectator, 17/24 December 1994. p. 78.

C491 GOKU [short story]
Independent on Sunday, 26 February 1995.

C492 WHEN CROW WAS WHITE [poem]
Paris Review (134:54), Spring 1995
Facsimile of ms. of unpublished poem.

C493 SYLVIA PLATH: *THE BELL JAR* AND *ARIEL* [essay]
Thumbscrew, vol. 2, pp. 2–11, Spring 1995.

C494   THE OAK TREE [poem]
Daily Telegraph, 4 August 1995. p. 2.

C495   *WHAT IS THE TRUTH?* AND *THE COLLECTED ANIMAL POEMS*
Classroom Choice, issue 2, Poetry Book Society, Autumn 1995.

D. TRANSLATIONS

We have not attempted to list every poem by Ted Hughes which has appeared in translation in a foreign anthology or periodical, only complete books and significant selections.

BULGARIAN

D1 *Pesterni ptici*, Navodna kultura, Sofija, 1983.

> *Cave Birds*, translated by Aleksandar Surbanov and Vladimir Trendafilov.

CATALAN

D2 *L'Home de Ferro*, Editorial Empúries, Barcelona, 1993.

> *The Iron Man*, translated by Marina Folch i Folch.

D3 [No entry]

DANISH

D4 Ted Hughes *Krage—Fra kragens liv og dens sange*, Udvalgt og gendigtet af Steen Thorborg. Illustrationer: Poul Allan. Husets Forlag/S.O.L., Århus, 1977.

> Contains 29 poems from *Crow*.

D5 *Årstiderne* Ted Hughes, Illustreret af Jean Elizabeth Langwadt, Oversat af Steen Thorborg. Forlaget Prometheus, Åbenrå, 1978.

> Contains all the poems in the Faber *Season Songs* except 'Autumn Nature Notes' and 'New Year Song'.

D6 *Snabeln og Andre Fortællinger fra da Verden Var Ny*, Host & Son, Copenhagen, 1995.

Tales of the Early World, translated by Bente Hansen.

DUTCH

D7 *Kraai*, Workshop Poezievertalen Amsterdam, 1975.

Contains parallel texts of eighteen poems from *Crow*: 'Two Legends', 'Lineage', 'Crow Hears Fate Knock on the Door', translated by Hans van Pinxteren; 'Examination at the Womb Door', 'A Disaster', 'Oedipus Crow', translated by Benno Karkabé; 'The Door', 'Crow Tries the Media', 'Dawn's Rose', translated by George de Bruin; 'Crow's First Lesson', 'Crow's Fall', 'Crow's Vanity', translated by Hilda Dijk; 'A Grin', 'Crow Goes Hunting', 'Apple Tragedy', translated by Gijs Hoetjes; 'Crow on the Beach', 'Crow's Undersong', translated by Elisabeth Key; and 'Littleblood', translated independently by all six translators.

D8 *Hoe Walvis een alwis werd: meer verhalen uit de vroege wereld*, Querido, Amsterdam, 1995.

How the Whale Became, translated by Rob Scholten, illustrated by Sylvia Weve.

FARSI (PERSIAN)

D8a *Âdam-e Âhani*, Nâder-e Ebrâhimi, Tehrân: Sâzemân-e Hamgâm bâ Kudakân va Nowjavânân bâ sarmâye-ye Amir Kabir, 1972.

The Iron Man.

FRENCH

D9 *La Discordance*, no. 1, 1978.

Contains 'Hawk Roosting', 'View of a Pig', 'Thrushes', 'Pike', 'Ghost Crabs', 'The Howling of Wolves'.

D10 Ted Hughes *Corbeau*, 8 dessins de Jan Lebenstein, traduction et préface de Claude Guillot, suivi d'une note sur Claude Guillot par Joaquim Vital. Éditions de la Différence, 1980.

Contains all the poems in the second edition of *Crow* except 'Littleblood'.

D11 *Le Géant de Fer*, Gallimard, Paris, 1984.

The Iron Man, translated by Sophie de Vogelas.

D12 *Cave Birds*, Orphée/La Différence, 1991.

Translated by Janine Mitaud.

GERMAN

D13 *Neue Zürcher Zeitung* (Zurich), 4 December 1965.

Contains 'The Thought-Fox', translated by Ursula Spinner.

D14 *Ted Hughes: Der Eisenmann*, Bilder von Rüdiger Stoye, Loewes Verlag Ferdinand Carl, Bayreuth, 1969.

The Iron Man, translated by Marita Moshammer-Lohrer.

D15 *Ted Hughes: Gedanken-Fuchs, Gedichte, Englisch–Deutsch*, Literarisches Colloquium, Berlin, 1971; rev. edn 1981.

Contains 'The Thought-Fox', 'The Horses', 'Hawk Roosting', 'An Otter', 'Sunstroke', 'Lupercalia', 'Still Life', 'Her Husband', 'Wino', 'Stations', 'The Bear', 'Theology', 'Out', 'New Moon in January', 'The Knight', 'The Rat's Dance', 'Skylarks', 'Pibroch', 'Gnat-Psalm', 'Full Moon and Little Frieda'.

Translated by Ekbert Faas in collaboration with Martin Seletzki.

D16 *Erkundungen—23 Englische Erzähler*, Verlag Volk und Welt, 1971.

Contains 'The Rain Horse'.

D17 *Philip Larkin, Thom Gunn, Ted Hughes, Gedichte*, Verlag Volk und Welt, Berlin, 1974. Edited and with a foreword by Karl Heinz Berger. Translators: Karl Heinz Berger, Klaus-Dieter Sommer, Ekbert Faas and Martin Seletzki.

Contains 'Song', 'The Hawk in the Rain', 'The Horses', 'Parlour-Piece', 'September', 'Bayonet Charge', 'Everyman's Odyssey', 'Acrobats', 'November', 'My Uncle Dan', 'Grandma', 'My Brother Bert', 'The Adaptable Mountain Dugong', 'Tree-Disease', 'Moon-Freaks', 'A Moon Man-Hunt', 'Her Husband', 'Second Glance at a Jaguar', 'Boom', 'The Bear', 'Theology', 'Out', 'New Moon in January', 'Skylarks', 'Wodwo', 'Full Moon and Little Frieda'.

D18 *Ensemble: Internationales Jahrbuch für Literatur, 6* (1975).

Contains 'Wind', 'Six Young Men', 'Hawk Roosting' and 'Pibroch'.

D19 *Moderne englische Lyrik*, Willi Erzgräbner (editor). Philipp Reclam Jun., Stuttgart, 1976. Translators Ute and Werner Knoedgen.

Contains 'The Thought-Fox', 'Hawk Roosting', 'View of a Pig', 'Snowdrop', 'Thistles', 'Full Moon and Little Frieda'.

D20 *Wie der Wal erschaffen wurde*, Lesen-und-Freizeit-Verlag, Ravens-burg, 1982; Otto Maier, Ravensburg, 1989.

How the Whale Became, translated by Karin Polz, illustrated by F. Chocholo.

D21 *Krähe*, Klett-Cotta, Stuttgart, 1986.

Parallel text of *Crow* introduced and translated by Elmar Schenkel.

D22 *Der Eisenmann*, Otto Maier, Ravensburg, 1987.

The Iron Man, translated by Uwe-Michael Gutzschhahn. Illustrated by J. Capek.

D23 *Der Rüssel*, Otto Maier, Ravensburg, 1991.

Tales of the Early World, translated by Uwe-Michael Gutzschhahn.

D24 *Ted Hughes: Gedichte*, translated with introduction and notes by Ulrich Horstmann, Mattes Verlag, Heidelberg, 1995.

Contains 'The Thought-Fox', 'The Jaguar', 'Famous Poet', 'The Horses', 'Meeting', 'Wind', 'Hawk Roosting', 'The Bull Moses', 'View of a Pig', 'Relic', 'Sunstroke', 'Thistles', 'Still Life', 'Her Husband', 'The Green Wolf', 'Stealing Trout on a May Morning', 'Kreutzer Sonata', 'The Warriors of the North', 'Skylarks', 'Gnat-Psalm', 'Full Moon and Little Frieda', 'Two Legends', 'Lineage', 'Examination at the Womb-Door', 'A Childish Prank', 'Crow's First Lesson', 'Crow Alights', 'A Disaster', 'Crow's Theology', 'Crow's Vanity', 'Crow Goes Hunting', 'Owl's Song', 'Crow's Elephant Totem Song', 'Crow's Song of Himself', 'Song for a Phallus', 'Apple Tragedy', 'Truth Kills Everybody', 'Notes for a Little Play', 'King of Carrion', 'Littleblood', 'Deceptions', 'Swifts', 'Apple Dumps', 'The Knight', 'Bride and Groom Lie Hidden for Three Days', 'Hillstone was Content', 'When Men Got to the Summit', 'Familiar', 'Crown Point Pensioners', 'Heptonstall Old Church', 'Heptonstall Cemetery', 'Tractor', 'February 17th', 'March Morning Unlike Others', 'Coming Down Through Somerset', 'A Motorbike', 'High Water', 'Low Water', 'In the Dark Violin of the Valley', 'The Kingfisher', 'October Salmon', 'Narcissi', 'Cyclamens in a Bowl', 'Where I Sit Writing My Letter', 'The Honey Bee', 'In the Likeness of a Grasshopper', 'Big Poppy', 'Dust as we Are', 'The Black Rhino'.

HEBREW

D25 *Anthologia Anglit*, Shocken, Tel Aviv, 1972.

Contains 'Full Moon and Little Frieda', translated by Shimon Sandbank.

D26 *Eton 1977*, Tel Aviv, January 1983.

Contains 'Remembering Teheran', translated by Yehuda Amichai.

HUNGARIAN

D27 *Nagyvilag*, no. 12, 1976.

Contains 11 poems from *Crow*.

D28 *Egtajak 1978–1979*, Europa Publishers, 1979.

Contains 'Sunday'.

D29 Ted Hughes: *A Vasember*, Móra Konyvkiadó, 1981.

The Iron Man, translated by Damokos Katalin.

D30 *A Szűz és az Egyszarvú: Contemporary English Poets* [*The Virgin and the Unicorn: Contemporary English Poets*], ed. István Tótfalusi, Készült, 1983.

Contains 'The Thought-Fox', 'Macaw and Little Miss', 'Soliloquy of a Misanthrope', 'The Dove-Breeder', 'The Jaguar', 'Witches', 'Cleopatra to the Asp', 'An Otter', 'Her Husband', 'Ghost Crabs', 'Bowled Over', 'Reveille', 'Kreutzer Sonata', 'Wodwo', 'Lineage', 'Crow's First Lesson', 'The Black Beast', 'A Disaster', 'Crow's Theology', 'Crow's Nerve Fails', 'Magical Dangers', 'Crow Goes Hunting', 'Crow Blacker Than Ever', 'Crow's Song of Himself', 'Apple Tragedy', 'Crow and Stone', 'King of Carrion', 'She Seemed So Considerate', 'The Plaintiff', and 'Only a Little Sleep, a Little Slumber', translated by István Tótfalusi.

D31 [No entry]

ITALIAN

D32 *Poesia Inglese del '900*, Con testo a fronte, introduzione, versioni e note di Carlo Izzo. Guanda, Parma, (third edition) 1967.

Contains 'The Jaguar', 'Wind', 'Song', 'Soliloquy of a Misanthrope', 'Six Young Men'.

D33 *Almanacco dello Specchio*, no. 2, Mondadori, Milan, 1973.

Contains 'Two Legends', 'A Kill', 'The Door', 'A Childish Prank', 'Crow's First Lesson', 'Crow's Theology', 'Crow and the Birds', 'Crow on the Beach', 'Glimpse', 'Two Eskimo Songs', 'Littleblood'.

Introduced and translated by Camillo Pennati.

D34 Ted Hughes: *Pensiero-volpe e altre poesie*, A cura di Camillo Pennati, Arnoldo Mondadori Editore, 1973.

Contains 6 poems from *The Hawk in the Rain*, 16 from *Lupercal*, 27 from *Wodwo*, and the poems from *Crow* in D33.

D35 Ted Hughes, *L'uomo di ferro*, Traduzione di Sandra Giorgini, Biblioteca Universale Rizzoli, Milan, 1977.

The Iron Man.

D36 Ted Hughes: *La balena e altre storie*, Illustrazioni di Claudio Benzoni, Emme Edizione, 1981.

How the Whale Became, translated by Grazia Viale Biscaretti.

D37 *Arsenale*, no. 2, April–June 1985.

Contains 'Poor Birds', 'New Year Exhilaration', 'Couples Under Cover', and 'Roe-deer', translated by Maria Stella.

D38 *Reporter*, 17/18 August 1985.

Contains 'Coming Down Through Somerset', 'Foxhunt', and 'Struggle', translated by Maria Stella.

D39 *Lingua e Letteratura*, 6, 1986.

Contains 'Dehorning', 'Foxhunt', and 'The Knight', translated by Maria Stella.

D40 *L'Uomo di Ferro*, Arnoldo Mondadori Editore, Milan, 1988.

The Iron Man, translated by Ilva Tron.

D41 *Linea d'Ombra*, VI, no. 33, December 1988.

Contains 'Feeding Outwintering Cattle at Twilight', 'Bringing in New Couples', 'Ravens', 'February 17th', 'Birth of Rainbow', and 'A Memory', introduced and translated by Maria Stella.

D42 *Storie del Mondo Primitivo*, Arnoldo Mondadori Editore, Milan, 1989.

Tales of the Early World, translated by Francesca Lazzarato.

D43 *Altri Termini*, January–April 1991.

Contains the following poems from the *Gaudete* Epilogue translated by Mauro Ferrari: 'In a world . . .', 'Collision with the earth', 'Trying to be a leaf', 'Once I said lightly', 'She rides the earth', 'The sea grieves', 'A bang—a burning', 'Glare out of just crumpled grass'.

D44 *Com'è Nata la Balena*, Arnoldo Mondadori Editore, Milan, 1992.

How the Whale Became, translated by Glauco Arneri.

D45 *Nessi il Mostro senza Complessi*, Arnoldo Mondadori Editore, Milan, 1993.

Nessie the Mannerless Monster, translated by Glauco Arneri.

D46 *Tzanne il Vampistrello e il Bacio di Verità*, Arnoldo Mondadori Editore, Milan, 1993.

Ffangs the Vampire Bat and the Kiss of Truth, translated by Francesco Saba Sardi.

D47 *La Donna di Ferro*, Arnoldo Mondadori Editore, Milan, 1994.

The Iron Woman, translated by Riccardo Duranti.

D48 *Per Mario Luzi*, ed. Giorgio Tabbanelli, Edizione del Leone, Venezia, 1994.

Contains 'Descent', translated by Riccardo Duranti.

JAPANESE

D49 Ted Hughes: *Tetsu no Kyojin to Uchū Kōmori*, Kōdansha, Tokyo, 1971.

The Iron Man, translated by Teruo Jingū.

D50 *Ted Hughes: The Hawk in the Rain*, Etude 2, Kyoto, 1975.

A private edition of 250 copies produced by the Etude Group for use in Doshisha University, Kyoto. Translated by members of that group: Jitsuyō Kodama, Tatsuo Murata, Kanshun Sakamoto, Kōichi Yakushigawa, Tōru Sugino.

Contains all the poems in *The Hawk in the Rain*.

D51 *Ted Hughes: Crow*, translated by Akira Minami, Eichosha, Tokyo, 1978.

Contains all the poems from the first edition of *Crow*.

D52 *World Literature (37) A Collection of Contemporary Poems*, edited by Hajime Shinoda, Shueisha, Tokyo, 1979.

Contains 'Gog', 'Dick Straightup', 'Pike', 'November', 'Ghost Crabs', and 'Thistles', translated by Einosuke Tamura.

D53 *Ted Hughes: The Iron Man*, translated by Yuuichi Hashimoto, Shinozaki Shorin, Tokyo, 1980.

D54 *Ted Hughes: Nesoko no Nesshi Ohabare*, Shogakukan, 1980.

Nessie the Mannerless Monster, translated by Saiichi Maruya.

D55 *The Iron Man*, translated by Hayato Mizuwaki, Sinozaki Shorin, Tokyo, 1981.

D56 *Ted Hughes shishu* [*Ted Hughes' Poems*], Doyoubijutsusha, 1982.

D57 *Shino umareru toki* [*Poetry in the Making*], translated by Junnosuke Sawasaki, Nan'undo, Tokyo, 1983.

KOREAN

D58 *Si jagbeob* [*Poetry in the Making*], translated by Han Gi Chang, Cheongha, Seoul, 1982.

MACEDONIAN

D59 See A105.

POLISH

D60 *Ted Hughes, Wiersze Wybrane*, translated by Teresa Truszkowska and Jan Rostworowski, Wydawnictwo Literackie, Kraków, 1975.

Contains 8 poems from *The Hawk in the Rain*, 8 from *Lupercal*, 20 from *Wodwo* and 26 from *Crow*.

D61 *Deszczowy kón i inne opowiadania*, Wydawnictwo Literackie, Kraków, 1982.

Wodwo, translated by Teresa Truszkowska.

D62 *Akcent*, 2(24), 1986.

Contains *Prometheus on his Crag*, translated by Ireneusz Szkamruk.

D63 *Piesni Czterech pór Roku*, Zysk I S-ka Wydawnictwo, Posnan, 1995.

Season Songs, translated by Marek Obarski.

PORTUGUESE

D64 *Leituras: Poemas do ingles*, edited and translated by João Ferreira Duarte, Relogio d'Agua, Lisboa 1993.

Contains 'Prometheus on his Crag Pondered the Vulture'.

ROMANIAN

D65 *Ted Hughes: Din Cîntecele Lui Kra*, Traducere şi prefaţă de Vasile Nicolescu, Editura Univers, Bucureşti, 1977.

Contains all but 14 of the poems in the first edition of *Crow*.

RUSSIAN

D66 *Robert Graves, Dylan Thomas, Ted Hughes, Philip Larkin; perevod s angliiskogo*, compiled and introduced by V. A. Skorodenko, 'Progress', Moskva, 1976.

Contains 'The Thought-Fox' (translated by A. Kistiakovsky), 'The Jaguar' (N. Bannikov), 'Famous Poet' (S. Bytchkov), 'The Man Seeking Experience Enquires his Way of a Drop of Water' (N. B.), 'Wind' (S. B.), 'The Martyrdom of Bishop Farrar' (N. B.), 'Mayday on Holderness', (A. K.), 'Hawk Roosting' (N. B.), 'Cat and Mouse' (N. B.), 'View of a Pig' (N. B.), 'The Retired Colonel' (S. B.), 'November' (S. B.), 'An Otter' (N. B.), 'Thistles' (S. B.), 'Cadenza' (A. K.), 'Second Glance at a Jaguar' (N. B.), 'Fern' (S. B.), 'Stations' (A. K.), 'The Bear' (A. K.), 'Warriors of the North' (S. B.), 'The Rat's Dance' (A. K.), 'Heptonstall' (A. K.), 'Pibroch' (A. K.), 'Kafka' (A. K.), 'Gnat Psalm' (A. K.), 'Wodwo' (S. B.), 'Two Legends' (A. K.), 'Lineage' (A. K.), 'Crow's Account of the Battle' (A. K.), 'Crow's Vanity' (A. K.), 'Dawn's Rose' (A. K.), 'Littleblood' (A. K.).

SERBIAN

D67 Ted Hughes, *Muzika za Gajde* [*Pibroch*], translated by Vladimir Žunjević, Kruševac, 1966.

Contains 13 poems from *The Hawk in the Rain*, 14 from *Lupercal*, 'Pibroch', 'The Howling of Wolves', 'Theology' and 'Gog', which were to be in *Wodwo*, and 'The Lake' and 'Unknown Soldier' which were to be in *Recklings*.

D68 *Književna reč*, 1, April 1972.

Contains 'Lineage', 'Crow's First Lesson', 'Crow Communes', 'Crow Blacker than Ever', and 'Crow's Song of Himself', translated by David Albahari, Raša Livada and Elizabeth J. Thomas.

D69 *Antologija savremene engleske poezije*, eds. S. Brkić and M. Pavlović, Beograd, 1975.

Contains 'Everyman's Odyssey' translated by Mirko Magarašević; 'Thistles' and 'The Horses' translated by Svetozar Brkić; 'Crow's Vanity' and 'Two Legends' translated by David Albahari and Raša Livada.

D70 *Književna reč*, 97, 25 March 1978.

Contains 'The Dove-Breeder', 'Full Moon and Little Frieda', 'The Door', 'The Bear', 'Crow's Theology', and 'The Judge', translated by David Albahari and Raša Livada.

D71 *Svetska Poezija Danas* [*World Poetry Today*], *Gradac*, 39–40, ed. Raša
Livada, Čačak, 1981.

Contains 'Two Legends', 'A Kill', 'Crow's First Lesson', 'Crow
Alights', 'Crow Communes', 'A Disaster', 'Crow's Theology', 'Crow's
Vanity', 'A Childish Prank', 'Crow's Nerve Fails', 'Dawn's Rose',
'Crowego', 'Crow's Playmates', 'Crow Blacker than Ever', 'Crow
Sickened', and 'Crow's Last Stand', translated by David Albahari
and Raša Livada.

D72 *Moderno svetsko pesnistvo* [*Modern World Poetry*], ed. Raša Livada,
Prosveta, Belgrade, 1983.

Contains 'Two Legends', 'Crow's First Lesson', 'Crow's Theology',
and 'Crow's Vanity', reprinted from D71.

D73 *Književna reč*, I, 15 July 1988.

Contains 'Theology', 'That Moment', 'Speech Out of Shadow', and
'Do Not Pick Up the Telephone', translated by Aleksandra
Jovanović.

D74 *Savremena Britanska Poezija*, eds. Mario Susko and David Harsent,
Sarajevo, 1988.

Contains 'Life is Trying to be Life', 'Coming Down Through
Somerset', 'Narcissi', 'And Owl' and 'New Year', translated by Mario
Susko.

D75 *Mostovi* [XX.1.], Belgrade, 1989

Contains 'The Tiger's Bones', 'Beauty and the Beast', and 'Sean, the
Fool, the Devil and the Cats', translated by Borivoj Gerzić.

D76 *Književne novine*, no. 829, 1 November 1991.

Contains 'Crow and Mama', 'Crow's First Lesson', and 'Tiger
Psalm', translated by Milos Komadina and David Albahari.

D77 *Sveske*, vol. 7, no. 24, Pancevo, June 1995.

Contains two translations of 'Emily Brontë', one by Gordana Pesić,
one by Zlatoje Martinov.

SLOVAK

D77a *Príbehy z Pociatku Sveta*, Knizná Dielna Timotej, Kosici, 1994.

Tales of the Early World, translated by Marián Andricík.

SPANISH

D78 Ted Hughes, *Antología poética*, Version de Jesus Pardo, Plaza & Janes, S.A., Barcelona, 1971.

Contains 15 poems from *Lupercal*, 21 poems from *Wodwo*, 13 from *The Hawk in the Rain*, and 26 from *Crow*.

D79 *Poemas: Ted Hughes: Poems*. A selection translated and introduced by Ulalume González de León. Ediciones El Tucán de Virginia y Penélope, Mexico, 1984.

Contains 'The Jaguar', 'September', 'Wind', 'February', 'Crow Hill', 'Hawk Roosting', 'The Voyage', 'Relic', 'Thistles', 'The Green Wolf', 'The Bear', 'Skylarks', 'Pibroch', 'Gnat-Psalm', 'Full Moon and Little Frieda', 'Wodwo', 'Two Legends', 'The Door', 'Crow's First Lesson', 'Crow's Theology', 'Crow and the Birds', 'Robin Song', 'Conjuring in Heaven', 'Crow Improvises', 'Crowcolour', 'Crow's Song of Himself', 'Crow's Last Stand', 'Lovesong', 'How Water Began to Play', 'The Knight', 'Life is Trying to be Life', 'Night Arrival of Sea-Trout', 'Tiger-Psalm', 'The Wild Duck', 'The Song', 'Crown Point Pensioners', 'Widdop', 'Light Falls Through Itself', 'In April', 'Do Not Pick Up the Telephone', 'Goose'.

D80 *De Como Las Ballenas Llegaron A Ser Las Ballenas*, Mexico. [Details lacking.]

How the Whale Became.

D81 *La Violencia de la Palabra*, Servicio de publicaciones Universidad de Cadiz, 1992.

Bilingual text of *Selected Poems 1957–1981*, translated by Manuel Alvarez de Toledo Morenés.

SWEDISH

D82 *Ted Hughes: Kråka*, Svensk tolkning av Eva Bruno, Tuppen På Berget 1, Coeckelberghs, Stockholm, 1975.

Contains all the poems from the second edition of *Crow*.

D83 *Järnmannen*, Sjöstrands Förlag, Stockholm, 1986. Reissued in 1994 in the En Bok för Alla series.

The Iron Man, translated by Berit Skogsberg.

D84 *Hur Valen Blev Till*, Sjöstrands Förlag, Stockholm, 1988.

How the Whale Became, translated by Sven Christer Swahn.

D85 *Järnkvinnan*, Sjöstrands Förlag, Stockholm, 1993.

The Iron Woman, translated by Sven Christer Swahn.

E. INTERVIEWS AND COMMENT

For radio and television interviews see section G. Broadcasts.

E1 'The Poet Speaks (XVI): Ted Hughes talks to Peter Orr'. pp. 87–92.

A duplicated document circulated by the British Council in 1963.

E2 'Desk Poet' by John Horder.

Guardian, 23 March 1965. p. 9.

E2a Interview with Hughes in *Good Talk: An Anthology of BBC Radio*, ed. Derwent May, Gollancz, London, 1968.

E3 'Ted Hughes' *Crow*'.

Listener, 30 July 1970. p. 449.

Extract from an interview on *Poetry Now* [G63].

E4 'Ted Hughes and Crow: An interview with Ekbert Faas'.

London Magazine (10:5–20), January 1971.

This interview is reprinted in B101 together with a previously unpublished interview on *Gaudete*.

E5 'Interview with Ted Hughes: Author of Orghast' by Peter Wilson.

5th Festival of Arts Shiraz Persepolis, 1 September 1971.

E6 'Orghast'.

Times Literary Supplement, 1 October 1971. p. 1174.

Incorporating an interview by Tom Stoppard.

E7 'The Persepolis Follies of 1971' by Geoffrey Reeves.

Performance (1:61–2, 66), December 1971.

Incorporates comments by Hughes drawn from Tom Stoppard's interview, but including some material not used by Stoppard himself in E6.

E8 'Playing with Words at Persepolis' by Ossia Trilling.

Theatre Quarterly (2:35), January–March 1972.

Contains her transcript of her own tape recording of remarks made by Hughes at an impromptu press-conference in Shiraz shortly before the first performance of the first part of *Orghast*.

E9 'An Interview with British Poet, Ted Hughes, Inventor of Orghast Language' by Jean Richards.

Drama and Theatre (10:4), 1972.

E9a *Contemporary Poetry in America*, ed. Robert Boyers, Schocken Books, New York, 1974. p. 19.

Quotes letter to M. L. Rosenthal on *Crow*.

E10 *A Conversation with Ted Hughes about the Arvon Foundation*.

A 20-page booklet in brown wrappers, published by the Arvon Press, Hebden Bridge, Yorkshire, in 1976. The interview with Ted Hughes occupies 9 pages.

E11 'The Art of Being Artless' by Tom Davis.

Observer, 9 November 1980.

An interview about judging the Observer London Weekend Poetry Competition.

E12 'Poet's Battle Against Pollution'.

Observer Colour Supplement, 9 December 1984. p. 29.

E13 The Laureateship.

Hughes' response to his appointment as Poet Laureate on 19 December 1984 was quoted in several newspapers the following day, most fully in the *Times*, *Western Daily Press*, and *Yorkshire Post*.

E14 'Your Poems Are So Impressive'.

Western Independent, 18 May 1986.

E15 'Poet Laureate Backs Grammar'.

Sunday Times, 15 November 1987. p. 7.

E16 'In Search of the £5000 Poem'.

Observer, 28 February 1988. p. 21.

E17 'Under the Bell Jar'.

Independent, 12 March 1988. p. 21.

Quotes Hughes on Linda Wagner-Martin's biography of Sylvia Plath.

E18 'Poet's Fury at Plath Story'.

Sunday Times, 13 March 1988. p. A3.

E19 'Truth and the Painful Voice of Hurt'.

Sunday Telegraph, 18 November 1990.

'Ted Hughes tells Vic Allen about drama's crucial role in green issues'.

E20 'Poet Claims Laurels in Clear-Water Battle'.

Guardian, 16 April 1992.

E21 'Master of an Island Universe'.

Times, 25 July 1992.

Article on George Mackay Brown contains comments by Hughes.

E22 'Figure in a Landscape II'. Frank Galligan interviews Ted Hughes.

Poetry Ireland Review [37:19–22], Winter 1992–3.

E23 'Moods and Memories', and 'Valley's Famous Sons Return for Opening'.

Halifax Evening Courier, 24 March 1993.

Hughes dedicates new technology centre to Billy Holt.

E24 'Babel Questionnaire—Ted Hughes'.

Babel VII, 1993. pp. 6–7.

E25 'Man of Mettle'.

Independent on Sunday, 5 September 1993. pp. 32–4.

Interviewed by Blake Morrison, largely about *The Iron Woman*.

E26 'Heavy Mettle'.

Sunday Times, 14 November 1993.

Letters to Heather Neill concerning the rock opera *Iron Man*.

E27 'Ted Hughes' in *Poets Talking* by Clive Wilmer, Carcanet, 1994.

Reprinted from G88.

E28 'Shakespeare's Little England' by Michael Kustow.

Independent, 19 November 1994.

Contains comments by Hughes on Suzuki's *The Tale of King Lear* at the Barbican.

E29 'Harmonizing at the Moon' by Michael Glover.

Independent, 11 March 1995.

Contains quotations from Hughes' reading at the Bath Festival of Literature, notably on 'Sheep' and 'Hawk Roosting'.

E30 'The Art of Poetry LXXI'.

Paris Review (134:55–94), Spring 1995.

Interviewed by Drew Heinz.

F. RECORDINGS

F1 Hughes and Plath recorded a joint reading for the Woodberry Poetry Room, Lamont Library, Harvard University, at Fassett Recording Studio, Boston, 13 June 1958.

CONTENTS: 'Crow Hill', 'Acrobats', 'To Paint a Water Lily', 'Witches', 'Relic', 'Dick Straightup', 'Historian', 'Thrushes', 'Bullfrog', 'View of a Pig', 'Of Cats'.

F2 *Poetry at the Mermaid.* 17 July 1961. National Sound Archive.

The first extant recording of a live public reading by Hughes.

F3 *Listening & Writing: Two Talks by Ted Hughes, 'Capturing Animals' & 'Learning to Think'.*

BBC records. Study Series. RESR 19M. 1971.

One 12 in. $33\frac{1}{3}$ r.p.m. disc. Matrix: RESR + 19 + 1.

CONTENTS: Side 1 'Capturing Animals'. First transmitted 6.10.61. Side 2 'Learning to Think'. First transmitted 10.5.63.

Notes: Two of the nine talks Hughes gave between 1961 and 1964 for the BBC radio schools series 'Listening and Writing'. The producer of that series was Moira Doolan, who has a note on the sleeve. The record was produced by Alan Lawson, and the sleeve designed by Andrew Prewett. In the course of these talks Hughes reads 'The Thought-Fox', 'Pike', 'View of a Pig', 'Wodwo', and D. H. Lawrence's 'Bare Almond Trees'. A few sentences were edited out of these talks when they were published in *Poetry in the Making* [A14].

F4 *Poets Reading No. 5: John Wain, Ted Hughes.*

A Jupiter Recording jep OC27. 1962.

One 7 in. 45 r.p.m. extended play disc. Matrix: JEP OC27 B.

CONTENTS: Side 2 'The Thought-Fox', 'Soliloquy of a Misanthrope', 'Mayday on Holderness', 'Pibroch'.

Notes: The recordings were directed by V. C. Clinton-Baddeley and made by Edgar A. Vetter, Spring 1962. Also available as a cassette OC27 from Audio-Visual Productions, London.

F5 *The Poet Speaks: Record Five, Ted Hughes, Peter Porter, Thom Gunn, Sylvia Plath.*

Argo Record Company, London RG 455. 1965. Reissued as PLP 1085.

One 12 in. 33⅓ r.p.m. disc. Matrix: side 1: ARG–2713–1A.

CONTENTS: Side 1 'Her Husband', 'Bowled Over', 'Still Life', 'Wodwo', 'Mountains', 'The Warriors of the North', 'Gog', 'Out, Part 1—The Dream Time, Part 2, Part 3—Remembrance Day', 'Full Moon'.

Notes: Recorded 29 August 1962, in association with the British Council and the Poetry Room in the Lamont Library of Harvard University. Edited by Peter Orr. The text of 'Full Moon' is longer than 'Full Moon and Little Frieda', in *Wodwo*, but the same as C148 and B26. The interview with Ted Hughes by Peter Orr recorded on the same day is available as a National Sound Archive tape.

F6 *Here Today: Poems by 45 Contemporary Authors, Part 1.*

A Jupiter Recording JUR 00A6. 1963. Also available as a cassette from Audio-Visual Productions, London.

One 12 in. 33⅓ r.p.m. disc. Matrix: B/2v420 11 1.

CONTENTS: Side 2 'View of a Pig'.

Notes: The recordings were directed by V. C. Clinton-Baddeley and edited by Edgar A. Vetter, Autumn 1962–Spring 1963. The sleeve was designed by John Seares Riley.

F7 *The Jupiter Anthology of 20th Century English Poetry*, Part III.

A Jupiter Recording JUR 00A8. 1963.

One 12 in. 33⅓ r.p.m. disc. Matrix: side 2: B 1/420 1 11.

CONTENTS: Side 2 'The Hawk in the Rain', 'Hawk Roosting'.

Notes: The recordings were directed by V. C. Clinton-Baddeley and edited by Edgar A. Vetter, 1963. Sleeve-note by Anthony Thwaite. This recording was reissued by Folkways Records, New York in 1967 as FL 9879. Also available as a cassette from Audio-Visual Productions, London.

F8 *Poetry 1900 to 1965.*

A Longmans Recording 34155. 1967.

One 12 in. 33⅓ r.p.m. disc. Matrix: LG 34155.A and B.

CONTENTS: Side 1 D. H. Lawrence 'Humming Bird'. Side 2 Keith Douglas 'Vergissmeinnicht'; 'Hawk Roosting'.

Notes: The recordings were directed by George MacBeth.

F9 *The Battle of Aughrim By Richard Murphy.*

Claddagh Records CCT 7. 1969.

One 12 in. 33⅓ r.p.m. disc. Matrix: Side 1: REZ 39/YC/68. A.2. Side 2: REZ 39/7C/681/B2.

Read by: Cyril Cusack, C. Day-Lewis, Ted Hughes, Niall Toibin, Margaret Robertson.

Notes: Recorded by the B.B.C. Third Programme, August 1968. With sleeve notes by Richard Murphy, Daniel Hoffman, and Ted Hughes.

F10 *Crow read by Ted Hughes.*

Claddagh Records CCT 9–10. 1973. Stereo.

Two 12 in. 33⅓ r.p.m. discs. Matrix: Side 1: CCT 9 A–1U; Side 2: CCT 9 B–1U; Side 3: CCT 10 A–1U; Side 4: CCT 10 B–1U.

CONTENTS: All the poems in the first English edition of *Crow* except 'Robin Song' and 'Crow Improvises'.

Notes: Recorded at Angus McKenzie Studios, London, by Ioan Allen. The sleeve has a drawing by Barrie Cooke and a note by Ted Hughes.

F11 *Cambridge Poetry Festival.* 21 April 1975.

Recording of Hughes' complete reading. National Sound Archive.

F12 *The Poetry and Voice of Ted Hughes.*

Caedmon TC 1535. 1977. Stereo.

One 12 in. 33⅓ r.p.m. disc. Matrix: Side 1: TC 1535 A–1. Side 2: TC 1535 B–1.

CONTENTS: Side 1: 'The Thought-Fox', 'The Jaguar', 'Wind', 'Six Young Men', 'Mayday on Holderness', 'The Retired Colonel', 'View of a Pig', 'Sunstroke', 'Pike', 'An Otter', 'Hawk Roosting'. Side 2: 'Icecrust and Snowflake', 'Sheep (Part 1)', 'His Legs Ran About', Fragments from *Lumb's Remains*: 'What Will You Make of Half a Man', 'The Sea Grieves', 'A Primrose Petal's Edge', 'Once I Said Lightly', 'Collision with the Earth', 'When the Still-Soft Eyelid', 'The Dead Man Lies', 'This Is the Maneater's Skull', 'Every Day the World', 'Waving Goodbye', 'A Bang—A Burning', 'Calves'; 'Bride and Groom'.

Notes: Recorded at CBS Studios, London, directed by Ward Botsford. Produced in Association with the Poetry Center of the 92nd Street YM-YWHA, New York. *Lumb's Remains* was Hughes' original title for the Epilogue of *Gaudete*. The sleeve has a photograph of Ted Hughes and of a holograph manuscript of 'A Bang—A Burning'. The sleeve-note is by Grace Schulman. Also available as a cassette: Caedmon CDL 51535.

F13 *Ted Hughes and R. S. Thomas read and discuss selections of their own poems.*

Norwich Tapes Ltd, London: The Critical Forum. 1978.

One standard cassette.

CONTENTS: Side 1: Hughes reads and discusses six poems from *Moortown*: 'Earth-Numb', 'Couples Under Cover', 'Ravens', 'Orf', 'February 17th', 'Birth of Rainbow'.

F14 *Selections from Crow and Wodwo read by the Poet Ted Hughes.*

Caedmon TC 1628. 1979. Stereo.

One 12 in. $33\frac{1}{3}$ r.p.m. disc. Matrix: Side 1: TC 1628 A–1. Side 2: TC 1628 B.

CONTENTS: Side 1: from *Crow*, 'Crow and Mama', 'A Childish Prank', 'Crow's First Lesson', 'Crow Hears Fate Knock on the Door', 'Crow's Fall', 'The Contender', 'A Horrible Religious Error', 'Crow's Elephant Totem Song', 'Song for a Phallus', 'Apple Tragedy', 'Crow Paints Himself into a Chinese Mural', 'Notes for a Little Play', 'Lovesong', 'The Lovepet', 'How Water Began to Play'. Side 2: from *Wodwo*, 'Thistles', 'Her Husband', 'Second Glance at a Jaguar', 'The Green Wolf', 'Theology', 'Gog', 'Kreutzer Sonata', 'Out (I, II and III)', 'Heptonstall', 'Pibroch', 'The Howling of Wolves', 'Gnat-Psalm', 'Full Moon and Little Frieda'.

Notes: Recorded at CBS Recording Studios, London, directed by Ward Botsford. The sleeve has Leonard Baskin's crow from the cover of the

American edition of *Crow*, on a yellow square. The sleeve-note is by Grace Schulman. Also available as a cassette: Caedmon CDL 51628.

F15 Cheltenham Festival of Literature. 17 October 1982. National Sound Archive.

Hughes reads the following poems from *The Rattle Bag:* 'The Rattlebag' (Gwilym), 'If I might be an ox' (trad. Ethiopian), 'The wicked who would do me harm' (trad. Gaelic charm), 'It is late last night' (trad. Erse, trans. Lady Gregory), 'Bullfight', 'The Benign Fly' and 'The Seventh' (Holub), 'Face of the Force' (Zabalotsky), 'Would I cast a sail on the water' (Yeats), 'This Lunar Beauty' (Auden), 'The Wind Suffers of Blowing' (Riding), 'The Garden Seat' (Hardy), 'Mad Tom's Song' (Graves), 'John Barleycorn' (Burns).

F16 *Ted Hughes and Paul Muldoon.* Faber Poetry Cassettes 0571130909, 23 May 1983.

One standard cassette with booklet of texts.

CONTENTS: 'Whiteness', 'Life is Trying to be Life', 'Bride and Groom Lie Hidden for Three Days', 'Do Not Pick Up the Telephone', 'Emily Brontë', 'Ravens', 'February 17th', 'Apple Dumps', 'When Men Got to the Summit', 'An October Salmon'.

F17 *For Frances Horovitz: A Celebration of Poetry.*

Talktapes, London TPL 001. 1985. One standard cassette, recorded at the Colston Hall, Bristol, 30 October 1983.

CONTENTS: Hughes introduces and reads 'River', 'The Risen', 'The Howling of Wolves', 'Narcissi', 'A Sunstruck Foxglove', 'Watching a Skylark' [section v of 'Skylarks'].

The complete recording is held at the National Sound Archive. In addition to the above Hughes reads 'Full Moon and Little Frieda', and section iv of 'Skylarks'.

F18 *Whales—A Celebration*

National Sound Archive recording of a reading at the Barbican Cinema 1, London, 1 December 1983. Hughes reads 'Little Whale Song' and Holub's 'There's a Shortage of Whales'.

F19 *John Clare*

Service in Westminster Abbey to mark the unveiling of a memorial to John Clare in Poets' Corner, 13 June 1989. Hughes reads 'The Nightingale's Nest' on the cassette sold to members of the John Clare Society.

F20 *The Thought-Fox and Other Poems*

One standard cassette. Faber and Faber Audio Poetry 0571 17501 5. 1994.

CONTENTS: Hughes introduces and reads 'The Thought-Fox', 'Song', 'The Jaguar', 'Hawk Roosting', 'Pike', 'Full Moon and Little Frieda', 'Pibroch', 'The Howling of Wolves', 'Examination at the Womb Door', 'A Childish Prank', 'Crow's First Lesson', 'A Horrible Religious Error', 'Apple Tragedy', 'Notes for a Little Play', 'Lovesong', 'The Lovepet', 'Bride and Groom', 'How Water Began to Play', 'The Harvest Moon', 'Do Not Pick up the Telephone', 'Ravens', 'Sheep', 'Night Arrival of Sea-Trout', 'Tiger-Psalm', 'October Salmon', 'Sunstruck Foxglove', 'On the Reservations', 'Telegraph Wires', 'Lines about Elias'.

F21 *The Lake Poets.* W. H. Smith video produced in collaboration with the Wordsworth Trust. 1994.

CONTENTS: Hughes reads (voice-over) selected passages from Wordsworth.

G. BROADCASTS

Programmes in which Hughes himself has participated, or in which works by him have made their first appearance. The National Sound Archive (at the British Library) has recordings of many of the broadcasts listed here (to which it provides the only public access).

G1 *The Poet's Voice*

14 April 1957. Third Programme.

Hughes reads 'The Martyrdom of Bishop Farrar'.

G2 *Ted Hughes*. A Selection of his published and unpublished poems.

Introduced by Karl Miller and read by Michael Atkinson.

27 August 1958. Third Programme.

The poems were 'Crow Hill', 'Dick Straightup', 'Pike', 'Witches', 'The Retired Colonel', and 'Crag Jack's Apostasy' (all to be collected in *Lupercal*).

G3 *Themes*: 'Creatures'.

Ted Hughes talks about creatures and makes a selection of poems suggested by this theme.

Readers: Keltie MacLeod and Bruce Stewart.

8 May 1960. Home Service.

The poems were: Dafydd ap Gwilym—'The Fox' (trans. Daniel Huws); Christopher Smart—'My Cat Jeoffry'; John Clare—'Badger'; Keith Douglas—'The Marvel'; Marianne Moore—'The Frigate Pelican'; Ted Hughes—'Hawk Roosting'.

G4 *The Rain Horse*. Written and read by Ted Hughes.

29 July 1960. Third Programme. Recorded 20 May 1960.

'Ted made his second BBC program this week, a recording of his story "The Rain Horse", a program which should bring in over $100 or so, with its rebroadcasting payment. Very nice. He has several projects going with them now—possibly a verse play when he finishes it [G7] (he's doing another now [G18]), a poem and talk for high school students with other poets and critics [G10], a long poem, etc. The BBC is the one organization that pays excellently for poetry—$3 a minute for reading.' Sylvia Plath, *Letters Home*, 21 May 1960.

G4a *Poetry and Performance* IV, 2 August 1960.

G5 *The Poet's Voice*

21 August 1960. Third Programme.

Hughes reads 'The Captain's Speech' from *The House of Aries* [G7] and 'Thistles'.

G6 *The Odyssey* (Homer). Translated in 12 parts by different poets.

Part 6 'The Storm' (Book V), translated by Ted Hughes.

10 November 1960. Third Programme. Recorded 26 October.

G7 *The House of Aries*. Play by Ted Hughes.

Produced by Sasha Moorsom. 16 November 1960. Third Programme.

G8 *The Harvesting*. Story written and read by Ted Hughes.

17 December 1960. Third Programme. Recorded 2 December.

'Ted has the best story he's done yet, about a fat man shooting rabbits at harvest-time, accepted by the BBC today, which will mean a nice sum. He'll read it, and then it will probably be played twice, once in Christmas week. I'm going to send it to magazines in America now.' Sylvia Plath, *Letters Home*, 25 November 1960.

G9 *Two of a Kind*: 'Poets in Partnership'.

Ted Hughes and Sylvia Plath interviewed by Owen Leeming.

31 January 1961. Home Service. Recorded 18 January.

Hughes reads 'Bullfrog'.

G10 *Talks for Sixth Forms*: 'Poetry and Performance IV—Ted Hughes.'

10 February 1961. Home Service (Schools). Recorded 2 August 1960.

Hughes reads 'An Otter' and discusses it at length with A. Alvarez.

G11 *The World of Books*: 'The Gentle Art' by Ted Hughes.

25 February 1961. Home Service. Recorded 24 February.

Hughes compares thinking with fishing.

G12 *Meet My Folks!* by Ted Hughes.

6 September 1961. Home Service. Recorded 26 June.

Hughes reads the whole book without introduction or comment.

G13 *In Football Playing*.

11 September 1961. Home Service. Recorded 25 August.

Hughes reads poems and prose about sport by A. E. Housman, Philip Stubbes, John Arlott, William Blake, John Scroggins, John Clare, Lewis Carroll, and D. H. Lawrence.

G14 *Woman's Hour*: 'The Elements'. Four short talks.

1—Fire. 25 September 1961. Light Programme. Recorded 22 September.

2—Air. 2 October 1961. Recorded 28 September.

3—Earth. 9 October 1961. Recorded 28 September.

4—Water. 16 October 1961. Recorded 28 September.

G15 *Listening and Writing*: 'Capturing Animals', by Ted Hughes.

6 October 1961. Home Service (Schools).

Collected in *Poetry in the Making*. See also C100 and F3.

G16 *Listening and Writing*: 'Writing a Novel—Beginning'.

20 October 1961. Home Service (Schools).

Collected in *Poetry in the Making*. See also C100.

C17 *Listening and Writing*: 'Writing a Novel—Going On'.

24 November 1961. Home Service (Schools).

Collected in *Poetry in the Making*.

G18 *The Wound*. Play by Ted Hughes (collected in *Wodwo*).

Produced by Douglas Cleverdon. Music by Alexander Goehr.

1 February 1962. Third Programme.

G19 *Listening and Writing*: 'Meet My Folks!'

30 March 1962. Home Service (Schools).

Collected in *Poetry in the Making*.

G20 *The Poetry of Keith Douglas*. Talk by Ted Hughes.

31 May 1962. Third Programme. Recorded 16 April. See C118.

G21 *Listening and Writing*: 'Creatures of the Air'.

29 June 1962. Home Service (Schools). Recorded 26 June.

This is the only talk in this series not collected in *Poetry in the Making*. In the course of it Hughes reads: 'A Robin' by Walter de la Mare, 'The Owl' by Edward Thomas, 'The Dove' by Ruth Pitter, his own 'Hawk Roosting', and 'The Wild Swans at Coole' by W. B. Yeats.

G22 *The Poet's Voice*.

24 August 1962. Third Programme. Recorded 10 August 1962.

Hughes reads 'The Road to Easington' and 'Out'.

G23 *Listening and Writing*: 'Wind and Weather'.

2 November 1962. Home Service (Schools).

Collected in *Poetry in the Making*.

G24 *Snow*. Story written and read by Ted Hughes.

8 January 1963. Third Programme. Recorded 9 November 1962.

G25 *Difficulties of a Bridegroom*. Play by Ted Hughes.

Produced by Douglas Cleverdon. Music by Nicholas Maw.

21 January 1963. Third Programme.

G26 *New Comment*: 'On Writing for Radio'.

24 January 1963. Third Programme. Recorded 16 January.

Hughes interviewed by Anthony Thwaite about his three plays for radio.

G27 *Listening and Writing*: 'Learning to Think'. (Includes Hughes' readings of 'View of a Pig', 'Wodwo' and D. H. Lawrence's 'Bare Almond Trees'.)

10 May 1963. Home Service (Schools). Recorded 6 May 1963.

Collected in *Poetry in the Making*. See also F3.

G27a *Harold Massingham*. BBC. 12 June 1963.

Hughes reads poems by Massingham.

G28 *Writers on Themselves*: 'The Rock'.

11 September 1963. Home Service. [C146.]

G29 *Listening and Writing*: 'Writing About People'.

   27 September 1963. Home Service (Schools).

   Collected in *Poetry in the Making*.

G30 *Talks for Sixth Forms*: 'Modern Poetry 4. Ted Hughes'.

   18 October 1963. Home Service (Schools). Recorded 24 May.

   Hughes on the history of his interest in poetry and on what makes genuine poetry. He introduces and reads 'Thistles', 'Unknown Soldier', 'Dream Time' ['Out' I], 'Pibroch', 'Wodwo', 'Her Husband', and 'Full Moon and Little Frieda'.

G31 *Listening and Writing*: 'Moon Creatures'.

   25 October 1963. Home Service (Schools). Recorded 21 October 1963.

   Collected in *Poetry in the Making*.

G32 *The Novel Today*: 4. *Voss* by Patrick White. Talk by Hughes.

   23 January 1964. Third Programme. [C151.]

G33 *Dogs: A Scherzo*. Play by Hughes.

   Produced by Douglas Cleverdon.

   12 February 1964. Third Programme.

G34 *Reading and Rereading*: 1. *The Worst Journey in the World* by Apsley Cherry-Garrard. Talk by Hughes.

   10 April 1964. Third Programme. [Much longer than C129.]

G35 *Zbigniew Herbert*.

   26 April 1964. Third Programme. Recorded 27 November 1963.

   A selection of his poems introduced and read in English by A. Alvarez with Ted Hughes.

G36 *Listening and Writing*: 'Writing About Landscape'.

   1 May 1964. Home Service (Schools).

   Collected in *Poetry in the Making*.

G37 *New Poetry*.

   13 July 1964. Third Programme. Recorded 7 July.

   Poems by Thomas Blackburn, Elizabeth Jennings, Donald Davie, Ken Smith, Jon Silkin, and D. M. Thomas, read by Caroline Hunt and Ted Hughes.

G38 *A Citizen's War 1939–45.*

Compiled and arranged by George MacBeth.

3 September 1964. Home Service.

Readers: Gene Baro, Hugh Dickson, Ted Hughes, and Zelia Morris.

G39 *Listening and Writing*: 'The Coming of the Kings'. Play by Hughes.

Part 1, 27 November 1964. Home Service (Schools).

Part 2, 4 December 1964. Home Service (Schools).

Collected in *The Coming of the Kings.*

G40 *The Poet's Voice.*

17 February 1965. Third Programme. Recorded 25 January.

Hughes reads the extract from *Eat Crow* later published as 'X' [C175] and 'Crow Wakes' in *Crow Wakes.*

G41 *Books, Plays, Poems*: 'Poems by Living Poets'.

16 June 1965. Home Service (Schools). Recorded 17 May.

Talk by Hughes about 'Stealing Trout on a May Morning'.

G42 *Poets in Public.* Recordings made at the Edinburgh Festival.

3 September 1965. Third Programme.

Hughes reads 'Hawk Roosting' and 'Full Moon and Little Frieda'.

G43 *The House of Donkeys.* A Chinese folktale retold by Ted Hughes.

30 September 1965. Home Service.

G44 *Poetry Now.*

17 October 1965. Third Programme.

Hughes reads 'Nightfall' and 'The Knight' ('Ghost Crabs' and 'Gog III' in *Wodwo*), described here as 'detachable poems' from *Difficulties of a Bridegroom.*

G45 *Poetry Now.*

22 November 1965. Third Programme.

Hughes reads 'The Brother's Dream'.

G46 *Listening and Writing*: 'The Tiger's Bones'. Play by Hughes.

Part 1, 26 November 1965. Home Service (Schools). Recorded 22 November.

Part 2, 3 December 1965. Home Service (Schools). Recorded 29 November.

Collected in *The Coming of the Kings*.

G47 *Living Language*: 'Beauty and the Beast'. Play by Hughes.

2 December 1965. Home Service (Schools).

Collected in *The Coming of the Kings*.

G48 *Poetry Now*.

31 July 1966. Third Programme.

Hughes reads 'Gnat-Psalm' and 'Second Glance at a Jaguar'.

G49 *Living Language*: 'The Price of a Bride'. Play by Hughes.

22 September 1966. Home Service (Schools).

G50 *The Poetry of Vasco Popa*. Talk by Hughes.

24 October 1966. Third Programme. Recorded 24 June. [C188.]

G51 *Religion in its Contemporary Context*: 'Words and Experience'.

24 January 1967. Home Service (Schools).

Collected in *Poetry in the Making*.

G52 *Poetry International '67*. The final readings.

16 July 1967. Third Programme.

Here, and in a programme of excerpts, 22 July, Hughes appears as speaker and reader.

G53 *Living Language*: 'The Head of Gold'. Play by Hughes.

Part I: 'The Fiery Furnace'. 21 September 1967. Home Service (Schools).

Part II: 'The World of the Holy Ones'. 28 September 1967.

Part III: 'Daniel and the Lions'. 5 October 1967.

G54 *Living Language*: 'Sean, the Fool, the Devil and the Cats'. Play by Hughes.

2 May 1968. Radio 4 (Schools).

Collected in *The Coming of the Kings*.

G55 *Isaac Rosenberg*. A selection of his poems introduced by Jon Silkin and read by Ted Hughes.

8 July 1968. Radio 3.

G56 *The Battle of Aughrim*, by Richard Murphy.

Produced by Douglas Cleverdon.

25 August 1968. Radio 3.

Readers: Cyril Cusack, C. Day-Lewis, Ted Hughes, Margaret Robertson, Niall Toibin.

G57 *Yehuda Amichai*. Poems translated and introduced by Assia Gutmann and read by Ted Hughes.

12 December 1968. Radio 3. Recorded 28 June.

G58 *Something to Say*.

4 May 1969. BBC TV. Recorded at Holly Royde College, Manchester, 18 March.

Hughes introduces and reads 'The Thought-Fox', 'Wind', 'Her Husband', 'The Retired Colonel', 'An Otter', 'Wodwo', 'Hawk Roosting', 'Six Young Men', 'View of a Pig', 'Pibroch', 'Theology'.

G59 *Stories and Rhymes*: 'The Iron Man', by Ted Hughes.

Adapted by Zoe Bailey. Produced by Elizabeth Ornbo.

3 October 1969. Radio 4.

G60 *The Living Poet*: Yannis Ritsos.

Presented by Paul Merchant. Poems read by Ted Hughes.

1 February 1970. Radio 3.

G61 *Poetry D-Day*.

23 May 1970. Radio 3. Recorded 18 May at the Roundhouse.

Hughes introduces and reads 'Notes for a Little Play' and 'How Water Began to Play'.

G62 *Down to Earth*: 'Man's Needs'.

26 May 1970. Radio 3. Recorded 4 May.

Hughes reads 'Moss' by Jon Silkin, 'Voices' by Ted Walker.

G63 *Poetry Now*.

6 July 1970. Radio 3. Recorded 24 June.

A conversation about *Crow* between Hughes and George MacBeth. Hughes reads 'A Kill', 'A Childish Prank', and 'Notes for a Little Play'. An extract was published in C252.

G64 *Crow*, by Ted Hughes.

Produced by Douglas Cleverdon.

9 October 1970. Radio 3.

Crow read by Hughes, Michael Hordern, Denis Goacher, and Sean Barrett.

G65 *Now Read On.*

30 December 1970. Radio 4. Recorded 17 December.

Hughes gives a brief synopsis of *Crow*, and reads 'Crow's Nerve Fails'.

G66 *Listening and Writing*: 'Orpheus'. Play by Hughes.

29 January 1971. Radio 4 (Schools).

Collected in *The Tiger's Bones*.

G67 *Crossing the Water*. Poems by Sylvia Plath with commentary by Hughes.

Produced by Douglas Cleverdon.

5 July 1971. Radio 3. Recorded 13 June.

Narrator Denis Goacher, reader Margaret Drabble.

G68 *Larkin at 50*. Eight poets read their favourite Larkin verse.

9 August 1972. Radio 3.

Hughes reads 'Absences', 'Going', and 'Days'.

G69 *Poems for the BBC*. Verse specially commissioned for the 50th anniversary of the BBC.

13 November 1972. Radio 3.

Hughes reads a poem from *Prometheus on his Crag*.

G70 *Jackanory*: 'The Iron Man', by Ted Hughes.

18, 19, 20, 21 December 1972. BBC 1 TV.

Read by Denholm Elliott.

G71 *Jackanory Playhouse*: 'The Coming of the Kings', by Ted Hughes.

22 December 1972. BBC 1 TV.

G72 *The Story of Vasco*. Opera by Gordon Crosse. Libretto by Hughes.

21 March 1974. Radio 3.

G73 *Cambridge Poetry Festival.*

   5 May 1975. Radio 3. Recorded 18, 19 and 21 April.

   Hughes introduces and reads 'Lovesong'.

G74 *Cave Birds*, by Ted Hughes.

   Directed by George MacBeth.

   23 June 1975. Radio 3. Recorded 26 May.

   Readers: Harvey Hall, Frances Horovitz, Peter Marinker, Gary Watson. Linking commentary by Hughes. Two of the poems in this reading, 'What is the legal position' and 'Your mother's bones', were not included in either edition of *Cave Birds*. Two others were revised almost beyond recognition to become 'The Plaintiff' and 'A Riddle'.

G75 *Pilinszky's Poetry.*

   6 February 1976. Radio 3.

   Hughes introduces his translations.

G76 *Yehuda Amichai.* A selection of recent work introduced by Hughes.

   26 May 1976. Radio 3. Recorded 12 November 1975.

   Similar in content to but verbally different from B83.

G77 *Season Songs*, by Ted Hughes.

   6 and 13 September 1977. Radios 3 and 4.

   Hughes introduces and reads poems from *Season Songs*.

G78 *South Bank Show: Remains of Elmet.*

   20 May 1979. ITV.

   Hughes reads a selection of poems from *Remains of Elmet* voice over film of the Calder Valley.

G79 *Crossing Lines.*

   18 December 1979. Radio 4.

   Children's poetry recorded at Fitzjohn's Primary School, London NW3. Presented by Ted Hughes.

G80 *Capital Set Books: Selected Poems 1957–67*, by Ted Hughes.

   2 March 1980. Capital Radio, London.

   Comments by Ted Hughes on his early poems, particularly 'Horses', 'Bull Moses', 'Pike' and 'Thrushes'.

G81 *Elmet.*

3 May 1980. Radio 3.

Hughes presents a selection of poems from *Remains of Elmet*: 'Football at Slack', 'Wild Rock', 'For Billy Holt', 'When Men Got to the Summit', 'The Long Tunnel Ceiling', 'Mount Zion', 'Dead Farms, Dead Leaves', 'Cock Crows', 'Heptonstall Old Church'.

G82 *Moortown.*

10 May 1980. Radio 3.

Hughes presents a selection of poems from the title sequence of *Moortown*: 'Teaching a Dumb Calf', 'Tractor', 'Orf', 'February 17th', 'Happy Calf'.

G83 *Earth-Numb.*

17 May 1980. Radio 3.

Hughes introduces and reads the following poems from *Moortown*: 'Earth-Numb', 'A Motorbike', 'The Lovepet', 'Funeral', 'The Song', 'And the Falcon Came', 'The Swift', 'The Dove', 'Life is Trying'.

G84 *For Frances Horovitz—A Celebration of Poetry*

28 July 1984. Radio 3. Recorded 30 October 1983.

Hughes introduces and reads 'River', 'The Risen', 'The Howling of Wolves', 'Narcissi', 'A Sunstruck Foxglove', 'Watching a Skylark' [section v of 'Skylarks'].

G85 *Jackanory*: 'The Iron Man', by Ted Hughes.

First episode 20 January 1986. BBC 1 TV.

Read by Tom Baker.

G86 *Poets International: Ted Hughes.*

15 February 1988. ITV Schools [Thames].

Hughes introduces and reads 'The Jaguar', 'The Thought-Fox', 'Full Moon and Little Frieda', 'The Motorbike', 'The Contender'.

Video available from Thames Television International, London W1P 9LL.

G87 *Bookshelf.* Interview with Nigel Forde.

20 March 1992. Radio 4.

Hughes reads 'Full Moon and Little Frieda', 'Littleblood', 'Dust As We Are', and 'Widdop'.

G88 *Poet of the Month.*

5 April 1992. Radio 3.

Interview with Clive Wilmer recorded North Tawton, Devon, 23 March 1992. [Subsequently published in E27.]

G89 *Poet of the Month.*

12 April 1992. Radio 3.

Hughes introduces and reads 'Rain-Charm for the Duchy'.

G90 *Poet of the Month.*

19 April 1992. Radio 3.

Hughes introduces and reads poems from *Capriccio*: 'Laws of the Game' [in *New Selected Poems* as 'The Other'], 'Folk Tale', 'Descent', 'Opus 131'.

G91 *Poet of the Month.*

26 April 1992. Radio 3.

Hughes introduces and reads poems by Emily Dickinson: 'That Love is all there is', 'A still—Volcano—Life', 'Of Consciousness her awful Mate', 'A Clock stopped', 'Safe in their Alabaster Chambers', 'After great pain, a formal feeling comes', 'It was not Death, for I stood up', 'There's a certain slant of light', 'A Wind that rose', 'How slow the Wind'.

G92 *Jackanory*: 'The Dreamfighter', by Ted Hughes.

Beginning 27 February 1995. BBC 1 TV.

Read by Bill Paterson.

G93 *Stanza.*

8 April 1995. Radio 4.

Hughes recorded at the Lyttelton Theatre, London, reading from *New Selected Poems.*

G94 *Stanza on Stage. After Ovid.*

22 April 1995. Radio 4.

Hughes reads 'Among those demi-gods ...', recorded at the 1994 Poetry International.

H. MISCELLANEOUS

Largely dust-wrapper, record-sleeve and programme notes, and ephemera.

H1 *Poetry International '67*. Broadsheet.

The Festival took place at the Queen Elizabeth Hall and Purcell Room, South Bank, London, 12–16 July 1967. The broadsheet used to advertise it (29.8 × 20.8 cm. printed in black and brown with hand-done lettering and heavy ornamentation) carried on the verso a statement on the aims of the Festival by Ted Hughes, who was co-director with Patrick Garland.

H2 *Poetry International '67*. Programme.

Four pages stapled into black and brown wrappers; 33.1 × 22.9 cm.

Published by the Poetry Book Society.

Nine of the seventeen capsule biographies of participating poets are signed 'T.H.'.

H3 *Poetry International 1969*. Boxed set of two 12 in. discs. Argo MPR 262–3.

Hughes was again co-director with Patrick Garland. The sleeve carries a statement by him [which is the same as H1]. This is also incorporated into the enclosed booklet.

H4 *The Battle of Aughrim*, by Richard Murphy. 12 in. disc. Claddagh CCT 7. 1969.

The sleeve has two paragraphs about the piece by Ted Hughes, who is also one of the readers. [See F9.]

H5 *Flying*, by Jeni Couzyn. Workshop Press, 1970.

The back cover has a paragraph by Hughes.

H6 *Noth*, by Daniel Huws. Secker and Warburg, 1972.

The dust-wrapper has a paragraph by Ted Hughes.

H7 *On the Coast*, by Wayne Brown. André Deutsch, 1972.

The dust-wrapper has a paragraph by Hughes.

H8 *Song of Long-Time Lovers*, by Shusha. 12 in. disc. Tangent TGS 114. 1972.

The sleeve has a paragraph by Hughes about Shusha.

H9 *Crow*, by Ted Hughes. Two 12 in. discs. Claddagh CCT 9–10. 1973.

The sleeve has a paragraph by Hughes about Crow's quest. [See F10.]

H10 *Earth Erect*, by Vasko Popa. Anvil Press Poetry, 1973.

The dust-wrapper has a paragraph by Hughes about the collection.

H11 'A Premium Poet', by Peter Dunn. *Sunday Times*, 26 January 1975.

Contains a paragraph by Hughes about Havelock Hudson, the new chairman of Lloyd's.

H12 *Ilkley Literature Festival 24–31 May 1975 Souvenir Programme.*

48 pp. stapled into green wrappers printed in blue. Contains Hughes' introductions to *Cave Birds* (three paragraphs) and the Epilogue to *Gaudete* (four paragraphs), pp. 3–4. The latter is the first printing of the Argument to *Gaudete* and remains the fullest and clearest version.

H13 'Public Lending Right'. Letter to *The Times*, 28 July 1975.

Hughes was one of the signatories to this letter from the Writers' Action Group.

H13a *Some Unease and Angels: Selected Poems*, by Elaine Feinstein. Hutchinson, 1977.

The cover has two paragraphs by Hughes.

H14 Platform Performance of *Gaudete* at the National Theatre. Synopsis.

This reading by Brian Cox, Ann Firbank and Struan Rodger, directed by Michael Kustow, took place in the Lyttelton Theatre 18 and 25 July 1977. A seven-paragraph synopsis by Hughes was distributed free in the form of photocopies of an A4 typescript. It is a slightly fuller version of the Argument in the American edition of *Gaudete*.

H14a *The Wise Wound*, by Penelope Shuttle and Peter Redgrove. Gollancz, 1978.

The dust-wrapper has a paragraph by Hughes.

H15 *Earth Hold*, by Jennifer J. Rankin. Secker and Warburg, 1978.

The back cover has an introductory note by Hughes.

H16 'Praise for Pupil Poets', by Richard Keeble. *Teacher*, 1 June 1979.

Contains quotations about poetry in schools from a speech made by Ted Hughes at the Silver Jubilee of the Poetry Book Society.

H17 *The Pig Organ*, with music by Richard Blackford and libretto by Ted Hughes. Programme.

At the world première at the Roundhouse, London, 3–12 January 1980, the programme, a card in the shape of a pink pig, carried an eight-paragraph synopsis by Hughes.

H18 *On the Beach at Cambridge*, by Adrian Mitchell. Allison and Busby, 1984.

The wrapper has a paragraph by Hughes.

H19 *About the Arvon Foundation*. Lumb Bank, 1986.

A4 fly-sheet by Hughes.

H20 *Leaseholder*, by Daniel Weissbort. Carcanet, 1986.

Paragraph by Hughes on cover.

H21 *Whale Nation*. Cape, 1988.

Brochure advertising Heathcote Williams' forthcoming book. Contains facsimile letter from Hughes to Williams dated 12 July 87. This letter is also quoted on the dust-wrapper of Williams' later book *Falling for a Dolphin*.

H22 *News of the World: Selected Poems*, by Peter Fallon. Wake Forest University Press, 1993.

The back cover has a paragraph by Hughes.

H23 *Selected Poems*, by Elaine Feinstein. Carcanet, 1994.

The cover has a paragraph by Hughes.

H24 *The Occasions of Love*, by Simon Fletcher. Pennine Pens, 1995.

The dust-wrapper has a few lines by Hughes.

H25 *R. S. Thomas: Collected Poems 1945–1990*. Phoenix Giant edn, 1995.

The back cover has a quotation from Hughes' letter: 'This is a book I've been waiting for'.

I. Settings

Many settings of Hughes poems have been performed. We list here only those which have been published or recorded.

I1 *Meet My Folks!* Gordon Crosse. Oxford University Press, 1965.

Recorded HMV XLP 40001, 1965; sung by the Finchley Children's Music Group with percussion and instrumental ensemble.

I2 *Three Choruses*, Hugh Wood. Universal Edition, 1967.

Includes a setting of 'The Hawk in the Rain' for unaccompanied chorus.

I3 *The Horses*, Hugh Wood. Universal Edition, 1967.

Settings of 'The Horses', 'Pennines in April', and 'September'. First performed 13 November 1967. Broadcast 24 October 1971. Recorded Argo ZRG 750, 1974.

I4 *The Demon of Adachigahara*, Gordon Crosse. Oxford University Press, 1969.

A Cantata for junior choir, narrator, and instruments, with optional mime. Based on a Japanese folk-tale. This work was commissioned by The Walker Trust and The Arts Council of Great Britain and was given its first performance, in its original full version, on 27 March 1968 in Shrewsbury as part of the Shropshire Education Committee's Schools' Music Festival, by combined Shropshire school choirs and orchestras with Michael Derry as Narrator. The conductors were the composer and John Stephens, and the mime was produced by Diana Griffiths.

15 *The New World*, Gordon Crosse. Oxford University Press, 1975.

Six poems by Hughes [see B60] set for medium voice and piano. These songs, commissioned by Lord Dynevor, were completed in February 1969, and were given their first performance by Meriel Dickinson and Peter Dickinson at an SPNM concert on 30 August 1972 during the Three Choirs Festival at Worcester. There is also a version for high voice. Meriel and Peter Dickinson recorded the cycle on 18 September 1974 on Argo ZRG 788, 1975.

16 *Water-song*, Stanley Myers.

Recorded by Shusha, *Song of Long-Time Lovers*, Tangent TGS 114, 1972.

17 *No. 2 sangbec I*, Richard D. Hames. Edition Modern, 1978.

Settings for six voices of 'King of Carrion' and 'Eros'. Commissioned by the Purcell Consort with funds provided by the Arts Council. Written between 1968 and 1970, and first performed at the Edinburgh Festival in 1970. 'Eros' is in *Crow* as the second of the 'Two Legends'. Hughes has no recollection of the poem ever having the title 'Eros'.

18 *Thomas the Rhymer's Song*, Shusha.

Recorded by Shusha on *Durable Fire*, Linnet Records, LIN 1.

19 *Adam and Eve*, Shusha.

Recorded by Shusha on *Strange Affair*, Linnet Records, LIN 2, 1986.

J. Books and Articles
About Ted Hughes

BOOKS AND PAMPHLETS

J1 Sagar, Keith. *Ted Hughes*. Writers and their work no. 227. London, Longman for the British Council, 1972. 50pp. Revised second edition, Profile Books, 1981. 57pp.

J2 Mitgutsch, Waltraud. *Zur Lyrik von Ted Hughes: Eine Interpretation Nach Leitmotiven*. Salzburg studies in English literature: poetic drama and poetic theory 22. University of Salzburg, 1974. 282pp.

J3 Sagar, Keith. *An exhibition in honour of Ted Hughes*. Ilkley Literature Festival, 1975. 12pp.

J4 Sagar, Keith. *The art of Ted Hughes*. Cambridge, Cambridge University Press, 1975. 213pp. Second edition, revised and extended, 1978. 280pp.

J5 Probyn, Hugh. *Ted Hughes' Gaudete*. Preston, Lancs., Harris Press, 1977. 32pp.

J6 Johnson, Rosanna Autera. *Ted Hughes's 'The Hawk in the Rain' and 'The Jaguar'*. Pisa, Editrice tecnico scientifico, 1978. 36pp.

J7 Haworth-Booth, Mark. *Illustrations to Ted Hughes' poems*. Exhibition catalogue. London, Victoria and Albert Museum, 1979. 9pp.

J8 Sagar, Keith. *Ted Hughes*. Hull, Norman Jackson and Martin Horrox, 1979. Extracts from J1, second edition. 8pp.

J9 Faas, Ekbert. *Ted Hughes: the unaccommodated universe*. Santa Barbara, Calif., Black Sparrow Press, 1980. 225pp.

J10 Sagar, Keith. *The art of Ted Hughes*. Descriptive catalogue of an exhibition to mark Ted Hughes' fiftieth birthday. Manchester, City Art Gallery, 1980. 12pp.

J11 Crivelli, Renzo. *L'Universo Indifferente: Miti de Aggressione nella Poesia di Ted Hughes*. Pisa, Editrice tecnico scientifico, 1980.

J12 Gifford, Terry and Roberts, Neil. *Ted Hughes: a critical study*. London, Faber and Faber, 1981. 288pp.

J13 Hirschberg, Stuart. *Myth in the poetry of Ted Hughes*. Totowa, N.J., Barnes and Noble, 1981. 239pp.

J14 Wilson, Jane. *Backing horses: a comparison between Larkin's and Hughes's poetry*. Aquila essays 16. Portree, Isle of Skye, 1982.

J15 Sagar, Keith (ed.) *The achievement of Ted Hughes*. Manchester, Manchester University Press, 1983. 377pp.

Contains the following previously unpublished essays:

Bradshaw, Graham. Hughes and Shakespeare.

Bradshaw, Graham. Creative mythology in *Cave Birds*.

Cushman, Keith. Hughes' poetry for children.

Faas, Ekbert. Chapters of a shared mythology: Sylvia Plath and Ted Hughes.

Gifford, Terry and Roberts, Neil. Hughes and two contemporaries: Peter Redgrove and Seamus Heaney.

Jacobs, Fred Rue. Hughes and drama.

Parker, Michael. Hughes and the poets of Eastern Europe.

Robinson, Craig. The good shepherd: *Moortown Elegies*.

Sagar, Keith. Fourfold vision in Hughes.

Schofield, Annie. Hughes and the Movement.

Schofield, Annie. The Oedipus theme in Hughes.

Scigaj, Leonard M. Oriental mythology in *Wodwo*.

Sweeting, Michael. Hughes and shamanism.

J16 Sagar, Keith and Tabor, Stephen. *Ted Hughes: a bibliography 1946–1980*. London, Mansell, 1983. 260pp.

J17 West, Thomas. *Ted Hughes*. Contemporary writers. London, Methuen, 1985. 126pp.

J18 Scigaj, Leonard M. *The poetry of Ted Hughes*. Iowa City, Iowa, Iowa University Press, 1986. 369pp.

J19 Walder, Dennis. *Ted Hughes*. Open guides to literature. Milton Keynes, Open University Press, 1987. 108pp.

J20 Minami, Akira. *Shijin no sugao: Sylvia Plath to Ted Hughes*. [*The true faces of Sylvia Plath and Ted Hughes*.] Tokyo, Kenkyusha, 1987.

J21 Stella, Maria. *L'Inno e l'Enigma: saggio su Ted Hughes*. Roma, Bibliotheca Ianua, 1988. 221pp.

J22 Robinson, Craig. *Ted Hughes: shepherd of being*. London, Macmillan, 1989. 220pp.

J23 McEwan, Neil. *York notes on selected poems: Ted Hughes*. Harlow, Essex, Longman, 1989. 80pp.

J24 Dyson, A. E. (ed.) *Three contemporary poets: Thom Gunn, Ted Hughes and R. S. Thomas*. Macmillan Casebook Series. Macmillan, 1990. 294pp.

J24a Paulin, Tom. *Ted Hughes: Laureate of the Free Market?* Kenneth Allott Lectures No. 7. Liverpool Classical Monthly, 1991.

J25 Bishop, Nicholas. *Re-making poetry: Ted Hughes and a new critical psychology*. Brighton, Harvester/Wheatsheaf, 1991. 276pp.

J26 Scigaj, Leonard M. *Ted Hughes*. Twayne's English Authors. Boston, Twayne, 1991. 183pp.

J27 Scigaj, Leonard M. (ed.) *Critical essays on Ted Hughes*. New York, G. K. Hall, 1992. 277pp.

Contains the following previously unpublished essays:

Sagar, Keith. 'The poetry does not matter'.

Scigaj, Leonard M. Introduction [a survey of criticism of Hughes].

Skea, Ann. Wolf-masks: from *Hawk* to *Wolfwatching*.

J28 Sagar, Keith (ed.) *The challenge of Ted Hughes*. London and New York, Macmillan/St. Martin's Press, 1994. 190pp.

Contains the following previously unpublished essays:

Anderson, Nathalie. Ted Hughes and the challenge of gender.

Bishop, Nicholas. Ted Hughes and the death of poetry.

Brandes, Rand. Hughes, history and the world in which we live.

Davis, Alexander. Romanticism, existentialism, patriarchy: Hughes and the visionary imagination.

Elkin, Roger. Neglected auguries in *Recklings*.

Gifford, Terry. Gods of mud: Hughes and the post-pastoral.

Roberts, Neil. Hughes, narrative and lyric: an analysis of *Gaudete*.

Sagar, Keith. The evolution of 'The Dove Came'.

Scigaj, Leonard M. Ted Hughes and ecology: a biocentric vision.

Skea, Ann. Regeneration in *Remains of Elmet*.

J29 Skea, Ann. *Ted Hughes: the poetic quest*. Armidale, New South Wales, University of New England Press, 1994. 269pp.

J29a Strotmann, Birgit. *Natur- und Dichtungskonzeption im lyrischen Gesamtwerk von Ted Hughes*. Trier, Wissenschaftlicher Verlag Trier, 1995, 236pp.

J29b Kupferschmidt-Neugeborn, Dorothea. *'Heal into time and other people': Shamanismus und analytische Psychologie in der poetischen Wirkungsästhetik von Ted Hughes*. Tübingen, Narr, 1995, 286pp.

PARTS OF BOOKS

J30 Cox, C. B. and Dyson, A. E. Ted Hughes: 'The Casualty'. In *Modern poetry*, pp. 142–6. London, Edward Arnold, 1963.

J31 Press, John. Metaphysics and mythologies. In *Rule and energy*, pp. 181–91. Oxford, Oxford University Press, 1963.

J32 Grubb, F. Thinking animal: Ted Hughes. In *A vision of reality*, pp. 214–25. London, Chatto and Windus, 1965.

J33 Rosenthal, M. L. Ted Hughes. In *The new poets*, pp. 224–33. Oxford, Oxford University Press, 1967.

J34 Oppel, Horst. Ted Hughes' 'Pibroch'. In Oppel, H. (ed.), *Die Moderne Englische Lyrik: Interpretationen*. Berlin, 1968.

J35 Grant, Allan. Ted Hughes. In Hussey, M. (ed.), *Criticism in action*, pp. 97–104. London, Longman, 1969.

J36 May, Derwent. Ted Hughes. In Dodsworth, M. (ed.), *The survival of poetry*, pp. 133–63. London, Faber and Faber, 1970.

J37 Faas, Ekbert. Ted Hughes. In Drescher, H. W. (ed.), *Englische Literatur der Gegenwart*. Stuttgart, Kroner, 1970.

J38 Melchiori, Giorgio. La Poesia Inglese dal 1950 al 1970. In *I Funambuli*. Torino, Einaudi, 1970.

J39 Lombardo, Agostino. Thom Gunn e il Nuovo Movimento. In *Ritratto di Enobarbo*. Pisa, Nistri Lischi, 1971.

J40 Smith, A. C. H. *Orghast at Persepolis*. London, Eyre Methuen, 1972.

J41 Swinden, Patrick. On 'Ghost Crabs'. In Cox, C. B. and Dyson, A. E. (eds), *The twentieth century mind*, pp. 391–8. Oxford, Oxford University Press, 1972.

J42 Hamilton, Ian. Ted Hughes: *Crow*. In *A poetry chronicle*, pp. 165–70. London, Faber and Faber, 1973. First appeared as a review of *Crow* in the *Times Literary Supplement*, 8 January 1971.

J43 Lodge, David. *Crow* and the cartoons. In Robson, J. (ed.), *Poetry dimension I*, pp. 30–9. London, Robson Books Ltd., 1973. First appeared in *The Critical Quarterly*, Spring 1971.

J44 Sonne, Jorgen. Natur, Dyr, Djævelskab: om Ted Hughes' Lyrik. In *Horisonter, Introduktioner og Essays*. Copenhagen, 1973.

J45 Bedient, Calvin. Ted Hughes. In *Eight contemporary poets*, pp. 95–118. Oxford, Oxford University Press, 1974. First appeared in *The Critical Quarterly*, Summer 1972.

J46 Hogg, James. Ted Hughes and the drama. In Mitgutsch, Waltraud, *Zur Lyrik von Ted Hughes*, pp. i–xiii. University of Salzburg, 1974. [See J2.]

J47 Stratford, Jenny. 21 Ted Hughes. In *The Arts Council collection of modern literary manuscripts 1963–1972*, pp. 61–2. London, Turret Books, 1974.

J48 Thurley, Geoffrey. Beyond positive values: Ted Hughes. In *The ironic harvest*, pp. 163–89. London, Edward Arnold, 1974.

J49 Dyson, A. E. Ted Hughes. In Martin, C. and Furbank, P. N. (eds), *Twentieth century poetry*, pp. 423–31. Milton Keynes, Open University Press, 1975. First appeared in *The Critical Quarterly*, Autumn 1959.

J50 Holbrook, David. Ted Hughes's *Crow* and the longing for non-being. In Abbs, P. (ed.), *The black rainbow*, pp. 32–54. London, Heinemann, 1975.

J51 Walder, Dennis. *Ted Hughes Sylvia Plath*. A 306 29. pp. 7–30. Milton Keynes, Open University Press, 1976.

J52 Bold, Alan. *Thom Gunn and Ted Hughes*. Edinburgh, Oliver and Boyd, 1976. pp. 1–15, 45–75, 99–136.

J53 Bold, Alan. Ted Hughes. In *Cambridge book of English verse 1939–1975*, pp. 228–37. Cambridge, Cambridge University Press, 1976.

J54 Liberthson, Daniel. *The quest for being: Theodore Roethke, W. S. Merwin and Ted Hughes*. New York, Gordon, 1976.

J55 Oliva, Renato. Introduzione. *Giovani Poeti Inglesi*. Torino, Einaudi, 1976.

J56 Lengeler, R. Ted Hughes: 'Crow's First Lesson'. In Lengeler, R. (ed.), *Englische Literatur der Gegenwart: 1971–1975*. Düsseldorf, Bagel, 1977.

J57 Ries, Lawrence, R. Ted Hughes: acceptance and accommodation. In *Wolf masks*, pp. 92–129. Port Washington, N.Y., Kennikat, 1977.

J58 Holbrook, David. From 'vitalism' to a dead crow: Ted Hughes's failure of confidence. In *Lost bearings in English poetry*, pp. 101–63. London, Vision Press, 1977.

J59 Forrest-Thomson, Veronica. Ted Hughes and John Ashberry; or The triumph of artifice. In *Poetic artifice*, pp. 146–63. Manchester, Manchester University Press, 1978.

J60 Wieselhuber, F. Ted Hughes: 'Gnat-Psalm'. In Platz-Waury, E. (ed.), *Moderne Englische Lyrik*. Heidelberg, Quelle und Meyer, 1978.

J61 Oliva, Renato. Ted Hughes. In *I Contemporanei della Letteratura Inglese*. Roma, Lucarini, 1978.

J62 Uroff, Margaret Dickie. *Sylvia Plath and Ted Hughes*. Champaign, Ill., University of Illinois Press, 1979.

J63 Bradshaw, Graham. Ted Hughes' *Crow* as trickster-hero. In Williams, P. V. A. (ed.), *The fool and the trickster*, pp. 83–108. Cambridge and Totowa, N.J., D. S. Brewer/Rowman and Littlefield, 1979.

J64 King, P. R. Elemental energy, the poetry of Ted Hughes. In *Nine contemporary poets*, pp. 107–51. London, Methuen, 1979.

J65 Schmidt, Michael. Ted Hughes. In *Fifty modern British poets*, pp. 383–91. London, Pan Books, 1979.

J66 Adams, John. Dark rainbow: reflections on Ted Hughes. In Chambers, N. (ed.), *The Signal approach to children's books*, pp. 101–8, 121–5. London, Kestrel Books, 1980. First appeared in *Signal*, May 1971.

J67 Morse, Brian. Poetry, children and Ted Hughes. In Chambers, N. (ed.), *The Signal approach to children's books*, pp. 109–21. London, Kestrel Books, 1980. First appeared in *Signal*, September 1971.

J68 Heaney, Seamus. Englands of the mind. In *Preoccupations*, pp. 150–69. London, Faber and Faber, 1980. First appeared in *Critical Inquiry*, Summer 1977, as 'Now and in England'.

J69 Stuart, Robert. Ted Hughes. In Jones, P. and Schmidt, M. (eds), *British poetry since 1970*, pp. 75–84. Manchester, Carcanet Press, 1980.

J69a Inglis, Fred. Rumours of angels [on *The Iron Man*]. In his *The promise of happiness: value and meaning in children's fiction*. Cambridge University Press, 1981.

J70 Roberts, Neil. Ted Hughes. In Wintle, Justin (ed.), *Makers of modern culture*, pp. 237–8. London, Routledge, 1981.

J70a Abbs, Peter. The revival of the mythopoeic: a study of R. S. Thomas and Ted Hughes. In Anstey, Sandra (ed.), *Critical writings on R. S. Thomas*, Poetry Wales Press, 1982 and 1993.

J71 Smith, Stan. Night is always close: Gunn and Hughes. In *Inviolable voice: history and twentieth-century poetry*, pp. 150–69. Dublin, Gill and Macmillan, 1982.

J72 Rosenthal, M. L. and Gall, Sally M. Ted Hughes's *Crow* and Galway Kinnell's *The Book of Nightmares*. In their *The modern poetic sequence: the genius of modern poetry*, pp. 460–76. New York, Oxford University Press, 1983.

J73 Dodsworth, Martin. Ted Hughes and Geoffrey Hill: an antithesis. In *The new Pelican guide to English literature, vol. 8: the present*, pp. 281–93. Harmondsworth, Middlesex, Penguin, 1983.

J74 Trotter, David. Playing havoc: pathos and anti-pathos in the poetry of Ted Hughes, Geoffrey Hill and J. H. Prynne. In *The Making of the Reader*, pp. 196–230. London, Macmillan, 1984.

J75 Göller, Karl Heinz. Ted Hughes's 'Apple Tragedy': eine Verkehrung des biblischen Schöpfungsmythos. In Höltgen, Karl Josef et al., *Tradition und Innovation in der englischen und amerikanischen Lyrik des 20. Jahrhunderts*. Arno Essch zum 75. Geburstag. Tübingen, Niemeyer, 1986.

J76 Lengeler, R. Tomlinson, Hill and Hughes. In Hagenbüchle, Roland and Skandera, Laura (eds), *Poetry and epistemology: turning points in the history of poetic knowledge*. Papers from the International Poetry Symposium at Eichstäff, November 1983. Eichstäff Beiträge 20. Regensburg, Pustet, 1986.

J77 Butler, Michael. Ted Hughes and the links to German expressionism. In Böhn, Rudolf and Wode, Henning (eds), *Tagungsberichte des Anglisten Tags* 8 (Kiel, 1986). Giessen, Hoffman, 1987.

J78 Erzgräbner, Willi. Die Welt aus der Perspektive einer Krähe: Zu Ted Hughes' Crow. In Ahrends, Gunter and Seeber, Hans Ulrich (eds), *Englische und amerikanische Naturdichtung im 20. Jahrhundert*, pp. 151–70. Tübingen, Gunter Narr, 1985. Also in Erzgräbner, Willi, *Von Thomas Hardy bis Ted Hughes: Studien zur modernen englischen und anglo-irischen Literatur*. Freiburg im Breisgau, Rombach, 1995.

J79 Booth, Martin. In *British poetry 1964–1984*, pp. 143–54. London, Routledge and Kegan Paul, 1985.

J80 Roeffaers, Hugo. *Engels kwintet: essays over Ted Hughes, Geoffrey Hill, Seamus Heaney, Craig Raine en Robert Graves.* Leuven, Amersfoort/Acco, 1986.

J80a Sagar, Keith. Ted Hughes. In Scott-Kilvert, Ian (ed.), *British Writers, Supplement I.* New York, Ch. Scribner's Sons, 1987. [Reprints second edn of J1.]

J81 Perkins, David. Ted Hughes. In *A history of modern poetry: modernism and after.* Cambridge, Mass., Harvard University Press, 1987.

J82 Moody, David. Telling it like it's not. In *Yearbook of English Studies* 17, 1987.

J83 Davie, Donald. 'Ferocious Banter': Clarke and Hughes. Bunting, Tomlinson and Hughes. Poet's Prose: Hughes and Hill. Hughes as Laureate. In *Under Briggflatts: a history of poetry in Great Britain 1960–1988*, pp. 74–9, 127–31, 164–6, 223–8. Manchester, Carcanet, 1989.

J84 Mole, John. In *Passing judgements.* Bristol, Bristol Classical Press, 1989.

J84a Csokits, János. János Pilinszky's *Desert of love*: a note. In Weissbort, Daniel (ed.), *Translating poetry: the double labyrinth.* Iowa University Press, 1989.

J85 Brandes, Rand. Ted Hughes in and out of time: *Remains of Elmet* and *Moortown Elegies.* In Trawick, Leonard M. (ed.), *World, self, poem*, pp. 37–43. Kent, Ohio, Kent State University Press, 1990.

J86 Larrissy, Edward. Ted Hughes. In his *Reading twentieth-century poetry: the language of gender and objects.* Oxford, Blackwell, 1990.

J87 Smallwood, Philip. Creators as critics I: Ted Hughes. In his *Modern critics in practice.* Brighton, Harvester/Wheatsheaf, 1990.

J88 Göller, Karl Heinz. Towards a new mythology: the poetry of Ted Hughes. In Gibinska, Marta and Mazur, Zygmunt (eds), *English and American literature: continuity and change.* Proceedings of the 4th International Conference of English Studies, Cracow, 8–11 April 1987. Zeszyty Naukowe Uni Jag CLMIV, Prace Historycno-literackie 73. Cracow: Uniwersytet Jagiellonski, 1989.

J89 Anderson, Nathalie. Ted Hughes and women. In O'Gorman and Orr, Leonard (eds), *British poetry since 1960.* Penkvill, 1991.

J90 Brandes, Rand. Behind the bestiaries: the poetry of D. H. Lawrence and Ted Hughes. In Cushman, Keith (ed.), *D. H. Lawrence's literary heritage.* New York: St. Martin's Press, 1991.

J91 Moulin, Joanny. Ted Hughes, poète postmoderne? In Haberer,

Adolphe (ed.), *De Joyce à Stoppard: écritures de la modernité*. Lyon, Presses Universitaires de Lyon, 1991.

J91a Underhill, Hugh. Ted Hughes. In his *The Problem of consciousness in modern poetry*. Cambridge University Press, 1992.

J92 Paulin, Tom. Laureate of the free market? Ted Hughes. In his *Minotaur: poetry and the nation state*. London, Faber, 1992.

J92a Short, Mick. To analyse a poem stylistically: 'To paint a water lily' by Ted Hughes. In Verdonk, Peter (ed.), *Twentieth century poetry: from text to context*. Routledge, 1993.

J93 Corcoran, Neil. Negotiations: Ted Hughes and Geoffrey Hill. In his *English poetry since 1940*. Harlow, Essex, Longman, 1993.

J93a Moulin, Joanny. 'Out there': le réel dans la poésie de Ted Hughes. In Labbé, Evelyne (ed.), *L'altérité dans la littérature et la culture du monde anglophone*. Le Mans, University of Maine, 1993.

J94 Paul, Anthony. The Poet Laureate's national poet. In Hoenselaars, A. J. (ed.), *Reclamations of Shakespeare*. Dutch Quarterly Review Studies in Literature 15, 1994.

J95 Paulin, Tom. Ted Hughes. In Hamilton, Ian (ed.), *The Oxford companion to twentieth-century poetry*, pp. 241–2. Oxford, Oxford University Press, 1994.

J96 Gauthier, Dominique. Moortown Diary de Ted Hughes: le corps dans tous ses états. In Rouyer, Marie-Claire (ed.), *Le corps dans tous ses états*. Bordeaux: Presses Universitaires de Bordeaux, 1995.

J97 Moulin, Joanny. La jouissance dans les poèmes de Ted Hughes. In Rouyer, Marie-Claire (ed.), *Le corps dans tous ses états*. Bordeaux: Presses Universitaires de Bordeaux, 1995.

J98 Draper, R. P. Lawrence, Hughes and the Black Mountain poets. In his *An introduction to twentieth-century poetry in English*. London, Macmillan, 1995. [Delayed until 1998.]

J99 Gifford, Terry. Laureate of nature: the poetry of Ted Hughes. In his *Green voices: understanding contemporary nature poetry*. Manchester and New York, Manchester University Press/St. Martin's Press, 1995.

ARTICLES IN PERIODICALS

J100 Ghose, Zulfikar. The hawk above London zoo. *Western Daily Press*, 22 February 1961.

J101 Cox, C. B. The violence of Ted Hughes. *John O'London's*, 13 July 1961.

J102 Hainsworth, John. Poets and brutes. *Essays in Criticism* (XII:98–104), January 1962.

J103 Lundkvist, Artur. En Stark Vind: om Englands nye poet, Ted Hughes. *Ord och Bild* (LXXI:1–5), 1962.

J104 Holbrook, David. The cult of Hughes and Gunn. *Poetry Review* (LIV:167–83), Summer 1963.

J105 Hainsworth, John. Extremes in poetry: R. S. Thomas and Ted Hughes. *English* (XIV:226–30), Autumn 1963.

J106 Backström, Lars. Ted Hughes och månskräcken [Fear of the moon]. *Lyrikvännen* (XI:10–12), 1964.

J107 Rawson, C. J. Ted Hughes: a reappraisal. *Essays in Criticism* (XV:77–95), January 1965.

J108 Hainsworth, John. Ted Hughes and violence. *Essays in Criticism* (XV:356–9), July 1965.

J109 Rawson, C. J. Ted Hughes and violence. *Essays in Criticism* (XVI:124–9), January 1966. [A rejoinder to J108.]

J110 Lewis, Peter Elfred. The new pedantry and 'Hawk Roosting'. *Stand* (8:58–65), 1966.

J111 John, Brian. Ted Hughes: poet at the master-fulcrum of violence. *Arizona Quarterly* (23:5–15), Spring 1967.

J112 James, G. Ingli. The animal poems of Ted Hughes: a devaluation. *Southern Review* (II:193–203), 1967.

J113 Rawson, C. J. Some sources of parallels to poems by Ted Hughes. *Notes and Queries* (15:62–3), February 1968.

J114 Ferns, John. Over the same ground: Ted Hughes' 'Wodwo'. *Far Point* 1, 1968.

J115 Hoffman, D. Talking beasts: the 'Single Adventure' in the poems of Ted Hughes. *Shenandoah*, Summer 1968.

J116 Tamura, Einosuke. Ted Hughes, *Oberon*, 32, 1968.

J117 Rife, David. Rectifying illusion in the poetry of Ted Hughes. *Minnesota Review* (X:95–9), 1970.

J118 Gitzen, Julian. Ted Hughes and elemental energy. *Discourse*, Autumn 1970.

J119 Peel, Marie. Black rainbow. *Books and Bookmen*, February 1971.

J120 Porter, Andrew. Orghast. *Financial Times*, 14 September 1971.

J121 Stoppard, Tom. Orghast. *Times Literary Supplement*, 1 October 1971.

J122 Reeves, Geoffrey. The Persepolis Follies of 1971. *Performance* (1:47–71), December 1971.

J123 Combecher, Hans. Ted Hughes: 'The Thought-Fox'. *Literatur in Wissenschaft und Unterricht*, 4, 1971.

J124 Trilling, Ossia. Playing with words at Persepolis. *Theatre Quarterly* (II:33–40), January–March 1972.

J125 Mollema, A. Mythical elements in the poetry of Ted Hughes. *Dutch Quarterly Review of Anglo-American Letters* (2:2–14), 1972.

J126 Sinnege-Breed, Afra. Plucking bark: an interpretation of Ted Hughes's 'Wodwo'. *Dutch Quarterly Review of Anglo-American Letters* (2:15–20), 1972.

J127 Harrison, Martin. Poetry and appearance: a note on Ted Hughes. *Granta*, Easter 1972.

J128 Watt, Donald J. Echoes of Hopkins in Ted Hughes' *The Hawk in the Rain*. *Notes on Contemporary Literature*, 2, 1972.

J129 Strauss, P. The poetry of Ted Hughes. *Theoria* (38:45–63), 1972.

J130 Blodden, H. and Kaussen, H. Structural analyses of modern English poetry for classroom teaching: 'The Windhover' by G. M. Hopkins and 'Owl's Song' by Ted Hughes. *Der fremdsprachliche Unterricht* (6:24–40), 1972.

J131 Gitzen, Julian. Ted Hughes and the triumph of energy. *Southern Humanities Review* (7:67–73), Winter 1973.

J132 Libby, Anthony. Fire and light: four poets to the end and beyond. *Iowa Review*, Spring 1973, 111–26.

J133 Fowkes, Rosalind. Pass, Crow: a discussion of Ted Hughes's last published collection of poetry. *UNISA English Studies* (11:51–6), June 1973.

J134 Kano, Hideo. Ted Hughes no Shi-Gendaishi no ichi-men. *Oberon* (14:2–8), 1973.

J135 Okubo, Naoki. On Ted Hughes' animal poems. *Studies in English Literature*, 1974, 239–40.

J136 Bouson, J. Brooks. A reading of Ted Hughes's *Crow*. *Concerning Poetry* (7:21–32), 1974.

J137 Libby, Anthony. God's lioness and the priest of Sycorax: Plath and Hughes. *Contemporary Literature* (XV:386–405), Summer 1974.

J138 Porter, David. Beasts/Shamans/Baskin: the contemporary aesthetics of Ted Hughes. *Boston University Journal* (XXII:13–25), Fall 1974.

J139 Hedetoft, Ulf. Ted Hughes, 'Pennines in April': the universal poem in the 20th century. *Language and Literature* (2:iv), 1974.

J140 Ries, L. R. Hughes' 'The Hawk in the Rain'. *Explicator* (33:item 34), December 1974.

J141 Hirschberg, Stuart. Myth and anti-myth in Ted Hughes' *Crow*. *Contemporary Poetry* (2:i), 1975.

J142 Kimball, Arthur S. Ted Hughes's Crow: chaos and the fool. *UNISA English Studies* (13:9–17), 1975.

J143 Poole, Richard. Dylan Thomas, Ted Hughes and Byron—two instances of indebtedness. *Anglo-Welsh Review* (25:119–24), 1975.

J144 Kirkham, Michael. Ted Hughes' *Crow*. *Sphinx*, 3, 1975.

J145 Novak, R. Ted Hughes' *Crow*: incarnation and the universe. *Windless Orchard* (21:40–2), Spring 1975.

J146 Porter, David. Ted Hughes. *American Poetry Review* (4:13–18), 1975.

J147 Smith, Stan. Wolf masks: the early poetry of Ted Hughes. *New Blackfriars* (56:414–26), September 1975. Reprinted in J71.

J148 Fernandez, Charles V. *Crow*: a mythology of the demonic. *Modern Poetry Studies* (6:144–56), Autumn 1975.

J149 Abbs, Peter. The revival of the mythopoeic imagination—a study of R. S. Thomas and Ted Hughes. *Poetry Wales* (10:10–27), 1975. Reprinted in J70a.

J150 Bedient, Calvin. Absentist poetry: Kinsella, Hill, Graham, Hughes. *P.N Review* (4:18–24), 1976.

J151 Keutsch, Wilfred. A reading of Ted Hughes' 'Thrushes'. *Literatur in Wissenschaft und Unterricht* (9:2), 1976.

J152 Hirschberg, Stuart. An encounter with the irrational in Ted Hughes' 'Pike'. *Contemporary Poetry* (9:63–4), 1976.

J153 Sprusiński, Michał. Najoczwiściej ja: niezarnie opierzony człowiek. [Of course it's I: an awkwardly feathered man.] *Twórczość* (32:92–102), 1976.

J154 Weatherhead, A. K. Ted Hughes, *Crow*, and pain. *Texas Quarterly* (XIX:95–108), Autumn 1976.

J155 [No entry]

J156 Law, Pamela. Poetry as ritual: Ted Hughes. *Sydney Studies in English* (2:72–82), 1976/7.

J157 Hahn, Claire. *Crow* and the Biblical creation narratives. *Critical Quarterly* (19:43–52), Spring 1977.

J158 Davies, Norman F. The poetry of Ted Hughes. *Moderna Språk* (71:121–7), 1977.

J159 Hughes, Geoffrey. Crow: myth or trickster? *Theoria* (48:25–36), 1977.

J160 Megerle, Brenda. Ted Hughes: his monsters and critics. *Southern Humanities Review* (11:184–94), 1977.

J161 Wood, Michael. We all hate home: English poetry since World War II. *Contemporary Literature* (18:305–18), 1977.

J162 Kramer, Lawrence. The Wodwo watches the water clock. *Contemporary Literature* (18:319–42), 1977.

J163 Roberts, Neil. Ted Hughes: encounters with death. *Dutch Quarterly Review of Anglo-American Letters* (8:2–17), 1978.

J164 Gifford, Terry. Return to 'The Wound' by Ted Hughes. *Kingfisher* (I:46–53), 1978.

J165 Goto, Akio. Ningen to Dobutsu no aida: Ted Hughes to Hyogen no Mondai. [Between man and animals: Hughes' poetic diction.] *Eigo Seinen* (124:204–8), 1978.

J166 Hirschberg, Stuart. Hughes' new 'Rough Beast': the malevolent new order in 'Song of a Rat'. *Contemporary Poetry* (11:59–63), 1978.

J167 Kano, Hideo. Ted Hughes no Shi: *Yorokobi* o ni tsuite no Shiron. [On *Gaudete*.] *Oberon* (17:76–93), 1978.

J168 Moyle, Geraldine. Hughes' *Gaudete:* a poem subverted by its plot. *Parnassus* (6:199–204), 1978.

J169 Pocock, Janet H. An addition to the Ted Hughes bibliography. *Bulletin of Bibliography* (35:15–18), 1978.

J170 Ramsey, Jarold. Crow: or the trickster transformed. *Massachusetts Review* (19:111–27), Spring 1978.

J171 Battiglia, Susan Payne. Alliteration, assonance and phonosymbolism in Ted Hughes' 'Wind'. Annali Istituto Universitario Orientale. *Anglistica*, 21, 1978.

J172 Johnson, Rosanna Autera. Alliteration, assonance and phonosymbolism in Ted Hughes' 'The Hawk in the Rain'. Annali Istituto Universitario Orientale. *Anglistica*, 21, 1978.

J173 Wain, John. Signal Poetry Award Citation: The Winner [*Moon-Bells*]. *Signal* (29:63–6), May 1979.

J174 Stevenson, Anne. The recognition of the Savage God: poetry in Britain today. *New England Review* (Middlebury College, Vermont), 2, 1979.

J175 Williams, A. Hughes' 'Hawk Roosting'. *Explicator* (38:39–41), 1979.

J176 Currie, Felicity. Poet as maker: reflections on Ted Hughes's 'To Paint a Water-Lily'. *Critical Quarterly* (21:43–9), Winter 1979.

J177 Sagar, Keith. The last inheritance: Ted Hughes and his landscape *Poetry Wales* (15:61–77), Winter 1979/80.

J178 Witte, John C. Wotan and Ted Hughes' *Crow*. *Twentieth Century Literature* (126:38–44), Spring 1980.

J179 Worthington, Brian. The best living poet? *New Universities Quarterly*, 199–207. Spring 1980.

J180 Howard, Ben. Terror's ambassador. *Parnassus* (8:253–65), 1980.

J181 Latané, David. Two Eskimo songs from *Crow*. *Notes on Contemporary Literature* (10:7–9), 1980.

J182 Villa, Fernando. Dall'ansia alla consaperolezza: Ted Hughes e la poesia inglese contemporanea. *Lettore di Provincia* (43:45–55), 1980.

J183 Nuttall, Jeff. A levelling. *The Artful Reporter* (32:7), October 1980.

J184 Sagar, Keith. In defence of a poet. *The Artful Reporter* (34:13), December 1980. [An answer to J183.]

J185 Iwasaki, Souji. Ted Hughes shouron—shishu *Crow* no sekai. [An essay on Ted Hughes—the world of *Crow*.] *Aichi University Poiesis* (10:23–37), 1980.

J186 Minami, Akira. *Crow* no kigeki to higeki. [Comedy and Tragedy in *Crow*.] *Bulletin of Konan University* (Literature) (34:141–59), 1980.

J187 Nishihara, Katsumasa. Ted Hughes no *Crow*—Ankoku no hyumaa. [Ted Hughes' *Crow*—black comedy.] *Nebyuras* (8:61–8), 1980.

J188 Owen, Elizabeth. Facing the unacceptable face of nature: the poetry of Ted Hughes. *New Poetry* (51–2:21–4), Winter 1980–1.

J189 Vanson, Frederic: Violence mythologised: some aspects of the poetry of Ted Hughes. *Magma*, 6, 1981?

J190 Gifford, Terry and Roberts, Neil. Ritual and goblin: *Cave Birds* by Ted Hughes. *Pacific Quarterly* (VI i:17–25), 1981.

J191 Bere, Carol. Remains of Elmet. *Concerning Poetry*, 14, Spring 1981.

J192 McKay, Don. Animal music: Ted Hughes's progress in speech and song. *English Studies in Canada*, 7, Spring 1981.

J193 Preda, Ioan Aurel. Two versions, two modes of expressions: Philip Larkin and Ted Hughes. *Revista de istorie și teorie literara* (30:529–35), 1981.

J194 Ito, Jiro. Ningen no seikatsu wo anisuru yaseitekina doubutsu no imeiji—Ted Hughes. [Analogues of human life in wild animal imagery.] *Jidoubungakusekai* [*The World of Children's Literature*], 3, 1981.

J195 Saito, Mamoru. Kakumei no tooi uminari: Ted Hughes no Shakespeare. [Far sea-sound of revolution: Ted Hughes' Shakespeare.] *Shin Bungaku Fuukei* [*New Literature Landscape*] (4:11–25), 1981.

J196 Sanazaro, Leonard. Note on Ted Hughes' 'An Icon' and Sylvia Plath's 'Medallion'. *Notes on Contemporary Literature*, 12, May 1981.

J197 Ahrens, Rudiger. Transzendenz und lyrisches Ich in Ted Hughes' 'Gnat-Psalm' und Geoffrey Hill's 'Mercian Hymns'. *Literaturwissenschaftliches Jahrbuch im Auftrage der Görres-Gesellschaft* (23:265–96), 1982.

J198 Cluysenaar, Anne. Formal meanings in three modern poems [including 'Hawk Roosting']. *Dutch Quarterly Review* (12:4:302–20), 1982.

J199 McPherson, Sandra. Ted Hughes's *Moortown*, real and imagined. *American Poetry Review* (11:1:18–22), January–February 1982.

J200 Takachi, Junnichiro. Uchi ni mukerareta kotoba—Ted Hughes. [Inward-turned words]. *Shigaku* [*Poetics*] (37:2), 1982.

J201 Yoshino, Masaaki. Muishikino fukami e: Ted Hughes ron. [Into the depths of the unconscious]. *Utsunomiya University's Gaikoku Bungaku* (30:14–20), 1982.

J202 Schlesinger, Sheila. Hawk, thrush and crow: the bird poems of Tomlinson and Hughes. *Theoria* (59:53–61), 1982.

J203 Bradshaw, Graham. The cult of irrationality: Ted Hughes and his critics. *Encounter*, June 1982, pp. 71–81.

J204 Zivley, Sherry Lutz. Ted Hughes's apologia pro matrimonio suo. *New England Quarterly* (55:187–200), June 1982.

J205 Blackburn, Thomas. End-stopped poets: Sylvia Plath and Ted Hughes. *Temenos* (2:161–81), 1982.

J206 Rees, David. Ted Hughes as a writer of children's books. *San Jose Studies* (9:2:6–16), 1982.

J207 Devoize, Jeanne. 'The Rain Horse': approche psychoanalytique. *Les Cahiers de la Nouvelle* (I:17–21), 1983.

J208 Hashimoto, Masanori. Ted Hughes kansho nouto 1—doubutsusi ni tsuite. [Appreciations of Ted Hughes' poetry 1: On his animal poems.] *Annual Report of Gakushuin University Faculty of Arts* (30:59–91), 1983.

J209 Nakada, Tamotsu. Seimei eno shinrai: Ted Hughes no shi. [Trust in life: Ted Hughes' poetry.] *Senshu English and American Studies* (1:30–43), 1983.

J210 Takachi, Junnichiro. 'Tsuyoi shi' to gendai bungaku hihyo—Ted Hughes, Geoffrey Hill oyobi Seamus Heaney. ['Mighty poem' and modern literary criticism.] *Bulletin of Oobirin University* (English language and literature), 23, 1983.

J211 Scigaj, Leonard. Genetic memory and the three traditions of *Crow. Perspectives on Contemporary Literature*, 9, 1983.

J212 Dickie, M. Ted Hughes: the double voice. *Contemporary Literature* (23:51–65), Spring 1983.

J213 Larrisy, Edward. Ted Hughes, the feminine, and *Gaudete. Critical Quarterly* (25 ii:33–41), Summer 1983.

J214 Hulse, Michael. Deeper into language: a note on Ted Hughes. *Quadrant* (27 11:48–51), 1983.

J215 Stella, Maria. The snow-screen vision: apparazione e scomparsa nella poesia di Ted Hughes. *Studi di Estetica* (Bologna), 4/5, 1984.

J216 Motto, Anna Lydia and Clark, John R. Grotesquerie ancient and modern: Seneca and Ted Hughes. *Classical and Modern Literature* (5:13–22), 1984.

J217 Schmitz, Götz. Schöpfung und Zerstörung in Ted Hughes früher Lyrik. *Germanische-romanische Monatsschrift* (34:431–53), 1984.

J218 Webster, Richard. 'The Thought-Fox' and the poetry of Ted Hughes. *Critical Quarterly* (26 iv:35–45), Winter 1984.

J219 Philip, Neil. The Signal Poetry Award [*What is the Truth?*]. *Signal*, 47, May 1985.

J220 Ahrends, Günter. From God to Gog? Ted Hughes, Gary Snyder und die romantische Naturkonzeption. *Anglistik und Englischunterricht* (26:69–86), 1985.

J221 Heuser, Alan. Creaturely inseeing in the poetry of G. M. Hopkins, D. H. Lawrence, and Ted Hughes. *Hopkins Quarterly* (12:35–51), 1985.

J222 Heaney, Seamus. The new Poet Laureate. *Belfast Review* (10:6), March/April/May 1985.

J223 Roberts, Neil. Ted Hughes and the Laureateship. *Critical Quarterly* (27 ii:3–5), Summer 1985.

J224 Schmitz, Götz. Lähmung und Bewegung in Gedichten von Philip Larkin und Ted Hughes. *Literatur in Wissenschaft und Unterricht* (18:115–35), 1985.

J225 Smith, Stan. Crow rides again: Thatcher's laureate. *Cencrastus* (20:19–20), 1985.

J226 von Lutz, Bruno. Die Auseinandersetzung mit dem britischen Empire in der zeitgenössischen englischen Lyrik. *Arbeiten aus Anglistik und Amerikanistik* (10:109–21), 1985.

J227 Haberstroh, Patricia Boyle. Historical landscape in Ted Hughes's *Remains of Elmet. Clio*, 14, Winter 1985.

J228 Richman, Robert. A crow for the queen. *The New Criterion* (3 6:90–2), February, 1985.

J229 Scigaj, Leonard M. The ophiolatry of Ted Hughes. *Twentieth Century Literature* (31:380–98), Winter 1985.

J230 Skea, Ann. Understanding Ted Hughes. *English in Australia* (74:i–viii), December 1985.

J230a Singh, Charu Sheel. The poetics of Ted Hughes. *The Literary Criterion* (Mysore) (20 2: 56–69), 1985.

J231 Harris, Richard W. The savage amazement of life—consistency and development in the poetry of Ted Hughes. *Bulletin of Nagoya University of Commerce* (30:669–84), 1985.

J231a Bromwich, David. Ted Hughes. *Grand Street* (5 1:244–56), Autumn 1985.

J232 Paul, Lissa. Inside the lurking-glass with Ted Hughes. *Signal* (49:52–63), January 1986.

J233 Gotou, Meisei. Ted Hughes—*Crow* igo 1. [After *Crow* 1.] *Eigo Seinen* [*The Rising Generation*] (132:332–3), 1986.

J234 Ponsford, Michael. Christianity and myth in Ted Hughes's 'The Golden Boy'. *Notes on Contemporary Literature* (16:4:11–12), 1986.

J235 Sym, Myung-Ho. Ted Hughes eui dongmul si. [Ted Hughes' animal poems.] *Journal of English Language and Literature* (32 4:625–45), 1986.

J236 Wandor, Michelene. When the muse refuses to appear in public. *Listener* (116:22), 31 July 1986.

J237 Maslin, Elizabeth. Counterpoint: collaborations between Ted Hughes and three visual artists. *Word and Image*, 2, January–March 1986.

J238 Holbrook, David. The Crow of Avon: Shakespeare, sex and Ted Hughes. *Cambridge Quarterly* (15:1–12), 1986.

J239 Lombardo, Agostino. La poesia di Ted Hughes. *Lingua e Letteratura* (Milano), 6, 1986.

J239a Bratini, Sergio. I lucci, il toro Moses ed altri animali. *Quaderni Lingue e Letterature* (11:51–73), 1986.

J240 Runcie, Catherine. On figurative language: a reading of Shelley's, Hardy's and Hughes's skylark poems. *Journal of the Australasian Universities Modern Language Association* (66:205–17), November 1986.

J240a Ahrens, Rüdiger. Ted Hughes' 'Gnat-Psalm': the poet in search of a new transcendence. *Fu Jen Studies* (Taipei) (19:15–36), 1986.

J241 Lomas, Herbert. The poetry of Ted Hughes. *Hudson Review* (XL 3:409–426), Autumn 1987.

J242 Le Bon-Dodat, Anne-Marie. Dissonances dans la poétique de Ted Hughes. *Repérages* (9:21–35), 1987.

J243 Gustavsson, Bo. Ted Hughes' quest for a hierophany: a reading of *River*. *Studia Neophilologica* (59:2), 1987.

J244 Schricker, Gale C. 'Madam, I'm Adam': managing mother earth in *Moortown*. *Thought* (62 245:176–89), 1987.

J245 Ishihara, Takeshi. Buta no fuukei—Ted Hughes to Sylvia Plath no shi no fuukei. [Landscape of pigs—the landscape of death in Hughes and Plath.] *Bunkyo University English Language and Literature* (14:25–9), 1987.

J246 Minami, Akira. 'I' to 'eye' no kincho: Hughes to Plath ni okeru tasha no imi. ['I' versus 'eye': the meaning of the 'other' in Hughes and Plath.] *Bulletin of Kansai University of Foreign Studies* (5:4:1–12), 1987.

J247 Mizuwaki, Hayato. Ame no naka no taka ron. [On *The Hawk in the Rain*.] *Report of Tokyo University of Fisheries* (22:71–86), 1987.

J248 Shimizu, Hideyuki. Eishi kenkyu ni okeru shiteki kyoyou to eigo kyoiku no kanousei—Ted Hughes no 'The Thought Fox'. [Poetry and poetic licence as a means of English teaching—Ted Hughes' 'The Thought Fox'.] *Bulletin of Shizuoka Jogakuin Junior College* (19:205–18), 1987.

J248a Lutz, Bruno von. Ted Hughes' 'Heptonstall Old Church'. *Literatur in Wissenschaft und Unterricht* (20 2:352–63), 1987.

J249 Ahrens, Rüdiger. The modern poet in view of Nature: Ted Hughes' 'Gnat-Psalm'. *Poetica* (28:60–73), Tokyo, 1988.

J249a Lenz, Olivia Bottum. Landscape of our dreams: Ted Hughes' *Moon-Whales*. *Children's Literature Association Quarterly* (13 1:22–5), Spring 1988.

J250 Miki, Toru. Ted Hughes' hawks—a bird as a symbol of violence. *Bulletin of National College of Maritime Technology*, 31, 1988.

J250a Gough, John. Experiencing a sequence of poems: Ted Hughes' *Season Songs*. *Children's Literature Association Quarterly* (13 4:191–4), Winter 1988.

J251 Shimizu, Hideyuki. Gendai shijin kou (2): Ted Hughes. [Modern British Poets (2): Ted Hughes.] *Alphalfa of Gakushuin University*, 11, 1988.

J251a Crafton, John Michael. Hughes' 'Crow's First Lesson'. *Explicator* (46 2:32–4), Winter 1988.

J252 Nakada, Tamotsu. Ted Hughes ni okeru mittsu no me. [Three types of 'eye' in Ted Hughes.] *Annual Bulletin of Senshu University Institute for Humanities*, 19, 1989.

J253 Nakada, Tamotsu. Ted Hughes—Jung—mizu. [Ted Hughes—Jung—water.] *Senshu English and American Studies* (7:1–14), 1989.

J254 Sasakura, Sadao. Ted Hughes no shi ni tsuite—chi no ronri wo megutte. [Ted Hughes' poetry—on the logic of blood.] *Shi to Shisou* [*Poetry and Thought*] (74–77), December 1989.

J255 Tomii, Toshirou. Shinwa ni miru sekaikan—Ted Hughes' *How the Whale Became* wo chuushin ni 1. [The world view in myths—Ted Hughes' *How the Whale Became* 1.] *Bulletin of Shimane Women's Junior College* (27:59–69), 1989.

J256 Murphy, Richard. Sylvia Plath and Ted Hughes: an Irish visit in 1962. *London Magazine* (29 3/4:31–43), June/July 1989.

J256a Myers, Lucas. Ah, youth ... Ted Hughes and Sylvia Plath at Cambridge and after. *Grand Street* (8 4:86–103), Summer 1989.

J257 Cox, C. B. British poetry since 1945: Philip Larkin and Ted Hughes. *Youngeo Youngmunhak* (5:1–13), 1989.

J258 Dienhart, John M. Form and function in Ted Hughes's poem 'The Jaguar'. *English Studies* (70 3:248–52), 1989.

J258a Fisher, Mathew D. Hughes' 'Pike'. *Explicator* (47 4:58–9), Summer 1989.

J259 Herbert, Hugh. Watching the Lone Wolf. *Guardian*, 15 September 1989.

J259a Vetrova, E. I. Svoeobrazie vozzrenii na prirodu Teda Kh'iuza. *Filologicheskie Nauki* (6:67–71), 1989.

J260 Wigboldus, Roelf. Isis and satori: an interpretation of Ted Hughes's *Gaudete*. *Neophilologus* (73 3:458–69), 1990.

J261 Bockting, Ineke. Worlds apart—pragmatics and poetry: an analysis of Ted Hughes' 'Her Husband'. *Dutch Quarterly Review* (20 4:268–76), 1990.

J262 Mizuwaki, Hayato. *Lupercal* sai ni tsuite. *Report of Tokyo University of Fisheries*, 25, 1990.

J263 Tomii, Toshirou. Shinwa ni miru sekaikan—Ted Hughes' *How the Whale Became* wo chuushin ni 2. [The world view in myths—Ted Hughes' *How the Whale Became* 2.] *Bulletin of Shimane Women's Junior College* (28:1–10), 1990.

J263a Raine, Craig. Profile: Ted Hughes. In his *Haydn and the Valve Trumpet*. Faber and Faber, 1990.

J264 Haberer, Adolphe. De *Hawk in the Rain* à *Crow*: oiseaux et bêtes mythiques dans la poésie de Ted Hughes. *Études Anglaises* (44: 4:413–27), 1991.

J264a Ráes, Istvan D. The realm between life and death in Ted Hughes. *Hungarian Studies in English* (22:121–6), 1991.

J265 Ferrari, Mauro. Poesie da *Gaudete*, 'Epilogue'. *Altri Termini* (Napoli), January–April 1991, pp. 51–6.

J265a Hamada, Kazuie. The emptiness in Ted Hughes' 'Wodwo'. *Journal of Kyoritsu Women's Junior College* (35:25–36), February 1992.

J266 Moulin, Joanny. Le mimologisme de Ted Hughes. *Études Britanniques Contemporaines*, April 1992, pp. 89–103.

J267 Hendry, Diana. Up with the lark(s). *Critical Survey* (4 1:67–9), 1992.

J268 Gammage, Nick. Casualties of war: Ted Hughes' war poetry. *Acumen* (Brixham, Devon) (15:40–5), 1992.

J269 Hughes, Olwyn. Ted Hughes and the Plath estate. *Times Literary Supplement*, 27 March 1992.

J270 Elkin, Roger. Ted Hughes: *Gaudete*. *Envoi* (103:116–18), Autumn 1992.

J271 Galea, Ileana. Ted Hughes şi poezia engleza moderna. *Tribuna* (Cluj-Napoca, Romania), 1 July 1993.

J272 Gervais, David. Ted Hughes: an England beneath England. *English* (42 172:45–73), 1993.

J273 Hamada, Kazuie. Seamus Heaney: seeing things—a comparative essay on Heaney and Ted Hughes. *Kyoritsu Women's Junior College Bulletin for Humanities*, 36, 1993.

J274 Miki, Toru. Ted Hughes as a war poet—human existence on the verge of total annihilation. *Ohtani Women's University Studies in English Language and Literature*, 20, 1993.

J275 Nagae, Yoshio. Ted Hughes no shoki no shi. [Early poems of Ted Hughes.] *Research Bulletin of Sugiyama Jogakuen University*, 24, 1993.

J276 Nakada, Tamotsu. Yorkushamua—Ted Hughes to Emily Brontë. [Yorkshire moor—Ted Hughes and Emily Brontë]. *Monthly Newsletter of Senshu University Institute for Humanities*, 151, 1993.

J277 Horiuchi, Toshimi. Fire and ice in Ted Hughes' poetry. *Bulletin of Sendai Shirayuri Junior College*, 22, 1994.

J278 Whiting, Alan. A reading of Ted Hughes's Jaguar Poems I. *Envoi*, 107, February 1994.

J279 O'Brien, Sean. On the shelf [on *Wodwo*]. *Sunday Times*, 3 April 1994.

J280 Whiting, Alan. Ted Hughes's 'Second Glance at a Jaguar'. *Envoi*, 108, June 1994.

J280a Schmitz, Götz. Local myth in the poetry of Ted Hughes. *Sewanee Review*, 1994, pp. 470–81.

J281 Moulin, Joanny. Ted Hughes, le chaman lauréat. *Études Anglaises*. April–June 1995, pp. 173–83.

J282 Minami, Akira. Ted Hughes no laureate poems. *Bulletin of Notre Dame Women's University*, 25, 1995.

TAPES

J283 Morrison, Blake and Raine, Craig. Ted Hughes: The Dark Forces. Audio Learning ELA 065, 1979.

THESES

J284 Haefner, Gerhard. Formen surrealistischer und realistischer Lyrik in England, 1910–1970: T. S. Eliot, Samuel Beckett, "The Movement", Ted Hughes. Köln, 1972.

J285 Mitgutsch, W. Zur Lyrik von Ted Hughes und Thom Gunn: Eine Interpretation nach Leitmotiven. Salzburg University, 1973.

J286 Gibson, John. A thematic analysis of the poetry in Ted Hughes' major works. Ph.D. University of Northern Colorado, 1974. University Microfilms DCJ74-24484.

J287 Liberthson, Daniel. The quest for being: Roethke, Merwin, and Hughes. Ph.D. Buffalo. [See J54.]

J288 Zwerdling, Florence. Man and beast in the poetry of Ted Hughes. Ph.D. Berkeley, 1976.

J289 Scigaj, Leonard. Myth and psychology in the poetry of Ted Hughes. Ph.D. Wisconsin, 1977. University Microfilms DDK77-19787.

J290 Elkin, Roger. A study of Ted Hughes' *Recklings* (1966). Ph.D. Keele University, 1982.

J291 Bubbers, Lissa Paul. Telling stories for children and adults: the writings of Ted Hughes. York University, Ontario, 1984. DA (45) 3134A.

J292 Robinson, Craig. The poetry of Ted Hughes. Ph.D. University of Lancaster, 1984.

J293 Sweeting, Michael. Patterns of initiation in the poetry of Ted Hughes from 1970 to 1980. Ph.D. Durham University, 1984.

J294 Truebell, Beth Linda. A blending of opposites: the evolution of Ted Hughes's mythological poetry. Ph.D. University of Maryland, 1985. DA (46) 433A-4A.

J295 Wallat, Rainer. Mensch zwischen Natur und Gesellschaft. Zur Lyrik von Ted Hughes. Ph.D. University of Rostock, 1985.

J296 Anderson, Nathalie. Survivor beast, politicized terrain: mythic approaches in the poetry of Ted Hughes and Seamus Heaney. Ph.D. Emory University, 1985. University Microfilms NBG85-16561. DA (46) 1622A.

J297 Brandes, Rand. The myth of the fall in the poetry of D. H. Lawrence and Ted Hughes. Ph.D. Emory University, 1985. DA (46) 2697A. University Microfilms NBG85-26289.

J298 Rice, Samuel. The function of metaphor in contemporary English-language poetry: the case of Ted Hughes. Ph.D. Catholic University of America, 1985. University Microfilms NBG85-06726. DA (46) 432A-3A.

J299 Barnden, Saskia. Voice in contemporary British poetry with special attention to Philip Larkin, Ted Hughes and Geoffrey Hill. Ph.D.

Indiana University, 1988. University Microfilms NFZ88-24152. DA (49) 2664A.

J300 Skea, Ann. Sources in the work of Ted Hughes. Ph.D. University of New England at Armidale, New South Wales, 1988.

J301 Bishop, Nicholas. Poetry and Grace: the dynamics of self in Ted Hughes's adult poetry. Ph.D. Exeter University, 1988. IT (38:1)30. DA (49) 1460A.

J302 Nickel, Claudia. Das motif der Gefangenschaft in den Geschichten von Ted Hughes. M.A. Erlangen-Nürnberg University, 1988.

J302a Montgomery, Mary Ann. Musical and poetical structures in Olivier Messiaen's *Couleurs de la cité céleste* and Ted Hughes' *Crow*. Ohio University, 1989. DAI 50(8) 2279A.

J303 Davis, Alexander T. An examination of the notions of 'masculinity' and 'femininity' in the poetry and prose of Ted Hughes and Seamus Heaney. Ph.D. Sheffield University, 1990.

J304 Johnson, Owen. Ted Hughes: speaking for the Earth. University of Durham, 1991. DA (53) 1993, 3919A.

J305 Head, Adrian. The resurgence of myth in the poetry of Ted Hughes and R. S. Thomas. Ph.D. Sheffield University, 1993.

J305a Strotmann, Birgit. Natur- und Dichtungskonzeption im lyrischen Gesamtwerk von Ted Hughes. Universität Köln, 1994.

J306 Pike, Jolyon. Ted Hughes and the visionary imagination. Ph.D. Sheffield University, 1995.

J307 Bentley, Paul. Language, self and reality in the poetry of Ted Hughes and Peter Redgrove. Ph.D. Sheffield University, 1995.

J308 Kupferschmidt-Neugeborn, Dorothea. 'Heal into time and other people': Shamanismus und analytische Psychologie in der poetischen Wirkungsästhetik von Ted Hughes. Universität Mannheim, 1995.

K. MANUSCRIPTS

Major collections in public and university libraries, arranged alphabetically by location.

Until 1997 the great majority of Hughes' manuscripts were in the poet's own hands. The bulk of these have now been bought by Emory University, Atlanta. It is estimated that it will take 'a year or two' before the collection is processed and opened for research use. The manuscripts listed below under K1 are those already possessed by Emory before this purchase.

K1 Atlanta. Robert Woodruff Library, Emory University.

Caprichos. Carbon typescripts of sixteen poems. These poems have nothing in common with *Capriccio* [A96]. Six of them appeared in *Moortown* (together with 'The Wolf') as Seven Dungeon Songs. 'He cast off the weight of space' is a version of 'For Leonard and Lisa' in *A Primer of Birds*. The remaining nine are unpublished. They are 'No came from the earth', 'He wanted to be here', 'The prisoners', 'When it comes down to it', 'When dawn lifts the eyelid', 'A man stepping from every tedious thing', 'A deathly sleep', 'He was frightened', and 'Nevertheless rejoice'.

Cave Birds. Three distinct versions, the first two in the form of carbon typescripts, the third a photocopy. The second and third have Hughes' autograph revisions and corrections. Together these include 'nine poems not included in the published versions'.

Crow. Typescripts with autograph revisions: 'The Black Beast', 'Bones', 'Crow Compromises', 'A Crow Joke', 'Fragment of an Ancient Tablet', 'I See a Bear', 'In Laughter', 'Song for a Phallus',

'Her Father's Enigma', 'Under the Gatepost of Heaven'. Other *Crow* typescripts: 'Crow Fails', 'Crow Goes Out to Play', 'Crow Outlawed', 'Carrion Tiresias Examines the Sacrifice'.

Miscellaneous revised typescripts: 'The New World', 'The Road to Easington', 'Scapegoats and Rabies'.

Other poems: 'A Near Thing', 'Full Moon and Little Frieda'.

22 letters from Hughes to W. S. and/or Dido Merwin. Poems included with this correspondence: 'The Ballad of the Burning of the Brothel', 'Bawdry Embraced', 'Lines to a Newborn Baby', 'My Father in the Night Commanding NO', 'Pibroch', 'You'll march along the vacant lanes', 'Morning Mist' or 'Cities in Mist', 'Fallen Eve', 'A man brought to his knees in the desert'.

20 letters to Peter Redgrove and/or Penelope Shuttle. Manuscripts included with this correspondence: 'An Alchemy', 'I had exploded ...', 'Crow Rambles', 'Crow's Song About Prospero and Sycorax', 'Genesis of Evil', 'Crow's Courtship', 'The Howling of Wolves', 'Kreutzer Sonata', 'Tutorial', 'Heptonstall', 'Cadenza', 'Waking', 'Out', 'The Hanged Man and the Dragonfly' (with author's revisions and notes).

12 letters to Michael Dawson.

Orts. Page proofs, with autograph corrections and revisions by Hughes.

Copies of Thoreau's *Walden*, and *Eight Plays by Molière*, containing extensive annotations by Hughes.

'Lobby from Under the Carpet'. Multiple versions, holograph and typescript, of this 1992 poem.

Typed notes by Hughes on eighty-four of his published works (varying in length from a single sentence to two single-spaced pages).

K2 Austin. Harry Ransom Humanities Research Center, University of Texas.

'Heatwave', 'Einstein Plays Bach', 'Song about love' (published as 'Birdsong'), 'Gnat-psalm', 'Still life'. TSS in the *London Magazine* Collection.

'Second Glance at a Jaguar'. TSC in the James Gibson Collection.

'Remembrance Day'. TS with letter to John Barrett, uncatalogued.

'Poetry and the Opposition'. 5pp. TS of unpublished essay in the John Lehmann Collection.

There is an uncatalogued letter from Hughes to Jacob Schwartz, and further letters in the following collections: Thomas Marby Cranfill, Harpers, Michael Josselson, Alfred A. Knopf Inc., John Lehmann, *London Magazine, London Review*, Derek Parker, Peter Redgrove, Anne Sexton, Tom Stoppard, Eric Walter White.

K3 Birmingham. University of Birmingham Library.

'A Crow Hymn'. TS and revised page-proofs. Sceptre Press archive 296–303.

K4 Bloomington. Lilly Library, Indiana University

Autograph MS and corrected page-proofs of *The Hawk in the Rain*.

Drafts and notes for *Lupercal*.

Poems: 'Very pleased with himself was little Willie Crib' (1956); 'Whenever I am got under my gravestone' ['Soliloquy of a Misanthrope'] (1956); 'Dolly Topplebull mourns her ascendant Sanity' (1956); 'On his side, embrangled in adult passion, he had' (1956); 'Ridiculous to call it love' (1956); 'Crow Hill' (1958); 'Pennines in April' (1958); 'Meet my folks!' (1961); 'Nessie' (1961); 'Era of Giant Lizards' (1963); 'Heatwave' (1963); 'Many a weary, weary day'; 'Parlour-Piece'; 'Pike'; 'Squirrel in January'; 'Thistles'.

Letters to Dorothy Schober Benotti, Douglas Cleverdon, Ronald Frederick Henry Duncan, Gerald and Joan Hughes, Galway Kinnell, Aurelia Schober Plath (approx. 60), Sylvia Plath (20), Warren Joseph Plath (18), Henry Rago.

K5 Buffalo. The Poetry/Rare Books Collection, State University of New York at Buffalo.

Poems: 'Against Larks', 'Things Present' (four versions), 'View of a Pig' (two versions), 'February' (six versions), 'Of Cats' (six versions), 'Blackbird', 'Dully Gumption's Addendum', 'Plum Blossom', 'Scapegoats and Rabies', 'The Road to Easington', 'Stealing Trout on a May Morning'.

Letters to Tom Pickard, Mac Hammond, David Posner, Ted Walker, Robert Graves.

K6 Exeter. University of Exeter Library.

Cave Birds. Complete archive, autograph and TS.

K7 Leeds. Brotherton Library, University of Leeds.

Letters from Ted Hughes to Anthony Thwaite, and three other letters.

K8 Liverpool. University of Liverpool Library.

MS.22.7(1–13). Revised TSS of nine poems from *The Hawk in the Rain*: 'The Martyrdom of Bishop Farrar' (two drafts), 'Lust and Desire' (two drafts: 'Lust' unpublished; 'Desire' became 'Incompatibilities'), 'Six Young Men' (three drafts), 'Egg-head', 'The Horses', 'Famous Poet', 'Wind', 'Bayonet Charge', 'Macaw and Little Miss'.

MS.26.1(68–73). Early holograph drafts from the *Wodwo* period: 'Gog II' (four drafts), 'Fern' (four drafts), 'The Rat's Dance', 'A wire, wobbingly long …' (includes 'To Be A Girl's Diary'), 'Bald had always imagined bald …' (two drafts, unpublished).

MS.22.18. *Bedtime Stories*. A projected but unpublished pre-*Crow* collection—'earlyish drafts' (T.H.) of twelve poems all but one of which subsequently appeared in *Crow* or elsewhere in revised form and with different titles: 'First Bedtime Story' ['Song of Woe'], 'Second Bedtime Story' ['Lovesong'], 'Crow Twice Born' ['Crow and Mama'], 'Third Bedtime Story' ['A Bedtime Story'], 'Fourth Bedtime Story' ['Criminal Ballad'], 'Fifth Bedtime Story' ['Crow's Account of the Battle'], 'Crow was so much blacker …' [unpublished], 'Seventh Bedtime Story' ['Elephant Totem Song'], 'Eighth Bedtime Story' ['Existential Song'], 'Magical Dangers', 'Ninth Bedtime Story' ['Anecdote'], 'Conjuring in Heaven'. Also 'Rocket to Venus'. All TSS.

MS.13.1(51). 'Revenge Fable'. TS.

MS.23.8. 'Crow goes to the movies'. [Unpublished poem.] Two autograph drafts.

MS.3.56(13). *The Demon*. An unpublished autograph play first performed at the Orchard Theatre, Bideford, Easter 1970.

MS.24.55–58. *Oedipus of Seneca*. Complete archive including autograph drafts, typescripts, theatre copies, correspondence, and Hughes' edition of Seneca heavily annotated.

MS.22.19. B.B.C. duplicated TSS of *The House of Donkeys* [G43] and *The Tiger's Bones* [G46].

MS.22.8. Three untitled scenarios for television. TS.

MS.22.6(1–3). Three letters from Hughes to Philip Hobsbaum, autograph and TS.

MS.13.1. Two letters from Hughes to Vernon Watkins, three to Ian Hamilton, and three to Charles Osborne, autograph and TS.

K9 London. The British Library Department of Manuscripts.

Revised autograph and TS drafts of *Nessie the Mannerless Monster*.

Autograph drafts of two poems from *Recklings*, 'The Lake' and 'Tutorial'.

Wodwo: numerous autograph drafts of three poems, 'The Green Wolf' (as 'Mid-May', 'Evening Star' and 'Dark Women'), 'Mountains' and 'Gog', and of the short story 'The Harvesting'.

TS drafts of 'Squirrel in January', 'Gulls' and 'Snails'.

Autograph fragment beginning 'At grammar school teachers ...'

TS fragment of 'Air' [G14]; autograph fragment of 'Difficulties of a Bridegroom' [G25].

Revised TS fragments of an unpublished play, *The Calm*. Add.Mss.53784.

Two autograph letters from Hughes to Marie Douglas. Add.Mss.59833,ff.61–4.

Various drafts, including Crow poems, and letters in the Al Alvarez archive.

K10 London. Adam Archive, Dept. of French, King's College, London.

Letters from Hughes in the files of *Adam International Review*.

K11 Manchester. Carcanet Press Archive, John Rylands University Library.

Revised proofs of contributions to *Poetry Nation Review*, with notes and letters from Hughes.

TS and revised proofs of *Selected Poems* by János Pilinszky [B79].

Revised TS introduction to *Collected Poems* of Vasco Popa [B90].

Autograph and TS letters from Hughes to Michael Schmidt.

K12 New York. Butler Library, Columbia University.

Five autumn songs for children's voices. MS. 11 pp. together with corrected page proofs. 1968.

Animal Poems. Corrected page proofs. 1968.

'Apple Tragedy'. TS dated February 1970.

TSS and corrected galley proofs of four poems submitted to *Grand Street* in 1986: 'Sacrificed Head', 'Halfway Head', 'Lamenting Head', 'Reckless Head'.

Letters to Robert Wallace, Barry Hall, Jeni Couzyn, Kenneth Bernard, Ben Sonnenberg.

K13 Newcastle. Northern Arts Manuscript Collection, Literary and Philosophical Society.

Four autograph letters to Tom and Connie Pickard. In Morden Tower Correspondence.

K14 Northampton, Massachusetts. Smith College.

'Lines to a newborn baby', 'Lines for a new daughter', TSS on verso of drafts of 'Stings' by Sylvia Plath.

Correspondence with Peter Davison about and corrections to *Bitter Fame*, by Anne Stevenson, in the Houghton Mifflin Co. papers.

K15 Reading. BBC Written Archives Centre.

Correspondence between Hughes and members of staff of the BBC (1956–62).

K16 Reading. University of Reading Library.

Duplicated TSS: 'Bayonet Charge', 'Famous Poet', 'The Horses', 'Macaw and Little Miss'.

Letters from Ted Hughes to Ian Fletcher.

Three letters from Hughes in the Bodley Head Adult Editorial File.

K17 St Louis. Washington University Library.

Three letters to Lee Anderson. Eight carbon typescripts enclosed with letter of 11 May 1958: 'Things Present', 'Relic', 'To paint a water-lily', 'Dick Straightup', 'Crow hill', 'The acrobats', 'Witches', 'Bullfrog', 'Thrushes'.

One letter each to Graham Ackroyd, Ian Hamilton, and Alexander Trocchi.

One joint card from Sylvia Plath and Ted Hughes to Olwyn Hughes.

Page proofs of *Recklings*.

K18 Victoria. University of Victoria Library, British Columbia.

Drafts of 'Dully Gumption's Addendum', 'Fishing at Dawn', 'New Moon', and 'Remembrance Day' [collected as 'Out III'].

In the Robin Skelton archive there are TSS of 'Ballad of the Burning of the Brothel', 'Bawdry Embraced' and 'Wodwo', and nine letters to Skelton.

Four letters to Graham Ackroyd, 1960–1.

INDEX

Titles of works by Ted Hughes are printed in capital letters, with separately printed works in bold caps; broadcasts, recordings, and other titles are in italics. References for Hughes' works are arranged chronologically; thus the index gives the order of the appearances of each title in books, periodicals, recordings, and broadcasts. Some of the poems have appeared under different titles; we have found it expedient to call each poem by a single title—usually the latest, or that by which the poem has become generally known. In the case of untitled poems, first lines have been treated as titles.

References are to item numbers, not pages.

417